The Implications of the Racial Equality Directive for Minority Protection within the European Union

THE IMPLICATIONS OF THE RACIAL EQUALITY DIRECTIVE FOR MINORITY PROTECTION WITHIN THE EUROPEAN UNION

by

M.J. Busstra

eleven international publishing

Published, sold and distributed by Eleven International Publishing
P.O. Box 85576
2508 CG The Hague, The Netherlands
Tel.: +31 70 330 70 33
Fax: +31 70 330 70 30
www.elevenpub.com

Sold and distributed in USA and Canada
International Specialized Book Services
920 NE 58th Avenue, Suite 300
Portland, OR 97213-3786, USA
Tel.: +1 800 944 6190 (toll-free)
Fax: +1 503 280 8832
orders@isbs.com
www.isbs.com

Printed on acid-free paper.

ISBN: 978-90-77596-96-8

Printed in The Netherlands

Acknowledgements

The author would like to thank in particular the two persons who have shared the whole proces from projet proposal to publication and who have become friends for life: Dr. Kristin Henrard and Dr Mónika Ambrus.

A special 'thank you' also to all the persons in Belgium, Hungary, Estonia and the Netherlands who were willing to share their experiences and expertise. Without your input it would have been impossible to get a grasp of the various national legal systems. I sincerely hope that the final result of this project can in some way pay back to you what you have given me.

This book is dedicated to my heavenly Father, from whom all blessings flow.

Table of Contents

List of Acronyms and Abbreviations

ABET	Advisory Body on Equal Treatment, Hungary
AC	Arbitration Court, Belgium
ACFCNM	Advisory Committee to the Framework Convention on National Minorities
ADA	Anti-Discrimination Act, Belgium
AET	Authority on Equal Treatment, Hungary
ARA	Anti-Racism Act, Belgium
CC	Constitutional Court, Hungary
CCSC	Constitutional Chamber of the Supreme Court, Estonia
CEOOR	Centre for Equal Opportunities and Opposition to Racism, Belgium
CERD	Committee on the Elimination of Racial Discrimination
CESCR	Committee on Economic and Social Rights
CoS	Council of State, The Netherlands
ECA	Employment Contract Act, Estonia
ECHR	European Convention on Human Rights
ECJ	European Court of Justice
ECRI	European Commission against Racism and Intolerance
ECtHR	European Court of Human Rights
EETA	Equal Treatment Act, Estonia
EFTA	European Free Trade Association
ETC	Equal Treatment Commission, the Netherlands
ETD	Equal Treatment Directive (76/207/EEC)
FD	Framework Directive on equal treatment (2000/78/EC)
FCNM	Framework Convention on National Minorities
GEA	Gender Equality Act, Estonia
GEC	Gender Equality Commissioner, Estonia
GETA	General Equal Treatment Act, the Netherlands
HC	High Council, the Netherlands
HETA	Equal Treatment Act, Hungary
HoL	House of Lords, United Kingdom
HRC	Human Rights Committee
IA	Implementation Act, the Netherlands

ICERD	International Convention on the Elimination of Racial Discrimination
ICCPR	International Covenant on Civil and Political Rights
ICESCR	International Covenant on Economic, Social and Cultural Rights
LC	Legal Chancellor, Estonia
LCA	Legal Chancellor Act, Estonia
RED	Racial Equality Directive (2000/43/EC)
SC	Supreme Court, Hungary
TEC	Treaty of the European Communities

Chapter 1

The Racial Equality Directive and Minority Protection: An Exploration

1.1. Introduction

Over the past decades the focus of European law has gradually expanded from a purely economic perspective towards a more encompassing vision on European integration, whereby fundamental rights have gained increasing importance. The adoption of the Racial Equality Directive (RED) in June 2000 constituted an important step in this process, and marked the transformation of the principle of equal treatment from "market unifier to fundamental right".[1] The directive integrated the prohibition of racial and ethnic discrimination in the European equality paradigm that, until then, only comprised nationality and sex discrimination. It was soon followed by the Framework Directive (FD), which further broadened the scope to religious, sexual orientation, disability and age discrimination.[2]

The RED was considered remarkable for its broad and inclusive approach to racial and ethnic discrimination, in addition to its very swift adoption, which was spurred by concern for increasing xenophobic tendencies in Europe. The RED's wide material scope was unprecedented at the time, and the directive moreover introduced discrimination concepts that had not yet been regulated in European equality law. It was in particular received as an important instrument for furthering the cause of minority groups throughout Europe and for compensating for the absence of a European minority protection regime.

---

1 Gijzen (2006), at 20; More (1999).

2 *Council Directive 2000/78/EC of 27 November 2000 establishing a general framework for equal treatment in employment and occupation.*

In the words of one commentator: "[t]he Race Directive (…) is innovative and quite radical in a number of respects which may lead it to become the most efficient minority protection tool in the EU for the years to come".[3]

An effective minority protection regime is generally considered to rest on two pillars: a pillar of effective protection of general human rights with special relevance for minorities, particularly the right to non-discrimination, and a pillar of special minority rights for minority groups.[4] Broadly speaking, the first pillar aims at securing full and effective equality in practice, which is commonly understood by the notion of "substantive equality". Substantive equality entails a levelling of the playing field in order to ensure that all persons can effectively participate in society, on an equal footing. This involves accounting for specific needs and circumstances that put persons belonging to minorities at a structural disadvantage compared to persons belonging to the majority group in society. Opposite to substantive equality stands the perspective of "formal equality", which aims at the formal equal treatment of all persons, regardless of their particular needs and circumstances.[5]

The second pillar of minority protection aims at accommodating the needs of minority groups that arise from their interest in maintaining a separate identity. Examples of typical second pillar rights are the right to provide for education in the minority mother tongue, the right to communicate with official authorities in the minority mother tongue, the right to maintain a traditional way of life and the right to exercise some degree of self-government.[6]

The pillars are not mutually exclusive, and depending on the particular way in which the first pillar is applied and interpreted, the second pillar decreases or increases in relevance. Thus, the greater the extent to which identity-related interests of minority groups are met by general human rights and the right to non-discrimination, the less the need for special minority rights.[7]

It should be clarified at this juncture that there is no generally accepted definition of 'minority' as of yet. It is one of those concepts that is mainly construed empirically and consequently finds its meaning in its practical application, by those who have to work with it. Still, scholars and international supervisory bodies more or less agree on a number of characteristics that need to be present among the members of a particular group in order for this group to qualify as a 'minority' in the context of the minority protection paradigm. Thus, groups need to:

- share stable ethnic, religious or linguistic characteristics that are not present among the rest of the population

[3] Toggenburg (2005), at 729; De Witte (2004), at 116.
[4] Henrard (2007), at 14.
[5] Fredman (2002), at 7-15.
[6] Henrard (2007), at 15-16.
[7] Henrard (2007), at 15.

- be in a numerical minority position
- be in a non-dominant position
- and have the wish to preserve a separate identity[8]

Whereas it used to be traditional minority groups that had historical ties with the host state that were targeted by the minority protection paradigm, there is nowadays growing recognition of the phenomenon of 'new' minorities. These groups are constituted by migrants' communities, whose members do not necessarily have the nationality of the host state.[9] This study takes an equally inclusive approach, and considers both traditional and 'new' minorities to be deserving of "minority protection", while not denying that differentiation between types of groups may in some instances be appropriate.[10]

Scholars have noted a steady development at the international level towards more and better protection of minorities, whereby both pillars of minority protection are accounted for.[11] Thus, the supervisory organs of non minority-specific human rights instruments, notably those of the European Convention for Human Rights (ECHR), the International Convention on the Elimination of All forms of Racial Discrimination (ICERD) and the International Covenant on Economic, Social and Cultural Rights (ICESCR) have increasingly paid particular attention to minority protection issues. A number of minority-specific instruments have moreover been adopted in recent years, which are likely to have triggered the shift in jurisprudence of the aforementioned bodies. The Council of Europe's Framework Convention for the Protection of National Minorities (FCNM) and European Charter for Regional or Minority Languages (Language Charter) lay down detailed rules in this respect. These treaties have not been ratified by all Member States of the EU, however, and their supervisory bodies cannot issue legally binding decisions, which diminishes their impact, despite the undeniable de facto authority of these bodies.

For this reason, the RED has been appraised as an important means of not only putting minority protection higher on the European agenda, but also of providing a body of legally binding rules that will potentially enhance the level of minority protection in the European Union. As an anti-discrimination

8 Pentassuglia (2003), at 57-58; Henrard (2000), at 30-48.

9 Cholewinski (2005), at 699-700; Thornberry & Estebanez (2004), at 93 and 95; Toggenburg (2003), at 277; *Opinion on Possible Groups of Persons to which the Framework Convention for the Protection of National Minorities Could be Applied in Belgium*, Venice Commission, March 2002, CDL-AD (2002) 1; *General Comment No. 23: The rights of minorities (Art. 27),* Human Rights Committee, 8 April 1994, UN Doc. CCPR/C/21/Rev.1/Add.5, paras. 5.1-5.2.

10 See Medda (2008), at 93-243 for an elaborate discussion of differentiated levels of protection for different types of minorities.

11 Henrard (2005).

instrument, the RED can be placed within the first pillar of minority protection, and its effectiveness in this respect will depend on the degree to which it is able to further the aim of substantive equality. In addition, to the extent that it is employed to serve identity-related interests of minority groups, it will decrease the need for additional second pillar rights within the EU and/or the Member States.

By its nature, the directive does not impose a set of detailed rules that have to be copied integrally into national law, but leaves Member States with some leeway as to how they implement its provisionsand adapt them to the particular national context.[12] It thus sets in place a framework of anti-discrimination rules that still need some degree of further elaboration. In the first place it will be up to national legislators and courts to fill in the gaps, but the actual amount of freedom they have is not unlimited. Over time, it can be expected that the European Court of Justice will set boundaries and accordingly determine the minimum baseline of protection required by the RED. Member States are allowed to go beyond this baseline and to provide for a higher level of protection against racial or ethnic discrimination, as is expressly recognised in Article 6 RED.

One can therefore expect that the following picture will emerge at a certain point in time: there will be a default level of protection against racial or ethnic discrimination visible throughout the Member States that has been developed by the Member States in dialogue with the ECJ.[13] In addition, there will be a higher level of protection in some Member States, which will perhaps exert an encouraging influence on other Member States to also increase their levels of protection.

Against this background, the present study aims at exploring the potential impact of the RED on the level of minority protection throughout the European Union, in particular at the Member State level. It forms part of a broader project funded by the Netherlands Organisation for Scientific Research (NWO) under the VIDI programme,[14] and is one of two connected studies, which build on the work of the project leader, who will also draw the various strands together.[15] This study analyses a particular aspect of the RED, namely its substantive anti-discrimination provisions (Articles 2-5), and focuses specifically on national implementation in four Member States: Belgium, Estonia, Hungary and the Netherlands, while the second study analyses the procedural provisions of the RED (Articles 7-15) in the same manner.[16] The project leader examines the RED's implications for minority protection at the European level, measured

---

[12] McInerney (2000), at 316.

[13] McCrudden (2003), at 36.

[14] *The Race Directive's implications for minority protection both at the level of the EU and at the level of the Member States*, initiated by K.A.M. Henrard (projectleader).

[15] The groundwork for the present study was set in place by the projectleader, and is laid down in Henrard (2006a), Henrard (2006b), Henrard (2007) and Henrard (2007b).

[16] Ambrus (2010).

against the developments in relation to equality and minority protection at the international level, and identifies synergies regarding these respective developments.

It is expected that the overall VIDI project will produce a thorough and comprehensive initial assessment of the impact that the RED has and will have on the level of minority protection throughout the European Union, both at the European level and the Member State level. This will provide steady input for further research regarding the status of minority protection in the European Union, and regarding the question whether further action is needed.

In the remainder of this chapter, the present study will be further outlined. In Section 1.2, the main research question is dissected into a number of sub-questions that guide the analysis in the following chapters. Section 1.3 subsequently presents the methodology followed throughout this study, and Section 1.4 offers a brief introduction to the four Member States that are examined in the case study part.

1.2. Questions for analysis

With a view to assessing the implications of the substantive section of the RED for minority protection in the European Union, more particularly at the Member State level, the following sub-questions have been examined in the present study:

1) Which minimum requirements can be distinguished within the substantive section of the RED and how do they relate to minority protection?

2) Which aspects of implementation are still obscure, and how can these be resolved best from a minority protection perspective?

3) Which opportunities does the substantive section of the RED offer for Member States that are willing to offer a higher level of minority protection than required by the RED?

4) In which way have the four Member States approached the aforementioned minimum requirements, obscurities and opportunities when implementing the substantive section of the RED?

5) Are there parallels and trends visible regarding the manner in which the Member States have implemented the substantive section of the RED?

For reasons of practicality, a number of questions have been deliberately left aside. Thus, this research project does not separately explore the meaning of fundamental minority protection concepts, such as 'minority', 'effective minority protection', 'identity' and 'substantive equality'. These notions have been amply examined and reflected upon elsewhere, and this study applies them in accordance with their generally accepted meanings, as explained above.[17] It should furthermore be emphasised that the present study focuses on the RED only, and does not separately examine other instruments of European equality law. These instruments will only be used to the extent that they provide relevant input for the interpretation of certain aspects of the RED. The study will in particular not contribute to the very interesting and topical debate on the alleged 'hierarchy of grounds' within European equality law.[18] While not denying the relevance of this debate, it is considered not to be of added value for the central question examined in this study, which only intends to examine the effects of the RED on minority protection.

1.3. Methodology

The present study follows the structure of the RED, and consists of six substantive chapters, each of which deals with one aspect of the substantive section of the RED. The first two chapters focus on the personal and material scope of the RED (Chapters 2 and 3), and the remaining four chapters are each centered around one or two concepts of discrimination, namely direct discrimination (Chapter 4), indirect discrimination (Chapter 5) , harassment and the instruction to discriminate (Chapter 6), and positive action (Chapter 7).

Since implementation of European law is a dynamic process in which there is an ongoing dialogue between the national and European levels, the present study has assessed the impact of the RED on minority protection at two levels: the theoretical as well as the practical, national level. It was deemed valuable not only to assess the current status quo of implementation at the national level, but also to set the agenda for future interpretation and implementation of the RED by way of providing a comprehensive theoretical outline of what is the optimal use of the RED in order to set in place a solid minority protection framework. Each chapter therefore contains a twofold analysis: a theoretical analysis of the provisions of the RED, and a practical analysis of

---

17 See inter alia the groundwork for this project as developed by Henrard (2006a), Henrard (2006b), Henrard (2007) and Henrard (2007b).

18 See on this topic inter alia Howard (2006); Holzleithner (2005), at 943; Bell & Waddington (2003); Waddington (2003), at 47-49; Schiek (2002), at 300; Bell & Waddington (2001); O'Hare (2001), at 144; Fredman (2001), at 151; Bell (2000), at 80; Flynn (1999), at 1127-1152.

the implementation of these provisions in Belgium, Estonia, Hungary and the Netherlands. The methodology for these two parts, a theoretical framework and a case study part, are discussed separately in the following subsections.

1.3.1. Theoretical framework

The theoretical framework entails a systematic analysis of all relevant aspects of the particular provision of the RED that is studied in the respective chapter. Whereas a thematic approach with special attention for the more relevant topics would have arguably produced a slightly more exciting version of the theoretical framework, a final choice has been made for a comprehensive and technical approach. The main reason for this lies in the fact that legal developments within the Member States were found to be very slow, and there was not yet enough material at the end of the fact-finding phase to produce an interesting thematic presentation. Moreover, in view of the relative inexperience we encountered on the ground, it was felt that a handbook-type of framework would better contribute to the development of a robust, effective and transparent anti-discrimination regime in the Member States.

As the present study is centered around the implementation of the RED at the national level, the theoretical framework of each chapter is set up from a particular angle, namely the individual Member State perspective. This means that the central question asked for each topic in the theoretical framework is the following: what is the ideal approach to be taken by the national legislator or the national court in order to maximize the minority protection impact of this particular aspect? This question is clearly of a normative nature, which makes it necessary to outline the presuppositions on which the normative reasoning in this study rests.

The theoretical framework is built upon the basic assumption that the (potential) minority protection impact of a particular provision is determined on two levels. At a very proximate level, the minority protection impact is determined by the degree to which the provision can be used to achieve substantive equality and to accommodate identity-related interests of persons belonging to minority groups. From a quantitative perspective this means that the provisions of the RED are to have as broad a reach as is legally possible. From a qualitative perspective this means that the provisions are to be interpreted and applied in such a way that they most closely connect to the particular needs and interests of minority groups. At a slightly more distant level, the minority protection impact of a provision greatly depends on certain procedural conditions, such as conceptual clarity and consistency, practicability and transparency.

The normative reasoning in the theoretical framework is construed by means of the traditional tools of theoretical legal research. The basis of each separate analysis is formed by the text of the relevant provision of the RED, which is subsequently analysed with the help of other legal instruments, jurisprudence, doctrine, international reports and policy documentation. This analysis provides the input for a discussion of the preferable interpretation or application of the particular provision from a minority protection perspective, whereby the abovementioned presuppositions of effective minority protection are applied.

Concerning the choice to make use of the jurisprudence of the ECJ, it should be mentioned that this court has so far rendered only one judgment on the basis of the RED.[19] Since it is generally expected that ECJ jurisprudence in the fields of nationality and sex equality law will to a large extent inform its interpretation of the RED, the theoretical framework gives prominent consideration to the various judgments rendered in this field.[20] It is realised, however, that the RED portrays a number of specific features that may lead the ECJ to apply and interpret differently certain aspects of this instrument in comparison with nationality and sex equality law. Relevant features of the RED in this respect are its very wide material scope, the particularities of the grounds 'racial' and 'ethnic' origin compared to nationality and sex, and differences in wording of the definitions of the substantive discrimination concepts. In view of these special characteristics of the RED, the case law of the ECJ in other fields is only regarded as a strong indication of the way in which a particular provision may be interpreted, and is not taken as conclusive. Where this is deemed relevant, potential differences in interpretation and application in regard to nationality and sex equality law are expressly mentioned in the theoretical framework.

1.3.2. Case study: comparative research

The case study part of each chapter contains an overview of the way in which four Member States, Belgium, Estonia, Hungary and the Netherlands, have implemented the particular provisions of the RED. In view of limited time and means and the intention to perform a comprehensive and in-depth analysis, it was decided not to study all 27 Member States of the European Union. The selection of countries for the present study rests on the assumption that a representative sample of the variety of Member States of the EU would yield the most interesting and reliable results. In addition to criteria of accessibility and feasibility, it accordingly seemed appropriate to apply the following criteria:

[19] *Centrum voor gelijkheid van kansen en racismebestrijding v. Firma Feryn NV*, Case C-54/07, 10 July (2008).

[20] Tobler (2008), at 9; Henrard (2007), at 22; Gijzen (2006), at 38; Parmar (2004); Caruso (2003), at 3.

- the countries under study should be drawn from both old and new Member States, as the relative experience of old Member States vis-à-vis new Member States with regard to the implementation and application of European equality law is expected to have some bearing on the respective modes of implementation

- the societies of the countries under study should be different regarding their demographic design, because the particular societal context is likely to exert an ongoing influence on the way in which implementing measures are drafted and applied in practice

- the countries under study should possess different track records in terms of national non-discrimination and minority protection measures present at the time of implementation, as the relative degree of experience with these types of measures is likely to impact on the formulation and application of implementing measures

The brief overview in the next section of the four countries selected for the present study will reveal that they show cross-cutting differences and similarities in respect of these three criteria and therefore are considered to provide a representative sample for the case study part of this study.

The structure of the case study part of each chapter largely follows the structure of the preceding theoretical framework, but is slightly more concise at some points, which is caused by the lack of relevant jurisprudence or quasi-jurisprudence and/or doctrine at the national level. During the course of the research project, it was found that legal developments in the Member States were much slower than expected beforehand, which means that many aspects of implementation have yet to crystallise.[21] To the greatest extent possible the case study part draws from other sources of information to predict the way in which implementation of the RED will go, but in many instances open-ended questions remain.

As the case study part proceeds from the findings that were formulated in the theoretical framework, it is of an analytical rather than of a normative nature. In other words, the case study part examines in a legal-factual way to what extent the Member States have followed the preferred approach that was outlined in the theoretical framework. It follows an integrated comparative structure, which means that the various national implementation measures are not examined separately, but are jointly analysed per topic, so as to make the similarities and differences between the national frameworks more

[21] The implementation deadline of the RED was 19 July 2003, and it was expected that quite a few developments would have taken place at the national level by the end of the period covered by the research in April 2009.

pronounced. This in turn makes it easier to discern trends and parallels in the national implementation processes, which are presented in the conclusion at the end of each chapter.

The sources that provided the input for the case study analysis are primarily the traditional legal sources, i.e. national legislation, jurisprudence and quasi-jurisprudence, national policy documents, doctrine and national and international reports. It should be mentioned that these sources have been consulted not only with regard to racial equality law, but also with regard to equality law more generally, as it was considered that the manner in which other discrimination grounds are approached provide a reliable indication of how the same matter will be dealt with in the context of racial discrimination. Naturally, the differences between racial equality law and equality law for other grounds that were outlined above were taken into consideration.

In addition to the traditional legal tools, the case study part made use of the less common tool of in-depth interviews that were conducted over a period of three years in each Member State with national policy makers, lawyers, judges, supervisory organs, NGO's and academics. The input of these interviews is mainly of an indirect nature, which means that they were generally used as an important means of obtaining a good understanding of the particular national contexts and of getting access to more objective legal sources. In the very few instances where the interviews are drawn upon to directly support a legal argument, it is explicitly mentioned in the text. This approach was chosen in the first place because it was considered desirable to support an argument with objective legal evidence rather than with a subjective opinion expressed by an expert. Second, many of the interviews were of a confidential nature in order to allow the interviewees to speak freely, which means that their output could not be directly used.

At certain points the case study analysis proved to be a complex exercise, which was caused by certain particularities of the national frameworks. In addition to the aforementioned problems of a lack of relevant practice and/or doctrine, the following difficulties need to be mentioned.

In Belgium, the complex federal structure proved to be a considerable obstacle. Since all of the six federated entities have some competence in domains covered by the RED, each of them had to adopt implementing instruments, in addition to the instruments that were adopted at the federal level. Over time they more or less complied with this obligation, and the result is a complex patchwork of legal instruments that are different in many respects. As a detailed analysis of each Belgian instrument would have produced an overly complex presentation, it was decided to focus on the instruments that were adopted by the federal legislator, and to mention only those aspects of the federated instruments that differed from these instruments in an important way.

In the Netherlands there is a clear division line visible between the practices of the quasi-judicial Equal Treatment Commission (ETC) on the one hand, and Dutch courts on the other. As the former body deals with the bulk of Dutch discrimination cases, it has developed a comprehensive, consistent and transparent equality framework. The opposite is true for the courts, which only sporadically come across discrimination cases, and therefore have an ad-hoc attitude that has not yielded a consistent approach. Even though the ETC cannot issue binding decisions, its practice is generally considered to constitute the baseline of Dutch equality law, which is reflected in the fact that 80 per cent of its decisions are followed up by the parties.[22] Therefore, it was decided to take the ETC's practice as the point of departure for the Dutch framework, and to refer to the Dutch courts' practice only where it was considered to provide useful insight into this framework.

In the following section, the four Member States under study are briefly introduced.

1.4. Belgium, Estonia, Hungary and the Netherlands: a brief introduction

1.4.1. Belgium

Belgium is one of the oldest Member States of the European Union and was one of the founding parties of the European Communities. At that time it was a unified state, but since the 1980s it has developed into a federal state, in a continuous movement towards more competence for the federated entities, and less competence for the federal state. The federated entities are structured along territorial and personal lines. There are three Regions that each administer a part of Belgian territory and are competent in structural areas such as infrastructure, transport and economy: the Walloon Region, the Flanders Region and the Brussels Capital Region. In addition, the population is divided into three linguistic groups that each fall under the competence of a Community as regards matters such as employment policy, education and healthcare: The French Community, The Flemish Community and the German Community.[23]

Demographically, Belgian society is first and foremost self-perceived as being composed of linguistic groups, the most prominent of which are the French and Flemish communities, who account for 57 and 32 per cent of the population respectively. Compared to these two groups, the German community

[22] *Jaarverslag 2008*, CGB, available at www.cgb.nl (accessed July 2009), at 40. Also see Asscher-Vonk & Hendriks (2005), at 173.

[23] See Van Drooghenbroeck (2004), at 97-121 for a detailed overview of the division of competences and its relation with the implementation of the RED.

is hardly visible and consists of only 70,000 persons.[24] The relations between the French and Flemish communities are strained, and linguistic matters are highly sensitive in Belgian society.[25] The burdensome ratification process of the FCNM by Belgium is illustrative in this respect: Belgium signed the Convention in 2001, but has so far failed to ratify it, as many fear that it will interfere with the delicate regulatory framework regarding the use of language within the public domain.[26] In addition, Belgium has not signed or ratified the Charter for Regional Minority languages. It has, however, signed and ratified all important general human rights instruments, notably the ECHR, European Social Charter, ICERD, ICCPR and ICESCR.

From the 1960s onwards large numbers of immigrant labourers moved to Belgium, which led to a growing number of 'new' minorities. Most of these groups originate from other EU Member States, and have not really caught the public eye. Other groups that originate from outside the EU, mainly Turkey, Morocco and former Belgian colonies in Africa, are more visible, however, and frequently encounter xenophobic and racist attitudes in society.[27] The members of these minorities are generally at a structural disadvantage compared to ethnic Belgians (regardless of their linguistic affiliation), as some studies show.[28] Racism and xenophobia have been noted to be on the rise in Belgium, in particular Islamophobia.[29]

Prior to implementation of the RED there was some Belgian anti-discrimination legislation in place at the federal level. As early as 1981, an Anti-Racism Act (old ARA) was adopted, penalizing certain forms of racial discrimination, in accordance with the obligations imposed by ICERD. This Act was amended a number of times, mostly on grounds of improving its effectiveness and of adapting it to changing national and international circumstances.[30] The general equality principle of the Belgian Constitution furthermore provided some protection against discrimination. Articles 10 and 11 of the Constitution contain the principles of equality before the law and of non-discrimination of all Belgian citizens.[31]

The Belgian implementation of the RED took place in two phases, the first of which involved the adoption of an Anti-discrimination Act (ADA) in 2003.

---

24 http://www.minorityrights.org/1507/belgium/belgium-overview.htl#1 (accessed June 2009).

25 http://www.minorityrights.org/1507/belgium/belgium-overview.htl#1 (accessed June 2009).

26 Swenden (2003), at 355.

27 http://www.minorityrights.org/1507/belgium/belgium-overview.htl#1 (accessed June 2009).

28 *Rapport Alternatif 2005 d'ENAR, Le Racisme en Belgique*, ENAR (2005).

29 *Third Report on Belgium*, European Commission against Racism and Intolerance (ECRI), June 2003, paras. 73-76.

30 For a detailed overview see De Prins et al (2005), at 295-301.

31 For a detailed analysis of these provisions see De Prins et al (2005), at 235-290.

This Act attracted much criticism from scholars and politicians, culminating in a landmark judgment issued by the Arbitration Court in 2004, which annulled certain aspects of this Act.[32] This judgment was one of the reasons for the Belgian legislator to propose new anti-discrimination legislation, which was furthermore instigated by a reasoned opinion of the European Commission that deemed certain aspects of the ADA in violation with European law, and the concern to show more respect for the exclusive competences of the federated entities.[33] Thus, in 2007 the legislator proposed a set of anti-discrimination measures, which entailed a comprehensive amendment of the 1981 Anti-Racism Act (new ARA) in order to implement the RED.[34] The new version of this Act was adopted in May 2007, and the ADA of 2003 was repealed at the same time.

The federated entities have adopted their own decrees in order to implement the RED. As was mentioned before, these decrees and ordinances are only mentioned in the present study to the extent that they show a remarkable feature that differs from the federal legislation in an important respect.

1.4.2. Estonia

Estonia is one of the newer EU Member States and joined the European Union in 2004, after having functioned as an independent republic for just over a decade. After its independence from the Soviet Union in 1992 it was faced with a large number of ethnic Russians who had been forced to migrate to the Republic under Soviet rule and who had established lasting ties with Estonia. As they could not rely on historic ties with Estonia before Soviet annexation they were denied immediate Estonian citizenship, which was made dependent on a number of restrictive conditions, amongst which their passing of a language test. As an immediate consequence, the political foundations of the newly independent state were determined by ethnic Estonians only, excluding ethnic Russians. In the intermediate and long term, the exclusive policy has brought about the situation that a large part of the population inhabiting Estonian territory does not have Estonian citizenship, a significant proportion of which does not have any citizenship at all. Needless to say, all of these persons are of non-Estonian ethnic origin.[35]

The citizenship policy received much criticism from NGO's, supervisory organs and states, as did the restrictive Estonian language policy pursued by the state.[36] The latter policy entailed strict regulation of the level of Estonian

32 Court of Arbitration, no. 157/2004, 6 October 2004; De Prins et al (2005), at 445-447.

33 Tojerow (2008).

34 *Act of 30 July 1981 to penalise certain acts motivated by racism or xenophobia*, as amended on 10 May 2007, BS 30 V 07.

35 http://www.minorityrights.org/2443/estonia/estonia-overview.html (accessed July 2009).

36 See for example *Linguistic minorities in Estonia: Discrimination must end,* Amnesty

required for certain posts, and the progressive introduction of Estonian as the main language of instruction in all schools in the territory. Both policies have been relaxed and/or improved over time.[37] Still, many ethnic Russians still do not have Estonian citizenship, and the relations between ethnic Estonians and ethnic Russians are somewhat strained.[38] Territorially, these groups are not evenly distributed. The eastern part of the country is mainly inhabited by ethnic Russians, who also constitute a large proportion of the population of the capital city: Tallinn. Tallinn's population is said to be marked by a high level of segregation along ethnic dividing lines, comprising in fact an ethnic Estonian society and an ethnic Russian society. Depending on whether one is in the North or another part of the country, the minority is constituted by either Estonians or by ethnic Russians. Still, most ethnic Russians are not considered by the state to constitute a national minority, as citizenship was declared to be a constitutive element of the notion 'national minority' at the occasion of FCNM ratification.[39] They are recognised, however, as making up an 'ethnic minority', and are the focus of a number of official language training programmes.[40] In addition to the FCNM, Estonia has signed and ratified the ECHR, the European Social Charter, ICERD, ICCPR and ICESCR. It has not signed or ratified the Language Charter of the Council of Europe.

The demographic make-up of Estonian society as assessed in 2005 is as follows: 68 per cent of the population are ethnic Estonians and 26 per cent are ethnic Russians, approximately half of which have Estonian citizenship.[41] In addition, there are small minorities of Ukrainians, Byelorussians and Finns, who each make up 1 or 2 per cent of the population. Aside from the ethnic Russians, there are hardly any migrant communities, or so-called 'new minorities' in Estonian society.[42] Of these groups, it is mainly the ethnic Russians who experience discrimination and who are economically and socially less well off than the rest of society.[43] Still, their situation has steadily

International (2007); *Concluding Observations of CERD on Estonia*, 22 August 2006, CERD/C/EST/CO/7, paras. 14-16; *Second opinion on Estonia*, Advisory Committee on the Framework Convention for national minorities, 24 February 2005, ACFC/OP/II(2005)001; *Racism in Estonia*, ENAR shadow report (2005), at 15.

37 *Third Report on Estonia*, ECRI, 24 June 2005, at 10-11; *Second opinion on Estonia adopted on 24 February 2005*, Advisory Committee on the Framework Convention for national minorities, ACFC/OP/II(2005)001, para. 17; *Second Report on Estonia*, ECRI, 22 June 2001, at 6-10.

38 http://www.minorityrights.org/2443/estonia/estonia-overview.html (accessed July 2009).

39 Cholewinski (2005), at 698-699. According to this declaration Estonian citizenship was a necessary condition to be fulfilled by members of a minority.

40 See for example the explanation of 'ethnic minority' on the official website of the Ministry of Population Affairs, at http://www.meis.ee/eng/minorities (accessed July 2009).

41 *Racism in Estonia*, ENAR Shadow Report (2005), at 9.

42 *Racism in Estonia*, ENAR Shadow Report (2005), at 12.

43 *Report on Estonia in 2005*, EU network of independent experts on fundamental rights, CFR-CDF/Rep[EE]2005, at 32-44.

improved over the years and is not as serious as that of many other minority groups in the CEE states. Moreover, in those parts of the country where this group forms the majority on a local level, they are liable to be perpetrators of discrimination towards ethnic Estonians.

Prior to the implementation of the RED, there were hardly any anti-discrimination provisions in the Estonian legal framework. There was article 12(1) of the Constitution, which contains the principle of equality before the law and prohibition of discrimination, but which is generally considered to be ineffective, despite the fact that it supposedly applies even in horizontal relations.[44] In addition, there is a generally worded criminal law prohibition of discrimination, which has never been applied in practice.[45] It should furthermore be mentioned that as early as 1993 an Act on the Cultural Autonomy of National Minorities was adopted.[46] This Act provides national minorities with the possibility of setting up particular organs to regulate certain cultural matters, and has hardly been made use of. According to experts on the ground, the Act is more or less redundant, as minorities can make use of normal civil law provisions to set up legal persons that deal with cultural matters.[47]

The implementation of the RED was a laborious process in Estonia, which only produced a more or less satisfying result in December 2008, more than five years after the due implementation date of 19 July 2003. In the beginning of 2002 the Ministry of Justice prepared a Draft Law on Equality and Equal Treatment, which was later repealed because of political reasons, and was not resubmitted to Parliament. In 2003 the Act on the Legal Chancellor was amended, so as to give this body the competence to mediate in horizontal discrimination conflicts and to investigate complaints of discrimination by public bodies. In 2004, an anti-discrimination provision was inserted in the Employment Contracts Act, which implemented the provisions of the RED for the field of employment.[48] Even though the Estonian government considered these implementing exercises to be sufficient, the European Commission made

[44] The ineffectiveness of the Constitutional equality provision is illustrated by the decision of the Supreme Court, 3-2-1-37-05, 24 May 2005, in which the Supreme Court dismissed a discrimination claim because there was not a statutorily recognised ground at stake. The court did not even consider the possibility of applying the Constitutional equality provision, which applies an open-ended list of grounds.

[45] Article 152 of the Criminal Code prohibits the "unlawful restriction of the rights of a person or granting of unlawful preferences to a person on the basis of his or her nationality, race, colour, sex, language, origin, religion, political opinion, financial or social status". See the *Combined sixth and seventh periodic reports of the Republic of Estonia to the Commission on the Elimination of Racial Discrimination*, 1 April 2005, CERD/C/465/Add.1, para. 62, in which the government states that this provision has not yet been applied in practice.

[46] *Act on the Cultural Autonomy of Minorities*, adopted on 26 October 1993.

[47] *Second opinion on Estonia adopted on 24 February 2005*, Advisory Committee on the Framework Convention for national minorities, ACFC/OP/II(2005)001, para. 8.

[48] Poleshchuk (2006), at 54-55.

clear that further action had to be taken. From 2007 onwards, a number of Draft Equal Treatment Acts were submitted to Parliament, and were rejected by very small majorities. Finally, in 2008 the Equal Treatment Act (EETA) successfully passed Parliament and entered into force in 2009.[49] This Act implements the provisions of the RED and the FD and is the object of analysis in the following chapters. Where deemed relevant, mention is made of the provisions that were in place before the adoption of the EETA.

1.4.3. Hungary

Hungary entered the European Union in 2004, similarly to Estonia. Unlike Estonia, however, it had been a separate Republic under Soviet rule, and therefore its transition to a truly independent state was less disruptive. For instance, Hungary did not face complicated citizenship questions, and merely altered its existing constitution in order to align it with the Western European conception of a democratic society. The German Constitution provided important inspiration in this respect, and much of the current Hungarian Constitutional regime has been directly derived from the German framework, including the jurisprudence of the *Bundesverfassungsgericht*.

Demographically, the make-up of Hungarian society has been fairly stable throughout the Soviet period and thereafter. The greater part of its society consists of ethnic Hungarians (95 to 98 per cent); the second largest group are the Roma, who account for 2 to 5 per cent of the population, depending on the figures used. In addition, various small minorities from surrounding nations reside in Hungary, such as Germans, Slovaks, Croats, Romanians, Ukrainians and Serbs. Furthermore, the number of immigrants, mainly of Chinese origin, is growing steadily in Hungary.[50]

Most of these minorities are well integrated into society, and do not experience any particular problems. The big exception in this respect are the Roma, who are at the margins of society, both socially and economically, and whose very disadvantaged position is a cause of great concern for both the Hungarian state and the international community.[51] Many studies have been published as regards the high level of discrimination experienced by this

---

49 *Act 384 SE III on Equal Treatment*, adopted on 11 December 2008.

50 See http://www.minorityrights.org/5804/hungary/hungary-overview.html (accessed July 2009).

51 See for instance *ECRI Report on Hungary (fourth monitoring cycle)*, ECRI, 20 June 2008, paras. 75-150; *Roma: Discrimination starts with primary education*, Amnesty International, 2006, EUR 05/004/2006; *Resolution ResCMN(2005)10 on the implementation of the Framework Convention for the Protection of National Minorities*, Council of Europe, Committee of Ministers, 14 December 2005, para. 1(b). The European Roma Rights Center has furthermore published a number of reports on Roma discrimination throughout the European Union, see www.errc.org (accessed July 2009). See also the special website on this issue of the

group, in all important spheres of society, and as regards their overall backward position in society. The Hungarian state has initiated many programmes and measures to tackle this persistent problem, but so far this has not led to a measurable improvement. There are currently voices calling for intensifying European policy concerning the Roma, arguing that an integrated approach is necessary for this group, which is spread over many EU Member States,.[52] At the regional level, there has been some action already, notably the institution of a "Roma Decade of Inclusion".[53]

Prior to the implementation of the RED, Hungarian law contained a number of anti-discrimination provisions, none of which were considered to be very effective. Article 70/A of the Hungarian Constitution provided for the principle of non-discrimination, and an obligation for the state to endeavour to create equal opportunities for all.[54] In addition, Articles 75 sub 1 and 76 of the Civil Code provided a right not to be discriminated against, under the guise of the "protection of personal rights.[55] Various cases of discrimination have been brought before national courts on the basis of these provisions. However, the difficulty in proving discrimination and the lack of a clear definition of the concept of discrimination severely limited the practical relevance of the Civil Code provision.[56] Other generally worded anti-discrimination provisions could be found in the Labour Code, the decrees on the labour and consumer protection inspectorates, the Act on radio and television and the Public Education Act. The problem with most of these provisions was that they did not provide any clarification on the concept of discrimination and that their scope was limited. Moreover, many of these provisions were conceived as being merely

European Commission at http://ec.europa.eu/social/main.jsp?catId=518&langId=en (accessed July 2009).

52 O'Nions (2007), at 222; *Thematic comment no. 3, The protection of minorities in the European Union*, EU Network of Independent Experts on Fundamental Rights, 2005, CFR-CDF.ThemComm2005.en, at 52; De Schutter (2005), at 27-30.

53 See www.romadecade.org. The current participating countries in this initiative are Albania, Bosnia and Herzegovina, Bulgaria, Croatia, the Czech Republic, Hungary, Macedonia, Montenegro, Romania, Serbia, Slovakia and Spain.

54 The article reads as follows: "(1) [t]he Republic of Hungary shall respect the human rights and civil rights of all persons in the country without discrimination on the basis of race, color, gender, language, religion, political or other opinion, national or social origins, financial situation, birth or on any other grounds whatsoever. (2) The law shall provide for strict punishment of discrimination on the basis of Paragraph (1). (3) The Republic of Hungary shall endeavor to implement equal rights for everyone through measures that create fair opportunities for all."

55 Article 76 of the Civil Code provides that "the violation of civil rights is explicitly defined as any form of discrimination against private individuals in relation to their gender, race, ethnicity or religion, as well as the violation of their freedom of conscience, the unlawful restriction of their individual freedom, the violation of physical integrity and health, and human dignity."

56 Examples can be found in the various white booklets of the NEKI at www.neki.hu (accessed August 2009).

declaratory and were not acted upon by the competent authorities.[57] Hungarian criminal law furthermore contained provisions against discrimination, which were hardly applied in practice.[58] Despite the fact that they were very difficult to effectively rely on in practice, these provisions do reveal a relatively high level of attention for the principle of non-discrimination by the Hungarian legislator.

In a similar way, the Hungarian framework shows a high degree of minority sensitivity, which was mostly born of a concern for the situation of fellow ethnic Hungarians constituting minority groups in surrounding states.[59] Thus, Article 68 of the Constitution expresses the principle of effective participation of minorities in public life. In addition, the 1993 Act for National Minorities provides inter alia the right to local minority self-government for cultural matters and certain linguistic rights. This Act only applies to the officially recognised minorities, however. In order to be recognised as an official minority, a minority group needs to fulfil a number of criteria, and needs inter alia to reside on Hungarian territory for at least 100 years. There are currently thirteen of these recognised minorities which have received an official minority status.[60] Hungary has been criticised by the Advisory Committee on the FCNM for its restrictive approach in this respect, but has so far refused to abolish it.[61]

In 1995 a Parliamentary Commissioner for Minorities was appointed, who monitors compliance with the rights of minorities, and more generally represents their interests with the Hungarian authorities.[62] At the policy level, the Hungarian government has adopted a number of programmes to improve the situation of the Roma in fields such as employment, housing and education. Even though these various measures are criticised for not being sufficiently effective on some points, they do reveal that minority protection is relatively high on the Hungarian public agenda. This impression is reinforced by the fact that Hungary has signed and ratified all important international minority protection instruments, notably the FCNM and the European Charter for Regional or Minority Languages.[63]

[57] See the white booklets of the NEKI at www.neki.hu (accessed August 2009) for examples of the practical difficulties in applying the provisions.

[58] *CERD country report Hungary*, 2002, CERD/C/431/Add.1.

[59] Sasse (2004), at 73.

[60] http://www.minorityrights.org/5804/hungary/hungary-overview.html (accessed June 2009).

[61] *Second Report on Hungary*, Advisory Committee on the Framework Convention on the Protection of National Minorities, December 2004, ACFC/INF/OP/II(2004)003, at 8.

[62] http://www.kisebbsegiombudsman.hu/hir-189-the-parliamentary-commissioner-for.html (accessed June 2009).

[63] See Balázs (2004), at 131-148 for more elaborate discussions of the Hungarian minority protection regime. Also see Kovács (2002), at 207-217.

The implementation of the RED in Hungary took place in phases, the first of which entailed a piecemeal adaptation of a number of existing acts, such as the Labour Act and the Act on education. According to some critical voices, this basic implementation exercise did not suffice, and a comprehensive equality act was needed. Their criticism found resonance with the new socialist government that came to power in 2002, which successfully steered through Parliament a Draft Equal Treatment Act (HETA) that entered into force in 2004.[64] In the first years of application of this Act, a number of flaws were identified, which were remedied in one comprehensive amendment exercise in 2007, producing the 2007 version of the HETA that is analysed in this study. In addition to Hungarian courts, the main monitoring body for this Act is the Hungarian Authority on Equal Treatment (AET), an administrative institution that is competent to issue binding decisions and impose fines.[65]

1.4.4. The Netherlands

The Netherlands is one of the six founding Members of the European Union. Until the 1960s, Dutch society was very homogenous and there were no noticeable minority groups other than the Frisians, who live in the Northern part of the country and speak a different language from the rest of the population. Despite their different language, however, this group is considered as being part of the Dutch nation. Dutch society fundamentally altered when numerous migrant workers were recruited from Turkey, Morocco and Indonesia, many of whom settled permanently in the Netherlands. Currently, the Turkish, Moroccan and Indonesian minorities each account for approximately 2 per cent of the population. In addition, there are a number of migrants from Surinam and the Dutch Antilles, and immigrants from all over the world. Persons belonging to these 'new' minorities are structurally at a disadvantage compared to the rest of the population. They face for instance higher levels of unemployment, worse housing conditions and more discrimination in all areas of public life. Since 9/11 and two high-profile cases of political murders, anti-Islamism has been on the rise in the Netherlands, and public discourse on the integration of foreigners into Dutch society has sharpened considerably. Consequently, tensions between Muslims and the rest of the population have increased.[66]

The Netherlands has traditionally not maintained any specific legislation or policy for minority groups. In the beginning of the 1990s, a limited minority

64 *Act CXXV of 2003 on Equal Treatment and Promotion of Equal Opportunities*, of 28 December 2003. Also see Bitskey & Gyulavári (2004), at 3-6 for a more detailed overview of the Hungarian implementation process.

65 Ambrus (2010).

66 http://www.minorityrights.org/5246/netherlands/netherlands-overview.html (accessed June 2009).

policy was developed, which was focused on ensuring full participation of minorities in Dutch society, and not at safeguarding their separate identities. From the beginning of the new millennium onwards, the notion of 'minority policy' was abolished, and it was decided to develop thematic policies, aimed at vulnerable groups in particular domains of public life.[67] In addition, a fairly strict 'integration' policy was set in place, so as to ensure that newcomers in Dutch society had a sufficient level of knowledge of the Dutch culture and language.[68] All of this reflects a rather pragmatic attitude that mainly aims at achieving a stable and integrated society, with equal opportunities for all, and not at serving the identity-related needs of minority groups. Thus, it is mainly the first pillar of minority protection that is accommodated in the Dutch context.

The Dutch track record with regard to minority-relevant international instruments confirms this impression. The Netherlands has signed and ratified all general human rights and non-discrimination instruments, amongst which the ICCPR, ICERD and ECHR. It has been more reserved with regard to minority-specific instruments. On the occasion of the ratification of the FCNM, the Netherlands declared that it regards only the Frisians as a national minority, excluding the many immigrant groups in the country. Similarly, as regards the Language Charter of the Council of Europe, it declared that most provisions of this Charter were only applicable to the Frisian population.[69]

The strong focus on the first pillar of minority protection becomes furthermore visible in the strong Dutch anti-discrimination regime that was set in place in 1994, with the adoption of the General Equal Treatment Act (GETA), which protected against different forms of discrimination, amongst which racial and ethnic discrimination, in various domains of public life. As this Act provided for an elaborate anti-discrimination regime, the implementation of the RED did not require much adaptation. Those changes that were deemed necessary by the Dutch legislator were effectuated by the Implementation Act (IA), which entered into force in April 2004.[70] In addition to the Dutch courts, the Dutch Equal Treatment Commission (ETC) is the main monitoring body for the GETA. The ETC can only issue non-binding opinions, and cannot impose any sanctions.[71]

---

[67] Fernandes Mendes (2004), at 624-625.

[68] See for a detailed description of the Dutch policy in this regard *Integratienota 2007-2011: zorg dat je erbij hoort!* ("Memo on Integration 2007-2011: make sure you participate!") of the Dutch Ministry of Public Housing, Environmental Planning and Environment at www.minvrom.nl (accessed June 2009).

[69] For the full text of the declaration see the website of the Council of Europe at www.coe.int (accessed June 2009).

[70] *Act amending the General Equal Treatment Act and some other acts implementing directive 2000/43/EC and directive 2000/78/EC*, published on 30 March 2004.

[71] Ambrus (2010).

Chapter 2

Personal Scope

For the purposes of this Directive, the principle of equal treatment shall mean that there shall be no direct or indirect discrimination based on racial or ethnic origin (Article 2(1) RED)

This directive shall apply to all persons, as regards both the public and private sectors, including public bodies (Article 3(1) RED)

This directive does not cover difference of treatment based on nationality (Article 3(2) RED)

Part one: Theoretical framework

2.1. Introduction

The personal scope provisions of the RED designate the addressees and beneficiaries of the provisions contained in this instrument. These provisions constitute one of the preliminary barriers to a successful claim of discrimination: if a claim is targeted against a non-addressee or submitted by a non-beneficiary, it will not be examined on the merits. The personal scope of the RED is regulated by Articles 3(1) and 3(2), the implementation of which raises a number of theoretical questions that will be discussed in this section.

Section 2.2 explores the circle of addressees of the RED, and examines two distinct issues. First, the exact delineation of the circle of addressees targeted by the RED is to some extent dependent on the manner in which the material scope provisions of the RED are interpreted. The formulations used in Article 3(1) to circumscribe the material scope raise the impression that a limited number of particularly responsible persons are targeted, whereas the reference in Article 3(1) to 'all persons' would seem to suggest that simply all persons active in a particular field are covered. This complexity is more closely analysed in section 2.2.1. Second, seeing that 'all persons' refers to both public and private actors, the potential differentiation in the application of anti-discrimination law to these different types of actors is examined in section 2.2.2.

In section 2.3 the beneficiaries of the anti-discrimination provisions of the RED are looked upon in more detail. Here also, a number of more specific questions arise. First of all, 'racial' and 'ethnic' origin can be interpreted in various ways, involving a complex of sociological realities that in some way must be integrated into legally workable concepts. The proper conceptualisation of 'racial' and 'ethnic' origin is discussed in section 2.3.1.

Second, practice has shown that various protected characteristics can interact in different ways and consequently complicate the application of anti-discrimination law, which assumes neatly separated grounds of discrimination. Section 2.3.2 explores the most pressing questions in this regard. Thirdly, Article 3(2) RED poses a potentially important obstacle for the effective application of the provisions of the RED, by excluding differences in treatment based on nationality from its scope. In reality, such differences in treatment are not easily distinguished from racial discrimination, in particular indirect racial discrimination. Section 2.3.3 examines the implications of this exception clause for the application of the provisions of the RED.

Finally, it needs to be clarified which types of victims of discrimination are envisaged by the RED, which is the topic of section 2.3.4.

2.2. Addressees of anti-discrimination legislation

2.2.1. 'All persons'

Article 3(1) RED applies what would appear to be a straightforward approach to the circle of addressees of the RED. By mentioning 'all persons' as the target group, it would seem to include all possible actors, both legal and natural.[1] However, the 'all persons' phrase is deceptively simple, as it stands in a complex relationship to the material scope provisions of Article 3(1) RED, which point to certain specific actors.

[1] Even though 'all persons' could also be read as referring to the beneficiaries of the RED, rather than to the addressees, it is submitted that the present interpretation is the most likely one. This proposition is supported by the fact that the personal scope provision of *Council Directive 2004/113/EC implementing the principle of equal treatment between men and women in the access to and supply of goods and services* clearly employs the 'all persons' phrase as referring to the addressees of this directive. Article 3(1) of this directive provides that it "shall apply to *all persons who provide* goods and services" (emphasis added, MB). Moreover, most authors who comment on the 'all persons' aspect of Article 3 regard it as referring to

A few examples may clarify this. Article 3(1)(a) refers to "conditions for access to employment", and formally keeps silent on who has to uphold the anti-discrimination provisions in this domain. Inadvertently however, the phrase points to a specific kind of actor, since most people will assume that the envisaged actor is the employer, and perhaps the intermediary that mediates between employer and employee. What to do then with situations in which other persons than the employer/intermediary discriminate in this field of application? For example, a co-worker could try to undermine the work of his colleague, or even harass him, in order to ensure that their superior does not consider him for a promotion. It is not certain that such instances of discrimination fall under Article 3(1)(a). In a similar way, it is a matter of argumentation whether subsections 3(1)(e) (healthcare), 3(1)(g) (education) or 3(1)(h) (provision of goods and services) are intended to target discriminatory actions of patients, students or service recipients. These persons are after all not the principally envisaged actors in the respective fields of application.

The question therefore arises how broadly the 'all persons' phrase should be interpreted. A broad interpretation would simply bring everybody doing anything in the enumerated domains within the scope of the non-discrimination provisions. With regard to the given examples, co-workers, students and patients/clients would all have to adhere to the non-discrimination principle. A narrow interpretation on the other hand would take 'all persons' to mean in practice 'all persons principally envisaged within the enumerated fields of application', covering only employers, school boards, teachers and service providers.

From a viewpoint of effectiveness, a broad interpretation of 'all persons' seems to be called for. After all, the behaviour of non-principally envisaged actors can have serious repercussions for members of minority groups, and the applicability of anti-discrimination law to these actors would clearly enhance the level of protection offered by anti-discrimination law.[2] The ECJ indeed tends to interpret equality law provisions extensively for reasons of

the addressees of the Directive. See Gijzen (2006), at 152; Holtmaat (2004), at 97; Whittle (2002), at 316. Also see contra Van den Berghe (2003), at 176. As regards the inclusion of legal persons as potential perpetrators of discrimination, see *Amended proposal for a Council Directive implementing the principle of equal treatment between persons irrespective of racial or ethnic origin*, Commission of the European Communities, 1999/0253 (CNS), 31 May 2000, in which it is stated that the term 'persons' has been chosen over 'individuals' so as to cover legal persons as well.

2 Compare *ECRI General Policy Recommendation no. 7 on national legislation to combat racism and racial discrimination*, 13 December 2002, para. 24 of the Explanatory Memorandum, which provides that: "[t]he prohibition of discrimination should not only target those who make goods and services available to others, but also those who receive goods and services from others, as would be the case of a company which selects the providers of a given good or service on the basis of one of the enumerated grounds". See for a clear example of the impact of actions of non-principally envisaged actors ECtHR *Sampanis and others v. Greece*, no. 32526/05, 5 June 2008, paras. 18-23, in which a description is given of the manner in which parents of

effectiveness,[3] which, in addition to the fact that the word 'all' in itself points to an inclusive approach, would support a broad reading of 'all persons' to be adopted in the future.[4]

Still, there are indicators pointing to a narrow understanding of 'all persons' at the European level. First, pre-RED European equality law mainly focused on public actors, and applied only to a very limited category of private actors, all of which were principally envisaged actors. In gender equality law, employers and social partners were targeted.[5] In the field of free movement, employers were targeted by Regulation 1612/68, and the ECJ applied the prohibition of nationality discrimination to the actions of employers or other "powerful collective actors", such as international sports associations.[6] A second indicator of a narrow interpretation is found in the formulation of the personal scope provisions of one of the more recent gender equality directives. Recital 13 and Article 3 of the Directive on gender equality in the provision of goods and services refer to "persons *providing*" and "persons who *provide*" goods and services respectively (emphasis added, MB).[7] The use of the verb 'provide' suggests that receivers of services are not targeted by the prohibition of discrimination, and that only the principally envisaged actors in this field, that is, providers of goods and services, are covered.

The relevance of the issue admittedly depends to some extent on the broader national framework in which the provisions implementing the RED are embedded. A narrow understanding of 'all persons' does not necessarily mean that persons other than the principally envisaged persons can discriminate at will. A lack of direct liability of these actors could be mitigated in a number of ways. One alternative would be to provide for attributed or vicarious liability of principally envisaged actors for discrimination perpetrated by subordinates

---

non-Roma students harassed Roma parents and their children, in order to prevent them from enrolling in a local school.

3 Barrett (2003), at 121; McCrudden (2003), at 7.

4 Gijzen (2006), at 152; Holtmaat (2004), at 97; Whittle (2002), at 316.

5 See specifically Articles 3, 4 and 5 of *Council Directive 76/207/EEC of 9 February 1976 on the implementation of the principle of equal treatment for men and women as regards access to employment, vocational training and promotion, and working conditions*, and Articles 4 and 5 of *Council Directive 92/85/EEC of 19 October 1992 on the introduction of measures to encourage improvements in the safety and health at work of pregnant workers and workers who have recently given birth or are breastfeeding* for the obligations imposed on employers. See furthermore *Council Directive 86/378/EEC of 24 July 1986 on the implementation of the principle of equal treatment for men and women in occupational social security schemes* on the implementation of the principle of equal treatment for men and women in occupational social security, which applies also to social partners.

6 Craig & De Búrca (2003), at 771; Davies (2002), at 224-227; Preedy (2000), at 130. The term "powerful collective actors" is borrowed from Craig & De Búrca (2003), at 771.

7 *Council Directive 2004/113/EC of 13 December 2004 implementing the principle of equal treatment between men and women in the access to and supply of goods and services.*

or third parties.[8] A second alternative would be to expand the direct liability of principally envisaged persons, holding them directly responsible for making sure that their subordinates or clients do not discriminate.[9] These types of liability regimes could to a large extent undo the disadvantages of not being able to hold non-principally envisaged actors accountable for discriminatory behaviour. Even more generally, these regimes can be said to enhance the effectiveness of anti-discrimination law, by attributing responsibility to those who are relatively more powerful and resourceful.

It should not be overlooked, however, that these liability regimes cannot remedy all disadvantages connected to a lack of liability of non-principally envisaged actors. Especially in the more serious discrimination cases victims have the psychological need to see the actual perpetrator held accountable. In this regard, direct liability of non-principally envisaged actors is still desirable, and is ideally combined with extended liability regimes for principally envisaged actors.[10]

2.2.2. 'As regards both the public and private sectors, including public bodies'

2.2.2.1. Applicability of the RED in the case of incorrect or untimely implementation

The RED envisages application of national anti-discrimination law to both public and private actors. The latter aspect is a novelty: whereas the greater part of EC equality law had focused on the obligations of Member States and public authorities,[11] the RED in 2000 introduced far-reaching obligations for private actors as regards non-discrimination. However, this feature of the RED only comes fully into play in the case of timely and correct implementation by the Member States. To the extent that Member States do not fulfil their implementation task correctly or timely, the RED provisions cannot be invoked against private actors, since provisions of directives do not have direct horizontal effect.[12] Victims of discrimination perpetrated by private

[8] See for example Roberts (2001) on the regulation liability in the UK, and White (1996) on the regulation of liability in American anti-discrimination law.

[9] See sections 4.8, 5.3, 6.2.3 and 7.2.4 that discuss the possibility of inferring positive duties from the provisions of the RED.

[10] See also Ambrus (2010) on liability matters in the context of the RED.

[11] To a limited extent a number of principally envisaged actors were covered: see section 2.2.1.

[12] Jans et al (2007), at 78. To some extent, though, provisions of directives can have indirect horizontal effect, when an individual's reliance on the direct effect of a provision against a public authority has repercussions for other private persons (Jans et al (2007), at 78-82). However, since this still entails the involvement of a public actor, it cannot be said to fill the

actors then have no other option than to claim damages from the State for not having properly implemented the provisions of the directive, which is not a very desirable situation.[13]

Conversely, public actors are presumably covered by the RED, regardless of the manner in which implementation takes place at the national level. This follows from the doctrine of direct effect, which entails that those provisions that are sufficiently clear and precise can be applied vis-à-vis public actors after the expiration of the implementation date.[14] Since the provisions of the RED are generally considered to be sufficiently clear and precise, actions of public actors will probably be governed by the provisions of the RED, even if correct and timely national implementation has not taken place.[15]

2.2.2.2. Differentiation between public and private actors

In the case of appropriate implementation by the Member States, the aforementioned rules on direct effect are not relevant, and public and private actors are equally bound by the national provisions on racial and ethnic discrimination. This raises the question whether these provisions should be applied in a similar fashion to both types of actors. There are after all essential differences between private persons and public actors, which could and perhaps should have an impact on the manner in which the provisions of the RED are applied to them. In this section, three possibilities are mentioned: the consideration of fundamental rights and freedoms of private actors; the application of a margin of appreciation for public actors; and the imposition of further-reaching obligations on public actors.

void of the absence of a doctrine of direct horizontal effect. See also Arnull (2006), at 239-252. According to Jans (2007), at 63, fundamental principles of Community law do have direct horizontal application. Thus, if the ECJ would recognise that the principle of racial and ethnic equality is a fundamental principle of Community law, as it has done in ECJ *Werner Mangold v. Rüdiger Helm*, Case C-144/04, 22 November 2005, for the principle of non-discrimination based on age, the RED could potentially be indirectly applied in horizontal settings, as laying down the principle of racial and ethnic equality. The ECJ has not yet pronounced on this matter.

13 Jans et al (2007), at 78.

14 Jans et al (2007), at 63-96.

15 Ellis (2005), at 215. See also the opinion of A-G Colomer in ECJ *Tadao Maruko v. Versorgungsanstalt der deutchen Bühnen*, C-267/06, 6 September 2007, para. 33, in which he argues that the provisions of the FD have direct effect. This could apply, mutatis mutandis, to the provisions of the RED, which to a large extent resemble those of the FD. As to the ECJ's approach to what constitutes a public body, see Craig & De Búrca (2003), at 209-210.

2.2.2.2.1. Fundamental rights and freedoms of private actors

Private actors have fundamental rights and freedoms that should be respected, as opposed to public authorities. These rights and freedoms of private actors are bound to influence the interpretation of some of the concepts of the RED.[16] This does not only flow from the fact that the first recitals of the RED firmly place the directive within the international human rights framework, but also from the case law of the ECJ, which has committed itself to uphold international human rights in its own jurisprudence.[17] This court will therefore take note of the broader human rights framework when applying the RED, which can occur at two levels.

First, fundamental rights and freedoms can have an impact on the interpretation of certain elements of the material scope. It could for instance be argued that certain actions of religious institutions are too closely connected to the freedom of religion to be covered by anti-discrimination law. Similarly, it is defensible that a decision to employ a personal care-taker is covered by the right to privacy and should not be covered by anti-discrimination law. Along similar lines of thought, Article 3(1)(h) RED contains an 'available to the public' clause, which delineates the field of goods and services in order to safeguard the freedom of association and the right to privacy.[18] Section 3.2.2. further discusses the manner in which fundamental rights and freedoms of private actors can impact on the material scope of the RED.

Second, fundamental rights and freedoms can be taken on board in the application of the substantive discrimination concepts of the RED, especially the justification possibilities for direct and indirect discrimination. For instance, the right to privacy of a private employer could inform the interpretation of the genuine and determining occupational requirement (GDOR) of Article 4 RED. Similarly, in a case in which a person wants a resident tenant to speak her native language, her right to privacy could be taken into account in the application of the objective justification test for indirect discrimination. In addition, the freedom of expression of a person who is accused of having created a hostile environment by making certain remarks could be considered in the application of the concept of harassment. The relevance of fundamental rights and freedoms for the substantive discrimination concepts will be

---

16 Compare Bell (2008), at 12, who points out that conflicts of rights that may emerge in the application of some of the anti-discrimination provisions, the resolution of which should be brought into line with international human rights instruments.

17 De Witte (1999), at 867-869. This does not mean, however, that the ECJ is bound by the interpretation of the various international supervisory bodies that oversee compliance with international human rights treaties. Still, it does take their quasi-jurisprudence into account when interpreting these rights. See Henrard (2007), at 32-33; Rosas (2004), at 488-489.

18 See section 3.3.5.

discussed in the relevant chapters in this study. For the GDOR, see section 3.5.2; for the objective justification test, see sections 5.2.4.2, 5.2.4.4; for harassment, see section 6.2.2.3.

It should be emphasised that, even though concern for fundamental rights and freedoms is requisite, it cannot lower the minimum baseline of protection required by the RED. This arguably means that the tool of interpretation can and should be used to safeguard these rights in the application of the RED's provisions, but that no additional delineations of the material scope, nor additional justification possibilities for the substantive concepts, may be set in place.

2.2.2.2.2. Margin of appreciation for public actors

Public actors have particular qualities for which they are often granted a margin of appreciation as regards the way in which they carry out their human rights obligations. The underlying rationale of a margin of appreciation doctrine is that states are expected to be acting in the interest of society as a whole, which should put more weight to their interest in comparison with that of self-serving individuals. Moreover, public actors are generally regarded as primary responsible for the observance of human rights and as better placed than supervisory organs to assess facts and perform balancing acts.[19]

Traces of margin of appreciation-thinking have already appeared in the ECJ's judgments in the field of gender equality, where the Court so far has been relatively lenient vis-à-vis public actors as regards social policy matters.[20] It is not unlikely that the ECJ will in a similar way be more lenient with regard to public actors when applying the provisions of the RED, especially in those fields that for the greater part belong to the competence of Member States.[21] The ECJ has already applied the margin of appreciation doctrine in the context of the FD, which was adopted a few months after the RED and resembles the RED in many respects. In *Mangold*, involving a claim of age discrimination, the ECJ affirmed the 'broad discretion' that Member States have in designing social policy.[22]

In a similar fashion, national courts may grant public authorities a margin of appreciation as to the fulfilment of their duties under the RED. It is to be

[19] Van de Lanotte & Haeck (2005), at 205; Benvenisti (1999), at 846; Schokkenbroek (1998), at 31. Also see Arai-Takahashi (2002) for an overview of the margin of appreciation doctrine as developed and applied by the ECtHR.

[20] Tobler (2005), at 245. See also the opinion of A-G Sharpston in ECJ *Bartsch v. BSH*, Case C-427/06, 22 May 2008, para. 118, in which she mentions "the broad discretion which Member States enjoy in the field of social and employment policy".

[21] See section 3.2.1 on the potential impact of the division of competences between the EU and Member States on national implementation of the material scope of the RED.

[22] ECJ *Werner Mangold v. Rüdiger Helm*, Case C-144/04, 22 November 2005, para. 63.

hoped that they will use prudence when doing so, since too much leeway for public actors could seriously undermine the effectiveness of the RED. This risk is especially present in those Member States where there is little knowledge of and attention for the situation of minorities. In such contexts there is a real danger of structural and systemic forms of discrimination going undetected, or even being expressly permitted.

2.2.2.2.3. Further-reaching duties for public actors

Whereas the margin of appreciation doctrine implies more leeway for public actors, there are also strong arguments for applying stricter scrutiny vis-à-vis public actors as compared to private actors. After all, public actors represent the Member State in their actions, and this exemplary function could call for further-reaching obligations for these actors than for private actors. In addition, the State, as represented by public actors, has primary responsibility for the application of human rights and must exclusively serve the general interest and the individual interests of its citizens. Individuals, to the contrary, are allowed to exclusively pursue their own interests, and to be irrational, within the limits of the law.[23] Moreover, public actors generally have more expertise and more resources at their disposal than private individuals, which should affect the way in which their respective actions are assessed.

These arguments could be used to set in place a higher level of protection against discrimination perpetrated by public actors. For instance, the justification possibilities of the RED could be applied with stricter scrutiny for these actors. In addition, positive duties to promote the principle of equality or to undo the effects of past discrimination could (primarily) be imposed on public actors, who are generally best suited for these kinds of obligations. Both scholars and experts have strongly emphasised the need to impose such duties on public actors in order to make anti-discrimination law more effective.[24] Imposing stricter requirements and perhaps even positive duties on public actors would clearly enhance the level of protection of national anti-discrimination law.

---

[23] Lerner (2003), at 32; Alexander (1992), at 154.

[24] See the *Ninth Report of the House of Lords Select Committee on the European Union,* 16 May 2000, paras. 154-60; Fredman (2005) and (2005a); Waddington (2003), at 51-2; Hepple et al (2000), at 59-64; Howard (2005), at 480; *ECRI General Policy Recommendation no. 7*, on national legislation to combat racism and racial discrimination, 13 December 2002, paras. 7, 8 and 9 of Chapter III. Compare Reddy (2006), at 301, who discusses the South-African antidiscrimination system, which entails stricter positive duties for public actors than for private ones.

2.3. Beneficiaries of anti-discrimination legislation

2.3.1. Conceptualisation of 'racial' and 'ethnic' origin

Only persons who are targeted in relation to the grounds racial or ethnic origin can invoke the implemented provisions of the RED. The circle of beneficiaries of this Directive is therefore determined by the meaning of 'racial' and 'ethnic' origin. In this regard it is a missed opportunity that the RED does not offer a definition of 'racial' and 'ethnic' origin, which refer to vague notions that are not easily delineated.[25] Even though the ECJ made clear in *Chacón Navas* that it prefers uniform and autonomous definitions of the grounds of discrimination, it can take a long time before this Court gets the opportunity to pronounce on the matter.[26] Thus, the conceptualisation of 'racial' and 'ethnic' origin will primarily take place at the national level.

2.3.1.1. Race and ethnicity as social constructs

It is important in this respect to recognise that 'racial' and 'ethnic' origin do not refer to clearly delineable categories. Racism is commonly understood as being connected to a notion that only exists in the minds of the persons committing it. Obviously, there are certain real characteristics that trigger racist behaviour, such as skin colour or other physical traits. However, the characteristic they are considered to be proxies for, i.e. race, does not exist from an objective point of view. It is beyond dispute that the notion of different human races is not a biological reality.[27] It is a psychological and social construct, called into existence in people's minds, and through societal patterns.[28]

In a similar way ethnicity is recognised to be a socially constructed concept; not so much because it would not exist at all, but rather because it is in essence highly indeterminable and not easily tied back to neatly distinguishable groups. There are many factors involved in determining which ethnic groups exist, which moreover can change over time. Moreover, different people have

25 Many authors have criticised this lack of definition. See inter alia Jones (2003), at 517; Brennan (2003), at 320-324; Brown (2002), at 204; Barnard (2001), at 968; Guild (2000), at 418.

26 ECJ *Chacón Navas v. Eurest Colectividades*, Case C13/05, 11 July 2006, para. 40.

27 Winant (2006), at 987; Ford (1994), at 1239.

28 Howard (2008), at 10; Fredman (2001a), at 9-10; Bulmer and Solomos (1998), at 822-825; Banton (1996), at 76-82; Ford (1994), at 1232. See also Recital 6 in the preamble of the RED: "The European Union rejects theories which attempt to determine the existence of separate human races. The use of the term 'racial origin' in this Directive does not imply an acceptance of such theories".

different perspectives on what ethnic groups a society is made of. In this sense, ethnicity cannot be fixed in scientific terms: it is determined by those who have to deal with it in everyday practice.[29]

Racial or ethnic discrimination in this respect is different from discrimination on the basis of nationality or gender, which are characteristics that can be *objectively* established. 'Racial' or 'ethnic' origin, to the contrary, are *subjectively* established, depending on particular conceptions of in-groups and out-groups in society. Since these conceptions vary in time and space, different proxies are used to single these groups out. For example, in Dutch society a person's adherence to Islam is an obvious proxy for membership of the Turkish or Moroccan community, since most members of these communities are Muslims. Similarly, since in Estonia the most prominent minority group is constituted by Russian speakers, the characteristic of speaking Russian is often used to single out persons belonging to this minority group.

Any conceptualisation of 'racial' or 'ethnic' origin should build on this reality and should not aim for once-and-for-all delineation of the groups connected to these grounds. National legislators and judges should be attentive to the governing perception of the racial and/or ethnic relations in a given society, and should beware of understanding 'racial' and 'ethnic' origin in an absolute or essentialist way.[30] This means that they must have regard for public perceptions as to which in-groups and out-groups exist in society at a given time, involving both self-perception of the members of the presumed groups, and perception by society as a whole.[31] Moreover, they should be alert with regard to the particular proxies used in a particular society to identify

[29] Brubaker (2004), at 79-85; Bulmer and Solomos (1998), at 822-825; Poulter (1998), at 6.

[30] McColgan (2007), at 76; Lerner (2003), at 56; Schiek (2002), at 313; Choudry (2000), at 167-168; Guild (2000a), at 75.

[31] Lerner (2003), at 39; Schiek (2002), at 313; Compare A-G Geelhoed in the *Chacón Navas* case, C-13/05, para. 66, in which he argues that: "in developing a uniform interpretation of 'disability', account should be taken of the (…) dynamic aspect of society's perception of the phenomenon 'disability'." See for an example of such a dynamic approach *An intersectional approach to discrimination: addressing multiple grounds in human rights claims*, Ontario Human Rights Commission, Policy Paper, at www.ohrc.on.ca/english/consultations/intersectionality-discussion-papers.html, (accessed August 2009): "In Canada, the focus is increasingly on a contextualized approach to discrimination: less emphasis on characteristics of the individual and more on society's response to the person. Also move towards an analysis of discrimination that takes into account the lived realities of individuals and the social context of discrimination." Another well-known example is the judgment of the House of Lords (HoL) of the United Kingdom *Mandla v. Dowell Lee and Others* 1983, IRLR 209, according to which 'race' should be attributed a broad meaning, covering a wide range of factors. The HoL mentioned inter alia the consciousness of the members of the group of a long-shared history as distinguishing it from other groups, and the characteristic of being a minority or being an oppressed or a dominant group within a larger community. These latter factors clearly were meant to take into account societal realities. However, the manner in which the HoL applied this approach has been criticised for not including religiously-affiliated groups such as Muslims and Rastafarians, see inter alia Brennan (2003), at 322, and infra in this section.

persons belonging to perceived out-groups.[32] In this respect, national courts and bodies can draw from the international human rights framework, which provides insight into the proxies that are commonly employed to construct racial or ethnic groups in modern societies.

2.3.1.2. Proxies for racism recognised in international human rights law

The relevant international instruments apply different lists of grounds regarding racial discrimination. The International Convention on the Elimination of all forms of Racial Discrimination (ICERD) lists "race, colour, descent, or national or ethnic origin", whereas the two general UN human rights treaties (ICCPR and ICESCR) refer to "race, colour, national or social origin". The ECHR also applies this latter list, with the additional ground of "association with a national minority". The ILO Convention C.111 concerning Discrimination in Respect of Employment and Occupation lists "race, colour, national extraction or social origin".

The interpretation of these grounds by the various supervisory bodies is tightly connected to the contemporary perception of what constitutes racism. According to this perception, racist behaviour is firstly triggered by visual, biological characteristics of persons, such as their skin colour, or certain physiological traits.[33] These physiological proxies employed for perpetrating racism are commonly understood to be captured by the ground 'race' in its narrow understanding, and partially by the ground 'colour'.[34]

Secondly, it is increasingly understood that racism is about treating persons differently on account of non-physiological characteristics, such as their cultural, religious, linguistic, historical or geographical affiliations.[35] Especially culture[36] and religion[37] have recently received much attention as

[32] O'Cinnéide (2003), at 77. For an application of this argument to American anti-discrimination law in employment, see Rich (2004).

[33] Howard (2008), at 12; Schiek (1999), at 79.

[34] Schiek et al (2007), at 46; Henrard (2000), at 49. See also ECtHR *Timishev v. Russia*, no. 55762/00 and 55974/00, 13 December 2005, para. 55.

[35] Howard (2008), at 11-14; Van Dooren (1997), at 29-34; Modood (1992), at 227-228; Van Dijk (1988), at 7.

[36] Makkonen (2004), at 166; Brennan (2003), at 324; Poulter (1998), at 10.

[37] Alves (2008); Poulter (1998), at 10. The UN Special Rapporteur on contemporary forms of racism, racial discrimination, xenophobia and related intolerance has devoted a number of recent reports on the regained role of religion in contemporary forms of racism. See E/CN.4/2005/18/Add.4, E/CN.4/2003/23, and E/CN.4/2006/17. The CERD has also referred to the link between race and religion in its concluding observations numerous times. Examples can be found in *Concluding Observations on Ghana*, 2003, CERD/C/62/C)/04, para. 16; *Concluding Observations on the United Kingdom*, 2003, CERD/C/63/CO/ 11, para. 20; *Concluding Observations on Turkmenistan*, 2003, CERD/C/TKM/CO/5, para. 17. Even at the European level, the close link between racism and religion has been recognised, especially with regard

proxies employed to perpetrate racist behaviour. Adherence to Islam is for instance often used to single out persons belonging to Arab communities. Moreover, nowadays even socio-economic origin or class is sometimes considered to be a factor involved in racism.[38] For example, if a particular ethnic group is known to live in a particular area of the city, postal codes can be used to covertly target this group. These non-physiological proxies for racism are captured at the international level by the grounds 'ethnic origin' or 'national origin/extraction', 'association with a national minority' or 'descent'. More specifically, 'ethnic origin' refers to a combination of cultural, linguistic, historical ties,[39] and is capable of covering the modern proxy of religion as well.[40] 'National origin' and 'association with a national minority' are connected to the ethnic – as opposed to civic – notion of a nation, which generally refers to the state people originate from, and can comprise more than one ethnic group.[41] 'Descent' points to caste-like systems and other structures of social stratification, and thus accommodates the modern proxy for racism of social origin or class.[42] The latter factors are probably also captured by the ground 'social origin'. 'Race' in its broad understanding is considered to cover all of the aforementioned proxies, both the physiological and the non-physiological.[43]

2.3.1.3. Interpretation of 'racial' and 'ethnic' origin of Article 2(1) RED

National interpretations of 'racial' and 'ethnic' origin of Article 2(1) RED should preferably follow the inclusive international understanding of race-related grounds. 'Racial origin' should accordingly be interpreted as broadly as the term 'race' in the international context, referring to physiological and non-physiological characteristics that are used to single out persons belonging to perceived out-groups.

---

to Muslims, see *Muslims in the European Union: Discrimination and Islamophobia*, EUMC 2006. See also Schiek (2002), at 312, who points out that religion may not only sometimes be involved in direct racial discrimination, but also with indirect racial discrimination. See section 2.3.2.1 on this point.

38 Howard (2008), at 12; Banton (1996), at 70-71; Modood (1992), at 229. See also *CERD General Recommendation No. 29, on Descent*, 1 November 2002, according to which relevant factors to recognise descent-based communities are, amongst others, private and public segregation, including in housing and education and access to public spaces.

39 Schiek et al (2007), at 47; Henrard (2000), at 49; Van Dooren (1997), at 29; Weis (1979), at 3. See also ECtHR *Timishev v. Russia*, no. 55762/00 and 55974/00, 13 December 2005, para. 55.

40 Safran (2008), at 178 and 184-187; Schiek et al (2007), at 60-61.

41 Schiek et al (2007), at 56-57 and 66; Van Dijk (1988), at 7.

42 Van Dooren (1997), at 29. See also *CERD General Recommendation No. 29, on Descent*, 1 November 2002.

43 Henrard (2008), at 243; Schiek et al (2007), at 47.

'Ethnic origin' would then refer to the non-physiological characteristics mentioned above, and could be interpreted as capturing cultural, linguistic and historical characteristics.[44] In addition, the more recently used proxies for racism, such as religion and social status, could be included in this ground.

It has been submitted that coverage of the characteristic of religion is doubtful, since this ground is separately regulated by the FD.[45] Still, it should be emphasised that inclusion of the proxy of religion for racism does not undermine any separate regulation of religious discrimination, because religious discrimination is essentially different from racial discrimination perpetrated by making use of the proxy of religion. Whereas the latter type of discrimination is essentially about disadvantaging persons because they belong to a perceived out-group for which the proxy happens to be religion, religious discrimination is about disadvantaging persons exactly on account of their religion. In other words, there is a difference between discriminating against a Muslim because he belongs to a group of persons that are believed to be unreliable or less intelligent than others, i.e. racism, and discriminating against a person because one rejects his religion, i.e. religious discrimination. Even though it may sometimes be difficult to apply this distinction in practice, it is a conceptually valid one. This argument is supported by Article 1(3) of the *Framework Decision on Racism and Xenophobia* adopted by the Council in the pillar of Judicial and Home Affairs. This article explicitly recognises the possibility of religion being used as a proxy for race, and provides that: "the reference to religion is intended to cover, at least, conduct which is a *pretext* for directing acts against a group of persons or a member of such group defined by reference to race, colour, descent, or national or ethnic origin" (emphasis added, MB).[46]

It is repeated here that, in addition to the proxies recognised at the international level, national understandings of 'racial' and 'ethnic' origin should preferably include those proxies that are used in the particular national societies. For example, in the Netherlands out-groups are often defined in terms of 'foreigners' or 'asylum seekers', and these designations should therefore be considered as being covered by 'racial' or 'ethnic' origin.

2.3.1.4. Alternatives in the case of an inflexible approach

It should be noted that, in the case of a narrow and/or inflexible interpretation of 'racial' and 'ethnic' origin at the national level, there are a number of alternatives available in order to bring relevant proxies under the scope of anti-discrimination law.

---

44 Ellis (2005), at 30.

45 Howard (2008), at 26; Henrard (2007), at 23; Guild (2000), at 418.

46 *Council Framework Decision on combating certain forms and expressions of racism and xenophobia by means of criminal law*, adopted on 28 November 2008, 2008/913/JHA.

First, the concept of indirect racial discrimination could be used to cover distinctions based on a characteristic that is a potential proxy for 'racial' or 'ethnic' origin but is not recognised as such by the national legislator and/or courts. After all, these proxies generally refer to groups that are predominantly composed of persons that have a different racial or ethnic origin from the majority of the population, and any distinction based on these proxies thus disproportionately disadvantages a racial or ethnic group. The UK context provides an example of this option. In the UK, the particular interpretation of 'race' by the House of Lords excluded religiously affiliated groups that did not share a particular geographic background, and therefore ruled out the possibility of the proxy of religion being used to perpetrate racism against, for instance, Muslims.[47] UK courts compensated for this lack of protection by qualifying discrimination based on a person's Muslim religion as indirect racial discrimination.[48] Scholars have pointed out that a similar mechanism could be used in the context of the RED in the case of a strict interpretation of 'racial' or 'ethnic' origin. The concept of indirect racial discrimination could accordingly be used to protect persons against racism perpetrated by making use of the proxies of language and religion.[49] However, this option is of a second-best nature, in view of the lower level of protection that applies to indirect racial discrimination: the RED permits hardly any justification possibilities for direct discrimination, while providing for an open justification possibility for indirect racial discrimination.[50]

Second, separate regulation of discrimination based on proxies that are commonly used to designate out-groups could provide a meaningful alternative in the case of a narrow interpretation of 'racial' and 'ethnic' origin. For instance, the problems related to a narrow understanding of 'race' in the UK context more or less evaporated with the adoption of separate protection against religious discrimination.[51] Similarly, additional regulation of discrimination on race-related grounds both at the national and European level would mitigate the effects of a narrow understanding of 'racial' and 'ethnic' origin in the RED context. In this regard, mention should be made of the FD, which regulates discrimination based on religion, and which is likely to be complemented in the future with a directive expanding the scope of protection against religious discrimination to all fields covered by the RED.[52] The next

[47] See Brennan (2003), at 322; Gearty (2000), at 336-339.

[48] Monaghan (2007), at 227. See for example House of Lords, *J.H. Walker Limited v. Hussain*, 1996, ICR 291.

[49] Howard (2005), at 475-476; Brown (2002), at 204-205.

[50] See sections 4.4 and 5.2.4 on the justification possibilities for direct and indirect discrimination respectively.

[51] Monaghan (2007), at 229.

[52] *Proposal for a Council Directive on implementing the principle of equal treatment between persons irrespective of religion or belief, disability, age or sexual orientation*, COM(2008) 426 final, 2008/0140 (CNS).

section discusses this option and reveals that it can only offer limited redress, at least at the European level, in view of the current differences in the level of protection for the different grounds of discrimination in European law.

Third, it has been submitted that an open-ended list of grounds of discrimination in national anti-discrimination law could mitigate the effects of a strict interpretation of racial and ethnic origin.[53] In practice this would require the list of grounds in national legislation to contain a non-specified reference to 'other grounds', to be filled in by courts and supervisory bodies. This would give courts the opportunity to tackle those disadvantageous treatments that raise the suspicion of racial discrimination, but cannot easily be traced back to narrow interpretations of racial or ethnic origin. It depends on the actual level of protection offered for discrimination on such unspecified grounds whether this option constitutes a satisfactory alternative.

2.3.2. Interaction of grounds of discrimination

Given that the grounds 'racial' and 'ethnic' origin involve a cluster of different personal characteristics, practical application of these concepts is somewhat problematic in anti-discrimination frameworks that presuppose neatly distinguishable categories. First of all, grounds of discrimination can be interlinked to such an extent that direct discrimination based on one ground can simultaneously be qualified as indirect discrimination on another ground. As was mentioned before, this relationship between grounds can be used to soften the edges of a narrow conception of 'racial' or 'ethnic' origin. At the same time, it is liable to raise difficult qualification issues. Secondly, persons belonging to more than one protected group sometimes suffer discrimination that is targeted at a specific combination of grounds, which cannot easily be classified as discrimination on either ground in play. This complexity has been coined 'intersectional discrimination', and poses a real challenge for legislators and courts. Thirdly, the reality that the provisions of the RED are embedded in a broader framework of discrimination law means it is possible that conflicts may arise between grounds, when persons belonging to a protected group invoke their right to non-discrimination in order to justify an interference with other persons' right to non-discrimination. All three complexities are discussed consecutively in the following subsections.

[53] Howard (2008), at 26. Compare McColgan (2007), at 76, who opposes lists of grounds because of the danger that modern types of discrimination cannot be fitted into one of the explicitly mentioned grounds.

2.3.2.1. Direct v. indirect discrimination

Some of the proxies that play a role in the perception of 'racial' and 'ethnic' origin constitute separate grounds of discrimination in the legal framework of European and/or national anti-discrimination law.[54] In some cases a particular situation can therefore be qualified in terms of a separately recognised ground of discrimination, as well as in terms of racial or ethnic discrimination. This is primarily true for the grounds religion, nationality and language. The first two grounds are separately regulated in EC equality law,[55] whereas the latter has been recognised as a separate protected ground in some Member States.[56]

When one of these grounds is used as a basis for differential treatment, and is not employed as a proxy for race,[57] two options are possible: the situation can either be qualified as direct discrimination on the particular ground, or as indirect racial or ethnic discrimination. For example, if a Muslim man is not hired because the employer does not want to work with a non-Christian, this can be qualified as direct discrimination based on religion, since his Islamic religion was the apparent reason for which he was not hired. At the same time, it is obvious that Muslims tend to come from particular geographical areas in the world and that a refusal to hire a Muslim person will disproportionately affect more persons that do not belong to the majority ethnic group of the population. Thus, the situation could also be qualified as indirect discrimination based on racial or ethnic origin.

The choice of qualification matters if the particular legal framework does not provide equal levels of protection for the different grounds involved. The

---

54 Many authors have pointed to this close link between racial discrimination and other forms of discrimination. See for example Ellis (2005), at 108; Howard (2005), at 475; Schiek (2002), at 311; Brown (2002), at 204-205; O'Hare (2001), at 145. During the negotiation process on the text of the RED, the European Parliament proposed to insert a recital in the preamble of the RED, providing that: "discrimination on the basis of racial or ethnic origin which is presented as a difference in treatment on the grounds of religion, conviction or nationality is covered by the scope of this RED". For unclear reasons, however, the Member States rejected this proposal, see the *Amended proposal for a Council Directive implementing the principle of equal treatment between persons irrespective of racial or ethnic origin*, Commission of the European Communities, 1999/0253 (CNS), 31 May 2000.

55 Discrimination based on religion is regulated by the FD, which is likely to be complemented by a new directive in the future, see *Proposal for a Council Directive on implementing the principle of equal treatment between persons irrespective of religion or belief, disability, age or sexual orientation*, COM(2008) 426 final, 2008/0140 (CNS). Discrimination on grounds of nationality is regulated by Article 12 TEC and the various free movement provisions in the TEC. See also section 2.3.3 on the interaction between race and nationality, and the implications of the Article 3(2) RED exclusion of nationality discrimination from the scope of the RED.

56 See for instance the Belgian and Estonian frameworks as discussed in section 2.5.2.

57 In case of a person's religion being used as a proxy for race, the label of direct racial discrimination is appropriate, as was already explained in section 2.3.1. See also section 4.2.3 on the notion of covert direct discrimination.

refusal to accept a student of the Muslim faith into a Christian school is for instance not covered by the prohibition of direct religious discrimination in current EC equality law, because the material scope of the FD does not extend to education. It is, however, covered by the prohibition of indirect discrimination on grounds of racial or ethnic origin, as the RED applies to education.[58]

For victims of these forms of discrimination the preferable qualification is obviously the one that provides the highest level of protection. The level of protection can be higher in terms of material scope of the anti-discrimination legislation, but also in terms of substantive protection, for example with regard to levels of scrutiny or available justification possibilities. Thus, in the aforementioned example the refusal of the Muslim student is preferably qualified as indirect racial discrimination.

It has furthermore been submitted that integrated national anti-discrimination legislation, covering all grounds of discrimination in a single instrument, would facilitate a flexible approach in this regard.[59] This is not necessarily true, since separate instruments can still afford the same level of protection for different grounds, whereas different levels of protection can exist within one single instrument.

2.3.2.2. Intersectional discrimination

A slightly more complex form of interaction of grounds than the one discussed in the previous subsection involves discrimination that is simultaneously based on two or more clearly distinguishable grounds. This type of discrimination has been labelled 'intersectional discrimination', a concept that was introduced in the United States in the 1980s by American feminist scholars. They drew

[58] See more elaborately on the differences between the various European regimes for discrimination in Howard (2008), at 20-23. The FD allows more justifications for direct discrimination based on religion, does not foresee in the establishment of a national body overseeing compliance with its provisions, and moreover has a narrower material scope than the RED. The adoption of the *Proposal for a Council Directive on implementing the principle of equal treatment between persons irrespective of religion or belief, disability, age or sexual orientation*, COM(2008) 426 final, 2008/0140 (CNS), would narrow this gap and would equalise the material scope for racial and religious discrimination. Protection against discrimination based on nationality in EU law does not extend to non-EU citizens. See more generally on the 'hierarchy' of discrimination grounds constituted by the different levels of protection in EC equality law in Howard (2006); Holzleithner (2005), at 943; Bell & Waddington (2003); Waddington (2003), at 47-49; Schiek (2002), at 300; Bell & Waddington (2001); O'Hare (2001), at 144; Fredman (2001), at 151; Bell (2000), at 80; Flynn (1999), at 1127-1152.

[59] Sierra (2002), at 16; Bell (1999), at 162, who makes a similar claim for European anti-discrimination law.

attention to the specific disadvantages suffered by non-white females in American society. Since then, the concept has increasingly gained importance at the international and European levels.[60]

Intersectional discrimination occurs when a person displaying more than one protected characteristic is adversely treated on the basis of the interaction of these characteristics, which means that persons who display only one of the characteristics do not experience the same disadvantage.[61] The typical example is the disadvantageous treatment of a woman belonging to a certain ethnic group, which is not experienced by male members of her ethnic group or by female members of other ethnic groups.

Practice reveals that adequate protection against intersectional discrimination is not easily provided by the traditional anti-discrimination paradigm, which presupposes discrimination to take place on one ground at a time. Persons suffering from intersectional discrimination often find that they cannot succesfullly invoke anti-discrimination law, as they cannot trace back the disadvantage they suffered to a single ground of discrimination.[62] Even if they can overcome this hurdle, the victim's particularly detrimental position within the protected groups is often not adequately recognised, which does not do justice to their experience.[63]

Effective protection against intersectional discrimination is of particular importance for minorities, since this problem concerns their more vulnerable members: those who display other characteristics that are liable to trigger discriminatory behaviour, in addition to their belonging to a particular ethnic or racial group. Besides the typical example of women belonging to ethnic minority groups (interaction between gender and racial or ethnic origin), one can think of persons adhering to a different religion or belief than most

---

60 Schiek et al (2007), at 174-175; Verloo (2006); Fredman (2005b); McInerney (2003), at 12-13; Carasco (1993). See inter alia *Tackling multiple discrimination. Practices, Policies and Laws*, European Commission, September 2007; *2006 Resolution on non-discrimination and equal opportunities for all*, European Parliament, P6_TA(2006)0261, para. 27; *Communication from the Commission to the European Parliament, the Council, the European Economic and Social Committee and the Committee of the Regions – Non-discrimination and equal opportunities: a renewed commitment*, COM/2008/0420 final, para. 3.2; *CERD General Recommendation No. 25, on Gender related dimensions of racial discrimination*, 20 March 2000; *CERD General Recommendation No. 29, on Descent*, 1 November 2002, paras. 11-13. Furthermore, on 7 March 2006, the UN Independent Expert on Minority Issues called for the application of a gender lens on minority issues on the UNHCR website (no longer available).

61 Makkonen (2002), at 11. This type of discrimination is also often referred to as 'multiple discrimination' (Makkonen (2002), at 9-10). However, the latter term can also point to situations in which two or more separate discriminations on distinct grounds take place at the same time, see Schiek et al (2007), at 171; Hannett (2003), at 68; Makkonen (2002), at 10. In order to avoid confusion, the concept of 'intersectional discrimination' is used in this study.

62 O'Cinnéide (2003), at 82-86; Hannett (2003), at 67; Makkonen (2002), at 13; Spiliopoulou Åkermark (1999), at 98-99.

63 Hannett (2003), at 67.

members of the ethnic minority they belong to (interaction between racial or ethnic origin and religion), or persons with a disability who belong to an ethnic minority (interaction between disability and ethnic or racial origin).[64]

Despite the relevance of the topic, recognition of the problems surrounding intersectional discrimination at the European level has not yet resulted in proper legal regulation. Recital 14 of the RED reveals that the problem is known to some exent, and provides that: "[i]n implementing the principle of equal treatment irrespective of racial or ethnic origin, the Community should (…) aim to eliminate inequalities, and to promote equality between men and women, especially since women are often the victims of multiple discrimination". A similar recital is found in the preamble of the FD.[65] These recitals only concern one form of intersectional discrimination, namely discrimination based on sex and another ground, and do not make clear how the concept can be practically addressed in the anti-discrimination frameworks.

The ECJ so far has not yet explicitly addressed the issue in its jurisprudence. Still, this court has in some cases recognised sub-groups within protected groups as potential victims of discrimination, which to some extent opens the door for an explicit intersectional discrimination approach to be developed in the future.[66] In *Liefting*, a rule according to which women married to civil servants received a lower pension benefit than male and unmarried female civil servants was qualified as a violation of the principle of equal pay for men and women.[67] In *Worringham*, the ECJ considered that a rule disadvantaging women under a certain age constituted a breach of the principle of equal pay.[68] The latter case in fact constitutes intersectional discrimination *avant la lettre*, combining the protected grounds of sex and age.

These judgments show that the ECJ is sometimes willing to broadly define the group protected by sex discrimination law and is willing to speak of sex discrimination when sex is clearly in play, regardless of the relevance of another ground of discrimination. However, they do not reveal particular sensitivity to the problem of intersectional discrimination, and it is uncertain whether the approach in these cases will be repeated for other discrimination grounds. In any event, it must be noted that even the most intersectionality-sensitive approach could not avoid the obstacle constituted by different levels of protection for various discrimination grounds in European equality law.[69]

---

64 Ontario Human Rights Commission, *An intersectional approach to discrimination: addressing multiple grounds in human rights claims*, Discussion and Policy paper, accessible at http://www.ohrc.on.ca (accessed August 2009).

65 Recital 3 FD.

66 Ellis (1998), at 16.

67 ECJ *Liefting v. Directie van het AZA*, Case 23/83, 18 September 1984, para. 14.

68 ECJ *Worringham and Humphreys v. Lloyds Bank*, Case 69/80, 11 March 1981, paras. 2 and 25.

69 Schiek (2007), at 172-173; *Tackling multiple discrimination. Practices, Policies and Laws*, European Commission, September 2007, at 28.

In view of the lack of guidance at the European level, it will primarily be up to national legislators and courts to formulate an adequate response to the problem of intersectional discrimination. Explicit regulation of intersectional discrimination in anti-discrimination law, allowing for such discrimination to be dealt with in accordance with the regime that offers the highest level of protection, is the best way to ensure adequate protection.[70] Otherwise, it is up to individual courts to recognise the phenomenon of intersectional discrimination and not too rigidly apply the compartmentalised anti-discrimination provisions, by providing protection for sub-groups within the nominally protected groups.[71] Integrated or harmonised national anti-discrimination legislation, which deals with the various grounds of discrimination in a single instrument, or at least uses similar terms and concepts for all grounds of discrimination, would greatly facilitate such a flexible approach.[72] Furthermore, an open-ended list of grounds of discrimination would be beneficial, since it would allow for recognition of grounds of discrimination consisting of cumulative vulnerable characteristics without having to fit them within one of the specified grounds of discrimination.[73]

2.3.2.3. Conflicts of grounds

Persons belonging to particular ethnic or racial groups are sometimes perpetrators of discrimination instead of victims. For example, cultural practices or rules that differentiate on the basis of sex can be challenged in the framework of sex equality law. Furthermore, it is conceivable that claims of racial or ethnic discrimination are countered with a claim of discrimination on another ground. For example, if a hospital refuses to treat a Muslim woman who does not want to be treated by a male physician, this could result in a claim of indirect discrimination on racial or ethnic origin versus a claim of direct discrimination based on sex. As the RED is part of a broader European equality law framework, it can be expected that cases of conflicting grounds will appear occasionally.[74]

Such cases call for a balancing act, which takes into account both rights to non-discrimination. It is submitted that the extent to which balancing is possible depends and should depend on the exception/justification possibilities

[70] Tobler (2008), at 45; Moon (2006), at 93.

[71] This was the approach taken by a number of American courts when confronted with discrimination of black women. They considered black women as a distinct group in need of protection by anti-discrimination law, see Fredman & Szyszczak (1992), at 221-225. See also Moon (2006), at 95, who mentions Canadian anti-discrimination law, in which combinations of protected grounds are recognised as constituting new distinct protected grounds.

[72] Schiek (2005), at 440; O'Cinnéide (2003), at 82-85; Flynn (1999), at 1148.

[73] Schiek (2007), at 176-177; Moon (2006), at 98.

[74] Bell (2008), at 12; Ellis (2005), at 108; Fredman (2002), at 75.

offered by the RED.[75] For cases of direct racial discrimination this means that other rights to non-discrimination should only be taken into account for direct racial discrimination if the claim can be framed in terms of a genuine and determining occupational requirement or positive action.[76] For cases of indirect racial discrimination, the objective justification test provides a balancing opportunity in the necessity test.[77]

2.3.3. The nationality exception of Article 3(2) RED

Article 3(2) RED stipulates that:

> This Directive does not cover difference of treatment based on nationality and is without prejudice to provisions and conditions relating to the entry into and residence of third country nationals and stateless persons on the territory of Member States, and to any treatment which arises from the legal status of the third-country nationals and stateless persons concerned

This exclusion has a personal scope component (exclusion of differences of treatment based on nationality) and a material scope element (exclusion of immigration, visa and asylum policies). The latter component is discussed in the next chapter, in section 3.4. The first component, the exclusion of differences of treatment based on nationality,[78] is discussed in this section.

According to the Explanatory Memorandum to the RED, this exclusion was called for because nationality discrimination was considered to be sufficiently regulated by Article 12 TEC and free movement law.[79] The insertion of Article 3(2) was furthermore motivated by Member States' desire to maintain certain instances of nationality differentiation in their social protection systems.[80]

Even though the Community legislator's intention presumably was to make a neat distinction between nationality discrimination and racial discrimination, such a distinction is not workable in practice.[81] Differences in treatment based on nationality entail a disproportionate disadvantageous impact on groups of

---

[75] Ellis (2005), at 108.

[76] See section 4.4.1.

[77] See section 5.2.4.4. There is no justification possibility for harassment, and it can be assumed that the justifications that apply for direct and indirect discrimination apply in the same way to instructions of direct or indirect discrimination.

[78] 'Nationality' refers to the legal notion of citizenship, and does cover 'national origin', which refers to the ties that a person may have with a particular nation or country, without necessarily having the matching citizenship, see Schiek et al (2007), at 65-66; Van Dooren (1997), at 32; Weis (1979), at 3.

[79] *Explanatory Memorandum*, Commission for the European Communities, 1999/0253, 25 November 1999.

[80] Tyson (2004), at 120-121.

[81] NicShuibhne (2003), at 273; Kimber (2003), at 247-248; O'Hare (2001), at 14.

a different racial or ethnic origin than the rest of the majority population.[82] This raises the question of the relationship between the prohibition of indirect racial and ethnic discrimination and the nationality exception clause. Is it permitted to scrutinise differences in treatment based on nationality as indirect racial discrimination if they produce a disparate disadvantageous impact on ethnic or racial minorities, which they almost inevitably do? The question is all the more relevant in view of the fact that the existing branch of EC law on nationality discrimination provides a lower level of protection than the RED. It has for instance limited application in disputes between private parties,[83] and offers no protection to non-EU citizens.[84]

As the RED makes part of the broader international human rights framework, there are strong reasons to assume that distinctions based on nationality should be deemed to fall within the scope of the RED, to the extent that they constitute indirect racial or ethnic discrimination. There is a development visible at the international level towards stricter scrutiny of nationality discrimination, in view of its clear connection to racial discrimination. International supervisory bodies such as the Human Rights Committee and the European Court of Human Rights have always been critical as regards the distinctions made by states between nationals and non-nationals.[85] In more recent times this

[82] Goldston (2006), at 327.

[83] Preedy (2000), at 130.

[84] NicShuibhne (2003), at 277-288; Cholewinski (2002), at 41; Brown (2002), at 209; Rodrigues (2001), at 105-106. There has been a development at the European level towards more and better protection of third-country nationals (TCN), culminating in the adoption of *Council Directive 2003/109/EC of 25 November 2003 concerning the status of third-country nationals who are long-term residents*. However, the protection afforded by this directive is still considered to be limited. See for a more detailed discussion of the legal position of TCN Doukas (2008); Goldstone (2006); *ENAR General Policy Paper No. 3, November 2006, on Third Country Nationals*, at http://www.eunet-integration.eu/content/view/33/21/ (accessed August 2009); Boelaert-Suominen (2005). Tridimas (2006), at 68 argues that this lower level of protection might be compensated for by making use of the general principle of equality in EC law. However, the ECJ so far has not opted for this approach.

[85] Henrard (2007), at 38. See for example *Gueye v. France*, Human Rights Committee, 6 April 1989, Communication 196/1989, CCPR/C/35/D/196/1985, in which the HRC examined a distinction based on nationality made by the French government with regard to pension rights of ex-soldiers in the light of the requirements of the prohibition of non-discrimination in ICCPR. The HRC found the distinction to be unjustifiable discrimination based on nationality, but emphasised that the distinction could not be considered to constitute racial discrimination, and classified it as amounting to prohibited discrimination based on 'other status', thus making use of the open-endedness of the list of grounds contained in the non-discrimination provision of ICCPR. See also ECtHR *Gaygusuz v. Austria*, no. 17371/90, 16 September 1996, para. 42, in which the ECtHR states that: "very weighty reasons would have to be put forward before the Court could regard a difference in treatment based exclusively on the ground of nationality as compatible with the Convention". It must be mentioned, however, that the ECtHR is not fully consistent. In ECtHR *Niedzwiecki v. Germany*, no. 58453/00, 25 October 2005, for example, the Court did not mention the 'weighty reasons' test at all.

critical attitude seems to be coupled with recognition of the close link between nationality discrimination and racial and ethnic discrimination.[86]

The practice of the Committee on the Elimination of Racial Discrimination (CERD) shows the clearest evolvement in this regard. In two cases in 1991, CERD interpreted the nationality exception clause of ICERD, which is broadly similar to Article 3(2) of the RED,[87] as meaning that distinctions based on nationality could not be scrutinised under the prohibition of discrimination.[88] More than ten years later, in 2004, CERD appeared to have altered, or at least qualified, its point of view. In its *General Recommendation on discrimination against non-citizens*, CERD makes clear that any instance of nationality discrimination has to comply with the prohibition of racial discrimination, regardless of the nationality exception clause. According to CERD, "under the Convention, differential treatment based on citizenship or immigration status will constitute discrimination if the criteria for such differentiation, judged in the light of the objectives and purposes of the Convention, are not applied pursuant to a legitimate aim, and are not proportional to the achievement of this aim".[89] Attention for the implications of nationality discrimination for racial discrimination is furthermore found in a number of final comments that CERD has issued with regard to State Reports.[90] CERD has thus taken a clear stance, granting the prohibition of indirect racial or ethnic discrimination supremacy over the nationality exception clause in ICERD. This development can be expected to impact the ECJ's perception of the relationship between Article 3(2) of the RED and the prohibition of indirect racial or ethnic discrimination.

In addition, most scholars consider that the exception clause of Article 3(2) does not exclude application of the prohibition of indirect racial or ethnic discrimination to distinctions based on nationality.[91] Their point of view sits well with the principle that exception clauses should be narrowly interpreted, as well as with the principle of effectiveness. After all, in the case of a broad

[86] Henrard (2007b), at 104-105; Van Dooren (1997), at 32. See also the Report of the UN Independent Expert on Minority Issues, Gay McDougal, *Promotion and protection of all human rights, civil, political, economic, social and cultural rights, including the right to development*, A/HRC/7/23, February 2008, para. 29.

[87] Article 1(2) of ICERD stipulates that: "[t]his Convention shall not apply to distinctions, exclusions, restrictions or preferences made by a State Party to this Convention between citizens and non-citizens."

[88] *GAC Enkelaar v. France*, CERD 2/1989, 18 March 1991; *Diop v. France*, CERD 2/1989, 10 May 1991.

[89] *CERD General Recommendation No. 30, on Discrimination Against Non Citizens*, 1 October 2004, para. 4.

[90] Van Dooren (1997), at 157.

[91] Henrard (2007), at 23; Tridimas (2006), at 67; De Schutter & Verstichel 2005, at 31; Howard (2005), at 486 et seq.; Kimber (2003), at 248-249; Cholewinski (2002), at 45; Toggenburg (2002), at 231; Rodrigues (2001), at 105.

interpretation of the exception clause, the prohibition of racial discrimination could be easily circumvented by simply applying nationality as a criterion instead of racial or ethnic origin.

In any case, it should be noted that Member States do not have to follow Article 3(2) RED, and are allowed to include in national legislation a prohibition of nationality discrimination. From a minority perspective, such an inclusionary approach is preferable, since it is mostly persons belonging to new minorities that are disadvantaged by distinctions made on the basis of nationality.[92] If Member States choose to maintain the nationality exception clause, however, discrimination based on nationality can be tackled with the concept of indirect racial or ethnic discrimination at the domestic level as well.

2.3.4. Types of victims

A final point of interest that deserves attention concerns the manner in which anti-discrimination law conceives of the actual person to be protected in concrete cases. A number of questions come up in this regard. First of all: are legal persons protected? Secondly, can persons who do not belong to a protected group, but are perceived as such or are associated with its members, invoke the anti-discrimination provisions?

2.3.4.1. Legal persons as victims

The extent to which legal persons are protected by the provisions of the RED may vary. Recital 16 RED provides that: "it is important to protect all natural persons against discrimination on grounds of racial or ethnic origin. Member States should also provide, where appropriate and in accordance with their national traditions and practice, protection for legal persons where they suffer discrimination on grounds of the racial or ethnic origin of their members." The Member States therefore have a certain margin of discretion in determining to what extent legal persons can invoke anti-discrimination norms.

Extending the scope of protection to include legal persons would enhance the effectiveness of anti-discrimination law, as some instances of discrimination are targeted at legal entities rather than at their distinct members. This would be the case, for example, if a Turkish Cultural Center is refused a rental contract by a racist landlord. It should be mentioned that the concept of discrimination by association could come to the rescue in a case

92 At least two-thirds of non-EU citizens resident in the EU belong to visible ethnic minorities, see *European Union Anti-discrimination policy: from equal opportunities between women and men to combating racism*, Directorate-General for Research, Working Document, LIBE 102 EN, European Parliament 1997, at 4.

of inapplicability of anti-discrimination law to legal persons. This concept is capable of catching situations in which legal persons are discriminated against on account of their association with a particular racial or ethnic group, and is discussed in the next subsection.[93]

2.3.4.2. Discrimination by association and by assumption

Persons experiencing negative consequences of discriminatory prejudices and behaviour do not always actually possess the relevant characteristics that are used as proxies by the discriminator. Persons are for instance sometimes treated adversely simply because of their association with someone else who displays a protected characteristic. A white person going out with a group of black persons can be harassed because of his association with this latter group. This form of disadvantageous treatment is referred to as discrimination by association.[94] In *Coleman*, the ECJ determined that this type of discrimination was covered by the prohibition of discrimination in the FD. The case involved less favourable treatment of a mother on account of the fact that her child was disabled. According to the ECJ, it did not follow from the provisions of the FD that the principle of equal treatment only applied to people who themselves portrayed the protected characteristic. Seeing that the FD protected against discrimination *on grounds of* disability, the ECJ found that the FD protected against any kind of less favourable treatment based on disability, regardless of whether the disadvantaged person herself was disabled. To exclude this particular instance of discrimination by association from the scope of the FD would, according to the ECJ, greatly reduce the level of protection offered by the FD.[95] The same reasoning fits the framework of the RED, and it can therefore safely be assumed that discrimination by association is covered by the RED.

Persons can furthermore be treated adversely for being perceived as belonging to a particular racial or ethnic group. For example, a relatively dark-skinned non-Roma person can be assumed to be of Roma origin and consequently be treated disadvantageously. This type of disadvantageous treatment is commonly referred to as discrimination by assumption.[96]

According to the European Commission the definitions of discrimination in the RED are intended to cover this type of discrimination.[97] As the reasoning

---

[93] See also Ambrus (2010) on the extent to which the RED allows for class actions.

[94] Schiek et al (2007), at 169.

[95] ECJ *S. Coleman v. Attridge Law and Steve Law*, Case C-303/06, 17 July 2008, paras. 33-56.

[96] Schiek et al (2007), at 163.

[97] *Explanatory Memorandum*, Commission for the European Communities, 1999/0253, 25 November 1999, at 6. Also see Ellis (2005), at 283; Bell (2004a), at 469.

employed by the ECJ in *Coleman* would appear to be applicable to this type of discrimination as well, it is likely that the RED covers discrimination by assumption.

Part two: Case study

2.4. Addressees of anti-discrimination legislation

2.4.1. 'All persons'

2.4.1.1. Applicability to principally and non-principally envisaged actors

All four Member States display some preference for a narrow approach to the 'all persons' phrase of Article 3(1) RED, albeit not equally strongly. Whereas the Estonian and the Belgian frameworks only show some initial signs that a narrow approach may be developed in the future, the Dutch and Hungarian frameworks unambiguously target only principally envisaged actors.

The Dutch GETA is generally understood to proceed from a particular rationale, according to which anti-discrimination law should only apply to actors who are in a relatively powerful position vis-à-vis potential victims of discrimination. These are public actors and private actors exercising authority over others, such as employers.[98] On the basis of this rationale the ETC draws the circle of addressees of the GETA quite narrowly.[99] For example, the ETC once refused to entertain a claim against a job applicant, as he could not be considered to be a 'provider' within the particular field of application, in this case employment.[100] Similarly, a company that performed psychological tests on job applicants as a service for employers was considered by the ETC not to be an addressee of the GETA as regards the prohibition of non-discrimination in the field of employment.[101]

The ETC does not apply this rule fully consistently, however. It has for instance already accepted a case against a recipient of services. The fact that

[98] Holtmaat (2007), at 36; Waaldijk (2004), at 355; Cremers-Hartman (2004), at 137. See also the statement of the government during the parliamentary proceedings on the IA in TK 2002-3, 18 770, nr. 5, at 28.

[99] *Het verschil gemaakt. Evaluatie AWGB en werkzaamheden CGB 1999-2004*, Commissie Gelijke Behandeling 2005, at 43-44.

[100] Opinion 2006-204 ETC, paras. 3.3-3.4.

[101] Opinion 2008-109 ETC, para. 3.4, in which the ETC considered that the assessment company merely fulfilled an advisory role, and did not or could not affect in any way the applicant's employment position. It was therefore not an addressee of the GETA's provisions.

the recipient hindered his contractual partner in the execution of his legal obligations was enough reason for the ETC to accept the case.[102] This clearly goes against the standard rule that the GETA targets 'providers' only, and shows that the ETC is willing to take a flexible approach if it considers this called for in the particular situation. It has not developed a clear policy in this regard, so that it is impossible to predict to what extent this more flexible approach will actually broaden the circle of addressees of the GETA. The point of departure therefore remains that only the relatively powerful, providing side of society is covered by the provisions of the GETA.

The Hungarian HETA has a similarly restrictive personal scope, which is moreover regulated in a complicated way, and applies different rules for different kinds of actors. Article 4 HETA stipulates that all official organs or bodies, all entities offering some kind of public service (e.g. schools, museums, health and social care institutions, mutual insurance or pension funds) and political parties have to uphold the provisions of the HETA in all of their activities.[103] According to Article 5 HETA, other persons are only covered if:

- they are employers or instructors acting within the employment or instruction relationship
- they offer a contract to persons not previously selected or invite such persons for tender
- they provide services or sell goods at their premises open to customers
- they carry out activities for which they have received state aid.

Here also, a particular rationale underlies the choice for limited applicability to private actors, according to which equal treatment is mainly a public actor responsibility and application of the equality principle to private actors should not go any further than necessary.[104] In line with this rationale the Hungarian AET only applies the principle of equal treatment to principally envisaged actors, and it has not so far accepted any exceptions in this regard. For example,

[102] Opinion 2003-142 ETC, para. 6.6.

[103] The only entity enumerated in Article 4 to which a limited scope applies, is "any other budgetary organ", which has to observe the requirement of equal treatment "in the course of establishing their relationships, in their relationships, in the course of their procedures and measures".

[104] Bitskey and Guylavári (2004), at 6.

in a harassment case it decided not to apply the prohibition of harassment against the actual harasser, because it considered that only his employer was obliged to observe the principle of equal treatment.[105]

The Estonian framework shows mixed signals concerning the approach to the 'all persons' phrase. After the first implementation phase, the anti-discrimination provisions of the ECA targeted employers, and thus only applied to principally envisaged actors in the field of employment. It is unclear whether the more recently adopted EETA takes a broader perspective. Article 2 EETA provides that the prohibition of racial discrimination shall apply:

> 1) in *establishing* conditions for employment, becoming a self-employed person, including in *establishing* recruitment and selection criteria, as well as in *promoting*; 2) in the conclusion of the contract of employment or for the provision of services or in the assignment or election to a post, in the establishment of work working conditions, *giving* orders, earnings, in termination or cancellation of the contract of employment or for the provision of services, in *releasing* from office; 3) in vocational training, career counselling, in *enabling* retraining or refresher course, in acquiring practical work experience; 4) in the affiliation with the employees or employers association, including the membership in the trade association and in *giving* benefits by these organizations (emphasis added, MB).

The emphasised words point to a narrow approach, since they refer to actions that are associated with employers, not with co-workers or third parties. The fields outside of employment are laid down in more neutral formulations, however, and to some extent even would seem to include non-principally envisaged actors. Article 2 EETA refers to the fields outside of employment as follows:

> 5) in *receiving* social welfare, health care and social security service, including *receiving* welfare benefit; 6) in education; 7) in the availability of goods and services, including lodging offered to the public

The verb 'receive' in this provision typically applies to non-principally envisaged actors. As there is no doctrine or jurisprudence on the matter, it is still unclear to what extent the EETA will apply to non-principally envisaged actors.

The Belgian framework is also ambiguous as regards the applicability of the anti-discrimination provisions to non-principally envisaged actors. The new ARA does not give any indications in this respect,and its personal scope provision in Article 5 wholly follows the wording of Article 3(1) RED, stipulating that the law applies to "all persons in both the public and private sectors, including public bodies".[106] Belgian case law moreover shows a

[105] See EBH 69/2006. Also see Gyulavári (2007), at 31.

[106] This provision constitutes an improvement with regard to the situation under the old ADA, which did not contain a separate personal scope provision, and was applied by a number of courts in such a way as to not cover persons who merely 'communicated' discriminatory treatment of

mixed picture. Some cases ruled under the old ADA reveal a narrow approach to the circle of addressees. For instance, the Ghent Labour Court stated in an employment discrimination case that, in addition to employers, persons representing the employer were required to act in conformity with the ADA. It thereby implied that persons not representing the employer were not covered by the provisions of the ADA.[107] This is indicative of a narrow approach to the circle of addressees, according to which only principally envisaged actors are targeted. There are, however, also indicators of a broader approach in Belgian anti-discrimination law. In a case under the old ARA, a person who had refused the service of a doctor for discriminatory reasons was punished for unlawful discrimination.[108] By including recipients of services as addressees of anti-discrimination law this judgment thus applies a lenient approach with regard to the personal scope of the old ARA. The cases show that the question as to how broadly the circle of addressees of the new ARA will be drawn is still out in the open. It should be mentioned that the debate that was prompted by the implementation of the RED and FD as regards the appropriateness of the imposition of anti-discrimination duties on private actors does not provide a favourable climate for the adoption of a broad approach.[109]

2.4.1.2. Alternatives available for direct liability of non-principally envisaged actors

There are quite a few differences between the four Member States with regard to the way in which they make up for the lack or potential lack of direct liability of non-principally envisaged actors that was identified in the previous subsection.

their instructors, despite suggestions in literature that this was too narrow an approach (De Vos (2004), at 74; Kusters (2003), at 555). For instance, in a judgment of the Ghent Court of Appeal, 30 November 2005, para. 6, a real estate agent who communicated the discriminatory refusal of the landlord and thus refrained from establishing a rental contract could not be held accountable, since he himself did not discriminate. These rulings denied the own responsibility that intermediary organisations have vis-à-vis their clients and therefore lowered the level of protection offered by anti-discrimination law. The Belgian government apparently wanted to improve this situation, and copied Article 3(1) RED into the new ARA, while emphasising the personal responsibility of those who execute discriminatory orders see the parliamentary proceedings on the new ARA, Doc 51. 2720/009, at 42-43.

[107] Ghent Labour Court, 26 March 2007.

[108] De Prins et al (2005), at 360.

[109] Thiery (2007), at 749; De Prins et al (2005), at 445-446; Van Drooghenbroeck (2004), at 133-135; Some of the critics of the ADA even went to the Arbitration Court in order to annul the ADA because they found that it unjustifiably interfered with the fundamental rights and freedoms of private actors. The Arbitration Court pronounced on the issue in its judgment of 6 October 2004, No. 157/2004, which partially annulled the ADA, inter alia because of its disproportionate impact on the freedom of expression of individuals.

The most elaborate regime is found in the Netherlands, where the disadvantages of the narrow circle of addressees have to quite an extent been compensated for by the development of extensive positive duties for principally envisaged actors. The ETC requires of these actors that they protect the persons within their sphere of influence against discrimination, and that they offer adequate procedural mechanisms for complaints of discrimination. This applies even if the discrimination is not perpetrated by subordinates, but by third persons.[110] In addition, Dutch law provides possibilities for victims of discrimination to invoke the general tort law provisions against non-principally envisaged perpetrators of discrimination. There is furthermore a rule of vicarious liability for employers for the actions of their employees.[111] To our knowledge, these latter avenues have so far not been explored, and they are therefore of limited importance.

It should be mentioned that the ETC considers the current Dutch approach to be satisfactory and to provide an even higher level of protection than a system with a broader personal scope but without positive duties.[112] The positive duties developed by the ETC have indeed greatly enhanced the level of protection offered by the GETA framework. However, in some cases, the limited personal scope could still constitute a problem for victims, since they are not always able to hold accountable the particular person who has done them harm. Scholars have been especially critical of the lack of personal liability of colleagues, students or other third parties in the context of harassment.[113] Still, The Dutch framework sets a high level of protection compared to the other frameworks.

The Hungarian and Estonian frameworks do show favourable signs as regards the development of positive duties, but these are not as far-reaching as the ones imposed by the Dutch ETC. In Hungary, positive duties as regards the elimination of educational segregation of Roma children have been recognised in the framework of the HETA, which could be further developed into a more general duty of care of principally envisaged persons.[114] In Estonia, Article 12 of the EETA provides for a positive duty of employers to "take all appropriate measures to protect the employee from discrimination". Depending on how this duty is applied in practice, it could mitigate the effects of a narrow approach to the 'all persons' phrase, but only in the field of employment. The Hungarian and Estonian frameworks furthermore provide some avenues of

[110] See sections 4.8, 5.4 and 6.4.3.

[111] Holtmaat (2007), at 36; Waaldijk (2004), at 355. The government also pointed to these alternatives during the parliamentary discussions of the implementation of the RED, see TK 2002-03, 18 770, no. 5, at 28.

[112] See evaluation report *Het verschil gemaakt. Evaluatie AWGB en werkzaamheden CGB 1999-2004*, Commissie Gelijke Behandeling 2005, at 43-44.

[113] Holtmaat (2007), at 36; Gijzen (2006), at 196-198.

[114] See sections 4.8 and 5.4.

vicarious liability of principally envisaged actors and direct liability of other actors under general civil law provisions, but these so far have not proved to be very effective.[115]

The Belgian framework does not include any positive duties for principally envisaged actors, save for harassment in the field of employment.[116] It furthermore only provides for limited personal or vicarious liability of these actors. In the field of employment employers are vicariously liable for acts of their employees, but employers are exempt if they can prove that the employee acted recklessly or intentionally.[117] Instances of intentional discrimination, one of the most serious forms of discrimination, would in this way slip through the net. In the field of education victims could invoke the rule that teachers are liable for damage caused by their students under their supervision.[118] To our knowledge, Belgian law does not provide for other ways to compensate for the lack of applicability to non-principally targeted actors.

2.4.2. 'As regards both the public and private sectors, including public bodies'

2.4.2.1. Applicability of the RED in the case of incorrect or untimely implementation

With the exception of Estonia, which only adopted a comprehensive anti-discrimination law at the end of 2008, the Member States under study have all implemented the RED in a timely manner. The doctrine of direct effect would therefore at first glance not seem to be relevant for Belgium, Hungary and the Netherlands. Nevertheless, these states have all to a certain extent excluded

---

[115] In Hungary there is a provision for liability of employers for damages caused by employees in the Civil Code, see Kádar (2007), at 34. Furthermore, kindergartens, schools, boarding schools and organisers of occupational training are fully liable for damages caused to their students during classes, regardless of culpability, according to Article 77(3) of the Public Education Act. More generally, non-principally envisaged actors can be held directly liable for discrimination on the basis of the protection of personal rights as provided by Article 76 of the Civil Code. However, the AET is not competent to apply this provision and it is generally difficult to obtain a favorable ruling under this provision, as can be inferred from the white booklets of NEKI, to be found at www.neki.hu (accessed August 2009). Estonian legislation also contains a few vicarious liability schemes that could mitigate the lack of direct liability of non-principally envisaged actors. Instructors and employers are to some extent liable for the actions of their contractors/subordinates, if the damage is caused during the execution of the contractual/employee's duties, see Poleshchuk (2007), at 26.

[116] See sections 4.8, 5.4 and 6.4.3.

[117] De Schutter (2007a), at 51-52.

[118] De Schutter (2007a), at 51-52.

certain public acts from the scope of their national anti-discrimination legislation, which could in some cases lead to claims based on the alleged direct effect of the RED.

In Hungary, the HETA does not cover regulatory acts enacted by public authorities. The Hungarian constitutional system does not permit one public actor to scrutinise regulatory acts adopted by another public actor, as the Constitutional Court is solely competent in this respect. Thus, the AET does not have the competence to rule on any acts adopted on the basis of the exclusive competence of other public actors.[119] A comparable approach can be found in the Netherlands, where the ETC is generally only allowed to rule on acts of public actors to the extent that they participate in social life in a similar fashion to private actors. Thus, acts stemming from their specific public powers are excluded, save for the field of social protection.[120] Even in this latter field the ETC has sometimes been reluctant to scrutinise typically public acts.[121]

In Belgium, Article 11 of the new ARA excludes federal legislative acts from the scope of this act, which was deemed necessary by the legislator to safeguard legal certainty. The Belgian government stressed, however, that legislative acts still had to comply with international anti-discrimination norms, including those of the RED.[122] The aim of Article 11 was thus presumably to leave the examination of the legality of legislative acts to the exclusive competence of the Arbitration Court, and not to let lower courts rule on the compliance of these acts with the RED. The Belgian framework furthermore has a protective leak that is caused by the exclusive competences of the federated entities. Some of these entities have not entirely fulfilled their implementation obligation under the RED, as is further explained in the case-study section of Chapter 3.

Depending on the degree to which the provisions of the RED are deemed to be directly effective, the doctrine of direct effect could be used by individuals for each of the aforementioned gaps of protection. To our knowledge, this has not yet happened in practice.

119 *Report on the activities of the Equal Treatment Authority and the experiences of the implementation of Act nr. 125 of 2003 on equal treatment and the promotion of equal opportunities*, AET, July 2006.

120 See sections 3.6.2 and 3.6.5.

121 Davidovic & Van Walsum (2009), at 46-47.

122 *Explanatory Memorandum to the Draft law amending the law of 30 July 1981 that penalises certain acts motivated by racism and xenophobia*, Doc 51. 2720/001, 24, at 53.

2.4.2.2. Differentiation between public and private actors

2.4.2.2.1. Fundamental rights and freedoms of private actors

As was explained in section 2.2.2.2, fundamental rights and freedoms of private actors can be taken into account on two levels of application: the level of the material scope and the level of the substantive concepts. As for the level of the material scope, the impact of fundamental rights and freedoms in the Member States is discussed in section 3.5.2. This section will only discuss the degree to which fundamental rights and freedoms have an impact on the application of the substantive discrimination provisions in the Member States.

In all four Member States it is clear that fundamental rights and freedoms are perceived as relevant factors for the interpretation of the various substantive concepts of the RED. The Belgian, Estonian and Hungarian frameworks appear to respect the boundaries of the RED in this respect, which means that the system of justification as provided for by the RED is not undermined, in particular the closed system of justification for direct discrimination. To the contrary, the Dutch framework contains a number of justification possibilities motivated by fundamental rights that are not in line with the RED.

In Belgian doctrine it is generally assumed that the fundamental rights and freedoms of private actors will influence the application of the provisions of the new ARL, in particular the genuine and determining occupational requirement,[123] the objective justification test of the concept of indirect discrimination,[124] and the remedy provisions.[125] The previous ADA even contained an explicit provision that made clear that the anti-discrimination provisions had to be applied in accordance with fundamental rights and freedoms.[126] It is not entirely clear, however, how such differentiated application will take place.

As for the Estonian framework, the Explanatory Memorandum to the EETA points out that it is important to take into account fundamental rights and freedoms of private actors in the application of the justification possibilities for discrimination, and that conflicts of rights should be resolved by applying

[123] According to the government in the *Explanatory Memorandum to the Draft law amending the law of 30 July 1981 that penalises certain acts motivated by racism and xenophobia*, Doc 51. 2720/001, 41, at 48-49, fundamental rights and freedoms could constitute a legitimate aim in the framework of the justification of a genuine and determining occupational requirement.

[124] Velaers (2003a), at 307; Foubert (2004), at 6; Van Drooghenbroeck (2003), at 237.

[125] Vrielink et al (2003), at 267.

[126] Article 3 of the ADA provided that the ADA was without prejudice to the fundamental rights and freedoms of individuals. According to the government, the provision made clear that strictly private relationships were not addressed by the ADL. The Arbitration Court, however, explained it more broadly in its judgment of 6 October 2004, No. 157/2004, para. B.51, as meaning that the provisions of the law were to be interpreted and applied in accordance with fundamental rights and freedoms.

the proportionality principle. At the same time it stresses that the RED does not allow for any other justifications for direct racial discrimination than the GDOR and positive action, and thus appears to recognise that no additional justifications are permitted.[127] There is no case-law or doctrine available to shed further light on the matter.

The Hungarian HETA makes explicit provision for the consideration of fundamental rights and freedoms of private actors in the application of justification possibilities in Article 7(2) a). This article stupultates that, if such right or freedom is at stake, a three-tiered proportionality test should be carried out in order to determine which right should prevail. This possibility does not apply to instances of direct racial discrimination, however, which is in line with the closed system of justification of the RED.[128]

The Dutch GETA contains a number of additional justification possibilities for private actors. Thus, Article 5(2) GETA permits religious and ideological institutions to make certain distinctions in order to safeguard their religious or ideological foundations. As is explained in section 4.7.1, this justification possibility can to some extent be reconciled with the requirements of the RED, but still goes beyond what is permitted. The provision of Article 5(3) GETA is somewhat less problematic, as it allows for requirements imposed in the employment relationship that are reasonable in view of the private nature of such a relationship, and is as such likely to be reconcilable with the GDOR of Article 4 RED. This justification possibility is also discussed in section 4.7.1. The Dutch ETC has furthermore developed an extra-textual justification possibility for direct discrimination on the basis of reasonability and equity. According to the ETC, one of the reasons for applying this exceptional justification possibility is the concern to safeguard a fundamental right or freedom of a private actor.[129] To the extent that it is applied in cases of direct racial or ethnic discrimination, the provision is not in conformity with the requirements of the RED, as is further explained in section 4.7.1. The ETC has furthermore recognised the potential occurrence of conflicting fundamental rights in the application of the substantive provisions of the GETA, and has

127 *Explanatory Memorandum to Act 384 SE III on Equal Treatment,* with regard to Article 9 EETA: "As the prohibition of discrimination collides with another legal value, the justifiability or prohibition of differentiation in the final degree is decided by the principle of proportionality (§ 11 of the Constitution). (…) According to Directive 2000/43/EC the discrimination on the grounds of racial origin or nation (ethnic origin) cannot be justified in any other case, other than if it regards genuine and determining occupational requirements or indirect discrimination". Still, despite the apparent intention to comply with the RED, the EETA does contain a justification possibility for direct racial discrimination that is not permitted by the RED: see section 4.7.1.

128 See section 5.5.4.6 for an explanation of this justification possibility. See also section 2.5.2.3 on conflicting grounds of discrimination and section 6.4.2.3 on conflicting rights in the context of harassment.

129 Opinion 2006-61 ETC, para. 3.11.

made clear that it will apply a proportionality test in order to determine which right should prevail. The way in which the ETC approaches the matter would seem to be in line with the RED.[130]

2.4.2.2.2. Margin of appreciation for public actors

There is quite some divergence between national frameworks as regards the degree to which they grant public actors leeway in the fulfilment of their obligations under the RED.

The strictest approach towards public actors is found in the Hungarian framework, which so far has not shown any traces of a margin of appreciation doctrine. One case of the AET rather reveals stricter scrutiny for public actors as compared to private actors. In the particular case, which concerned accessibility of a courthouse for users of wheelchairs, the AET considered that: "the court subjected to these proceedings, as an organ of the justice system, one of the main institutions in place to ensure respect of the rule of law, should have set an example by being one of the first institutions to fulfil its legal obligation and ensure equal access to the justice system".[131] This consideration indicates stricter scrutiny when it comes to public actor responsibility for equal treatment. This reading of the decision is supported by the underlying rationale of the HETA, according to which public actors are the primarily responsible actors for ensuring equal treatment.[132]

The Belgian and Dutch frameworks are less strict, and grant public actors a certain margin of appreciation. The Belgian approach in this respect is not yet fully developed. The jurisprudence of the Arbitration Court on the constitutional equality provision reveals that this court applies a lower level of scrutiny for legislative acts, in order to respect the division of powers between the legislature and the judiciary.[133] It is possible that this practice will develop into a more full-blown doctrine of a margin of appreciation for public actors, but it is still too early to draw conclusions in this regard.

The Dutch framework shows a more developed margin of appreciation doctrine, which was created over time by the ETC. Whereas the ETC in 2006 still claimed that it would not apply this doctrine in cases of racial or ethnic discrimination,[134] it did exactly the opposite in a 2007 case. The particular case involved a claim of indirect racial discrimination, allegedly committed by the legislator when differentiating between resident and non-resident

[130] See section 2.5.2.3 on conflicting grounds of discrimination and section 6.4.2.3 on conflicting rights in the context of harassment.
[131] EBH/13/5/2005, 20 February 2006.
[132] See section 2.4.1.1.
[133] Arbitration Court, Case No. 23/89, 13 October 1989; Arbitration Court, Case No. 18/90, 23 May 1990. See also De Prins et al (2005), at 264-266.
[134] *Jaarverslag Commissie Gelijke Behandeling 2006*, ETC, at 70.

citizens as regards pension benefits. The ETC commenced its decision by granting the state a margin of appreciation, while emphasising that the margin would have been much stricter in a case of direct racial discrimination. It then proceeded to apply an attenuated proportionality test and concluded that, even though there were alternatives available that would be more favourable to non-residents, it was up to the legislator to choose in this regard, and the latter had not come to an unreasonable choice.[135] The application of a reasonability test instead of a necessity/proportionality test in this case clearly amounted to less strict scrutiny than normally applied by the ETC. It is doubtful that such an attenuated form of the objective justification test for indirect discrimination would be accepted by the ECJ, but this still needs to be cleared out.

Whereas the Dutch approach can at least still be argued to remain within the boundaries of the RED, the Estonian EETA clearly goes beyond what is permitted with regard to the leniency it applies to public actors. Article 9(1) of this Act contains a general justification possibility for these actors and provides that: "[t]his Act does not restrict the application of such measures that are in compliance with the law, which are necessary for guaranteeing public order and security, the prevention of crime, the protection of health, or the rights or freedom of other people. The measures applied in such manner must be in proportion to the objective to be attained". This rather openly worded justification possibility is clearly at odds with the closed system of justification for direct racial discrimination set in place by the RED.[136] In addition, it is not unlikely that a margin of appreciation will be granted to public actors acting under the EETA. The jurisprudence of the Constitutional Chamber of the Supreme Court on the constitutional equality provision reveals that this court accords the legislator a wide discretion.[137] The Estonian Chancellor of Justice has furthermore emphasised the need to grant the executive power a margin of appreciation in the context of the general principle of equal treatment.[138]

2.4.2.2.3. Differentiated application of duties

The national frameworks show a few, yet weak, signs of stricter demands being imposed on public actors than on private actors as regards the duties they have. The clearest example is found in the Estonian framework, which provides for a mainstreaming duty for the Estonian ministries. Article 14 of the EETA provides that "[e]ach ministry will supervise within its area

[135] Opinion 2007-4 ETC, paras. 3.7 and 3.16.

[136] See section 4.7.1.

[137] See for instance Decision of the Constitutional Chamber of the Supreme Court, 3-4-1-2-02, 3 April 2002, para. 17 and Decision of the Constitutional Chamber of the Supreme Court, 3-4-1-33-05, 20 March 2005, para. 26.

[138] *Position Paper on the violation of the principle of equal treatment*, No. 7-5/070340/00705874, Legal Chancellor 2007.

of administration the compliance with the requirements of this Act and will cooperate with the other persons and authorities in promoting the principle of equal treatment." As is explained in section 7.2.2.1, mainstreaming can be a powerful instrument for tackling structural and institutionalised forms of discrimination. There is no monitoring mechanism for the duty of Article 14 EETA, however, and it is unclear to what extent it is complied with.

The Belgian and Hungarian frameworks both show an interesting form of special responsibility for public actors. Both frameworks approach positive action as being something to be pursued mainly by public actors, and require a legislative basis for most measures of positive action. As is explained in section 7.6.2, this emphasis on public actor responsibility makes it harder for positive action measures to be adopted, and is therefore regrettable. It should be mentioned, on the other hand, that the Hungarian HETA contains an obligation for state-funded bodies to devise an equal opportunities plan, which is a positive asset of the Hungarian framework.[139]

The Belgian framework displays another particular form of special responsibility of public actors. All discriminatory acts of public actors are criminally sanctioned by the new ARA, whereas discriminatory acts of private actors are only criminally sanctioned if perpetrated in the field of employment or the provision of goods and services.[140] A benevolent reading would interpret this stricter regime for public actors as an affirmation of the exemplary function of persons acting on behalf of the state.

In the Dutch context, finally, differentiation between public and private actors is hardly visible. The ETC has developed extensive positive duties for private actors and public actors alike, and does not generally apply differentiated standards in this respect. Still, one set of cases could be read so as to show that duties to accommodate the special needs of minorities are more easily acknowledged for public than for private actors. Both cases involved the situation in which a person living in a trailer camp asked for special consideration of his particular way of life. In the first case, the ETC ruled that a private insurance company was not required to develop a special insurance policy tailored to the situation of persons living in trailers, because this would put too much of a strain on the individual company.[141] In the second case, the ETC decided that a local government had the duty to provide suitable social housing for persons living in trailers, even if this required adaptation of their policy.[142] The difference between the two cases is perhaps explained by the notion of a special responsibility that public actors have vis-à-vis citizens. Further practice of the ETC should reveal whether this was indeed the underlying reasoning of the ETC.

[139] Article 63(4) of the HETA.
[140] Articles 23-25 of the new ARA.
[141] Opinion 2006-5 ETC.
[142] Opinion 2006-222 ETC.

2.5. Beneficiaries of anti-discrimination legislation

2.5.1. Conceptualisation of 'racial' and 'ethnic' origin

The four Member States have included in their national laws grounds of discrimination that could capture most of the aforementioned proxies nowadays used to perpetrate racism, and have drawn inspiration from the list provided by ICERD in this respect.

The Dutch and Belgian frameworks have most clearly followed this list, and cover all the grounds mentioned therein. Article 1(1) of the Dutch GETA refers to 'race' as the only ground for racial discrimination, but the practices of the ETC and the courts make clear that the complete ICERD list of racial grounds is covered by 'race'.[143] 'Race' is accordingly considered to refer to groups that share a number of characteristics, which are of a physical, ethnic, geographical, cultural, historical or religious nature.[144] The practice of the ETC furthermore shows that the modern proxies of language and religion are comprised by 'race'. Thus, distinctions based on language or religion are often expressly recognised to be connected to 'race',[145] and are sometimes even classified as direct racial discrimination.[146]

Article 4(4) of the new Belgian ARA applies the following list of protected characteristics: "nationality, so-called race, skin colour, descent, national or ethnic origin". This list intentionally follows the ICERD list, adding to it the ground 'nationality'.[147] The word 'so-called' was put before 'race' in order to

---

143 Holtmaat (2007), at 16. At the time of the implementation of the RED the Dutch government stressed that 'race' should indeed be interpreted in accordance with ICERD, see the *Explanatory Memorandum to the Draft Amendment of the General Act on Equal Treatment and certain other acts in order to implement directive 2000/43/EC and directive 2000/78/EC*, TK 2002-03, 28 770, No. 3, at 3.

144 See for instance High Council 13 June 2000, NJ 2000/513, para. 3.5.1.

145 See for example Opinion 2007-14 ETC, in which a person claimed to be rejected for a position because of his Arab name; the ETC dealt with the case as pertaining to "race and/or religion". A similar case is Opinion 2007-83 ETC, in which an Iranian man was asked during a job interview about his religious beliefs. Here also, the ETC dealt with the case as concerning potential racial or religious discrimination. See furthermore High Council 13 June 2000, NJ 2000/513, para. 3.5.1, in which the High Council acknowledged the relationship between 'race' and religious characteristics. Furthermore, the ETC frequently deals with language requirements as potentially amounting to indirect discrimination on the basis of race, see for example Opinion 2007-173 ETC and Opinion 2007-127 ETC.

146 See Opinion 2003-142 ETC and Opinion 1997-69 ETC, in which a language requirement was considered to amount to direct racial discrimination. In Opinion 1998-57 ETC, discrimination against Muslims was qualified as direct racial discrimination.

147 Formally, the full range of grounds of all three anti-discrimination acts of 2007 are based on the EU Charter on Fundamental Rights, as is explained by the government in the *Explanatory Memorandum to the Draft law amending the law of 30 July 1981 that penalises*

make clear that the State rejected any theory of different human races.[148] The interpretation of the grounds of Article 4(4) of the new ARA is closely related to the interpretation that they have received in the framework of ICERD. Thus, 'race' is taken to refer to physiological characteristics, as is 'skin colour',[149] whereas 'ethnic' and 'national' origin are seen as referring to characteristics that are not visible on the outside. 'Ethnic origin' is understood to link back to a group of persons that are connected by a number of factors that makes them a community, for example language or culture.[150] A common religion could furthermore play a part in the interpretation of this concept, as jurisprudence reveals that Belgian courts seem willing to qualify distinctions made on the basis of religion as direct racial discrimination if they consider that covert racial discrimination is in play.[151]

'National origin' is considered to refer to the ethnic notion of a nation, just as its international counterpart.[152] Finally, 'descent' appears to be interpreted in a somewhat different way than at the international level. Under the old ARA this ground was mainly associated with descent from the Jewish nation,[153] and it is therefore unclear whether 'descent' in the new ARA covers proxies related to social stratification. The twin Act to the new ARA, the Act combating certain forms of discrimination, regulates discrimination based on 'social origin', which would appear to cover such proxies. The regime of this latter Act is more lenient than the regime for racial discrimination in the new ARA, however, and in that respect a broad interpretation of 'descent' in Article 4(4) of the new ARA would be welcome.[154]

The Estonian and Hungarian frameworks have not completely followed the list of ICERD, and/or apply to some extent separate conceptions of the grounds that are mentioned in Article 1(1) of this treaty. Article 1(1) of the

certain acts motivated by racism and xenophobia, Doc 51. 2720/001, at 17. The old ARA, however, contained an identical list of grounds to that of the new ARA, with the exception of 'nationality', and this list was intentionally based on the one contained in ICERD. See De Prins et al (2005), at 307.

148 De Prins et al (2005), at 308-309; Brems (2004), at 37-38; Vrielink (2003), at 200-201.

149 See the parliamentary proceedings on the draft old ARA that was adopted in 1981 in Gedr. St. Kamer, B.Z. 1979, nr. 214/9, at 11.

150 Gedr. St. Kamer, B.Z. 1979, nr. 214/9, at 11.

151 De Prins et al (2005), at 312-313.

152 See Hand. Senaat 18 July 1981, 2234. See also the explanation of this ground given by CEOOR on its website at http://www.diversiteit.be/?action=onderdeel&onderdeel=119&titel=Nationale+afstamming (accessed August 2009).

153 Gedr. St. Kamer, B.Z. 1979, nr. 214/9, at 22.

154 See the *Act of 10 May 2007 combating certain forms of discrimination*, BS 30 V 07. This act provides for an open-ended justification possibility for direct discrimination, whereas the new ARA applies a closed system of justification for direct racial discrimination in line with the RED, see section 4.7.1.

Estonian EETA mentions the grounds of 'ethnic origin',[155] 'racial origin' and 'colour'. According to the Explanatory Memorandum to the EETA, 'racial origin' is understood as referring to "certain hereditary characteristics that are not chosen by the persons who have them", which should probably be taken to mean that it envisages mainly physiological characteristics.[156] This corresponds to 'race' in its narrow understanding at the international level. For unclear reasons, the Explanatory Memorandum to the EETA does not define or exemplify 'ethnic origin'. This ground is likely to be interpreted in accordance with the Estonian understanding of what constitutes a national or ethnic minority, as put forward by the Act on the cultural autonomy of national minorities. Article 1 of this Act defines minorities as groups that differ from Estonians by their ethnic affiliation, cultural and religious idiosyncrasies, or language.[157] If 'ethnic origin' in Article 1(1) EETA is defined along these lines, it would largely conform to its international counterpart, and would cover the modern proxies for racism, such as religion, language and culture. The Estonian framework therefore appears to cover the same grounds and proxies as the ICERD list, except for the ground of 'descent', for which no equivalent is provided by Article 1(1) EETA.

Article 8 of the Hungarian HETA lists the following race-related grounds: 'racial origin', 'colour', 'nationality' and 'belonging to a national or ethnic minority'. 'Racial origin' is understood largely in the same way as the narrow understanding of 'race' at the international level. Thus, it refers to physiological characteristics, and therefore covers 'colour' as well.[158] 'Nationality' does not refer to legal nationality, in terms of citizenship, but rather to nationality in its historical, cultural meaning. It could be said to cover what is in the international context understood under 'ethnic origin', since it also comprises ethnic groups within nations. Substantively, the ground 'nationality' refers to the same kind of groups as 'belonging to a national or ethnic minority', the single difference being that the latter only comprises officially recognised minorities in Hungary. This means inter alia that the proxies of language and religion are comprised by 'nationality', as these characteristics are mentioned in the definition of 'national or ethnic minority' in the Act on national

[155] The Estonian word used is 'nation' or 'nationality', which in the Estonian context means 'ethnic origin', see Poleshchuk (2005), para. 2.1.1. In order to avoid confusion with the word 'national origin' as it is understood in the international context, the notion of 'ethnic origin' is used here.

[156] *Explanatory Memorandum to Draft 262 SE.*

[157] Even though this definition formally only applies to 'national minority', it can also be used to explain what is meant by 'ethnic minority'. The latter term is understood to refer to the same kind of groups as those covered by the Act on cultural autonomy of national minorities, except for the fact that they arrived in Estonia after the Second World War, see Poleshchuk (2007), at 12.

[158] *White Booklet 2006, Legal Defence Bureau for National Ethnic Minorities (NEKI) 2007,* at 36.

minorities.[159] Similarly to the Estonian framework, the Hungarian framework thus covers the grounds listed in Article 1(1) ICERD, except for 'descent'. Contrary to the Estonian framework, however, it provides for a remedy for this omission in the open-endedness of the list of grounds in Article 8 HETA, which is reflected in the reference to "any other status, characteristic feature or attribute". This phrase is filled in by the Hungarian courts and the AET on the basis of the principle that all personal characteristics connected to human dignity are to be protected by the HETA.[160] Practice of the AET so far shows that this body does not impose very high standards in this respect. Grounds that have been recognised include for example the existence of a conflict between the applicant's husband and the headmaster of the school where the client worked;[161] having a different opinion from a superior;[162] residing in a particular village;[163] being in foster care;[164] being an association which provides social assistance to prostitutes.[165] The HETA has therefore a fairly indeterminate reach in terms of the grounds of discrimination it applies to, and it is not likely that particular minority groups will be excluded from its scope in the future.

The lack of practice in most Member States makes it difficult to draw any conclusions as to whether the discrimination grounds are applied in a way that recognises contemporary proxies associated with 'racial' and 'ethnic' origin and that is sensitive to the particular national context. It is at least positive that the minorities most in need of protection in Belgium, Estonia and Hungary would seem to be covered by national anti-discrimination law. For Belgium, case law under the previous ARA and ADA reveals that persons belonging to

[159] Kádar (2007), at 9-10. Article 1 of the *Act on National Minorities* defines national and ethnic minorities as follows: "any ethnic group with a history of at least one century of living in the Republic of Hungary, which represents a numerical minority among the citizens of the state, the members of which are Hungarian citizens, and are distinguished from the rest of the citizens by their own language, culture and traditions, and at the same time demonstrate a sense of belonging together, which is aimed at the preservation of all these, and the expression and the protection of the interests of their communities which have been formed in the course of history." There are currently twelve recognised minority groups, amongst which the Roma. Not recognised are the Jewish community (Farkas (2006), at 54) and immigrant groups, such as Chinese persons.

[160] This practice is based on a judgment of the Constitutional Court, Decision no. 61/92. See for example Debrecen Court of Appeal, PF.II. 20.513/2005/4, 28 October 2005, in which the Court ruled that: "a precondition for bringing an action because of violation of the principle of equal treatment is that the violation has to be based on a characteristic deemed an essential feature of personality, meaning that it is directly connected to the essence of personality." See also EBH 188/2008 and EBH 482/2005, in which the AET referred to human dignity as determining which personal characteristics are covered by Article 8.t) HETA.

[161] EBH 226/2007.

[162] EBH 231/2008.

[163] EBH 419/2007.

[164] EBH 30/2007.

[165] EBH 482/2005.

immigrant communities are covered by the list of race related grounds.[166] In Hungary the AET has already examined many cases involving discrimination of Roma persons, which it approaches as racial discrimination.[167] Moreover, the Advisory Body to the AET has made clear that characteristics such as language and social origin should be recognised as potential proxies for Roma origin, which makes clear that this body recognises modern proxies and embraces a context-sensitive approach.[168] As regards the Estonian context, finally, the minority that has attracted the most concern from NGO's and the international community, the group of ethnic Russians, is assumed to be covered by 'ethnic origin', since they constitute an officially recognised ethnic minority.[169]

The practice of the ETC provides a good example for the other Member States with regard to the context-sensitivity and flexibility it displays in the interpretation of 'race'. It was already mentioned that the modern proxies of religion and language are covered by 'race' as it is interpreted by the ETC. The ETC furthermore shows regard for proxies that are specific to the Dutch context, and has for example ruled that differential treatment of 'asylum seekers' could qualify as covert direct racial discrimination, if in reality a racial or ethnic group was targeted.[170] The Dutch High Council showed a similarly sensitive approach by ruling that the refusal to allow asylum seekers from a particular asylum centre to enter a disco should be dealt with as racial discrimination.[171] The ETC furthermore shows regard for the self-perception of the group, as well as perceptions and prejudice existing in society. For instance, persons living in mobile homes are considered by the ETC to constitute a 'race', because they consider themselves to constitute a separate group with their own culture and are perceived as a separate group in society and are met with prejudice by others.[172]

[166] See the list of cases at www.diversiteit.be, under '*rechtspraak*' ('case law') (accessed August 2009).

[167] See the various examples mentioned in *Report on the activities of the Equal Treatment Authority and the experiences of the implementation of Act nr. 125 of 2003 on equal treatment and the promotion of equal opportunities*, AET, July 2006.

[168] *Position Paper of the Advisory Body on Equal Treatment on the requirement of Equal treatment in Public Education*, 23 March 2007.

[169] See for example the explanation of 'ethnic minority' on the official website of the Ministry of Population Affairs at http://www.meis.ee/eng/minorities (accessed July 2009).

[170] Opinion 2001-70 ETC, para. 4.4.

[171] High Council 13 June 2000, NJ 2000/513, para. 3.6.

[172] See for instance Opinion 2007-157 ETC, paras. 3.6-3.8; Opinion 2007-109 ETC, paras. 3.7-3.9.

2.5.2. Interaction of grounds of discrimination

2.5.2.1. Direct v. indirect discrimination

All four Member States have to some extent set in place separate anti-discrimination frameworks for grounds that are closely connected to racial grounds, sometimes involving considerably diverging levels of protection.

In Belgium and Hungary there are mainly differences in protection between the regime for direct racial discrimination and the regime for direct discrimination on other grounds, amongst which religion, language, nationality and social status. Indirect racial discrimination, on the contrary, is regulated on more or less equal terms as direct discrimination on other grounds.[173] The qualification issue of direct discrimination on one ground versus indirect racial discrimination is therefore not relevant for these member states.

In Estonia and the Netherlands, on the contrary, the regime for indirect racial discrimination is stricter than the regime for some of the separately regulated race-related grounds, and the choice for qualification in terms of indirect racial discrimination or direct discrimination on another ground therefore has important consequences in these Member States.

In Estonia the grounds of 'language' and 'social status' are very weakly regulated in the Legal Chancellor Act (LCA), which does not provide for substantive protection but only sets in place procedural mechanisms such as official investigation and/or non-compulsory mediation services. There is a stronger regime for religious discrimination, which is regulated in the

[173] In Belgium, the new ARA sets in place a different regime for direct nationality discrimination than for direct racial discrimination, providing for an open justification possibility for the former, which resembles the objective justification test for indirect racial discrimination. The regime for nationality discrimination is further discussed in section 2.5.3. Furthermore, the Belgian *Act of 10 May 2007 combating certain forms of discrimination, BS 30 V 07* (ACFD), MB 30 V 07, regulates discrimination based on religion, language and social origin. For religion this Act maintains a closed system of justification similar to the one for racial direct discrimination, and there are no relevant differences in that regard (Articles 8 and 13). For language and social origin the ACFD provides for a regime that differs from the regime for racial discrimination in that it allows for an open justification possibility for direct discrimination (Article 7). In Hungary, the HETA separately regulates discrimination on the following race-related grounds: 'religious or ideological conviction' and 'social status'. Moreover, the ground of nationality is implicitly covered, since it is comprised by the phrase "any other status, characteristic feature or attribute". Initially the HETA applied a single regime for all the grounds contained therein, but this changed in 2007. The 2007 amendments introduced a closed justification system for direct racial discrimination, which means that the level of protection for this type of discrimination is now higher than for direct discrimination on other grounds. However, the regime for indirect racial discrimination remained exactly the same as the regime for direct discrimination on any of the other grounds.

EETA alongside racial discrimination. The EETA still offers a higher level of protection for racial discrimination, however, particularly with regard to the width of the material scope.[174] Similarly, the Dutch framework applies a wider material scope for racial discrimination than for religious and nationality discrimination.[175] Substantively, the level of protection for these various types of discrimination would not seem to be much lower than for racial discrimination. Even though the GETA provides for different justification possibilities for each ground, the different regimes appear to be comparably strict.[176]

The direct versus indirect qualification controversy is thus clearly relevant for the Estonian and Dutch frameworks. For example, religious discrimination in the field of social protection, such as refusing particular social protection services to persons who do not shake hands with women on grounds of their religion, would only be covered by Estonian and Dutch anti-discrimination law if qualified as indirect racial discrimination. Unfortunately, no discrimination cases have appeared in Estonia so far, which makes it impossible to know in which way the courts will approach this issue. In the Netherlands, the ETC has not yet applied the concept of indirect racial discrimination for distinctions on the ground of religion or nationality.[177] The ETC could possibly change this

[174] Article 2(2) EETA provides for a less expansive material scope for religious discrimination than does Article 2(1) EETA for racial and ethnic discrimination, and does not extend to education, social protection or the provision of goods and services. Moreover, in the *Explanatory Memorandum to Act 384 SE III on Equal Treatment*, the drafters emphasise that discrimination based on racial or ethnic origin is hardly ever justifiable, without making a similar statement with regard to religious discrimination. This apparently points to higher scrutiny for racial discrimination.

[175] Article 7a GETA extends the material scope of the prohibition of discrimination to the field of social protection for racial discrimination only.

[176] For *racial discrimination*, Article 2(4) GETA allows for using racial appearance as the basis for a difference in treatment if it constitutes a determining criterion, see section 4.7.2. Moreover, Article 2(3) GETA allows for positive action measures on behalf of disadvantaged ethnic groups, see section 7.5. For *nationality discrimination*, Article 2(5) GETA provides for a similar justification possibility for nationality as a determining criterion, and moreover allows for differences in treatment based on nationality that are based on generally binding regulations or written or unwritten rules of international law, see section 2.5.3. Finally, for *religious discrimination*, Articles 5(2), 6a(2) and 7(2) GETA allow institutions based on a particular ideology/philosophy to set requirements in accordance with that ideology/philosophy, as long as this does not result in a difference in treatment on the sole ground of race, gender, nationality, sexual orientation or civil status, see section 4.7.1. All provisions thus proceed from the premise that direct discrimination is only permissible in limited and neatly circumscribed circumstances, and do not seem to entail greatly diverging levels of protection.

[177] Examples drawn from the ETC's practice in 2007 include: Opinion 2007-2 ETC, in which a higher enrollment fee was applied to non-EU/EEA students, which was qualified as direct nationality discrimination; Opinion 2007-92 ETC, in which a telecom company refused clients who did not have Dutch nationality, which was qualified as direct nationality discrimination;

approach when confronted with such cases in the field of social protection, in which only the prohibition of racial discrimination applies. So far, such a case has not yet presented itself.

2.5.2.2. Intersectional discrimination

Consciousness of the problem posed by intersectional discrimination is so far only really found in the Netherlands, where it is recognised in doctrine as well as by the ETC.[178] Still, a thorough and consistent practical approach is yet to be developed in the Dutch context.

In the earlier intersectionality cases the ETC took an ad-hoc approach and did not explicitly pay attention to the intersectional aspect. For instance, in a case in which a woman of Surinam origin complained of discrimination based on sex and race, the ETC took a compartmentalised view, and decided to deal with the case as involving two types of discrimination: it first examined the sex discrimination aspect, and then it turned to racial discrimination.[179] In another case the ETC dealt with both grounds simultaneously. The particular case involved harassment that was connected to ethnic origin as well as religion, which the ETC considered to amount to discrimination based on 'race and/or religion'.[180]

In more recent cases the ETC explicitly recognised the intersectional aspect of the claim. One case involved a job applicant of Iranian origin, who was asked during a job interview about his religion. Since he could not substantiate his claim, the ETC did not get to apply any particular regime, but it nevertheless explicitly recognised the intersectionality of ethnic origin and religion.[181] The other claim involved a complaint brought by a blind Turkish woman, who complained of discrimination as regards a test assessing her professional skills. The ETC acknowledged that the test was conducted in such a way that it disadvantaged her on account of her Turkish origin as well as her disability. It did not further examine the justifiability of this instance of intersectional discrimination, and it is therefore not clear in which way the ETC would solve the different regimes for disability discrimination and racial discrimination.[182] The cases at least reveal that the ETC is willing to expressly recognise intersectionality, which means that victims of this type of

Opinion 2007-137 ETC, in which a woman was not hired because she wore a headscarf, which was qualified as direct religious discrimination.

178 Holtmaat (2007), at 17; Rodrigues & Van Walsum (2006), at 21; Evaluation report *Het verschil gemaakt. Evaluatie AWGB en werkzaamheden CGB 1999-2004*, Commissie Gelijke Behandeling 2005, at 40.

179 Opinion 2005-189 ETC.

180 Opinion 2005-75 ETC.

181 Opinion 2007-83 ETC, para. 3.1.

182 Opinion 2006-256 ETC.

discrimination receive acknowledgement of their specific disadvantage. It is therefore to be hoped that the ETC will continue to apply this more outspoken approach, and that it will develop a mechanism for solving differences in the level of protection for different grounds.

In Hungary and Belgium the problem of intersectional discrimination has been picked up by one or two public organs. In Belgium the Explanatory Memorandum of the new ARA contains a remark as to the benefits of a single instrument for the various grounds of discrimination from the viewpoint of effective protection against intersectional discrimination.[183] There is, however, no mention of intersectional discrimination in any of the federal anti-discrimination laws. Interestingly, the recently adopted decree of the Flemish Community on equal treatment contains a specific provision for cases of intersectional discrimination. The definition of direct discrimination in this decree refers to less favourable treatment on grounds of 'one or more' of the protected grounds.[184] This provision makes it easier for courts to deal with cases of intersectional discrimination, since they are no longer hindered by the confines of single grounds of discrimination. Moreover, the provision enables explicit acknowledgment of the specific disadvantage experienced by the victim of intersectional discrimination. Still, it does not give any guidance as to how differences in the level of protection for different grounds should be reconciled.

In Hungary the Ombudsman for national and ethnic minorities gave ample attention to intersectional discrimination in his 2007 annual report, but did not provide any concrete guidelines for a solution to this problem.[185] The AET has already encountered cases involving interplay between more than one ground of discrimination, but the intersectional aspect of these cases seems to have escaped the attention of this body. For instance, in a case in which the applicant claimed to have been discriminated on the basis of his Roma origin as well as his being in foster care, the AET decided not to examine the former aspect, because 80 per cent of those who were in foster care were Roma.[186] It thus denied one important aspect of the complaint, which does not show sensitivity to the victim's personal experience.

It should be mentioned that the open-endedness of the list of grounds in the HETA could in the future facilitate an inclusive approach to cases involving intersectional discrimination. If a victim of intersectional discrimination is able to show that his/her particular combination of grounds has a connection

[183] *Explanatory Memorandum to the Draft law amending the law of 30 July 1981 that penalises certain acts motivated by racism and xenophobia*, Doc 51. 2720/001,11.

[184] Article 16(1) of the Decree containing a framework for the Flemish equal opportunities and equal treatment policy of 10 July 2008.

[185] *Report on the activity of the Parliamentary Commissioner for the rights of national and ethnic minorities 2007,* at http://www.kisebbsegiombudsman.hu/data/files/121643856.pdf (accessed July 2009), at 105-107.

[186] EBH 30/2007.

with human dignity, the complaint should be judged admissible for involving discrimination on 'any other status, characteristic feature or attribute'. Not only would cases of intersectional discrimination in this way hardly risk falling outside of the scope of anti-discrimination law; victims of intersectional discrimination would also receive acknowledgement of their particular disadvantage. Still, it remains to be seen how the AET and the Hungarian courts will deal with the dilemma as to the appropriate level of protection in the case of the intersection of race and another ground of discrimination, given that the level of protection for the former ground is higher than that for any other ground of discrimination.

2.5.2.3. Conflicts of grounds

The issue of conflicting grounds has so far only played a part in the Hungarian and Dutch frameworks. The Hungarian HETA is rather unique in expressly regulating situations of conflicting rights, which is understood to also cover conflicts between discrimination grounds. Article 7(2) a) HETA provides that: "the principle of equal treatment is not violated by such disposition, which limits a basic right of the entity brought into a disadvantageous position in order to enforce another basic right in an unavoidable situation, assuming that such a limitation is suitable for this purpose and is also in proportion to it". This is a difficult way of saying that, if allegedly discriminatory treatment affects a fundamental right of the victim and the perpetrator invokes a fundamental right to justify his behaviour, a proportionality test should be carried out. Article 7(3) HETA subsequently clarifies that this proportionality rule does not apply to cases of direct racial discrimination or racial segregation, meaning that for these forms of discrimination, no justification is possible, not even if it is based on another fundamental right. This bold provision should be played down somewhat, since Article 22 (1) a) HETA provides for the application of race as an occupational requirement under certain conditions.[187] Still, the article makes clear that the closed system of justification for direct racial discrimination needs to be respected even in case of a conflict of grounds, which is in line with the requirements of the RED. In cases of indirect racial or ethnic discrimination, the proportionality rule of Article 7(2) HETA regains importance. If the discrimination does not concern a so-called basic right of the disadvantaged racial or ethnic group, the test is even more lenient, requiring only a reasonable explanation directly related to the legal relationship at stake (Article 7(2) b) HETA). As is explained in section 5.5.4.6, this test is overly lenient, as it does not require a balancing act to be carried out. In this respect, the Hungarian regime for conflicting grounds would seem to fall short of what is required by the RED, but this needs to be confirmed in practice.

---

[187] See section 4.7.2.

The Dutch framework is the only one where the problem of conflicting grounds has already appeared in practice, apart from being recognised in literature.[188] Since the cases so far involved only claims of indirect discrimination, the ETC has been able to solve them by applying the objective justification test for one of the grounds, which entails a test of appropriateness, necessity and proportionality.[189] In practice, this means that the ETC thoroughly assesses the interests at stake and balances them against each other.

For instance, in a case in which a man was not employed because he refused to shake hands with female customers, the ETC applied the objective justification test for indirect religious discrimination and balanced the right to non-discrimination of women with the right to non-discrimination on grounds of religion. In the end, it found that the requirement to shake hands was not proportionate in relation to the aim of protecting women from discrimination, since there were viable alternatives available that the employer had not used.[190]

Interestingly, the Rotterdam District Court subsequently came to the opposite conclusion, by considering that the requirement of the employer was necessary, because they were allowed to abide by the normal societal politeness rules. Formally, however, the Court applied the same approach as the ETC: it concluded that there was indirect distinction based on religion, which it found to be objectively justified in view of the need to ensure equal treatment between men and women.[191] This shows that cases of conflicting grounds involve difficult choices that are not of a legal nature, which makes it hard to make a general assessment of the way in which cases of conflicting grounds are dealt with. Still, the formal aspect of the judgments in these cases can be assessed. In this regard it is remarkable that the court simply stated that the obligation to shake hands was appropriate and necessary, without explaining in any way why. The ETC, to the contrary, applied more meticulous reasoning, by extensively going through all phases belonging to the objective justification test: the requirements of a legitimate aim, appropriateness and necessity. This approach is obviously preferable over that of the court.

A second example involves a case in which a man was turned down for the job of civil servant because he refused to marry same-sex couples, on religious grounds. Here also the ETC made use of the objective justification test, because the case involved indirect discrimination on grounds of religion. The ETC again applied meticulous reasoning, arguing that the aim of protecting against discrimination of homosexuals was legitimate; that the measure (refusal to

---

188 Goldschmidt & Hendriks (2003), at 1283; Loenen (2003), at 267-268.

189 See section 5.2.4.

190 Opinion 2006-202 ETC, paras. 3.22-3.25.

191 Rotterdam District Court, 6 August 2008, LJN: BD 9643, paras. 5.2.2-5.2.3.

hire) was appropriate; and that the interest of being able to marry persons was trumped by the interest of not being discriminated against, which made the measure necessary/proportionate.[192]

On the whole, the approach of the ETC seems satisfactory; especially its tendency to make a thorough assessment of the case and to apply all aspects of the objective justification test. A case of conflicting grounds involving racial discrimination has so far not emerged, which makes it impossible to say whether this ground is given sufficient weight, and whether the ETC remains within the boundaries of the RED.

2.5.3. The nationality exception of Article 3(2)

Of all four Member States under study, only Estonia has followed the RED in its restrictive approach to nationality discrimination. The EETA does not cover nationality discrimination, and the Explanatory Memorandum to this Act reveals that this was a deliberate choice, by providing that: "[t]he norms of international law and the legal acts in force in Europe specify the principle that the distinction of people on the grounds of citizenship is not deemed to be discrimination on grounds of ethnic origin or race."[193] This remark apparently proceeds from a flawed understanding of the international legal state of affairs with regard to nationality discrimination, which was discussed in section 2.3.3. Moreover, if it correctly reflects the Estonian legal climate, it makes clear that it is not very likely that the concept of indirect racial or ethnic discrimination will be used to protect against nationality discrimination. This impression is reinforced by a decision of the Administrative Chamber of the Supreme Court on the constitutional equality provision, which suggests a rather permissive approach to the differential treatment of foreigners. In the particular case, it was asserted that the strict official policy with regard to the granting of permanent residence permits to former Soviet military servicemen and their relatives was discriminatory on the basis of social status. The Administrative Chamber disagreed, and stated that: "[a]ccording to international law a State possesses the right to decide the presence of a foreigner on its territory. The Constitution does not provide a foreigner with the basic right to live and stay in Estonia. There will be no discrimination according to the meaning of Article 12 of the Constitution if the requirements for granting a permanent residence permit are related to the membership of a particular group".[194] This ruling comes down to giving the state complete freedom in designing its residence policy, which is not in conformity with international law. It appears to proceed from the same line of thinking as the previously mentioned remark in the

[192] Opinion 2008-40 ETC, paras. 3.18-3.30.

[193] *Explanatory Memorandum to Act 384 SE III on Equal Treatment.*

[194] As reproduced by Poleshchuk (2007), at 38.

Explanatory Memorandum of the EETA, according to which the Estonian state is considered to have more or less unrestricted power to deal with non-nationals in a way it sees fit. Perhaps courts will draw some boundaries in the future, but for now it would seem that there is little protection for non-nationals. This is all the more serious in the Estonian context, where the position of a large group of non-citizens of Russian origin is a sensitive issue that has received attention from many NGOs and international supervisory bodies.[195]

Contrary to Estonia, the other three Member States have included the ground of nationality in their anti-discrimination laws. The Netherlands and Belgium in particular provide quite a high level of protection against nationality discrimination.

The Belgian anti-discrimination framework has included nationality as a protected ground since 1981, when the old ARA entered into force.[196] After the first phase of implementation of the RED, the old ADA implicitly protected against nationality discrimination, since this ground was understood to be covered by the ground 'national origin'.[197] It thus received a level of protection similar to the regime for racial grounds, which involved an open justification possibility for direct as well as indirect discrimination. When the new ARA was adopted, the government decided to set up a separate regime for nationality discrimination, so as to retain the open justification possibility for this ground.[198] Article 7(2) of the new ARA prohibits any distinction based on nationality that cannot be justified by a legitimate aim and is not appropriate and necessary.

It is expected that this open justification possibility will be strictly interpreted by Belgian courts, since previous jurisprudence reveals that they are rather suspicious with regard to nationality discrimination, in view of its close relation with racial discrimination. For instance, the Arbitration Court emphasised in a 2003 case that differential treatment of foreigners was only allowed if carried out by law.[199] Even though this decision involved a vertical relationship, it could impact on the interpretation of the horizontally applicable

[195] See for example Poleshchuk (2005), para. 4.4; *Second opinion on Estonia*, Advisory Committee on the Framework Convention for the Protection of National Minorities, 24 February 2005, ACFC/OP/II(2005), in particular para. 37 on the omission of a prohibition of nationality discrimination; *Report by Mr. Alvaro Gil-Robles, Commissioner for Human Rights on his visit to Estonia*, 12 February 2004, CommDH(2004)5; *Third Report on Estonia*, European Commission against Racism and Intolerance, 24 June 2005, CRI(2006)1, especially paras. 9-13 on citizenship regulation; *Concluding Observations Estonia*, CERD, 2006, CERD/C/EST/CO/7, especially paras. 9, 14 and 15 on the position of non-citizens.

[196] De Prins et al (2005), at 310-312.

[197] De Prins et al (2005), at 453-455.

[198] *Explanatory Memorandum to the Draft law amending the law of 30 July 1981 that penalises certain acts motivated by racism and xenophobia*, Doc 51. 2720/001, at 23.

[199] Court of Arbitration, no. 106/2003, 22 July 2003, para. B.5.3-B.5.4, which contains an interpretation of Article 191 of the Constitution, according to which: "[a]ll foreigners on Belgian

regime of the new ARA. The Court's emphasis on the need for a legal basis at least conveys appreciation of the seriousness of nationality discrimination, which could translate into the requirement that private actors act on a legal basis when differentiating on grounds of nationality.

Another indication for strict scrutiny can be found in a 2004 decision of the Court of Cassation, which was ruled under the regime of the old ARA. In this decision the Court supported the reasoning of a lower court, according to which private actors were not allowed to make distinctions based on nationality. The Court moreover confirmed that the nationality exception of Article 2(1) ICERD was applicable to public actors only.[200] Even though the old ARA is no longer applicable, this judgment is arguably still relevant for Article 7(2) new ARA in that it confirms that Belgian courts are particularly strict vis-à-vis nationality discrimination perpetrated by private actors.

The Dutch framework also applies a strict approach as regards nationality discrimination, and provides an even higher level of protection than the Belgian framework. The GETA, which has covered nationality discrimination since 1994, applies a closed system of justification and only allows permits distinctions on grounds of nationality that are based on a legal provision (national or international),[201] or for which nationality constitutes a determining characteristic.[202] The former requirement reminds of the insistence of the Belgian Arbitration court on a legal basis for nationality discrimination. The latter requirement has been further developed in a Royal Decree, which only allows for differentiation on grounds of nationality when rules or practice of a sport association require that persons of Dutch nationality partake in a competition to represent their country.[203] The ETC furthermore applies strict scrutiny with regard to nationality discrimination, which it considers to be as serious as racial discrimination.[204]

In practice this means that nationality discrimination is not reformulated in terms of covert or indirect racial discrimination, because both types of discrimination are considered to be equally serious. Still, there is a difference in material scope between the regulations for both types of discrimination:

soil benefit from that protection provided to persons and property, save for those exceptions provided for by law."

200 Court of Cassation, 9 November 2004, para. 11.1.

201 'Legal provision' in this context actually only extends to those provisions that contain generally binding rules, as Article 2(5)a makes clear. The ETC follows the general Dutch legal approach to the concept of generally binding rules: the provision concerned must contain independent rules, which do not simply further elaborate another rule or regulation, and which can be applied to consecutive situations. See for example Opinion 2006-110 ETC, and the note on this opinion by Zoontjens 2006c. In view of its technicality, the matter is not further discussed in this study.

202 Article 2(5) GETA.

203 Article 3 of the *Royal Decree of 18 August 1994*, Stb. 657.

204 See the 2007 Annual Report of the ETC, *Jaarverslag 2007*, Commissie Gelijke Behandeling, at 65.

the scope of the prohibition of nationality discrimination follows the material scope of the FD, not of the RED.[205] In line with what was said before on the qualification issue of direct versus indirect discrimination, it is not clear whether the ETC will more often resort to the notion of indirect racial discrimination when confronted with nationality discrimination in the field of social protection, which is only covered by the prohibition of racial discrimination.[206]

The Hungarian framework also protects against nationality discrimination, albeit at a lower level. Nationality is considered to be one of the "other grounds" as referred to in Article 8.t) of the HETA.[207] Differences in treatment based on nationality should therefore comply with the general justification clause of Article 7(2) HETA.[208] This test resembles the objective justification test applied by the Belgian framework for nationality discrimination. Still, Hungarian courts will perhaps not be as strict on nationality discrimination as their Belgian counterparts. A decision of the Metropolitan Court in 2006 in any case reveals a rather lenient attitude. In the particular case, a local spa granted permanent residents with Hungarian nationality a discount on entry tickets. A German man who had lived in the town for five years was denied the discount, which according to him and the AET constituted discrimination based on an 'other ground' (i.e. nationality). The Metropolitan Court disagreed in quite an unstructured judgment. The Court commenced by stating that the right of the defendant to primarily advantage the permanent residents of the town could not be disputed, since these persons as inhabitants of the town obviously contributed to making their town better and more pleasant. Moreover, the Court considered that European law did not preclude a national authority or operator from providing discounts for the inhabitants of its own town in particular cases. The Court then went on to deny that nationality was even actually used as a factor, because the applicant could not be regarded as a permanent resident and Hungarian citizens who were not permanent residents were disadvantaged as well. The Court felt that it had no reason to doubt the defendant's statement that the lack of Hungarian nationality in itself would not have prevented issuance of the discount card, despite the fact that it was a formal criterion.[209] This judgment clearly does not reveal a critical attitude towards differences in treatment based on nationality.

[205] *Explanatory Memorandum to the Draft Amendment of the General Act on Equal Treatment and certain other acts in order to implement directive 2000/43/EC and directive 2000/78/EC*, TK 2002-03, 28 770, No. 3, at 13. It should be noted, however, that the material scope for nationality discrimination was slightly less comprehensive than it is now. The implementation of the FD has therefore reinforced the level of protection against nationality discrimination.

[206] See section 2.5.2.1.

[207] EBH 10/2006; EBH 46/2007; EBH 56/2007.

[208] Since the justification clause of Article 7(2) is rather complicated, it is not dealt with here. See section 5.5.4.6 for a more detailed analysis.

[209] Metropolitan Court, 8.K. 33.297/2006/5, 11 December 2006.

If this judgment is representative for the manner in which Hungarian courts look upon nationality discrimination, it can be expected that many distinctions made on the basis of nationality will slip through the net. Moreover, seeing that the concept of indirect discrimination is new and unfamiliar to Hungarian courts, it is not very likely that nationality discrimination will appropriately be recognised as constituting covert or indirect racial discrimination. Therefore, it remains to be seen to what extent Hungarian law will effectively protect against nationality discrimination. Since it in any case does not go against the requirements of the RED, one can at most speak of a missed opportunity.

2.5.4. Types of victims

2.5.4.1. Legal persons as victims

The anti-discrimination laws of the four Member States are not very generous with regard to legal persons as potential victims of discrimination. In Hungary and the Netherlands the supervisory bodies in principle reject claims of legal persons as victims of discrimination.[210] However, the Hungarian AET does allow for legal persons to file a complaint if there is a connection to the human dignity of a natural person. For instance, the AET accepted a complaint of an association that set up an integration programme for former prostitutes. The association was refused as a client by a conference centre for the accommodation of a press conference announcing the integration programme. The AET decided that the conference centre had violated the principle of equal treatment with respect to the association, because: "[t]o indirectly stand in the way of such activities by not allowing an official event to take place without any reasonable objective justification (…) can contribute to a violation of human dignity".[211] This flexible approach enhances the level of protection offered by the HETA. No similar approach is discernable in the quasi-jurisprudence of the Dutch ETC.

In Belgium and Estonia there is no clear approach yet. It has been argued that the new Belgian ARA will probably provide protection for legal persons, but this has not yet been confirmed in practice.[212] In Estonia, there are contradictory indications as to the manner in which the question will be solved. On the one hand, the constitutional equality provision has been applied by the Constitutional Chamber of the Supreme Court in cases involving claims

[210] *Report on the activities of the Equal Treatment Authority and the experiences of the implementation of Act nr. 125 of 2003 on equal treatment and the promotion of equal opportunities*, AET, July 2006; Evaluation report *Het verschil gemaakt. Evaluatie AWGB en werkzaamheden CGB 1999-2004*, ETC 2005, at 41. This is not to say that legal persons cannot institute proceedings on behalf of natural persons as victims, see Ambrus (2010).

[211] EBH/482/2005.

[212] De Schutter (2007a), at 50; De Schutter (2004), at 29.

of legal persons.[213] Reasoning per analogy, one would expect that the more specific anti-discrimination legislation would then provide protection for legal persons as well. On the other hand, it has been submitted that only natural persons can be victims of discrimination according to local legal tradition, and that anti-discrimination law will thus not be available for legal persons.[214] Practice has not yet revealed which line of argument will prevail.

2.5.4.2. Discrimination by assumption or by association

The problem of discrimination by assumption has been recognised in the Member States under study, save for Estonia. In the latter state, the concept has so far not come up in doctrine or other documentation. It is of course possible that courts will apply the concept in the future. In the other Member States, the possibility of discrimination by assumption has been explicitly recognised, and the concept has already been applied in practice.[215]

As regards discrimination by association, the Belgian, Hungarian and Dutch frameworks all accommodate this type of discrimination. In Belgium, the matter was connected to developments at the European level. During the parliamentary proceedings on the new ARA, the government refused to decide whether discrimination by association was covered, and referred to the *Coleman* case, which was pending before the ECJ at the time.[216] Since the ECJ has subsequently unequivocally included discrimination by association as a prohibited form of discrimination in this case, it can be expected that Belgian courts will follow suit.

In Hungary, it seems fairly certain that discrimination by association is effectively covered by the HETA, even though this has not happened explicitly.[217] The aforementioned case of the discrimination of an association that organised integration activities for former prostitutes could be viewed as an implicit application of this concept.[218] Moreover, discrimination by association can easily be tackled by making use of the open-endedness of the list of grounds of Article 8 HETA: being associated with persons that have a protected characteristic could be seen as one of the 'other grounds'.

---

213 Decision of the Constitutional Chamber of the Supreme Court, 3-4-1-1-02, 6 March 2002, para. 13. See also Poleshchuk (2007), at 26.

214 Poleshchuk (2005), para. 3.1.2.

215 For Belgium, see the *Parliamentary proceedings on the new ARA*, Doc 51, 2720/009, at 41, and Ghent Correctional Tribunal, 10 May 2005. For Hungary, see Kádár & Farkas (2005), at 9; Pest Central District Court, 20.AT85.346/2003/10, 1 July 2003 and Szabolcs-Szatmár-Bereg County Court, 1.AT 21.752/2004/26, 13 June 2005. For The Netherlands, see Hendriks (2003), at 56; Opinion 2005-4 ETC, p 6-7 and Opinion 2002-84 ETC.

216 *S. Coleman v. Attridge Law and Steve Law*, Case C-303/06, 17 July 2008. Also see section 2.4.3 for a discussion of this judgment.

217 Kádár & Farkas (2005), at 9.

218 See previous section 2.5.4.1.

Finally, the Dutch ETC has taken a very clear standpoint with regard to discrimination by association, stating explicitly in a 2002 case that it is not necessary that the complainant himself has the protected characteristic, and that it suffices that he is disadvantaged by a distinction made on the basis of another person's protected characteristic.[219]

2.6. Summary and conclusion

The relevance of the personal scope provisions of the RED for minority protection is quite straight-forward and is primarily quantitative in nature: the more persons are covered by the RED, the more persons are obliged to uphold its provisions (addressees) and the more persons can invoke its provisions (beneficiaries). The basic premise of this chapter was therefore that the positive scope provisions should be interpreted as extensively as legally possible. Seeing that the personal scope provisions of the RED are very summarily worded, referring to 'all persons' (addressees) and 'racial or ethnic origin' (beneficiaries), there is quite some room to manoeuvre in this respect. Consequently, for lack of guidance at the European level so far, the impact of the personal scope provisions of the RED on the level of minority protection in the first place depends on the choices made at the national level.

Minimum baseline of protection

In view of the many remaining open-ended questions that were identified in the theoretical framework the minimum baseline of protection required by the RED can only partially be construed.

As regards the circle of addressees, it is at least sufficiently clear that both public and private actors must be targeted by national anti-discrimination law, and that differentiation between these actors is possible only to a limited extent. The RED arguably leaves some room to grant public actors a margin of appreciation and to interpret the provisions of the RED in line with fundamental rights and freedoms of public actors. Still, it seems clear that additional justification possibilities or delineations of the material scope in order safeguard fundamental rights and freedoms for private actors are not permissible, other than those already provided for in the RED.

Unfortunately, not all Member States under study have respected these boundaries. The Dutch framework provides for a number of justification possibilities for private actors that are not permitted by the RED. In a mirror-wise manner, the Estonian framework provides for an overly broad additional

[219] Opinion 2002-204 ETC, para. 5.1. For another case of discrimination by association see Opinion 2001-78 ETC.

justification possibility for public actors, which also clearly overstretches the limits set in place by the RED. In a similar fashion, the Dutch ETC grants public actors what would appear to be an overly broad margin of appreciation.

Even the fairly basic requirement of full applicability of the RED to both public and private actors has not been completely fulfilled. Thus, Belgium, Hungary and the Netherlands have to a greater or lesser extent excluded a portion of public actor activity from their national anti-discrimination acts. The doctrine of direct effect could be used to remedy this lack of applicability, but it would have been preferable for national anti-discrimination law to be applicable to all public actor activity that falls within the material scope of the RED.

As regards the circle of beneficiaries, the one thing that is unmistakably clear is that the RED requires the grounds 'racial' and 'ethnic' origin to be covered by national anti-discrimination law. All Member States have met this relatively low threshold.

Obscurities and opportunities for providing a higher level of protection

It was pointed out in this chapter that one of the most pressing unanswered questions with respect to the circle of addressees is whether persons other than the actors that have particular responsibilities within the material fields of application, such as employers, school boards, shops, service providers, etcetera, can be viewed as addressees of the prohibition of discrimination. Due to lack of guidance at the European level so far, Member States have the liberty of taking either a broad or a narrow approach to this question.

The four Member States have generally opted for the narrow approach, and thus have excluded the possibility of holding co-workers, co-students, clients and other third parties directly responsible for discriminatory behaviour. The new Belgian ARA and Estonian EETA are still potentially applicable to these types of actors, but future practice needs to show whether this will be the case.

The Dutch framework is the only one that has compensated for the lack of liability of non-principally envisaged actors to a high degree, by setting in place extensive positive duties for principally envisaged actors. The Hungarian and Estonian frameworks have some openings for similar duties of principally envisaged actors, but it is uncertain whether these opportunities will be made use of. In addition, most Member States provide for some form of liability of employers and/or schools for unlawful behaviour of their subordinates, but these are not sufficiently developed to provide a strong remedy in cases of discrimination perpetrated by non-principally envisaged actors.

As regards the circle of beneficiaries, it was pointed out in the theoretical framework that it is greatly important that the grounds of 'racial' and 'ethnic' origin are interpreted in a flexible manner, with special consideration for the modern proxies that are used in contemporary societies to designate racial and ethnic in-groups and out-groups. For instance, not only physiological characteristics are nowadays used as markers for racial or ethnic origin, but also characteristics such as religion, language, social class etcetera. These proxies are all covered by the list of grounds covered by the International Convention on the Elimination of All Forms of Racial Discrimination (ICERD), as interpreted by the ICERD supervisory organ, CERD, which was therefore presented as an exemplary model for the Member States.

The case-study revealed that the four Member States have generally taken a generous approach with regard to the conceptualisation of these grounds, and have largely followed the inclusive list of grounds contained in ICERD. Moreover, it was shown that the most important minority groups in the Member States' societies are covered by the grounds contained in the national acts. It should in particular be mentioned that the Dutch ETC has developed a flexible and inclusive approach, by showing regard for perceptions within society as regards out-groups and in-groups and for contemporary proxies used in Dutch society to designate out-groups.

It was furthermore explained that various grounds of discrimination can interact in complex ways. This presents a challenge for anti-discrimination frameworks, which presuppose instances of discrimination to involve one ground at a time. The concept of intersectional discrimination is particularly difficult to accommodate in the traditional anti-discrimination paradigm. This type of discrimination occurs if a person is discriminated against on grounds of a particular interplay of characteristics, such as race combined with gender or disability. No satisfactory approach has yet been developed at the European level for this particular type of discrimination.

Since most national frameworks are still in the initial stages of development, it is unsurprising that intersectional discrimination was also found not to have been specifically regulated in the Member States. There is growing attention for the problems posed by intersectional discrimination, however, and these will hopefully be resolved in a satisfactory manner. This would at least involve formal recognition of the particular intersection of grounds as being the ground for the discriminatory treatment, as well as application of the anti-discrimination regime that offers the highest level of protection.

One of the most interesting findings of this chapter was the fact that the four Member States have hardly made use of Article 3(2) RED, which excludes nationality discrimination from the scope of the RED. This exception is problematic in view of the close ties between nationality and racial discrimination, and it was expected by many to seriously restrain the impact of national anti-discrimination law. The case study part revealed that only one Member State, namely Estonia, has effectively excluded nationality discrimination from the scope of its anti-discrimination Act. The other three Member States, to the contrary, have included the ground of nationality. The Dutch framework provides a particularly high level of protection for this ground, which hardly differs from the level of protection for the ground of race. In Belgium nationality discrimination also appears to be strictly scrutinised. In Hungary, to the contrary, nationality discrimination appears to be protected to quite a lesser degree than racial discrimination. In any event, it is very positive that Article 3(2) RED has by far not had as undermining an effect as was expected.

In conclusion, it is clear that the RED provides for sufficient opportunity for generous and inclusive personal coverage of anti-discrimination law, even though it does not give Member States much guidance in this respect. To some extent Member States have made use of this opportunity, but they have clearly not fully maximised the reach ratione personae of their national anti-discrimination laws.

It is especially regrettable that they have in some instances not respected the minimum baseline of protection required by the RED. It was particularly remarkable that the Netherlands has crossed the boundaries of the RED, by providing for a number of justification possibilities that are not permitted by the RED, which seems to stem from the wish to maintain the Dutch anti-discrimination acquis that was in place prior to the RED. Clearly, the existence of a well-developed anti-discrimination framework prior to implementation does not always produce a higher quality of implementation. In contrast, the Belgian framework, which operates in a context of much less experience with anti-discrimination law and sensitive minority issues, has to a high degree adhered to the minimum requirements of the RED, and has even provided for a higher level of protection than required by prohibiting nationality discrimination.

It should not be overlooked, however, that the Dutch framework shows some particularly positive features, such as protection against nationality discrimination, extensive positive duties for principally envisaged actors and a context-sensitive approach to the conceptualisation of 'racial' and 'ethnic' origin. To a lesser extent, the Hungarian framework, which operates in the context of a relatively high level of minority protection shows similar positive features, in particular positive duties for principally envisaged actors and a prohibition of nationality discrimination.

Of all four Member States, Estonia is clearly the least progressive: not only has this Member State not fully respected the minimum requirements of the RED; it has also hardly made use of the considerable leeway granted by the RED to provide for a higher level of protection than required.

Chapter 3

Material Scope

Within the limits of the powers conferred upon the Community, this Directive shall apply to all persons, as regards both the public and private sectors, including public bodies, in relation to:

(a) conditions for access to employment, to self-employment and to occupation, including selection criteria and recruitment conditions, whatever the branch of activity and at all levels of the professional hierarchy, including promotion;
(b) access to all types and to all levels of vocational guidance, vocational training, advanced vocational training and retraining, including practical work experience;
(c) employment and working conditions, including dismissals and pay;
(d) membership of and involvement in an organisation of workers or employers, or any organisation whose members carry on a particular profession, including the benefits provided for by such organisations;
(e) social protection, including social security and healthcare;
(f) social advantages;
(g) education;
(h) access to and supply of goods and services which are available to the public, including housing (Article 3(1) RED)

This Directive does not cover difference of treatment based on nationality and is without prejudice to provisions and conditions relating to the entry into and residence of third country nationals and stateless persons on the territory of Member States, and to any treatment which arises from the legal status of the third-country nationals and stateless persons concerned (Article 3(2) RED)

PART ONE: THEORETICAL FRAMEWORK

3.1. Introduction

The material scope provisions of the RED determine which domains of social life are covered by the RED and, in setting the second preliminary barrier for persons who want to invoke the RED's substantive provisions, complement the personal scope provisions. The wide material reach of the RED as compared to other European equality instruments creates a relatively favourable starting position in this respect.[1] However, the fact that the RED treads to some extent upon hitherto unknown territory will undoubtedly produce some difficulty in practice. This chapter discusses the various issues that can be expected to arise in this respect.

The actual discussion of the separate elements of the list contained in Article 3(1) RED in the following sections is preceded by an examination of two factors that are of general relevance for the RED's material scope. The first of these factors involves the 'within the limits of the powers conferred upon the Community' clause of Article 3(1), which touches on the complex relationship between Community and Member State competence. The second factor relates to the question whether the material scope can to some extent be further delineated by fundamental rights and freedoms of private actors. Both factors are discussed in section 3.2.

Section 3.3 discusses the interpretation of the different domains mentioned in Article 3(1) RED. It should be underscored from the outset that the link with effective minority protection is rather straightforward and can be summarised as follows: the more expansive the material scope, the higher the level of protection for persons belonging to minority groups. A broader material scope makes for more possibilities of bringing alleged instances of discrimination before the courts. This rather obvious link will not be repeated in each of the following subsections.

Finally, section 3.4 explores the implications of Article 3(2) RED, which excludes immigration, visa and asylum policies from the material scope of the RED.

---

1 The FD, which was adopted months after the RED, regulates equal treatment on grounds of religion, age, disability and sexual orientation, and only applies to the field of employment. In 2008 a proposal was made by the Commission to align the material scope of anti-discrimination law for these grounds with that of the RED, see *Proposal for a Council Directive on implementing the principle of equal treatment between persons irrespective of religion or belief, disability, age or sexual orientation*, European Commission, 2 July 2008, COM(2008) 426 final. Until 2004, sex equality law only applied in employment-related fields: see Directive 2006/54/EC, which integrates and synchronises the various instruments that existed in this field. Since the adoption of Directive 2004/113/EC, sex equality law now also extends to access to and provision of goods and services.

3.2. Factors that potentially qualify the material scope of the RED

3.2.1. Division of competences between Member States and the EU

The first phrase of Article 3(1) RED emphasises that the RED operates "within the limits of the powers conferred upon the Community". This clause is similar to a clause contained in Article 13(1) TEC, which provides the legal basis for the adoption of the RED, and which reads as follows:

> [w]ithout prejudice to the other provisions of this Treaty and *within the limits of the powers conferred by it upon the Community*, the Council, acting unanimously on a proposal from the Commission and after consulting the European Parliament, may take appropriate action to combat discrimination based on sex, racial or ethnic origin, religion or belief, disability, age or sexual orientation (emphasis added, MB).

At the time of the insertion of Article 13 TEC by the Treaty of Amsterdam, the reference to 'powers' was considered remarkable for its deviation from Article 12 TEC, which contains the prohibition of nationality discrimination. Article 12 TEC does not refer to the limits of the competences of the Community, but to the limits of the scope of application of the TEC instead, and provides that:

> *[w]ithin the scope of application of this Treaty,* and without prejudice to any special provisions contained therein, any discrimination on grounds of nationality shall be prohibited (emphasis added, MB).

On the basis of this particular clause, the ECJ adopted quite an extensive approach to the material scope of the prohibition of nationality discrimination. Thus, if Member States acted within a domain that fell within the scope of the TEC, they were required to act in compliance with Article 12 TEC, even when acting in a field that belonged to their exclusive competence. As a result, very few domains remained in which Member States were not obliged to uphold Article 12 TEC.[2] For example, the ECJ ruled that, even though the Community had no competence to act in the field of criminal law, the prohibition of nationality discrimination should still be upheld by Member States when they regulated in this field, if they acted within the scope of the Treaty.[3] In this context, the reference to 'powers' instead of 'scope of application' in Article 13 TEC was received by scholars as being prompted by

---

2 Bell (2002), at 131-132.

3 ECJ *Bickel and Franz*, Case C-274/96, 24 November 1998, paras. 13-19. See also Bell (2002), at 132; Flynn (1999), at 1134-1135.

a wish to curtail the interpretative creativity of the ECJ, and to ensure that the material scope of instruments adopted on the basis of Article 13 TEC was not overly broadly interpreted.[4]

This particular history of the 'within limits' clause in Article 3(2) RED raises the question as to what impact the division of competences in European law could or should have on the material scope of the RED. The Explanatory Memorandum of the RED apparently approaches the clause solely as a reminder of the fact that the RED provides a minimum baseline of protection for racial discrimination, and that Member States are still fully competent to provide a higher level of protection.[5] Along similar lines of thinking, it has been submitted that the clause is a reminder of the subsidiarity principle, according to which regulation at the European level should only concern those matters that are not better regulated at the member state level.[6] According to this view, the limitation clause is meant to emphasise that the RED's provisions are not intended to have any substantive legal impact in fields belonging to Member State competence, other than ensuring the absence of racial discrimination.[7] The most recent Commission proposal for an equality directive on the basis of Article 13 TEC aligns with this latter interpretation.[8]

An important objection against these interpretations is that they would seem to strip the 'within limits' clause of real meaning. After all, both the minimum baseline of protection rule and the subsidiarity principle are applicable in the

---

[4] Van den Berghe (2003), at 172-173; Bell (2002), at 131-135; Flynn (1999), at 1134; Waddington (1999), at 137.

[5] *Amended proposal for a Council Directive implementing the principle of equal treatment between persons irrespective of racial or ethnic origin*, Commission of the European Communities, 1999/0253 (CNS), 31 May 2000, at 15: "European legislation must, of course, respect the *limits of the powers conferred on the Community* by the Treaty. The proposed Directive *therefore* lays down general principles, providing a common minimum level of protection within the limits of Community competence, while allowing Member States to maintain a higher standard of protection in accordance with their political and historical choices and traditions." (emphasis added, MB)

[6] See Article 5(2) TEC, which provides that: "[i]n areas which do not fall within its exclusive competence, the Community shall take action, in accordance with the principle of subsidiarity, only if and in so far as the objectives of the proposed action cannot be sufficiently achieved by the Member States and can therefore, by reason of the scale or effects of the proposed action, be better achieved by the Community."

[7] Van der Mei (2005), at 188; Knook (2005), at 391-392.

[8] *Proposal for a Council Directive on implementing the principle of equal treatment between persons irrespective of religion or belief, disability, age or sexual orientation*, European Commission, 2 July 2008, COM(2008) 426 final, at 8: "[t]he areas are covered only to the extent that the subject matter falls within the competences of the Community. Thus, for example, the organization of the school system, activities and the content of education courses, including how to organize education for persons with disabilities, is a matter for the Member States, and they may provide for differences in treatment in access to religious educational institutions. For example, a school could arrange a special presentation just for children of a certain age, while a faith based school would be allowed to arrange school trips with a religious theme."

context of the RED anyway, and do not need an express reminder to that effect.[9] Some have therefore taken a different stance and argue that the clause has an actual substantive impact on the reach of the material scope of the RED. The clause would in their opinion exclude from the RED's material scope those aspects of domains listed in Article 3(2) that exclusively belong to the competence of Member States. This would mainly be the case for some parts of the fields of education, housing and healthcare.[10] Social advantages would for instance only be covered in so far as they are provided in domains that fall within Community competence.[11] However, this interpretation of the qualification clause is no less problematic than the previous one, because it is nearly impossible to neatly define the boundaries between Member State and Community competence.[12] There are no clear-cut parameters to determine the limits of the scope of application of the RED in the above-mentioned areas, which would lead to the unsatisfactory situation in which no one would know which aspects of for example education or healthcare would be covered until the ECJ pronounced on it.

So far, the ECJ has appeared to side with the first interpretation of the clause and has not accepted any substantive material scope delineations on the basis of the 'within limits' clause. This is the picture emerging from the currently developing body of case law on the FD, which contains a clause similar to that of Article 3(2) RED. In *Palacios*, Advocate General Mazák referred to the competence of the Member States in order to justify a restrictive interpretation of the concept of 'dismissal'. He argued that Recital 14 of the preamble to the FD, which provides that the Directive is without prejudice to national provisions laying down retirement ages, implied that a rule of national law ending an employment contract automatically when a person reaches the statutory retirement age fell outside the material scope of the Directive. In other words, he considered that the exclusive competence of Member States to lay down retirement ages had to shape the interpretation of the concept 'dismissal'.[13] The ECJ refused to go along with this argument,

---

9 Flynn (1999), at 1135. See Article 6(1) RED, which provides that: "Member States may introduce or maintain provisions which are more favorable to the protection of the principle of equal treatment than those laid down in this Directive", and thus lays down the minimum baseline of protection rule. See furthermore Article 5(2) TEC, which lays down the subsidiarity principle for all legal activity of the European Community.

10 Bell (2002), at 136-144; Brown (2002), at 214-215.

11 Howard (2005), at 478; Ellis (2003), at 656-657.

12 Davies (2006), at 65; Bell (2002), at 143.

13 ECJ *Félix Palacios de la Villa v. Cortefiel Servicios SA*, Case C-411/05, Opinion of Advocate-General Mazák, 15 February 2007, paras. 56-60. A-G Mazák actually does not refer explicitly to the 'within limits' phrase, but does so implicitly by referring to the opinion of A-G Geelhoed in the *Chacón Navas* case, *Sonia Chacón Navas v. Eurest Colectividados SA*, Case C-13/05, 16 March 2006, paras. 52-22, in which the call for a restrictive interpretation of the concept of 'disability' was partly based on the 'within limits' clause.

and simply considered that the legislation at issue affected the duration of the employment relationship between the private parties, and thus fell within the material scope of the FD.[14]

The *Palacios* ruling raised the impression that the ECJ does not easily accept material scope restrictions based on exclusive Member State competence, which was reinforced by its judgment in *Maruko*. Mr Maruko contested a national rule on survivor's benefits, which was in a complex way connected to national marital status law, and claimed that it constituted discrimination on grounds of sexual orientation. The UK government submitted, however, that the FD was not applicable, and referred to the 'within limits' clause and the affirmation in Recital 22 that the directive was without prejudice to national marital status law. The ECJ dismissed the UK's argument by repeating its long-standing line of case law in the field of nationality discrimination, according to which Member States had to exercise their own competences in accordance with Community law. It then decided that the benefit indeed constituted pay and that the FD was applicable.[15] This standpoint would appear to end all conjecture as to the relevance of the 'powers' versus 'scope' terminology, since it reveals that the ECJ does not take any notice of the difference in wording of these two qualifying clauses. Translated to the context of the RED, this would mean that the 'within limits' clause does not have a substantive impact on the material scope as listed in Article 3(2), and that the domains mentioned are fully covered. This is still to be confirmed by future case law, however.

Regardless of what the 'within limits' clause might turn out to mean at the European level, the relevant question in the framework of this study is whether Member States will act upon it. They could perhaps take it to mean that public actors have a margin of appreciation or that additional justification possibilities are allowed in those fields that belong to their exclusive competence. This could lead to a lower level of protection for minorities, especially in those Member States that display less sensitivity to the needs of minorities. It is to be hoped that they follow the ECJ and do not understand the 'within limits' clause as giving them the opportunity to lower the standards set by the RED.

[14] ECJ *Félix Palacios de la Villa v. Cortefiel Servicios SA*, Case C-411/05, 16 October 2007, paras. 42-47.

[15] ECJ *Tadao Maruko v. Versorgungsanstalt der Deutschen Bühnen*, Case C-267/06, 1 April 2008, para. 59. The cases referred to by the Court in order to support its argument were both cases on the freedom to provide/receive services as provided for by Article 49 TEC (ECJ *Watts v. Bedford Primary Care Trust*, Case C-372/04, 16 May 2006 and ECJ *Stamatelaki,* Case C-444/05, 19 April 2007). Advocate-General Colomer had defended the same position as the ECJ in his opinion of 6 September 2007, paras. 74-77.

3.2.2. Fundamental rights and freedoms

It was mentioned in the previous chapter that fundamental rights and freedoms of private actors are expected to have some bearing on the manner in which the provisions of the RED are implemented.[16] More particularly concerning the material scope of the RED, fundamental rights and freedoms could to some extent qualify the provisions of Article 3(1) RED. The Community legislator perceived for instance the provision of goods and services to be a domain in which a potential conflict with the rights and freedoms of private actors could arise. This resulted in the insertion of the qualifying clause "available to the public" in Article 3(1)(h). Similar conflicts of rights are likely to arise in other domains, as was mentioned in section 2.2.2.2. For example, if someone wishes to hire a personal caretaker and has a preference for a person of his or her own ethnic origin, the right to privacy is arguably at stake. In the field of education, a Sunday school organised by members of a specific minority could for religious reasons want to admit students belonging to that minority only, which implicates their freedom of religion. In these cases, it could be argued that non-discrimination provisions should not apply, or should not apply to the full extent, which could be a reason for Member States to insert additional safeguards in material scope provisions of their national laws.

As was mentioned before, the RED would to some extent seem to leave open room to interpret the provisions of the RED in accordance with fundamental rights and freedoms. However, it is uncertain whether this means that the material scope can be further delineated on the basis of these rights. After all, the lack of 'available to the public' – like phrases in the other provisions of Article 3(1) RED would seem to indicate that the Community legislator did not want to delimit other fields than goods and services. It therefore remains to be seen to which extent the ECJ will permit Member States to exclude certain matters that are closely connected to fundamental rights and freedoms from fields other than goods and services.

In any event, it seems clear that it is not permissible to set in place general delineations of the material scope in addition to the 'available to the public' clause in Article 3(1)(h). A general restriction of the material scope of anti-discrimination law appears to be too crude an instrument, since it entails blanket exclusion with no consideration for individual circumstances. From an effectiveness perspective it would be preferable to take into account fundamental rights and freedoms of private actors on a case-by-case basis, determining in each instance whether the particular fundamental right or freedom calls for non-application of anti-discrimination law.[17] In this way, accommodation of fundamental rights and freedoms would go no further than necessary.

16 See section 2.2.2.2.

17 See sections 4.4 and 5.2.4 on the justification possibilities for prima facie cases of direct and indirect discrimination.

This argument is supported by a judgment of the ECJ in the field of sex equality law stemming from 1983. The case involved a procedure initiated by the Commission against a provision in UK legislation implementing the Equal Treatment Directive,[18] which excluded from the material scope of national anti-discrimination law all employment relationships in private households and in small undertakings with less than five employees. The UK justified this provision by invoking Article 2(2) of the Directive, which permitted acknowledging particular genuine and determining occupational requirements based on sex (GDOR).[19] The ECJ acknowledged that the fundamental right of respect for private life was a factor that should be taken into account in determining the meaning of the GDOR in a particular case. However, exclusion of the aforementioned types of employment from the material scope went too far, and the ECJ considered that:

> [w]hilst it is undeniable that, for certain kinds of employment in private households, that consideration may be decisive, that is not the case for all the kinds of employment in question. (..) Consequently, *by reason of its generality*, the exclusion provided for in the contested provision of the 1975 Act goes beyond the objective which may be lawfully pursued within the framework of Article 2(2) of the directive (emphasis added, MB).[20]

The ECJ therefore apparently accepts consideration of fundamental rights and freedoms on a case-by-case basis, but not a general exclusion clause.

3.3. The material scope as regulated by the RED

3.3.1. Employment (Article 3(1) (a)-(d))

The extensive list of Article 3(1) (a) to (d) reveals the intention of the Community legislator to bring within the scope of the RED all activities and aspects that can be associated with labour, and is rather broad in nature. The four subdomains, access to employment, vocational guidance and training, work conditions and membership of professional organisations, are discussed here in consecutive order.

---

18 *Council Directive 76/207/EEC of 9 February 1976 on the implementation of the principle of equal treatment for men and women as regards access to employment, vocational training and promotion, and working conditions.*

19 The RED has a similar provision in Article 4. See section 4.4.2.

20 ECJ *Commission v. UK,* Case 165/82, 8 November 1983, paras. 13-16.

3.3.1.1. Access to employment

> Conditions for access to employment, to self-employment and to occupation, including selection criteria and recruitment conditions, whatever the branch of activity and at all levels of the professional hierarchy, including promotion; (Article 3(1)(a) RED)

This provision pertains to circumstances relevant for entering the labour market and acquiring a particular job. The term 'access to employment' has received a rather extensive interpretation from the ECJ in the field of sex equality law, as not only envisaging the conditions existing before an employment relationship comes into being, but also the factors that influence a person's decision as to whether or not to accept a job offer. All kinds of contextual factors that make taking on work a more attractive option thus fall under this description, as long as they are sufficiently directly linked to employment.[21] This case law is probably also valid for the RED, even though this would arguably create some overlap between 'access to employment' and the notions of 'social protection' and 'social advantages' of Article 3(1) (e) and (f).[22]

By referring to 'self-employment' and 'occupation', the provision makes clear that not only work carried out within an employment relationship is targeted, but also other ways of making a living.[23] This raises the question whether access to activities that are not performed for remuneration are covered, such as voluntary work, or work in sheltered workplaces. The second draft of the RED included a reference to unpaid or voluntary work that somehow disappeared from the final version,[24] which could be interpreted to mean that only activities performed for remuneration are covered by Article 3(1) (a-d). Such a restrictive interpretation is moreover supported by case law in free movement law, according to which working for remuneration is an

---

[21] See for example ECJ *Meyers v. Adjudication Officer*, Case C-116/94, 13 July 1995, paras. 17-25, in which the ECJ accepted that a family benefit that intended to keep poorly paid workers in employment belonged to the category 'access to employment'. See furthermore ECJ *Jackson and Cresswell v. Chief Adjudication Officer*, Cases C-63/91 and 64/91, 16 July 1992, paras. 27, 28 and 31, in which the ECJ found that social security benefit schemes that provided income support for single mothers were not sufficiently directly linked to employment in order to qualify as falling under 'access to employment'.

[22] See sections 3.3.2 and 3.3.3.

[23] See also Article 2(a) of *Council Directive 86/613/EEC of 11 December 1986 on the application of the principle of equal treatment between men and women engaged in an activity, including agriculture, in a self-employed capacity, and on the protection of self-employed women during pregnancy and motherhood*, which defines self-employment as "gainful activities pursued by persons for their own account".

[24] *Amended proposal for a Council Directive implementing the principle of equal treatment between persons irrespective of racial or ethnic origin*, Commission of the European Communities, 1999/0253 (CNS), 31 May 2000.

essential aspect of being a 'worker'.[25] However, in view of the different aim pursued by the RED compared with economically motivated free movement law, it is arguable that remuneration should not be an essential factor for employment in the context of the RED. To the contrary, the possibility of performing unpaid work is a relevant factor for participation in society and from that perspective is preferably included in the material scope of the RED. Should the ECJ not accept this argument and maintain the remuneration requirement for the RED framework, other categories of Article 3(1) such as 'practical work experience' of subsection (b), and 'social advantages' of subsection (f) could perhaps cover access to unpaid activities.

The reference to "selection criteria and recruitment conditions…" has not yet been exemplified at the European level, but the broad formulation can be considered to underline that the Community legislator wanted to include all relevant circumstances that impact on an individual's opportunity of obtaining a particular job. Thus, this provision does not only refer to formal criteria that are applied by a prospective employer/contractor/partner, but also to contextual factors impacting on the recruitment process. It probably extends, for example, to the communication channels chosen to launch the job advertisement, the questions asked during the job interview and the assessment test carried out in order to assess the person's capabilities. Research has revealed that these aspects of the application process can involve serious barriers for persons belonging to minority groups, and their inclusion thus enhances the effectiveness of anti-discrimination law.[26]

3.3.1.2. Vocational guidance and training

> Access to all types and to all levels of vocational guidance, vocational training, advanced vocational training and retraining, including practical work experience;(Article 3(1) (b) RED)

The second employment-related provision aims at facilities that help people acquire new skills and gives them guidance so as to enhance their chances on the job market. Again, this gives evidence of an expansive vision of which factors influence an individual's career path and need to be covered by anti-discrimination law.

'Vocational guidance' presumably refers to all activities, either in the private or public sector, which are aimed at helping people to find employment.

'Vocational training' has been interpreted broadly by the ECJ in free movement law, as comprising "[a]ny form of education which prepares for a qualification for a particular profession, trade or employment or which provides the necessary training and skills for such a profession, trade or employment

[25] Craig & De Búrca (2003), at 705-712.

[26] Craig (2007), at 95-118; Liegl et al (2005), at 4-5.

is vocational training, whatever the age and the level of training of the pupils or students and even if the training programme includes an element of general education".[27] This broad understanding is likely to overlap with 'education' in Article 3(1) (g) RED. Apparently, the material difference with 'education' is to be found in the motivation of the student, as can be inferred from the judgment of the Court in *Blaizot*. Thus, training is no longer vocational if it is pursued in order to improve one's general knowledge rather than to prepare for an occupation.[28] The difference is not likely to be relevant in the context of the RED, which covers 'vocational training' as well as 'education', and provides for a single same regime for both fields.

The reference to "practical work experience" probably includes internships, traineeships and the like. Moreover, this category could be interpreted so as to extend to unremunerated forms of work, as was mentioned before.

3.3.1.3. Work conditions

> Employment and working conditions, including dismissals and pay; (Article 3(1) (c) RED)

This reference makes clear that the RED envisages the conditions under which work is performed, in addition to those factors that are material to acquiring work. 'Conditions' should probably be read to mean not only aspects of the working contract, but also broader circumstances that have a bearing on the work environment, such as company culture and social activities with colleagues. These informal and contextual conditions can involve serious structural forms of discrimination, and their inclusion would therefore enhance the effectiveness of the regime of the RED.[29]

'Dismissal' has been broadly interpreted in sex equality law as covering, for instance, voluntary redundancy schemes[30] and compulsory retirement.[31] It was furthermore applied with regard to age discrimination in the previously mentioned *Palacios* case, which concerned the automatic termination of an employment contract after the statutory retirement age had been reached.[32] It thus appears to refer to any situation in which an individual is forced by someone else to quit his job.

[27] ECJ *Françoise Gravier v. City of Liège,* Case 293/83, 13 February 1985, para. 30.
[28] ECJ *Blaizot v. University of Liège*, Case 24/86, 2 February 1988, para. 15.
[29] Craig (2007), at 95-118.
[30] ECJ *Burton v. British Railway Board*, Case 19/81, 16 February 1982, para. 9.
[31] ECJ *Marshall v. Southampton and South-West Hampshire Area Health Authority*, Case 152/84, 26 February 1986, para. 34.
[32] ECJ *Félix Palacios de la Villa v. Cortefiel Servicios SA*, Case C-411/05, 16 October 2007, paras. 42-46. The ECJ simply referred to "employment and working conditions, including dismissals and pay", but it can be inferred from the opinion of Advocate-General Mazák of 15 February 2007, paras. 53-67, that it was in fact 'dismissal' that was envisaged.

The meaning of 'pay' has often come up as the object of dispute before the ECJ in the field of sex equality, and has been broadly interpreted, so much so that the question has been posed whether simply all benefits conferred by employers constitute pay.[33] In sex equality law, the delineation of pay versus other benefits was relevant because the regime for pay was different than for other benefits. Especially the delineation with regard to pensions proved to be a highly contentious issue, resulting in a complex body of case law.[34] Since the RED imposes a single regime for pay and social security, including pensions, this jurisprudence is not relevant in this context and will not be discussed here. Moreover, as the RED also applies to social advantages, which comprise advantages conferred by employers, it appears to be sufficiently clear that the RED covers all benefits conferred by employers, even though it is perhaps not entirely clear yet which aspect will fall under which element of the material scope.

3.3.1.4. Membership of professional organisations

> Membership of and involvement in an organisation of workers or employers, or any organisation whose members carry on a particular profession, including the benefits provided for by such organisations (Article 3(1) (d) RED)

The fourth employment-related provision refers to all associations and networks of a professional nature, the membership of which and participation in which can be determining for a successful career. Its inclusion is an important asset of the RED, since this is a field that can involve important structural barriers for persons belonging to minority groups. Especially participation in bodies that are involved in negotiation of collective agreements and other employment conditions is an important aspect that is now covered by this provision.

3.3.2. Social protection, social security and healthcare

> Social protection, including social security and healthcare (Article 3(1) (e) RED)

Article 3(1) (e) covers the social domains and does so in an inclusive way, just as Article 3(1)(a) to (d) does with regard to the employment-related fields. The umbrella concept of 'social protection' is very broad, and is understood to cover all kinds of benefits and policies targeted at keeping persons above subsistence level and enhancing their wellbeing. Policies aimed at

---

33 Ellis (2005), at 156-157.

34 For an extensive overview see Ellis (2005), at 121-158; Craig & De Búrca (2003), at 865-884.

social inclusion, the prevention of poverty and welfare more generally are therefore most likely covered.[35] In other words, the whole realm of social and economic rights seems to be comprised by 'social protection', and it is not clear where the limits should be drawn. This broad coverage greatly enhances the level of protection offered by the RED, since research reveals that racial discrimination is widespread in this field. For instance, members of ethnic and racial minorities frequently come across negative attitudes and inferior treatment within social service institutions.[36] Moreover, structural forms of disadvantage, such as lack of cultural accommodation and linguistic problems exist in this field.[37]

The formulation of Article 3(1) (e) lacks any reference to official or state policies, so it is likely and certainly preferable that private initiatives in the field of social protection are covered. The phrase "all persons, as regards both the public *and private* sectors" (emphasis added, MB) of Article 3(1) RED lends support to such an inclusive interpretation.

'Social security' is an aspect of 'social protection', and covers those situations in which compensation is offered to persons for the impossibility of continuing in paid work.[38] In the field of sex equality, the ECJ has consistently interpreted 'social security' as comprising those benefits that constitute the whole or part of a statutory scheme providing protection against the risks of sickness, invalidity, old age, accidents at work and occupational diseases and unemployment, or a form of social assistance having the same objective, and that are directly and effectively linked to protection against one of these risks.[39] 'Social security' in sex equality law also extends to private sector initiatives, as can be inferred from *Council Directive 86/378/EEC of 24 July 1986 on the implementation of the principle of equal treatment for men and women in occupational social security schemes*, which regulates equal treatment between men and women in *occupational* social security schemes.[40]

---

[35] Van der Mei (2005), at 183.

[36] *Migrants experiences of racism and xenophobia*, Pilot Study, EUMC, May 2006, at 21.

[37] Lynch (2005), at 20-22.

[38] Ellis (2005), at 346.

[39] ECJ *The Queen v. Secretary of State for Social Security, ex parte Smithson*, Case C-243/90, 4 February 1992, paras. 12 and 14; ECJ Joined Cases *Jackson and Cresswell v. Chief Adjudication Officer*, Cases C-63/91 and 64/91, 16 July 1992, paras. 15 and 16; and ECJ *R. v. Secretary of State for Health, ex parte Richardson,* Case C-137/94, 19 October 1995, paras. 8 and 9.

[40] Article 2(1) of this Directive defines occupational social security schemes as: "schemes not governed by Directive 79/7/EEC whose purpose is to provide workers, whether employees or self-employed, in an undertaking or group of undertakings, area of economic activity or occupational sector or group of such sectors with benefits intended to supplement the benefits provided by statutory social security schemes or to replace them, whether membership of such schemes is compulsory or optional". See also the proposal of the Commission to amend this Directive: *Proposal for a Directive of the European Parliament and of the Council on the application of the principle of equal treatment between men and women engaged in an activity in a self-employed capacity and repealing Directive 86/613/EEC*, COM/2008/0636 final.

The explicit reference to 'healthcare' is positive, since this is a field which has proved to be tainted with racial discrimination. The European Union Agency for Fundamental Rights has recently expanded its monitoring focus to this sector, and it has identified the following problems of racial and ethnic minorities: bureaucratic constraints, such as documentation requirements that are difficult to fulfil; denial of services or provision of substandard levels of care; segregation and accessibility problems in terms of geographical distance.[41] All of these difficulties are in particular experienced by persons of Roma origin.[42]

'Healthcare' has not yet been defined at the European level. *General Comment No. 14* of the Committee of Economic, Social and Cultural Rights (CESCR) could provide some inspiration in this regard. The description of the right to health in section 4 of this Comment suggests a very broad understanding and provides that:

> the right to health embraces a wide range of socio-economic factors that promote conditions in which people can lead a healthy life, and extends to the underlying determinants of health, such as food and nutrition, housing, access to safe and potable water and adequate sanitation, safe and healthy working conditions, and a healthy environment.[43]

This description includes contextual factors that impact on a person's ability to secure an appropriate level of healthcare, which is positive. If not deemed to be covered by 'healthcare' in Article 3(1) e RED, most of these aspects are in any case covered by the broader notion of 'social protection'. It should be said that it is desirable here too that private healthcare institutions and initiatives are covered.

It has been submitted that not only the quality of the services and benefits provided in the field of social protection, social security and healthcare should be covered, but also the way in which beneficiaries are treated by officials and other persons dealing with clients or patients in this field.[44] The same can be said with regard to accessibility issues: a useful interpretation of the concepts of Article 3(1) (e) should cover geographical and other obstacles to gaining access to social protection, social security and healthcare.[45]

---

41 *Annual Report 2008*, European Union Agency for Fundamental Rights, at 82-90.

42 *Ambulance not on the way. The disgrace of healthcare for Roma in Europe*, ERRC 2006; *Social inclusion through social services. The case of Roma and Travellers*, ERRC 2007.

43 *General Comment No. 14 on the right to the highest attainable standard of health*, Committee on Economic, Social and Cultural Rights, E/C.12/2000/4.

44 *ECRI General Policy Recommendation No. 7 on national legislation to combat racism and racial discrimination*, 13 December 2002, paras. 22 and 23 of the Explanatory Memorandum.

45 See on the requirement of physical accessibility also *General Comment No. 19 on the right to social security*, Committee on Economic, Social and Cultural Rights, E/C.12/GC/19, para. 27; *General Comment No. 14 on the right to the highest attainable standard of health*, Committee on Economic, Social and Cultural Rights, E/C.12/2000/4, para. 12(b).

Extrapolation of the ECJ's reasoning as regards the meaning of 'access to employment' as mentioned in the previous subsection would support such a broad understanding.

3.3.3. Social advantages

Social advantages (Article 3(1) (f) RED)

Whereas social protection, social security and healthcare concern measures and mechanisms that aim to protect persons against certain risks, social advantages would rather seem to comprise benefits that are not directly connected to any risks, but simply advantageous for those enjoying them. There is some overlap between these concepts, however, and it is not entirely clear where the division line should be drawn.[46]

'Social advantages' is a concept borrowed from Article 7(2) of Regulation 1612/68 on the free movement of workers, which has been extensively interpreted by the ECJ.[47] In a progressive line of case law, the Court took a purposeful approach to the meaning of the concept, considering the determining factor to be the extent to which a particular benefit could further the integration of workers who did not have the nationality of the state in which they performed work or resided.[48] It thus adopted a very broad interpretation, the exact boundaries of which are still unclear. Examples of social advantages recognised by the ECJ are study grants, reduced prices for public transport or for social/cultural activities and subsidised meals.[49] It is moreover clear that 'social advantages' in the field of free movement do not necessarily have to be of economic value, but can also be of immaterial value. In *Mutsch*, for example, the ECJ ruled that the right to use one's own language in court proceedings under the same conditions as national workers constituted a social advantage.[50] These non-economical rights are particularly relevant for minority groups, as they are capable of serving identity-related interests.

The free movement meaning of 'social advantages' was considered to be the point of departure for the interpretation of the similar concept in the RED, as the Explanatory Memorandum to the RED makes clear.[51] Still, Member States

46 Van der Mei (2005), at 192; Ellis (2003), at 650.

47 Article 7(2) of *Regulation 1612/68 on the free movement of workers* contains the right to enjoy the same social advantages as enjoyed by nationals of the host state.

48 For a brief overview of this development see Ellis (2003), at 642-653; Craig & De Búrca (2003), at 737-739.

49 *Explanatory Memorandum*, Commission of the European Communities 1999, COM/99/0566 final, at 7.

50 ECJ *Ministère Public v. Mutsch*, Case 137/84, 11 July 1985, paras. 15-18.

51 *Explanatory Memorandum*, Commission of the European Communities 1999, COM/99/0566 final, at 7.

emphasised during the deliberations on the draft of the RED that the meaning of the concept was still not entirely clear, and could be further developed over time.[52] Thus, it is possible that 'social advantages' in the context of the RED will acquire a different meaning from 'social advantages' in free movement law.

According to some, the fundamental rights rationale of the RED will spur a broader interpretation of 'social advantages' than the one developed in the context of the economically oriented Regulation 1612/68.[53] In other words, the aim of putting into effect the principle of equal treatment should result in a broader interpretation than the one that was built on the aim of the full integration of a worker into society, which was the aim followed by the ECJ in interpreting Article 7(2) of Regulation 1612/68.[54] Their claim is not substantiated, however, and it is difficult to see in what way these different aims could lead to different conceptions of 'social advantages', especially since this concept is already very extensively interpreted.

Others have pointed to the extensive material scope of the RED, which according to them should produce a more extensive interpretation of 'social advantages' than in free movement law.[55] After all, the RED confers protection not only on workers and those dependent on them, as does Regulation 1612/68, but to all persons residing within the territory of the Member States, and in many more areas than employment. The argument seems to hold value to the extent that 'social advantages' in the RED do not necessarily have to be accorded to workers. Substantially, however, it is very difficult to conceive of any way in which the meaning of 'social advantages' can be further expanded, in view of the very broad interpretation the concept already has been given in free movement law. It should be mentioned that there is even a possibility that the ECJ will restrict the meaning of 'social advantages' in the context of the RED, rather than expand it. Thus, it has been asserted that the exclusion in Article 3(2) RED as regards immigration matters could lead to a stricter interpretation. Residence rights for partners, which have in the field of free movement law been recognised as social advantages,[56] would thus arguably not be covered by the RED.[57] Future case law will reveal whether the ECJ will

---

52 Tyson (2004), at 119-120.

53 Ellis (2003), at 653; Brown (2002), at 213; House of Lords Select Committee on the European Union, *Ninth Report on the EU proposals to combat discrimination*, 16 May 2000, para. 102.

54 See Article 1 RED, which provides that: "[t]he purpose of this Directive is to lay down a framework for combating discrimination on the grounds of racial or ethnic origin, with a view to putting into effect in the Member States the principle of equal treatment."

55 Ellis (2003), at 653-655; Kimber (2003), at 252-253.

56 ECJ *Netherlands v. Reed*, Case 59/85, 17 April 1986.

57 Van der Mei (2005), at 190. Also see section 3.4 on the material scope aspect of Article 3(2) RED.

indeed opt for this more restrictive reading. It may in any case be clear that it is desirable from a minority protection perspective to maintain as broad an interpretation of 'social advantages' as possible.

3.3.4. Education

Education (Article 3(1) (g) RED)

The term 'education' has not yet been defined or exemplified at the European level. It will preferably be interpreted so as to extend to all facilities that offer the opportunity to learn something, and not only officially recognised and publicly funded institutions. Moreover, it is desirable to extend the meaning of 'education' beyond entry to training facilities, so as to include contextual factors, such as teacher attitudes, content of learning material and examination requirements. Similarly, broader matters of access, such as social or geographical obstacles to participating in education are preferably covered.[58]

An inclusive interpretation of 'education' is clearly necessary in view of the many instances of discrimination that have been identified in this field. A very serious and recurring problem that was found to exist is educational segregation, which involves separate or substandard education for children from a minority background.[59] Especially Roma children encounter this type of disadvantage.[60] More generally, racial discrimination in enrolment and in testing, as well as racial harassment within schools has been noted to exist throughout the EU.[61] At a deeper level, studies have shown that children from minority backgrounds tend to be disadvantaged by certain structural factors in the educational system of Member States, such as the maintenance of highly stratified systems of education instead of comprehensive school systems. Children of a minority background are apparently disproportionately represented in the lower echelons of stratified school systems, and find it much harder to change to the higher and more prestigious ranks of education.[62] Also, lack of access to preschool facilities tends to disproportionately disadvantage children of a minority background, especially because of their tendency to

[58] See *General Comment No. 13 on the right to education*, Committee on Economic, Social and Cultural Rights, E/C.12/1999/10, para. 6b on the need for the provision of physical accessibility to education.

[59] *Annual Report 2006*, EUMC, at 74 and 82; *Annual Report 2008*, European Agency for Fundamental Rights, at 76-77.

[60] *Separate and unequal: combating discrimination against Roma. A source book*, Public Interest Law Institute 2004, at 64-65; *Annual Report 2006*, EUMC, at 74; *The impact of legislation and policies on school segregation of Romani children*, ERRC 2007; *Stigmata: segregated schooling of Roma in Central and Eastern Europe*, ERRC 2004.

[61] *Annual Report 2008*, European Agency for Fundamental Rights, at 67-73; *Annual Report 2006*, EUMC, at 76.

[62] *Annual Report 2006*, EUMC, at 74 and 82.

have a linguistic disadvantage.[63] Finally, certain disciplinary rules within the school, such as language requirements and dress codes disproportionately affect students belonging to minority groups.[64]

3.3.5. Goods and services

> Access to and supply of goods and services which are available to the public, including housing (Article 3(1) (h) RED)

The meaning of 'goods and services'

'Goods' and 'services' are familiar concepts in the European equality framework, occupying a prominent place in free movement law. 'Goods' have been defined by the ECJ as: "products which can be valued in money and which are capable, as such, of forming the subject of commercial transactions".[65] Subsequent case law has shown that the term is very broadly interpreted, and covers for instance artistic and historic articles, waste and electricity.[66]

Article 50 TEC defines 'services' as follows:

> Services shall be considered to be 'services' within the meaning of this Treaty where they are normally provided for remuneration, in so far as they are not governed by the provisions relating to freedom of movement for goods, capital and persons. 'Services' shall in particular include: (a) activities of an industrial character; (b) activities of a commercial character; (c) activities of craftsmen; (d) activities of the professions.

Case law of the ECJ reveals that an important distinguishing criterion for determining whether a service constitutes a 'service' is whether making a profit is the objective of the service provider. Thus, public services, such as the provision of courses in the framework of the general education system, do not constitute 'services' in their free movement understanding, since by offering them the government does not pursue any gainful activity, but merely fulfils its task in the general interest.[67]

Both 'goods' and 'services' have therefore a strong economic connotation in free movement law, in that they have to be commercially valuable, or provided on the basis of an economic motive. Holding on to this economic aspect in the framework of the RED would, however, entail a loss in terms of effective protection against racial and ethnic discrimination. This is especially

[63] *Annual Report 2008*, European Agency for Fundamental Rights, at 67-73.
[64] *Annual Report 2006*, EUMC, at 76; *Annual Report 2008*, European Agency for Fundamental Rights, at 79-80.
[65] *Commission v. Italy*, Case 7/68, 10 December 1968, para. B.1.
[66] Horspool & Humphreys (2006), at 285-286.
[67] O' Leary (1999), at 398-399.

the case for 'services', which in its popular understanding extends to a wide range of activities that are not economically motivated: public services, such as policing, resource allocation services and services provided by non-profit organisations. Research shows that racial discrimination in the provision of these non-economically motivated services is unfortunately widespread. Members of minorities are for example often subjected to ethnic profiling by the police[68] and to condescending or insensitive attitudes by public officials.[69] Furthermore, instances of discrimination have been discovered in the domain of charity work. An example is the deliberate policy choice to offer pork soup only to homeless persons, which makes it impossible for Muslims to benefit from free meals.[70] A broad interpretation of 'services', extending to services provided not with the aim of making a profit, would therefore be preferable.[71] Similarly, 'housing' should be taken to refer not only to accommodation offered by private landlords, but also to municipal housing and other public housing schemes.[72]

Even though the Commission has made clear that it adheres to the free movement understanding of 'goods and services',[73] a broader meaning in the context of the RED is defensible in view of the fundamental rights rationale of this instrument. Whereas the aim of economic integration pursued by free movement law understandably led to an economically coloured understanding of 'goods' and 'services', the aim of ensuring equal treatment between persons irrespective of racial or ethnic origin would seem to call for as broad an interpretation as possible.[74]

Moreover, the negotiations on the draft RED reveal that Member States did not want to retain the narrow understanding of services in free movement law, which is why they did not include the 'normally provided for remuneration' proviso of Article 50 TEC.[75] Even though it is not clear which alternative

68 De Schutter (2008); *I can stop and search whoever I want,* Open Society Justice Initiative 2007; *ECRI General Policy Recommendation no. 11, on combating racism and racial discrimination in policing*, ECRI 2007.

69 *Migrants experiences of racism and xenophobia*, Pilot Study, EUMC, May 2006, at 21.

70 A. Sandford, *French row over charity pork soup*, BBC news, 23 December 2005, available at http://news.bbc.co.uk/2/hi/europe/4557034.stm (accessed June 2009).

71 Howard (2005), at 477; O'Cinneíde (2004), at 7; Brown (2002), at 215; Compare ECRI's *General Policy Recommendation no. 7 on national legislation to combat racism and racial discrimination*, ECRI 2002, which proposes 'public services' be included in the scope of national legislation on racial discrimination.

72 Ellis (2005), at 256.

73 In its *Proposal for directive 2004/113/EC implementing the principle of equal treatment between men and women in the access to and supply of goods and services*, COM(2003) 657 final, 12-13, the Commission makes clear that these concepts should be interpreted in accordance with their interpretation in free movement law, and that it considers this to apply also to the framework of the RED.

74 Kimber (2003), at 254-255.

75 Tyson (2004), at 120.

meaning of 'services' they had in mind exactly, the point that the meaning of 'services' does not have to keep in line with the interpretation in free movement law creates some room for interpretation. Therefore, there do not seem to be any real barriers to a more extensive interpretation of 'goods' and 'services' in the context of the RED as compared with their meaning in free movement law.

It should be mentioned that to some extent the concepts of 'social protection' and 'social advantages' could act as a safety net in case of a narrow understanding of 'services', since they cover a number of services that are provided in view of a social rather than an economic aim.

Even aside from the economic aim controversy, it is to be hoped that 'goods' and 'services' will be accorded as wide a meaning as possible. For example, they should be interpreted as referring not only to conditions of access to certain products, but also to the quality of the product, or its provision, and the situational conditions governing the relationship between provider and recipient. A broad interpretation of 'housing' is furthermore desirable, extending not only to access to housing, but also housing conditions, as well as the termination of renting contracts and evictions.[76]

The 'available to the public' clause

It was mentioned before that Article 3(1)(h) contains a qualification clause that was inserted out of concern for fundamental rights and freedoms of private actors, more particularly the right to privacy and the freedom of association. The exact interpretation of this 'available to the public' clause is difficult to pin down, however.

According to some authors, the clause should be taken to exclude those goods and services that are offered to a closed and fixed group of recipients, such as members of an association.[77] However, this understanding of the clause is not very useful, because it leaves too much leeway for private actors to dodge the requirements of the RED. It is only too easy to come up with an arbitrary set of criteria and to draw one's circle of recipients accordingly, in order to avoid application of anti-discrimination law. It is for example a well-known trick of disco-owners to claim that persons of a particular racial background were not refused entry because of their racial origin, but because they did not have membership cards. Indeed, the very act of discrimination comes down to the application of particular arbitrary selection criteria.

In its most recent proposal for an equality directive, which broadens the material scope for the prohibition of discrimination on grounds of

[76] *ECRI General Policy Recommendation no. 7 on national legislation to combat racism and racial discrimination*, ECRI 2002, para. 21 of the Explanatory Memorandum. See also *General Comment No. 7 on forced evictions*, Committee on Economic, Social and Cultural Rights, E/1998/22 Annex IV.

[77] O'Cinnéide (2004), at 6; Bell (2002a), at 22-23.

religion, disability, age and sexual orientation, the Commission approaches the 'available to the public' clause as referring to the quality of the goods/ service provider. According to the Commission, transactions between private individuals acting in a private capacity are excluded, and consequently all activities of a professional or commercial nature are covered.[78] Still, it is not wholly clear what 'private capacity' means. For instance, does it extend to a person that rents out a room in her own house? It would seem that a residents' right to privacy extends to the decision as to who to choose for a tenant in one's own house, but the commercial aim of renting out a room could according to the Commission's interpretation bring the situation within the material scope of the RED. Moreover, it is questionable whether associations can act in a 'private capacity', whereas Recital 4 of the RED makes sufficiently clear that the freedom of association should at least to some extent be accounted for.

It is submitted that the aforementioned approaches to the 'available to the public' clause wrongly apply a subjective perspective, by focusing on the person providing the goods or service: the determining factor according to these approaches is either his choice of addressees/channels of communication, or the extent to which he acts on a commercial basis. It would be preferable to take a more objective perspective, and to focus on the particular goods or service provided: do these particular goods or service belong to the private life/ freedom of association of the person providing them? For instance, renting out a room in one's own home would seem objectively to belong to the private sphere of the home-owner, regardless of whether his motives are commercial or personal in nature. This approach entails a thorough assessment of the extent to which the service or goods provider would be hampered in exercising his right to privacy/freedom of association if obliged to accept applicants in a non-discriminatory manner, which can be complex at times.

In fact, it seems inevitable that the practical meaning of 'available to the public' is determined on a case-by-case basis, which would involve a balancing act for each particular case. It is to be hoped that courts will in this respect have sufficient regard for the seriousness of racial discrimination, while of course not overlooking the importance of respecting the right to privacy and the freedom of association. In view of the difficulty in striking the right balance between these rights, it is essential that they apply thorough, consistent and transparent reasoning.

It should be mentioned with regard to the freedom of association that courts could draw inspiration from the practice of the American Supreme Court, which has extensive experience in dealing with the conflict between the right to non-discrimination and the freedom of association. Activities of private associations are normally covered by American anti-discrimination

[78] *Proposal for a Council Directive on implementing the principle of equal treatment between persons irrespective of religion or belief, disability, age or sexual orientation*, European Commission, 2 July 2008, COM(2008) 426 final, at 8.

law, unless they are carried out by a so-called 'expressive association'. By 'expressive association', the American Supreme Court envisages associations that proceed from a particular ideology or philosophy. These associations are required to act in line with the principle of non-discrimination, unless this would amount to an unreasonable burden for the association, which is determined by carrying out a proportionality test.[79] Thus, only those activities that are in the specific case deemed to be sufficiently closely connected to the freedom of association are excluded from the scope of anti-discrimination law. This clear-cut and balanced approach provides a good starting point for the ECJ and national courts when interpreting the 'available to the public' clause with regard to activities of private associations.

3.4. The exception of immigration, visa and asylum policies (Article 3(2) RED)

> This Directive does not cover difference of treatment based on nationality and is without prejudice to provisions and conditions relating to the entry into and residence of third country nationals and stateless persons on the territory of Member States, and to any treatment which arises from the legal status of the third-country nationals and stateless persons concerned (Article 3(2) RED)

As was mentioned before, Article 3(2) RED has a personal scope component (exclusion of differences of treatment based on nationality), which was discussed in section 2.3.3, and a material scope component, which is discussed in this section. The material scope component of Article 3(2) excludes immigration, visa and asylum (hereafter IVA) policies from the RED. This sensitive domain is usually closely examined by NGOs and supervisory bodies for being in line with human rights law, since it is of great importance for vulnerable groups such as refugees, certain non-citizens and stateless persons.[80] Unsurprisingly, therefore, the exception clause has been criticised by a number of authors for withdrawing from the scope of the RED a field of application that is particularly important for racial and ethnic minorities.[81] In

---

[79] De Prins (2003), at 531-532.

[80] Bell (2008), at 11-12. See for example the thematic websites of Human Rights Watch, at http://www.hrw.org/en/topic/migrants; Amnesty International, at http://www.amnesty.org/en/refugees-and-migrants; and Justice Initiative, at http://www.justiceinitiative.org/activities/ec/ec_noncitizens (all accessed May 2009). CERD also scrutinises national practice and policy as regards non-citizens; see *CERD General Recommendation No. 30, on Discrimination Against Non Citizens*, 1 October 2004, paras. 13-17 and 25-28.; See also the Human Rights Committee's *General Comment No. 15, The position of aliens under the Covenant,* 11 April 1986. More particularly for the European context, see *Racism in Europe, Shadow Report 2004*, ENAR, at 58-67.

[81] Brennan (2003), at 325; McInerney (2003), at 14; Brown (2002), at 210.

this regard it should be emphasised that Member States are not obliged to take over Article 3(2), and are free to decide to include IVA policies in the material scope of their national anti-discrimination legislation.

If, however, they choose to implement Article 3(2), and thus to exclude IVA policies, the interpretation of Article 3(2) becomes greatly important. The broad wording of the clause gives reason for concern in this respect, since it can be interpreted so as to exempt all distinctions based on a non-national's legal status, regardless of the actor with whom it originates.[82] This would mean that all differentiations made by private actors on the basis of the legal status of foreigners would be excluded from the scope of the RED. For example, a refusal by a telecommunication company or by a landlord to enter into a contract with a person who does not have a permanent residence permit would be excluded. Such a broad interpretation of Article 3(2) is clearly not desirable, since it entails a serious limitation of the material scope of the RED. The clause is thus preferably interpreted so as to exclude only official IVA law and policy, and not differentiations made by private actors on the basis of legal status.[83]

The drafting history of the RED supports the narrower interpretation, as it reveals that the aim of the exclusion clause was not to exclude all differences in treatment based on legal status, but rather to safeguard Member State discretion in the field of IVA policies.[84] Thus, the clause should probably be taken to mean that only official IVA law and policy is excluded, and that private actor activity relying on the legal status of persons is fully covered by the RED. The tendency of the ECJ to interpret exception clauses restrictively lends further support to such a narrow interpretation.[85]

Part two: Case study

3.5. Factors that could potentially qualify the material scope of the RED

3.5.1. Division of competences between Member States and the EU

The 'within limits' clause has not played any part in the national contexts, at least not as regards the material scope of national legislation. In all four Member States, the material scope provisions of the RED were apparently taken as a given and implemented, even though this sometimes took several

82 Ellis (2005), at 289-290; Brown (2002), at 211; Cholewinski (2002), at 44.
83 Henrard (2007), at 23.
84 Tyson (2004), at 120-121.
85 Howard (2005), at 479; Tobler (2003), at 3; Sierra (2002), at 24.

implementation phases. Clearly, the fear of some that the clause would lead to additional delineations of the material scope has proven to be unjustified, at least for the four countries under examination.

The only instance in which the 'within limits' clause was actually expressly mentioned, albeit not with regard to any material scope provisions, is provided by the Netherlands. The Dutch government invoked the 'within limits' clause in order to justify Article 7(2) GETA, which accords ideologically or religiously founded educational institutions a specific justification possibility as regards enrolment requirements.[86] As is explained in section 4.7.1, this provision could perhaps be reconciled with the positive action provision of Article 5 RED, but this is doubtful. It remains to be seen whether the ECJ will follow the Dutch government and will interpret the 'within limits' clause as permitting additional justification possibilities in the fields that belong mainly to Member State competence.

Interestingly, whereas the division of competences between Member States and the EU has hardly proven relevant at the domestic level, matters of internal competence division have caused problems in one Member State, namely in Belgium. The very complicated division of competences between the Belgian federal government, the Regions and the Communities has caused much controversy as regards the implementation of the RED and the FD. At the time of the adoption of the Belgian ADA, the federal competence issue hardly came up, but it was subsequently raised by a number of authors, who claimed that particular fields covered by the ADA fell under the competence of the Communities or the Regions.[87] In fact, one of the reasons for the revision of federal anti-discrimination law in 2007 was the desire to regulate matters in accordance with the Belgian competence structure.[88] The Explanatory Memorandum to the new ARA indeed emphasises that the material scope provisions of the new ARA have to be interpreted in line with the federal competence structure.[89]

All in all, the following sectors fall outside the scope of the new ARA: the status of Community and Region personnel, including staff in education (Communities' and Regions' competence); employment policies (Regions' competence); vocational training (Communities' competence); healthcare, with the exception of the general structure of the healthcare system and healthcare insurance (Communities' competence); cultural policies (Communities'

[86] *Advice and Report on the Amendment of the General Act on Equal Treatment and certain other acts in order to implement directive 2000/43/EG and directive 2000/78/EG,* TK 2002-3, 28 770, A, at 12. See section 4.7.1 for a more detailed discussion of this justification possibility.

[87] Foblets & Velaers (2006), at 124-127; Van Drooghenbroeck (2004), at 97-114; Velaers (2003), at 298-305.

[88] *Explanatory Memorandum to the Draft law amending the law of 30 July 1981 that penalises certain acts motivated by racism and xenophobia*, Doc 51. 2720/001, at 8-9.

[89] *Explanatory Memorandum to the Draft law amending the law of 30 July 1981 that penalises certain acts motivated by racism and xenophobia*, Doc 51. 2720/001, at 21.

competence); economic and housing policies (Regions' competence).[90] Even though the list thus seems rather clear, it is not yet exactly certain where some of the boundaries are to be drawn in concrete cases. The situation seems especially blurry as regards healthcare. Unfortunately, the Communities and Regions have not yet fully implemented the provisions of the RED in their respective fields of competence, which means that there are gaps of protection within the Belgian legal framework.[91] In the following sections, the persisting gaps will be separately mentioned for the relevant material scope provisions.

3.5.2. Fundamental rights and freedoms

It was already mentioned in the previous chapter that fundamental rights and freedoms of private actors influenced the implementation process in all four Member States.[92] The extent to which this has led to the adoption of additional limitation clauses of the material scope of national anti-discrimination legislation greatly differs, however. Neither in Belgium nor in Estonia have there been any such additional delineations in the national laws. In Belgium, however, the Explanatory Memorandum to the new ARA states that the material scope provisions have to be interpreted in accordance with the guideline that strictly personal matters are not covered.[93] It has been submitted by Belgian scholars that this guideline can only be applied in a way that respects the requirements of the RED. Thus, strictly private matters outside the sphere of goods and services can only be excluded if this can be framed in terms of the justification possibilities provided for by the RED.[94] This would indeed seem to be the only interpretation that would comply with the RED, but practice needs to show whether it will be followed by Belgian courts.

The concern to ensure respect for fundamental rights and freedoms has had a more discernable impact on the material scope of the Dutch GETA, albeit still a limited one. More particularly, the freedom of religion has been accommodated by Article 3 GETA, which excludes relations within religious

[90] De Schutter (2007a), at 7-11.

[91] For a clear overview of the states of affairs in 2007 see De Schutter (2007a), at 11. Since then, matters have improved, because both the Flemish government and the French Community have adopted decrees that cover the full material scope of Article 3(1) RED, see *Decree of the French Community with regard to the combat against certain forms of discrimination*, 12 December 2008; *Decree of the Flemish Community containing a framework for the Flemish equal opportunities and equal treatment policy*, 10 July 2008.

[92] See section 2.4.2.2.

[93] *Explanatory Memorandum to the Draft law amending the law of 30 July 1981 that penalises certain acts motivated by racism and xenophobia*, Doc 51. 2720/001, 41, at 21.

[94] Bayart & Bosmans (2008), at 557.

communities.[95] According to the Explanatory Memorandum to the IA, this provision was permissible on the basis of Article 6 TEU, which requires the EU to respect the ECHR, of which Article 9 enshrines the freedom of religion.[96] However, it would seem that this provision is incompatible with the RED, to the extent that it excludes actions of religious entities that impact on the fields listed in Article 3(1) RED.[97] As was explained before, wholesale material scope exemptions appear to be too crude an instrument, and consideration at the level of justification possibilities is to be preferred. The European Commission has indeed notified the Dutch government of its failed obligations in this regard.[98]

In Hungary, finally, one can see a rather big impact of fundamental rights and freedoms on the material scope of the HETA, which applies only to a limited extent to private actors.[99] These actors are covered only insofar as they act in the field of employment, provide goods or services at their premises open to customers, or make a proposal for a contract to persons not defined preliminarily.[100] This limited material scope with regard to private actors is not in line with the requirements of the RED. To be true, the most important areas in which private actors can act, that is in employment and the provision of goods and services, are covered. Still, private actors can and do also discriminate in other areas mentioned by Article 3(1) RED, and the HETA

[95] This article provides that: "[t]his Act does not apply to: a. legal relattions within religious communities, independent sections or associations thereof and within other associations of a spiritual nature; b. the office of minister of religion."

[96] *Explanatory Memorandum to the Draft Amendment of the General Act on Equal Treatment and certain other acts in order to implement directive 2000/43/EC and directive 2000/78/EC*, TK 2002-03, 28 770, No. 3, TK 2002-3, 28 770, No. 3, at 5. See also Vermeulen (2006), at 235-237.

[97] See *Advice and Report on the Amendment of the General Act on Equal Treatment and certain other acts in order to implement directive 2000/43/EG and directive 2000/78/EG,* TK 2002-3, 28 770, A, at 9, in which the Council of State argues that the provision is not in line with Article 3(1) of the RED.

[98] See the reasoned opinion of the Commission of 31 January 2008 with regard to the Dutch compliance with the requirements of the FD, C(2008) 0115. It is unclear why the Commission has not issued a similar opinion with regard to the RED. Still, the same reasoning should apply for this instrument, especially because the material scope provisions of the RED are more extensive than those of the FD. In its reaction to the reasoned opinion in Recommendation 2008/02, at 6-7 the ETC agrees with the Commission that this provision, combined with the additional justification possibility for religious institutions in Article 5 GETA, is perhaps incompatible with the requirements of the FD.

[99] See also Bitskey & Gyulavári (2004), at 7-8 who report that the application of anti-discrimination norms to private actors was one of the most debated issues in the implementation process.

[100] Article 5 HETA.

falls short of the requirements of the RED in this respect.[101] In the following sections, the problems in this respect will be pointed out for each domain mentioned in Article 3(1) RED separately.

In addition to the limited material scope for private actors of Article 5 HETA, Article 6 of this Act contains a number of additional delineations of the material scope that were added in order to safeguard fundamental rights and freedoms. The following fields are thus expressly kept outside the material scope of the HETA: family law relationships; relationships between relatives; relationships of ecclesiastical entities directly connected to the activities of the religious life of churches; relationships between members of NGOs, legal entities and organisations without legal personality, with the exception of the establishment and cancellation of membership; internal affairs of political parties.

These exclusions are for the larger part compatible with the requirements of the RED, because most of them involve fields of application that are anyway outside of the material scope of the RED, such as family law relationships and internal affairs of political parties. Moreover, the requirement that private actors act at their premises or towards persons not preliminarily defined can – to some extent at least – be reconciled with the 'available to the public' phrase. Section 3.6.5 discusses this in more detail. However, the full exclusion of internal affairs of religious institutions and of internal affairs of associations, which resembles Article 3 of the Dutch GETA, is not in line with the RED.

3.6. The material scope as regulated by the RED

Most Member States had some anti-discrimination law in place prior to the implementation of the RED. In the following analysis it will be mentioned which anti-discrimination provisions already existed in the particular fields.

3.6.1. Employment (Article 3(1) (a)-(d))

3.6.1.1. Provisions implementing Article 3(1) (a)-(d)

In all four Member States, legislation against discrimination in employment existed prior to the implementation of the RED, but the level of protection offered by these provisions was considerably lower than that offered by the RED, at least in Belgium, Estonia and Hungary.

[101] Kádár & Farkas (2005), at 2; Farkas et al (2003), at 122.

Belgian law provided only for a very basic level of protection against discrimination in employment, which only covered the hiring phase.[102] The first implementation phase brought about considerable improvement, and the ADA contained an employment-related material scope provision largely identical to that of the RED.[103] At the occasion of the 2007 amendments, the government wanted to further reinforce the level of protection in employment, by adopting an even more comprehensive material scope provision.[104] Thus, the following employment-related aspects are now mentioned in Article 5 of the new ARA:

> All relations with regard to employment (Article 5(1)(5) of the new ARA, which is extensively exemplified in Article 4(1) of the new ARA).
>
> Membership of or involvement in an employers' or employees' organization or any organization of which the members exercise a particular profession, including the advantages offered by these organizations (Article 5(1)(7) of the new ARA).

Similarly to Belgium, Estonia provided for a very basic level of protection against employment discrimination before the implementation of the RED, and the relevant provisions were never applied in practice.[105] The insertion of Article 10 ECA as an implementing measure of the RED in the field of employment introduced more detailed protection against racial and ethnic discrimination, and constituted an improvement in that sense. Still, the ECA did not cover all aspects of Article 3(1) (a)-(d). For instance, it did not extend to self-employment or membership of professional organisations.[106] The EETA in 2008 introduced a more extensive field of application as regards employment and now covers the following employment-related aspects, according to Article 2(1):

102 Collective Agreement no. 38 prohibited discrimination in the hiring phase. Moreover, discrimination in employment was criminally sanctioned by the old ARA. Both regimes were considered not to be very effective. See De Prins et al (2005), at 361-363; Cuypers (2003), at 455 and 460-461; Verhelst & De Wilde (2003), at 442; Bayart (2002), at 323.

103 Article 2(4), second bullet of the ADA referred to: "[...] the conditions for access to gainful, unpaid employment or self-employment, including the selection and appointment criteria, irrespective of the branch of activity, on all levels of the occupational hierarchy, including promotion opportunities, as well as employment and working conditions, including dismissal and pay, in both the private and public sector." Membership of and involvement in professional organisations, as well as benefits provided by them, were considered to be an implicit part of this provision, De Schutter (2004), at 35.

104 Bayart & Bosmans (2008), at 553.

105 The 1972 Labour Code prohibited "to allow or give preferences, or to restrict rights in a direct or indirect way on the grounds of sex, race, ethnic origin and attitude towards religion". Since 1992, the ECA contained a provision for an extended list of grounds, amongst which ethnic origin, color, race, native language, social origin and religion, see Poleshchuk (2005), para. 2.

106 For a more detailed overview, see Poleshchuk (2005), paras. 3.2.1-3.2.5.

> Establishing conditions for employment, becoming a self-employed person, including in establishing recruitment and selection criteria, as well as in promotion; the conclusion of the contract of employment or for the provision of services or in the assignment or election to a post, in the establishment of working conditions, giving orders, earnings, in termination or cancellation of the contract of employment or for the provision of services, in releasing from office; vocational training, career counselling, in enabling retraining or refresher course, in acquiring practical work experience; affiliation with an employees' or employers' association, including the membership in trade associations and in giving benefits by these organisations.

In Hungary, protection against discrimination in employment prior to the implementation of the RED was provided for by a generally worded provision in the Labour Code, which only envisaged discrimination of employees, not of job seekers, and was hardly applied in practice.[107] In the first phase of implementation of the RED, this provision was altered so as to include a prohibition of indirect discrimination and to extend to the hiring phase.[108] A real substantive change came, however, with the adoption of the HETA at the occasion of the second implementation phase. The relevant provisions of the HETA are somewhat complicated. First of all, there is no delineation of the material scope for public actors, which means that all relevant fields listed in Article 3(1) RED are covered for these actors. For private actors, however, the HETA provides for a limited material scope, which is described by a combination of articles. Article 5(d) HETA stipulates that private actors have to abide with the provisions of this Act to the extent that they act as employers in respect of employment relationships, or as persons entitled to give instructions in other relationships aimed at work or relationships directly related thereto.

Contrary to the three aforementioned national frameworks, the Dutch framework provided extensive protection against employment-related discrimination prior to the implementation of the RED. The RED had therefore a modest impact in this field, leading only to the insertion of references to intermediary services in the labour market, working conditions and membership of/involvement in professional organisations. The full employment-related list now comprises:

> Advertisements for job vacancies and procedures leading to the filling of vacancies; *job placement*; the commencement or termination of an employment relationship; the appointment and dismissal of civil servants; terms and

[107] Article 5 of the Labour Code provided that: "[i]n connection with an employment relationship, no employee shall be discriminated against on the basis of sex, age, family status, disability, nationality, race, origin, religion, political conviction or membership in organizations representing employees or activities connected therewith, as well as any other circumstances that have no relation to employment." See furthermore Kádár (2007), at 8.

[108] Bitskey & Gyulavári (2004), at 3.

> conditions of employment; permitting staff to receive education or training during or prior to employment; promotion; *working conditions* (Article 5 GETA, emphasis added, MB).
>
> The conditions for and access to the professions and opportunities to pursue such professions or for development within them (Article 6 GETA).
>
> *Membership of or involvement in an employers' or employees' organisation, or a professional association, or with regard to the benefits which arise from such membership or involvement* (Article 6A GETA) (emphasis added, MB).
>
> Providing services, educational or careers guidance if such acts of discrimination are committed: a. in the course of carrying on a business or practicing a profession; b. by the public sector; c. by institutions which are active in the fields of housing, social services, health care, cultural affairs or education, or d. by private persons not engaged in carrying on a business or practicing a profession, insofar as the offer is made publicly (Article 7 GETA).

The emphasised parts are the provisions that were adopted in 2003 in order to implement the RED. The other fields have been covered by the GETA since 1994, and have generally received a generous interpretation by the ETC.[109]

3.6.1.2. Access to employment

Most national frameworks are as inclusive as Article 3(1)(a) RED with respect to the types of employment-related activities covered by the material scope. For Estonia, this is true only since the EETA came into force in 2009. Article 10 ECA did not cover all aspects of Article 3(1)(a) RED, and excluded public sector employment and self-employment.[110] This deficiency was remedied by the EETA. Article 2(1) of this Act refers to:

> [e]stablishing conditions for employment, becoming a self-employed person, including in establishing recruitment and selection criteria, as well as in promotion; The conclusion of the contract of employment or for the provision of services or in the assignment or election to a post.

[109] For example, the term 'labour conditions', that now is explicitly mentioned in the GETA, was already read into 'conditions for employment' by the ETC. National courts did not always employ a similarly broad interpretation, however, which is why the government opted for an explicit reference in the amended GETA. See *Explanatory Memorandum to the Draft Amendment of the General Act on Equal Treatment and certain other acts in order to implement directive 2000/43/EC and directive 2000/78/EC*, TK 2002-03, 28 770, No. 3, TK 2002-3, 28 770, No. 3, at 11; *Het verschil gemaakt. Evaluatie AWGB en werkzaamheden CGB 1999-2004*, Commissie Gelijke Behandeling 2005, at 47.

[110] Poleshchuk (2005), paras. 3.2.1-3.2.5.

This provision clearly extends to self-employment, and Article 4 EETA furthermore makes clear that public sector employment is covered as well.[111]

The other national frameworks have covered public sector employment and self-employment for a much longer time than the Estonian framework. The Hungarian HETA explains in Article 3(a) that 'employment relationship' covers private as well as public employment relationships, professional and contracted service relationships.[112] Article 3 (b) exemplifies 'other relations aimed at work', which comes down to forms of self-employment.[113] Similarly, Article 5 of the Dutch GETA expressly refers to employment relationships in both the private and public sectors, and Article 6 GETA mentions 'professions', which covers all forms of self-employment.[114] Finally, Article 4(1) of the new Belgian ARA makes clear that 'employment relations' cover

> the private and the public sector; with regard to paid as well as unpaid labour, traineeships, internships and self-employment; at all levels of the professional hierarchy and for all branches of activities; regardless of the statutory or contractual regulation, with the exception of personnel of the Federated entities.

The express reference to unpaid labour in this provision is remarkable and constitutes a positive feature of the Belgian framework compared to the other national frameworks, which do not expressly cover unremunerated forms of work.

At the same time, it should be mentioned that the Belgian federated entities have not yet fully complied with their obligations in the field of employment. Given their competences, they should have acted to implement the provisions of the RED as regards their own officials. To some extent, they have done

[111] Article 4 EETA provides as follows: "[f]or the purposes of this Act: 1. an employee is a person working under a contract of employment or a contract for the provision of services and a public servant in the meaning of the Public Service Act. Employment or public service applicants are also treated as employees; 2.an employer is a natural or legal person, who enables work under a contract of employment or a contract for the provision of services, as well as a state or local government authority." See furthermore Article 29 EETA, which inserts a prohibition of discrimination in the Public Service Act.

[112] The exact list reads as follows: "employment, public service relationship, civil service relationship, judicial service relationship, legal service relationship, prosecution service relationship, professional and contracted service relationship, professional foster parent relationship."

[113] The exact list reads as follows: "work-from-home relationship, relationship created pursuant to a contract for work, membership in a professional group and elements of the co-operative membership and partnership activities under economic and civil law involving personal contribution and aimed at work."

[114] See Asscher-Vonk & Hendriks (2005), at 24 and 45. Also see Waaldijk (2004), at 355 and Holtmaat (2007), at 38, who argue that the term 'professions' could refer to a slightly narrower notion than 'self-employment' and 'occupation' in Article 3(1) (a) RED, but it is generally expected that the ETC and Dutch courts will follow the European interpretation in this regard.

so.[115] However, there is currently no protection against discrimination for those who are pursuing employment as an official of the Walloon Region or the Region of Brussels-Capital.[116]

The various aspects of access to employment as circumscribed in Article 3(1)(a) RED are sufficiently covered by the four national frameworks under study. Most frameworks have adopted somewhat more elaborate descriptions of the type of situations that fall into this category. The exception is provided by the Estonian EETA, which refers to:

> [e]stablishing conditions for employment, becoming a self-employed person, including in establishing recruitment and selection criteria, as well as in promotion,

and thus does not provide more detail than Article 3(1)(a) RED.

The three other national frameworks are more elaborate than the RED, however, and in particular provide more clarity as regards the inclusion of conditions other than formal selection criteria that impact on a person's opportunities for employment. Thus, Article 5(2) of the new Belgian ARA provides a non-exhaustive list of matters that are understood to fall in the category of 'access to employment', and mentions:

> *job offers, job advertisements*, formulation and application of selection criteria, *choice of particular selection channels*, and accession to professional partnerships(emphasis added, MB).

Similarly, Article 21 of the Hungarian HETA contains an exemplary list of actions that are considered to be discriminatory in the field of employment, and provides inter alia that:

> [i]t is considered a violation of the principle of equal treatment in particular if the employer inflicts direct or indirect negative discrimination upon an employee, especially when the following dispositions are defined or applied: a) for access to work, especially in *public job advertisements*, hiring, and regarding the conditions of employment; b) for *a disposition made before the establishment*

[115] See *Decree of the Walloon Region of 27 May 2004* for vocational guidance and vocational training in the Walloon Region; *Ordinance of the Brussels Capital Region of 26 June 2003* for vocational guidance in the Region of Brussels-Capital; *Decree of the French Community of 19 May 2004* for access to employment as an official with the French Community; *Decree of the German Community of 17 May 2004* for access to employment as an official with the German Community, vocational guidance and vocational training in the German Community; *Decree of the Flemish government of 8 May 2002* for access to employment as an official with the Flemish Community, vocational training in the Flemish Community, and vocational guidance in the Flemish Region. In 2008, the French Community and the Flemish government furthermore adopted comprehensive anti-discrimination decrees, which more or less follow the material scope of the RED. See *Decree of the French Community of 12 December 2008; Decree of the Flemish Community of 10 July 2008*.

[116] De Schutter (2007), at 11.

> *of the employment relationship or other relationship related to work, related to the procedure facilitating the establishment of such a relationship* (...) h) in the promotion system (emphasis added, MB).

Finally, the Dutch GETA mentions in Article 5:

> *[a]dvertisements for job vacancies and procedures leading to the filling of vacancies* (...); the commencement (...) of an employment relationship; the appointment (...) of civil servants; terms and conditions of employment; (...) promotion (emphasis added, MB).

With regard to self-employment, Article 6 GETA refers to:

> [t]he conditions for and access to the professions and *opportunities to pursue such professions* or for development within them (emphasis added, MB).

As was explained before, these contextual factors for access to employment are of great importance for minorities, since they often occasion structural forms of discrimination. Their express inclusion is therefore an asset of the Belgian, Hungarian and Dutch frameworks.

3.6.1.3. Vocational guidance and training

Vocational guidance and training are for the greater part sufficiently covered by the national frameworks, with a few problems remaining in the Belgian framework. The domains of vocational guidance and training belong to the competence of the Belgian Regions and Communities, which have not all adopted comprehensive anti-discrimination decrees yet. More particularly, the Walloon Region and the Region of Brussels-Capital have not fulfilled their obligations under the RED: both have adopted decrees that cover vocational guidance (and vocational training, as regards the Region of Brussels-Capital), but these fall substantively short of the requirements of the RED.[117]

In Estonia, Article 2(3) of the Estonian EETA refers to:

> vocational training, career counselling, in enabling retraining or refresher course, in acquiring practical work experience.

In Hungary, the domains of vocational guidance and training are not spelled out in the HETA. According to Articles 4 and 5 HETA, vocational guidance and

[117] The French, German and Flemish Communities have all included vocational guidance and training in their anti-discrimination decrees, which moreover substantively comply with the requirements of the RED. See the *Decree of the French Community of 12 December 2008*; the *Decree of the Flemish Community of 10 July 2008*; and the *Decree of the German Community of 17 May 2004*. The *Decree of the Walloon Region of 27 May 2004* covers vocational guidance and vocational training in the Walloon Region, but only prohibits direct and indirect discrimination, and does not mention harassment or the instruction to discriminate. The *Ordinance of the Brussels Capital Region of 26 June 2003* covers vocational guidance in the Region of Brussels-Capital.

training offered by employers, public actors and publicly subsidised actors are fully covered; other actors are covered only in so far as they offer vocational guidance or training from premises open to customers, or are the object of a publicly made offer.[118] These qualifications for private actors seem acceptable as the RED itself sets in place a similar qualification for the provision of services in general ('available to the public' in Article 3(1)(h)RED), which would seem to comprise vocational guidance and training services.

The Dutch GETA sets in place a similar qualification clause with regard to vocational guidance and training offered by a body other than the employer. These domains are covered by Article 7 GETA, which pertains to the provision of services in general, and which applies to services offered by private actors only to the extent that these are publicly offered.[119] Insofar as vocational training and guidance are offered by the employer, they are covered by Article 5 f) GETA, which expressly mentions "job placement" and "permitting staff to receive education or training during or prior to employment". During the deliberations on the IA, the government made clear that the reference to 'job placement' is intended to cover all services aimed at enhancing someone's opportunities in the labour market, which includes the offering of internships.[120] This interpretation is in line with 'practical work experience' of Article 3(1)(b) RED, and appears moreover suitable to bring unremunerated forms of work within the scope of the GETA.

3.6.1.4. Work conditions

All four national frameworks sufficiently cover work conditions as circumscribed by Article 3(1)(c) RED. The new Belgian ARA is especially elaborate, and contains in Article 5(2) a very extensive list with examples of aspects of employment that belong to this category, which is simply too elaborate to reproduce here. The list mentions all kinds of conditions relating to entry into employment, pay, promotion, representation of employees, leave and dismissal. As it makes abundantly clear to both lawyers and the public which aspects of employment can be tainted by discrimination, it can be said to enhance the practicability and effectiveness of the law.

---

[118] For vocational guidance, see also Article 27 (2) h) HETA, which stipulates in combination with Article 27 (1) HETA that the principle of equal treatment shall be enforced with regard to access to vocational guidance by state regulated or state subsidised educational institutions.

[119] See section 3.6.5.

[120] *Explanatory Memorandum to the Draft Amendment of the General Act on Equal Treatment and certain other acts in order to implement directive 2000/43/EC and directive 2000/78/EC, TK 2002-03, 28 770, No. 3*, TK 2002-3, 28 770, No. 3, at 11.

The Estonian, Hungarian and Dutch provisions are less elaborate than the Belgian one, but do capture the various elements of Article 3(1)(c) RED. Article 2(1) of the Estonian EETA mentions the following employment-related aspects:

> the establishment of work conditions, giving orders, pay and dismissal.

The Hungarian HETA, in Article 21, mentions the following fields of employer activity:

> the determination and application of work conditions; the establishment and provision of allowances, the determination of pay or other work-related benefits; the determination of disciplinary sanctions.

Article 5 of the Dutch GETA, finally, mentions:

> dismissal, terms and conditions of employment and work conditions.

This provision is very broadly applied in the Dutch context, and extends to all matters related to the entire employment trajectory: from access to the ending of the employment relationship.[121] A similarly broad interpretation will hopefully be adopted in the Estonian and Hungarian frameworks in the future.

3.6.1.5. Membership of professional organisations

With the exception of the Hungarian framework, the national laws sufficiently cover membership of professional organisations of Article 3(1)(d) RED. The Belgian, Estonian and Dutch laws have all more or less copied Article 3(1)(d), and therefore fully comply with the RED.[122] In Hungary, the limited application of the HETA to private actors constitutes a problem, since membership of and involvement in professional organisations is only covered to the extent that such organisations are public bodies, receive a state subsidy, make an offer available to the public, or are provided for by the employer or contractual partner.[123] Even aside from this restrictive coverage, Article 6 (1) d and (2) HETA makes clear that only the membership policies of associations are covered, not any other aspects of their internal relations, which ignores the 'involvement' and 'benefits' aspects of Article 3(1)(d) RED.

121 Asscher-Vonk & Hendriks (2005), at 31; Cremers-Hartman (2004), at 13-20.
122 See Article 2(1) of the Estonian EETA, Article 5(7) of the new Belgian ARA and Article 6A of the Dutch GETA.
123 Kádár (2007), at 35.

3.6.2. Social protection, social security and healthcare

Prior to the implementation of the RED, there was limited protection for discrimination in social protection, social security and healthcare in the Member States under study, and the RED has thus had a considerable impact in these fields.

In Belgium the old ARA contained a general prohibition of discrimination in the provision of services, which extended to healthcare and public services, such as for instance garbage collection.[124] Application of the criminal provisions of the old ARA was difficult, however, particularly with regard to issues of proof, and these provisions were therefore not often applied in practice.[125] The first instrument of implementation, the ADA, did not contain a specific provision with regard to social matters. These were considered to be comprised by the general reference in Article 2(4) to:

> [t]he provision of goods and services to the public and the access to and participation in, as well as any and all other exercise of an economic, social, cultural or political activity accessible to the public.

It was not entirely clear to what extent these generally worded provisions covered all of the aspects mentioned by Article 3(1) (e) RED.[126] The new ARA has improved matters by containing explicit references to social protection, social security and healthcare in Article 5(1)(2) and to occupational schemes of social security in Article 5(1)(4).[127] In addition, the French and Flemish Communities have adopted comprehensive anti-discrimination legislation in the field of healthcare policy, which complies with the requirements of the RED.[128] The German Community has not yet acted in this field, which means that there is a minor lack of protection in the Belgian framework for this domain.

In Estonia, there was no specific anti-discrimination law in place for the social domains prior to the implementation of the RED. The EETA now expressly applies to the fields of social protection, social security and healthcare, as Article 2(1) mentions:

> receiving social welfare, health care and social security service, including receiving welfare benefit.

[124] De Prins et al (2005), at 359-360.

[125] De Prins et al (2005), at 445.

[126] De Schutter (2004), at 36.

[127] Article 5(1)(4) actually refers to "additional regulations for social security", which in Article 4(16) are defined as occupational social security schemes as regulated by Directives 96/97/EC and 86/378/EEC in the field of gender equality law.

[128] *Decree of the French Community with regard to the fight against certain forms of discrimination*, 12 December 2008; *Decree of the Flemish Community containing a framework for the Flemish equal opportunities and equal treatment policy*, 10 July 2008.

The Hungarian framework also lacked any specific anti-discrimination law for the social domains prior to the implementation of the RED, which changed with the adoption of the HETA. Articles 4(h) and 4(k) of this Act require compliance with anti-discrimination law by:

> persons providing social care and child protection services, as well as child welfare services [and] entities providing healthcare.

The field of social protection and social security is one of the few in which the RED has actually had a big impact on the Dutch anti-discrimination framework. Prior to implementation of the RED, the GETA did not cover this field, except for healthcare, which was covered by the general provision on goods and services. Article 7a GETA now prohibits discrimination in the field of social protection, including social security.

As regards the interpretation of the three aspects of Article 3(1)(e) RED, 'social security' has received most attention, and has been interpreted in line with the ECJ's jurisprudence in all Member States, save for Estonia. Article 4(14) of the new Belgian ARA explains that social security comprises all statutory provisions protecting against risks of loss of income due to for instance disability, sickness, dismissal, etcetera, as well as provisions regulating paid leave and child benefits. The Explanatory Memorandum to the HETA provides for a similar interpretation of social security, as does the Explanatory Memorandum of the Dutch IA.[129]

The HETA furthermore contains two provisions that further elaborate the practical meaning of the prohibition of discrimination in the fields of social security and healthcare. Article 24 HETA thus provides that:

> [t]he principle of equal treatment shall be enforced in respect of social security, particularly in the course of claiming and ensuring a) benefits financed from the social security systems, and b) social benefits, financial and in-kind child protection or personal care.

'Social benefits' and 'personal care' are especially broad notions that can probably cover even more than 'social security' in its European law understanding. Article 25(1) HETA provides that:

> [t]he principle of equal treatment shall be enforced in respect of health care, particularly in respect of the provision of health services, including a)

[129] For Hungary, see *Explanatory Memorandum to Act CXXV of 2003 on Equal Treatment and Promotion of Equal Opportunities,* with regard to Articles 24 and 25 HETA, which expressly refer to Directives 97/7/EC and 86/3/78 on sex equality in social security and occupational social security schemes. For The Netherlands, see *Explanatory Memorandum to the Draft Amendment of the General Act on Equal Treatment and certain other acts in order to implement directive 2000/43/EC and directive 2000/78/EC*, TK 2002-03, 28 770, No. 3, TK 2002-3, 28 770, No. 3, at 15, which describes social security as extending to those measures taken to alleviate loss of income due to unemployment, disability, sickness, etc.

> participation in preventive programmes and medical check-ups, b) preventive medical care, c) use of premises for residence, d) the satisfaction of dietary and other needs.

These exemplifying provisions enhance the level of protection offered by the HETA, by making it easier for inexperienced persons to detect discrimination.

The notion of 'social protection' has so far only been further exemplified in the Dutch framework, where it has received a very broad interpretation. The Explanatory Memorandum to the IA considers this concept to extend to all measures aimed at tackling poverty and social exclusion, furthering social integration and the inclusion of most vulnerable groups.[130] The National Action Plan against poverty and social exclusion of 2003, which is explicitly referred to in the Explanatory Memorandum, reveals that the list of aspects thus covered is virtually endless. Participation in the labour market, income levels, housing, education, healthcare, IT, public transport, integration, homelessness and violence in the private sphere are all policy areas that come within the ambit of 'social protection'.[131] The mention of 'integration' is especially interesting, in view of the exception of Article 3(2) RED, which excludes immigration, visa and asylum policies from the scope of the RED and which is discussed in sections 3.4 and 3.7. It may be clear in any case, that a very broad interpretation of social protection is envisaged.

Practice of the ETC confirms this broad reach. Cases ruled under Article 7a GETA have so far concerned all kinds of financial social benefits,[132] assistance in setting up a company for persons receiving social benefits,[133] housing policy,[134] preschool facilities for disadvantaged children,[135] and dismissal schemes for subsidised jobs.[136] In view of the legal uncertainty that could arise concerning the exact delineation of the scope of Article 7a, section (2) of this Article leaves open the possibility of providing a more detailed description of the concept, as well as of social security, in an Order in Council, which has not yet been adopted.

---

130 *Explanatory Memorandum to the Draft Amendment of the General Act on Equal Treatment and certain other acts in order to implement directive 2000/43/EC and directive 2000/78/EC*, TK 2002-3, 28 770, No. 3, at 14-15.

131 *Nationaal Actieplan ter Bestrijding van Armoede en Sociale Uitsluiting 2003* (National Action Plan to Combat Poverty and Social Exclusion 2003), Dutch Ministry of Social Affairs 2003. The plan referred to in the Explanatory Memorandum is the one from 2001; both plans cover similar policy areas, however.

132 Opinion 2008-122 ETC (benefit for young disabled persons); Opinion 2007-132 ETC (benefit for war victims); Opinions 2007-91, 2007-12 and 2006-257 ETC (welfare); Opinion 2007-4 ETC (benefit for elderly persons).

133 Opinion 2008-107 ETC.

134 Opinion 2006-222 ETC.

135 Opinion 2006-206 ETC.

136 Opinion 2008-1 ETC.

Finally, as regards the application of private sector initiatives in the fields of social protection, social security and healthcare, it seems that only the Estonian framework is ambiguous, by not making clear whether the material scope provisions apply to both the public and private sectors. The new Belgian ARA states in Article 5(1) that the law is applicable to all persons in both the private and public sectors, in line with the first phrase of Article 3(1) RED. Moreover, the express reference to occupational social security schemes in Article 5(1)(4) of the new ARA shows that the legislator had no objection against including private sector initiatives in the field of social security, which could also impact on the understanding of 'social protection' and 'healthcare'. The Hungarian framework also comprises private sector activity, since Articles 4 h) and k) HETA simply refer to 'persons' and 'institutions' and thus extend to private actors as well. The government's commentary to Articles 24 and 25 in the Explanatory Memorandum supports this broad reading.[137] Therefore, the limited applicability of the HETA to private actors does not seem to be an issue in social matters. Finally, the Explanatory Memorandum to the Dutch IA reveals that private sector initiatives are covered.[138]

3.6.3. Social advantages

Social advantages constitute another domain in which the RED has had a relatively far-reaching impact in the four Member States, none of which had in place specific anti-discrimination provisions in this field prior to the implementation of the RED. In Belgium, the provision in the old ARA on discrimination in the field of goods and services probably covered social advantages, but this is not certain. After the first implementation phase the ADA did not explicitly refer to social advantages, but these were considered to be covered by the general provisions on the provision of goods and services to the public and the access to and participation in economic, social, cultural or political activities accessible to the public (Article 2(4) ADA).[139] Only with the adoption of the new ARA were social advantages explicitly regulated in Belgian anti-discrimination law. The new ARA mentions social advantages as a separate component of its material scope in Article 5(3).

---

137 *Explanatory Memorandum to Act CXXV of 2003 on Equal Treatment and Promotion of Equal Opportunities,* with regard to Articles 24 and 25 HETA, in which the government emphasises that the provisions apply to private and public actors alike. See also the Healthcare Act, *Act CLIV of 1997*, which in Article 7(1) orders compliance with the principle of equal treatment, and which applies to public and private healthcare providers alike (Article 3 f).

138 *Explanatory Memorandum to the Draft Amendment of the General Act on Equal Treatment and certain other acts in order to implement directive 2000/43/EC and directive 2000/78/EC*, TK 2002-03, 28 770, No. 3, TK 2002-3, 28 770, No. 3, at 15.

139 De Schutter (2004), at 36.

In the Netherlands, social advantages were regulated by the GETA only after implementation, and Article 7A GETA now expressly mentions social advantages as a field in which the prohibition of discrimination must be upheld.

In Estonia, regulation of social advantages came about after a relatively long period of incomplete implementation of the RED, and the EETA of 2008 now mentions social advantages as an element of its material scope in Article 2(1).

In Hungary, finally, social advantages were not mentioned in anti-discrimination provisions prior to the implementation of the RED. The HETA now mentions 'social benefits' in Article 24 as a field in which the principle of equal treatment must be observed. Articles 4 and 5 make clear that these benefits are fully covered insofar as they are offered by public or publicly subsidised actors and employers. Social advantages offered by private actors other than employers are, however, only covered to the extent that they are offered publicly.[140] Seeing that social advantages in their current understanding at the European level usually concern advantages that are accorded on a general rather than on an individual basis, the requirement of a public offer will probably not be problematic in practice. Nevertheless, it cannot be ruled out that some social advantages will be considered not to be offered publicly and therefore not to be covered by the HETA. Practice will need to reveal whether there is a real problem in this respect.

As regards the interpretation of 'social advantages', only the Belgian and Dutch frameworks have provided some guidelines, and both point to European law in this respect. Article 4(15) of the new Belgian ARA makes clear that social advantages should be interpreted in line with the similar concept in Article 7(2) of Regulation 1612/68 on the free movement of workers within the Community. Similarly, the Explanatory Memorandum to the Dutch IA emphasises that the interpretation of Article 7(2) of Regulation 1612/68 should be followed, and furthermore explains that social advantages are all advantages of an economic or cultural nature offered by public as well as private institutions.[141] As was mentioned before, interpretation along the lines of Regulation 1612/68 ensures a broad understanding of social advantages, and the Belgian and Dutch affirmations that such a broad interpretation is called for in the context of racial discrimination are therefore to be welcomed.

[140] See for a more detailed discussion of how the HETA approaches the 'available to the public' clause section 3.6.5.

[141] *Explanatory Memorandum to the Draft Amendment of the General Act on Equal Treatment and certain other acts in order to implement directive 2000/43/EC and directive 2000/78/EC*, TK 2002-03, 28 770, No. 3, TK 2002-3, 28 770, No. 3, at 14-15.

3.6.4. Education

The four Member States show a mixed picture as regards the implementation of the RED in the field of education. In the Netherlands, racial discrimination in education was covered by the GETA from 1994, and the RED therefore did not have a real impact in this Member State.

In Estonia, to the contrary, regulation of discrimination in this field came about only in 2008, with the adoption of the EETA. Article 2(1)(6) of this Act mentions education as part of the material scope.

In Hungary, discrimination in education was covered by a general provision in the Public Education Act prior to implementation of the RED, but this provision was hardly applied in practice.[142] The HETA now provides in Articles 4 (g) and (i) that the principle of equal treatment must be upheld by all institutions of public education and of higher education, as well as by general educational institutions.

In Belgium, finally, implementation is not complete, since education belongs to the competence of the Communities, which have not all fulfilled their implementation duties under the RED in this respect.[143] The Flemish and French Communities adopted comprehensive anti-discrimination decrees in 2008, both of which cover education as organised by these Communities.[144] The German Community, however, has not enacted any anti-discrimination legislation in this field. Forms of education offered by the private sector are covered by Article 5(8) of the new Federal ARA, which mentions "access to and participation in any economic, social, cultural or political activity" as an aspect of the material scope.

The meaning of 'education' has so far only been further elaborated in the Netherlands and in Hungary. The Dutch Explanatory Memorandum to the IA emphasises that the provision on education needs to be interpreted broadly, covering all entities that offer education, whether endowed with legal personality or not. Moreover, it makes clear that education extends beyond

[142] Article 4 sub 7 and 77 sub 3 of *Act LXXIX of 1993 on Public Education*. See also Farkas (2003).

[143] Under the ADA some scholars asserted that the general provision on economic, social, cultural and political activities in Article 2(4) extended to education, but the Antwerp Court of Appeal in *A. e.a. v. Provincie Limburg*, 14 June 2005, *Rechtskundig Weekblad* 2006, at 136-144, refused to adopt this broad interpretation. In view of the fact that the Communities are competent with regard to all educational matters, to the exclusion of the Federal legislator, the Antwerp Court's approach would seem to be the right one (see Schutter (2007a) at 4-6; Foblets & Velaers (2006), at 125-127; Veny (2004), at 118). The Explanatory Memorandum of the new ARA in any case supports it, making clear that the provision in Article 5(1)(8), which applies similar wording as the previously applicable Article 2(4) ADA, does not cover education (*Explanatory Memorandum to the Draft law amending the law of 30 July 1981 that penalises certain acts motivated by racism and xenophobia*, Doc 51. 2720/001, 41, at 21).

[144] Articles 3(13) and 3(14) of the *Decree of the French Community of 12 December 2008*; Article 20(5) of the *Decree of the Flemish Community of 10 July 2008*.

the public education system, and should be read so as to cover all kinds of courses, seminars, etcetera. Finally, it stresses that all intermediary and information services in the field of education are covered by Article 7(1)(c) GETA.[145] The Hungarian Explanatory Memorandum to the HETA makes clear that the prohibition of discrimination does not only relate to matters of entry into education, but applies to the overall quality of education, as well as all broader measures that are relevant for education.[146] Article 27 of the Hungarian HETA furthermore exemplifies the prohibition of discrimination in education, providing that equal treatment shall be ensured as regards, inter alia, performance evaluation, providing and using services related to education and access to benefits related to education. These inclusive approaches to education of the GETA and HETA, which embrace contextual factors, enhance the level of protection offered by anti-discrimination law, as was explained before. It is to be hoped that an equally broad interpretation will be adopted in Belgium and Estonia.

In most Member States it is clear that not only public education, but also private sector initiatives in this field are covered. Only the Estonian EETA remains silent in this respect, and application of this Act in the future needs to show whether private sector activity is actually covered by 'education'. In Belgium, the general provision of Article 5(1)(8) of the new ARA on the access to and participation in any economic, social or cultural activity is clearly broad enough to comprise private sector education initiatives. Article 7(1)(a) of the Dutch GETA on the provision of services fulfils a similar function in the Dutch framework, and practice of the ETC confirms that this Article covers courses offered by private institutions.[147] In Hungary, the Explanatory Memorandum to the HETA reveals that the provisions on education cover private institutions and other institutions providing courses outside of the general educational system.[148] The limited applicability of the HETA to private actors therefore does not apear to constitute a problem in this field.

It is remarkable that the Hungarian HETA is unique in showing a regard for the particular interests of minority groups in the field of education in Hungarian society. The Act contains an express prohibition of segregation as a particular form of discrimination, which is a well-known structural problem for the Roma community in Hungary.[149] Moreover, Articles 28 and 29 HETA regulate positive action in education, and allow ethnic minorities to set up

[145] *Memo sent to the Parliament with regard to the implementation of the RED*, TK 2001-2, 28 187, No. 1, at 10-13.

[146] *Explanatory Memorandum to Act CXXV of 2003 on Equal Treatment and Promotion of Equal Opportunities*, with regard to Article 27 HETA.

[147] See for instance Opinion 2002-157 ETC, which involved courses offered by a Jewish institution on the Jewish religion. See also *Memo sent to the Parliament with regard to the implementation of the RED*, TK 2001-2, 28 187, No. 1, at 10-13.

[148] *Explanatory Memorandum to Act CXXV of 2003 on Equal Treatment and Promotion of Equal Opportunities*, with regard to Article 27 HETA.

[149] Articles 7(1), 10 (2) and 27 (3) HETA.

education in line with their own cultural, linguistic and other group-related standards.[150] This special attention for the interests of minorities suggests a substantive equality perspective and a sensitivity to the identity-related interests of minority groups, which enhances the quality of the HETA anti-discrimination framework.

3.6.5. Goods and services

Prior to the implementation of the RED, there was limited protection for discrimination in the field of goods and services in the Member States, with the exception of the Netherlands. The Dutch GETA provided extensive protection against discrimination in this field since 1994. Implementation of the RED produced a mainly cosmetic change, and brought about an express reference to *access* to goods and services.[151] Thus, Article 7(1) GETA now provides that:

> It is unlawful to discriminate in offering *or providing access to* goods or services, in concluding, implementing or terminating agreements thereon, (...) if such acts of discrimination are committed: a. in the course of carrying on a business or practicing a profession; b. by the public sector; c. by institutions which are active in the fields of housing, social services, health care, cultural affairs or education, or d. by private persons not engaged in carrying on a business or practicing a profession, insofar as the offer is made publicly (emphasis added, MB).

According to the government, the word 'access' made clear that all kinds of information and intermediary services with regard to the obtainment of certain goods or services were covered.[152] However, this would seem self-evident, even without an explicit reference to 'access', seeing that information and intermediary services constitute 'services' in its normal understanding.

The old Belgian ARA contained a prohibition of discrimination in the provision of goods and services, which was to a limited extent applied in practice.[153] In this regard, Article 5(1)(1) of the new ARA does not entail considerable substantive changes. This Article mentions:

> the access to and the provision of goods and services that are publicly available.

[150] Article 28 HETA allows for the voluntary participation in/setting up of education for ethnic minorities of which the objective or program justifies the creation of separate classes or groups, provided that this does not result in any disadvantage for those participating in such education and the education complies with public requirements on education.

[151] *Explanatory Memorandum to the Draft Amendment of the General Act on Equal Treatment and certain other acts in order to implement directive 2000/43/EC and directive 2000/78/EC, TK 2002-03, 28 770, No. 3,* TK 2002-3, 28 770, No. 3, at 13.

[152] *Explanatory Memorandum to the Draft Amendment of the General Act on Equal Treatment and certain other acts in order to implement directive 2000/43/EC and directive 2000/78/EC, TK 2002-03, 28 770, No. 3,* TK 2002-3, 28 770, No. 3, at 13.

[153] De Prins et al (2005), at 353-360.

Still, because of the procedural and remedial tools offered by the new ARA the prohibition of discrimination in this field has more force now than under the old ARA.[154] Even though this is not specified, housing is considered to be comprised by 'services' in Article 5(1)(1).[155] In view of the competence of the Belgian Regions concerning public housing policy, it is only the private housing market that is envisaged here.[156] The Regions have not yet acted to implement the RED in the field of public housing, which means that there is a lack of protection in this field.[157]

Similarly to the Belgian framework, the Hungarian anti-discrimination framework offered limited protection in the field of the provision of goods and services before the implementation of the RED. Consumer protection law provided for a general prohibition of discrimination, but it was hardly ever relied upon successfully, mainly due to problems of proof.[158] The HETA now covers discrimination in the field of goods and services in a more extensive way. Given the unlimited material scope of this Act for public actors, all public services are covered.[159] Furthermore, activities of private actors in this field are covered to a large degree. Article 4 HETA lists a number of private actors that have to abide by the anti-discrimination requirements in all aspects: museums, libraries, general educational institutions, voluntary mutual insurance funds and private pension funds. In addition, the provisions in Article 5 (a) and (b) HETA require compliance with the principle of equal treatment by:

> those who make a proposal to persons not defined preliminarily to enter into contract or those who invite such persons to tender; those who provide services or sell goods at their premises open to customers.

Finally, in Estonia there was no protection against discrimination in the field of goods and services prior to the implementation of the RED.[160] The EETA now covers this field, and in Article 2(1)(7) mentions:

> the availability of goods and services, including housing, available to the public.

[154] Ambrus (2010).
[155] Van Drooghenbroeck (2004), at 113.
[156] Van Drooghenbroeck (2004), at 113-114.
[157] De Schutter (2007a), at 62. See Bernard (2008), at 829-832, who mentions a draft decree of the Brussels-Capital Region implementing the RED in the field of housing, which was not yet available at the end of the research period for this study.
[158] According to Article 25 sub 2 of *Act No. 1 of 1978 on Domestic Trade* it was prohibited to unlawfully discriminate against customers. See the White Booklets on the website of NEKI at www.neki.hu (accessed July 2009), in which the experiences of this NGO with the application of this provision are recounted.
[159] See also Articles 37 and onwards of the HETA, which contain amendments to a number of acts on particular public services/activities, and introduce the HETA's anti-discrimination regime for these particular domains, among which, inter alia: the treatment of prisoners; public procurement; military personnel; cemeteries and burials; copyrights and public utilities.
[160] Poleshchuk (2007), at 33-34.

The interpretation of 'goods and services' is not the same in all four Member States. First of all, some Member States have taken a broader approach to the meaning of these concepts as compared to their economically coloured meaning in free movement law. In the Netherlands, the ETC does not require a remunerative aim.[161] The practice of Belgian courts under the old ARA reveals a similarly broad approach.[162] It should be mentioned, however, that the Explanatory Memorandum to the Belgian new ARA refers to European free movement law as providing guidelines for the interpretation of 'goods and services'. In this respect, Belgian courts could decide to apply a narrower approach in the future and to require a remunerative aim, which is clearly not desirable. In Hungary and Estonia, it is not clear yet whether such an aim will be imposed.

Secondly, the extent to which 'goods and services' cover goods and services offered by public actors differs greatly between the Member States. In the Hungarian framework the unlimited material scope of the HETA as regards public actor activity makes for extensive coverage of these goods and services. The Belgian framework again is ambiguous in this respect. Case law under the old ARA reveals that public services, such as garbage collection, were covered by 'services'.[163] Still, the Explanatory Memorandum to the new ARA states that 'goods and services' are to be interpreted in line with their meaning in free movement law, which would mean that public services are not covered.[164] The Dutch framework, unfortunately, clearly does not extend to public services. Despite the confusing formulation of Article 7 GETA ("by the public sector"), 'goods and services' in the Dutch context are generally understood not to extend to services or goods typically provided by public actors. The GETA thus only covers goods and services provided by public actors that could also normally be provided by private actors. The only exception to this general principle concerns the fields of social protection, social security and social advantages (Article 7a GETA), in which services typically provided by public actors are covered.[165] In 2006 a study commissioned by the Dutch government on the potential expansion of the GETA to all acts of public actors was published, which was rather sceptical as to the benefits of such an opening-up.[166] On the basis of this report the government decided not

161 Gerards & Heringa (2003), at 71.

162 De Prins et al (2005), at 352 and 503.

163 De Prins et al (2005), at 352 and 503.

164 *Explanatory Memorandum to the Draft law amending the law of 30 July 1981 that penalises certain acts motivated by racism and xenophobia*, Doc 51. 2720/001, at 44.

165 Van der Mei (2005), at 191; Gerards & Heringa (2003), at 71-72.

166 See Zoontjens (2006a). According to the author, an expansion of the GETA with regard to public actors should be accompanied by certain safeguards; legislative action should not be covered. Moreover, an open system of justification should be retained and the competence of the ETC should be limited with regard to these actors. So far there have been no initiatives by the government to act upon the findings of this report.

to expand the GETA in this respect and emphasised that the constitutional, administrative and international legal obligations of public actors provided sufficient protection against discrimination.[167] The Estonian framework does not provide any information as to whether public services are covered.

Thirdly, not all Member States have expressly included contextual factors pertaining to the provision of goods and services, such as issues of accessibility. The Estonian framework does not provide any indications in this respect. In Belgium, to the contrary, it is generally understood that the terms 'access to' and 'provision of' are intended to cover all relevant aspects of contractual relationships with regard to goods and services.[168] A similarly broad interpretation is found in the Netherlands, as can be inferred from the practice of the ETC.[169] It should particularly be mentioned that, when interpreting 'access to' and 'provision of' services, the ETC takes into account the relevance of the particular activity or opportunity to full participation in society. For instance, being able to donate blood for altruistic reasons is, according to the ETC, covered by Article 7a GETA, because of its relevance to full participation in society.[170] This concern for participation in society reveals a clear substantive equality outlook.

In Hungary, the regard for contextual factors can be seen particularly in the exemplifying provisions on goods and services, as contained in Article 26 HETA on housing and Article 30 HETA on goods and services. Article 26 mentions the following relevant aspects with regard to housing: housing subsidies, benefits, interest subsidies by the state or a municipality, the conditions of sale or leasing of state-owned or municipal housing and plots, occupancy and other building permits. Moreover, in section 3, it prohibits public authorities to pursue ethnic segregation in their housing policy. In Article 30 HETA the following examples of discriminatory behaviour are listed: denial of the provision of goods or services by catering, commercial, cultural and entertainment establishments; provision of offering goods or services of a lower quality; display of a notice or sign according to which particular individuals are excluded from the provision of services or sale of goods at the premises.

Article 30(2)-(3) HETA furthermore permits minority groups to set up institutions to preserve their own culture and traditions in the field of goods and services, and provides that:

---

[167] *Letter of the government with regard to the third evaluation of the GETA*, TK 2008-9, 28 481, at 5-6.

[168] Van Drooghenbroeck (2004), at 134-135; De Boeck (2003), at 435. For detailed discussions of the impact of Belgium anti-discrimination law with regard to goods and services see Bernard (2008) (housing market); De Boeck (2003) (contract law generally); Kusters (2003) (housing market).

[169] Gerards & Heringa (2003), at 71.

[170] Opinion 2007-85 ETC, paras. 3.6-3.8.

> [e]ntry into premises established for a group defined by [a protected characteristic, MB] for the purposes of preserving traditions or maintaining cultural or self identity and open to the immediate public may be limited or subject to membership or specific conditions. The limitation [...] must be obvious from the name of the establishment and the circumstances of the use of the service; and this shall not be done in a manner humiliating and defamatory to individuals who do not belong to the particular group, and further it must not provide an opportunity for abusing the law.

This provision again suggests a special regard for the identity-related interests of minorities, which is a very positive feature of the Hungarian framework.

The 'available to the public' clause

There is quite some divergence visible as regards the approach to the 'available to the public' clause in the four Member States. As far as a preliminary assessment goes, the most restrictive approach would appear to be present in the Hungarian framework, and more particularly in Article 5(a)-(b), which regulates the applicability of the HETA to private actor activity. This provision reveals that the determining factor is whether the provider of a good or service approaches the public in general – in other words no person in particular – with his offer. Housing offered by private persons is for example only covered insofar as they make their offer in publicly accessible premises or advertise the offer publicly.[171] Similarly, Article 6 HETA determines that goods or services offered by associations to their members are not covered by the HETA. As was explained before, this approach, which focuses on the choice of addressees and/or channels of communication, is not satisfactory, since it is very easy to establish a 'closed' group of recipients in order to circumvent anti-discrimination law provisions.

The Belgian approach to the 'available to the public' clause is not yet clearly spelled out. A number of Belgian authors have submitted that the distinguishing factor in interpreting 'available to the public' is whether the particular provider has made his offer to the broader public, by way of an advertisement, poster, etcetera.[172] This approach, which resembles the Hungarian one, was supported by the Belgian government in 2003 during the deliberations on the draft ADA, when it stated that associations were only covered by the provisions of the ADA to the extent that they provided goods and services in a way that was open to the general public. Moreover, this approach found some resonance in practice, more specifically in a case ruled by the Brussels Tribunal of First Instance in 2005. The Tribunal decided that the rental offer of an apartment within the building in which the landlady lived was 'publicly available' because she had approached a real estate agency

171 Kádár & Farkas (2005), at 26.

172 De Schutter (2004), at 38; Dambre (2004), at 325-326.

to find a tenant, and had made use of internet advertisements and posters to make the offer.[173] Thus, the Tribunal apparently considered the choice of communication channels to be determining.

The Explanatory Memorandum to the new ARA, however, would appear to require a stricter approach, and states that only *strictly private* matters are excluded from the scope of this Act.[174] This consideration could be interpreted so as to require that courts look further than communication channels, and only exclude those activities that are very closely linked to the right to privacy and the freedom of association. One author submits in this respect that the application of the clause should entail individual assessment of each case separately, and more particularly the exercise of a balancing act.[175] This is indeed the preferable approach, as was explained in section 3.3.5, but it remains to be seen whether it will be followed in practice by Belgian courts.

The Dutch framework so far seems to provide a rather satisfactory approach, which can be inferred from the way in which the ETC approaches the import of the freedom of association on the provisions of the GETA. The 'available to the public' clause as contained in Article 7(1)(d) has not yet been applied in practice. Nevertheless, the ETC has already on many occasions had the opportunity to rule on the applicability of the GETA to private association activity, and its approach in this regard has become increasingly strict.

For a long time, the ETC took the point of view that private association activity was only covered to the extent that the association concerned was of an open and business-like character. In practice this meant that not only goods and/or services offered to the general public were covered, but also goods or services that were considered essential for participation in an important aspect of public life, regardless of the fact that they were provided to members only.[176] There is clearly an underlying concern for the effective participation of vulnerable groups in society here, which underlines the ETC's focus on substantive equality. Moreover, this line of practice shows that the ETC does not only look at the choice of addressees and/or communication channels, but balances the interests involved in each particular case.

In 2006 the ETC decided to apply even stricter scrutiny with regard to activities of private associations. Thus, it made clear that it would from then scrutinise the provision of goods and services exclusively available to members, unless the reason to exclude non-members was connected to the particular aim pursued by the association.[177] This change of attitude makes clear that the ETC only excludes from the scope of the GETA those activities that it finds to be sufficiently closely connected to the freedom of association,

---

173 *MRAX v. S.A. IMMO MDH*, Brussels Court of First Instance, 3 June 2005.

174 *Explanatory Memorandum to the Draft law amending the law of 30 July 1981 that penalises certain acts motivated by racism and xenophobia*, Doc 51. 2720/001, at 44.

175 Van Droogenbroek (2003), at 231.

176 De Kluiver (2006), at 171. See for instance Opinion 2005-52, para. 5.4.

177 Opinion 2006-258 ETC, paras. 3.1-3.14.

which is the preferable approach, as was explained before. It is to be hoped that the ETC will be equally strict vis-à-vis individual private actors that invoke the 'available to the public' clause of Article 7(1)(d).

3.7. The exception of immigration, visa and asylum (IVA) policies

It is interesting to note that none of the four Member States have included references similar to Article 3(2) RED in their national legislation. This is particularly remarkable for the Estonian framework, where the previous draft of an equal treatment act did include such exclusionary provision.[178] The absence of provisions similar to Article 3(2) RED in national law means that the question to what extent private actors distinguishing on the basis of legal status are covered is fairly easily answered: to the extent that private actor distinctions based on legal status fall within the scope of national anti-discrimination law, they are covered.

It should furthermore be mentioned that some of the national frameworks appear to cover public actor activity in the field of IVA policies. This is very clear for the Hungarian HETA, which applies an unlimited material scope for any public actor activity not amounting to regulatory acts.[179] Furthermore, some elements of the material scope provisions of the Belgian and Dutch frameworks could be interpreted so as to cover certain IVA aspects. Article 5(1)8 of the new Belgian ARA mentions "access to and participation in, as well as all other exercise of an economic, social cultural or political activity that is available to the public". The Belgian legislator intended this provision to be a catch-all phrase, so as to make sure that all aspects of public life were covered by anti-discrimination law.[180] As such it will probably be interpreted broadly, which opens the door for certain aspects of IVA policy to be included. At the same time, inclusion of IVA matters is not self-evident, seeing that these policies do not address the public in general, but rather a more limited target group, that is foreigners wanting to reside/work in the country. It is therefore uncertain whether the new Belgian ARA will be applicable to this policy field.

In a similar way, it is uncertain to what extent the Dutch GETA covers IVA policies. The social protection provision of this Act, contained in Article 7a, could be interpreted so as to extend to certain matters of IVA policy. As was mentioned before, the concept of social protection of Article 7a is very broadly interpreted in the Dutch context, extending inter alia to integration

178 Poleshchuk (2007), at 25.
179 Kádár (2007), at 48.
180 Van Drooghenbroeck (2004), at 137.

policies.[181] Such policies naturally have strong links with IVA policies, which could induce the ETC to include certain immigration matters. Practice needs to confirm whether the ETC will be willing to use this option.

3.8. Additional domains covered by national anti-discrimination law

Of the four Member States, only Belgium and Hungary have opted for a wider material scope than the one prescribed by Article 3(1) RED. For Hungary, this follows from the already frequently mentioned unlimited material scope for public actors.

In Belgium, two provisions have been added to the list required by Article 3(1) RED. Article 5(1)8 of the new ARA refers to "access to and participation in, as well as any and all other exercise of an economic, social, cultural or political activity accessible to the public". This inclusive formulation brings within the material scope of the new ARA virtually anything that is going on in the public sphere,[182] and in this regard the new Belgian ARA is more inclusive than the RED.

Perhaps less obviously extending beyond the requirements of the RED, but still relevant, is the mention in Article 5(1)(6) of "the reference in an official document or in a report" as being part of the material scope of the new ARA. The wording of this provision is a bit clumsy, because it appears to cover all references to protected characteristics in official documentation, which would greatly complicate communication and policy making with regard to protected groups. A number of authors have indicated, however, that the provision is only intended to tackle harmful and unnecessary references to a person's protected characteristic in official documents or reports; it is not meant to prohibit all data collection on the basis of these characteristics.[183] According to this understanding, the provision would tackle instances of discrimination which not so much directly cause material damage to individuals, but rather cause immaterial damage by sending out negative messages about particular groups. Still, this raises the question as to exactly when mention of someone's ethnic or racial origin is harmful, which complicates the application of this provision. Symbolically, however, it could have a positive effect, by emphasising that prudence is called for as regards the mention of racial or ethnic origin in official documents.

[181] *Explanatory Memorandum to the Draft Amendment of the General Act on Equal Treatment and certain other acts in order to implement directive 2000/43/EC and directive 2000/78/EC*, TK 2002-3, 28 770, No. 3, at 15.
[182] Van Drooghenbroeck (2004), at 137.
[183] Van Drooghenbroeck (2004), at 136; Vrielink et al (2003), at 270.

3.9. Summary and conclusion

The implications of the RED's material scope provisions for minority protection are mainly measurable in quantitative terms, in the same way as for the personal scope provisions. As discrimination occurs in all aspects of public life, the greater the extent to which public life is covered by anti-discrimination law, the higher the level of protection against discrimination. Thus, the point of departure of this chapter was that the material scope provisions of the RED should be interpreted as extensively as legally possible. It was pointed out in the theoretical framework that the RED covers a considerable portion of public life and in this respect provides a relatively high level of protection, especially in comparison to other European equality instruments, which until recently mainly focused on the field of employment. Article 3(1)(a)-(h) RED extends the reach of the RED far beyond employment, to the fields of social advantages, social protection, education and the provision of goods and services.

Minimum baseline of protection

The discussion of the various elements of Article 3(1) RED in the theoretical framework revealed that the meaning of the concepts is for the greater part fairly straightforward, and the minimum baseline of protection is therefore to a relatively high degree identifiable. Hence, to the extent that the meaning of 'employment', 'social security', 'healthcare', 'social advantages', 'education', 'goods and services', et cetera is clear, they have to be covered by the national anti-discrimination frameworks.

In the case study part of this chapter it was shown that the four Member States have to a high degree complied with this minimum baseline, and have included all aspects mentioned in Article 3(1) RED in their national material scope provisions. It is particularly remarkable that the Member States have hardly paid any attention to the qualification clause of Article 3(1) RED, which provides that the material scope should remain within the limits of the competences of the Community. Thus, the expectation of some authors that the clause would have a restrictive effect on the material scope of national anti-discrimination law proved to be unfounded for the Member States under study.

It furthermore turned out that, with the exception of the Estonian EETA, most national frameworks provide for more elaborate descriptions of the domains covered, and generally display a generous and inclusive interpretation of the various elements of Article 3(1) RED. For instance, the new Belgian ARA contains an extensive list of the various aspects of employment that are covered. Similarly, the Hungarian HETA contains a number of provisions that further exemplify the meaning of the prohibition of discrimination in particular fields such as healthcare, education and the provision of goods and services. These elaborations of Article 3(1) are helpful in a national context where there is a lack of experience with anti-discrimination law and pre-empt overly restrictive interpretations. The Belgian, Dutch and Hungarian frameworks furthermore expressly mention a number of contextual factors, such as matters of access, communication and procedure, which can greatly impact on persons' opportunities in employment, education, healthcare etcetera.

Still, a few deficiencies were notable. The Belgian implementation of the RED has clearly been hindered by the internal competence division between the federal state and the federated entities, which has resulted in a patchwork of protection constituted by the Federal ARA and the various anti-discrimination decrees enacted by the federated entities. Consequently, not all domains listed in article 3(1) RED are fully covered by anti-discrimination regimes that comply with the requirements of the RED.

It became furthermore clear that the underlying rationale of the Hungarian HETA, according to which anti-discrimination is mainly a responsibility of public actors, has had a restrictive impact on the material scope with regard to private actor activity. Moreover, Hungary and the Netherlands have set in place delineations of the material scope in order to safeguard fundamental rights and freedoms of private actors that go beyond what is permitted by Article 3(1) RED. Thus, they have both excluded the internal affairs of religious institutions from the scope of their anti-discrimination laws. The Hungarian HETA furthermore expressly excludes internal affairs of private associations.

Obscurities and opportunities for providing a higher level of protection

Despite the relative clarity of the various aspects of Article 3(1) RED, the theoretical section of this chapter revealed that a number of obscurities remain concerning the required level of protection. Especially with respect to certain concepts that were borrowed from free movement law, it is not entirely clear whether the economically oriented interpretations of this latter body of law should be upheld in the context of the RED. It was argued that some of the employment-related aspects and the concepts of goods and services should preferably be interpreted more extensively than in free movement law.

The four Member States have not invariably opted for such a broad interpretation, however. The Belgian framework is for instance the only one that clearly covers unremunerated forms of work. Similarly, only the Dutch ETC so far has made clear that a remunerative aim is not a constitutive element of 'services'. In addition, the essential field of public services is only unambiguously covered by the Hungarian framework. While the Estonian framework does not provide any clarity in this respect, the Belgian framework sends out mixed signals and the Dutch GETA only covers public services that are provided in the context of social protection.

Another obscurity concerns the interpretation of the 'available to the public' clause in Article 1(h) RED with regard to the field of goods and services. The theoretical section pointed out that the clause is intended to safeguard the right to privacy and the freedom of association of private actors, and consequently touches on the difficult question as to how far anti-discrimination law can penetrate into the private sphere of persons. It was argued that the clause should not be applied in a way that only focuses on the degree to which the circle of recipients is closed or open, or the degree to which the goods- or service provider has made use of public communication channels. Instead, it would be preferable to determine the meaning of 'available to the public' on a case-by-case basis, performing a balancing act that takes into account the fundamental right of the private actor, as well as the interest of the affected person in not being discriminated against.

The case study part showed that the Dutch ETC has seemingly opted for this latter approach. Practice reveals that this body seriously investigates whether the freedom of association calls for non-applicability of the GETA, and it is not unlikely that it will apply a similar approach to the right to privacy. In contrast to the ETC, the Hungarian HETA clearly focuses on the communication channels chosen by the goods- or service provider, and excludes all activity that is not aimed at the broader public. Unfortunately, the Belgian framework shows some signs of a similar approach to be adopted in the future.

Finally, it was interesting to note that none of the four Member States has taken over the provision of Article 3(2) RED that excludes matters of immigration, visa and asylum (IVA) from the scope of the RED. As a result, distinctions made by private actors on the basis of legal status are not excluded from the scope of national anti-discrimination law. A potential easy escape route for perpetrating discrimination against foreigners has thus effectively been closed down, which is fortunate. Moreover, Member States have also to some extent taken a less restrictive approach to public actor activity in the IVA field than Article 3(2) RED. The Hungarian HETA is for instance fully applicable to all non-regulatory public actor activity in this field. Moreover, in The Netherlands certain matters of integration policy are likely to be covered by the GETA, and the Belgian new ARA also shows some openings in this respect.

In conclusion, the broad material scope of the RED clearly has created a very favourable starting point for extensive protection of minority groups against discrimination. Since most Member States had no anti-discrimination provisions in place for a substantial portion of the fields covered by the RED, it is clear that this instrument has in this regard had a big impact on the level of protection at the national level. The Netherlands constitutes an exception in this respect, since the GETA has since 1994 applied to most of the fields covered by the RED.

A number of general observations can be made with regard to some of the aspects of implementation that were examined in this chapter. The Belgian competence complexity shows that certain structural factors in national legal systems can hinder effective implementation of the RED.

It is furthermore remarkable that the Hungarian system defaulted on account of the particular national perspective on who is the main responsible actor for ensuring non-discrimination. The restricted applicability of the HETA to private actor activity reveals that a pre-existing anti-discrimination paradigm is not invariably advantageous and can even negatively impact on the quality of implementation. At the same time it must be emphasised that a number of Hungarian particularities have actually increased the level of protection offered by the Hungarian framework instead of lowering it. Thus, the provisions that elaborate the prohibition of discrimination for particular domains, as well as the provisions that show regard for specific minority group interests are important assets of the Hungarian HETA.

Similarly, the elaborations in the Belgian and Dutch laws of certain material scope aspects, and particularly the attention for certain contextual factors, can be considered to have increased the quality of these instruments. These generous approaches would seem to reveal an intention to set in place a truly effective framework against racial and ethnic discrimination.

It is finally notable that the Estonian EETA is the single framework that more or less repeats the wording of Article 3(1) RED and does not show any particularities. This perhaps underlines the relative inexperience in the Estonian context, not only with anti-discrimination law, but also with European law more generally.

Chapter 4

Direct discrimination

> Direct discrimination shall be taken to occur where one person is treated less favourably than another is, has been or would be treated in a comparable situation on grounds of racial or ethnic origin (Article 2(2)(a) RED)
>
> Notwithstanding Article 2(1) and (2), Member States may provide that a difference of treatment which is based on a characteristic related to racial or ethnic origin shall not constitute discrimination where, by reason of the nature of the particular occupational activities concerned or of the context in which they are carried out, such a characteristic constitutes a genuine and determining occupational requirement, provided that the objective is legitimate and the requirement is proportionate (Article 4 RED)
>
> With a view to ensuring full equality in practice, the principle of equal treatment shall not prevent any Member State from maintaining or adopting specific measures to prevent or compensate for disadvantages linked to racial or ethnic origin (Article 5 RED)

Part one: Theoretical framework

4.1. Introduction

The concept of direct discrimination constitutes one of the foundational pillars of European equality law, and covers the most blatant and obvious forms of discrimination.[1] Despite its central importance, it only received a formal definition in 2000, at the occasion of the adoption of the RED. Prior to the adoption of this statutory definition the concept mainly gained its meaning

1 Schiek et al (2007), at 185-186.

from case by case application by the ECJ, often by being contrasted with the concept of indirect discrimination.[2] This did not produce a fully consistent and transparent understanding, however. The conceptualisation of direct and indirect discrimination in the European equality framework took place on an ad hoc basis, depending on the needs and questions arising in practice, rather than departing from a clear theoretical principle. The obscurities that resulted from this unsteady development can be expected to confuse the application of the seemingly clear-cut definitions of direct and indirect discrimination of the RED and subsequent European equality instruments.

For this reason, section 4.2 first explores the manner in which the concepts of direct and indirect discrimination should be delineated. The subsequent sections build on the insights gained from this analysis and set a normative framework for the implementation of the concept of direct discrimination as defined by the RED. Section 4.3 examines the various elements of the definition of direct discrimination of Article 2(2)(a) RED. In section 4.4 the justification possibilities for prima facie cases of direct discrimination are discussed, with a particular focus on the open versus closed system dichotomy and the genuine and determining occupational requirement (GDOR) of Article 4 RED. Finally, section 4.5 assesses to what extent direct discrimination offers potential for the development of positive duties vis-à-vis vulnerable groups in society.

4.2. Proper delineation of direct discrimination v. indirect discrimination

4.2.1. Delineation of direct v. indirect discrimination from a theoretical perspective

In line with the sex equality paradigm of European law, the RED approaches direct discrimination differently from indirect discrimination, which becomes clear throughout Chapters 4 and 5. The most important difference between the regimes for these two concepts is the closed system of justifications for direct discrimination, as opposed to an open justification possibility for indirect discrimination.[3] In practice this means that prima facie cases of direct discrimination are much harder to justify than prima facie cases of indirect discrimination, which in turn implies a difference in the level of protection for both types of discrimination. The manner in which direct discrimination is delineated vis-à-vis indirect discrimination therefore has an immediate impact on the level of protection applying in particular situations, and should be

[2] Ellis (2005), at 88.

[3] See sections 4.4. and 5.2.4.

supported by thorough reasoning. In addition, a clear conceptual delineation of both concepts does justice to the principle of legal certainty, since it helps lawyers and individuals to determine which legal regime is applicable to their case. This section thus examines in which way direct discrimination should be conceptually distinguished from indirect discrimination, and proceeds from the premise that any theory in this respect should be based on thorough conceptual reasoning, so as to enable consistency and transparency in its application in practice.

It appears essential to take as a starting point the prima facie meaning of the concepts of direct and indirect discrimination that stems from their names and definitions. This entails consideration of two circumstances. First of all, the term 'direct discrimination' implies a *direct* causal link between the protected ground and the treatment complained of, whereas 'indirect discrimination' points to an *indirect* link.[4] The former type of causal link can be understood as a link that can be established without the help of an additional circumstance that connects the measure to the protected ground. For example, a sign above a store saying that "Turks cannot enter" involves a direct causal link, because there is no intermediary circumstance necessary to ascertain that it is a Turkish person who cannot enter the premises. In other words, there is a direct connection between being Turkish and the disadvantage of not being able to enter the store. One does not need to look at the particular situation of Turkish persons in general, or at the effects that the sign has in practice in order to know that it disadvantages persons on the basis of their racial or ethnic origin.

In indirect discrimination cases there is no direct causal link and additional circumstances are therefore needed to establish the causal connection with the protected ground. Take for example a language requirement for a particular job. It is necessary to take into account the additional circumstance that it is usually persons of foreign origin that do not speak the majority language in order to establish a causal link between the disadvantage of not qualifying for the job and the protected characteristic of being of a foreign origin. This link is indirect, since it is constituted by the interplay of the characteristic of not speaking the majority language and the circumstance that being of foreign origin often implies a lesser command of the majority language.

Secondly, the definitions of direct and indirect discrimination as provided by the RED and the subsequently adopted European equality directives reveal that direct discrimination is about the underlying *motive or cause* for some difference in treatment, whereas indirect discrimination rather focuses on the *effects* of a particular treatment.[5] The definition of direct discrimination speaks of a less favourable treatment *on grounds of* a protected ground, whereas the

---

4 De Vos (2004), at 75.

5 Gijzen (2006), at 58; De Prins et al (2005), at 83-84; Fredman (2001), at 161-163.

definition of indirect discrimination refers to an apparently neutral provision, criterion or practice that *would put at a particular disadvantage* certain protected groups.

These two considerations warrant the conclusion that 'direct discrimination' should be reserved for those instances of disadvantageous treatment for which the underlying motive or cause is a protected ground, and which can therefore be directly causally linked to this ground. 'Indirect discrimination' instead covers measures that do not rely on the motive or the cause of a protected characteristic, but have a disadvantageous impact on members of a particular racial group and in that way are indirectly causally connected to the protected characteristic. In other words, if taken in isolation, an indirectly discriminatory measure is not causally connected to the protected ground; the causal link only appears when one sees its effects or takes into account information about the characteristics of the persons belonging to the protected group.

This delineation makes of direct and indirect discrimination mutually exclusive concepts, which enhances their applicability in practice. It is acknowledged that this theoretical delineation cannot change the reality that issues of proof can make it difficult in specific cases to know whether direct or indirect discrimination is at play. From a conceptual viewpoint, however, the delineation as proposed in this section produces two neatly separated categories of discrimination.

Advocate General Maduro applied the same line of argumentation in his opinion in *Coleman*, which concerned a disability discrimination case under the FD. His statement on the delineation of direct versus indirect discrimination in section 19 of the opinion is reproduced in its entirety here, so as to support the argument made in this section and to sharpen the contrast with the ECJ's approach to the matter in sex equality law, which is discussed in the next section. According to the Advocate General:

> [t]he distinguishing feature of direct discrimination and harassment is that they bear a necessary relationship to a particular suspect classification. The discriminator relies on a suspect classification in order to act in a certain way. The classification is not a mere contingency but serves as an essential premise of his reasoning. An employer's reliance on those suspect grounds is seen by the Community legal order as an evil which must be eradicated. Therefore, the Directive prohibits the use of those classifications as grounds upon which an employer's reasoning may be based. By contrast, in indirect discrimination cases the intentions of the employer and the reasons he has to act or not to act are irrelevant. In fact, this is the whole point of the prohibition of indirect discrimination: even neutral, innocent or good faith measures and policies adopted with no discriminatory intent whatsoever will be caught if their impact on persons who have a particular characteristic is greater than their impact on other persons. It is this 'disparate impact' of such measures on certain people that is the target of indirect discrimination legislation. The prohibition of such discrimination ties in with the obligation of employers to accommodate those groups by adopting measures and designing their policies in a way that does

> not impose a burden on them which is excessive compared with that imposed on other people. In this way, while the prohibition of direct discrimination and harassment operates as an exclusionary mechanism (by excluding from an employer's reasoning reliance on certain grounds) the prohibition of indirect discrimination operates as an inclusionary mechanism (by obliging employers to take into account and accommodate the needs of individuals with certain characteristics).[6]

4.2.2. Delineation of direct v. indirect discrimination in the jurisprudence of the ECJ on equal treatment between men and women

The original equality provisions in European law prohibited 'discrimination' as such, without referring to different types of discrimination.[7] From quite early on, however, the ECJ developed the two-tiered approach of direct and indirect discrimination, following the examples of American and UK anti-discrimination law.[8] After a shaky start of ambiguous judgments in which the direct versus indirect distinction was used in more than one sense,[9] the ECJ arrived at a single conception of direct discrimination, which it continued to use throughout the years. According to this understanding, direct discrimination is present if the *fundamental reason* for the disputed treatment is one which applies without distinction to persons of either sex or, conversely, whether it *applies exclusively to one sex*.[10] The words in italics reveal that this understanding of direct discrimination actually hinges on two thoughts, since it focuses on the underlying motive for a difference in treatment (*fundamental reason*) as well as on its effects in practice (*applies exclusively to one sex*).

This ambiguity comes back in the ECJ's practical application of direct discrimination, which reveals that the label of direct discrimination is not uniquely used for differences in treatment for which the fundamental reason is a protected characteristic. First of all, the ECJ sometimes applies the qualification of direct discrimination in cases in which the disadvantage

6 Advocate-General Maduro in ECJ *S. Coleman v. Attridge Law and Steve Law*, Case C-303/06, 31 January 2008, para. 19.

7 Davies (2002), at 31; Fredman (2002), at 93-94.

8 For an extensive overview of this development, see Tobler (2005), at 101-277.

9 In the very first judgments, the direct v. indirect distinction was sometimes used to distinguish overt vs. covert discrimination, or to distinguish discrimination that could be established without the need of further specification in national law and discrimination that did need such further specification. See Bell (2007), at 192; Ellis (2005), at 89-90; Tobler (2005), at 116-121. See on the notion of overt vs. covert discrimination section 4.2.3.

10 ECJ *Dekker v. Stichting Vormingscentrum voor Jong Volwassenen*, Case C-177/88, 8 November 1990, para. 10; ECJ *Habermann-Beltermann v. Arbeiterwohlfahrt*, Case C-421/92, 5 May 1994, para. 14; ECJ *Katharine Rinke v. Ärztekammer Hamburg*, Case C-25/02, 9 September 2003, para. 32.

exclusively affects a protected group, but is not based on the particular protected characteristic. The pregnancy cases provide the best-known example in this regard. According to a consistent line of practice of the ECJ, disadvantageous treatment on account of pregnancy or pregnancy-related characteristics constitutes direct discrimination of women, because it "affects only women".[11]

A more recent sex equality case provides another clear example of this effects-based approach. *Nikoloudi* involved a rule which reserved established staff positions only for persons with full-time jobs, while part-timers at the company were only women, as staff regulations made it possible only for women to obtain a part-time contract for the particular job category. The ECJ ruled that the rules for becoming an established staff member amounted to direct discrimination based on sex, even though the criterion for obtaining the established staff status was "ostensibly neutral as to the worker's sex." The determining factor for the Court was the fact that the measure impacted negatively on a category of workers that could only be composed of women.[12]

The same effects-based reasoning is visible in *Maruko*, in which the ECJ considered that a rule granting survivor's pensions only to surviving spouses, thus excluding a category of 'life partners', constituted direct discrimination on grounds of sexual orientation.[13] This was remarkable because the rule in itself did not distinguish according to sexual orientation. The most obvious explanation for the ECJ's choice is the circumstance that 'life partners' in German law are necessarily partners of the same sex, which means that the criterion of being married excluded a category uniquely composed of homosexual persons.

Secondly, the ECJ sometimes employs the label of direct discrimination for cases in which there is not a disadvantageous treatment based on a protected characteristic, but a lack of provision for the special needs of particular vulnerable groups. In *Kiiski*, a woman requested interruption of the childcare leave she was enjoying, because she had become pregnant. The employer refused, because the relevant regulations did not allow for interruption of childcare leave on grounds of a new pregnancy. Even though this refusal was

---

[11] Schiek et al (2007), at 3-192; Ellis (2005), at 107. See inter alia ECJ *Dekker v. Stichting Vormingscentrum voor Jong Volwassenen*, Case 177/88, 8 November 1990, para. 12; ECJ *Brown v. Rentokil*, Case C-394/96, 30 June 1998, para. 24; ECJ *Mahlburg*, Case 207/98, 3 February 2000, para. 20; ECJ *Sari Kiiski v. Tampereen kaupunki*, Case C-116/06, 20 September 2007, para. 55.

[12] ECJ *Nikoloudi v. Organismos Tilepikinonion Ellados AE*, Case 196-02, 10 March 2005, paras. 31-36.

[13] ECJ *Maruko v. Versorgungsanstalt der deutschen Bühnen*, Case C-267/06, 1 April 2008, paras. 65-73. The ECJ left the final word to the national court, however, saying that there would only be direct discrimination if that court would find that national law treats spouses and life partners as comparable. See for a discussion of the appropriateness of applying a comparability test section 4.3.4.

clearly not based on the reason that Mrs Kiiski was a woman, or even because she was pregnant, the ECJ still considered that the case amounted to direct discrimination on grounds of sex. It considered that the relevant provisions should have allowed for alteration of the childcare leave period in the case of a new pregnancy, since such a circumstance seriously influences the extent to which a mother can achieve the aims sought after by childcare leave.[14] Thus, the ECJ in fact considered the lack of provision for the special needs of pregnant women to amount to direct discrimination.

Along a similar line of argumentation, the ECJ developed a principle of special consideration of the needs of transsexuals in the context of the prohibition of direct discrimination. In *Richards*, a male-to-female transsexual claimed to have been discriminated against on sex because she was denied a retirement pension after having reached the age upon which other women received a pension. The ECJ acknowledged that the disadvantageous treatment was "based on Ms Richards' inability to have the gender which she acquired following surgery recognised", and thus implicitly acknowledged that the fundamental reason for the denial of the pension was not her change of gender. Still, it considered that this lack of provision for the special situation of transsexuals constituted discrimination on grounds of sex, with which it apparently envisaged direct discrimination, since it did not mention or explore any objective justification possibilities.[15] This judgment was more strongly formulated than the one in *K.B.*, which had been rendered two years before, and had more or less concerned the same subject matter. In *K.B.*, a female-to-male transsexual could not obtain survivor's benefit on account of his life partner's employment contract, because they were not married. The reason they were not married, however, was that UK law did not permit change of the birth registry in accordance with a person's new gender. The ECJ considered that there was unequal treatment with regard to the right to get married, which subsequently affected the Community right of equal pay for men and women. It therefore found that the legislation which prevented them from getting married was "in principle incompatible with Article 141 TEC".[16] The Court thus remained vague as to the proper qualification of this 'incompatibility', not even explicitly referring to 'discrimination'. Advocate General Colomer, however, had qualified the case as amounting to direct discrimination based on sex.[17] With *Richards*, the ECJ appears to have moved in the same direction. The important point to stress here is that in both *K.B.* and *Richards* it was

[14] ECJ *Sari Kiiski v.Tampereen kaupunki*, Case C-116/06, 20 September 2007, paras. 49-55.

[15] ECJ *Richards v. Secretary of State for Work and Pensions*, Case C-423/04, 27 April 2006, paras. 27-38. The individualised wording of the ECJ's judgment, not referring at all to a group that is disproportionately affected, also points to the applicability of the concept of direct discrimination.

[16] ECJ *K.B. v. National Health Service Pensions Agency*, Case C-117/01, 7 January 2004, paras. 28-36.

[17] Opinion of Advocate-General Colomer in *K.B.*, 10 June 2003, para. 76.

obvious that the fundamental reason for the disadvantage suffered was not transsexuality. In fact, the complaint was not so much about transsexuality being applied as a prohibited criterion, but rather about the lack of consideration of transsexuality and the needs arising from having this characteristic.

Substantively speaking, one is perhaps inclined to sympathise with the ECJ's choice to include in the category of direct discrimination disadvantageous treatments based on characteristics that are very closely connected to a protected characteristic as well as certain omissions to provide for the special needs of vulnerable groups. These forms of disadvantage after all have serious repercussions for the victims, and call for a high level of protection, which the regime for direct sex discrimination offers. Still, as these disadvantages are not actually based on a protected characteristic, but rather entail serious effects for protected groups, they should be grouped under the heading of indirect discrimination from a conceptual point of view.

The ECJ's approach actually obfuscates the difference between direct and indirect discrimination, which is harmful from a standpoint of legal certainty, since no one is able anymore to determine where the exact boundary between direct and indirect discrimination is situated. The fact that the Advocates General in *Nikoloudi* and *Maruko* actually applied the qualification of indirect discrimination, and even concluded that there was no discrimination at all in *Kiiski*, is telling in this respect.[18]

Moreover, the ECJ's own jurisprudence reveals that it does not consistently apply its effects-based approach as manifested in the aforementioned cases. For example, the ECJ in *Larsson* refused to qualify as directly discriminatory the situation in which a woman was dismissed because of her incapability of performing her job due to an illness which was caused by her pregnancy but had occurred after she had given birth.[19] Unsurprisingly, the judgment was criticised by some scholars for being inconsistent and incomprehensible, seeing that other instances of disadvantageous treatment of women because of pregnancy-related illnesses or maternity leave had been qualified as direct discrimination.[20] Another example is provided by *Schnorbus*, in which the ECJ classified a rule benefiting persons who had fulfilled military service as indirect discrimination based on sex, which necessarily exclusively benefited men. According to the ECJ, the benefit could not be regarded "as being directly based on the sex of the persons concerned".[21] Again, the ECJ's approach invited criticism by scholars, who claimed that the fact that the rule de facto excluded all women warranted a label of direct discrimination.[22]

[18] Opinion of Advocate-General Stix-Hackl in *Nikoloudi*, 29 April 2004, para. 45; Opinion of Advocate-General Colomer in *Maruko*, 6 September 2007, para. 102; Opinion of Advocate-General Kokott in *Kiiski,* 15 March 2007, paras. 31-47.

[19] ECJ *Larsson v. Dansk Handel & Service*, Case C-400/95, 29 May 1997, paras. 17-19.

[20] Wintemude (1998), at 23-28; Ellis (1998), at 206 ; Sczyszczak (1996), at 54.

[21] ECJ *Julia Schnorbus v. Land Hessen*, Case C-79/99, 7 December 2000, paras. 32-33.

[22] Gijzen (2006), at 231; Tobler (2005), at 314.

It may be clear that the ECJ's approach in sex equality law is preferably not followed in the context of the RED, and it is therefore to be hoped that a conceptually more appropriate delineation of direct and indirect discrimination will be developed. The next section discusses the practicalities of such a conceptually sound approach for the RED.

4.2.3. Delineation of direct v. indirect discrimination as regards racial and ethnic origin

On the basis of the foregoing, it is proposed that the qualification of direct racial discrimination is used only if racial or ethnic origin is the actual motive or cause for a disadvantageous treatment. A few considerations are relevant in this respect.

First of all, it is repeated that the grounds of racial and ethnic origin are identified in practice by making use of proxies.[23] Some of these proxies concern characteristics that are inextricably linked to the protected ground, in that they invariably come with membership to a protected group and cannot be thrown off by their bearers. This is for example the case for skin colour as a proxy for race: a person cannot choose to have a particular skin colour. Distinctions made on the basis of these inextricably linked characteristics should therefore automatically be categorised as distinctions on the basis of the protected ground they are proxies for. Thus, if a person is treated differently because of his dark skin colour, or because of the shape of his nose, he is de facto treated differently on the basis of racial or ethnic origin.

However, most proxies involve characteristics that are less strictly connected to a protected ground, because they involve an element of choice.[24] For example, speaking a foreign language or adhering to a minority religion are proxies that are often used in daily life to establish a person's different racial or ethnic origin, but they are not inextricably linked to these protected grounds: some persons belonging to the particular ethnic group will speak the majority language fluently, or adhere to a different religion. In this regard, one could be inclined to treat disadvantageous treatments based on these proxies as indirect discrimination, since they would appear not to be directly based on racial or ethnic origin. Still, if language, religion or a similar characteristic is actually used as a proxy for racial or ethnic origin, the label of direct discrimination is the more appropriate one. After all, in such a case the individual is not treated on the basis of his own characteristics and capabilities, but as a member of

[23] See section 2.3.1 on the conceptualisation of racial and ethnic origin.
[24] Gear-Rich (2004), at 1158-1171.

a group that is considered to portray a particular characteristic. His group membership is therefore the real reason for the way in which he has been treated, which justifies speaking of a direct causal link.[25]

Secondly, in line with general anti-discrimination theory, it is emphasised that intent is not required for a qualification of direct discrimination. In other words, it is not necessary that the alleged perpetrator of direct discrimination is consciously seeking to disadvantage persons belonging to a particular racial or ethnic group. It is nowadays generally accepted that the intention to discriminate is not a prerequisite for a finding of direct discrimination,[26] since prejudiced beliefs about persons belonging to particular racial or ethnic groups can operate at a subconscious level.[27] It is therefore possible that a person's action amounts to direct discrimination, because of its reliance on a stereotypical or biased belief, without the person actually wanting to disadvantage persons belonging to a particular racial or ethnic group.[28]

Whereas discriminatory intent is therefore not requisite, it should be stressed that where such intent is present, the qualification of direct discrimination should automatically be applied, regardless of the formal reason given by the alleged perpetrator for his behaviour. If an employer claims, for instance, that the real reason for his refusal to hire a particular person was the person's insufficient command of the majority language, whereas evidence shows that he did not want to hire the person for being of a foreign ethnic origin, his behaviour should be qualified as direct discrimination. After all, the real motive for the rejection of the person's application was his different ethnic origin. These cases are often referred to as covert direct discrimination, since

---

25 Compare Advocate-General Jacobs in ECJ *Lindorfer v. Council*, Case C-227/04, 27 October 2005, para. 59, on the application of higher actuarial factors for women than for men in the determination of the amount of pensionable years, where he states that: "discrimination of the kind in issue involves ascribing to individuals average characteristics of a class to which they belong. In relation to the individual, I do not think that such average characteristics can in any way be described as 'objective'. What is objectionable (and thus prohibited) in such discrimination is the reliance on characteristics extrapolated from the class to the individual, as opposed to the use of characteristics which genuinely distinguish the individual from others and which may justify a difference in treatment."

26 Bayart & Deiteren (2008), at 195; Ellis (2005), at 103.

27 Lee (2005), at 483-488; Bertrand, Chug & Mullainatthan (2005); Banton (1996), at 65.

28 See Lord Nicholls' argumentation in the United Kingdom House of Lords case *Nagarajan v. London Regional Transport* [1999], 15 July 1999, ICR 877: "human beings have perceptions, beliefs, attitudes and prejudices on many subjects. It is part of our make-up. Moreover, we do not always recognise our own prejudices. Many people are unable, or unwilling, to admit even to themselves that actions of theirs may be racially motivated. An employer may genuinely believe that the reason why he rejected an applicant had nothing to do with the applicant's race. After careful and thorough investigation of a claim members of an employment tribunal may decide that the proper inference to be drawn from the evidence is that, whether the employer realised it at the time or not, race was the reason why he acted as he did."

the discriminatory component is not visible at first glance.[29] Covert direct discrimination should, however, not be confused with indirect discrimination, which also involves cases where the discriminatory component only becomes visible when one considers additional circumstances of the case. In cases of covert direct discrimination, there is a direct causal link with the protected characteristic, since the *real* reason behind the facially neutral measure was to disadvantage persons belonging to a particular group. Such a direct causal link is not present in a case of indirect discrimination, which concerns facially neutral measures for which the underlying reason is not connected to a person's racial or ethnic origin.

In summary, direct racial discrimination is the appropriate label for those cases that involve:

- a measure for which the underlying motive or cause is immediately identified to be racial or ethnic origin or a characteristic inextricably linked to these grounds (overt direct discrimination)

- a measure for which the underlying motive or cause is established by proof to be racial or ethnic origin or a characteristic inextricably linked to these grounds (covert direct discrimination). This includes cases in which a characteristic is used as a proxy for racial or ethnic origin (i.e. some stereotype or generalised assumption is at play)[30]

An example of the first category is the refusal to serve a person in a restaurant because he is of Roma origin. An example of the second category is the refusal to serve a person in a restaurant because he allegedly does not adhere to the dress code, which in reality turns out to be because he is of Roma origin, as other persons who are not Roma and who are similarly dressed are accepted as customers.

In contrast, the label of indirect racial discrimination should be applied for all measures that do not fall in either category and are thus less directly causally linked to the protected ground. Indirect discrimination is especially the proper label for cases in which the particular needs of vulnerable ethnic groups are not appropriately provided for.[31] Unless an omission to accommodate for a particular characteristic that is shared by the members of a protected group is in fact deliberately intended to disadvantage these persons *because of* their group membership, it should be seen as indirect discrimination. Moreover,

[29] Schiek et al (2007), at 185-186.

[30] Compare Barmes (2003), who describes a development in the case law of the United Kingdom House of Lords on direct discrimination from the application of the simple 'but for' test to the search for the real underlying reason of a particular treatment.

[31] Wintemude (1998), at 28-34. See section 5.3 in which the possibilities offered by the concept of indirect discrimination in this respect are discussed.

indirect discrimination should comprise those measures that were not adopted because of a protected characteristic, but in practice exclusively affect persons belonging to a protected group. For example, even if a ban on religious expressions in the workplace turns out to disadvantage only persons of a minority ethnic origin, indirect discrimination is the appropriate label, unless the motive behind the ban was to disadvantage persons of the particular ethnic minority. Since the causal link in these cases is indirect, and is established by looking at the effects in practice rather than by looking at the measure itself, these measures are more appropriately classified as indirectly discriminatory.

Again it is emphasised that this proposed delineation is only intended to create conceptual clarity and consistency. It does not change the fact that, in reality, it may be very difficult to establish what kind of causal link is in play. For a more elaborate discussion of the various means of proof in this respect, see Ambrus 2010.

4.3. Definition of direct discrimination in the RED

> Direct discrimination shall be taken to occur where one person is treated less favourably than another is, has been or would be treated in a comparable situation on grounds of racial or ethnic origin (Article 2(2)(a) RED)

In the following sections, direct discrimination as defined by Article 2(2)(a) of the RED is examined. The definition shows quite some similarity with the definition of direct discrimination in UK anti-discrimination law, which predates the RED, and which reads as follows:

> [a] person discriminates against another in any circumstances relevant for the purposes of any provision of this Act if on racial grounds he treats that other less favourably than he treats or would treat other persons.[32]

The extensive UK practice and case law can thus provide some insight into the practical implications of the definition of direct discrimination of the RED, and are discussed in the following sections where deemed relevant.

4.3.1. 'One person'

The first element of the definition refers to the persons who can invoke the anti-discrimination provisions as introduced by the RED. The personal scope aspect of this element was discussed in section 2.5, and the discussion will not be reproduced here. Instead, attention should be drawn to the individual focus of this element, which is conveyed through the reference to *one* person. Despite the suggestion of the European Parliament during the

[32] Article 1(1)(a) of the *Race Relations Act* 1976 (c. 74).

proceedings on the draft RED to add a reference to *groups* of persons, the Member States resolved to maintain an individualised understanding of direct discrimination.[33] This reduced the chances of using the concept for tackling collective manifestations of direct discrimination, which are typically detected by looking at a pattern of disadvantageous treatment of individuals that reveals the existence of prejudiced behaviour, and which are difficult to discern at the individual level.[34] As was explained in the previous section, behaviour that is based on stereotypes or generalised assumptions should be classified as direct discrimination, and it should not matter in this regard that these stereotypes or assumptions can only be ascertained by looking at the broader picture rather than at individual cases.

The UK context provides a good example of the way in which the concept of direct discrimination can be applied to these collective manifestations of discrimination. In *R (European Roma Rights Centre) v. Immigration Officer at Prague Airport*, British immigration officers were claimed to have perpetrated racial discrimination against Roma persons. Statistics showed that Roma persons were questioned much more thoroughly and for a much longer time by these officers regarding their prospective journey than persons of another ethnic origin.[35] Moreover, Roma persons were 400 times more likely to be refused permission to board an airplane which was headed to the UK.[36] All of this clearly indicated that the Roma origin of the disadvantaged persons was the underlying reason for their disadvantageous treatment. Indeed, the House of Lords, having recognised that the discrimination could only be discerned by looking at the statistics concerning the entire operation, acknowledged that the operation carried out at the airport was directly discriminatory.[37] It is noteworthy in this regard that the definition of direct racial discrimination in UK law is equally individually worded as the definition in the RED.

It is unclear whether the ECJ will be similarly alert to such collective manifestations of direct discrimination. So far, it has not yet dealt with cases involving statistics in the context of direct discrimination. In the field of equal pay a number of cases appeared that involved a statistical disparity that could not be traced back to one particular source, which were examined in terms of

[33] *Report on the proposal for a Council directive on implementing the principle of equal treatment between persons irrespective of racial or ethnic origin,* European Parliament, Committee on Citizen's freedoms and rights (COM(1999)) 566 – C5-0067/2000 – 1999/0253/ (CNS)), A5-0136/2000, 16 May 2000.

[34] Craig (2007), at 94.

[35] *R. (European Roma Rights Centre) v. Immigration Officer at Prague Airport*, 9 December 2004, [2004] UKHL 55.

[36] Para. 34 per Lord Steyn.

[37] Para. 97, per Baroness Hale of Richmond. See also para. 110, per Lord Carswell, who points out that: "[i]t is important therefore to appreciate that the complaint is one of a discriminatory system, not of discrimination which prevented any specified individual from traveling to the United Kingdom."

indirect discrimination.[38] Given the fact that there were no indications of gender prejudice playing a part, it is understandable that the ECJ did not consider the possibility of direct discrimination, which would have been nearly impossible to prove.[39] One can therefore not infer from these judgments an unwillingness to detect direct discrimination in statistical disparities. It is to be hoped that the ECJ and the national courts will follow the lead of the House of Lords as regards collective manifestations of direct discrimination against particular racial or ethnic groups. Even though the presence of collective data may throw them off course, it is desirable that they remain alert to the possibility of racial prejudice having caused the disparity, which should lead them to apply the label of direct discrimination.

4.3.2. 'Is treated less favourably'

The second element of the definition makes clear that discrimination in substance entails less favourable treatment. The implementation of this element raises two questions. First, 'treatment' can refer to various kinds of behaviour, and it is not yet clear how far its meaning can be stretched. A broad interpretation is clearly preferable, which would not only include active forms of behaviour, but also attitudes and omissions.[40] Moreover, in line with the approach taken by the UK House of Lords, tangible loss should not be a prerequisite: deprivation of choice, or words or acts of discouragement should also be considered to amount to 'treatment'.[41]

The interpretation of 'treatment' has so far hardly come up in the ECJ's practice, but there is one case ruled under the RED that touched upon the matter. In *Feryn* the ECJ pointed out that the announced intention to discriminate against a particular ethnic group constitutes direct racial discrimination, without it being necessary to identify a particular victim. This would logically mean that a statement in itself is considered to constitute 'treatment'. At the

---

[38] See section 5.2.1.3.

[39] It should be noted that some authors have been critical in this respect. See Schiek et al (2007), at 385, who submit that the qualification of these cases in terms of indirect discrimination is perhaps not wholly appropriate. See also Forshaw & Pilgerstorfer (2008), who claim that the Enderby type of discrimination portrays characteristics of direct and indirect discrimination, and should therefore be labeled as 'quasi-direct discrimination'.

[40] T. Makkonen, *Main causes, forms and consequences of discrimination*, at http://action.web.ca/home/narcc/attach/Causes,%20Forms,%20Consequences%20of%20Discrimination%20paper%5B1%5D.pdf (accessed June 2009), at 8. See however Burri (2001), at 435, who doubts whether the word 'treatment' can extend to omissions. As was pointed out before, omissions should only be accepted as constituting direct discrimination if they are based on a choice to exclude members of protected groups, because only then would a direct causal link with a protected ground exist. Purely needs-based claims are more appropriately dealt with as indirect discrimination.

[41] Monaghan (2007), at 290-291.

same time, however, the ECJ acknowledged that factual evidence showing that the person making the statement had not carried out his intention in practice could refute the presumption of direct discrimination, which would imply that a mere statement in itself is not enough to constitute direct discrimination.[42] The Court thus clearly hinged on two thoughts, and it remains to be seen whether it will in the future unambiguously include statements in its interpretation of 'treatment'.

The second question concerns the interpretation of the disadvantageous aspect, the 'less favourable' part, of the treatment. Case law of the ECJ in the field of sex equality law shows that the disadvantageous element is not an empty requirement. In *Nikoloudi* the ECJ required that a category composed exclusively of women should actually be treated less favourably, because the "creation of a category of exclusively female workers (…) does not constitute in itself direct discrimination against women".[43] Thus, the ECJ would appear to find a mere difference in treatment to be insufficient: the differentiated category should also be treated disadvantageously.

The validity of similar reasoning in the context of racial or ethnic discrimination is highly questionable. Distinctions based on racial or ethnic origin have nowadays come to be considered as being ipso facto disadvantageous, because of the symbolic message of unworthiness and indignity they convey.[44] There are very limited accepted possibilities of exceptions to this basic principle, as the closed system of justification of the

---

[42] *Centrum voor gelijkheid van kansen en racismebestrijding v. Firma Feryn NV*, Case C-54/07, 10 July 2008. In para. 28, the ECJ stated that: "the fact that an employer states publicly that it will not recruit employees of a certain ethnic or racial origin constitutes direct discrimination in respect of recruitment within the meaning of Article 2(2)(a) of Directive 2000/43, such statements being likely strongly to dissuade certain candidates from submitting their candidature and, accordingly to hinder their access to the labour market." It is subsequently pointed out in paras. 31 and 32 that: "[s]tatements by which an employer publicly lets it be known that, under its recruitment policy, it will not recruit any employees of a certain ethnic or racial origin may constitute facts of such a nature as to give rise to a presumption of a discriminatory recruitment policy. It is, thus, for that employer to adduce evidence that it has not breached the principle of equal treatment, which it can do, inter alia, by showing that the actual recruitment practice of the undertaking does not correspond to those statements."

[43] ECJ *Nikoloudi v. Organismos Tilepikinonion Ellados AE*, Case C-196/02, 10 March 2005, para. 34.

[44] Monaghan (2007), at 291. Illustrative is the rejection by the US Supreme Court of the 'separate but equal' doctrine for racial discrimination as early as 1954 in *Brown v. Board of Education of Topeka*, 347 U.S. 483 (1954). See in the ECHR framework also ECtHR *Timishev v. Russia*, no. 55762/00 and 55974/00, 13 December 2005, para. 58: "the Court considers that no difference in treatment which is based exclusively or to a decisive extent on a person's ethnic origin is capable of being objectively justified in a contemporary democratic society built on the principles of pluralism and respect for different cultures"; ECtHR *D.H. v. Czech Republic*, no 57325/00, 13 November 2007, para. 196: "[w]here the difference in treatment is based on race, colour or ethnic origin, the notion of objective and reasonable justification must be interpreted as strictly as possible."

RED illustrates.[45] In addition, the universal rejection of segregation along racial lines reflects a consensus on the immorality of any differences in treatment based on racial or ethnic origin.[46]

As the use of racial and ethnic origin as distinguishing criteria is in itself disadvantageous, because of the immaterial damage it causes, the 'less favourable treatment' aspect of the direct discrimination should not be accorded much weight. It should in other words not be applied in such a manner that it is burdensome for an applicant to show that he has actually experienced disadvantageous treatment, in addition to his racial or ethnic origin being used as a reason for the manner in which he has been treated differently.[47] The focus should rather be on determining whether the differential treatment was actually based on racial or ethnic origin. It is thus to be hoped that the ECJ will not extend its *Nikoloudi* reasoning to the field of racial discrimination.

4.3.3. 'On grounds of racial or ethnic origin' (causal aspect of direct discrimination)

The 'on grounds of' element of the definition of direct discrimination makes clear that a causal link between the less favourable treatment and the protected ground of racial and ethnic origin is required. It was pointed out before that this link is a direct one, which means that racial or ethnic origin is the underlying cause or motive for this disadvantageous treatment.[48] As the underlying cause or motive is not always immediately obvious, it can be difficult in practice to establish causality.

In the UK, courts have developed the 'but for' test for establishing causality, and this test has been brought up by some scholars as relevant also for the European context.[49] The central question of this test is whether the victim would have been treated differently, had he or she not portrayed the protected characteristic.[50] This test is acceptable in principle, as long as it is applied in

---

45 See section 4.4.

46 See Article 3 of ICERD, according to which "States Parties particularly condemn racial segregation and apartheid and undertake to prevent, prohibit and eradicate all practices of this nature in territories under their jurisdiction". See also *CERD General Recommendation No. 19, Racial segregation and apartheid (Art. 3),* A/50/18, of 18 August 1995.

47 In this respect I disagree with the standpoint of the EU Network of independent experts on fundamental rights, forwarded in *Thematic comment no. 3, The protection of minorities in the European Union*, EU Network of Independent Experts on Fundamental Rights, 2005, CFR-CDF.ThemComm2005.en, at 54, according to which segregation is not addressed by the RED, because of the 'less favorable' requirement. It really depends on how much weight will be given to this requirement by the ECJ and national courts, as to whether it will constitute a problem for tackling segregation with the provisions of the RED.

48 See section 4.2.3.

49 Monaghan (2007), at 314; Ellis (2005), at 103-104; Gerards (2005), at 75-76.

50 Monaghan (2007), at 314.

line with the delineation of direct v. Indirect discrimination that was outlined above. The 'but for' test should in particular not be used in order to apply an effects-based approach to direct discrimination similar to the one applied by the ECJ in the field of gender equality law.[51] If it is clear that the underlying cause or motive for the less favourable treatment was not a person's racial or ethnic origin, it should not matter that all persons affected by the measure happen to be of a particular racial or ethnic origin.

A remark must be made regarding the tightness of the causal link between the treatment complained of and the protected ground. Practice has revealed that differences in treatment can often not be traced back to one single characteristic of the disadvantaged individual, but rely on a number of characteristics taken together, the individual weight of each separate one being difficult to determine. The notion of intersectional discrimination that was discussed in section 2.3.2.2 is a case in point. It is submitted that courts should not require racial or ethnic origin to be the sole or even the decisive reason for the less favourable treatment, because this would make it fairly easy to circumvent the prohibition of direct discrimination. In view of the invidiousness of using race or ethnicity as a distinguishing criterion, it seems appropriate to conclude to a prima facie case of direct discrimination in *each* instance in which race or ethnicity is used as a reason for treating someone less favourably.

The ECJ has so far not adopted an outspoken standpoint with regard to this topic,[52] but its jurisprudence that was discussed in the framework of intersectional discrimination would seem to indicate that it will be rather lenient. These decisions after all show that the ECJ does not require gender to be the only distinguishing criterion for the treatment complained of to qualify as sex discrimination.[53] It can be expected that it will therefore also not require racial or ethnic origin to be the single reason in the context of direct racial discrimination. National courts will hopefully follow suit.

4.3.4. 'Than another is, has been or would be treated in a comparable situation' (comparative aspect of direct discrimination)

The third element of the definition adds a comparative aspect to the concept of direct discrimination, and stems from the general principle of equal treatment, which plays a prominent part in the ECJ's equality jurisprudence.[54] The comparative element of direct discrimination gives a certain colour to the concept, because it introduces an implicit preference for similar treatment

[51] See section 4.2.2.
[52] De Prins et al (2005), at 87; De Vos (2003), at 247.
[53] See section 2.3.2.2.
[54] Schiek et al (2007), at 191-192; Gerards (2002), at 9.

of persons, rendering differential treatment the exception that needs to be justified.[55] In a way, therefore, it calls for the elimination of the factor of racial or ethnic origin in any decision-making process, and is completely neutral as to the material effect of such elimination. In this sense direct discrimination is biased towards a formal conception of equality rather than a substantive conception.[56] This is not necessarily disadvantageous from a minority protection perspective, as long as other discrimination concepts and provisions of the RED allow for a more substantive conception of equality to be realised. In the following chapters, it will be shown that the concepts of indirect discrimination and positive action embrace the notion of substantive equality and in that respect complement the concept of direct discrimination in an important way.

This is not to say that the comparative aspect as put forward by Article 2(2)(a) RED is wholly unproblematic. More particularly, the comparability requirement raises difficulties, especially because the definition maintains a separate causality requirement, which was examined in the previous section. As was explained before, a direct causal link between a disadvantage and racial or ethnic origin should suffice to constitute a prima facie case of direct discrimination. If the cause or motive for the treatment was someone's racial or ethnic origin, there is a direct causal link. By additionally requiring that the less favourably treated person was in comparable circumstances to those who did not receive the same treatment, the definition suggests that there could be relevant circumstances that would remove the discriminatory aspect of the less favourable treatment based on racial or ethnic origin. This in turn implies that, in addition to the two justification possibilities allowed for by the RED, that is the genuine and determining occupational requirement and positive action, there are other circumstances in which a less favourable treatment on grounds of racial or ethnic origin can be justified. In other words, the comparability test can be used to create a de facto open justification possibility for direct racial discrimination.[57]

The previously mentioned *Nikoloudi* case provides a good example of how comparability can fulfil a disguised justificatory function. In this case the ECJ first held that a criterion for becoming an established member of staff affected a group exclusively composed of women, and therefore constituted direct discrimination. It subsequently left open the possibility of justifying this direct discrimination by establishing that the excluded group was not

[55] Tobler (2005), at 27; Alexy (2001), at 271; Vierdag (1973), at 12. A different conception of direct discrimination is conceivable, which does not require any comparative element. According to such a conception direct discrimination is the imposition of a disadvantage on grounds of racial or ethnic origin. See Réaume (2005), at 549; Holmes (2005), at 186; Schiek (2002), at 306.

[56] O'Cinnéide (2006), at 352; Fredman (2002), at 94; Hepple & Barnard (2000), at 562.

[57] This disguised justificatory function of the comparability test has been recognised by a number of authors at a more general level. See Arnardóttir (2003), at 89; Loenen (1992), at 212.

comparable to the advantaged group, and stated that: "[i]n order for there to be no direct discrimination on grounds of sex, the factor characterising the category to which the excluded worker belongs must be such as to place that worker in a situation that is *objectively different,* with regard to appointment as an established member of staff, from the situation of those who are eligible to become established" (emphasis added, MB).[58] Interestingly, the words used by the ECJ, particularly those in italics, resemble the words used by the ECJ in earlier nationality discrimination cases to describe the objective justification for *indirect* discrimination.[59]

Clearly, a similar use of the comparability test in the context of racial discrimination would be in contradiction with the closed system of justification for direct discrimination of the RED.[60] Moreover, it would be detrimental in terms of legal certainty, making it very difficult to know in advance whether particular circumstances are capable of justifying less favourable treatment on grounds of racial or ethnic origin. Scholars have furthermore pointed out that the use of comparability in this particular way threatens to lower the quality of decision making, for two reasons. First of all, by speaking in terms of comparability, courts raise the impression that they are making factual judgments rather than normative ones, which means that their considerations in this respect are likely to be less critically scrutinised. Secondly, there are no set requirements for determining comparability, which gives much discretion to courts, whereas justification tests for discrimination are generally carried out according to set criteria, such as the requirements of legitimacy of the aim and proportionality.[61]

In the light of the above, there are cogent reasons to assume that the only appropriate function to be fulfilled by the comparability test in the context of direct racial discrimination is to help establish the causal link between the less favourable treatment and the racial or ethnic ground. Consider for example a person who claims to have been denied a pay rise on account of his ethnic origin, and who supports his claim by pointing to the pay rise that his colleagues, who are of a different ethnic origin, have received. The comparability of his colleagues should then be assessed in the light of the requirements for granting a pay rise, so as to be able to determine whether the denial of a rise in pay was indeed based on the applicant's ethnic origin. Such use of comparability is acceptable and even necessary for a meaningful evidentiary role to be played by the comparison.

---

[58] ECJ *Nikoloudi v. Organismos Tilepikinonion Ellados AE*, Case 196-02, 10 March 2005, para. 40.

[59] ECJ *Sotgiu v. Deutsche Bundespost*, Case 152/73, 12 February 1974, para. 12; ECJ *Caisse régionale d'assurance maladie de Lille (CRAM) v. Diamante Palermo, née Toia*, Case 237/78, 12 July 1979, paras. 15-17. Also see Tobler (2005), at 186-187.

[60] See section 4.4.1 for a more detailed discussion of the closed system of justification for direct discrimination.

[61] Bayart & Deiteren (2008), at 194; Prechal (2004), at 544; Gerards (2002), at 59.

Comparability should not, however, be used in such a way so as to establish that persons with the protected characteristic are relevantly different from other persons, leading to the conclusion that there is no direct discrimination.[62] It is for instance not permissible for an employer to claim that the lower level of pay of employees of a minority ethnic origin can be explained by the fact that persons of this ethnic group differ from their colleagues as to the manner in which they adapt to the company culture and approach the clients. This is a justification claim in disguise and should be rejected, since it cannot be made to fit into either the genuine and determining occupational requirement or the positive action justification of Articles 4 and 5 RED respectively.

It should be stressed that, in view of its supportive function vis-à-vis the causality element, the comparative aspect should not be made a constitutive part of the concept of direct discrimination. Thus, if the causal link with the protected characteristic can be established in another way, it is not necessary and could even be counterproductive to demand that a comparison is carried out.[63]

In this regard it should be pointed out that the RED provides for a useful mechanism for situations in which it is difficult to find a real life comparator who shows appropriate features to identify racial or ethnic origin as the real cause or motive for an instance of less favourable treatment. The words 'would be' in the definition of Article 2(2)(a) RED open up the possibility of forwarding a hypothetical comparator. A crucial difference between this hypothetical comparator and a real life one is that the hypothetical comparator can be used in highly unique situations where the alleged discriminator does not deal with other persons, and does not intend to make a *difference* in treatment between persons, but only to disadvantage the person who claims to have been discriminated against. In other words, the hypothetical comparator can *replace* the person who has experienced the disadvantage in a theoretical exercise, instead of being placed alongside this person in order to show that they have been treated differently.[64]

Even though it is to be welcomed that in cases of absent actual comparators a case of discrimination can still be made, such cases can be very difficult to prove. It can be hard to establish enough facts from which it can be presumed that a person of a different racial or ethnic origin would have been treated differently.[65] The hypothetical comparator is therefore certainly not a panacea that will remedy all difficulties experienced by alleged victims of discrimination, since it does not solve the contentious issue of proving discrimination in practice.[66]

62 Monaghan (2007), at 295-296.
63 Bell (2007), at 209; McColgan (2005), at 53.
64 Bayart & Deiteren (2008), at 190.
65 Monaghan (2007), at 302.
66 Ambrus (2010).

4.4. Justification possibilities for prima facie cases of direct discrimination

The RED applies a closed system of justification for prima facie cases of direct discrimination, which means that only those justifications that are explicitly provided for are acceptable.[67] Two possible justifications are envisaged: racial or ethnic origin as a genuine and determining occupational requirement (GDOR) in Article 4 and positive action in Article 5. The closed system of justification of the RED is in line with the traditional approach in European nationality and sex discrimination law. In this section, this justification system will be explored in more detail.

4.4.1. Open v. closed system of justification

In the UK, there has been some debate as to the stringency with which the closed system should be applied in the context of sex equality law. A number of authors argued in favour of a more lenient approach in specific cases, which would come down to a limited possibility of a reasonable and objective type of justification for direct discrimination, which has hitherto only been explicitly recognised for indirect discrimination.[68] The merits of this argument have apparently been recognised at the European level, since the directive on equal treatment between men and women in the provision of goods and services allows for an open justification possibility for direct sex discrimination in this field.[69]

It is not likely that the same debate would arise in the context of racial or ethnic discrimination. After all, as was pointed out before, differentiation on the basis of race is universally condemned and regarded as not capable of being justified, save in very exceptional cases. Even if calls for an open justification system for racial discrimination would arise at the national level, Member States arguably are not allowed to set in place such a system. An open-ended justification mechanism goes directly against the wording of the RED, as well as its drafting history. For instance, the fear of some Member

[67] For an extensive discussion of the open vs. closed system dichotomy see Sottiaux (2008), at 230-235.

[68] Bowers & Moran (2002); Gill & Monaghan (2003); Bowers, Moran & Honeyball (2003).

[69] Article 4(5) of *Council Directive 2004/113/EC of 13 December 2004 implementing the principle of equal treatment between men and women in the access to and supply of goods and services* provides that: "[t]his Directive shall not preclude differences in treatment, if the provision of the goods and services exclusively or primarily to members of one sex is justified by a legitimate aim and the means of achieving that aim are appropriate and necessary."

States that too broad a formulation of the GDOR risked legalising racial discrimination resulted in a very strict formulation of article 4 RED.[70] This does not reveal any sympathy towards an extra-textual justification possibility.

Moreover, the ECJ has so far held tightly to the texts of equality instruments, refusing to allow extra-textual justification possibilities for direct discrimination in either sex or nationality discrimination law.[71] For instance, in *Johnston*, which involved a sex discrimination claim based on the Equal Treatment Directive (ETD), the Commission had proposed that a number of provisions in the TEC that contained exceptions based on public safety could be applied analogously to the ETC, so as to permit an extra-textual justification possibility for reasons of public safety. The ECJ considered that the relevant provisions only allowed for specific exceptions based on public order, and could not simply be extrapolated to apply for instance in the framework of the ETD. According to the Court, "[i]f every provision of Community law were held to be subject to a general proviso, regardless of the specific requirements laid down by the provisions of the Treaty, this might impair the binding nature of Community law and its uniform application". It concluded that the only possible justifications for the case at hand had to be those that were provided for by the ETD.[72] The issue came furthermore to the fore in *Birds Eye Walls*, an equal pay case in which the Commission suggested that the distinction directly based on gender in the particular case could be justified, in view of the aim behind it, which was to ensure substantive equality between the sexes. Article 119 (currently Article 141) TEC did not, however, provide for such justification possibility. The Court did not go into the Commission's argumentation and instead used the comparability test in a justificatory way to be able to conclude that the prohibition of direct discrimination was not violated.[73]

These judgments reveal that the ECJ so far has not formally opened up to the possibility of reading additional justification possibilities into Community law. At the same time it should be kept in mind that improper use of the comparability test could open the back door for such justifications, as *Birds Eye Walls* illustrates.

Since the original design of the RED is that of a closed system, it will be the point of departure in this study that there are only two possible justifications

---

70 Tyson (2004), at 122.

71 Ellis (2005), at 111-113; Gerards (2002), at 225.

72 ECJ *Johnston v. Chief Constable of the RUC*, Case C-222/84, 15 May 1986, para. 22-28.

73 ECJ *Birds Eye Walls Ltd v. Friedel M Roberts*, Case C-132/92, 9 November 1993, paras. 15 and 20. After considering the incomparability of the cases, the ECJ also emphasised the neutral character of the measure complained of, and considered that the similar treatment of women in this case would amount to the illegal discrimination of men. See further section 4.3.4 on the use of a comparability test.

for prima facie cases of direct discrimination: a GDOR or positive action. As Chapter 8 will extensively dwell on positive action, the following subsection only discusses the GDOR.

4.4.2. Genuine and determining occupational requirement (GDOR)

> Notwithstanding Article 2(1) and (2), Member States may provide that a difference of treatment which is based on a characteristic related to racial or ethnic origin shall not constitute discrimination where, by reason of the nature of the particular occupational activities concerned or of the context in which they are carried out, such a characteristic constitutes a genuine and determining occupational requirement, provided that the objective is legitimate and the requirement is proportionate (Article 4 RED)

4.4.2.1. Introduction

The GDOR allows for the use of racial or ethnic origin and related proxies as a requirement for a particular job or function in certain circumstances. The formulation of the GDOR in Article 4 RED strongly resembles the 'sex as a determining factor' justification, which until recently was applicable in the field of sex equality law. Article 2(2) of the Equal Treatment Directive (ETD) provided that:

> [t]he Directive shall be without prejudice to the right of Member States to exclude from its field of application those occupational activities and, where appropriate, the training leading thereto, for which, by reason of their nature or the context in which they are carried out, the sex of the worker constitutes a determining factor.

This formulation was altered in 2006, and Article 2(6) of Directive 2006/54/EC of the European Parliament and of the Council of 5 July 2005 on the implementation of the principle of equal opportunities and equal treatment of men and women in matters of employment and occupation (recast) (recast directive) now provides that:

> Member States may provide, as regards access to employment including the training leading thereto, that a difference of treatment which is based on a characteristic related to sex shall not constitute discrimination where, by reason of the nature of the particular occupational activities concerned or of the context in which they are carried out, such a characteristic constitutes a genuine and determining occupational requirement, provided that the objective is legitimate and the requirement is proportionate.

Although the more recent formulation of the RED and the recast Directive is stricter than Article 2(2) ETD and adds the 'determining' criterion, it is generally expected that the jurisprudence on Article 2(2) of the ETD is applicable also in the context of the RED, and it will therefore be drawn from in the following analysis.[74] In addition, use will be made of the ECJ's jurisprudence on the objective justification test of the concept of indirect discrimination.

4.4.2.2. Genuine and determining

It is difficult to disentangle the various conditions imposed by Article 4 RED, which appear to overlap to a considerable degree, as will be shown below. The reference to proportionality means that suitability and necessity tests need to be carried out, which apparently cover the same load as the 'genuine' and 'determining' conditions.[75] Overall, it would appear that the words 'genuine' and 'determining' were not added in order to impose additional conditions, but rather to emphasise that a claim of the relevance of racial or ethnic origin for the fulfilment of a particular job has to be supported by very convincing arguments.[76] These conditions thus mainly appear to be intended to impose a high level of scrutiny for a claim of a racial or ethnic GDOR. This also clearly comes back in Recital 18 of the RED, which provides that the GDOR should apply only in "very limited circumstances".[77]

4.4.2.3. Legitimate aim

When determining the legitimacy of the aim pursued by the occupational requirement, courts should be open to consideration of both intrinsic and extrinsic factors for the particular occupational activity, since Article 4 speaks of the *nature* of the particular occupational activity and the *context* in which it is carried out. An example of an extrinsic factor (context) is the fact that a social service worker would predominantly work with persons belonging to a particular ethnic origin. An intrinsic factor (nature) would be present in the case of a movie or play, the script of which requires a black person to play a particular part.[78]

'Legitimate' in indirect discrimination case law furthermore is interpreted as prohibiting discriminatory aims, which is equally applicable in the context

[74] Ellis (2005), at 277; Thüsing (2003), at 193.
[75] Sottiaux (2008), at 237.
[76] Sottiaux (2008), at 243.
[77] The drafting history of the RED also reveals that Member States were determined to very strictly confine the possibilities of justifying direct racial or ethnic discrimination, see Tyson (2004), at 122.
[78] See the *Explanatory Memorandum*, Commission for the European Communities, 1999/0253, 25 November 1999, at 8.

of the GDOR. Thus, the author of the GDOR may not be motivated by racist intentions.[79] The 'genuine' condition of Article 4 RED can also be considered to capture this requirement.

The ECJ's judgment in *Commission v. UK* makes clear that a GDOR for whole categories of jobs in general is not acceptable. The legitimate aim of the protected characteristic as a job requirement must therefore be assessed separately for each particular occupational activity.[80]

4.4.2.4. Suitability

'Suitability' is a factual notion, which requires that the contested measure is practically capable of attaining the aim sought after.[81] In the context of the GDOR, this should mean that race or ethnicity is indeed a relevant requirement for the particular job, which also comes back in the conditions captured by 'genuine' and 'determining'.

Another aspect of 'suitability' has to do with the particular way in which the occupational requirement is framed and applied, as can be inferred from case law on Article 2(2) ETD. In *Commission v. France* the ECJ required that the use of gender as a determining factor complied with the principle of transparency, so as to make judicial review possible. The particular case involved a rule according to which French civil service recruitment agencies could establish a fixed percentage of posts to be filled in by women. France invoked the 'sex as a determining criterion' exception, which was rejected by the ECJ. The Court found it unacceptable that the rule did not provide any criteria for the setting of the percentages, because this violated the requirement of transparency.[82]

The ECJ has furthermore recognised that the question as to which kinds of occupational requirements are deemed acceptable and reasonable can receive different answers over time.[83] Therefore, it is important that the acceptability of a GDOR is not decided on for once and for all when the issue comes up in a particular case, but is reviewed periodically in view of social developments. The obligation that Recital 18 RED imposes on Member States to communicate to the Commission which kinds of GDOR have been recognised in their national legal systems in their five-yearly reports could be helpful in this regard, allowing periodic assessment of the appropriateness of particular GDORs.[84]

---

[79] Sottiaux (2008), at 238.

[80] ECJ *Commission v. UK*, Case C-165/82, 8 November 1983, paras. 12 -16.

[81] Gerards (2002), at 286, 300; Emiliou (1996), at 25-26.

[82] ECJ *Commission v. France*, Case C-318/86, 30 June 1988, paras. 25-27.

[83] ECJ *Commission v. France*, Case C-318/86, 30 June 1988, paras. 25; Burri (2006), at 1.

[84] See Article 17 of the RED, which requires that "Member States shall communicate to the Commission by 19 July 2005, and every five years thereafter, all the information necessary

4.4.2.5. Necessity

'Necessity' in European law generally requires that there are no alternatives available that would have a less serious impact than the contested measure. It furthermore entails a balancing act of the various interests involved in the particular case, in line with the principle of proportionality stricto sensu.[85] In the context of the GDOR, 'necessity' would therefore require that there is no other way of pursuing the aim pursued by the occupational requirement, and that the various interests involved justify the use of as far-reaching a criterion as racial or ethnic origin. 'Determining' in its normal, everyday understanding would appear to capture the same conditions.[86]

The balancing element of the necessity test is of great importance, since it allows the GDOR to be placed in a broader perspective, taking into account the interests of the targeted minority group, as well as other relevant contextual factors. It provides a safeguard against essentialist and harmful stereotypical requirements,[87] and furthers the aim of substantive equality.[88]

4.5. Direct discrimination and positive duties

The discussion of the delineation of direct versus indirect discrimination in section 4.2.1 made clear that direct discrimination is not the first instrument that comes to mind when one considers the possibilities of developing positive duties for the benefit of minority groups. After all, needs-based complaints are more appropriately dealt with under the heading of indirect discrimination. Still, the concept of direct discrimination offers a limited possibility of creating positive duties, namely by way of imposing levelling-up instead of levelling-down as a remedy for direct discrimination. Levelling-up entails granting the discriminated person the same preference that was denied to him/her on account of his/her protected characteristic. Levelling-down entails the exact opposite, that is undoing the advantages that were granted in a discriminatory way to the persons who did not have the protected characteristic.

Formally, the concept of direct discrimination does not require levelling-up, because unequal treatment can equally be remedied by levelling-down.[89] From the victim perspective, however, levelling-up is clearly preferable, because this entails a material improvement in her situation. Moreover, levelling-up

for the Commission to draw up a report to the European Parliament and the Council on the application of this Directive."

85 Emiliou (1996), at 25-29.

86 Sottiaux (2008), at 243.

87 See Bell (2007), at 278, who points out that the GDOR justification carries some risk of facilitating essentialist or stereotyped thinking.

88 See section 5.5.4.4.

89 Fredman (2002), at 95.

generally attributes more to the effectiveness of anti-discrimination law. After all, levelling-down could in some cases 'reward' the discriminator for his discriminatory behaviour, by eliminating the costs incurred by him in granting the non-discriminated persons the discriminatory benefit.

In the field of sex equality law, the ECJ generally has considered levelling-up to be the only acceptable option to remedy past discrimination.[90] At the same time the ECJ has made clear that this does not preclude the adoption of new regulations or provisions by legislators or social partners that comply with the principle of equal treatment, and that take away the advantages enjoyed by the group that was not discriminated against.[91] The duty to level-up recognised by the ECJ as flowing from the principle of equal treatment is therefore a limited one, and does not guarantee any future results. This makes sense, since it indeed appears overly burdensome to leave employers, service providers and others with an eternal duty never to lower the level of pay, or set higher prices, and so forth. In any case, the explicit recognition of a duty to level up by the ECJ enhances the effectiveness of the principle of equal treatment and can be expected to apply in the context of the RED as well.

Part two: Case study

4.6. Definition of direct discrimination

4.6.1. Situation prior to the RED and the changes brought about by implementation

In order to put the discussion of the various national approaches to direct discrimination in the following sections into context, a brief overview is given here of the relevant provisions that existed at the time of the implementation of the RED in the domestic frameworks, as well as the definition that was adopted as a consequence of the RED.

In all four Member States some discrimination provisions were operable prior to the implementation of the RED, the most prominent of which are the Constitutional equality provisions, which approach discrimination as unjustified differences in treatment.[92] Moreover, all four Member States had

[90] See for example ECJ *National Pensions Office v. Emilienne Jonkman and others*, joined cases C-231-233/06, 27 June 2007, paras. 23-24; ECJ *Caballero v. Fogasa*, Case C-442/00, 12 December 2002, para. 42. See also Germain & Eyben (2008), at 347; Jans et al (2007), at 139.

[91] See for instance ECJ *Constance Christina Ellen Smith and others v. Avdel Systems Ltd*, Case C-408/92, 28 September 1994, paras. 17-21; ECJ *Maria Nelleke Gerda van den Akker and others v. Stichting Shell Pensioenfonds*, Case C-28/93, 28 September 1994, paras. 15-17.

[92] In Belgium, Articles 10 and 11 of the Constitution provide for the principles of equality before the law and non-discrimination, which are applied by the Arbitration Court as prohibiting

in place criminal anti-discrimination law, in conformity with their obligations under ICERD. The Belgian and Dutch criminal law provisions defined discrimination in line with Article 1(1) ICERD, which defines discrimination as:

> any distinction, exclusion, restriction or preference based on race, colour, descent, or national or ethnic origin which has the purpose or effect of nullifying or impairing the recognition, enjoyment or exercise, on an equal footing, of human rights and fundamental freedoms in the political, economic, social, cultural or any other field of public life.[93]

The Estonian criminal provision is less elaborate, and prohibits in Article 152 of the Criminal Code:

> the unlawful restriction of the rights of a person or granting unlawful preferences to a person on the basis of [protected characteristics, MB].

The Hungarian Criminal Code does not prohibit racial discrimination, but does contain prohibitions of genocide, apartheid and incitement to hatred and violence against ethnic groups in Articles 155, 157, 174/B and 269.

From 1994 onwards, the Dutch framework provided for civil law provisions on discrimination in the GETA, which defined direct discrimination in terms of direct distinction:

> a distinction between persons on the grounds of [a protected characteristic, MB] (Article 1(1)(b) GETA).

This definition was not altered at the occasion of the implementation of the RED, as this was not considered necessary by the government. The European Commission, however, disagreed and made clear in a letter of formal notice to the government that the deinition had to be aligned with the European

---

a difference in treatment that cannot be objectively justified (see De Prins et al (2005), at 250-266; De Boeck (2003), at 422-423; Tison 2002, at 697-710; Theunis 1997, at 135-146). In Estonia, Article 12(1) of the Constitution contains the principles of equality before the law and non-discrimination, which is interpreted in the same way as the Belgian provisions by the Constitutional Chamber of the Supreme Court (see Alexy (2001), at 73-87). Article 70/A(1) of the Hungarian Constitution contains the prohibition of discrimination, which has been described by the Constitutional Court as: "the differential treatment of persons, things or phenomena which from a certain well defined perspective can be regarded as equal" (Decision 45/2000 of the Constitutional Court). In The Netherlands, Article 1 of the Constitution contains the general principle of equal treatment of equal cases and the prohibition of discrimination. This article is hardly applied in practice, however, since Dutch courts tend to apply the international anti-discrimination provisions, such as Article 26 ICCPR and Article 14 ECHR (Henrard (2008a), at 280-281).

[93] Article 1(1) of the old ARA defined racial discrimination as follows: "any distinction, exclusion, restriction or preference, which has or could have the purpose or effect of nullifying, limiting or impairing the recognition, enjoyment or exercise, on an equal footing, of human rights and fundamental freedoms in the political, economic, social, cultural or any other field of public life." Article 90quater of the Dutch Criminal Code contains an identical definition.

law definition of direct discrimination. In 2009, therefore, the government proposed a draft amendment to Dutch Parliament that alters the definition of direct distinction. After entry into force of this draft act, a direct distinction will be deemed to exist:

> If a person is treated differently than another in a comparable situation is, has been or would be treated, on grounds of [a protected characteristic, MB].[94]

It is interesting to note that the Dutch definition uses the word 'distinction', and thus apparently considers discrimination to invariably amount to a *difference in treatment.* Belgium and Hungary have also opted for the 'distinction' perspective. In Belgium, the first implementation phase introduced a definition of direct discrimination which was similar to the Constitutional equality provision, and referred to:

> any difference in treatment that cannot be objectively and reasonably justified (emphasis added, MB).

Article 4(6) of the new ARA introduced a new definition, while maintaining the difference-based perspective. This article defines direct *distinction* as follows:

> the situation in which a person is treated less favourably than another person in a comparable situation has been, is, or would be treated on the basis of one of the protected grounds.

Article 7 of the new ARA subsequently makes clear that direct discrimination is constituted by unjustified direct *distinctions.*[95]

The Hungarian HETA also maintains the distinction terminology, even though this is not visible in the English translation. The translation speaks of direct *discrimination*, whereas the Hungarian words literally mean disadvantageous *distinction*. Thus, Article 8 HETA provides that a *direct disadvantageous distinction* is constituted by:

> any action (conduct, omission, requirement, order or practice) as a result of which a person or group based on its real or assumed [protected characteristic, MB] is treated or would be treated less favourably than another person or group in a comparable situation.

By applying distinction- or difference-based language, Belgium, Hungary and the Netherlands have arguably bridged the domestic understandings of discrimination as provided by the Constitutional equality provisions (unjustified *differences in treatment*) and the direct discrimination definition

---

[94] *Proposal for an amendment to the equal treatment acts in order to align with directive terminology*, TK 2008-9, 31 832, No.2.

[95] Article 7 of the new ARA specifies that "any direct distinction on the basis of a so-called race, skin colour, descent, or national or ethnic origin constitutes direct discrimination, except for the cases mentioned in Articles 8, 10 and 11." The latter articles contain exceptions for positive action, statutory distinctions, and the GDOR, see section 4.7.1.

of the RED. Since tailoring of the concept of direct discrimination to the national legal context is likely to facilitate its application, this move has perhaps enhanced the effectiveness of the anti-discrimination frameworks in these states.

Still, as is more elaborately explained in section 5.5.2, the distinction terminology threatens the effectiveness of the concept of indirect discrimination. Courts could interpret 'distinction' or 'difference in treatment' as requiring the establishment of a *formal* difference in treatment for indirect discrimination, which would exclude instances of formally equal treatment that still particularly disadvantage a racial or ethnic group from the scope of the prohibition of indirect discrimination. From this perspective, the 'distinction' terminology could actually lower the level of protection of national anti-discrimination law and is perhaps better abolished.

The matter has been the subject of debate in the Netherlands, where there has been an ongoing discussion as to whether the distinction terminology is in line with European law.[96] Until 2008, the standpoint of the Dutch government consistently was that European law does not necessitate a change in formulation, and that the Dutch acquis should be respected.[97] In its 2008 reaction to the second evaluation of the GETA it seemed to have departed from this standpoint,[98] but at the occasion of the amendment of the definition of direct distinction in 2009 it again emphasised that there was no need to leave the 'distinction' terminology, which was considered to ensure a higher level of protection against discrimination by only requiring a difference in treatment and not a disadvantageous treatment.[99]

The Estonian definition of direct discrimination does not apply the 'distinction' based perspective and follows the discrimination language of the RED. Article 3(2) of the EETA provides that:

> [d]iscrimination is direct, if based on a [protected characteristic, MB] one person is treated less favourably than another person has been treated, is treated or would be treated in a similar situation.

[96] See for a comprehensive overview of the debate and the various relevant considerations Holtmaat (2006), at 3-116.

[97] See for instance the *Memo sent to the Parliament with regard to the implementation of the RED*, TK 2001-2, 28 187, No. 1, at 5-6. The government maintained this position even after the Council of State had recommended to change the definitions of discrimination in the GETA in order to bring them into line with the European definitions, see the *Advice and Report on the Amendment of the General Act on Equal Treatment and certain other acts in order to implement directive 2000/43/EG and directive 2000/78/EG, TK 2002-3, 28 770, A*, at 3-4.

[98] *Letter of the government with regard to the third evaluation of the GETA*, TK 2008-9, 28 481, at 3.

[99] *Explanatory Memorandum to the Amendment to the equal treatment acts in order to align with directive terminology*, TK 2008-9, 31 832, No.3, at 3.

It should finally be mentioned that the Hungarian HETA maintains a separate definition and prohibition of racial segregation as a particular form of direct discrimination:[100] Article 10 (2) HETA defines 'unlawful separation' as:

> conduct that separates individuals or groups of individuals from other individuals or groups of individuals in a similar situation on the basis of their [protected characteristic, MB] without a reasonable explanation resulting from objective justification.

Given that racial segregation is a very pressing problem in Hungary, in particular for the Roma minority, this clear condemnation of treating racial or ethnic groups differently, without requiring disadvantageous treatment, is very welcome in that it shows special regard for the particular situation of vulnerable minority groups in Hungarian society. Moreover, it is clearly based on substantive equality thinking.

4.6.2. 'One person'

In most Member States it is not yet clear whether collective manifestations of direct discrimination that can only be discerned through quantitative evidence are covered by the definitions of direct discrimination. In the Netherlands and in Estonia, no such cases have yet presented themselves, and it is therefore uncertain whether the 'one person' terminology will constitute a problem in this respect.[101]

In contrast, there are some positive signs discernable in the Belgian and Hungarian frameworks, which indicate that these particular collective manifestations of direct discrimination are probably lcovered. In Belgium, the new ARA expressly accommodates the use of quantitative information for establishing direct discrimination. Article 30, which regulates matters of proof, provides in section 2(1) that a presumption of direct discrimination can be inferred from a *pattern* of consecutive instances of disadvantageous treatment of persons belonging to a protected group.[102] The provision has not yet been

---

[100] Gyulavári (2007), at 43.

[101] The definition of direct distinction in Article 1(1)(b) GETA currently does not refer to 'one person', but this will change with the adoption of the proposed *Amendment to the equal treatment acts in order to align with directive terminology*, TK 2008-9, 31 832, No.2. See section 4.6.1.

[102] The paragraph reads as follows: "[c]onsidered as facts from which the existence of a direct discrimination on grounds of a protected characteristic can be presumed are, although not exclusively, data that reveal a particular pattern of disadvantageous treatment with regard to persons who portray a particular protected characteristic; amongst others different, separate complaints submitted to the Center or one of the interest organisations."

applied in practice, but it arguably allows for establishing direct discrimination by making use of quantitative information, without the discrimination being visible in each separate case.[103]

The clearest example of provision for collective manifestations of direct discrimination is found in the Hungarian framework, where the definition in Article 8 HETA of direct discrimination contains a reference to *groups* of persons. Moreover, practice confirms that there is regard in the Hungarian context for collective manifestations of direct discrimination. Thus the AET finds direct discrimination where statistics show that persons with a particular characteristic are disadvantageously affected to a greater extent than other persons, for which no reasonable explanation can be found.[104] In principle, this approach can be positively evaluated. However, as is pointed out in section 4.6.4.1, a clear and consistent delineation of direct versus indirect discrimination has not yet been developed in the Hungarian legal framework. This means that both the AET and the courts in some cases conclude too easily that direct discrimination is present, where the label of indirect discrimination would be more appropriate. It is to be hoped that a more conceptually sound and consistent approach will be adopted in the future. Aside from this concern, however, it is a positive asset of the Hungarian framework that it recognises collective manifestations of direct discrimination.

4.6.3. 'Is treated less favourably'

For Belgium and Estonia, there is insufficient information available in order to determine how broadly 'treatment' will be interpreted in practice. In Estonia, there is no court practice at all, whereas in Belgium discrimination cases so far concerned refusal of goods or services or rejection of job applicants, all actions that are uncontroversially captured by the notion of 'treatment'.[105]

The Hungarian framework is unique in providing express guidance as to the meaning of 'treatment', and provides in Article 7(2) HETA the following enumeration of the types of behaviour: "conduct, measure, condition, omission, instruction or practice". The mention of 'omission' is particularly interesting, since it introduces the possibility for needs-based complaints to be brought under the heading of direct discrimination. A number of segregation cases indeed show that Hungarian courts, as well as the AET, consider the omission to take appropriate action against segregation to constitute direct discrimination.[106] As was explained in section 4.2.1, this approach is

[103] Rorive & Van der Plancke (2008), at 452.

[104] *Annual Report 2006*, EUMC, at 13.

[105] See De Prins et al (2005), at 353-360 and 362-363, discussing jurisprudence under the old ARA.

[106] See for example the landmark case of the Debrecen Court of Appeal, 9 June 2006, Pf. I. 20.683/2005/7, in which the Court admitted that the maintenance of a situation which resulted

conceptually flawed. However, the matter should arguably be assessed in the light of the particularities of the Hungarian context, in which there is not much experience with dealing with discrimination, especially not in the way as proscribed by European law. As was mentioned before, and will be explained in more detail in the next chapter, indirect discrimination is still an unknown concept that is not eagerly, nor properly used by the Hungarian bodies and courts. This means that banning needs-based complaints to the framework of indirect discrimination could actually heighten the threshold for succeeding in such complaints. Dealing with needs-based complaints under the heading of direct discrimination could therefore actually enhance the level of protection offered by Hungarian anti-discrimination law. Seen from this perspective, conceptual fuzziness is perhaps preferable over a conceptually clear framework that would entail a lower level of protection for minorities in practice.

As was previously mentioned, the Dutch framework is the only one that has not more or less copied the definition of direct discrimination of the RED, even though this will change with the adoption of the draft Amendment Act of 2009. After the adoption of this Act, the definition will speak of a difference in treatment, whereas the definition now only refers to 'distinction'. 'Distinction' in its normal understanding is broader than the word 'treatment', since it does not refer to the differentiating source and thus does not point to a particular type of action or behaviour.[107] This could mean that the amended definition will cover less types of behaviour than the current one. In any case, the ETC and Dutch courts closely follow the jurisprudence of the ECJ in anti-discrimination law, and the interpretation of 'treatment' at the Dutch level is therefore likely to conform to European standards.

Interestingly, *Feryn*-like cases have come up in all frameworks under study, and have produced more or less similar results, according to which an announcement of discriminatory behaviour is considered to constitute direct discrimination. The Dutch ETC and the Estonian Gender Equality Commissioner (GEC) have applied a particularly clear approach, making it unambiguously clear that subsequent non-discriminatory behaviour of the author of the statement does not uplift the discriminatory character of the statement. The case before the GEC involved an advertisement for an event for children, which referred to the event as being "for all small and big boys". The commissioner ruled that this constituted direct discrimination, and did not change this classification in view of the fact that in reality girls were also admitted.[108] In a similar way, the Dutch ETC ruled that an advertisement of

---

in a disadvantage for a particular group constituted discrimination, even though there was no active discriminatory behaviour. Similarly see EBH 23/2007, in which the AET ordered a local government to take measures to end a situation of educational segregation.

[107] Compare Holtmaat (2006), at 65, who points out that 'distinction' is an empty notion.

[108] This case is described on the website of the Gender Equality Commissioner at www.svv.ee (in Estonian).

rental apartments for foreign persons working temporarily in the Netherlands constituted direct discrimination. It then separately examined the question whether the agency had also discriminated when entering into rental contracts in practice, and ruled that there was no evidence of such discrimination.[109] Furthermore, in a case concerning a publicity campaign offering vaccinations for reduced rates on particular dates, which expressly only targeted Moroccan and Turkish children, the ETC ruled that this constituted direct discrimination on grounds of race, regardless of the fact that in practice other children were accepted as well.[110] The approach of the GEC and the ETC is less ambiguous than the ECJ's judgment in *Feryn*, and would moreover seem to be substantively correct, seeing that discriminatory advertisements can have a chilling effect on persons belonging to protected group, and therefore cause real damage.[111]

It is therefore unfortunate that the Hungarian framework has produced a judgment that is as ambiguous as the *Feryn* judgment of the ECJ. The particular case, commonly referred to as the *Károli* case, involved a declaration posted on the website of a Catholic university, which stated that the university would not admit homosexual students in its training programme for priests. According to a lower court, this could not be scrutinised under the prohibition of discrimination, since the freedom of expression of the institution was at stake.[112] The Supreme Court rejected this line of argumentation, and ruled that the statement did constitute discrimination. At the same time, it took note of the fact that the university had actually followed up on the statement, by refusing a particular student.[113] Thus, it is not entirely certain whether the judgment should be read to mean that an announcement of discriminatory behaviour in itself constitutes direct discrimination, or whether it merely establishes a presumption of direct discrimination that can be refuted by factual evidence.[114]

It is not yet clear how Belgian courts will interpret the ECJ's *Feryn* ruling, which concerned a Belgian case.

As regards the 'less favourable' aspect of direct discrimination, it is still uncertain in the Member States whether this implies a disadvantage requirement.

[109] Opinion 2006-11 ETC, paras. 4.9-4.11.

[110] Opinion 2006-55 ETC, para. 4.8.

[111] See for instance the opinion of Advocate-General Maduro in *Centrum voor gelijkheid van kansen en racismebestrijding v. Firma Feryn NV*, Case C-54/07, 12 March 2008, para. 15: "a public statement from an employer that persons of a certain racial or ethnic origin need not apply has an effect that is anything but hypothetical. To ignore that as an act of discrimination would be to ignore the social reality that such statements are bound to have a humiliating and demoralising impact on persons of that origin who want to participate in the labour market and, in particular, on those who would have been interested in working for the employer at issue."

[112] Metropolitan Court, 19.AT21.788/2004/10, 8 October 2004.

[113] Supreme Court PFv. IV.20.687/2005/5, 8 June 2005.

[114] According to Halmai (2005a), at 53-54, the judgment should be interpreted to mean that an announcement of discriminatory behaviour in itself constitutes discrimination.

This is particularly the case for Estonia, where lack of practice makes it impossible to say how the 'less favourable' aspect of direct discrimination will be interpreted. In Belgium and Hungary, the Constitutional Courts have read into the Constitutional equality provisions a disadvantage requirement, which could be expected to seep through into the frameworks of the new ARA and of the HETA.[115] Still, in both frameworks, the legislator has chosen to approach racial segregation as a particular form of direct discrimination, which implies a rejection of the 'separate but equal' doctrine and could impact on the interpretation of direct racial discrimination more generally.[116] Since the issue has not yet come up in practice, it remains unclear to what extent the disadvantage element of the concept of direct discrimination will constitute an actual hurdle for applicants.

The Dutch framework shows a slightly misleading picture, as the definition in Article 1(1)(b) GETA only requires a difference in treatment, which will not change after the entry into force of the draft Amendment Act of 2009.[117] Formally, therefore, no disadvantage is required for the establishment of direct discrimination. However, in practice the ETC does require a disadvantage to have occurred.[118] This is caused by the standing requirement of Article 12(2)(a) GETA, which requires that individual applicants are actually disadvantaged by the distinction complained of. Moreover, Article 14(1)(b) GETA determines that the ETC refrains from investigating a case when the interest of the applicant or the seriousness of the behaviour complained of is not sufficiently weighty.

Every now and then, Articles 12(2)(a) and 14(1)(b) GETA actually prove to be a stumbling block for individual applicants. For instance, the ETC considered that offering a taxi for women only by a large taxi company implied such a small inconvenience for men, who had plenty of alternatives for getting

[115] For Belgium, see the judgment of the Arbitration Court, Case no.157/2004, 6 October 2004. See also De Prins et al (2005), at 467. The Arbitration Court did not further explain what it meant by 'disadvantage'. For Hungary see the decisions of the Constitutional Court, Decision No. 45/2000 (XII.8.), para. 3-4 and Decision No. 71/2002, which interpret 'disadvantage' as the restriction of a particular right or the imposition of an obligation.

[116] As was mentioned before, the HETA contains an express prohibition of segregation in Article 10(2). See also Farkas et al (2006), at 67. In Belgium, there is no express prohibition of segregation, but the Explanatory Memorandum to the new ARA makes clear that the legislator deems this form of discrimination to be covered by the concept of direct discrimination. *Explanatory Memorandum to the Draft law amending the law of 30 July 1981 that penalises certain acts motivated by racism and xenophobia*, Doc 51. 2720/001, 41. See also Bayart & Deiteren (2008), at 222-224.

[117] The Dutch government even emphasised the usefulness of the lack of a disadvantage requirement in the *Explanatory Memorandum to the Proposal for an amendment to the equal treatment acts in order to align with directive terminology*, TK 2008-9, 31 832, No. 3, at 3.

[118] Holtmaat (2006), at 88-89; Asscher-Vonk & Hendriks (2005), at 54; Waaldijk (2004), at 351.

a taxi, that the complaint about the discriminatory character of this service was inadmissible.[119] It is uncertain whether the ETC will rule in a similar way when direct discrimination on racial or ethnic grounds is in play.

4.6.4. 'On grounds of racial or ethnic origin' (causal aspect of direct discrimination)

4.6.4.1. Delineation of direct v. indirect discrimination

Unsurprisingly, the delineation of direct versus indirect discrimination is problematic in all Member States, perhaps with the exception of Estonia, where the issue has not yet come to the fore.

The Netherlands holds the best track record in this respect, as the ETC applies a fairly transparent and consistent approach. The cases of the ETC reveal that it generally applies direct discrimination to distinctions that are either directly based on a protected ground, or on a ground inextricably linked to a protected ground.[120] In order to find the real underlying cause or motive, the ETC thoroughly investigates the arguments presented by the defendant, and consistently deals with covert use of a protected ground as direct discrimination.[121] For instance, in a case in which a list of entry criteria was applied in order to spread 'disadvantaged' children over various schools, the ETC ruled that there was direct racial discrimination, even though none of the criteria directly referred to racial or ethnic origin. It did so because it had inferred from the facts of the case that in reality the intention was to target only children of a non-Dutch background.[122] Similarly, the prohibition of wearing a headscarf amounts to either direct or indirect religious discrimination according to the ETC, depending on whether the author of the prohibition in reality wants to prevent the expression of religion (direct discrimination), or has other reasons, unrelated to religion (indirect discrimination).[123] According

[119] Opinion 2008-102 ETC, paras. 3.10-3.13. In paras. 3.14-3.16 the ETC also concludes that the complaint about the policy to only schedule female chauffeurs on the women's taxi should be dismissed for lack of seriousness of the distinction made.

[120] Asscher-Vonk & Hendriks (2005), at 58; Cremers-Hartman (2004), at 143; Wentholt (1999), at 107-108. The ETC describes the causal link inter alia as a distinction that: "directly refers to" (Opinion 2007-109 ETC, para. 3.9), "is directly based on or referring to" (Opinion 2007-91 ETC, para. 3.3) or is "on grounds of" (Opinion 2008-1 ETC, para. 3.7) one of the protected characteristics. All of these descriptions are centered on the notion of the protected characteristic as the fundamental cause or motive for the treatment complained of.

[121] Gerards (2006a), at 317; Cremers-Hartman (2004), at 34-35.

[122] Opinion 2005-25 ETC, paras. 6.11-6.13.

[123] In Opinion 2007-73 ETC the prohibition to wear religious dress, including headscarves, in a sports club was deemed to constitute direct discrimination based on religion, since the reason for the prohibition was to create a religiously neutral environment; in Opinion 2007-173 ETC the refusal of an intern because of her wearing a headscarf was considered to constitute indirect

to this approach, total exclusionary effects on a particular group are not enough to establish direct discrimination, and practice confirms that the ETC generally does not apply an effects-based approach. For example, a requirement of possession of a residence permit was considered by the ETC not to constitute direct racial discrimination, even though it exclusively affected non-Dutch nationals.[124] The ETC furthermore regards acting on the basis of prejudice against a particular group to constitute direct discrimination. For instance, in a case in which someone claimed to have been discriminated against because of his origin from the Northern part of the country, the ETC stated that it would only consider this to constitute direct racial discrimination if it could be established that certain prejudices with regard to 'Northerners' had played a part.[125]

This approach of the ETC corresponds with the one proposed in section 4.2.3 and the ETC usually applies it consistently, which is a very positive asset of the Dutch framework. However, the ETC has sporadically rendered decisions that do not fit the general approach. For example, a rule according to which only couples of mixed sex could participate in a dancing competition was considered by the ETC to constitute direct discrimination based on sexual orientation, because it imposed a non-neutral heterosexual norm.[126] However, the facts of the case did not reveal any underlying motivation of disadvantaging homosexuals or prejudice against such persons. Moreover, a requirement of couples being of mixed sex is not based on anybody's sexual orientation or a ground inextricably linked to it. Therefore, the more appropriate qualification would have been indirect discrimination on the basis of sexual orientation, since the rule in effect tends to disadvantage more homosexual than heterosexual persons. In 1997, the ETC had indeed in a similar case opted for the label of indirect discrimination.[127] An equally appropriate qualification would have been direct discrimination based on gender, since gender is clearly the distinguishing criterion used by the rule; interestingly, a later court decision on this case indeed qualified the case as amounting to direct sex discrimination.[128]

Another 'aberration' in the usually consistent quasi-jurisprudence of the ETC concerned a rule according to which soldiers that were married or were in a comparable relationship with persons from Bosnia could not

---

discrimination, since the underlying reason for the refusal was that the employer wanted his staff to dress fashionably.

[124] Opinion 2003-18 ETC, paras. 5.12-5.13. According to the ETC, there was no direct distinction, because the requirement did not directly refer to racial or ethnic origin.

[125] Opinion 2006-53 ETC, para. 4.5. See also Opinion 2006-153 ETC, in which the occurrence of unsubstantiated statements with regard to a job applicant's cultural background influenced the ETC's decision in qualifying the facts as constituting direct discrimination.

[126] Opinion 2004-116 ETC.

[127] Opinion 1997-29 ETC.

[128] The Hague District Court, 26 July 2006, LJN: AY5005.

participate in a peacekeeping mission in that region. According to the ETC, this constituted indirect racial discrimination, since not all persons living in the region were affected, with which it implied that an exclusive negative impact on persons from the particular region would have deserved the label of direct discrimination. This actually suggests an effects-based approach, similar to the one that is sometimes taken by the ECJ and was discussed in section 4.2.2.[129] A more appropriate qualification of the case would have been direct discrimination on racial origin, since the actual reason for refusing persons participation in the mission was the national origin of their partner. This was therefore a clear case of discrimination by association, directly based on a racial ground.[130] It is unclear why the ETC in these cases deviated from its normal line of reasoning, and it is to be hoped that similar deviations will not appear in the future.

It must furthermore be mentioned that the ETC's overall positive record is not replicated by Dutch courts, which so far have revealed not to be very sensitive as regards the conceptual difference between direct and indirect discrimination. A good example is found in a number of cases concerning the rule of insurance companies that self-employed women have to have been insured for at least two years with the company before they can claim compensation for maternity leave. The rule was examined by a number of courts, which applied different qualifications. According to the Utrecht District Court, the rule did not constitute direct sex discrimination, because only women can get pregnant, not men. It did not go into the question whether indirect discrimination was perhaps at stake.[131] To the contrary, the Amsterdam Court of Appeal qualified the rule as involving indirect sex discrimination, because it affected only women negatively.[132] Earlier on, the Injunction Judge of the Utrecht District Court had opted for the qualification of direct discrimination based on sex.[133]

The lack of a clear approach with regard to the difference between direct and indirect discrimination is probably due to the fact that Dutch courts do not often encounter discrimination cases, which are mainly dealt with by the ETC. Moreover, in addition to the discrimination concepts of the GETA, there are other discrimination concepts in the Dutch legal framework. This makes it understandably difficult for courts to apply the various discrimination concepts correctly. For instance, in criminal law, differences in treatment formally based on neutral grounds but in reality targeting a protected characteristic amount to indirect discrimination in criminal law, whereas the ETC would qualify

[129] Opinion 2002-204 ETC, paras. 5.1-5.11.

[130] See for the concept of discrimination by association section 2.3.4.

[131] Utrecht District Court, 10 January 2007, LJN: AZ7462, para. 4.6.

[132] Amsterdam Court of Appeal, 19 October 2006, LJN: AZ0509, para. 4.10.

[133] Injunction Judge of the Utrecht District Court, 15 November 2005, LJN: AU6168, paras. 4.7-4.8.

them as covert direct discrimination in the framework of the GETA.[134] In any case, the resulting legal uncertainty makes the adoption of a transparent and consistent approach by the Dutch courts in the future highly desirable.

The same is true for Belgium, where much remains to be clarified as regards the approach to the delineation of direct versus indirect discrimination. Belgian scholars that comment on the issue generally take the conceptually appropriate approach, according to which direct discrimination is constituted by actions that are openly or obviously based on a protected characteristic; actions that are based on characteristics that are inextricably linked to a protected characteristic; and actions based on prejudice or stereotypical beliefs about a group sharing a protected characteristic.[135]

However, it remains to be seen whether this approach will be followed in practice. First of all, the drafters of the new ARA have clearly opted for qualifying covert direct discrimination as indirect discrimination. According to the Explanatory Memorandum, the latter concept is intended to cover the deliberate use of a neutral criterion in order to circumvent the prohibition of direct discrimination.[136] As was explained above, it is more appropriate to qualify such cases as direct discrimination, because in reality they involve a direct causal link between disadvantage and protected characteristic. Unfortunately, the drafters' position finds support from some Belgian scholars, and it is very likely that courts will follow it as well.[137] Indeed, seeing that the criminal law part of the ARA expressly refers to "intentional indirect discrimination", which comes down to the deliberate use of a neutral ground in order to mask direct discrimination, it would seem that they have little leeway in this regard.[138]

On the other hand, the Arbitration Court in its landmark judgment of 2004 made clear that it is difficult to see how indirect discrimination can be intentional, which is why it rejected criminal law provisions prohibiting incitement to indirect discrimination.[139] Along the same lines of reasoning, the concept of intentional indirect discrimination of the new ARA could be considered to be unlawful. It should be said, however, that even though the 'intentional indirect discrimination' approach is conceptually not appropriate, it is at least advantageous that the legislator has drawn attention to the possibility of covert direct discrimination, and that it has underlined the seriousness of such discrimination by sanctioning it criminally, unlike the other forms of (so-called 'unintentional') forms of indirect discrimination.

---

[134] High Council 13 June 2000, NJ 2000/513, para. 3.5.2.

[135] Bayart & Deiteren (2008), at 195-198; De Prins et al (2005), at 469.

[136] *Explanatory Memorandum to the Draft law amending the law of 30 July 1981 that penalises certain acts motivated by racism and xenophobia*, Doc 51. 2720/001, 41, at 41.

[137] Bayart & Deiteren (2008), at 212-217.

[138] See Articles 19-25 of the new ARA, and the drafters' commentary in Doc. 51. 2720/001, at 29-31.

[139] Arbitration Court, Case no. 157/2004, 6 October 2004, para. B.55-6.

The conceptual confusion as regards direct versus indirect discrimination in Belgium does not only concern the qualification of covert direct discrimination as indirect discrimination. One judgment of the Antwerp Court of Appeal appears to reveal a misunderstanding of the fundamental difference between direct and indirect discrimination. The case concerned the prohibition of wearing headscarves in class by a public high school, and the Court stated that this could not constitute direct discrimination, since the school did not discriminate in providing access to education.[140] The Court thus apparently considered discrimination to be direct when it actually prohibits access to some opportunity or advantage, and indirect when it does not entail an absolute bar, but only makes it more difficult to benefit from an opportunity or advantage. Naturally, one cannot make too much of one phrase of one court, but the statement is nevertheless remarkable and does not convey a clear sense of what exactly makes direct discrimination direct.

In a similar way to Belgium, the Hungarian framework is governed by uncertainty as regards the delineation of direct versus indirect discrimination. One of the rare cases in which the concept of indirect discrimination has so far been used shows that the AET has not yet arrived at a clear conception of the boundary between the two concepts.[141] The case concerned the complaint by a person of Roma origin that her local council had failed for a long time to provide for representation of the local Roma community in a committee on minority issues. Moreover, she claimed that their refusal to appoint her as a member of this committee when it finally had been set up was discriminatory. The AET concluded that the case amounted to both direct and indirect discrimination. It found direct discrimination against the applicant, because "the suffered grievances were because of the Roma origin of the client". The indirect discrimination aspect allegedly lay in the manner in which the committee was set up: even though it was the legal prerogative of the corporation of the local government to set up such a committee and the decision did not aim to discriminate, the Roma minority was put in a very unfavourable position compared with other minority groups.[142]

The case was reviewed by the Supreme Court, which agreed with the AET on the indirect discrimination aspect of the case, because it considered the negligence in providing for representation in the committee to be in contravention with the fundamental right of minorities to representation of their interests at the local level. The direct discrimination part against the individual applicant could not be proven according to the Supreme Court, as it found that the local council had good reasons not to appoint the particular person as a member of the committee, and it could not be proven that the

---

[140] *A. e.a. v. Provincie Limburg*, Antwerp Court of Appeal, 14 June 2005, para. 2.2.2.

[141] This perception has been confirmed in our interviews with Hungarian lawyers that work with the AET.

[142] EBH 337/24/2005.

woman's Roma origin had been the reason for the refusal.[143] Interestingly, the facts of the case as described in the AET's decision show that the local Mayor had made racist remarks during the deliberations on the setting up of the committee, saying for instance that: "you Gypsies have to perform first". Despite this clear indication that the ethnic origin of the persons belonging to the Roma committee was at least one of the real reasons for the behaviour of the Mayor and the local government, both the AET and the Supreme Court opted for the classification of indirect discrimination. This would appear to be based on the assumption that indirect discrimination covers disadvantages that are not directed against any individual in particular, but affect all members of a protected group. Indeed, the disadvantageous treatment of the applicant herself was seen to constitute direct discrimination. This is not a conceptually sound approach, since direct discrimination can manifest itself in a disadvantage for a whole group, just as indirect discrimination can concern a disadvantage for a particular individual.

Another flawed perception of the delineation of direct and indirect discrimination in the Hungarian context is found in a handbook on the HETA published by a Hungarian NGO. In the comment on Article 26 HETA - which provides that it is a particular violation of the principle of equal treatment when, on the basis of one of the protected characteristics, a person is put in a disadvantageous position as regards the determination of the conditions of sale or as regards leasing of public housing property – the handbook explains this provision as targeting indirect discrimination, which it understands as comprising the imposition of requirements that are not essentially necessary, but have a disproportionate effect on persons with a protected characteristic. This explanation seems to propose that indirect discrimination is at stake when some action makes it harder, but not impossible, for persons of a particular characteristic to obtain a particular good. Arguably, the implication is that direct discrimination then covers those instances where persons are effectively banned from access at all to the particular good.[144] This perception of the delineation between direct and indirect discrimination is reminiscent of the approach taken by the Antwerp Court of Appeal as cited above.

4.6.4.2. Establishment of the causal link

In none of the four Member States a clear test has been developed in order to establish the causal link for direct discrimination, and the bodies/courts hardly pay attention to the matter. Nevertheless, an interesting pattern can be discerned in the practice of the Hungarian AET, which is worth mentioning.

---

[143] Supreme Court, Kfv.IV.37.450/2006/5, 11 July 2007.

[144] *White Booklet 2006*, Legal Defence Bureau for National Ethnic Minorities (NEKI) 2007, at 82-83.

The particular way in which the HETA approaches the division of burden of proof between applicant and defendant has impacted on the way in which the AET establishes the causal link. According to Article 19 HETA, it is up to the applicant to establish a presumption of discrimination, which implies the presence of a disadvantage and of a protected characteristic; if these elements are established, the burden of proof rests on the defendant to show that there was no breach of the principle of equal treatment.[145] The causal link is therefore usually established in a negative way: by the applicant being unable to convincingly establish that the protected ground was not the reason for the disadvantageous treatment.[146]

In line with this negative approach to the causal link, the AET has developed the curious practice of using the justification possibilities for direct discrimination for establishing the causal link. For instance, in a dismissal case the AET applied the GDOR justification in order to establish that the employer had a valid reason to dismiss the Roma applicant and that her Roma origin was therefore not the reason for which she was dismissed; the dismissal was consequently not qualified as discriminatory.[147] The GDOR was thus approached as some kind of open justification possibility that could help determine whether the reason for a disadvantageous treatment was a protected characteristic.

Apart from the flawed conception of the GDOR that this argumentation entails, it also mixes up the various stages for establishing direct discrimination that transpire from the RED and is therefore objectionable. According to the logic of the RED, direct discrimination is established first by finding the causal link with the protected ground, after which it should be examined whether any justification possibilities are available.[148] By using a justification possibility to establish causation, the AET opens the door to extra-textual justification possibilities for racial discrimination. After all, it suggests that justification arguments are relevant at the stage of determining the causal link, which invites defendants to submit all kinds of justifications for racist behaviour.

---

[145] See for a more detailed analysis Ambrus (2010).

[146] See for instance Miskolc Labour Court, 19 June 2007, 6.m.755/2006/22, in which the Court had to decide whether the refusal to prolong a temporary employment contract was based on pregnancy. After having established that there was a protected ground (pregnancy) and a disadvantage (refusal to prolong the contract), the Court examined the various defenses forwarded by the employer and decided that none of them were credible and therefore that there was discrimination on grounds of pregnancy.

[147] EBH/476/2008. See for another example EBH/271/2007, in which the AET used the GDOR to establish that there was no valid reason not to hire persons of Roma origin, and that the refusal of the job therefore amounted to racial discrimination.

[148] See Ambrus (2010) for an elaborate analysis in this regard.

4.6.4.3. Intent required?

The four Member States all appear to have recognised that discriminatory intent is not a constitutive element of discrimination. In the Netherlands this is presupposed in doctrine and in practice.[149] In Belgium this can be inferred from the fact that the criminal law section of the new ARA explicitly requires intent for both direct and indirect discrimination. According to an a contrario reasoning, this requirement does not apply to the civil law provisions on direct and indirect discrimination, which is confirmed in literature.[150] In Estonia, the GEC made clear in the aforementioned *boys' event* case that it did not matter for the qualification of direct sex discrimination that the organisation organising the event did not intend to discriminate between boys and girls.[151] Similarly, the Hungarian AET in a disability discrimination case made clear that this body does not consider discriminatory intent a necessary ingredient of direct discrimination. In the particular case, a man with sight impairment had to go through a very laborious procedure in order to obtain a signature for a contract for a financial loan: he had to travel to the local notary, who would read the contract out loud, and he had to sign an official notary act that acknowledged his debt, which had adverse legal consequences. According to the AET, this constituted discrimination on the basis of disability, even though the financial company did not intend to discriminate.[152]

4.6.4.4. Racial or ethnic origin as one of the reasons

The issue whether direct discrimination will be applied in cases where racial or ethnic origin is not the sole reason for the less favourable treatment has so far only really come up in the Dutch framework. Thus, in the Netherlands it is generally acknowledged in literature and in practice that the presence of other reasons for a disadvantageous treatment in addition to one of the protected grounds does not constitute an obstacle for a finding of direct discrimination.[153] For example, in a case in which a man was rejected for a client manager job, one of the reasons for which was his religious dress, the ETC reminded that it was a settled line of case law that it is sufficient for a finding of direct distinction that the protected ground played a role in the

[149] Gijzen (2006), at 191. See for instance Opinion 2007-57 ETC, para. 3.6.
[150] Bayart & Deiteren (2008), at 195.
[151] See section 4.6.3.
[152] EBH/553/2006.
[153] Holtmaat (2007), at 21; Cremers-Hartman (2004), at 144; Gerards & Heringa (2003), at 44-45.

decision-making process.[154] This test is rather lenient, which is appropriate in view of the fundamental violation of human dignity implicated by any use of racial or ethnic origin as a reason for differentiation.

In the other Member States no clear approach has been developed yet. In Belgium, a provision in the procedural part of the new ARA appears to indicate that racial or ethnic origin does not have to be the sole reason for the less favourable treatment. Article 16(2)(1) of this Act provides for a diminished amount of damages in case the defendant shows that the contested measure would have been applied even in the absence of the discrimination, because of non-discriminatory reasons. This can be read as an acknowledgement of the possibility that racial discrimination can exist even if there are other, non-discriminatory reasons in play.[155] Practice needs to confirm whether this approach will indeed be taken by the Belgian courts.[156]

In Hungary one case ruled by the Metropolitan court reveals that this court is not very alert to the possibility of direct discrimination being present where a protected ground is only one of the reasons for the treatment complained of. The case involved a rule of a local authority that permanent residents with Hungarian nationality were entitled to a reduced fee for the local spa. The Metropolitan Court rejected the claim of discrimination, because it found it justifiable to grant certain benefits to permanent residents only. Moreover, it accepted the local government's statement that the applicant's foreign nationality in itself would not have prevented him from obtaining the reduction benefit.[157] Seeing that the nationality criterion was expressly laid down as a requirement this simple acceptance of a statement by the local government representative is surprising. Indeed, the judgment raises the impression that the court did not really want to look into the nationality discrimination aspect of the case, because it found it reasonable to confer certain benefits on grounds of permanent residency. It thus effectively ignored one of the reasons for the disadvantageous treatment. One can easily imagine similar cases coming up involving publicly accepted forms of racism. The Metropolitan court's approach is thus preferably not to be followed by other courts.

As for the AET, we have been told by a member of this body that it will apply the concept of direct discrimination each time that a person's ethnic origin has played a part in a decision, even if this was not the only reason.[158] This more favourable approach has yet to appear in practice.

154 Opinion 2006-202 ETC, para. 3.10.

155 The author is grateful to M. Ambrus for pointing this out.

156 See Bayart & Deiteren (2008), at 200-204, who discuss the matter and conclude that there is no indication yet as to which way Belgian courts will go.

157 Metropolitan Court, 8.K. 33.297/2006/5, 11 December 2006.

158 For reasons of privacy the particular source is not revealed here.

4.6.5. 'Than another person is, has been or would be treated in a comparable situation'

4.6.5.1. Function of the comparative element

With the exception of the Dutch GETA, the national anti-discrimination laws have more or less copied the formulation of the comparative element of Article 2(2)a RED. The Belgian, Estonian and Hungarian definitions of direct discrimination furthermore expressly refer to the notion of comparability.[159]

The current definition of direct discrimination in the Dutch GETA makes no mention of a comparison or of comparability, but the ETC does use it every now and then. If the ETC uses the comparison, it does so in order to establish that the reason for a distinction was indeed a protected characteristic. In 2007, there were two cases on direct racial discrimination in which a comparison played a part. In the first case, a man claimed that his non-Dutch origin was the reason for which a housing corporation refused to install a shower in his home, whereas his neighbour, a Dutch woman, had obtained a shower before she moved in. The ETC compared the two cases, and concluded that the two persons differed as to the time at which they moved into their houses and thus fell under different rules, which explained the difference in treatment. Thus, there was no causal link with the man's ethnic origin.[160] In the second case, a man of Moroccan origin complained that he was refused membership of a gym, whereas his Dutch girlfriend and her father were admitted. The ETC compared the two cases, and decided that the gym could not explain why they were different, which established a presumption of direct racial discrimination.[161] Both decisions clearly reveal that the comparison was only used to establish causation and did not involve justificatory use of comparability, which is a positive asset of the ETC's practice.

This positive impression is confirmed by the advice issued by the ETC in 2001 on the implementation of the RED, which reveals that this body has a good grasp of the appropriate function of the comparability test. In its advice the ETC rejected an explicit reference to a comparison and comparability test in the definition of direct discrimination as this would potentially lower the level of protection offered by the GETA. According to the ETC, the insertion of a

[159] Article 4(6) of the Belgian new ARA follows the wording of the RED: "[...] than another person in a comparable situation has been, is, or would be treated." Article 3(2) of the EETA contains the phrase: "[...] than another person has been treated, is treated or would be treated in a similar situation." Article 8 HETA frames the comparative aspect as follows: "than another person or group in a comparable situation." Moreover, since the amendments of 2007, the definition of segregation in Article 10(2) contains an express reference to a comparative exercise, speaking of "other individuals or groups of individuals in a similar situation."

[160] Opinion 2007-126 ETC, para. 3.9.

[161] Opinion 2007-156 ETC, para. 3.8-9.

comparability test would open the door for justification possibilities for direct discrimination other than those expressly mentioned in the GETA.[162] This attitude of the ETC shows that it rejects the justificatory use of the comparison and the comparability test, which is fortunate, as the new definition of direct discrimination as proposed in the 2009 draft Amendment Act does refer to comparability.

In Belgium, there is no consistent practice of courts with regard to the comparative element of direct discrimination. It is interesting to note that the new Belgian ARA itself gives guidance as to how the comparability test is to be used. Article 30(2)(2) describes the application of the comparability test as a way of *proving* direct discrimination, which indicates that comparability should only be used to establish causation. This provision is accordingly explained by scholars as requiring an elimination exercise, according to which all factors of difference between persons are examined in order to determine whether they could reasonably account for a difference in treatment, and whether the protected characteristic is in reality the reason why persons were treated differently.[163]

In Hungary, the AET has on a number of occasions expressly applied the comparative element of direct discrimination. For instance, in a sexual orientation case, the AET compared the treatment of the applicant by immigration services with the treatment of other persons who had applied for the same kind of permit in the same period. On the basis of this comparison, it concluded that the applicant had been treated in the same way and on the basis of the same criteria as everyone else, and it therefore dismissed the complaint.[164] In a similar way, the AET dismissed the complaint of a Croatian man who claimed that he had been dismissed on account of his nationality because it turned out that a Hungarian employee had been dismissed for exactly the same reason.[165] These decisions show an appropriate use of the comparison, and do not reveal a justificatory use of comparability.

There is, however, one disconcerting decision of the AET in which it used comparability in a justificatory way. The case involved a complaint about a measure that denied a food allowance for persons on leave for a longer period. Since this tended to disadvantage women on maternity leave, it was claimed to be discriminatory on grounds of sex. This would appear to be a classic claim of indirect discrimination, since the measure itself did not distinguish between the sexes, but disproportionately affected women.[166] The AET, however, framed the facts in such a way so as to make it a case of direct discrimination,

[162] See Advice 2001/3, at 4 on the implementation of the RED, and Advice 2001/1, at 2 on the proposal for the recast directive.
[163] Bayart & Deiteren (2008), at 192.
[164] Case EBH/278/2007, as summarily described on the website of the AET, at http://www.egyenlobanasmod.hu/index.php?g=cases.htm (accessed July 2009).
[165] Case EBH/46/2007, also to be found on the website of the AET. See n. 637.
[166] See sections 4.2.1 and 5.2.2.

and it did so by making use of comparability. It decided that the women on leave had to be compared with other persons on leave for a longer period, thus implicitly saying that only the latter persons were comparable with the women. Unsurprisingly the comparison revealed no disadvantage based on sex, because all the persons compared were disadvantaged in the same way.[167] This comes down to a justificatory use of the comparison, since by drawing the comparison in this particular way, the ETC implicitly said that differentiation between workers not on leave and workers on leave is permissible. It thus compared between workers on leave for maternity and workers on leave for another reason, apparently because it considered that a difference in treatment between these two groups would not be appropriate. Clearly it is to be hoped that neither the AET nor the Hungarian courts will continue along this route.

In Estonia the lack of relevant jurisprudence makes it impossible to determine how the comparative element is and/or will be approached.

4.6.5.2. Hypothetical comparator

The hypothetical comparator has been inserted in all national laws except the Dutch GETA. In Belgium, the hypothetical comparator only appeared in the 2008 anti-discrimination laws, amongst which the new ARA. In Hungary, the hypothetical comparator was effectuated by the 2007 amendments to the HETA. Thus, the definition of Article 8 HETA now refers to "[a]ll dispositions as a result of which a person or a group is treated or *would be* treated less favourably than another person or group in a comparable situation" (italics added, MB). This adaptation was clumsy, since the formulation now rather points to potential discrimination ("I am not yet discriminated against, but I can/will be in the future") than to the possibility to use a hypothetical comparator ("someone else would have been treated differently from me"). Still, a favourable interpretation would permit using a hypothetical comparator, since this was the obvious intention of the phrase.

Article 3(2) of the Estonian EETA employs 'would be treated' language for direct discrimination, which was previously also part of the definition of direct discrimination in Article 10 ECA.

The lack of an explicit reference to the hypothetical comparator in the Dutch GETA is not a serious deficiency, since the ETC has in its practice allowed for the use of a hypothetical comparator, so that it clearly complies with the RED in this respect.[168] The ETC's practice will be codified by the 2009 Amendment Act, which provides for a hypothetical comparator in the new definition of direct distinction ('is, has been, or would be treated').

[167] See for a description of this case *Annual Report 2006*, AET 2006, and Demeter (2006), at 63.

[168] ETC Advice No. 2008/02, at 4-5. Nevertheless, the European Commission has criticised the GETA for the lack of an explicit reference to the hypothetical comparator in its Reasoned Opinion, No. 2006/2444, C(2008)0115, at 3.

4.7. Justification possibilities for a prima facie case of direct discrimination

4.7.1. Closed v. open system of justification

The influence of pre-existing constitutional equality provisions is particularly visible with regard to the manner in which the Member States have approached the justification system for direct discrimination. Three out of four Member States initially opted for an open system of justification, in line with their Constitutional equality frameworks. However, pressure from within and outside the national contexts finally led to the adoption of closed systems, in accordance with the RED. In these Member States the RED has therefore overturned the traditional approach to discrimination.

In Belgium, the Belgian legislator inserted an open system of justification into the ADA of 2003 for all discrimination grounds, including racial and ethnic origin. This move was heavily criticised by scholars, and was reversed at the occasion of the second implementation phase.[169] The new ARA now applies a closed system of justification for racial grounds, as Article 7(1) makes clear. According to this article, direct distinctions on the basis of one of these grounds can only be justified in accordance with one of the justification possibilities provided by Articles 8, 10 and 11 of the new ARA. Article 8 permits the use of a racial ground as a GDOR; Article 10 contains the positive action provision and Article 11 excludes scrutiny of legislative provisions. The commitment to a closed system that was spurred by the RED has furthermore produced positive spillover effects, since it induced the legislator to apply the closed system also for racial discrimination outside the material scope of the RED.[170]

The Estonian framework provided for a 'mixed' system of justification for quite some time, since the different instruments that were considered to implement the RED before the adoption of the EETA applied different systems of justification. The ECA maintained a fully closed system, in that it did not allow for any justifications of direct racial discrimination, not even for race as a GDOR.[171] At the same time, the Constitutional equality provision

[169] Criticism as regards the open system of justification has been expressed by Burri & Dorssemont (2005), at 552, 556 and 566; De Prins et al (2005), at 482; Foubert (2004), at 29-30; Van Drooghenbroeck (2004), at 145; Laurent (2003), at 622; De Schutter (2003), at 849.

[170] See the *Explanatory Memorandum to the Draft law amending the law of 30 July 1981 that penalises certain acts motivated by racism and xenophobia*, Doc 51. 2720/001, at 23.

[171] Article 101 of the ECA allowed for a number of justification possibilities, of which one is relevant for racial discrimination, and even then only for indirect discrimination: the possibility to make a distinction based on the level of language proficiency if this is an essential and determinative professional requirement arising from the nature of the professional activity or related conditions (section 101(4) ECA).

provided for an open system of justification.[172] This open-ended justification possibility was obviously not in line with the RED, and the introduction of a closed system of justification by the EETA in 2008 was therefore a clear improvement.

However, the system of the EETA is still overly permissive, since it not only permits positive action and the use of race as a GDOR,[173] but also the application of measures that are necessary for guaranteeing public order and security, the prevention of crime, the protection of health or the rights or freedom of other people, if they are in accordance with the law, pursue a legitimate aim and are proportionate.[174] This justification possibility is incompatible with the strict justification system of the RED. A possible remedy would be to interpret the article in line with the RED, which means that Estonian bodies and courts should only allow for using race as a GDOR or for positive action. It remains to be seen whether this approach will indeed be taken. It is at least a positive sign that the Explanatory Memorandum to the EETA stresses that the RED does not allow for any other justifications for direct racial discrimination than the GDOR and positive action, and thus appears to recognise that no additional justifications are permitted.[175]

Similarly to the Belgian and Estonian frameworks, the Hungarian framework only recently opted for the closed system of justification. Until the 2007 amendments, the HETA permitted all direct differences in treatment that were "found by objective consideration to have a reasonable explanation directly related to the relevant relationship".[176] The AET applied this provision in conformity with the RED, allowing only for the justification possibilities of the GDOR and positive action.[177] Nevertheless, in line with criticism expressed by legal scholars, the legislator decided to mend this shortcoming and introduced a closed system of justification for racial grounds at the occasion of the 2007 amendments. The newly inserted section (3) of Article 7 provides that the justification possibility contained therein does not apply to cases of direct discrimination and segregation based on racial grounds. Thus,

[172] See decision of the Constitutional Chamber of the Supreme Court, 3-4-1-2-02, 3 April 2002, para. 17; decision of the Constitutional Chamber of the Supreme Court, 3-4-1-33-05, 20 March 2006, para. 13, which shows that the Constitutional equality provision is interpreted by the CCSC as permitting all distinctions that are not 'arbitrary', which is taken to mean that they should pursue a legitimate aim and fulfill the proportionality requirement.

[173] Article 6 of the EETA provides for the possibility of positive action, see section 7.5. Article 10 (1) EETA contains the GDOR exception, which is discussed in the section 4.7.2.

[174] Article 9(1) EETA.

[175] *Explanatory Memorandum to Act 384 SE III on Equal Treatment,* with regard to Article 9 EETA: "[a]ccording to Directive 2000/43/EC the discrimination on the grounds of racial origin or nation (ethnic origin) cannot be justified in any other case, other than if it regards genuine and determining occupational requirements or indirect discrimination."

[176] Article 7(2) of the HETA in its pre-2007 version.

[177] EBH 314/2006.

the only justification possibilities that remain are those of positive action and the GDOR, which are discussed in the next chapter and the next subsection respectively.

The Dutch framework was unique in its application of a closed system of justification for direct racial discrimination prior to the implementation of the RED. In fact, the GETA of 1994 applied a sophisticated system of various justifications for different actors that was the result of an intensive deliberation process. At the occasion of the implementation of the RED this system was not adapted to the requirements of the RED; it was rather consolidated and expanded with a GDOR provision that followed the wording of the RED.[178] Thus, the GETA currently provides for a number of justification options for direct racial discrimination which, in addition to positive action and the GDOR,[179] include the following:

- a possibility in the field of employment and education for organisations with a religious or philosophical/ideological foundation to set requirements that are necessary for the realisation of their religion/philosophy/ideology, as long as this requirement does not come down to a distinction on the sole grounds of race and other protected grounds (Articles 5(2), 6a(2) and 7(2) GETA). This justification is commonly known as the 'sole grounds construction'

- a possibility to set requirements that can reasonably be imposed in the context of an employment relationship in view of the private nature of the relationship (Article 5(3) GETA)

- a possibility to set requirements related to political conviction that can reasonably be imposed with regard to functions in boards, advisory boards and positions of trust (Article 5(5) GETA)

The last two possibilities have so far not been applied in practice and, if interpreted sufficiently strictly, they can probably be reconciled with the GDOR provision of the RED. After all, both allow for setting occupational requirements that are linked to the nature of the employment relationship, which is in line with the rationale underlying the GDOR. However, both

[178] See *Parliamentary proceedings on the Amendment of the General Act on Equal Treatment and certain other acts in order to implement directive 2000/43/EC and directive 2000/78/EC*, TK 2002-3 28 770, 5, at 26, in which the government emphasised the importance of the sole grounds construction. It was the result of a long and laborious discussion, and lays down a careful balance between the right to non-discrimination and other fundamental rights and freedoms. Therefore, the government was determined to maintain this justification possibility in the GETA.

[179] Positive action is regulated in Article 2(3) GETA; the GDOR is regulated in Article 2(4) GETA.

provisions only require the requirement to be reasonable, whereas the GDOR provision in the RED requires it to be genuine, determining, appropriate and necessary, which is clearly stricter. Conformity with the RED would require the interpretation of 'reasonable' along the lines of this stricter test. This was recognised by the Dutch government at the occasion of the second evaluation of the GETA, where it announced an amendment of the reasonableness standard so as to incorporate the requirements of legitimacy and proportionality. At the same time the government emphasised that the reasonableness standard was already being interpreted in line with European law.[180]

The sole grounds construction has been applied quite a number of times already, albeit only once with regard to racial discrimination. The 'sole grounds' aspect of this justification has led some to conclude that it only applies to indirect discrimination cases: according to their reasoning, direct discrimination is a distinction on the sole ground of one of the protected grounds, and therefore is never permitted.[181] Still, if one considers that direct discrimination is present not only if the protected ground is the only reason for the difference in treatment, but also if it is *one of the reasons*, one should realise that the sole grounds justification can be relevant for cases of direct discrimination. Indeed, the one case on racial discrimination in which this justification was used concerned direct discrimination. In the particular case, a Jewish institution provided courses on the Jewish religion uniquely for Jewish persons. Non-Jewish persons could only participate if they were accompanied by a Jewish partner. According to the ETC, this amounted to a direct distinction based on race, which was nonetheless justified. It found that the requirement could be considered to be necessary in view of the realisation of the institution's Jewish-cultural identity, and that there was therefore no distinction on the sole ground of race.[182] The decision followed the model normally used by the ETC for 'sole grounds' construction cases, which entails examination of the following sub-questions: 1) does the institution have a real interest in setting the requirement; 2) is the requirement based on a consistent and purposeful policy; 3) is the requirement necessary in view of the purpose of the institution; and 4) is the distinction not solely based on one of the protected grounds.[183]

180 *Letter of the government with regard to the third evaluation of the GETA*, TK 2008-9, 5, at 5.

181 Heringa (1991), at 17; Mulder (1991), at 61.

182 Opinion 2002-157 ETC, para. 6.5-11.

183 Gerards & Heringa (2003), at 104-107; Monster et al (1999), at 175. Also see for instance Opinion 2007-61 ETC, para. 3.10; Opinion 2007-93 ETC, para. 3.8; Opinion 2007-96 ETC, para. 3.7.

This model could be fairly easily interpreted in line with the requirements of the GDOR of the RED, and the sole grounds justification in the field of employment is in that respect not very problematic.[184] In contrast, the 'sole grounds' construction in the field of education is less easily brought into conformity with the RED. Perhaps the positive action provision of Article 5 RED, in combination with Recital 17, which allows for the maintenance of identity-based institutions for racial and ethnic minorities, could be interpreted so as to permit this justification in this field. Moreover, it was argued by the Dutch government that the 'sole grounds' construction in education was legitimate in view of the Dutch State's exclusive competence in the field of education. To this end it invoked the 'within the limits of the powers conferred upon the Community' clause of Article 3(1) RED. As was mentioned in section 3.2.1, the ECJ so far has not been willing to further delineate the scope of equality law on the basis of this clause, so that it is doubtful that the Dutch government's argument will be accepted. In any case, it seems fair to preliminarily conclude that the sole grounds justification in education is going beyond what is permitted by the closed justification system of the RED.[185] The problem has been recognised by the Dutch government, which, at the occasion of the second evaluation of the GETA, announced that the Council of State would render an advice on the question whether the 'sole grounds' construction was compatible with European law.[186] This advice has not yet been made public, but it is clear that the Council recommends the abolishment of the 'sole grounds' construction in the GETA. It remains to be seen how the Dutch government will respond to this suggestion.[187]

Another problematic feature of the Dutch framework is the extra-textual justification possibility that has been developed by the ETC, in accordance with the normal jurisprudential rule in the Dutch legal system that courts can set aside legal provisions on grounds of reasonability and equity. Even though the legislator repeatedly refused to insert such a justification possibility

[184] Sewandono (2001), at 226. The European Commission considers the lack of a legitimate aim and proportionality requirement to be irreparable. See its reasoned opinion as regards the compliance of The Netherlands with the FD, 2006/2444, C(2008)0115, 31 January 2008, at 5-6. The ETC agrees with the Commission in this regard, see Advisory Opinion 2008-02 ETC, at 9-10. In the opinion of this author, however, the legitimate aim and proportionality requirements can be read into the sole grounds justification test. Moreover, the strictness with which the ETC usually applies this justification makes it difficult to see how it would allow for differences in treatment that would not simultaneously be allowed for by the GDOR.

[185] Sewandono (2001), at 226.

[186] *Letter of the government with regard to the third evaluation of the GETA*, TK 2008-9, 28 481, 5, at 2.

[187] See the following article in the Dutch newspaper NRC Handelsblad, *Council of State: Christian school may refuse gay teacher*, 9 June 2009, at http://www.nrc.nl/binnenland/article2265394.ece/Raad_christelijke_school_mag_homo_voor_de_klas_weren (accessed July 2009).

in the GETA,[188] the ETC proceeded to set in place such a possibility in its quasi-jurisprudence in 2006.[189] This means that the ETC will not conclude that a direct distinction has taken place if such a qualification would lead to consequences that are unacceptable in terms of reasonability and equity. So far, it has twice applied this test in practice, and in only one case it concluded that the distinction was indeed justified from the viewpoint of reasonability and equity. In the particular case the ETC ruled that it was justified to offer vaccination against hepatitis at a lower rate for homosexuals, because the latter group had an increased risk of attracting hepatitis and was difficult to reach.[190] The other case also involved a vaccination programme, which offered vaccinations at a reduced rate for Turkish and Moroccan children, who had an increased risk of attracting hepatitis on holiday in their countries of origin. In view of the fact that other public health institutions did not apply the same programme, and offered reduced rates for other persons as well, the ETC decided that this particular direct distinction did not fulfil the strict test of being necessary in terms of reasonability and equity. The ETC furthermore emphasised that it would only apply the extra-textual justification if there was no other way of achieving a particular legitimate aim than by way of making a direct distinction.[191] Despite this strict approach, the extra-textual justification developed by the ETC crosses the line. As was explained in section 4.4.1 the ECJ has so far refused to allow for any extra-textual justification possibilities in the field of sex equality law, and it is to be expected that it will take the same stance with regard to the RED.

4.7.2. Genuine and determining occupational requirement (GDOR)

All four Member States have inserted GDOR-like provisions in their national anti-discrimination laws, not all of which are fully in line with the RED.

The Belgian framework so far shows the best record of implementation, theoretically at least, since there is no relevant practice yet. Article 8(2) of the new ARA defines the GDOR as a characteristic related to one of the protected grounds that is:

[188] See the *Letter of the government with regard to the first evaluation of the GETA*, TK 2001-2, 28 481, no. 1,15, in which the government emphasised the importance of maintaining the closed system of justification for direct discrimination in the GETA.

[189] The ETC announced the adoption of such a justification possibility in its position paper on the second five-yearly evaluation of the GETA, *Het verschil gemaakt. Evaluatie AWGB en werkzaamheden CGB 1999-2004*, Commissie Gelijke Behandeling 2005, at 35-37. In Opinion 2006-20 ETC the justification possibility was applied in practice for the first time.

[190] Opinion 2006-20 ETC, para. 5.10-5.14.

[191] Opinion 2006-55 ETC, para. 4.8-4.10.

> 1) genuine and determining in view of the nature of the particular specific professional activities, or the context in which these are carried out; 2) relies on a legitimate aim and 3) is proportionate to this aim.

The starting point for the application of the GDOR is that each case should be examined on its own merits by the Belgian courts, as is stipulated by Article 8(3). In addition, Article 8(4) provides for the possibility of a list containing examples of situations in which the GDOR applies to be drawn up by the government. So far, such a list has not been adopted, which means that the concept of the GDOR will be filled in casuistically. Even though no cases so far have presented themselves, some elements of the GDOR have already been filled in by scholars and the drafters of the new ARA. Thus it has been submitted that the first element of the GDOR, the 'genuine and determining' aspect not so much adds additional requirements, but rather qualifies the subsequent tests of a legitimate aim and proportionality, in that they should be applied with stricter scrutiny.[192] As was explained in section 4.4.2.2 this indeed seems to be the most sensible reading of the 'genuine and determining' phrase.

As regards the legitimate aim requirement, it is generally recognised in the Belgian context that the aim of the GDOR must not be discriminatory or related to discriminatory preferences of others, such as customers.[193] At the very least, the aim should be authentic, as in truly important for the particular actor.[194] The Explanatory Memorandum to the new ARA mentions the following examples of aims that are considered to be legitimate: respect for privacy and other fundamental rights, feelings of patients, public security and maintaining military force.[195] This list reveals an expansive notion of what can be considered a legitimate aim, but in view of the fact that strict scrutiny applies, it is expected that Belgian courts will look critically at the aims forwarded.

The test of proportionality is carried out along the lines of the appropriateness, necessity and proportionality stricto sensu requirements. Here again, it is expected that strict scrutiny will be applied. Indeed, the Explanatory Memorandum stresses that the GDOR must be *strictly* necessary in view of the aim pursued; mere usefulness or appropriateness is therefore not enough.[196]

This rather strict approach to the GDOR in the Belgian framework can be positively evaluated. Especially the emphasis on strict scrutiny and on separate

[192] Sottiaux (2008), at 242-243. Compare *T.S.T. v. F.W.A.G.*, Tongeren Labour Court, Case no 199/2005, 6 March 2007, in which the Labour Court stressed the need to interpret the GDOR strictly.

[193] Sottiaux (2008), at 237; Bayart & Bosmans (2008), at 575.

[194] Sottiaux (2008), at 238.

[195] *Explanatory Memorandum to the Draft law amending the law of 30 July 1981 that penalises certain acts motivated by racism and xenophobia*, Doc 51. 2720/001, at 48-49.

[196] Sottiaux (2008), at 243.

examination of each particular case is promising. In the end, however, all depends on the manner in which the final balancing act is carried out, and lack of practical application makes it impossible to assess the quality of the Belgian approach in this regard.

The same is true for the Estonian framework, which theoretically adheres to the requirements of the RED. In Estonia, an explicit GDOR justification possibility exists only since recently, since the ECA did not permit any justifications of direct racial discrimination. This situation changed with the entry into force of Article 10(1) EETA, which provides that less favourable treatment based on a racial ground is:

> not deemed to be discrimination, if that feature is an important and determining occupational requirement, which results from the nature of the occupational activity or the conditions related to it and the purpose of the requirement is legitimate and the requirement proportionate.

With a few minor differences, which are probably due to translation issues rather than to deliberate choices of the drafters, this provision follows the language of Article 4 RED. It can be expected that the proportionality test mentioned in this provision will be applied in accordance with the CCSC's practice on the Constitutional equality provision, which entails the three-tiered tests of suitability, necessity and proportionality stricto sensu.[197] Since there is no case law and the Explanatory Memorandum does not exemplify the GDOR, the conclusion should be that in theory, the GDOR as regulated in the EETA is in conformity with the RED.

In contrast with the – at least theoretical – compliance of the Belgian and Estonian frameworks with the RED, the Hungarian framework does not live up to the strict requirements of Article 4 RED, particularly as regards the application of the GDOR by the AET. The GDOR in the HETA is regulated in Article 22, which is situated in the part of the act that specifies the anti-discrimination norms for particular fields of application, including employment. This article provides that:

> [t]he principle of equal treatment shall not be considered violated if the discrimination is proportional, justified by the characteristics or nature of the work and is based on all relevant and legitimate terms and conditions considered during the hiring.

This particular wording is less strict than Article 4 RED. The last phrase, "is based on all relevant and legitimate terms and conditions during the hiring", does not seem to add much to the requirement that the difference in treatment must be justified by the characteristics or nature of the work; it would therefore seem that Article 22(1)(a) HETA only requires a legitimate aim (from the viewpoint of the work to be carried out) and a proportionate relationship. The lack of 'genuine' and 'determining'-like criteria is not

[197] Supreme Court, 17 March 2003, 3-1-3-10-02, para. 30.

necessarily problematic, since the meaning of these criteria anyway appears to lie not so much in their substantive contribution, but rather in their impact on the level of scrutiny. Thus, if the AET and Hungarian courts apply Article 22(1)(a) HETA sufficiently strictly, it would most likely be in conformity with the RED. The provision has already been applied a few times by the AET, but the rather crude nature of the cases, involving so far only fairly obviously unjustified differences in treatment, means that the application of the GDOR does not involve detailed reasoning. It is therefore unclear whether the AET indeed opts for strict scrutiny when applying this provision.

What does become clear, however, is that this body lacks a clear and consistent approach. As was mentioned before, a number of decisions show that the GDOR is perceived as a kind of open justification possibility, not necessarily pertaining to a protected ground being used as a job requirement, but rather to any reason forwarded for a difference in treatment. For instance, in a case in which a Roma woman complained of discriminatory dismissal, the AET found that there was no causal link between the difference in treatment and the protected ground, since the dismissal was based on a legitimate reason and was proportionate. Even though it did not mention the GDOR explicitly in this part of its reasoning, it had listed the GDOR provision at the beginning of its decision as one of the relevant provisions.[198] This raises the impression that it was the GDOR that was applied when the AET looked at the legitimacy of the aim and the proportionality of the dismissal, which was confirmed in an interview conducted for this study.[199] It is to be hoped that the AET will abandon this practice in the future and limit itself to using the GDOR as it is intended: to allow in very limited circumstances for the use of a protected ground as an essential job requirement.

The Dutch framework finally shows a mixed record. Since the implementation of the RED, the Dutch GETA provides for two GDOR's, one of which is in fact a GDR, in the sense that it does not refer to an *occupational* requirement, but applies outside the sphere of employment. Article 2(4) GETA reads as follows:

> The prohibition on discrimination on the grounds of race contained in this Act does not apply: a) in cases in which a person's racial appearance is a genuine and determining requirement, provided that the aim is legitimate and provided that the requirement is proportionate to that aim; b) if the discrimination concerns a person's racial appearance and constitutes, by reason of the nature of the particular occupational activity in question or of the context in which it is carried out, a genuine and determining occupational requirement, provided that the aim is legitimate and the requirement is proportionate to that aim.

198 EBH/476/2008.

199 For reasons of privacy the particular source is not revealed here. For another example, see EBH/142/3/2007, which concerned a demotion based on motherhood. In a similar way as the aforementioned case, the AET applied the GDOR article to establish the causal link between the disadvantage and the protected characteristic.

The b) part of the provision was inserted in order to implement the RED. The government considered it desirable to maintain the a) part, even though this was not permitted by the RED, because in a very limited number of cases race was considered to constitute a relevant criterion outside the sphere of employment.[200]

As regards the substance of the GDOR of Article 2(4) GETA, this provision follows the wording of Article 4 RED, except for the fact that it only mentions racial *appearance*. In this regard, the Dutch GDOR is more strictly regulated than Article 4 RED, which allows for other aspects of racial and ethnic origin than physiological characteristics to constitute GDOR's. Moreover, a Royal Decree lays down an exhaustive list of situations in which racial appearance as a requirement is deemed permissible, which further limits the possibilities of successfully invoking the GDOR provisions in the Dutch context. According to this decree, racial appearance can be a relevant criterion for the following activities:

- the performance of a particular role that requires the actor, dancer or artist to be of a particular racial origin
- modelling or posing, to the extent that it is reasonable to apply appearance-related requirements
- participation in beauty contests insofar as racially determined traits are relevant in view of the aim of the contest
- the provision of services that can only be provided to persons with particular outward characteristics[201]

The ETC has made clear that it will strictly adhere to this decree,[202] and it is thus not surprising that very few cases have come up with regard to race as a GDOR, none of which resulted in a favourable ruling for the author of the requirement.[203] Especially the question whether it is justifiable to require a particular racial or ethnic origin for a job that entails working with particular racial or ethnic groups has been answered in the negative.[204] This is remarkable in view of the fact that the European Commission has expressly mentioned

---

[200] *Advice and Report on the Amendment of the General Act on Equal Treatment and certain other acts in order to implement directive 2000/43/EG and directive 2000/78/EG*, TK 2002-3, 28 770, A.

[201] Article 2 of the Decision on Equal Treatment, 18 August 1994, Stb. 657.

[202] Opinion 1997-99 ETC, para. 4.8.

[203] Up to 31 December 2008, only seven cases concerning race as a GDOR have come before the ETC.

[204] Opinions 2008-87 ETC, para. 3.13; 2006-61 ETC, para. 3.22.

this type of requirement as being permitted by the GDOR of the RED. The ETC's approach is therefore stricter than the RED and in this respect offers a higher level of protection.

Given the limited amount of relevant practice, it is difficult to assess the manner in which the various criteria listed in Article 2(4) GETA are applied. In the field of sex equality, the ETC has developed a model of review for applying the justification possibility of sex as a GDOR, which is probably also relevant for racial grounds. According to this test, the ETC will assess: 1) on the basis of up-to-date and objective data whether the activities can only be performed by a member of a particular sex; 2) whether it is possible to adjust the activities in such a way that they need not necessarily be performed by the members of a particular sex.[205] This model seems sufficiently strict so as to ensure that the GDOR will not be used lightly, but it lacks a proportionality stricto sensu test. As was mentioned before, the balancing act implied by proportionality stricto sensu is an essential element for ensuring that the interests of minority group members are taken into account, and this test is therefore preferably included in the model of review for Article 2(4) GETA.

4.8. Direct discrimination and positive duties

There is some divergence as regards the degree to which Member States have allowed for positive duties in the framework of direct discrimination. In Belgium and Estonia there is a mere theoretical possibility of such duties being adopted in the future, whereas the Hungarian and Dutch frameworks have clearly embraced the connection between direct discrimination and positive duties.

In Belgium, the Arbitration Court has recognised that the principle of equal treatment entails the rule that unequal cases should be treated unequally, which can in the future be developed into the recognition of certain positive duties for particular groups. However, it is doubtful that, should this happen, it will be done in the framework of the concept of direct discrimination. It is generally not expected that Belgian courts will infer positive duties from the prohibition of direct discrimination as contained in the new ARA.[206] It has been submitted that positive duties are to a limited extent possible, under the guise of the order of cessation of discriminatory behaviour, a remedy provided for in Article 18 of the ARA.[207] This remedy could in some cases amount to

[205] Opinions 2006-61 ETC, para. 3.14; 2005-08, para. 4.9.

[206] Bayart & Deiteren (2008), at 186-188. See in general Ambrus (2010) on the order of cessation.

[207] Taelman (2004), at 211. Also see Labour Court Brussels, Case no. KG-284, 6 April 2007.

the order to do something, rather than to stop doing something. However, it is generally expected that this duty cannot extend very far.[208] Indeed, the word 'cessation' rather points to a negative action than to a positive one.

In Estonia the EETA contains positive duties for employers, educational institutions and ministries.[209] These are not, however, conceptually linked to direct discrimination, but are separately regulated under the heading "The application and promotion of the principle of equal treatment". Similarly to its Belgian counterpart, the CCSC has recognised the rule that unequal cases must be treated unequally, and has even explicitly referred to substantive equality in that regard.[210] This has opened up the door for the recognition of positive duties in the future.

In contrast with the Belgian and Estonian frameworks, the Hungarian HETA clearly provides for positive duties to be inferred from direct discrimination, by making clear that direct discrimination can be constituted by omissions. So far, this possibility has mainly been used in the context of educational segregation. The duty to desegregate in the field of education has been imposed a number of times already. For instance, the Debrecen Appeals Court ruled that the maintenance of a situation of segregation could amount to a violation of the principle of equal treatment, regardless of the fact that the situation was not actively brought about by the respondent.[211] Similarly, the AET stated in a 2007 case: "[n]ot only can an authority actively segregate students, but those who tolerate or help the maintenance of existing segregation also violate the principle of equal treatment". It subsequently ordered the elimination of the segregation by the start of the next academic year.[212] Furthermore, the AET deals consistently with reasonable accommodation claims of disabled persons in the framework of direct discrimination,[213] which means that this concept could also be used more broadly for accommodation duties of racial or ethnic groups. So far, such a ruling has not yet been adopted.

In a similar way to its Hungarian counterpart, the Dutch ETC has recognised extensive positive duties in the framework of direct discrimination, which mostly come down to duties of ending or preventing direct discrimination.

---

208 Closset-Marchal & Van Drooghenbroeck (2008), at 372.

209 Articles 12, 13 and 14 EETA. See also sections 6.4.3 and 7.7.1.

210 Constitutional Chamber of the Supreme Court, 3-4-1-2-02, 3 April 2002, paras. 16 and 17; Constitutional Chamber of the Supreme Court, 3-1-3-10-02, 17 March 2003, para. 36.

211 Debrecen Court of Appeal, Pf.I.20.683/2005/7, 9 June 2006.

212 EBH/23/2007.

213 See for instance EBH/418/ /2007, in which a railway company was said to directly discriminate on the basis of disability because of the very limited accessibility of trains for disabled persons and the insufficient measures taken by the company in this regard. In case EBH/29/27/2006, two store owners were considered to directly discriminate on the basis of disability by not providing for a possibility for disabled persons to get to the second floor of a building. See also more generally *Position Paper of the Advisory Body on the obligation of providing accessibility, Position no. 10.007/3/2006. TT.*

Thus, Dutch employers have a duty to ensure a discrimination-free working environment, which extends not only to behaviour of co-workers, but also of third parties.[214] Moreover, employers have a procedural duty to set in place an effective complaint mechanism for discrimination on the work floor.[215] Similarly, landlords have the duty to protect their tenants against discrimination by fellow tenants[216] and schools have to protect their students.[217]

It may be clear that the manner in which positive duties are set up in the Hungarian and Dutch frameworks is not in line with the conceptually preferable approach that was outlined in section 4.2. At the same time the development of these duties has greatly enhanced the level of protection offered to racial and ethnic minorities by the HETA and GETA respectively. Moreover, in both frameworks the positive duties are not arrived at by way of applying the comparability test in a justificatory way, which would have opened the door for extra-textual justification possibilities. The approach taken by the ETC and its Hungarian counterparts is in this sense perhaps preferable over a conceptually flawless approach that does not entail any positive obligations at all.

As for the question whether a finding of direct discrimination should result in a duty to level-up, it is remarkable that there is no clear approach discernable in any of the four Member States.

Belgian courts are expected by scholars to opt for levelling-up, which would mean the imposition of a limited positive duty for discriminators.[218] Still, an unambiguous choice for levelling-up has yet to be made. The Tongeren Labour Court in 2007 discussed the matter in the theoretical section of its judgment, with no clear preference for either option.[219] Belgian scholars have pointed out that it is not possible to force private persons to enter into a contract with victims of discrimination as a remedy, since this would go against the fundamental freedom of contract.[220] Levelling-up duties will therefore probably not go so far as imposing the creation of a contractual relationship.

---

214 See for instance Opinion 2004-77 ETC, in which the ETC ruled that an employer had the duty to protect his employees against discrimination by third parties. See also Gerards (2004), at 630-631.

215 Opinion 2007-193 ETC, para. 3.23, in which the procedural duty of the employer is set out in more detail. Dutch courts have also recognised that employers have a duty of care vis-à-vis their employees, as part of their general duty of care vis-à-vis their employees. See for instance Amsterdam Court, 29 May 2008, LJN: BD8720, para. 4.9.

216 Opinion 2005-90 ETC, in which a duty was imposed on a caravan park owner to prevent discrimination from occurring between park visitors; Opinion 2003-132 ETC, in which a duty to provide for a discrimination-free living environment was imposed on a landlord.

217 Opinion 2005-91 ETC.

218 Germain & Eyben (2008), at 347.

219 *T.S.T. v. F.W.A.G., Tongeren Labour Court*, Case no. 199/2005, 6 March 2007, at 23.

220 Closset-Marchal & Van Drooghenbroeck (2008), at 372.

The Hungarian AET and the Dutch ETC have few to none sanction possibilities, which means that both are not in the position to order the perpetrator of direct discrimination to level-up the situation of the victims to that of other persons. The AET can only order that discrimination should end, but cannot give any concrete guidelines as to how to do this. The Dutch ETC does not have any competence to order any sanctions, which means that it limits itself to establishing whether discrimination has taken place. Case law of Dutch courts does not reveal a clear approach either in this respect.

In Estonia the lack of any relevant case law makes it impossible to know which approach will be taken by Estonian courts.

4.9. Summary and conclusion

This chapter was based on the premise that the contribution of the prohibition of direct discrimination to the overall level of minority protection should ideally work at two separate levels. First of all, the prohibition should target to the greatest extent possible and in the most effective way the real-life experiences of discrimination felt by minority group members. Secondly, the prohibition should be designed and applied in the conceptually most appropriate way, which, by enhancing the overall quality and robustness of the anti-discrimination framework, indirectly advances the cause of minority protection. Both assumptions came back in different guises in the theoretical framework, in which it was examined how the direct discrimination regime of the RED should preferably be interpreted. The theoretical framework made clear that the RED contains the necessary ingredients for an inclusive, effective and conceptually appropriate approach to the most serious form of discrimination experienced by minority group members: discrimination that is directly linked to their group membership.

Minimum baseline of protection

The inquiry could only determine to a limited extent the minimum baseline of protection set in place by the RED, as many obscurities still remain about the concept of direct discrimination. One relatively clear minimum condition concerns the closed system of justification for direct discrimination. It is more or less certain that Member States cannot allow for any other justification possibilities than the genuine determining occupational requirement (GDOR) of Article 4 RED and positive action of Article 5 RED.

In the case study part of this chapter it was found that this minimum condition was complied with by only two Member States, namely Belgium and Hungary. Estonia and the Netherlands have set in place justification possibilities that are not in line with the closed system of justification for direct discrimination of the RED. The Estonian EETA grants public actors an open justification possibility with regard to measures that are necessary in order to achieve certain public aims. In the Netherlands, the GETA contains a number of justifications that existed previously to the implementation of the RED, which the Dutch legislator did not want to abolish. In addition, the ETC has developed an extra-textual justification possibility for highly exceptional cases, in line with Dutch courts' practice in general civil law. Even if these additional justifications were to be interpreted in conformity with the RED, they would still unnecessarily obscure the fairly straightforward justification system of the RED.

It is remarkable that the lack of compliance with the RED in this respect was even greater in the initial stages of implementation, as the case study revealed. The Belgian, Estonian and Hungarian frameworks initially followed the traditional constitutional approach of an open system of justification for direct discrimination. Over time amendments were introduced in these Member States in order to introduce closed systems of justification for direct racial discrimination.

The case study furthermore revealed that, despite the fact that the national frameworks have not completely remained within the limits of the justification system of the RED, the GDOR provision in itself is complied with to a considerable extent. Thus, with the exception of the Hungarian HETA, the national laws approach this justification sufficiently strictly. The Belgian and Dutch frameworks provide a particularly high level of protection; in both frameworks strict scrutiny applies for the application of the GDOR. Moreover, the Dutch government has laid down an exhaustive list of situations in which the GDOR can be applied, which de facto greatly limits the playing field created by this justification possibility. In contrast, it was found that the Hungarian AET has adopted the disconcerting habit of applying the GDOR as if it constitutes an open justification possibility for employers accused of direct discrimination. It is expected that this practice is on its way out, however.

The minimum baseline that can be deduced from the theoretical framework furthermore requires the provision for a hypothetical comparator, which is captured in the words 'would be' in Article2(2)(a) RED. It was explained that this component of the definition of direct discrimination facilitates proof of discrimination and extends the scope of the concept to cases in which no real-life comparators are found. It is thus very positive that all Member States have provided for a hypothetical comparator in the national frameworks. Here also a development towards greater compliance with the RED was visible, since the hypothetical comparator only appeared in the Belgian and Hungarian laws after the second and third implementation phases respectively.

Obscurities and opportunities for providing a higher level of protection

It became clear throughout this chapter that many components of the minimum baseline of protection required for direct discrimination are yet to be fleshed out.

The most fundamental controversy that was found in this regard is the delineation of the concept of direct discrimination vis-à-vis the concept of indirect discrimination of Article2(2)(b) RED. Case-law of the ECJ in the field of sex-equality law makes clear that this Court does not apply a conceptually sound approach, and that it to some extent has mixed up both concepts. As a result, the concept of direct discrimination in its current form has not as much force as it should have, and its authority is attenuated by improper use of concepts such as causality and comparability.

A similar confusion was found to exist at the level of the Member States, where the majority of bodies and/or courts struggle with the delineation of these two discrimination concepts. The Dutch ETC constitutes an exception in this respect, and generally applies both concepts correctly, which entails reserving the label of direct discrimination only for those disadvantages for which the underlying cause or motive is the protected characteristic. Dutch courts, however, tend to mix up the concepts of direct and indirect discrimination in a similar way to the ECJ and the other national courts and bodies.

The fundamental uncertainty as to the actual boundaries of the concept of direct discrimination proved to be closely connected to a number of issues at the level of the practical application of this concept. It was for instance pointed out that it is not yet clear to what extent collective manifestations of direct discrimination, which can only be detected by looking at a bundle of individual cases taken together, will be recognised as direct discrimination, since quantitative evidence is usually associated with indirect discrimination. Whereas the ECJ so far has not given any guidance in this respect, it was positive to note that there are some favourable signs of an inclusive approach to be developed in Belgium, Hungary and The Netherlands. It was furthermore interesting to note that, whereas the RED does not explicitly cover racial segregation, the Hungarian HETA provides for an express prohibition of this type of discrimination, which is highly relevant for minority groups.

Another obscurity concerning direct discrimination relates to the proper function of the comparison. It was explained that it is possible to use the comparison, and more particularly the comparability test, in a justificatory function, in addition to its normal function of establishing the direct causal link between the disadvantageous treatment and the protected characteristic. Such use of comparability unnecessarily obscures the decision-making process and risks lowering the quality of the final outcome. Unfortunately, such improper use of comparability has appeared in the sex equality jurisprudence of the ECJ a number of times. In contrast, it was found in the case study that comparability is rarely used in a justificatory way at the national level. One clear case was found in the practice of the Hungarian AET, which did not involve racial discrimination, however. As more case-law becomes available in the future, it will hopefully become clear whether the function of the comparability test is rightly appreciated by national bodies and courts. So far, only the Dutch ETC has shown a clear insight in this respect.

It was finally interesting to note that direct discrimination has been used as an instrument for imposing positive duties of care on certain actors in the Hungarian and Dutch frameworks. In Hungary, duties to end racial segregation in education have been imposed on local councils and school boards. The Dutch ETC has developed far-reaching duties of care for all principally envisaged actors, who are obliged to protect their employees, clients or students against discrimination perpetrated by others. It was explained in the theoretical framework that direct discrimination is not the most appropriate concept to develop positive duties; still it is clear that these duties have greatly enhanced the level of protection of the Dutch and Hungarian frameworks, which obviously surpasses the minimum level of protection required by the RED.

In conclusion, much of the potential of Article3(2)(a) for minority protection is not yet realised, which to a considerable extent is due to the ECJ's incoherent approach to direct discrimination. It is perhaps unsurprising that the obscurities identified at the European level re-appeared in the national frameworks, as one can perhaps not expect of relatively inexperienced national bodies and courts to have a better grasp of the concept than the ECJ.

However, the relatively high degree of non-compliance of the Member States as regards those aspects of the RED that are not obscure and thus constitute the minimum baseline of protection raises concern. This should perhaps be seen against the background of previously existing anti-discrimination regimes at the national level. The initial preference for open systems of justification in Belgium, Hungary and Estonia is for instance likely to have been inspired by the national constitutional equality regimes, which all provide for an open system of justification. Moreover, Dutch non-compliance with the justification system of the RED was clearly directly related to the wish to maintain the national anti-discrimination acquis. This reveals that previous experience with anti-discrimination law can sometimes complicate the implementation process and does not invariably enhance the quality of implementation at the national level.

On the other hand, the Dutch example also shows that extensive experience with anti-discrimination law has produced a transparent, consistent and conceptually appropriate approach to direct discrimination, which is of a higher quality than the ECJ's framework. The far-reaching positive duties that form part of the Dutch direct discrimination regime are another example of how previous experience with anti-discrimination law has produced a higher level of protection than that required by the RED. In a similar way, lack of experience is liable to produce an incoherent approach to direct discrimination, as is illustrated by the misunderstanding displayed by the Hungarian AET with regard to certain aspects of direct discrimination. In contrast, the overall sensitivity to minority issues in the Hungarian context has positively affected the level of protection offered by the HETA. This act strongly and expressly protects against racial segregation, which entails inter alia positive duties to actively end racial segregation.

The two Member States with less affinity with minority protection and/or anti-discrimination law, Belgium and Estonia, have not opted for higher levels of protection than required by the RED. Still, there are important differences between these two states. The Belgian implementation of the minimum baseline of protection is generally of a high quality, and entails inter alia more specific rules for the proof of discrimination. Estonia, to the contrary, has not even fully complied with the minimum baseline of protection, by providing for an overly broad justification possibility for direct racial discrimination.

Chapter 5

Indirect discrimination

> Indirect discrimination shall be taken to occur where an apparently neutral provision, criterion or practice would put persons of a racial or ethnic origin at a particular disadvantage compared with other persons, unless that provision, criterion or practice is objectively justified by a legitimate aim and the means of achieving that aim are appropriate and necessary *(Article 2(2)(b) RED)*

Part one: Theoretical framework

5.1. Introduction

The concept of indirect discrimination is an essential component of EC non-discrimination law, which was developed over time by the ECJ in order to make the prohibition of discrimination more effective. According to the ECJ, the broad interpretation of the general non-discrimination principle as covering indirect discrimination was "necessary to ensure the effective working of one of the fundamental principles of the Community."[1] The prohibition of discrimination is indeed not of much use if it only tackles actions that expressly make a distinction on a prohibited ground, and not the ones that lead to similar effects, although formally not making such distinction. The concept of indirect discrimination captures those measures that have particularly detrimental *effects* on protected groups, and in that way covers a wider spectrum of types of behaviour than direct discrimination, which targets only measures for which the underlying *cause or motive* is a protected characteristic.

The concept of indirect discrimination is furthermore inherently focused on groups instead of on individuals: it requires reassessment of the legitimacy

---

1 ECJ *Sotgiu v. Deutsche Bundespost*, Case 152/73, 12 February 1974, para. 11.

of measures that negatively impact on a protected group as a whole.[2] As such, indirect discrimination is tightly linked to the notion of substantive equality, because it requires consideration of the specific situation of a particular protected group.[3] The power of the concept of indirect discrimination accordingly lies in the fact that it allows for recognising the different starting points in social, economic and cultural aspects of various groups in society and requires that these differences are accounted for in decision-making processes.[4]

These strengths of the concept are at the same time its main weakness: to a far greater extent than direct discrimination, indirect discrimination triggers a complex normative debate about the make-up of society. The concept has been appraised by some as operating at the boundaries of equality law, since it involves difficult questions as regards which measures or patterns that are considered to be 'normal' in a society should nevertheless be abolished due to their detrimental effect on particular groups.[5] Courts dealing with the concept are thus often faced with contentious issues, as reflected in the inconsistent and non-transparent manner in which they tend to apply indirect discrimination.[6] Even the ECJ has not yet come to a fully structured and transparent framework, as is shown throughout this chapter, despite the fact that this court has worked with the concept for a few decades already.

Seen from this perspective, the implementation of the concept of indirect racial discrimination as introduced by the RED involves a number of complexities, which are examined in this chapter. Section 5.2 discusses the component parts of the definition of indirect discrimination. It consecutively deals with the type of behaviour constituting indirect discrimination, the disadvantage requirement, the comparative aspect and the objective justification test, of which particularly the comparative aspect and the justification test are complex matters. Section 5.3 examines the extent to which the concept of indirect discrimination can be used to develop positive duties to the benefit of protected groups.

5.2. Definition of indirect discrimination in the RED

The definition of Article 2(2)(b) RED is the product of extensive deliberation among Member States, and differs from previously existing definitions in free movement and sex equality law. The leading definition in free movement law was formulated in the *O'Flynn* judgment, in which the ECJ stated that:

---

2 Henrard (2007), at 26.

3 Henrard (2008a), at 263.

4 McCrudden (1985), at 84.

5 Craig (2007), at 42-43; Réaume (2006), at 726; Sjerps (1999), at 241.

6 Compare Prechal (2004), at 536-537, who points out that experience shows that it may take a long time before indirect discrimination is properly understood and applied.

> [u]nless objectively justified and proportionate to its aim, a provision of national law must be regarded as indirectly discriminatory if it is intrinsically liable to affect migrant workers more than national workers and if there is a consequent risk that it will place the former at a particular disadvantage.[7]

In the field of sex equality law, a definition that was based on the ECJ's jurisprudence appeared in 1997 in the Burden of Proof Directive, which provided that:

> [i]ndirect discrimination shall exist where an apparently neutral provision, criterion or practice disadvantages a substantially higher proportion of the members of one sex unless that provision, criterion or practice is appropriate and necessary and can be justified by objective factors unrelated to sex.[8]

Despite these differences in wording it is generally expected that the case law of the ECJ in sex equality law and free movement law will be of relevance for the interpretation of the concept as defined by the RED.[9] In the following sections, jurisprudence of the ECJ in these connected fields will be drawn upon where this seems relevant.

Conceptually speaking, the application of the concept of indirect discrimination entails two separate investigations.[10] As a first step, it is examined whether there is a particular disadvantage for a protected group, after which it is determined whether the measure causing this disadvantage is objectively justified. Thus, the first phase is mostly technical in nature and is all about establishing facts amounting to a prima facie case of indirect discrimination. Conversely, the second phase involves more normative reasoning and is about determining whether a measure is acceptable or not. Seeing that the second phase entails critical scrutiny of the legitimacy of prima facie cases of indirect discrimination, there would seem to be no objection against a lenient approach to be applied in the first phase. To the contrary, an inclusive approach as to what constitutes a prima facie case maximises the restructuring effect of the concept of indirect discrimination on society. After all, it ensures that as many processes, patterns and structures as possible are critically reviewed and assessed in terms of their compatibility with non-discrimination standards,

---

7 ECJ *O'Flynn v. Adjudication Officer,* Case C-237/94, 23 May 1996, paras. 17-19. This was not the only formulation used by the Court, but it is generally considered to be the leading definition for indirect discrimination in free movement law. For a detailed account of the relevant case law see Tobler (2005), at 206-208.

8 Article 2(2) of *Council Directive 97/80/EC of 15 December 1997 on the burden of proof in cases of discrimination based on sex*. This definition was altered in 2006, and Article 2(1)(b) of *Directive 2006/54/EC of the European Parliament and of the Council of 5 July 2005 on the implementation of the principle of equal opportunities and equal treatment of men and women in matters of employment and occupation (recast)* now contains a definition similar to Article 2(2)(b) RED.

9 Tobler (2008), at 8.

10 From the perspective of proving discrimination the model of review is more elaborate, entailing a negation phase before the justification phase, see Ambrus (2010).

without risking disregard for the rights and freedoms of individual actors. Thus, it is the point of departure of this study that the first phase should be carried out leniently, and that the relevant elements of the definition should be interpreted in an inclusive fashion. In contrast, the second phase, consisting of the objective justification test, should be applied in a sufficiently strict manner, so as to do justice to both conflicting interests that are implicated in each particular case. In the following sections, this proposition will be worked out in more practical guidelines.

5.2.1. 'An apparently neutral provision, criterion or practice'

The first element of the definition describes which types of measures are envisaged by the concept of indirect discrimination. A number of considerations are relevant for an appropriate implementation of this element, which are discussed in the following subsections.

5.2.1.1. Formal differences in treatment and material differences in treatment

It is important to stress that this element in practice involves either formal differences in treatment or material differences in treatment. For example, imposing higher entrance fees in universities for foreign students entails a formal difference in treatment between nationals and foreigners, which at the same time particularly disadvantages persons who have a different racial or ethnic origin than the majority of society. It is also possible that universities require a basic knowledge of the national language, which applies to all students and thus does not entail a formal difference in treatment, but still particularly disadvantages students of a minority racial or ethnic background. The latter type of situation, in which a formally equal treatment de facto creates unequal results is often referred to as a "material difference in treatment". The concept of indirect discrimination should cover both formal differences in treatment and material differences in treatment.[11]

Unfortunately, this dual nature of indirect discrimination is not often well understood by courts. Even the ECJ sometimes requires the establishment of a formal difference in treatment before it is willing to see whether there is a disparate impact on a protected group. A clear example is found in *Helmig*, which involved a rule according to which overtime supplements were only paid for hours worked in excess of the working hours of a full time employee. This was claimed to constitute indirect discrimination of part-time employees, who did not receive overtime supplements for hours worked in excess of their contractual working time. The Court stated that it first needed to determine

[11] Bayart & Deiteren (2008), at 188; Henrard (2006), at 229-230; Tobler (2005), at 216; Hepple & Barnard (1999), at 399-401; Drijber & Prechal (1997), at 124.

whether there was different treatment for full-time and part-time employees and whether that difference in treatment affected considerably more women than men, before it could turn to the objective justification test. It found that there was no difference in treatment, because part-timers received the same amount of pay as full-timers, and that consequently there was no discrimination on grounds of sex.[12] A similar approach is found in *Voß*, which involved a regulation stipulating that overtime hours were paid less than normal working hours, even those worked by part-timers. This was claimed to be indirectly discriminatory vis-à-vis the part-time work force, which mainly consisted of women. Again the ECJ stated that it first needed to determine whether there was a difference in treatment, which it considered to be present in this case, in view of the fact that a part-timer working more than his usual hours was paid less than a colleague working the same amount of hours. This initial finding opened the way to further scrutiny of the measure in the light of the prohibition of indirect sex discrimination.[13]

By first requiring the establishment of a formal difference in treatment, the ECJ thus denied the possibility of formally equal treatment being able to produce disparate effects from a substantive equality viewpoint. Such an approach effectively excludes from scrutiny measures that at first glance treat everybody in the same way, but on looking closer tend to disadvantage a protected group, which is detrimental in terms of substantive equality. It is thus submitted that the 'provision, criterion or practice' phrase of Article 2(2)(b) RED should not be interpreted as requiring a formal difference in treatment. This should not be too difficult, seeing that the words 'provision' and 'practice' in their normal understanding do not necessarily point to measures that formally differentiate.

5.2.1.2. Broad interpretation of 'provision, criterion or practice'

In line with the premise that the first phase of review is carried out in a lenient way, the phrase 'provision, criterion or practice' is preferably interpreted broadly, as referring to all products of human agency that have an impact on others. Thus, in addition to formal rules and criteria, it is preferable that by-laws, informal codes of conduct, statements, attitudes, conditions within which persons are placed, processes, and so forth, are all covered. In this respect, the mention of the rather vague notion of 'practice' in Article 2(2)(b) RED would seem particularly helpful, since it seems capable of covering a

12 ECJ *Angelika Helmig and Waltraud Schmidt v. Deutsche Angestellten-Krankenkase et al*, Joined cases C-399/92, C-409/92, C-425/92, C-34/93, C-50/93 and C-78/93, 15 December 1994, paras. 16-31.

13 ECJ *Voß v. Land Berlin,* Case C-300/06, 6 December 2007, paras. 26-44.

very broad array of types of behaviour that negatively impact on protected groups.[14]

The UK context provides an example of how a restrictive interpretation in this regard immediately narrows the effective reach of the prohibition of indirect discrimination. UK anti-discrimination law originally defined indirect discrimination as being brought about by a 'requirement or condition'. This phrase was narrowly interpreted by UK courts, as referring to absolute bars. Provisions that merely made something more difficult to attain were thus excluded, while perfectly capable of producing disparate impacts on particular groups.[15] A similar approach in the framework of the RED would for instance exclude from scrutiny an ethnocentric knowledge test that makes up only one element of a recruitment process, and thus does not involve an absolute bar for access to the particular post. Such a restrictive approach is obviously not desirable from an effectiveness point of view.

5.2.1.3. No single identifiable cause required

Practice reveals that cases can come up in which a protected group finds itself in a clear structurally disadvantageous situation, which cannot be traced back to a single identifiable cause. A good example of such a complex form of indirect discrimination is found in *D.H. v. Czech Republic*, a case that was handled by the ECtHR and that involved the racial segregation of Roma children in education. The facts of the case revealed a disproportionate number (75 per cent) of Roma children that had been placed in special schools on account of their 'limited mental capabilities'. On average, Roma children constituted 80 per cent of all students receiving special education for the mentally challenged. This number was claimed to constitute indirect racial discrimination, even though the applicants could not establish which practices/regulations/criteria exactly had caused the disparate impact.[16] It was exactly because of this indeterminacy as to the exact cause of the serious disparate impact that the Chamber of the ECtHR ruled that no violation of the non-discrimination principle had taken place.[17] It is clear that the Chamber's strict approach excluded a very real and serious form of structural disadvantage experienced by a very vulnerable minority group.

[14] Tobler (2005), at 284; Fredman (2002), at 107-108.

[15] Monaghan (2007), at 331-332; Craig (2007), at 58; Schiek et al (2007), at 373.

[16] They did point to some possibilities, such as the inappropriateness of the tests used, but no clear cause could be established.

[17] ECtHR *D.H. and others v. the Czech Republic*, No. 57325/00, 7 February 2006, paras. 44-53. This judgment was overruled in a later judgment by the Grand Chamber of the ECtHR, which determined that there was indeed indirect racial discrimination. See ECtHR *D.H. and others v. the Czech Republic*, No. 57325/00, Grand Chamber, 13 November 2007, paras. 193-195.

Therefore, it is preferable that a broader approach is taken in the context of the RED. This would require the phrase 'provision, criterion or practice' to be interpreted as applying to situations in which a complex of human behaviour has caused a particular disadvantage, while the exact cause cannot be pinned down. Practically speaking, such an approach would entail interpreting 'provision, criterion or practice' as extending to structures, cultures and processes that cannot easily be disentangled into single decisions or actions.[18]

Case law of the ECJ in the field of equal pay shows some promise in this respect. In *Enderby*, two separate collective bargaining processes had led to a difference in pay between two different professions that were considered to be of equal value. The lower paid profession was mainly occupied by women, which made for a disparate impact on this group. The Court explicitly recognised that the source of this disparate impact could not be identified and considered that: "[f]irst, it is not a question of de facto discrimination arising from a particular sort of arrangement such as may apply, for example, in the case of part-time workers. Secondly, there can be no complaint that the employer has applied a system of pay wholly lacking in transparency since the rates of pay of NHS speech therapists and pharmacists are decided by regular collective bargaining processes in which there is no evidence of discrimination as regards either of those two professions." Nevertheless, the Court accepted that there was a prima facie case of indirect discrimination, despite the impossibility of establishing the exact cause for the disparate impact: "[h]owever, if the pay of speech therapists is significantly lower than that of pharmacists and if the former are almost exclusively women while the latter are predominantly men, there is a prima facie case of sex discrimination, at least where the two jobs in question are of equal value and the statistics describing that situation are valid."[19]

A similarly flexible approach is found in *Royal Copenhagen,* which involved a difference in average pay between men and women within one company. The exact cause of this disparate impact could not be established, as the determination of the level of pay depended on a number of criteria, one of which was individual output. The Court considered that, "[if] in a system such as that in the main proceedings (…) it is not possible to identify the factors which determined the rates or units of measurement used to calculate the variable element in the pay (…), the objective of not depriving workers of any effective means of enforcing the principle of equal pay may require the employer to bear the burden of proving that the differences found are not due to sex discrimination."[20] Thus, the court found the disparate impact in itself

---

[18] Sjerps (1994), at 89; Makkonen (2004), at 5.

[19] ECJ *Enderby v. Frenchay Health Authority and Secretary of State for Health*, Case 127-92, 27 October 1993, paras. 15-16.

[20] ECJ *Specialarbejderforbundet i Danmark v. Dansk Industri/Royal Copenhagen*, Case C-400/93, 31 May 1995, para. 26.

sufficient for a finding of a prima facie case, which still could subsequently be rebutted by the employer. He could do so by showing that the cause of the disparity was actually something beyond his control, such as "the choice by the workers concerned of their rate of work."[21]

Even though the issue is addressed in terms of proof in these cases, the ECJ's approach practically comes down to the employer having a duty to find out how a disparate impact has come about and to justify the way in which he has acted in the face of the disparate impact. If he cannot show that the structural disadvantage came about in such a way that he could not do anything about it, the concept of indirect discrimination is applicable.

Translated to the RED, this would mean that a structurally disadvantageous situation of a racial or ethnic group that occurs within the sphere of influence of a particular actor, who does not succeed in showing that the situation is caused by a factor beyond his control, is captured by Article 2(2)(b) RED. The word 'practice' in particular appears to be broad enough to be applied to these kinds of cases. For example, in a case such as *D.H. v. Czech Republic*, it could be argued that the 'practice' of the assessment process leading to the determination of which children were suitable for special education amounted to a prima facie case of indirect discrimination, in view of the disproportionately high number of Roma children in special education.

5.2.1.4. The 'single source' requirement

In the field of equal pay the ECJ has set in place an important limitation to the potential reach of the prohibition of discrimination, by determining that differences in pay have to originate from a single source, in other words, a single actor. The two cases in which this doctrine was developed, involved inequality in pay that was caused by outsourcing certain activities to another company. The applicants were employed by a new employer for a lower salary, while continuing to do the same work in the same place for their old employer. In view of the higher salary received by those persons who were not outsourced, they claimed that this constituted unequal pay for equal work. The ECJ rejected their claims, maintaining that the difference in pay could not be attributed to a single source, in the sense that it could not be remedied by one body or actor.[22]

The single source requirement proceeds from the generally applicable premise that the prohibition of discrimination is a tort-like concept, which requires a certain measure of human agency/negligence, as well as an

[21] ECJ *Specialarbejderforbundet i Danmark v. Dansk Industri/Royal Copenhagen*, Case C-400/93, 31 May 1995, para. 27.

[22] ECJ *A.G. Lawrence and others v. Regent Office Care Ltd and others*, Case C-320/00, 17 September 2002, paras. 11-19; ECJ *Debra Allonby v. Accrington & Rossendale College and others*, Case C-256/01, 13 January 2004, paras. 41-50.

identifiable responsible agent.[23] In this respect, the requirement is thought by some to be applicable also outside the field of equal pay, in European equality law more generally. According to these authors, the single source doctrine could diminish the effectiveness of the concept of indirect discrimination, by making it harder to apply in cases in which it is difficult to pinpoint the source of the disparate impact.[24]

It is debatable, however, that the single source doctrine will be applied in such a general way. The doctrine has so far only appeared in the field of the principle of equal pay, which is a very specific branch of equality law. The restrictive material scope of this branch of equality law has arguably obscured the true relevance of the doctrine. In the field of equal pay, claims of discrimination can only concern pay itself or conditions directly determining the level of pay. Other conditions of employment that have a more remote impact on the level of pay are not caught by the material scope.[25] Seen from this perspective, the Court's consideration that there was not a single responsible actor is understandable: the disparate impact in question could be traced back to the decision of the original employer to outsource some of his activities to another employer (outside the material scope), combined with the lower salary paid by the latter (inside the material scope); it was therefore not uniquely caused by the manner in which the new employer determined the applicants' salaries. Indeed, the new employer did not discriminate either directly or indirectly as regards the level of pay of his employees. One could wonder whether the ECJ would have rejected the applicant's claims in the context of a broader material scope, covering the entire field of employment conditions, including dismissal. The applicants could then have claimed that the outsourcing activity in itself was discriminatory, since it resulted in a lower level of pay for a group that was mainly made up by women. It is not unthinkable that the ECJ would have accepted such a claim. The specialty of these equal pay cases therefore makes it difficult to determine the impact of the single source doctrine on the regime of the RED, which covers a much more extended material scope.

In addition, it is arguable that the single source doctrine was necessary in the field of equal pay to make the principle of equal pay workable in practice, by determining under which circumstances a particular actor could be held accountable for an inequality in pay. After all, the formulation of the principle of equal pay in Article 141(1) TEC does not mention from which sources unequal pay can spring, and only mentions the effect of unequal pay:

---

23 Morris (1995), at 199-228.

24 Fredman (2005), at 390; Prechal (2004), at 546.

25 The ECJ has traditionally maintained a strict separation between the regime of Article 141 TEC (equal pay) and that of *Council Directive 76/207/EEC of 9 February 1976 on the implementation of the principle of equal treatment for men and women as regards access to employment, vocational training and promotion, and working conditions* (equal treatment in other conditions of work than pay and employment). See Craig & De Búrca (2003), at 895-899.

"Each Member State shall ensure that the principle of equal pay for male and female workers for equal work or work of equal value is applied."

In contrast, the definition of indirect discrimination mentions which kinds of measures are capable of producing indirect discrimination ('provision, criterion or practice'), and thus does not seem to 'need' the single source doctrine to be applicable in practice. Whenever a provision, criterion or practice is identifiable, it should logically be possible to identify the corresponding responsible actor. Seen from this perspective, it is doubtful that the single source doctrine will play a meaningful role in the context of indirect discrimination as defined by the RED. It is telling in this regard that the Community legislator deleted from the text of the draft recast directive on sex equality a general reference to the single source doctrine, which would have subjected the whole domain of sex equality law to this doctrine.[26]

In view of the foregoing it is submitted that the single source doctrine is preferably not applied in the context of Article 2(2)(b) RED, as it is not necessary and would only set in place an additional barrier to establishing a prima facie case of indirect discrimination.

5.2.2. 'Would put at a particular disadvantage persons of a racial or ethnic origin'

The second element of the definition describes the effect on a racial or ethnic group needed for the establishment of a prima facie case of indirect discrimination. Since indirect discrimination focuses on *effects*, intent is not a relevant factor for the establishment of the particular disadvantage.[27] Even in the absence of an intent requirement, however, practical application of this element can be quite difficult, as is shown in this section. Prior to the discussion of the relevant complexities in this respect, a preliminary matter needs to be addressed: the question whether this element requires a causal link between the contested measure and the characteristic of belonging to a particular racial or ethnic group.

[26] Article 4 of the *Proposal for a directive of the European Parliament and of the Council on the implementation of the principle of equal opportunities and equal treatment of men and women in matters of employment and occupation (recast version)*, COM (2004) 279 final, contained a reference to the single source doctrine, which had disappeared in the final version of *Directive 2006/54/EC of the European Parliament and of the Council of 5 July 2005 on the implementation of the principle of equal opportunities and equal treatment of men and women in matters of employment and occupation (recast).*

[27] Tobler (2008), at 31-32; Loenen (1999), at 210; Waldron (1985), at 95.

5.2.2.1. Causal link required?

It is possible to say that the second element of the definition lays down the causal aspect of indirect discrimination, that is, the connection between the contested measure and the protected characteristic.[28] As was mentioned in the previous chapter, this link is indirect, because it is connected to the protected characteristic through some other circumstance. For instance, a language requirement is indirectly linked to the protected characteristic of racial or ethnic origin, through the circumstance that persons of a particular racial or ethnic origin tend to speak a particular language.

If the connecting circumstance is very closely linked to the protected characteristic, the causal link comes close to a direct one and is easily visible. Differences in treatment based on nationality are for example very closely connected to the characteristic of racial or ethnic origin, because persons of a different nationality are almost invariably also of a different racial or ethnic origin than the majority of society. Differentiation on the basis of nationality therefore closely resembles direct discrimination on grounds of racial or ethnic origin. Other characteristics are less closely connected to racial or ethnic origin, such as for instance body height in the case of a height requirement for a particular job. Persons belonging to some ethnic groups tend to be less tall than persons of other ethnic groups, but this differs greatly from person to person, which makes for a more indirect causal link with racial or ethnic origin than the aforementioned nationality example. The more indirect the link with racial or ethnic origin, the more difficult it generally is to see the causal link. Especially since there is still much unknown about the dynamics that cause disadvantages for minority groups, it is likely that in some instances the causal link is not readily visible, but can only be inferred from the practical effect of a contested measure. The aforementioned case of *D.H. v. Czech Republic* provides a good example.[29]

In this respect, it is desirable that courts do not require applicants to establish the causal link between the contested measure and the particular racial or ethnic characteristic, in addition to the particular disadvantage experienced by this group. An additional causality requirement risks excluding from the scope of the prohibition of indirect discrimination those measures or practices for which we lack the particular knowledge that enables us to see how exactly the causal link is construed. If it is established that a provision, criterion or practice has created a particular disadvantage for a racial or ethnic group, the causal link should be taken as a given. Thus, the remainder of this section takes as a starting point the presupposition that the second element of the

---

28 Ellis (2005), at 104-106.

29 ECtHR *D.H. and others v. the Czech Republic*, No. 57325/00, 7 February 2006 and ECtHR *D.H. and others v. the Czech Republic*, No. 57325/00, Grand Chamber, 13 November 2007. See section 5.2.3.1.

definition of indirect discrimination only needs to be assessed in terms of what *effect* must be produced by a provision, criterion or practice for a prima facie case of indirect discrimination.

5.2.2.2. Establishing the particular disadvantage

5.2.2.2.1. Means of proof

At the time of the adoption of the RED the phrase "would put at a particular disadvantage persons of a racial or ethnic origin" was critically received for adding yet another formulation to the collection of formulations that already existed in Community law.[30] The *O'Flynn* definition in free movement law required the contested measure to be "intrinsically liable to affect migrant workers more than national workers", with the "consequent risk that it will place the former at a particular disadvantage".[31] In the field of sex equality law the Burden of Proof Directive required that the provision, criterion or practice "disadvantages a substantially higher proportion of the members of one sex".[32] The differences between the various definitions were considered not so much to be about the particular degree of disparity required, but rather about the manner in which the disparity should be established. Thus, in sex equality law a claim of indirect discrimination generally had to be corroborated with quantitative data, whereas in nationality law other means of proof, such as facts of general knowledge or other qualitative evidence were much more acceptable.[33]

The definition in the RED was intended to build upon these differences in proof options and was originally crafted in terms of the free movement definition. The Commission considered that a requirement of quantitative proof would make the prohibition of indirect discrimination less effective, in view of the huge lack of statistical data on ethnic or racial affiliation in the majority of the Member States.[34] It was expected that this lack of data would not be remedied any time soon, as the collection of such data was considered illegal

---

30 Tridimas (2006), at 69-70.

31 ECJ *O'Flynn v. Adjudication Officer*, Case C-237/94, 23 May 1996, paras. 17-19. This was not the only formulation used by the Court in the field of nationality law. For a comprehensive account of relevant case law, see Tobler (2005), at 206-208.

32 See Article 2(2) of *Council Directive 97/80/EC on the burden of proof in cases of discrimination based on sex*. The definition of indirect discrimination in sex equality law has been brought into line with the one of the RED in Article 2(1)(b) of *Directive 2006/54/EC of the European Parliament and of the Council of 5 July 2005 on the implementation of the principle of equal opportunities and equal treatment of men and women in matters of employment and occupation (recast)*.

33 Gerards (2002), at 266; Schiek (2002), at 296.

34 Tridimas (2006), at 70.

and morally unacceptable in quite a number of Member States.[35] However, the Member States did not want to completely rule out the possibility of using statistical proof, and slightly altered the formula in the final draft, which led to the current definition.[36] The unique wording of Article 2(2)(b) of the RED was therefore not intended to mark a substantive departure from the meaning of indirect discrimination in EC equality law as it was known until then, but to make it possible to use both qualitative and quantitative means of proof.[37]

Despite the clear preference of the Community legislator for the acceptability of both means of proof, Member States were left with some discretion. Thus, Recital 15 of the RED provides that:

> [t]he appreciation of the facts from which it may be inferred that there has been direct or indirect discrimination is a matter for national judicial or other competent bodies, in accordance with rules of national law or practice. Such rules may provide in particular for indirect discrimination to be established by any means including on the basis of statistical evidence.

The exact purport of this recital is unclear; even though it appears to leave it up to the Member States to decide which kinds of proof are acceptable, it is debatable whether the current state of EC equality law actually allows for much leeway in this regard. Since the use of statistical evidence is generally accepted in other fields of equality law and has in some instances even been required by the ECJ, it is questionable whether Member States can exclude claims of indirect racial discrimination solely based on statistical data. As one commentator argued, they may well be forced by the ECJ to accept statistics on grounds of ensuring the effectiveness of the general principle of equality.[38] It is indeed not desirable that Recital 15 be used to completely exclude the possibility of establishing a prima facie case of indirect discrimination by means of statistical evidence, because this would unnecessarily limit the possibilities of establishing a prima facie case of indirect discrimination.

5.2.2.2.2. The meaning of 'disadvantage'

Practice has shown that establishing the 'disadvantage' element of a prima facie case of indirect discrimination can be controversial, and is not merely a matter of getting the facts right. For instance, in *Helmig*, part-time workers

[35] The lack of statistical data is currently a concern that has been raised by a number of NGOs and experts, since it is often very difficult to find other means of proving disparate impact: see Ringelheim 2008; De Schutter (2007), at 22-33.

[36] Tyson (2004), at 114-116.

[37] Schiek et al (2007), at 424; Waddington & Bell (2001), at 594.

[38] De Schutter (2007), at 15-16. Additional support for this argument can be found in ECtHR *D.H. v. Czech Republic,* Grand Chamber, 13 November 2007, para. 188, in which the Grand Chamber considered that reliable and significant statistics are sufficient to constitute a prima facie case of indirect discrimination.

complained that they did not receive any overtime supplements for the hours worked by them on top of their contractual hours because these additional hours did not exceed the amount of hours worked by full-time employees. They claimed that this constituted a disadvantage for part-time workers and thus amounted to indirect sex discrimination, since the part-time workforce was predominantly made up of women. The ECJ, however, ruled that there was no disadvantage, as part-timers were treated in exactly the same way as full-timers.[39]

The Court's approach makes sense from a formal equality point of view, according to which all persons should always receive the same amount of pay for the same amount of hours worked. From a substantive equality perspective, however, there should at least be consideration for the argument that working overtime is for part-timers as burdensome as for full-timers, even though they remain within the amount of hours worked by full-timers. The Court did not even address this argument, therefore implicitly choosing to approach 'disadvantage' from a formal equality standpoint only. This approach denies the aforementioned reality that indirect discrimination can be constituted by either formally differential treatment or by formally equal treatment, and thus undermines the effectiveness of the prohibition of indirect discrimination. Interestingly, in a more recent case, the ECJ considered that a rule according to which additional hours were only compensated for if they exceeded three hours, which equally applied to part-timers and full-timers, imposed a greater burden for part-time teachers than for full-time teachers, and thus constituted indirect sex discrimination.[40] In this case the Court was thus sensitive to the argument that the same rule was more burdensome for part-time employees than for full-time employees, even if both were formally treated in the same way.

The cases clearly show that the interpretation of 'disadvantage' depends on the particular perspective on equality that the Court adopts, and to some extent involves normative reasoning. Translated to the context of the RED, this means that there is a risk that claims of indirect racial discrimination are dismissed too easily for lack of disadvantage, if the ECJ and/or national courts hold on too strongly to a formal equality viewpoint. For instance, a rule of having to wear the company uniform constitutes a disadvantage for a person who for religious reasons wears particular pieces of clothing, because he/she is no longer able to dress according to his/her religious identity. A court applying the formal equality perspective could rule, however, that the rule is not disadvantageous, because all employees have to wear the same uniform.[41]

---

[39] ECJ *Helmig and Schmidt v. Deutsche Angestellten-Krankenkasse et al*, Joined cases C-399/92, C-409/92, C-425/92, C-34/93, C-50/93 and C-78/93, 15 December 1994, paras. 25-30.

[40] ECJ *Elsner-Lakeberg v. Land Nordrhein-Westfalen*, Case C-285/02, 27 May 2004, para. 17.

[41] Compare Fredman (2002), at 96, who mentions a case that occurred in the UK, in which a court refused to see a disadvantage in the impossibility to get time off from work to go to

It may be obvious that a substantive equality perspective is preferable in such cases. In practice this means that the threshold should not be set very high and that a claimant's perception of a particular treatment as being disadvantageous be taken sufficiently seriously.[42]

5.2.2.2.3. The meaning of 'particular'

It is generally understood that the word 'particular' not so much refers to the intensity of the disadvantage, but rather to the special way in which persons belonging to a protected group are affected by it. In other words, 'particular' means that the disadvantage should disproportionately affect more persons belonging to a protected group.[43] Establishing this element can be difficult for different reasons, depending on which type of evidence is in play.[44]

In the face of qualitative evidence, courts have to decide to what extent the information revealed is actually representative for the whole group. Sometimes this is very easy, for example when legal facts or facts of general knowledge are used. *Schnorbus* provides a good example in this respect. The contested rule in this case was a provision that provided preferential access to traineeship places in the judiciary for persons who had experienced particular hardship, a separate category of which was constituted by men who had completed their military service. Whereas the Commission had forwarded statistical material in order to show that more women than men were disadvantaged by this provision, the Court decided that this evidence was not necessary because "the provisions at issue themselves are evidence of indirect discrimination since, under the relevant national legislation, women are not required to do military or civilian service and therefore cannot benefit from the priority accorded by the abovementioned provisions".[45] The legal fact that only men were required to perform military service made immediately clear that women were disproportionately impacted.

Sometimes, however, the qualitative evidence put forward by the applicant is less unambiguous. In those cases there is a danger that, by relying on this evidence, a court actually revives or perpetuates the use of harmful stereotypes or essentialist thinking.[46] It is therefore essential that courts seriously examine the evidence before them, and ascertain that it provides an objectively correct

the Mosque, because all persons adhering to minority religions had to conform to the majority religion.

42 Gerards (2005), at 78.

43 Tobler (2005), at 225.

44 Tobler (2008), at 31 and 40.

45 ECJ *Julia Schnorbus v. Land Hessen*, C-79/99, 7 December 2000, paras. 13 and 38.

46 Schiek et al (2007), at 435.

picture of the particular racial or ethnic group. Moreover, there is a clear need for relevant and thorough research of the position of minority groups in society and the disadvantages they encounter in daily life.[47]

Once it is established that the qualitative evidence is accurate, the establishment of the particular disadvantage is fairly easy, and is brought about by a common sense approach. The court or supervisory body should simply decide whether the particular situation of the protected group is such that the contested provision, criterion or practice is liable to particularly disadvantage persons belonging to this group.[48]

If a claim of indirect discrimination is based on quantitative evidence, courts are faced with the question as to which degree of disparity is required. Practice has shown that the establishment of this element of indirect discrimination can be very complicated. Unfortunately, it is generally acknowledged that it is not possible to formulate a clear-cut, definitive standard. The factual circumstances of indirect discrimination cases often do not fulfil the requirements for reliable statistical testing. Moreover, pools of comparators may be tainted by past discrimination, which means that by simply applying statistical standards with no regard for the broader context courts could miss the mark.[49]

In view of these complexities, it is perhaps not surprising that the ECJ has so far not adopted a clear approach for the establishment of the particular disadvantage. In *Seymour-Smith*, concerning a claim of unequal pay, the referring court explicitly asked the court to pronounce on the matter. The ECJ did not provide much clarity, however. The court acknowledged that two types of statistical disproportions merited a classification of a prima facie case of indirect discrimination: 1) a situation in which "a considerably smaller percentage of women than men" is able to satisfy the contested condition; or 2) a situation in which "the statistical evidence reveal[s] a lesser but persistent and relatively constant disparity over a long period between men and women" who satisfy the contested condition. This approach appears useful, since it shows regard for the concern that the prolonged character of a disparity should give it some additional weight. However, the ECJ did not give any guidance on how to establish both types of disparities. The court only stated that the disparity should not amount to a purely fortuitous or short-term phenomenon, which does not add anything useful, since the whole point of establishing the disparity for indirect discrimination is to decide whether a disproportion is fortuitous or not. In the case at hand, the ECJ ruled that the difference between 77.4% of men and 68.9% of women who could comply with the contested measure was too small, but that it was up to the national court to make the

47 De Schutter (2007), at 19.
48 Tobler (2008), at 40.
49 Monaghan (2007), at 345; Finlay (2003), at 140-141.

decision.[50] *Seymour-Smith* thus sheds a meagre ray of light on the issue, and it is actually still left to national courts to develop a practical approach to the manner in which the 'particular disadvantage' should be determined.

Academics have forwarded a number of approaches for determining whether a particular impact is sufficiently disproportionate, the choice for which depends on the data available in the particular case. A test that is particularly helpful in cases that concern a very large number of comparators is the rule of thumb approach, according to which a particular proportion, such as for instance four-fifths, is sufficient.[51] Similarly suitable for large pools is the impressionistic approach, which asks the question whether the disparity strikes as being considerable or suspicious.[52] In the face of smaller pools of comparators, a statistical significance standard is appropriate, which follows the rules of the science of statistics.[53] In those cases where the numbers of comparators are even too small for a statistical significance test, courts could try to see whether a relatively small quantitative disproportion is backed up by qualitative evidence. In this way, qualitative evidence can come to the rescue of ambiguous quantitative data.

It may be clear that no single approach is preferable, and that it depends on the facts of the case in which way the disparate impact can be established. Courts undeniably have quite some discretion in the matter. At the very least, national courts should adopt a consistent and transparent approach and thoroughly motivate their decisions in this regard, so as to ensure legal certainty. A relatively lenient approach is furthermore desirable, because the objective justification test provides a sufficient safeguard against fortuitous claims of indirect discrimination.

It should be emphasised that the disadvantage does not have to materialise before a claim of indirect discrimination can be submitted. In view of the 'would put' language of Article 2(2)(b) RED, it suffices that a disproportionate effect is liable to occur.[54]

5.2.2.2.4. The 'persons' controversy

The reference to 'persons' in Article 2(2)(b) RED has been criticised by a number of scholars, who point out that the 'particular disadvantage' should always be assessed in terms of the way in which the protected group as a

[50] ECJ *Regina and Secretary of State for Employment, ex parte Nicole Seymour-Smith and Laura Perez*, Case C-167/97, 9 February 1999, paras. 60-64.
[51] Hepple & Barnard (1999), at 405-406; Gijzen (2006), at 80.
[52] Hepple & Barnard (1999), at 406; Gijzen (2006), at 80.
[53] Hepple & Barnard (1999), at 406-407; Gijzen (2006), at 77. This is the common approach of US courts, see Craig (2007), at 45.
[54] Finlay (2003), at 149; Barnard (2001), at 969.

whole is affected, and not just some persons belonging to that group.[55] Their argument seems slightly redundant, as it is difficult to conceive of any other understanding of the concept of indirect discrimination. If the label of indirect discrimination would be applied to simply any case in which a few persons who happen to share a protected characteristic are disadvantaged, indirect discrimination would lose its distinctive meaning as a *discrimination* concept. Instead, it would become a concept that simply requires measures that have a disadvantageous impact on some persons to be scrutinised according to the objective justification test. It therefore seems quite obvious that one can only meaningfully speak of indirect *discrimination* in the case of a particular disadvantage for a protected group as a whole. This is not to say that the disadvantage must in reality be experienced by all members belonging to the protected group: it suffices that the statistical or qualitative evidence at hand makes clear that, within the relevant pool of comparators, the protected group is particularly disadvantaged. The comparison that is needed for this assessment is discussed in the next section.

5.2.3. Compared to other persons (comparative aspect of indirect discrimination)

Indirect discrimination is an inherently comparative concept, which means that its application in practice necessarily involves a comparison. The particular disadvantage on a racial or ethnic group can only be determined by comparing the situation of this group with other persons, since this is the only way of knowing whether the racial or ethnic group is disproportionately affected. In this respect the concept of indirect discrimination differs from direct discrimination, the application of which does not necessarily entail a comparison.[56] Despite its central importance for indirect discrimination, the comparative aspect poses a number of challenges in practice. More specifically, application of the comparative entails two complexities: the delineation of the appropriate pool of comparators, and the determination of the proper comparison to be carried out within the pool of comparators. Both issues are discussed in the two following subsections.

5.2.3.1. Establishing the pool of comparators

The step that precedes the actual comparison is the delineation of the appropriate pool of comparators. Logically speaking, the pool should consist

---

[55] See inter alia Gijzen (2006), at 79-80; Finlay (2003), at 150; Barnard (2001), at 969; Fredman (2001), at 163.

[56] See section 4.3.4.

of the entire circle of addressees of the particular provision, criterion or practice at hand: this ensures that a complete picture of the exact impact is obtained. The ECJ has underlined this in *Allonby,* stating that: "[w]hen it is necessary to consider whether a set of rules conforms with the requirements of [previously Article 119 TEC, now Article 141 TEC, MB], it is in principle the scope of those rules which determines the category of persons who may be included in the comparison."[57]

Depending on the nature of the particular provision, criterion or practice, this rule can be more or less easily applied. It will generally be easier to determine the scope of addressees of a provision or criterion than of a practice, since the former concepts usually target a certain audience more explicitly. For practices that do not target an expressly mentioned group of addressees, it is probably best to look at the actor with whom the practice originates, and to draw the pool of comparators in accordance with his/her sphere of influence as well as the nature and aim of the practice at hand.[58] For instance, in the field of equal pay, the 'practice' complained of often constitutes a complex body of rules and criteria, as well as some discretionary room for the employer. It is then best to look at the workforce of the employer (sphere of influence), and more particularly only those employees that fulfil work that is equal in terms of the required skills, experience etcetera (nature and aim of pay policy). This was indeed the approach taken by the ECJ in *Royal Copenhagen*, which involved a claim of indirect sex discrimination as regards pay. According to the Court, the appropriate pool of comparators comprised "all the workers who, taking account of a set of factors such as the nature of the work, the training requirements and the working conditions, can be considered to be in a comparable situation".[59]

The latter sentence reveals that in cases in which the circle of addressees cannot be easily deduced from the contested measure itself, it may be necessary to use a comparability test in order to establish the appropriate pool of comparators. Comparability should not, however, be used in a justificatory way. An example of such justificatory use of comparability is found in *Gruber,* which involved legislation that granted persons who gave up work in order to take care of children a lower termination payment than persons who gave up

[57] ECJ *Allonby v. Accrington & Rossendale College and others*, Case C-256/01, 13 January 2004, para. 73. This rule was repeated in ECJ *Ursula Voß v. Land Berlin,* Case C-300/06, 6 December 2007, para. 40.

[58] Compare the ECJ's consideration on comparability in the context of the general principle of equal treatment in ECJ *Société Arcelor Atlantique et Lorraine e.a. v. Premier Ministre e.a.,* Case C-127/07, 16 December 2008, para. 26: "the elements which characterise different situations, and hence their comparability, must in particular be determined and assessed in the light of the *subject matter and purpose* of Community act which makes the distinction in question" (emphasis added, MB).

[59] ECJ *Specialarbejderforbundet i Danmark v. Dansk Industri/Royal Copenhagen*, Case C-400/93, 31 May 1995, para. 33.

work for an 'important reason'. Mrs Gruber claimed that the legislation was indirectly discriminatory, since persons giving up work in order to take care of children were mainly women. The ECJ first examined whether the legislation put "a worker like Mrs Gruber at a disadvantage in relation to other workers who are in a situation identical to or similar to hers". It subsequently found that the 'important reasons' in the particular provision were all related to working conditions in the undertaking or to the conduct of the employer that would render continued work impossible, and that these situations were "in substance and origin different from that of a worker like Mrs Gruber". This led to the unsurprising conclusion that there was no indirect discrimination.[60] In this case, the ECJ did not make use of a comparability test in order to determine who should be compared to whom. To the contrary, it used comparability reasoning in order to establish that it was acceptable to pay persons giving up work in order to take care of their children less than persons giving up work for 'important reasons'. In doing so, it did not motivate its opinion that it is justified to make this distinction, and it did not follow the three-tiered approach of the objective justification test, which entails assessment of the legitimacy of the aim pursued, appropriateness and necessity.[61] This goes to show that justificatory use of comparability tends to obscure the decision-making process and lower the quality of decision-making, which is why it should be rejected.[62]

Comparability arguments are therefore preferably only used to delineate the pool of comparators, in case the circle of addressees of the contested measure is not immediately obvious. Moreover, it is essential that the test is carried out in a transparent way: the criteria deemed relevant should be expressly mentioned and supported by solid reasoning.

Courts should be alert as to the possibility that the circle of addressees of a contested measure is tainted by past discrimination, which could be a reason to adjust the pool of comparators accordingly.[63] An example of such a flexible approach is provided by a judgment of the High Court of Australia in a case in which the contested measure was a redundancy policy based on a last in, first out rule. The High Court accepted the lower court's standpoint that the pool of comparators had to include persons outside the workforce of the employer so as to comprise all persons who had applied for a job within a certain period, in order to adjust for past discriminatory hiring practices.[64]

60 ECJ *Gabriele Gruber v. Silhouette International Schmied GmbH & Co. KG*, Case C-249/97, 14 September 1999, paras. 25-35.

61 See for a discussion of these various elements section 5.2.4.

62 See section 4.3.4 for a similar argument in the context of direct discrimination. See furthermore Schiek et al (2007), at 471; Prechal (2004), at 543; Arnardóttir (2003), at 89; Gerards (2005), at 57-72.

63 Monaghan (2007), at 345; Finlay (2003), at 140-141.

64 *Australian Iron and Steel PTY v. Banovic* [1989] 168 CLR 165 FC 89/052, as commented on by Finlay (2003), at 140-141.

The scope of addressees rule can furthermore be difficult to apply when there is insufficient data on the particular group of addressees, which can make it necessary to look at data on a larger or smaller group. For instance, in *Lewark* the ECJ permitted applicants to adduce general statistics in order to establish a disparate impact within a subgroup for which no specific data was available.[65] This flexible approach is supported in literature in view of the fact that a single rule can have different effects for different sections of society; it would then seem reasonable to adjust the pool of comparators accordingly.[66] In order to avoid arbitrary decisions in this respect, it should be stressed here also that any adjustment of the pool of comparators should be supported by a thorough motivation.

5.2.3.2. Making the appropriate comparison within the pool of comparators

The comparison to be carried out within the pool of comparators should determine whether a racial or ethnic group is particularly disadvantaged in comparison with others. It should accordingly establish whether persons of a particular racial or ethnic origin are disproportionately represented in the group of persons that are disadvantaged by the contested measure.

In the case of qualitative evidence, the comparison is in fact a theoretical exercise, which seeks to answer the question whether the evidence reveals any particularities about the specific racial or ethnic group that causes the contested measure to particularly disadvantage them. Transparent and consistent reasoning is clearly requisite in this respect.

When courts are faced with quantitative evidence, on the other hand, they have to actually make a numerical comparison of those who are disadvantaged and those who are not disadvantaged by the provision, criterion or practice. To this end it is necessary to look at relative rather than absolute numbers, as was pointed out by the ECJ in *Seymour-Smith*. In the same judgment the ECJ made clear that the comparison should focus on two sets of proportions: 1) the number of persons who do not have the protected characteristic in the group that is not disadvantaged by the contested measure, in relation to their number in the group that is disadvantaged by the measure; and 2) the same proportion for persons who do have the protected characteristics.[67]

Take the example of a provision that stipulates that workers are not allowed to take time off to pray during office hours. The pool of comparators

[65] ECJ *Kuratorium für Dialyse und Nierentransplantation v. Lewark*, Case C-457/93, 6 February 1994, paras. 29-30. See also Bayart & Deiteren (2008), at 213-216.

[66] Schiek et al (2007), at 407.

[67] ECJ *Regina and Secretary of State for Employment, ex parte Nicole Seymour-Smith and Laura Perez*, Case C-167/97, 9 February 1999, para. 59; See also ECJ *Ursula Voß v. Land Berlin,* Case C-300/06, 6 December 2007, para. 41. See also Schiek et al (2007), at 412-414; Gijzen (2006), at 81.

is constituted by all workers within the company, 1000 persons in total, 100 of who are of Arab origin. 300 workers feel constrained by the measure, because they have a religious obligation to pray at set times, and 95 of these workers are of Arab origin. The appropriate comparison would proceed as follows: non-Arab persons make up slightly more than 99 per cent (695/700) of the group that is not disadvantaged, and 68 per cent of the group that is disadvantaged. Arab persons make up less than 1 per cent (5/700) of the group that is not disadvantaged and 32 per cent (95/300) of the disadvantaged group. These percentages should subsequently be scrutinised in accordance with the test for establishing the particular disadvantage, which was discussed in section 5.2.2.2.

It can be difficult for courts to know which percentages to compare. In the above example the following meaningful combinations are possible: 1) 32 per cent of Arab persons in the disadvantaged group versus 1 per cent of Arab persons in the non-disadvantaged group; 2) 1 per cent of Arab persons in the non-disadvantaged group versus 10 per cent of Arab persons in the overall workforce; 3) 32 per cent of Arab persons in the disadvantaged group versus 10 per cent of Arab persons in the overall workforce. The second and third options actually come down to the same substantive comparison, because both make clear what difference there is between the normal ethnic composition of the workforce and the way in which the contested measure has produced a different ethnic composition. These options are preferable, because they make it easiest to see that Arab persons have been affected to a greater extent than non-Arab persons. This means that courts should ideally look at the proportion of persons belonging to the racial or ethnic group in the overall pool of comparators as opposed to their proportion in either the non-disadvantaged or the disadvantaged group.

5.2.4. 'Unless that provision, criterion or practice is objectively justified by a legitimate aim and the means of that aim are appropriate and necessary' (justification aspect of indirect discrimination)

The final element of the definition of Article 2(2)(b) RED contains the objective justification test, which is applied when a particular disadvantage on a protected group has been established. This test consists of a number of subtests, which are preferably applied consecutively, for reasons of transparency and legal certainty.[68] The examination of these subtests in this section is preceded by a brief discussion on the proper qualification of the function of the objective justification test, which has been the object of debate in literature.

---

[68] Compare the opinion of Advocate-General Colomer in ECJ *Othmar Michaeler a.o. v. Arbeitsinspektorat der Autonomen Provinz Bozen*, Cases C-55/07 and C-56/07, 24 January

5.2.4.1. Justification or causation?

There is an ongoing debate with regard to the role played by the objective justification test within the model of review of indirect discrimination. According to some, it is a causation test in disguise, in the sense that an objectively justified measure is not causally linked to the protected ground, despite its disparate impact on a protected group.[69] According to others, justification considerations are to be conceptually distinguished from causality considerations.[70]

As became clear earlier, one of the premises of this chapter is that there is a clear conceptual difference between the more technical phase in which a prima facie case of indirect discrimination is established and the normative phase in which justification arguments are considered. This study therefore aligns with the second point of view. 'Causation' is conceptually best reserved for the indirect link between the disadvantage and the particular racial or ethnic origin, which after all corresponds to the understanding of causation in the framework of direct discrimination. As was explained in section 5.2.2.1, this causal link is established by showing that a racial or ethnic group is particularly disadvantaged by the contested measure. After the establishment of the indirect causal link between the contested measure and the racial or ethnic group, the objective justification provides the framework for critical review of the legitimacy of this measure. The arguments that play a part in the objective justification test are normative in nature, and are therefore essentially different from the arguments used for establishing causality, which are preferably only factual/evidentiary in nature, as was explained before.[71] It is thus preferable to keep a strict division between causation and justification. The basic design of indirect discrimination as understood in this study is therefore as follows: a disadvantage that can be indirectly causally linked to the membership of a particular group (causation) and that cannot be objectively justified (justification).

5.2.4.2. 'Objectively justified by a legitimate aim'

The first element of the justification test makes clear that the perspective of the defending party is not determining, but that an objective assessment is needed to determine whether the forwarded justification for a contested measure is

2008, para. 37, on the general proportionality test in Community law, according to which: "[u]sing that threefold evaluation, which is carried out in stages rather than cumulatively, the assessment of equality becomes more transparent and generates greater legal certainty."

[69] Schiek et al (2007), at 436-443; Ellis (2005), at 111-112. See also the overview of the debate as given by Tobler (2005), at 254-258.

[70] Tobler (2005), at 258.

[71] See the introduction to section 5.2.

acceptable or not. It furthermore makes clear that the author of the contested measure is not allowed to pursue just any aim with his measure.[72] In the first place this means that no discriminatory considerations may play a part in justifying a prima facie case of indirect discrimination.[73] This also means that stereotypes or unfounded generalisations about a protected group that exist in the background of an indirectly discriminatory measure are unacceptable,[74] which makes sense, since such presumptions could even cause the contested measure to qualify as direct discrimination, as was pointed out in the previous chapter.[75]

Even aside from the unacceptability of discriminatory considerations, the aim sought after by the contested measure still needs to be 'legitimate'. It is not exactly clear how this criterion should be interpreted in the framework of the RED. The case law of the ECJ for sex and nationality discrimination law shows a number of different considerations that can play a part,[76] but the picture is highly casuistic and the ECJ has hardly offered any clear benchmarks to national courts.[77] The only fairly consistent consideration to be found is the consideration that mere budgetary considerations are not acceptable.[78] This

[72] It should be mentioned that in cases in which the source of the disparate impact is not readily identifiable, the question will not so much be whether the alleged perpetrator pursued a legitimate aim, but rather whether he can forward a legitimate reason for the fact that he did not undertake any action to prevent or remedy the disparate impact.

[73] Schiek et al (2007), at 460; Tobler (2005), at 239.

[74] Gerards 2000, at 271. See inter alia ECJ *Erika Steinicke v. Bundesanstalt fur Arbeit*, Case C-77/02, 11 September 2003, para. 64; ECJ *Helga Kutz-Bauer v. Freie und Hansestadt Hamburg*, Case C-187/00, 20 March 2003, para. 58; ECJ *Specialarbejderforbundet i Danmark v. Danks Industri*, Case C-400/93, 31 May 1995, para. 43; ECJ *Ingrid Rinner-Kühn v. FWW Spezial-Gebäudereinigung GmbH & Co. KG*, Case C-171/88, 13 July 1989, para. 14; ECJ *Helga Nimz v. Freie und Hansestadt Hamburg*, Case C-184/89, 7 February 1991, para. 14.

[75] As was explained in the previous chapter, any decision or action against an individual based on a stereotype or generalisation about the protected group to whom he/she belongs should be qualified as direct discrimination, not as unjustified indirect discrimination. See section 4.2.3.

[76] See Gerards (2005), at 270-287.

[77] Tobler (2005), at 243-245. See also Tobler (2008), at 32-35, in particular at 34, where she lists the various social policy and business aims that have been accepted by the ECJ so far. The list does not show any remarkable aims and includes inter alia: offering protection against dismissal; finding qualified labour; encouraging employment; guaranteeing a minimum replacement income; ensuring sound public expenditure. This list is a clear illustration of the casuistic approach taken by the ECJ, which makes it impossible to draw any general conclusions as to how a legitimate aim is assessed.

[78] Tobler (2005), at 249-250; Geulette (2002), at 568, 570; Gerards (2002), at 274-275. See inter alia ECJ *Nikoloudi v. Organismos Tilepikinonion Ellados AE*, Case 196-02, 10 March 2005, para. 53; ECJ *Erika Steinicke v. Bundesanstalt fur Arbeit*, Case C-77/02, 11 September 2003, para. 68; ECJ *Hilde Schönheit v. stad Frankfurt am Main* Case 4/02 and 5/02, 12 November 2001, para. 85; ECJ *Helga Kutz-Bauer v. Freie und Hansestadt Hamburg*, Case C-187/00, 20 March 2003, para. 59; ECJ *B. Jørgensen v. Foreningen af Speciallæger*, Case C-226/98, 6 April 2000, para. 39; ECJ *Regina and Secretary of State for Employment, ex parte Nicole Seymour-Smith and Laura Perez*, Case C-167/97, 9 February 1999, para. 40.

consideration seems sensible and applicable in the context of racial indirect discrimination. Still, as will be shown below, it does not seem suitable for all cases of indirect discrimination, especially not if a positive duty is in play.

It is submitted here that it is possible to set some parameters for assessing the legitimacy of the aim a particular contested measure is intended to serve. First of all, it makes sense to take into account the quality of the actor at stake. In accordance with what was said about the differences between public and private actors in section 2.2.2.2, the different tasks and interests of public and private actors should be taken into account when determining which aims pursued by them are permissible.[79] For instance, making a profit is an acceptable aim for a private company that does not offer a specifically tailored insurance policy for trailers, but is not an acceptable aim for a public authority that does not provide for traveller communities in its housing policy.

The ECJ itself has to some extent differentiated between public and private actors in the field of sex equality. In the field of gender equality law, it required that the national legislator showed that he pursued a "necessary aim of social policy",[80] whereas it required private employers to put forward a "real need".[81] The latter test was perceived to be applied more strictly.[82] It is conceivable that similar differentiation will take place in the context of the RED.

Secondly, the nature of the contested measure should have some bearing on the assessment of the legitimacy of the aim. Positive duties should for instance be evaluated differently from negative duties.[83] In view of the cost element involved in positive duties, it is reasonable to more readily accept economic and budgetary aims with regard to these duties.[84] Such differentiation has thus far not been made by the ECJ, which is generally hesitant to accept budgetary aims, as was mentioned before. Still, it is unrealistic to assume that economic considerations cannot play a part, especially with regard to private actors who are generally expected and allowed to pursue self-serving interests, and especially in the context of positive duties, which can involve high costs.[85] This position is supported by Advocate General Geelhoed in *Chacón Navas*, who mentions the cost element as a relevant consideration in the application

[79] Sottiaux (2008), at 237; Velaers (2003), at 307.

[80] ECJ *Ingrid Rinner-Kühn v. FWW Spezial-Gebäudereinigung GmbH & Co. KG*, Case C-171/88, 13 July 1989, para. 14. Also see Gerards (2005), at 275-276.

[81] ECJ *Bilka Kaufhaus v. Karin Weber von Hartz*, Case 170/84, 13 May 1986, para. 36; Gerards (2005), at 274-275.

[82] Finlay (2003), at 143; Hepple & Barnard (1999), at 402.

[83] For a discussion of the relationship between the concept of indirect discrimination and positive duties, see section 5.3.

[84] Kelman (2001), at 836. See also Moon (2006a), at 13, who points out that the cost element is a relevant factor in the practice of the Canadian Supreme Court with regard to the duty of reasonable accommodation.

[85] Tobler (2005), at 248-250.

of the duty of reasonable accommodation for disabled persons of the FD.[86] Indeed, in order to make positive duties a reality in the broader European equality framework, and particularly in the context of indirect discrimination, it appears inevitable to accept financial considerations as legitimate aims in certain cases.

Thirdly, the legitimacy of the aim should be determined in the light of the context within which the contested measure operates. If, for instance, a particular aim is highly unusual or even considered inappropriate within a particular branch of business or sector of society, it should be less easily accepted.

Finally, it seems fairly obvious that the aim needs to be authentic, in that it is actually of worth to the author of the contested measure.[87] This criterion comes back in the ECJ's '*real* need' test for private employers in sex equality law, and seems generally applicable for all actors.

5.2.4.3. Appropriateness

Of the various components of the objective justification test, the appropriateness requirement lends itself most to objective assessment, because it concerns a relatively technical question of whether the contested measure is capable of attaining the legitimate aim sought after.[88] In the words of Advocate General Colomer in *Michaeler*, what is required is a "logical relationship" between the contested measure and the aim sought after.[89] Common sense and qualitative data are relevant here, rather than political or moral considerations.[90] Still, notwithstanding the rather factual nature of the assessment, courts have some leeway in finding the middle ground between mere usefulness and indispensability, which appropriateness is considered to cover.[91] So far, the ECJ has not yet taken the opportunity to give them specific guidelines in this regard.[92] Again it should be emphasised that a transparent and consistent approach is called for.

The appropriateness test can furthermore be used in order to take into consideration a number of quality requirements to be fulfilled by the author of the contested measure. Thus, if a measure is of low quality it should be

86 ECJ *Sonia Chacón Navas v. Eurest Colectividades SA*, Case C-13/05, Opinion of Advocate-General Geelhoed, 16 March 2006, para. 83: "[w]hat is reasonable is also determined by the cost of appropriate resources, the proportionality of those costs if they are not reimbursed by the authorities (…)."

87 Sottiaux (2008), at 238.

88 Gerards (2002), at 286 and 300; Emiliou (1996), at 25-26.

89 Opinion of Advocate-General Colomer in ECJ *Othmar Michaeler a.o. v. Arbeitsinspektorat der Autonomen Provinz Bozen*, Cases C-55/07 and C-56/07, 24 January 2008, para. 41.

90 Sottiaux (2008), at 238.

91 Jans et al (2007), at 153.

92 Gerards (2002), at 286 and 300.

more easily dismissed as inappropriate. For instance, courts may require that measures are sufficiently transparent and that target groups are appropriately delineated. This latter requirement ties in with the notions of over or under-inclusiveness: if a measure inappropriately excludes particular persons from its scope, it is under-inclusive; conversely, if it targets an overly large audience it is over-inclusive. Both over and under-inclusiveness undermine the quality of measures, which is why it is preferable that courts pay attention to this matter.[93]

5.2.4.4. Necessity

The necessity test of the objective justification test focuses on the weightiness of the interest that an actor has in maintaining the contested measure. Again the jurisprudence of the ECJ does not make entirely clear what the necessity test entails. At the very least, it involves a subsidiarity assessment, which entails the search for less intrusive alternatives for achieving the legitimate aim, as becomes clear from both nationality and sex discrimination law.[94] As one author has commented, it is possible to discern the traces of a duty of care in this aspect of necessity, since it implies a proactive attitude of the author of a contested measure to look for the least intrusive means of attaining his objective.[95]

Case law of the ECJ in the field of nationality discrimination shows that necessity does not invariably involve a subsidiarity test and can be assessed in a more general manner. For instance, the ECJ considered a rule limiting the possibilities to contract foreign language teachers for an indefinite period unnecessary because it simply did not further the aim sought after, which was to ensure high quality teaching staff.[96] According to AG Colomer in *Michaeler*, necessity in this understanding comes down to assessing the overall effectiveness of the contested measure.[97] This effectiveness aspect would appear to be also covered by the appropriateness test, at least to a large extent, which goes to show that the ECJ does not maintain strict boundaries between the various components of the objective justification test.

The general principle of proportionality in European law entails, in addition to the requirements of appropriateness and necessity, a requirement of proportionality stricto sensu, which demands a proportionate relationship

[93] Gerards (2002), at 46, at 304.

[94] Tobler (2005), at 242; Emiliou (1996), at 29.

[95] Jans et al (2007), at 158. See section 5.3 on a more extensive discussion of the possibility of inferring positive duties from the concept of indirect discrimination.

[96] ECJ *Allué and Coonan v. Università degli studi di Venezia*, Case 33/88, 30 May 1989, para. 15, as commented on by Gerards (2002), at 300.

[97] Opinion of Advocate-General Colomer in ECJ *Othmar Michaeler a.o. v. Arbeitsinspektorat der Autonomen Provinz Bozen*, Cases C-55/07 and C-56/07, 24 January 2008, para. 43.

between the advantages and the disadvantages caused by the contested measure.[98] This requirement of proportionality stricto sensu is not an express part of any of the formulations of the objective justification test in the ECJ's case law, and is equally absent in the definition of indirect discrimination in the RED. Still, a number of authors find that the balancing act associated with proportionality stricto sensu is implicitly present in the case law of the ECJ and is even an indispensable element of the objective justification test.[99]

From a substantive equality perspective, it is desirable to include a proportionality stricto sensu requirement in the objective justification test, because this makes sure that the interests of the members of the affected racial or ethnic group are taken into account. In other words, even if a measure is 1) pursuing a legitimate aim, 2) appropriate, and 3) necessary in terms of the unavailability of viable alternatives, it should still be possible to consider it unacceptable in view of the seriousness of the consequences for the particular vulnerable group.[100] Especially since cases of indirect discrimination often involve measures that at first glance seem rational and reasonable, it is important that the interest of the disadvantaged group is a real factor in the objective justification phase.

It is desirable that the application of the proportionality stricto sensu test involves inclusive and thorough consideration of all relevant circumstances. This means that the personal situations of the author of the measure and of the racial or ethnic group are thoroughly examined, in order to determine the weight of their respective interests. Since the other elements of the objective justification test are mainly focused on the interests of the author of the contested measure, it is likely that this exercise will to a large extent focus on mapping the interest of the racial or ethnic group. From a substantive equality perspective it is essential that the seriousness of the disadvantage implied by the contested measure for the racial or ethnic group is appropriately examined. This would entail inter alia consideration of the intensity of the disadvantage, the relative number of persons of the group affected by it, negative spillover effects that the measure could engender and the context within which the contested measure is applied.

An important question that has been raised in literature is the extent to which attention should be paid to the free choice of the members of a

[98] The general principle of proportionality in EU law follows the German model, according to which proportionality consists of three separate aspects: suitability, necessity and a proportionate relationship between the aim of the measure and the restrictions on individuals that it entails, see Craig & De Búrca (2003), at 372, and Emiliou (1996), at 23. The latter aspect is also known as 'proportionality stricto sensu' and requires a balancing act of the various interests involved.

[99] Baker (2008), at 309-310; Tobler (2005), at 240; Gerards (2002), at 288-289 and 302-304; Opinion of Advocate-General Colomer in ECJ *Othmar Michaeler a.o. v. Arbeitsinspektorat der Autonomen Provinz Bozen*, Cases C-55/07 and C-56/07, 24 January 2008, para. 37.

[100] Baker (2008), at 311.

disadvantaged group.[101] One could after all argue that a disadvantage that is wholly or partially attributable to the choices made by the alleged victims should be taken less seriously. For instance, whether or not to learn the majority language is something a person chooses to do, and it is arguable that this choice element should influence the examination of the proportionality of a contested measure that disadvantages persons not speaking the majority language. Obviously this is quite a sensitive issue, since many characteristics associated with minorities are not intrinsically linked to minority group membership but involve a personal choice.[102] The greater the extent to which courts are willing to leave room for these personal choices, the more they embrace a substantive concept of equality, which allows persons to be different from the majority. It is therefore desirable that the choice element is not perceived as rendering less weighty the interest of the racial or ethnic group, especially if it concerns something that is perceived as very closely connected to the minority identity.

The ECJ's nationality discrimination jurisprudence appears to endorse this standpoint.[103] In *O'Flynn*, a rule that provided for coverage of funeral expenses only for burials or cremations that took place within the territory of the UK was claimed to be indirectly discriminatory against migrant workers. The referring instance wanted to know whether it was relevant for which reasons the applicant had failed to meet the territorial criterion. The ECJ answered in the negative, and considered that: "the reasons why a migrant worker chooses to make use of his freedom of movement within the Community are not to be taken into account in assessing whether a national provision is discriminatory. The possibility of exercising so fundamental a freedom as the freedom of movement of persons cannot be limited by such considerations, which are purely subjective".[104] A similar standpoint is welcome in the framework of the RED regarding the freedom to embrace one's minority identity.

5.3. Indirect discrimination and positive duties

There is a clear connection between indirect discrimination and positive duties, seeing that the prohibition of indirect discrimination requires persons who enact provisions, criteria or practices to take into consideration the effects of these measures on vulnerable groups.[105] If they do not account for the interests

[101] De Schutter (2007), at 8; Davies (2002), at 59.

[102] This is for instance true for religion and language; see section 2.3.1 for a discussion of the various proxies that are relevant for racial and ethnic discrimination.

[103] Tobler (2005), at 188-189.

[104] ECJ *John O'Flynn v. Adjudication Officer*, Case C-237/94, 23 May 1996, paras. 12 and 21.

[105] *Thematic comment no. 3, The protection of minorities in the European Union*, EU Network of Independent Experts on Fundamental Rights, 2005, CFR-CDF.ThemComm2005.en, at 23; De Vos (2007), at 14; Monaghan (2006), at 445; Jolls (2001), at 642-699; Morris (1995), at 214; Gottesman (1991), at 1750; McCrudden (1985), at 87; Advocate-General Maduro in

of these groups, they risk a finding of unjustified indirect discrimination. For instance, if an employer decides to organise a collective entry exam for new employees on a Saturday, he should find ways to accommodate persons of the Jewish religion, who are not allowed to work on Saturday, in order to avoid a finding of indirect discrimination.[106] The inherent link with the duty to take into consideration the interests of vulnerable groups places the concept of indirect discrimination in the realm of substantive equality, and depending on how strictly courts apply the objective justification test, substantive equality is more or less generously served.

The impact of indirect discrimination in terms of substantive equality can reach a very high level if courts are willing to qualify as indirectly discriminatory situations in which no single cause for the particular disadvantage is identifiable. Deciding on the objective justification in such cases comes down to deciding to what extent an actor should have actively done something about a particular disadvantage for a racial or ethnic group, even if he perhaps did not cause that disadvantage himself. For example, if numbers show that within a particular company persons belonging to ethnic minorities tend not to move up to management positions, the employer could be required to take measures to tackle this disproportion. Similarly, schools in which many of the children have an insufficient command of the language of instruction could be required to offer language courses.

Whereas in literature the link between these proactive duties and indirect discrimination has been recognised,[107] the ECJ so far has not applied indirect

ECJ *Coleman v. Attridge Law and Steve Law*, Case C-303/06, 31 January 2009, para. 19. See furthermore a number of decisions of the European Committee on Social Rights, in which it explains that indirect discrimination is constituted by the failure to take "due and positive account of all relevant differences or by failing to take adequate steps to ensure that rights and collective advantages that are open to all are genuinely accessibly by and to all." See *Autism Europe v. France*, ECSR complaint no. 13/2002, 4 November 2003, para. 52; *ERRC v. Italy*, ECSR complaint no. 27/2004, 7 December 2005, para. 20; *ERRC v. Bulgaria*, 18 October 2006, ECSR complaint no. 31/2005, para. 26. For a slightly different view, see Tobler (2008), at 54, who submits that a duty of accommodation is not automatically connected to the concept of indirect discrimination. She mentions a case of indirect discrimination as regards equal pay for equal work, which simply entails a duty to equalise pay levels. Still, even in such cases, there is a reason for the inequality in pay, which had some connection with a protected ground. Thus, by equalising the levels of pay, this reason of inequality is eliminated or counteracted, and the motivation for this is to offset a particular disadvantage for a protected grouat Clearly, such an action breathes of consideration for the interests of the protected group, which is why even in the example mentioned it is possible to connect the concept of indirect discrimination to a positive duty.

[106] Compare ECJ *Vivien Prais v. Council*, Case 130/75, 27 October 1976, in which the ECJ determined that the European Commission should take into account the interests of a person who could not work on Saturday for religious reasons when setting the date for an entry exam.

[107] See for example *Thematic comment no. 3, The protection of minorities in the European Union*, EU Network of Independent Experts on Fundamental Rights, 2005, CFR-CDF. ThemComm2005.en, at 23; Jolls (2001), at 652-666, *House of Lords Select Committee on the*

discrimination in such a far-reaching way.[108] Proactive duties do fit European equality thinking, however, or at least are not at variance with it. After all, Article 5 RED allows Member States to take measures of positive action. Moreover, the European equality paradigm already entertains positive duties to provide for the special needs of certain vulnerable groups: the FD imposes on employers a duty to reasonably accommodate individual persons with a disability. The individual focus of this duty admittedly distinguishes it from positive duties that would flow from the group-focused prohibition of indirect discrimination.[109] Still, the notion of reasonable accommodation reveals substantive equality thinking, according to which proactively addressing the needs of vulnerable persons is called for. Similar thinking is visible in the various provisions in European sex equality law that protect women as regards special needs that they have on account of pregnancy and maternity.[110]

As Member States are allowed to set in place a higher level of protection than required by the RED, it is conceivable that they will open up the concept of indirect discrimination to proactive duties. This would seem particularly feasible with regard to public actors. After all, as agents of the state they indirectly already have an international duty to actively address the interests of racial and ethnic groups. This duty is explicitly laid down in ICERD, which is referred to by Recital 3 of the RED.[111] Moreover, the FCNM, which is ratified by some Member States, contains a number of positive duties towards minorities.[112] The practice of the Committee on the Elimination of Racial

European Union, Ninth Report on the EU proposals to combat discrimination, 16 may 2000, paras. 94-95.

[108] Asscher-Vos (1999), at 44; Tobler (2005), at 373. See also ECJ *Bilka Kaufhaus v. von Hartz*, Case 170/84, 13 May 1986, para. 43, in which the ECJ refused to infer such a positive duty from the concept of indirect discrimination.

[109] Gijzen (2006), at 396-397; Waddington (2004).

[110] Ellis (2005), at 285-289.

[111] Article 2(2) of ICERD reads as follows: "States Parties shall, when the circumstances so warrant, take, in the social, economic, cultural and other fields, special and concrete measures to ensure the adequate development and protection of certain racial groups or individuals belonging to them, for the purpose of guaranteeing them the full and equal enjoyment of human rights and fundamental freedoms. These measures shall in no case entail as a consequence the maintenance of unequal or separate rights for different racial groups after the objectives for which they were taken have been achieved."

[112] Article 4 FCNM contains a duty to promote full and effective equality; Art. 12(3) FCNM contains a duty to promote equal opportunities for access to education at all levels; Art. 5(1) FCNM contains a duty to promote the conditions necessary for persons belonging to national minorities to maintain and develop their culture and to preserve their essential elements of their identity, namely their religion, language, traditions and cultural heritage.

Discrimination (CERD),[113] the UN Human Rights Committee (HRC),[114] the European Committee of Social rights (ECSR)[115] and the Advisory Committee on the Framework Convention for National Minorities (ACFCNM)[116] of the Council of Europe furthermore all to some extent recognise such duties.

As was mentioned before, it makes sense to primarily target public actors with positive duties, who have to serve the interests of citizens and who generally have more expertise and resources than private actors.[117] Still, the possibility of setting up proactive duties for private actors should not be ruled out, especially not with regard to powerful actors or actors who have discriminated in the past. It should be kept in mind that the recognition of proactive duties for private actors would generally only find acceptance if it were accompanied with safeguards to alleviate concerns related to the limits set by the fundamental rights and freedoms of private actors.[118] As regards the limits set by the prohibition of discrimination, reference is made to section 7.3, where the limits to positive action posed by direct and indirect discrimination are discussed.

It should furthermore be emphasised that recognizing proactive duties vis-à-vis minority groups could have unintended negative effects by reinforcing stereotypes or disempowering minority groups. This is an important consideration to be taken on board in the decision-making process as to whether a proactive duty is called for.[119]

---

113 A few examples drawn from CERD's non-binding Concluding Observations include a call for comprehensive national strategies for implementing the Article 2(2) duty (*Concluding Observations on Guyana, 2006,* CERD/C/Guy/CO/14; *Concluding Observations on Slovenia*, 2003, CERD/C/62/CO/09, para. 11) and a call for accommodation of minority languages in media and education (*Concluding Observations on Morocco, 2003,* CERD/C/62/CO/05, para. 17; *Concluding Observations on Uzbekistan*, 2006, CERD/C/UZB/CO/5, paras. 18 and 19; *Concluding Observations on Albania*, 2003, CERD/C/63/CO/1, para. 7).

114 See *HRC General Comment No. 23, The rights of minorities (Art. 27), 8 April 1994*, para. 6.2: "positive measures by States may also be necessary to protect the identity of a minority and the rights of its members to enjoy and develop their culture and language and to practice their religion, in community with the other members of the group."

115 *ERRC v. Italy*, ECSR complaint no. 27/2004, 7 December 2005, para. 20; *ERRC v. Bulgaria*, ECSR complaint no. 31/2005, 18 October 2006, para. 26.

116 A small selection of the legally non-binding opinions of the ACFCNM shows the following picture: a duty of adopting special measures in education (*Second opinion on Germany,* 1 March 2006, *ACFC/OP/II(2006) 001*, para. 112); a duty to find suitable solutions to specific problems encountered by Roma in housing, employment and education as well as a duty to provide for education in minority languages (*Second opinion on Norway,* 5 October 2006, ACFC/OP/II(2006)006, paras. 48, 134, 136); a duty to ensure access to media for minorities and provide funding for media outlets, as well as a duty to provide for textbooks in minority languages (*Second Opinion on the Russian Federation*, 11 May 2006, ACFC/OP/II(2006)004, paras. 189 and 240).

117 See section 2.2.2.2.

118 See section 2.2.2.2.

119 Emiliou (1996), at 46.

PART TWO: CASE STUDY

5.4. Definition of indirect discrimination

5.4.1. Situation prior to the RED and the changes brought about by implementation

Indirect discrimination is one of the aspects of the RED that brought about quite a change in the national equality frameworks under study, which were all, except for the Netherlands, unfamiliar with this concept at the time of implementation. It is perhaps for this reason that the national definitions generally stay close to the wording of Article 2(2)(b) RED.

In Belgium and Hungary, the national definition of indirect discrimination was changed over time, in a move towards more conformity with Article 2(2)(b) RED. In Belgium, the first implementation phase produced the following definition in Article 1(2) ADA:

> an apparently neutral provision, criterion or practice that has harmful repercussions for persons [with a protected characteristic, MB], unless this provision, criterion or practice is objectively and reasonably justified.

The amendments of 2007 introduced a definition made up of a complex of articles, which distinguish between indirect *distinction* and indirect *discrimination*. Article 4(8) of the new ARA defines indirect *distinction* as:

> the situation in which an apparently neutral provision, criterion or practice can in particular disadvantage persons characterised by a [protected characteristic, MB] in comparison to other persons.

Article 4(9) of the new ARA defines indirect *discrimination* as follows:

> indirect distinction on [a protected characteristic, MB] that cannot be justified in accordance with the exception provisions.

The exception provision for indirect discrimination is provided by Article 9 of the new ARA, which stipulates that:

> any indirect distinction on the basis of one of the protected grounds amounts to indirect discrimination unless the apparently neutral provision, criterion or practice that underlies the indirect distinction can be justified by a legitimate aim and if the means for achieving that aim are appropriate and necessary.

In Hungary, the first step of implementation involved the insertion of a provision in the Labour Code, which defined indirect discrimination as follows:

> an employment-related provision, criterion, condition or practice that is apparently neutral or that affords the same rights to all, disadvantages a

> substantially higher proportion of the members of a particular group of employees, unless that provision, criterion, condition or practice is appropriate and necessary and can be justified by objective factors.

This definition, and in particular the implicit preference for quantitative data for the establishment of the disparate impact, reminds of the definition of indirect sex discrimination in the Burden of Proof Directive.[120] The second implementation phase altered this preference for quantitative data and produced a description of the disparate impact that more closely resembled the 'particular disadvantage' wording of the RED. Thus, Article 9 HETA provided the following definition:

> a provision not deemed as direct discrimination and ostensibly meeting the requirement of equal treatment is considered to be indirect discrimination if it puts individual persons or groups [with a protected characteristic, MB] in a significantly disproportionately disadvantageous situation compared to a person or group in a comparable situation.

This definition was criticised for lacking the 'would put' language of the RED, and was thus altered by the 2007 amendments. The new definition in Article 9 HETA now provides the following definition:

> Those dispositions are considered indirect negative discrimination, which are not considered direct negative discrimination and apparently comply with the principle of equal treatment but put any persons or groups having characteristics defined in Article 8 at a considerably larger disadvantage than other persons or groups in a similar situation were or would be (emphasis added, MB).

The 'would be' reference was intended to implement the 'would put' aspect of Article 2(2)(b) RED, but it is wrongly located, since it now refers to the comparators of the disadvantaged persons, instead of to the disadvantaged persons themselves. Still, as is pointed out in section 5.2.2.2, the 'would put' part of Article 2(2)(b) will most likely be appropriately applied in the Hungarian context.

In Estonia, implementation of the RED also came about in phases, the first of which produced the following definition of indirect discrimination in Article 10 of the ECA:

> Indirect discrimination shall be taken to occur where an apparently neutral provision, criterion or practice would put employees or persons applying for employment at a particular disadvantage compared with other employees or persons applying for employment based on [a protected characteristic, MB], unless that provision, criterion or practice is objectively justified by a legitimate aim and the means of achieving that aim are appropriate and necessary.

This definition closely follows Article 2(2)(b) RED, and so does its successor, Article 3(4) of the EETA, which provides that:

[120] See section 5.2.2.2.

> Discrimination is indirect, if a seemingly neutral provision, criterion or tradition places persons based on [a protected characteristic, MB] in a more disadvantageous situation, unless the stipulation, criterion or tradition has an objective legitimate purpose and the means of achieving this purpose are appropriate and necessary.

Contrary to the other national frameworks, the Dutch framework does not provide for a definition that resembles Article 2(2)(b) RED and has maintained the definition provided by Article 1(1)(c) GETA since 1994. This definition describes indirect discrimination as:

> distinction on the grounds of characteristics or behaviour other than [direct distinction, MB], which results in a direct distinction.

At the occasion of the implementation of the RED, the government decided to insert an explicit reference to the objective justification test for indirect discrimination, which is now provided in Article 2(1) GETA. This provision reads as follows:

> The prohibition on distinction contained in this Act does not apply to an indirect distinction which is objectively justified by a legitimate aim and where the means to achieve that aim are appropriate and necessary.

Even though the government for a long time resisted calls for adaptation of the definition of indirect discrimination, it decided in 2003 that it would change the definition to bring it in line with European law.[121] In January 2009, a draft amendment to the GETA was proposed to Parliament, which defines 'indirect distinction' as follows:

> if an apparently neutral provision, criterion or practice particularly affects persons with a [protected characteristic, MB] in comparison with other persons.[122]

As was pointed out in the previous chapter, in most Member States courts and bodies still wrestle with the meaning of indirect discrimination, which will be confirmed throughout the following assessment. The Dutch ETC is the sole body so far that has developed a clear and consistent approach to indirect discrimination, and its quasi-jurisprudence will thus often be referred to as providing a good example for the other frameworks.

[121] *Letter of the government with regard to the second evaluation of the GETA,* TK 2003-4, 29 311, no. 3, at 2-3. The commitment was repeated in the *Explanatory Memorandum to the Draft act implementing directive 2004/113/EC on equal treatment between men and women in the provision of goods and services*, TK 2006-7, 30967, no. 3, at 3. See also Holtmaat (2007), at 69.
[122] *Proposal for an amendment to the equal treatment acts in order to align with directive terminology*, TK 2008-2009, 31 832, No.2.

5.4.2. 'An apparently neutral provision, criterion or practice'

5.4.2.1. Formal differences in treatment and material differences in treatment

As was already observed in the previous chapter, the definitions of discrimination in the Belgian, Hungarian and Dutch frameworks make use of 'distinction' language, which reveals that they consider discrimination to be constituted by differences in treatment, in line with their constitutional traditions.[123] This 'distinction' approach arguably makes it more likely that national courts and/or bodies will require the establishment of a formal difference in treatment in the context of indirect discrimination, which lowers the level of protection offered by this concept.

Case law in Belgium and the Netherlands indeed reveals that such a requirement is sometimes imposed. For example, in a case involving the dismissal of a woman for refusing to remove her headscarf, which she wore for religious reasons, the Brussels Labour Court rejected the claim of indirect discrimination, because the prohibition of wearing religious symbols applied to all workers within the company, *without any distinction*.[124] In the Netherlands, the Central Appeal Council rejected a claim of indirect sex discrimination concerning a provision for maternity leave of teachers that did not compensate for overlap between school holidays and maternity leave. The Council could not see how the disadvantage was related to a *distinction* based on a prohibited criterion, as the disadvantage was rather an inherent aspect of the kind of employment performed by teachers.[125] In other words, the Council tried to find a difference in treatment that it could causally link to sex, after which it concluded that no such difference was present and that it was therefore not necessary to look at justification issues. This kind of reasoning produces an additional barrier for applicants and threatens to undermine the substantive equality focus of indirect discrimination, as was explained in section 5.2.1.1. Even though this difference-based reasoning does not consistently appear in indirect discrimination cases in the Belgian and Dutch frameworks, it does raise some concern. It is advisable for Belgian and Dutch courts to follow the example of the Dutch ETC, which has developed a clear approach that focuses on the establishment of the particular disadvantage and not of a difference in treatment.[126]

---

[123] See section 4.6.1.

[124] *Centrum voor gelijkheid van kansen en racismebestrijding v. Firma Feryn NV* Brussels Labour Court, no. 15091/07, 15 January 2008, as recorded in *European Anti-Discrimination Law Review* 2008, No. 6/7, at 79-80.

[125] Central Appeal Council, 17 May 2001, LJN: AB1704, para. 7.3. For another example of a difference-based approach, see Utrecht District Court, 24 May 2006, LJN: AY4333, para. 2.12, in which the Court explains the concept of indirect discrimination as a *distinguishing* criterion that leads to a disadvantage for a particular group.

[126] Gerards (2005), at 561-562.

It is to be hoped that the 'distinction' language of the HETA will not induce the Hungarian AET and Hungarian courts to follow the example of some of their Belgian and Dutch counterparts and to require a formal difference in treatment for indirect discrimination. It is fortunate in this respect that the particular model of review applied by the AET for discrimination cases does not comprise such a requirement. According to this model, it suffices to establish the existence of a disadvantage and the presence of a protected characteristic in order to establish a prima facie case of discrimination.[127] Still, the model has so far only been applied in direct discrimination cases, and it remains to be seen how it will be applied in indirect discrimination cases.

5.4.2.2. Broad interpretation of 'provision, criterion or practice'

Two out of four Member States, Belgium and Estonia, have replicated in their definitions of indirect discrimination the 'provision, criterion or practice' phrase. In both states there is no relevant case law with which to assess the manner in which this phrase is interpreted, and it thus remains to be seen whether an inclusive approach will be adopted.

In Belgium there is a favourable scholarly climate in this respect, because Belgian scholars have emphasised that courts should not put too much effort into trying to localise the particular source of a disparate impact and should instead focus on the disparate impact itself.[128] This approach is in line with the above-cited *Enderby* jurisprudence of the ECJ and extends the meaning of indirect discrimination to situations in which there is not a difference in treatment, but only a statistical disparity for which no single cause can be identified. If Belgian courts would indeed follow the academics' suggestion, they would contribute significantly to the effectiveness of the concept of indirect discrimination.

The Dutch framework provides an example of how such an inclusive approach works in practice. The Dutch GETA currently lacks an explicit reference to the measure causing indirect discrimination, but this will change with the adoption of the proposed amendment to the GETA, after which the 'provision, criterion or practice' phrase will formally be part of the definition of indirect discrimination. Even now, however, the words 'provision, criterion or practice' can be read into the current definition.

The ETC practice indeed shows that it is more concerned with establishing the *effect* of a disadvantage on a particular group than the particular source of this effect.[129] So far, a broad array of measures/actions have been presented to the ETC in the context of indirect discrimination, and this body has never

---

[127] EBH 384/4/2008. See more elaborately on the division of the burden of proof Ambrus (2010).
[128] Bayart & Deiteren (2008), at 206-207; De Prins et al (2005), at 471.
[129] Gerards (2005), at 561-562.

dismissed any of these cases for lacking an appropriate causing factor. The ETC has for example qualified a discouraging and obstructive attitude towards a woman who wanted to change her working hours as indirect discrimination.[130] Furthermore, in a social housing policy case, the ETC accepted the possibility that a bundle of criteria together could cause a disparate effect.[131] Sporadically, the ETC has even considered that the omission to provide for special provisions for protected groups could constitute indirect discrimination. Examples include the omission to take into account the special needs of travellers when drawing up a public housing policy, and the omission to provide for fire and theft insurance for mobile homes.[132] The inclusion of omissions as potential causes of indirect discrimination opens the door for proactive positive duties and thus has a strong substantive equality focus.

Similarly to the Dutch framework, the Hungarian HETA takes an inclusive approach to the potential sources of indirect discrimination, and mentions in Article 7(2) the following types of behaviour: "conduct, measure, condition, omission, instruction or practice". Again it should be emphasised that the inclusion of 'omission' is an important step in the direction of substantive equality. The favourable conditions set by the HETA have not yet led to a great number of cases on indirect discrimination, which is most likely due to unfamiliarity with the concept.

5.4.2.3. Single source doctrine

Traces of a single source doctrine have so far only appeared in the Netherlands. The ETC has applied this doctrine in the field of equal pay in the same way as the ECJ. For instance, it refused to scrutinise a difference in pay that was caused by two separate collective agreements as a potential case of indirect discrimination, for lack of a single source of the inequality.[133] It is to be hoped that the ETC will not further expand this particular use of the doctrine beyond the field of equal pay, for reasons that were explained in the theoretical framework.

The ETC has furthermore sometimes used the doctrine to determine whether a person was sufficiently connected to the author of discrimination to be held accountable for the discrimination. It has referred to the single source doctrine in the context of mother companies being held accountable for discriminatory actions of daughter companies, stating that it considered both companies to constitute a single source if the mother company exerted a sufficient degree of influence over the daughter company's policy.[134] This

[130] Opinion 2003-104 ETC, para. 5.14.
[131] Opinion 2002-159 ETC, para. 5.8.
[132] Opinion 2006-222 ETC, para. 3.20; Opinion 2006-5 ETC, para. 5.22.
[133] Opinion 2005-190 ETC, para. 5.8.
[134] Opinion 2008-19 ETC, paras. 3.3-4; Opinion 2007-171 ETC, paras. 3.13-16.

particular use of the single source doctrine is substantively different from the way in which the ECJ has applied it so far, and arguably further obscures the true meaning of the doctrine. It is advisable for the ETC to more clearly distinguish between the single source doctrine for the field of equal pay and the doctrine of liability for daughter companies or other associated persons.

5.4.3. Would put at a particular disadvantage persons of a racial or ethnic origin

5.4.3.1. Formulation of the 'particular disadvantage' element

The four Member States have each adopted their own formulations of the second element of indirect discrimination, which differ to a greater or lesser extent from the formulation of Article 2(2)(b) RED. The Dutch definition currently differs most from the RED's definition and simply refers to a distinction that results in a 'direct distinction'. The ETC and the Dutch courts, however, have consistently interpreted this phrase in line with the appropriate European law definition. Thus, they have followed the O'Flynn definition of free movement law or the definition in the Burden of Proof Directive in cases of nationality or sex discrimination respectively.[135] It is therefore expected that they will apply the definition of Article 2(2)(b) RED when examining indirect racial discrimination cases, especially since the definition of the GETA will be altered in the near future in line with the wording of the RED. After the entry into force of the proposed amendment, Article 1(1)(c) GETA will refer to a measure that 'particularly affects' a protected group.

Article 4(8) of the new Belgian ARA most closely resembles Article 2(2)(b) RED and refers to a provision, criterion or practice that "can in particular disadvantage persons characterised by a particular protected characteristic". This wording, as well as the 'particularly affects' wording of the Dutch Amendment Act, in a way is less ambiguous than Article 2(2)(b) RED, because it more clearly points out that 'particular' is not about the intensity of the disadvantage but about the disproportion in the number of affected persons with a protected characteristic.

The Estonian and Hungarian versions have instead retained the – admittedly minor – ambiguity of the RED by linking the qualification of 'particular' to the disadvantage and not to the disproportion of the impact on the protected group. Article 3(4) EETA refers to a provision, criterion or practice that "places persons based on a [protected characteristic, MB] in a more disadvantageous situation", and Article 9 HETA refers to measures that "put any persons or groups having [a protected characteristic, MB] at a considerably larger disadvantage".

135 Gerards (2005), at 542, 557 and 561.

5.4.3.2. Causal link required?

The Estonian definition is remarkable for the causality perspective that transpires from the words "*based on* [a protected characteristic, MB]" in Article 3(4) EETA (emphasis added, MB). This formulation could induce Estonian courts to require the establishment of a causal link between the contested measure and the protected ground, in addition to the establishment of the particular disadvantage. As was explained above, such an approach is not desirable.

Unfortunately, traces of such a causality approach have appeared in the Hungarian and Dutch contexts. In one of the scarce indirect discrimination cases of the Hungarian AET, this body appeared to make use of the notion of causality in order to assess the legality of the particular measure, and thereby bypassed the normal justification test for indirect discrimination. The case involved a salary scheme that was claimed to particularly disadvantage persons with health problems and persons taking care of dependents. The AET found this scheme to cause unreasonable harm to these persons, and it considered the scheme not to be sufficiently *explained by* the objective of increasing the motivation of employees. Moreover, it considered that the scheme was not transparent and was not well communicated to employees, which led it to conclude that the scheme amounted to indirect discrimination of the said persons.[136] The use of the verb *explain* in the decision points to a causality perspective, according to which there is no causal link if there is an acceptable justification for the contested measure. This impression is reinforced by the fact that the AET did not mention the justification test of Article 7(2)(b) HETA anywhere in its decision, whereas it normally enumerates all legal provisions that it applies. Thus, it would seem that the AET did not apply the Article 7(2)(b) test at all, having already considered the relevant justificatory arguments in terms of causality. One decision is obviously not conclusive, and perhaps only illustrates the difficulty that courts and bodies have in applying the unfamiliar concept of indirect discrimination. Future practice should indicate whether a causality approach indeed makes up part of the AET's toolbox.

In the Dutch context, an example of the causality approach is found in the aforementioned ruling of the Central Appeal Council on a provision that did not compensate for overlap between school holidays and maternity leave.[137] In this case the Council held that the alleged disadvantage was not *a consequence* of pregnancy, but was an inherent aspect of the employment contract of teachers. It thus viewed the concept of indirect discrimination through a causality prism, searching for a causal link between sex and the alleged disadvantage. The High Council in a similar case applied the exact same reasoning, and added that the measure could not be traced back to a distinction based on sex, which

[136] EBH 700/2007.

[137] Central Appeal Council, 17 May 2001, LJN: AB1704. See section 5.5.2.

underlines the causality perspective from which it reasoned.[138] Fortunately the Dutch ETC does not apply the causality approach for indirect discrimination cases: this body only requires the establishment of a particular disadvantage for a protected group.[139]

5.4.3.3. Establishing the particular disadvantage

5.4.3.3.1. *Means of proof*

All four Member States have permitted quantitative and qualitative evidence for the establishment of the particular disadvantage. The new Belgian ARA provides a particularly transparent framework, since the matter is expressly regulated in Article 30(3) of the new ARA. This article provides that:

> [f]acts that can raise the suspicion of the presence of indirect discrimination on grounds of a protected criterion are considered to comprise amongst others, though not exclusively: 1. general statistics about the situation of the group to which the victim of the discrimination belongs or facts of general knowledge; or 2. the use of an intrinsically suspicious criterion of distinction; or 3. elementary statistical data which reveal a disadvantageous treatment.

Thus, both qualitative and quantitative means of proof are permissible, and the non-exhaustive nature of this list makes clear that applicants have quite some room for forwarding all kinds of relevant data that they can find. The clarity thus created by the Belgian legislator pre-empts difficulties in practice, which reinforces the protective framework of the new ARA.

For Estonia, the permissibility of both types of evidence can be inferred from the Explanatory Memorandum to the EETA, which mentions qualitative and quantitative types of evidence in the context of indirect discrimination.[140] It remains to be seen whether Estonian courts will follow the Explanatory Memorandum's suggestion.

In Hungary, both quantitative and qualitative data have already been used in practice. The AET for instance points out in its 2006 year report that it sometimes looks at statistics when establishing the disadvantage for direct discrimination, which must mean that such evidence may also be used for

---

[138] High Council 23 April 2004, NJ 2008/393, para. 6.11.

[139] Gerards (2005), at 561-562.

[140] *Explanatory Memorandum to Act 384 SE III on Equal Treatment*: "[i]ndirect discrimination is mainly revealed by *statistical information or sociological studies*, which have been broken down in terms of possible grounds of discrimination. Thus the ethnic and racial groups living in Estonia, organizations or other persons in public law must be compared, dominant groups in different fields must be identified, etc for ascertaining discrimination" (emphasis added, MB). 'Statistical information' clearly points to quantitative evidence, while 'sociological studies' points to both quantitative and qualitative data.

indirect discrimination.[141] In addition, one indirect discrimination case that was handled by the Minorities Ombudsman appears to have been based on quantitative evidence. The case concerned a claim of educational segregation of Roma children. The Ombudsman considered the permanent closing-off of a corridor that connected a special needs class to the main school building as indirectly discriminatory, but did not explain or motivate this statement. It remains unclear how the Ombudsman established the particular disadvantage, but it can be assumed that a high percentage of Roma children in the special needs class led it to conclude that the measure was indirectly discriminatory.[142] To our knowledge, this case constitutes so far the only one where quantitative evidence was apparently used to come to a finding of indirect discrimination. The two other known cases of indirect discrimination involved qualitative evidence. The first case involved the negligent behaviour of a local council in ensuring representation of the local Roma minority in a committee for minority issues, which evolved around the circumstances surrounding the setting up of the committee.[143] The second case involved a rule that granted bonuses to employees who had an absence rate of less than 15 per cent, which the AET regarded to be indirectly discriminatory against persons of diminished health status and persons taking care of dependants. The AET drew this conclusion on the basis of the fact of general knowledge that these persons tend to be absent from work more often than other persons.[144]

The Dutch ETC has traditionally been very inclusive regarding the means of proof that can be used for establishing a prima facie case of indirect discrimination, and this has not changed with the implementation of the RED. Thus, the particular disadvantage can be established by quantitative as well as by qualitative evidence, which includes facts of general knowledge, social facts, and simply 'obviousness'.[145] In the context of indirect racial discrimination, obviousness is for instance used for language requirements, headwear requirements and criteria related to place of residence, all of which are considered to obviously disproportionately impact on ethnic minorities.[146]

141 *Report on the activities of the Equal Treatment Authority and the experiences of the implementation of Act nr. 125 of 2003 on equal treatment and the promotion of equal opportunities, AET, July 2006*, at 13.

142 The case is described in the *Annual Report on 2005* of the Parliamentary Commissioner for the Rights of National and Ethnic Minorities, to be found at www.kisebbsegiombudsman.hu (accessed August 2009). The description remains silent on the particular statistical data.

143 EBH 337/24/2005 and Supreme Court, Kfv.IV.37.450/2006/5, 11 July 2007. See for a more detailed description of this case section 4.6.4.1.

144 EBH 700/2007.

145 Gerards (2005), at 582-585.

146 Gerards (2005), at 583-585.

5.4.3.3.2. Establishment of the particular disadvantage

With the exception of the Dutch ETC, national courts and bodies have not yet come to develop a clear and consistent test for the particular disadvantage element of indirect discrimination, which moreover does not receive much attention.

The single known Belgian case on indirect discrimination, for instance, did not show any explicit consideration of this element. The case played before the Antwerp Court of Appeal and involved a prohibition of wearing headscarves in the classroom. The Court first stated that indirect discrimination was present where an apparently neutral provision, criterion or practice had a disadvantageous impact on persons, unless it was objectively and reasonably justified. It subsequently scrutinised the legality of the measure in the light of the freedom of religion. It thus simply took the particular disadvantage element for granted, which is not entirely surprising, since the link between headscarves and the Muslim religion is fairly obvious. Still, an express mention of the reasoning employed would have been welcome.

So far, no cases involving statistical material have presented themselves in the Belgian context, but it can be expected that courts will be rather lenient, seeing that Article 30(3) of the new ARA speaks of *elementary* statistical data, which indicates that they cannot set too high a standard.

The few cases in the Hungarian framework in which quantitative data was relevant involve direct discrimination, but are nevertheless likely to be relevant for indirect discrimination, especially because some of them arguably are indirect discrimination cases in disguise.[147] These cases reveal at any rate that there is not a consistent or systematic approach as to the assessment of quantitative data. In an age discrimination case mentioned in its 2006 Year Report, the AET considered that the fact that all of the dismissed employees were in the higher age category was not sufficient, in view of the fact that 86% of the total workforce consisted of this age category.[148] In this case the proportion of the older employees was thus only 1.163 (86/100) times higher than the proportion of these persons in the total workforce, and this factor was apparently considered too low to warrant a finding of discrimination, which seems a fair conclusion. Still, the fact remains that the AET did not apply a particular test or threshold in order to come to its finding.

Another case that involved quantitative evidence involved educational segregation of Roma children. In this case, the Hajdú-Bihar County Court deemed the following disparities sufficient to come to a finding of unlawful segregation: while 50% of the total student population was made up of Roma

---

[147] See section 4.6.2.

[148] *Report on the activities of the Equal Treatment Authority and the experiences of the implementation of Act nr. 125 of 2003 on equal treatment and the promotion of equal opportunities, AET, July 2006*. See also Kádár (2007), at 20.

students, only 28% of the students studying in the better equipped building were of Roma origin. Tellingly, 86% and 96% of the students in the lesser equipped schools were of Roma origin. This means that the proportions of Roma in the disadvantaged groups were respectively 1.72 (50/86) and 1.92 (50/96) times more than the proportion of Roma students in the total student population. In another school area, the factor was even 3.125.[149] The Court did not apply any particular test in order to determine whether these numbers established segregation, which is perhaps not surprising, since the disparity is simply overwhelming. The Supreme Court later confirmed the reasoning of the County Court.[150] The County Court and the Supreme Court thus looked at relative numbers, taking into account the normal demographic make-up of the local community in order to decide whether the proportions in the schools were disproportionate. As was explained before, it is essential to work with relative numbers in order to establish whether a racial or ethnic group was indeed particularly disadvantaged, and this approach is thus to be welcomed. Still, it is unfortunate that no specific test for the particular disadvantage was mentioned by either court.

The only test that has been forwarded so far is remarkably crude, the more so because it has been proposed by the Advisory Board on Equal Treatment, and expert body that advises the AET. According to its official opinion on discrimination in education, segregation is present if more than 50% of the students are of Roma origin.[151] This simple rule shows total disregard for the particular context of the case and for the relative numbers of the total student population. It is to be hoped that a more nuanced approacj will be adopted in practice.

The Dutch ETC stands out as regards its extensive quasi-jurisprudence on indirect discrimination, which shows to a large degree a consistent and thorough picture. The ETC has not refrained from performing complicated statistical tests and has developed a relatively objective and transparent approach to the 'particular disadvantage'. The ETC has not yet made a clear choice for one particular test to be applied, but it does consistently make use of objective and statistically valid methods to establish a disparate impact and it always describes in its decision the method that it has followed. In some cases it has applied a rule of thumb, according to which there is a disparate impact if the proportion of persons with the protected characteristic in the disadvantaged group is equal to or greater than 1.5 times their proportion in the non-disadvantaged group.[152] Furthermore, it has sometimes resorted to a very technical statistical method, by first establishing a correlation between

[149] Hajdú-Bihar County Court, 6.AT 20.341/2006/50, 2 May 2007.

[150] Supreme Court, Pfv.IV.20.936/2008/4, 19 November 2008.

[151] *Position Paper of the Advisory Body on Equal Treatment on the requirement of Equal treatment in Public Education*, 23 March 2007.

[152] Gijzen (2006), at 132; Gerards (2005), at 585-586.

the protected ground and the particular disadvantage and subsequently determining whether this correlation is statistically significant.[153] If these tests do not yield unambiguous results, the ETC is willing to consult with statistical experts, or to take into account supporting qualitative evidence.[154] This benevolent approach of the ETC means that the hurdle of establishing a prima facie case is kept as low as possible, while it respects the requirements of objectivity and transparency. It is thus a very positive asset of the Dutch anti-discrimination framework.

Unfortunately, the practice of Dutch courts does not provide a similarly positive picture, since it does not reveal a consistent or transparent approach. The courts often speak in generalities and do not apply a clear and transparent test. In the field of sex equality they have referred to the particular disadvantage aspect in the following terms: "many more women than men" should be affected;[155] "a considerable percentage of one sex [should be] disadvantaged with regard to the other sex";[156] a measure "exclusively or predominantly affects women";[157] or "disadvantages in fact more women than men".[158] None of these general statements were further elaborated. This adds weight to the claim of one author according to whom Dutch courts are generally not very willing to perform complicated statistical tests. The disproportionate impact therefore needs to be fairly obvious in order for them to conclude a prima facie case of indirect discrimination.[159]

It is interesting to see that the proposed amendment to Article 1(1)(c) GETA uses the more neutral verb *affect* instead of *disadvantage*, as in the RED. The Explanatory Memorandum to the draft amendment act reveals that the government deliberately chose this verb because it was broader than the verb *disadvantage*.[160] Still, reference should be made here to the standing requirement of the GETA according to which applicants must show that they have experienced an actual disadvantage, which was discussed in section 4.6.3. As was explained before, the disadvantage aspect of indirect discrimination is preferably not given too much emphasis at the stage of the establishment of a prima facie case and the use of the word *affect* is a positive asset in this regard.

153 See for more details on this test Gijzen (2006), at 131.
154 Gijzen (2006), at 132; Gerards (2005), at 586.
155 High Council, 13 February 1998, NJ 1999/58.
156 High Council, 23 April 2004, NJ 2008/393, para. 6.11.
157 High Council, NJ 2002/548, para. 3.3.
158 Central Appeal Council 17 May 2001, LJN: AB1704, para. 7.2.
159 Gerards (2005), at 581.
160 *Explanatory Memorandum to the amendment to the equal treatment acts in order to align with directive terminology*, TK 2008-2009, 31 832, No.3, at 3.

5.4.3.3.3. The 'would put' aspect of indirect discrimination

The 'would put' aspect of indirect discrimination has been appropriately implemented in most Member States, with the exception of Estonia. The definition of indirect discrimination in the Estonian EETA is framed in present tense wording ("places … in a more disadvantageous situation"), and it is uncertain whether Estonian courts will be willing to apply the concept of indirect discrimination in cases in which the particular disadvantage has not yet materialised.

Of the other three national anti-discrimination laws, the new Belgian ARA is the only instrument that expressly provides for this aspect of indirect discrimination, referring in Article 4(8) to a measure that "*can* in particular disadvantage" (emphasis added, MB).

As was mentioned before, the 'would put' aspect was clumsily inserted in Article 9 of the Hungarian HETA, which now contains a reference to hypothetical comparators and not to instances of non-materialised disadvantages. Still, given that the amendment was clearly intended to accommodate the 'would put' aspect of Article 2(2)(b) RED, it is expected that the AET and courts will interpret Article 9 in line with the RED. Additional support for such an interpretation is found in Article 19(1)(a) HETA, which allows for collective actions in the case of a direct danger of discrimination taking place. This article shows that actual disadvantage is not requisite for the application of the provisions of the HETA.

The definition of indirect discrimination in the Dutch GETA does not employ any 'would put language', and this will not change with the adoption of the proposed amendment of the definition of indirect discrimination. The new Article 1(1)(c) GETA will refer to a measure that *affects* a protected group. Still, the 'would put' aspect is appropriately accounted for in the practice of the ETC. If a particular disadvantage is liable to occur in the future, the ETC is willing to examine the case on the merits.[161] For instance, a complaint involving a ranking list that determined the order in which persons would be dismissed was accepted by the ETC, because it was not unlikely that the complainant would be directly affected by dismissal in the future.[162]

---

161 Gijzen (2006), at 128-129.

162 Opinion 2003-149 ETC, para. 5.2.

5.4.4. Compared to other persons (comparative aspect of indirect discrimination)

5.4.4.1. Reference to the comparison and use of comparability

There is quite some divergence between the national definitions of indirect discrimination concerning the reference to the comparative aspect. The Estonian and Dutch definitions do not mention this element at all, whereas Article 4(8) of the new Belgian ARA refers to a "comparison to other persons". Article 9 of the Hungarian HETA describes the comparison in the following words: "than other persons or groups in a similar situation were or would be".

It is remarkable that the Hungarian definition refers to comparability, which arguably increases the risk of this test being used in an improper way. As was mentioned in the previous chapter, the AET has used comparability in a justificatory way in one direct discrimination case, which was actually about indirect discrimination. It is briefly repeated here that the AET made use of comparability reasoning in order to reject the claim that a rule disadvantaging persons who were on prolonged leave was discriminatory. It thus wholly denied the particular disadvantage for women, who tend to be on prolonged leave more often than men, on account of maternity.[163] The reasoning applied by the AET effectively meant that a seemingly valid claim of indirect discrimination was not examined on the merits. This case hopefully belongs to the category of AET growing pains.

In this regard it should be mentioned that even the Dutch ETC, which has a longstanding practice on indirect discrimination, sporadically resorts to a justificatory use of comparability. For instance, in a case involving a residence requirement for obtaining a pension, the ETC first considered the question whether residents and non-residents were comparable in terms of their eligibility for social pensions before it turned to the question whether there was a particular disadvantage for persons of non-Dutch origin. According to the ETC, there was non-comparability only if constitutional or international law required differentiation between residents and non-residents without leaving the state any margin of appreciation.[164] Obviously this comparability reasoning is infused with the justificatory argument that a state cannot be reproached for making differences in treatment that are in compliance with constitutional or international law. The ETC thus apparently decided to take this argument into account in the first phase of review, instead of considering it at the more

[163] See section 4.6.5.1. For a description of this case see *Report on the activities of the Equal Treatment Authority and the experiences of the implementation of Act nr. 125 of 2003 on equal treatment and the promotion of equal opportunities, AET, July 2006*, and Demeter (2006), at 63.
[164] Opinion 2007-4 ETC, paras. 3.2-5.

appropriate objective justification phase. It is unclear why the ETC opted for this route, and it is to be hoped that it will not do so again.[165] It is fortunate in this respect that the proposed new definition of indirect discrimination does not refer to comparability, but only speaks of a "comparison with other persons".

Lack of practice makes it impossible to assess the Estonian and Belgian courts' approach to comparability. Belgian scholars have warned against the justificatory use of the comparability test for the same reasons as set out in sections 4.3.4 and 5.2.3.1, and it is to be hoped that their suggestion is followed in practice.[166]

5.4.4.2. Delineation of the pool of comparators and application of the comparison

There is hardly any relevant practice in the Member States to assess the actual application of the comparative element of indirect discrimination, with the exception of the Netherlands.

In Hungary, direct discrimination cases provide some indicators of how the AET will approach the comparison for indirect discrimination in the future. In direct discrimination cases involving quantitative evidence, the AET draws the pool in accordance with the sphere of influence of the respondent, such as the total workforce for an employer and the total student population in a municipality for a local council.[167] In cases of equal pay in which the contested measure is a collective agreement or a decree, the pool is drawn in accordance with the addressees of these measures.[168] The cases furthermore reveal that the AET and the courts compare in terms of relative numbers, as was mentioned before. It is to be hoped that these positive features are consolidated for indirect discrimination and that a consistent approach is developed in the future.

In the Netherlands the ETC has developed a rather consistent and transparent framework for the comparative element of indirect discrimination. In the practice of the ETC the pool of comparators is constituted by the persons who are directly affected by the measure at stake, which converges with the circle of addressees approach that was outlined in section 5.2.3.1.[169] In equal pay cases in which there is not an identifiable source for the disparity, the ETC follows the jurisprudence of the ECJ and draws the pool of comparators

[165] Gerards (2005), at 560-563.

[166] Bayart & Deiteren (2008), at 208; De Prins et al (2005), at 472.

[167] See *Annual Report 2006*, EUMC at 13.

[168] *Position Paper of the Equal Treatment Advisory Board on the Principle of Equal Pay for Equal Work*, Position No. 384/2008.

[169] Gerards (2005), at 579.

in terms of those who perform work of equal value for the defendant.[170] A fairly recent example involves a complaint of Polish workers who performed seasonal work in the horticulture sector and worked at a lower rate than their colleagues who were hired on a permanent basis. In this case, the ETC looked at all employees within the workforce who performed the tasks of gardening assistants, regardless of their official function, because these persons performed work of equal value. It subsequently concluded that the lower rate affected only Polish nationals and found that there was a prima facie case of indirect discrimination based on nationality and descent.[171] It thus made use of comparability arguments (work of *equal* value) in order to determine the pool of comparators. As was explained in section 5.2.3.1, this particular use of comparability is necessary for establishing a disparate impact in the absence of an identifiable single cause for the particular disadvantage and is therefore justified.

The cases furthermore reveal that the ETC takes an active approach, and adapts the pool of comparators in cases where the statistical test yields ambiguous results.[172] For instance, in a case where the particular workforce was too small for a proper assessment of the extent to which the disproportionate effect on members of a protected group was statistically significant, the ETC took into account national data in order to be able to better appreciate the proportions in the particular workforce.[173] The ETC's attitude is generally appreciated by scholars as benevolent towards applicants, as it is willing to thoroughly examine whether their claim of a disparate impact holds value.[174] As was explained before, such inclusive approach in the first phase of review is justified, in view of the fact that the objective justification phase offers enough safeguards against fortuitous claims.

Finally, as to the comparison to be carried out within the pool of comparators, the ETC consistently compares the proportion of all persons with the protected characteristic in the disadvantaged group with the proportion of these persons in the entire pool.[175] This exemplary approach is, unfortunately, not followed by the Dutch courts, which do not have a particular model or framework for the comparison in indirect discrimination cases and tend not to pay much attention to this element.[176]

[170] See in this respect also High Council, 12 April 2002, NJ 2002/411, in which the High Council accepted the application of a comparability test in a case of indirect discrimination as regards the principle of equal pay.

[171] Opinion 2008-127 ETC, paras. 3.6-13.

[172] Holtmaat (2007), at 27-28; Gijzen (2006), at 131; Gerards (2005), at 579; Cremers-Hartman (2004), at 145-148.

[173] Opinion 2005-144 ETC, paras. 5.21-5.22. See also Gijzen (2006), at 130-131.

[174] Holtmaat (2007), at 27-28; Gijzen (2006), at 131-132.

[175] Gerards (2005), at 578; Asscher-Vonk & Hendriks (2004), at 64.

[176] Gerards (2005), at 581.

5.4.5. 'Unless that provision, criterion or practice is objectively justified by a legitimate aim and the means of that aim are appropriate and necessary' (justification aspect of indirect discrimination)

5.4.5.1. Formulation of the objective justification test

With the exception of Hungary, the Member States have more or less copied the objective justification test as formulated by Article 2(2)(b) RED. For the Netherlands this is one of the few aspects of anti-discrimination law that were visibly impacted by the RED, as the GETA only explicitly mentions the objective justification test since the entry into force of the IA. Thus, Article 2(1) GETA resembles Article 2(2)(b) RED, and permits prima facie cases of indirect discrimination that are:

> objectively justified by a legitimate aim (…) where the means to achieve that aim are appropriate and necessary.

Before the insertion of this explicit formula, the objective justification test was applied *de facto* by Dutch courts and the ETC.[177]

The Belgian and Estonian definitions also follow the wording of the RED and require a legitimate aim, appropriateness and necessity. Article 9 of the new Belgian ARA requires the contested measure to be:

> 'justified by a legitimate aim' and the means to achieve that aim to be 'appropriate and necessary'.

Article 3(4) of the EETA requires the measure to have:

> an objective legitimate purpose and the means of achieving this purpose are relevant and necessary.

The Hungarian HETA applies a unique justification test for indirect discrimination, which is designed in accordance with the Constitutional Court's case law on the constitutional equality provision.

As to the other three frameworks, many aspects of the objective justification test were already known and applied prior to the implementation of the RED, mainly by the Constitutional Courts, in a way that more or less converges with the jurisprudence of the ECJ. It can be presumed that the relevant national case law in this respect will be replicated in the context of the objective justification test for indirect discrimination. The relevant practice of the Belgian, Estonian and Dutch courts will first be discussed in this section, after which the particular Hungarian system is examined.

---

177 Gerards (2005), at 545, 557, 563-564.

5.4.5.2. 'Objectively justified by a legitimate aim'

The decisions of the Estonian Supreme Court do not reveal much about the manner in which this court assesses the legitimacy of an aim forwarded by the actor of an unequal treatment. The only thing that can be inferred from the case law so far is that this Court does not easily accept financial reasons or aims resting on arguments of expediency,[178] which is in line with the ECJ's jurisprudence as outlined before.

In the Netherlands and Belgium the legitimacy criterion has already been further developed, and both frameworks show similar lines of reasoning. In line with ECJ jurisprudence, it is clear that the aim pursued by the contested measure needs to be non-discriminatory in nature.[179] For instance, the Dutch ETC rejected a rule to speak Dutch in a gym, which was claimed to be necessary because clients would feel intimidated by the use of a foreign language. According to the ETC, this aim fundamentally relied on xenophobic prejudice, and was thus not legitimate.[180]

Furthermore, in both Member States differences between private and public actors are reflected in the way in which their respective aims are assessed.[181] A good example of such differentiation is found in the ETC's 2007 annual report, in which it argues that the aim of maintaining religious neutrality is only acceptable for public actors. According to the ETC, it is appropriate for a state to pursue religious neutrality in order to respect the freedom of religion. However, private actors cannot rely on this aim, as it is most likely based on the anticipation of prejudiced reactions from clients or customers, and thus is discriminatory in nature.[182]

It should furthermore be mentioned that in both Belgium and the Netherlands there is attention for the authenticity of the aim put forward by the author of a contested measure.[183]

Finally, practice of the Dutch ETC reveals that this body scrutinises the general relevance of the aim rather strictly.[184] For instance, it does not

[178] Decision of the Constitutional Chamber of the Supreme Court 21 January 2004, 3-4-1-7-03, para. 39; Decision of the Constitutional Chamber of the Supreme Court 6 March 2002, 3-4-1-1-02, para. 15.

[179] For Belgium see *Explanatory Memorandum to the Draft law amending the law of 30 July 1981 that penalises certain acts motivated by racism and xenophobia*, Doc 51. 2720/001; Sottiaux (2008), at 237. For The Netherlands see Gerards (2005), at 596-600.

[180] Opinion 2008-12 ETC, para. 3.22.

[181] For Belgium see Sottiaux (2008), at 237; De Prins et al (2005), at 474-475; Velaers (2003), at 307; Vrielink (2003), at 209.

[182] *Jaarrapport 2007*, Commissie Gelijke Behandeling 2007, at 53-54.

[183] For Belgium see Sottiaux (2008), at 238; Velaers (2003), at 333-334. For The Netherlands see Gerards (2005), at 596-600.

[184] Gerards (2005), at 604-608.

easily accept financial arguments, and it expects actors to formulate aims in a sufficiently specific and objective fashion.[185] It remains to be seen to what extent Belgian courts will be equally strict.

5.4.5.3. Appropriateness

In Belgium, Estonia and the Netherlands, appropriateness is understood in its usual meaning, as requiring the contested measure to be capable of attaining the aim pursued.[186] There are hardly any Belgian and Estonian cases in which the appropriateness test received explicit attention, and it is therefore not yet clear how this test is applied in practice. It is expected that the test will be applied at an intermediate level of strictness in the Belgian context, which means that it suffices to show that one *can reasonably expect* the measure to further the aim pursued.[187]

In the Netherlands, practice of the ETC and the Dutch courts greatly diverges: the latter hardly pay attention to appropriateness, whereas the ETC scrutinises quite strictly.[188] For instance, the ETC tends to require objective and reliable data showing that the contested measure is capable of attaining the aim pursued.[189] The ETC also requires the contested measure to be sufficiently transparent, which means that it should be clear for outsiders how it is applied in practice. For instance, the ETC found a requirement that telephone operators should speak Dutch without an accent to be unsuitable, inter alia because it was applied subjectively and in a non-transparent way.[190] The ETC furthermore requires timely evaluation and adaptation of a particular measure in the light of societal developments.[191] Thus, while remaining fair, the ETC is relatively strict and sets quite a high threshold of legality for prima facie cases of indirect discrimination, which entails a high level of protection for protected groups.

5.4.5.4. Necessity

In the Belgian, Estonian and Dutch frameworks the necessity requirement clearly comprises a subsidiarity test, which entails a search for less intrusive

---

[185] Gerards & Heringa (2003), at 149.

[186] For Belgium see Sottiaux (2008), at 238. For Estonia see Decision of the Constitutional Chamber of the Supreme Court, 17 March 2003, 3-1-3-10-02, para. 30; For The Netherlands see Gerards (2005), at 615.

[187] Sottiaux (2008), at 238

[188] Gerards (2005), at 615-616.

[189] Gerards (2005), at 615. See for instance Opinion 2007-109 ETC, para. 3.14.

[190] Opinion 2007-127 ETC, para. 3.12.

[191] See for instance Opinion 2007-109 ETC, para. 3.14.

but viable alternatives to the contested measure.[192] The Dutch ETC furthermore interprets necessity as requiring measures to be carefully construed. This involves inter alia a test of the over or under-inclusiveness of the circle of addressees.[193] To some extent this aspect of the necessity test overlaps with the appropriateness test as applied by the ETC, which confirms the close relation between these two tests. For instance, the assessment of the extent to which the measure is periodically evaluated and adjusted to relevant societal developments is sometimes evaluated in the framework of necessity, instead of appropriateness.[194] In any case, the practice of the ETC shows that the necessity requirement involves a duty of due diligence of the author of the contested measure, which again entails a relatively high level of protection for protected groups.

In Belgium and the Netherlands, it is generally accepted that necessity also presupposes proportionality stricto sensu.[195] The Estonian Supreme Court regularly applies the principle of proportionality stricto sensu,[196] but it is not clear whether this principle will be read into the necessity aspect of the objective justification test in the EETA. As was explained before, the proportionality stricto sensu test brings the interests of minority groups into the equation and in that way facilitates a substantive equality approach to indirect discrimination. The Dutch ETC for instance considers the actual severity of the disadvantage experienced by the members of the protected group in the framework of the proportionality stricto sensu principle. This entails inter alia an assessment of whether there are viable alternatives available to these persons.[197] Some of its earlier decisions furthermore reveal that the ETC tends to give more weight to the interest of the protected group if the effect of the contested measure more closely resembles direct discrimination.[198]

192 For Belgium see Sottiaux (2008), at 238-240; Doc 51. 2720/001, at 50-51. For Estonia see Constitutional Chamber of the Supreme Court 17 March 2003, 3-1-3-10-02, para. 30; Constitutional Chamber of the Supreme Court, 6 March 2002, 3-4-1-1-02, para. 15.

193 Gerards (2005), at 617-620.

194 Opinion 2007-109 ETC, para. 3.17-3.18.

195 For Belgium see Sottiaux (2008), at 240. For The Netherlands see Gerards (2005), at 622-629; Cremers-Hartman (2004), at 152-154; Gerards & Heringa (2003), at 141-143, 151.

196 Constitutional Chamber of the Supreme Court 17 March 2003, 3-1-3-10-02, para. 30 and Constitutional Chamber of the Supreme Court, 6 March 2002, 3-4-1-1-02, para. 15, in which proportionality stricto sensu is approached as a separate element of the general proportionality principle.

197 Gerards (2005), at 622-624.

198 Gerards (2005), at 623; see Opinion 2001-90 ETC, para. 4.11; 1996-44 ETC, para. 4.4.

5.4.5.5. Need for consistency and transparency: a bad example drawn from the Belgian framework

At the end of this section, it seems appropriate to mention the single judgment on indirect discrimination rendered in Belgium so far, in order to underline the importance for national frameworks to develop a thorough and consistent framework for the objective justification test. The case concerned a rule prohibiting the wearing of headscarves in classrooms, which was considered by the Antwerp Court of Appeal to constitute a prima facie case of indirect discrimination. The court subsequently assessed whether the rule pursued a legitimate aim and was proportionate, and did so by first discussing the requirements of Article 9 ECHR on the freedom of religion. It then looked at the facts of the case, and decided that in the particular circumstances, involving unrest and intimidation of fellow students, the measure was objectively justified. However, it did not balance the opposing interests of the Muslim students versus the school: it only regarded the matter from the viewpoint of the school.[199] Moreover, critics of the decision have denounced the summary manner in which the court dealt with the relevant facts: it did not go into detail as regards the situation of unrest, which made it difficult to assess the thoroughness of the court's reasoning.[200] Application of the objective justification test preferably involves more meticulous reasoning, which would involve at least separate attention for each of the various elements of the objective justification test.

5.4.5.6. The Hungarian approach

The Hungarian HETA sets in place a justification scheme that was inspired by the Constitutional Court's jurisprudence on the constitutional equality provision. This scheme involves one justification mechanism for all types of discrimination other than direct racial and ethnic discrimination. The mechanism is divided into two tests, depending on whether the alleged discrimination affects a fundamental right of the applicant or not. If a fundamental right is at stake, Article 7(2)(a) HETA prescribes a rather strict regime, requiring:

1) that the defendant acts in order to enforce another fundamental right

2) that the conflict between both rights is unavoidable

199 Antwerp Court of Appeal, 14 June 2005, para. 2.2.2.

200 Foblets & Velaers (2005), at 131.

3) that the contested measure is suitable to enforce the other fundamental right, and

4) is in a proportionate relationship with the intrusion of the fundamental right of the applicant

If there is not a fundamental right at stake for the applicant, but some other interest, a more lenient regime applies. According to Article 7(2)(b) HETA, the contested measure should then be "found by objective consideration to have a reasonable explanation directly related to the relevant relationship."

The mechanism for fundamental rights appears to be stricter than the objective justification test forwarded by the RED. Not only does it narrow the interpretation of what constitutes a legitimate aim (another fundamental right), but it also requires a very strict application of the subsidiarity test (the conflict must be unavoidable) and it explicitly mentions the proportionality stricto sensu test ('proportionate relationship'). However, the mechanism for interests other than fundamental rights is in some respects more lenient than the objective justification test of Article 2(2)(b) RED. It appears to be sufficiently strict as regards the legitimacy of the aim: even though it is not exactly clear in which way the 'directly linked' criterion will be applied, it arguably makes clear that not just any aim is accepted, but only an aim that is considered to be objectively relevant for the particular relationship between the applicant and the defendant. However, the reasonability test would appear to be easier to fulfil than the appropriateness and necessity tests of Article 2(2)(b) RED, at least at a formal level.

At a practical level, sufficiently strict scrutiny could remedy to a great extent the weak wording of Article 7(2)(b) HETA. This can be illustrated by an educational segregation case, which was ruled under the pre-2007 version of the HETA and thus involved the application of the more lenient justification test as mentioned above, even though the case involved direct racial discrimination.[201] The county court examining the case first emphasised that the elimination of unequal treatment based on ethnic origin called for strict interpretation of the justification test. It then stated that the management and material equipment of the individual school buildings could not be considered to provide a reasonable and objective ground. In the same way it dismissed the defendant's expediency-related arguments. It considered that a situation existing due to decades of convention did not provide a reasonable and objective ground, nor did any economic consideration or lack of financial means.[202] The decision is remarkable, since one would expect the various aims invoked to pass a mere reasonability test. Thus, the county court, while formally applying the lenient justification test of Article 7(2)(b) HETA, de

[201] The closed system of justification for direct discrimination was only effectuated in the HETA by the 2007 amendments. See section 4.7.1.

[202] Hajdú-Bihar County Court, 2 May 2007, 6.AT20.341/2006/50.

facto applied a much stricter test. The strong wording used even raises the impression that the court was not prepared to accept any justification for an apparently serious case of racial segregation.

If the AET and Hungarian courts would be willing to apply equally strict scrutiny in indirect racial discrimination cases, the justification scheme of Article 7(2)(b) HETA would de facto comply with the requirements of Article 2(2)(b) RED. Future practice will indicate whether this is the case.

5.5. Indirect discrimination and positive duties

In view of the novelty of the concept of indirect discrimination in most of the Member States included in this study, it is unsurprising that there is hardly any relevant practice on positive duties in the national frameworks, with the exception of the Dutch framework. The practice of the Dutch ETC nicely shows how the concept of indirect discrimination is intertwined with duties to take into consideration the interests of protected groups, which in turn furthers the aim of substantive equality. For example, in a case that involved a complaint about the impossibility of fulfilling a particular job on a part-time basis, the ETC made clear that employers should critically determine in each case whether full-time availability is really necessary and actively investigate ways of making the job available on a part-time basis.[203] Another case involved a requirement that a non-Dutch parent speaks Dutch with his child within the premises of social protection services. According to the ETC the requirement was not objectively justified, because social protection services had not investigated the possibilities of hiring a translator and did not look for other ways of facilitating the communication between the parent and his child.[204]

The strong substantive equality outlook of the ETC is confirmed in the way in which it has proved willing to examine the need for proactive positive duties, by way of accepting omissions as potential causes of indirect discrimination. For example, it considered whether a local government should develop specific opportunities for travellers to apply for caravan dwelling places in its housing policy. In the particular case it decided that the lack of such a policy was objectively justified because of the small amount of applications for caravan dwelling places, but it still recommended that application forms were altered so as to invite persons to express an interest for such places, with a view to accommodating caravan owners in the future.[205] In other cases it considered duties of an insurance company and a financial institution to make special

[203] Opinion 2002-83 ETC, para. 5.6.

[204] Opinion 2004-22 ETC, paras. 5.13-5.21.

[205] Opinion 2006-222 ETC, paras. 3.22-3.28.

products for mobile home owners.[206] Even though it concluded in these cases that such a duty would impose too heavy a burden on the particular companies, the fact that it was willing to consider the question at all makes clear that it in principle accepts the possibility of far-reaching positive duties as flowing from the concept of indirect discrimination.

Of the three other national frameworks, the Hungarian one is the most likely to follow in the footsteps of the Dutch ETC. As was mentioned in the previous chapter, the AET and the Hungarian courts are not afraid of inferring far-reaching positive duties from the concept of direct discrimination, in particular with regard to racial segregation. They expect national councils to take action to end and prevent segregation of Roma students in education, even if they themselves have not caused the segregation.[207] It is likely that they will be similarly progressive in indirect discrimination cases, the more so because the HETA expressly mentions 'omissions' as potential causes of indirect discrimination. For Estonia and Belgium the picture remains obscure and future developments will have to be awaited.

5.6. Summary and conclusion

This chapter took the same starting point as the previous chapter, namely that the relevance of the concept of indirect discrimination for minority protection is determined on two separate levels. On one level it is important that indirect discrimination covers real-life experiences of discrimination to the greatest extent possible and in the most effective way. On another level conceptual clarity and consistency are essential. Both considerations informed the analysis in the theoretical part of this chapter, in which it was examined how national indirect discrimination regimes are ideally designed.

It was shown throughout this chapter that the concept of indirect discrimination holds great potential in terms of minority protection. It captures those forms of discrimination that are perhaps not immediately visible, but hinder participation of minority groups in public life in an important way. In this respect it not only provides a remedy for individual instances of unfair treatment, but it also targets structural discriminatory factors in society, which is essential for furthering the aim of substantive equality. It was also pointed out that the concept of indirect discrimination is greatly relevant to the goal of substantive equality because it inherently entails a positive duty to take into consideration the interests of vulnerable groups in society. This means that indirect discrimination can be used to restructure society in a way that does

[206] Opinions 2007-157 ETC; 2006-5 ETC.

[207] See section 4.8.

more justice to the interests of minority groups, which could even embrace identity-focused measures and thus serve the second pillar of minority protection.

Minimum baseline of protection

A number of aspects of indirect discrimination were found to be sufficiently clear so as to make up the minimum baseline of protection. Despite the general lack of experience with the concept of indirect discrimination, the Member States have complied with these aspects to a high degree.

Thus, all four Member States have – implicitly or explicitly – replicated the 'provision, criterion or practice' phrase, which ensures that nearly all conceivable products of human agency are covered by indirect discrimination, and not only formal rules or criteria. The Hungarian and Dutch frameworks proved to be especially inclusive, since they include omissions to act as potential causing factors of indirect discrimination. This opens up the door for far-reaching positive duties to be inferred from the concept of indirect discrimination, which in turn furthers the goal of substantive equality.

In addition, most Member States have complied with the formulation of "would put at a particular disadvantage". This particular formulation is significant, as it allows for the establishment of indirect discrimination with qualitative data, which makes up for the problem that there tends to be a lack of quantitative data broken down in terms of racial or ethnic origin in the Member States. It was furthermore found that all four Member States have allowed for the use of quantitative data in addition to qualitative data, whereas they are not formally obliged to do so under the RED. They have exceeded the minimum baseline of protection in this regard, which is fortunate, since quantitative evidence is essential in those cases in which it is impossible to know how exactly a disproportionate disadvantage for a protected group has come about.

Finally, the Member States have largely complied with the objective justification test for indirect discrimination, which makes up an important aspect of the minimum baseline of protection required by Article 2(2)(b) RED. Belgium, Estonia and The Netherlands have included all aspects of this test in their national regimes, and national practice in these Member States so far has proved to be in line with the ECJ's approach. It was especially positive to note that a proportionality stricto sensu requirement is included in the Belgian and Dutch objective justification tests, which ensures that the interests of the affected vulnerable group are a factor that co-determines the legitimacy of the contested measure. The Dutch ETC moreover has provided for a higher level of protection than the ECJ by developing a more detailed, transparent and relatively strict regime.

It was only the Hungarian HETA that was found to have deviated from the structure of Article 2(2)(b) RED concerning the objective justification. This act provides for a two-fold test of justification, which entails too lenient a test for cases involving non-fundamental rights of alleged victims of indirect discrimination. Even though practice so far has shown that the test is applied strictly, it is unfortunate from a viewpoint of legal certainty and transparency that the test is very loosely formulated.

Obscurities and opportunities for providing a higher level of protection

The theoretical part of the chapter made clear that the minimum baseline of protection for indirect discrimination is only partially identifiable, and that there are quite a few obscurities with regard to the application of the concept at the European level. In view of the relative unfamiliarity with the concept in the national legal contexts, it is unsurprising that these obscurities were for the greater part replicated at the national levels. Unfortunately, the case study on these topics was hindered by a general lack of relevant case-law in Belgium, Estonia and Hungary. It was accordingly difficult to determine in which direction national approaches would go, and the assessment could most of the time only put forward some indications of what future application would look like.

The Dutch framework, to the contrary, contains an extensive body of case-law, which greatly enabled the analysis. It was nevertheless shown that Dutch courts and even the ETC have at times stumbled over some of the complexities identified in the theoretical part. Dutch courts for instance sometimes require that the contested measure amounts to a formal difference in treatment, which denies the reality that indirect discrimination can equally be constituted by a material difference in treatment. The single known Belgian case of indirect discrimination unfortunately suggests a similarly restrictive approach.

In addition, it was shown that Dutch courts have sometimes required the establishment of a causal link between the contested measure and the protected characteristic, which unnecessarily increases the burden of proof for applicants. Traces of a similar approach were found in the Estonian and Hungarian frameworks.

The Dutch ETC and the Hungarian AET were furthermore found to have incidentally applied the comparability test in a justificatory way, which means that they applied justification arguments when determining whether a particular disadvantage could be established. It was pointed out that the ECJ has at times done the exact same thing, which undermines the indirect discrimination framework by obscuring the model of review and by potentially lowering the substantive quality of the final outcome of the case.

The establishment of the particular disadvantage on a protected group finally turned out to be a complex exercise that still raises many questions, even at the European level. In view of the fact that the ECJ has not yet developed a clear approach in this respect, it is unsurprising that no such approach was found at the national level, except for the practice of the Dutch ETC. The ETC takes into account the type of proof available when determining what test should be applied for the particular disadvantage, and moreover makes use of scientific expertise as regards the use of statistics. In addition, the ETC usually thoroughly motivates its approach to the establishment of the particular disadvantage, thus fostering transparency.

Finally, it was pointed out that the extent to which the substantive equality potential of indirect discrimination is realised, more particularly with regard to positive duties, greatly depends on the way in which the objective justification test is applied in individual cases. As the ECJ generally leaves the actual decision in this respect to the national courts, it can be expected that Member States will diverge to some extent as regards the strictness applied vis-à-vis authors of prima facie indirectly discriminatory measures. The lack of national case-law made it impossible to provide a full picture in this respect, and it is therefore still quite unclear to what degree the opportunity to further substantive equality will be seized in the Belgian, Estonian and Hungarian frameworks. By contrast, the Dutch ETC has been shown to go quite far, and generally examines strictly whether alleged perpetrators of indirect discrimination have done what could be reasonably expected of them to meet the needs of minority groups in society.

In conclusion, it became clear that the minority protection potential of indirect discrimination is not yet fully realised, neither at the European, nor at the national levels. This is not very surprising in view of the relative unfamiliarity and complexity of this concept. Still, it is regrettable that the ECJ has so far not given much guidance and has ducked complex conceptual questions, which has caused much uncertainty with regard to the conceptual framework for indirect discrimination. Even though it is unfortunate that the national frameworks have reproduced most obscurities, Member States can hardly be reproached for not going where the ECJ itself dared not tread. The Dutch ETC clearly stands out in this respect, and its generally consistent, transparent and minority-sensitive approach to indirect discrimination, with a few minor glitches, sets a very positive example. The ETC's intensive attention for substantive equality for vulnerable groups in society is a particularly valuable asset. The ETC's example shows that it is possible to set in place a coherent and high quality indirect discrimination regime without guidance from the ECJ, which holds promise as regards the approach to be developed in those Member States in which indirect discrimination has hardly or not yet been applied. It was interesting to see, however, that the Dutch picture in this chapter was ambiguous, with the Dutch courts greatly lagging behind the ETC and generally displaying a similar lack of coherence and transparency as the ECJ.

A question that is raised by the findings in this chapter is whether the relative ease with which the Member States have accepted quantitative evidence for indirect racial discrimination can be explained by the fact that indirect discrimination in European gender equality law was traditionally approached in terms of quantitative evidence. This could perhaps be taken to mean that the Member States are not overly dogmatic as regards the differences between the various European equality regimes, which in turn can produce meaningful interaction between them.

Chapter 6

Harassment and the Instruction to Discriminate

Harassment shall be deemed to be discrimination within the meaning of paragraph 1, when an unwanted conduct related to racial or ethnic origin takes place with the purpose or effect of violating the dignity of a person and of creating an intimidating, hostile, degrading, humiliating or offensive environment. In this context, the concept of harassment may be defined in accordance with the national laws and practice of the Member States (Article 2(3) RED)

An instruction to discriminate against persons on grounds of racial or ethnic origin shall be deemed to be discrimination within the meaning of paragraph 1 (Article 2(4) RED)

Part one: Theoretical framework

6.1. Introduction

One of the novelties of the RED at the time of its adoption in 2000 was its inclusion of new forms of discrimination that were until then not regulated by European equality law. The expansion of the concept of discrimination beyond direct and indirect discrimination, to harassment and the instruction to discriminate, was received as an important symbolic step.[1] Both concepts

[1] As regards harassment, however, it should be mentioned that some scholars have criticised its inclusion in the RED. They consider it inappropriate to approach harassment as a form of discrimination, since many instances of bullying or mobbing are not linked to a person's protected characteristics. See for instance Clarke (2007), at 175; Bacik (2003), at 169-175; Sinclair (1998). The Community legislator apparently disagreed with this vision, and rightly so in the view of the present author. To the extent that harassment is linked to a protected

underline the close connection between discrimination and uneven power relationships, as they regulate forms of discrimination that most often occur as a consequence of the misuse of a powerful position.[2] In this sense, they indirectly target structural factors of discrimination and thus contribute to substantive equality.[3] Moreover, the reference to human dignity and the lack of a comparator requirement in the definition of harassment sends out a clear message of what discrimination is really about: causing detriment to the very being of a person simply because of his or her affiliation with a particular group. Thus, the emphasis is not so much on formal equal treatment of all persons, but rather on equal concern and respect for each individual person, which is also indicative of a substantive equality perspective.[4]

The fact that the concepts of harassment and the instruction to discriminate are relatively new in the European equality framework means there are a number of questions regarding their proper implementation at the national level. This chapter will discuss these questions in the following order. The first part deals with the concept of harassment, focusing on the margin of discretion accorded to Member States in section 6.2.1, the various elements of the definition of harassment in section 6.2.2, and the particular duty of care associated with it in section 6.2.3. Section 6.3 contains an analysis of the instruction to discriminate, which is very brief in view of the ancillary nature of this concept.

6.2. Harassment

Prior to the adoption of the RED the concept of harassment played a limited role in the European equality framework, and there were only a number of soft law instruments that dealt with sexual harassment as a particular problem of sex discrimination.[5] The regulation in the RED finds its roots in American and

characteristic, it builds upon unequal power structures in society that disadvantage particular vulnerable groups, see section 6.2.2.1. This broader context of structural disadvantage justifies dealing with grounds-related harassment as a particular form of discrimination.

2 This is inherent in the notion of 'instruction'; several authors have furthermore stressed the link between harassment and unequal power relationships, see Gijzen (2006), at 144-146; Friedman (2003), at 250; Schultz (2001), at 424; Abrams (1998), at 23-24.

3 Gijzen (2006), at 143.

4 Fredman (2001), at 160-161.

5 See Gijzen (2006), at 147-149 for an overview of the relevant instruments that were adopted in this regard. Sexual harassment was regulated in a legally binding instrument for the first time in 2002, when *Council Directive 76/207/EEC on the implementation of the principle of equal treatment for men and women as regards access to employment, vocational training and promotion, and working conditions* was amended by *Directive 2002/73/EC of the European Parliament and of the Council of 23 September 2002.* A prohibition of sexual harassment is now also laid down in *Directive 2006/54/EC of the European Parliament and of the Council of 5 July 2005 on the implementation of the principle of equal opportunities and equal treatment*

UK equality law, where the concept of discriminatory harassment was first developed and applied.[6] In the following sections, reference will therefore be made to the relevant aspects of English and American law that shed light on particular features and problems of discriminatory harassment.

6.2.1. Margin of discretion for Member States

> In this context, the concept of harassment may be defined in accordance with the national laws and practice of the Member States.

The last sentence of Article 2(3) RED grants Member States a margin of discretion with regard to the definition of harassment in their own legal systems. The clause is remarkable, since the definition that precedes it is quite elaborate, which raises the impression that the definition has been very consciously crafted in this particular fashion. One would expect a much vaguer and more generally worded provision if the intention was to leave the definition of harassment to be determined by each Member State separately. Moreover, similar discretion clauses do not appear in the two most recently adopted sex equality directives with definitions similar to Article 2(3) RED. This raises doubts as to the actual import of the clause in Article 2(3) RED.[7]

From the deliberations in the Council on the draft RED it can be inferred that the discretion clause was inserted not so much because Member States wanted to maintain different substantive conceptions of harassment, but rather because they wanted to be able to determine autonomously to what extent employers should be liable for harassment perpetrated by employees.[8] Most scholars therefore take the clause to confer discretion as regards procedural matters as to who can be held liable and which type of legislation is best suited to regulate the concept (for example legislation on harassment in general or on safety in the workplace instead of anti-discrimination legislation).[9] According to this reading, the clause would not have substantive implications for the

---

of men and women in matters of employment and occupation (recast) and *Council Directive 2004/113/EC of 13 December 2004 implementing the principle of equal treatment between men and women in the access to and supply of goods and services.*

6 Gijzen (2006), at 140-141.

7 Article 2(c) and (d) in *Directive 2006/54/EC of the European Parliament and of the Council of 5 July 2005 on the implementation of the principle of equal opportunities and equal treatment of men and women in matters of employment and occupation (recast)*, and Article 2(c) and (d) in *Council Directive 2004/113/EC of 13 December 2004 implementing the principle of equal treatment between men and women in the access to and supply of goods and services* do not contain this clause. The FD, which was adopted only a few months after the RED, does contain a discretion clause for harassment, which is provided in Article 2(3) FD.

8 Tyson (2004), at 117-118.

9 Gijzen (2006), at 152; Bell (2001), at 26-27; Guild (2000), at 420.

conceptualisation of harassment. The definition of Article 2(3) RED would accordingly provide a minimum baseline on which Member States are allowed to build further, but which they cannot lower unilaterally.

However, a different, more substantive reading of the clause is possible, according to which Member States have some leeway in the conceptualisation of racial harassment. After all, the clause expressly refers to the *definition* of the concept of harassment, which points to a substantive focus rather than to a procedural one. Moreover, the procedural interpretation of the clause would make the clause more or less redundant, because the instrument of a directive ipso facto presupposes procedural freedom for Member States as to the choice of particular types of liability and types of implementing legislation.[10]

A substantive interpretation of the clause has difficulties of its own, however. In view of the effectiveness principle the prohibition of harassment cannot be eroded indefinitely: some minimum level of protection will most likely be required. Moreover, the fact that the most recent sex equality directives do not contain a discretion clause with regard to harassment complicates matters. It would seem to be very difficult for the ECJ to uphold a uniform concept of harassment related to sex, and simultaneously to allow for a fragmentised understanding of harassment related to racial or ethnic origin. The ECJ has so far not provided any guidance as to the proper interpretation of the clause. In *Coleman* the ECJ merely reaffirmed the importance of the clause, but did not further explain its meaning.[11]

If interpreted in a substantive way, the clause could work both ways as regards its effects on the level of minority protection at the national level. On the one hand, it is likely that a definition of harassment that suits the national legal context and applies concepts and notions known to national lawyers will be more effective than a definition that employs unfamiliar wording. On the other hand, it is conceivable that the harassment provision is watered down to such an extent that it fails to realise its substantive equality potential.[12]

In view of the obscure meaning of the discretion clause in Article 2(3) RED, the following discussion will take the complete definition contained in this Article as a starting point for the discussion of the conceptualisation of racial harassment.

---

10 Barmes (2007), at 456.

11 *Coleman v. Attridge Law and Steve Law*, Case C-303/06, 17 July 2008, para. 60.

12 Schiek (2002), at 290; Brown (2002), at 195; Guild (2000), at 420.

6.2.2. Definition of racial harassment

6.2.2.1. 'An unwanted conduct'

The first element of the definition describes the core aspect of discriminatory harassment: conduct that is unwanted by the person who is confronted with it. A number of remarks concerning the application of this element are in place, more particularly with regard to the meaning of the words 'conduct' and 'unwanted'.

The word 'conduct' seems sufficiently broad so as to comprise verbal, non-verbal, physical and passive behaviour.[13] This broad interpretation is confirmed in the Explanatory Memorandum to the RED, which provides with regard to harassment that: "[s]uch conduct can take different forms, ranging from spoken words and gestures to the production, display or circulation of written words, pictures, or other material".[14] All that a person could think of to do or not to do in order to make someone else's life miserable should therefore be covered.

An illustration of what 'conduct' can look like in practice is offered by Friedman, who specifically focuses on harassment in the working place, but whose list is applicable also in other fields.[15] He distinguishes between three categories of behaviour:

1) employing abusive communications or actions, such as screaming, berating, telephone terror, unjustified criticism, sexual harassment, violence

2) destructing the victim's status, through insults, spreading rumours, public humiliation, sabotage, physical isolation

3) giving degrading assignments, such as assigning senseless tasks or no tasks at all, or tasks for which the target is not qualified

[13] Gijzen (2006), at 155; Bell (2001), at 26. Some authors have expressed doubts in this regard; Driessen-Reilly & Driessen (2003), at 497, point out that the definition of sexual harassment in *Council Directive 76/207/EEC on the implementation of the principle of equal treatment for men and women as regards access to employment, vocational training and promotion, and working conditions* as amended by *Directive 2002/73/EC of the European Parliament and of the Council of 23 September 2002* explicitly refers to 'verbal, non-verbal and physical conduct', and argue that Article 2(3) RED a contrario would perhaps cover only relatively active forms of conduct, to the exclusion of non-verbal behaviour. Still, a normal reading of the word 'conduct' does not exclude non-verbal conduct and the travaux preparatoires of the RED moreover do not reveal any intention of the Member States to apply a restrictive interpretation of this word. See Tyson (2004), at 116-118.

[14] *Proposal for a Council Directive implementing the principle of equal treatment between persons irrespective of racial or ethnic origin*, COM/99/0566 final.

[15] Friedman (2003), at 249.

The word 'conduct' of Article 2(3) RED is preferably interpreted as covering all of these types of behaviour, so as to ensure effective protection against all forms of harassment that take place in practice. Especially because the second part of the definition of Article 2(3) requires a high degree of severity before the prohibition kicks in, which sufficiently safeguards against frivolous complaints, it does not make sense to interpret the word 'conduct' restrictively. This also means that it is preferably interpreted as covering sufficiently serious single incidents, not only recurring or persistent behaviour or a combination of events.[16]

The qualification 'unwanted' in the first element of the definition of harassment in Article 2(3) is the object of controversy. Although some have welcomed this adjective as adding an element of subjectivity and thus showing regard for the victim's personal experience,[17] it has been pointed out that it could actually backfire on the victim. Experience in other legal systems shows that the standard can be interpreted in such a way that victims of harassment need to prove that it was clear to the perpetrator that the conduct was unwanted, which constitutes a considerable hurdle.[18] A similar interpretation of the 'unwanted' standard of Article 2(3) RED would clearly lower the level of protection of the prohibition of discriminatory harassment. Moreover, it would deny the reality that harassment usually takes place in unequal power relationships, which makes it very difficult for a victim to express his/her discontent.

For these reasons, the 'unwanted' standard is preferably interpreted in a subjective sense, which means that the victim's perception of the conduct as being unwanted should suffice. Victims should not be required to establish that the perpetrator knew or should have known that the conduct was unwanted.[19] Objections that this subjective approach would violate the right to legal certainty of alleged offenders can be countered by pointing to the fact that Article 2(3) RED provides for strict requirements as to the seriousness of the unwanted conduct. The resulting high threshold of severity that must be attained before a harassment claim can succeed provides a sufficient safeguard for perpetrators' rights.

---

16 Gijzen (2006), at 157-159; Vickers (2006), at 582.

17 O'Hare (2001), at 148.

18 Schultz (2001-2002), at 427; Dine & Watt (1995), at 356-358.

19 Gijzen (2006), at 151. A similar position was taken by the Commission in the *Recommendation of 27 November 1991 on the protection of the dignity of women and men at work*, 92/131/EEC, in which it considers that "[i]t is for each individual to determine what behaviour is acceptable to them and what they regard as offensive."

6.2.2.2. 'Related to racial or ethnic origin'

The prohibition of harassment in the RED envisages only those forms of harassment that have a particular linkage to racial or ethnic origin, which is reflected in the second element of the definition. It is remarkable that the words 'related to' are used, instead of 'on grounds of' in the direct discrimination definition of Article 2(2)a RED. This points to a less strict causal link for harassment than for direct discrimination.[20] It is accordingly not necessary to establish that the person was harassed *because* of his/her racial or ethnic origin: a looser connection suffices. According to one author, whenever the harassing conduct is "dictated by and targeted at" a person's racial or ethnic origin the 'related to' criterion is fulfilled.[21] For example, racist posters on the walls in an office presuppose the inferiority of a particular racial or ethnic origin, and therefore target employees of that racial or ethnic origin. This should suffice for the establishment of the 'related to' requirement; employees belonging to the targeted group should not be required to show that persons of a different racial or ethnic origin would not have been targeted in a similar fashion. Similarly, racial abuse by teachers or co-students is sufficiently 'related to' the ethnic origin of particular students in order to qualify as discriminatory harassment, without these students having to establish that other students would not be treated in the same way.

This atypical approach to causality actually reflects strong substantive thinking, since it builds on the reality of unequal power structures between racial and ethnic groups in society. Power inequalities not only make particular groups more vulnerable than others in relation to harassing conduct, but also make it more likely that persons belonging to these groups are harassed with reference to their protected characteristics. For example, an employee who harasses his Turkish colleague out of dislike, and not because of his Turkish origin, is likely to employ his colleague's racial origin. After all, he knows that this is a sensitive issue and is bound to particularly hurt his colleague's feelings. If he were to harass a person belonging to the majority ethnic group, he would probably not pick this person's ethnic origin, but another characteristic that is sensitive to the person. Thus, because of the unequal power structures in society, persons belonging to protected groups are more easily targeted in a way that makes use of their protected characteristic, regardless of the underlying reason for the harassment.

The substantive equality outlook of the concept of harassment is furthermore reflected in the lack of a comparative element in Article 2(3) RED. Thus, it is not necessary to establish that another person was or would have been treated in a different way than the victim. This remarkable feature of the concept of harassment marks a departure from the traditional European

---

[20] Barmes (2007), at 453; Monaghan (2007), at 352.

[21] Monaghan (2007), at 352.

equality paradigm.[22] It is a fortunate departure, because experience in UK law shows that a comparator requirement makes it much harder to establish discriminatory harassment. Before the implementation of the RED, UK anti-discrimination law required victims to establish that the harassment would not have taken place vis-à-vis a person who did not have the protected characteristic.[23] This approach presupposed that there is only discriminatory harassment if the perpetrator actually harassed the person *because of* her protected characteristic, and thus required a much stronger causal link for discriminatory harassment than does the 'related to' element of Article 2(3) RED. As this significantly increases the burden of proof for applicants, it is desirable that Member States do not insert a comparison element in the definition of harassment.

6.2.2.3. 'With the purpose or effect of violating the dignity of a person and of creating an intimidating, hostile, degrading, humiliating or offensive environment'

The third element of Article 2(3) RED sets in place a threshold of severity that needs to be reached by unwanted conduct in order to qualify as harassment. The 'with the purpose or effect…' phrase provides a two-fold test in order to assess the severity of the conduct complained of: the violation of dignity, and the creation of an intimidating, hostile, degrading, humiliating or offensive environment (hereafter: hostile environment). Member States are presumably allowed to opt for an alternative enumeration instead of a cumulative one, according to which harassment is constituted either by the violation of dignity or by the creation of a hostile environment.[24] Such an alternative test arguably alleviates the burden of proof for the applicant and thus establishes a higher level of protection against harassment, which is permitted by Article 6(1) RED.

'With the purpose or effect'

The phrase 'with the purpose or effect' gives some guidance as to how the dignity and hostile environment tests need to be carried out. First of all, it makes clear that the intent of the perpetrator is immaterial: regardless of his intentions, his conduct constitutes discriminatory harassment if it violates dignity and creates a hostile environment.[25] Secondly, it suggests an objective

[22] Gijzen (2006), at 143 and 149. See sections 4.3.4 and 5.2.3 in which the comparative elements of the more traditional concepts of direct and indirect discrimination are examined.
[23] Clarke (2006), at 163-167; Bacik (2003), at 154-155; Dine & Watt (1995), at 345-347.
[24] This has for example been done in the UK, see Monaghan (2007), at 349.
[25] Gijzen (2006), at 151.

rather than a subjective perspective: the *effects* of the violation of dignity and the hostile environment suffice for a finding of harassment, regardless of the particular perceptions of the perpetrator and the victim. Most authors support such an objective perspective, which is usually applied by making use of a 'reasonable person' standard. This standard entails examination of the question whether a reasonable person would perceive the conduct as violating human dignity and creating a hostile environment.[26] A 'reasonable person'–like standard is indeed advisable, because it allows for striking a balance between the conflicting interests implicated in a harassment case, and avoids unjust bias in favour of either the victim or the perpetrator.

Nevertheless, application of this standard is not without difficulty, because what is 'reasonable' in particular circumstances is a matter of debate. Sexual harassment litigation in the United States for example produced the contentious question whether a 'reasonable woman' standard was called for, in view of the different perceptions of sexual behaviour that men and women tend to have. Some American courts indeed adopted a reasonable woman standard in order to account for this difference in perception.[27] Translated to the context of the RED: it is very likely that a person belonging to an ethnic minority perceives a racist joke differently from a person belonging to the majority population group. Should this inform the application of the dignity and hostile environment tests? Similarly, it could be argued that certain characteristics specific to the perpetrator, such as a low level of expertise or lack of experience with intercultural environments, should be taken into account. Since harassment is a very sensitive and serious matter, it is advisable for courts to construe a balanced perspective on the basis of the victim's perspective, as well as the perpetrator's perspective.[28] This means that each case should be judged on its own merits, with due consideration for all the particular circumstances involved.

In this context, two important considerations seem worth mentioning. First, it should be emphasised that regard must be had for structural power imbalances between ethnic groups in society.[29] In the words of the US Supreme Court in the *Oncale* case:

[26] Gijzen (2006), at 151; Clarke (2006), at 177; Dine & Watt (1995), at 359. This standard is used in the UK and in the United States. For the UK see Moon & Allen (2002), at 25. For the United States see Shoenfelt et al (2002), at 633-672; Gutek & O'Connor (1999), at 596-629; Goodman-Delahunty (1999), at 519-555.

[27] See inter alia Shoenfelt et al (2002), at 633-672; Gutek & O'Connor (1999), at 596-629; Goodman-Delahunty (1999), at 519-555.

[28] See more specifically on the issue of the victim vs. perpetrator perspective Mullender (1998), at 242-243.

[29] Monaghan (2007), at 354.

> Common sense, and an appropriate *sensitivity to social context*, will enable courts and jurors to distinguish between simple teasing or roughhousing (...) and conduct which a reasonable person in the plaintiff's position would find severely hostile or abusive (emphasis added, MB).[30]

This could mean that some form of behaviour that would not be offensive if perpetrated against a person belonging to the majority population group is considered to be offensive to a person belonging to a minority group that is structurally disadvantaged in society. In other words, an asymmetric approach, conferring more protection on vulnerable groups than on emancipated majority groups seems called for. This is for example the approach taken by the Canadian Supreme Court and the South African Constitutional Court in their equality jurisprudence.[31] In this way, protection against discriminatory harassment could more effectively contribute to the achievement of substantive equality.

Secondly, as for the perpetrator perspective, courts should at least take into account their fundamental freedoms, which are often implicated in harassment cases.[32] Rights that are prone to emerge are the freedom of expression and the freedom of religion: conduct of people venting their opinions or adhering to religious practices can be offensive to persons belonging to groups that are protected under anti-discrimination law. Persons belonging to an ethnic minority can feel threatened or offended when a co-worker expresses his strong opinions on immigration issues, or when a heated debate on the link between Islam and violence is taking place during the lunch break. In such cases, courts need to find a balance between acceptable exercises of fundamental freedoms and the right not to be harassed.[33]

6.2.2.3.1. 'Of violating the dignity of a person'

Human dignity is a very broad notion, as is confirmed by the various guises that the concept has taken on in European law so far. Aside from mere references,[34] actual consideration of the principle of human dignity in case law is found only in a small number of cases, which reveal an extensive meaning. In *The Netherlands v. European Parliament* the ECJ referred to human dignity in terms of the unavailability and inalienability of the human body, in the context

[30] *Oncale v. Sundowner Offshore Services*, Inc., 523 U.U. 75, 118 S. Ct. 998, 140 L. Ed.2d 201 (1998), at 1003.

[31] Grant (2007); Moon (2006a), at 4.

[32] See inter alia Barmes (2007), at 462; Vickers (2006), at 583-588, 603; Clarke (2006), at 172; Flauss (2001), at 509; Hepple (2000); Volokh (1995) and Volokh (1992).

[33] See for a more general discussion of the relevance of private actors' fundamental rights and freedoms section 2.2.2.2.

[34] See for examples of cases in which reference was made to human dignity the opinion of Advocate-General Stix-Hackl in ECJ *Omega Spielhallen- und Automatenaufstellungs-GmbH v. Oberbürgemeisterin de Bundesstadt Bonn*, C-36/02, 18 March, paras. 87 and 88.

of the question whether human tissue could be the object of a patent.[35] In *Omega* the ECJ accepted that the principle of human dignity was served by the prohibition of very violent computer games, which connects human dignity to physical as well as moral integrity.[36] In her opinion in *Omega*, Advocate General Stix-Hackl further linked human dignity to the notions of self-determination, freedom of mankind, identity and personality.[37] The link with physical and moral integrity and self-determination also appears in Articles 2-5 of the Charter of Fundamental Rights, which under the heading of human dignity protect the right to life, the right to mental and physical integrity, the right not to be tortured or undergo degrading treatment and the right not to be forced to slavery. Finally, in his opinion in *Coleman*, Advocate General Maduro associated human dignity with the principle of non-discrimination, by saying that being targeted because of a protected characteristic violates human dignity.[38]

In line with the – admittedly vague – picture emerging from these references, the violation of dignity test would be fulfilled when a person's physical or moral integrity is violated, or when a person is impeded in exercising his/her right to autonomy. Dignity can thus be violated in a physical manner, by way of physical violence or by way of withholding particular essential socio-economic goods necessary for a dignified life, but it can also be violated in an immaterial way.[39]

This very broad reach of the meaning of human dignity makes it difficult to assess its usefulness as separate from the other elements of the definition of harassment, which together seem quite capable of capturing the material aspect ('unwanted conduct', 'hostile environment') and the immaterial aspect ('unwanted conduct', 'related to ethnic or racial origin', 'hostile environment')

---

[35] ECJ *Kingdom of the Netherlands v. European Parliament and Council of the European Union*, C-377/98, 9 October 2001, paras. 69-77.

[36] ECJ *Omega Spielhallen- und Automatenaufstellungs-GmbH v. Oberbürgemeisterin de Bundesstadt Bonn*, C-36/02, 14 October 2004, paras. 34-39.

[37] Opinion of Advocate-General Stix-Hackl in ECJ *Omega Spielhallen- und Automatenaufstellungs-GmbH v. Oberbürgemeisterin de Bundesstadt Bonn*, C-36/02, 18 March 2004, para. 79.

[38] Opinion of Advocate-General Maduro in ECJ *S. Coleman v. Attridge Law and Steve Law*, C-303/06, 31 January 2008, para. 10. The Canadian Supreme Court has described this particular immaterial violation of dignity as taking place each time a person is treated in a way that reflects the stereotypical application of presumed group or personal characteristics, or that perpetuates or promotes the view that the individual is less capable or worthy of recognition or value as a human being. See Moon (2006a), at 3-4.

[39] Grant (2007); Réaume (2003), at 248. See for more elaborate descriptions and applications of the principle of human dignity Grant (2007); Moon (2006a); Moon & Allen (2002); Ehrenreich (1999). See for a well-known application of the socio-economic aspect of human dignity by the South African Constitutional Court *Government of the Republic of South Africa v. Grootboom*, 2001 (1) SA 46 (CC), in which the right to housing was connected to human dignity.

of human dignity. It remains to be seen whether national courts and the ECJ will develop a separate meaning in the future. Perhaps the real meaning of the dignity test is its implicit message that the behaviour complained of should truly be very serious in order to constitute harassment. In any case, the vagueness of the test, in combination with the discretion clause of Article 2(3) RED, ensures that Member States have considerable room to manoeuvre as regards its practical interpretation.[40]

6.2.2.3.2. 'And of creating an intimidating, hostile, degrading, humiliating or offensive environment'

The hostile environment test is complicated in its own way, being extensively formulated. The fear of some Member States that employers would be faced with overly burdensome anti-harassment duties spurred the use of an abundance of adjectives.[41] Even though these adjectives are rather concrete, in that most persons have an immediate grasp of what they mean, courts obviously have quite some discretion as to their application. In view of the apparent overlap between the words, the phrase should probably be taken as a whole, which means that it does not require separate application of each particular aspect.

The ECJ and national courts can find inspiration for the interpretation of this phrase in the practice of the American Supreme Court, which has extensive experience with the concept of harassment and applies a particular test for the establishment of a hostile environment. The basic rule according to the Supreme Court is that a hostile environment is created if the conduct substantively alters the conditions within which the harassed person carries out the relevant activity.[42] According to the Supreme Court, all circumstances of the case need to be assessed in order to determine whether this rule is fulfilled. Furthermore, it has mentioned the following relevant factors, in a non-exhaustive manner:

1) the frequency of the conduct (single versus multiple incidents)

[40] See also ECJ *Omega Spielhallen- und Automatenaufstellungs-GmbH v. Oberbürgemeisterin de Bundesstadt Bonn*, C-36/02, 14 October 2004, para. 37, where the ECJ acknowledges that different conceptions of human dignity can co-exist among the Member States: "[i]t is not indispensable in that respect for the restrictive measure issued by the authorities of a Member State to correspond to a conception shared by all Member States as regards the precise way in which the fundamental right (…) in question is to be protected."

[41] Gijzen (2006), at 150; Tyson (2004), at 117-118; Jones (2003), at 518. See also *Explanatory Memorandum*, Commission for the European Communities, 1999/0253, 25 November 1999, in which the Commission states that harassing conduct, "[t]o be caught by the Directive, must be of a serious nature, creating a generally disturbing or hostile working environment."

[42] *Oncale v. Sundowner Offshore Services, Inc.*, 523 U.S. 75, 118 S. Ct. 998, 140 L. Ed.2d 201 (1998), 1003.

2) the severity of the conduct

3) whether the conduct is physically threatening or humiliating or rather an offensive utterance

4) whether it interferes with an employee's work performance

The latter factor reveals that US case law only concerns working environments; the factors do seem valid beyond this context, though, and can be applied per analogy in other types of environments as well.

It should be pointed out that the word 'environment' suggests a demarcated context, which in turn implies a real connection between perpetrator and victim. Thus, for example, offensive remarks made on television are reasonably not considered to create a hostile environment for the person watching at home. On the other hand, if such a show is purposefully shown at work or in a cafeteria, there is an 'environment' in the sense of Article 2(3) RED. Moreover, the word 'environment' makes clear that the conduct complained of does not need to be directly aimed at the person complaining of harassment. Harassment can be constituted by behaviour targeting other persons who belong to the same racial or ethnic group as the applicant, or even targeting no-one in particular.[43] For instance, a workplace where the walls are covered with racist posters impacts on the overall environment, even if the posters were not put up to offend any particular person.

6.2.2.3.3. Need for transparency and consistency

The main conclusion of the foregoing discussion of the dignity and hostile environment tests is that national courts have a wide playground, seeing that there is a clear lack of concrete benchmarks at the European level. American case law can provide inspiration, but in the end it is up to national courts to find their way, until the ECJ speaks out on the matter. And even then it can be expected that the latter court will permit a certain margin of discretion, in view of the discretion clause of Article 2(3) RED. In view of this high degree of uncertainty, it is essential that courts respect legal certainty and develop transparent and consistent standards.

6.2.3. The duty of care implied by Article 2(3) RED

In section 2.2.1 the circle of addressees of the RED was discussed, with particular attention for the question whether non-principally envisaged persons, such as co-workers, students and patients, were covered by the RED.

[43] Barmes (2007), at 448; Thüsing (2003), at 210.

The issue comes particularly to the fore in the context of Article 2(3) RED, since this provision appears to be especially aimed at principally envisaged actors. This can be inferred from its wording, which points to a different perspective than the definitions of direct and indirect discrimination, which clearly target active personal behaviour. By employing the verb 'take place', Article 2(3) appears to target an actor that is not always the actual perpetrator. After all, the definition could just as easily have been formulated in more active terms, referring to harassment in words such as: "behaving with the intent or effect of." The impression that Article 2(3) is primarily intended to impose a duty of care on principally envisaged actors is supported by its drafting history, which shows that the deliberations of the Member States consistently focused on the particular duties that it would impose on employers.[44] Both the UK and American systems follow a similar logic of primary responsibility for principally envisaged actors, by recognising direct liability for employers who have not taken reasonable steps to prevent or end harassment in the workplace.[45]

It is repeated here that it is desirable that the victim can hold accountable not only the principally envisaged actor, but also the actual perpetrator of the discriminatory harassment. In practical legal terms this would entail direct liability for the actual perpetrator of harassment, in addition to direct liability on the basis of the duty of care for principally envisaged actors.[46]

As regards direct liability of principally envisaged actors, two types of duties are conceivable: a structural duty that aims at the problem of harassment in general, and an incidental duty that is concerned with the way in which the particular actor handles a specific case of harassment. Ideally, national frameworks should impose both types of duties on principally envisaged actors. Still, in view of the particular history of Article 2(3) RED and the discretion clause contained therein, it is expected that Member States have quite some leeway in determining which duties of care apply in their particular national context.

The structural duty could entail an obligation to set in place policies and procedures to prevent harassment from occurring and to solve claims of harassment in an appropriate way. The European framework offers two soft-law documents that provide useful input in this respect. In 1991, the Commission adopted a *Recommendation on the protection of the dignity of women and men at work,* which contains a code of conduct for employers.[47] In 2007, the European Social Partners adopted a *Framework agreement on*

[44] Tyson (2004), at 117-118.

[45] Driessen-Reilly & Driessen (2003), at 504; Thüsing (2003), at 210; Roberts (2001), at 388.

[46] Gijzen (2006), at 152.

[47] *Commission Recommendation of 27 November 1991 on the protection of the dignity of women and men at work*, 92/131/EEC.

harassment and violence at work.[48] Both documents focus on harassment in the workplace, but the guidelines contained therein are applicable in a broader context, such as for example in schools or hospitals.

The guidelines put forward by these documents focus both on prevention and on appropriate conflict resolution, and can be summarised as follows. Prevention ideally involves the development of clear rules and a clear company policy with regard to harassment, as well as effective communication of these measures and awareness-raising amongst employees. Training of managers and supervisors is furthermore an important aspect of an effective prevention policy. As regards effective conflict resolution, both documents emphasise the need for informal and confidential support channels that should be made available to victims in the preliminary stage of a harassment case. In addition, fair and thorough formal conflict resolution mechanisms should be set in place for formal resolution of harassment complaints.[49] Finally, effective and appropriate sanctions should be determined in advance and should be effectively applied if necessary.

The incidental duty of care would necessarily have to be determined for each case separately, with regard for the specific circumstances of the case. The assessment of whether the principally envisaged actor has fulfilled his duty in this respect could follow the lines of the 'reasonable steps' inquiry as developed by UK courts. Thus, it should be examined to what extent the particular actor has taken all reasonable steps that could be expected of him in order to prevent or end the particular instance of harassment.[50] An important factor that turned up in the UK context in this respect is the extent to which the actor knew or should have known what was going on.[51] It makes sense to take into account the knowledge level of the actor, since it is quite unreasonable to expect someone to do something about a problem he knew nothing about. It is difficult to provide more specific guidelines, since the application of the 'reasonable steps' inquiry is by its nature dependent on the circumstances of the case. It should therefore be emphasised that transparency and consistency are essential.

---

[48] This agreement is contained in the *Communication from the Commission to the Council and the European Parliament* of 8 November 2007, COM(2007) 686 final.

[49] See for a more detailed description of a proper procedure for harassment complaints Driessen-Reilly & Driessen (2003), at 505.

[50] Thüsing (2003), at 210; Roberts (2001), at 389-391.

[51] Roberts (2001), at 390.

6.3. Instruction to discriminate

> An instruction to discriminate against persons on grounds of racial or ethnic origin shall be deemed to be discrimination within the meaning of paragraph 1 (Article 2(4) RED)

The insertion of a prohibition of instructing to discriminate is an important addition to the toolbox of the RED, because it enlarges the reach of the provisions of the RED to persons that have not discriminated themselves but have caused discrimination to happen by making use of their relative power position. The concept can probably be traced back to the UK anti-discrimination framework, where courts have since long recognised that the instruction to discriminate against persons belonging to protected groups constitutes direct discrimination.[52] In this way, persons not belonging to protected groups who do not want to comply with an instruction to discriminate have a legal cause of action against the instructor, which enhances the effectiveness of the anti-discrimination framework.

The provision on the instruction to discriminate refers back to "discrimination within the meaning of paragraph 1", which could be either direct or indirect discrimination. The words 'on grounds of' would seem to indicate that direct discrimination was on the Community legislator's mind when drawing up this provision, which is also in line with the understanding of the instruction to discriminate in the UK context. Still, it is theoretically possible to include instructions to indirectly discriminate, which would de facto widen the reach of Article 2(4) RED, and would therefore not be objectionable. To the contrary, such an extension of liability for instances of indirect discrimination would only increase the level of protection of the RED framework.

In view of the ancillary nature of the provision, which links back to the concepts of Article 2(1) RED, there are not many features that need to be discussed separately in this section. Both direct and indirect discrimination have been amply examined in Chapters 5 and 6, and the points made there would seem valid also for the application of Article 2(4) RED. Two questions remain that merit separate attention in this section.

First of all, due to the lack of guidance at the European level, Member States have some leeway in determining the meaning of 'instruction'. The word can be interpreted more or less broadly, depending on how formally the concept is approached. A formal reading would require an express command that is issued in a hierarchical context. A less formal reading would include more implicit forms of coercion, and would perhaps also extend to instructions issued in the context of an unequal power relationship that does

[52] Schiek et al (2007), at 527-528. See for example *Showboat Entertainment Centre Ltd v. Owens* [1984] IRLR 7, EAT; *Weathersfield Ltd v. Sargent* [1999] IRLR 94, CA.

not necessarily fit in a particular hierarchical order. Naturally, a less formal interpretation would increase the scope of application of Article 2(4) and in that regard would be preferable. Still, the boundaries of 'instruction' should not be stretched too far, in view of the principle of legal certainty and the will of the Community legislator, who deliberately refused to insert references to incitement and pressurising to discriminate in Article 2(4) RED.[53]

It would at least seem reasonable to include non-verbatim forms of instruction, which means that any form of coercion exerted within a hierarchical context is preferably covered.[54] For example, if an employer does not literally instruct an employee to discriminate, but makes clear that he/she will have to bear the consequences of not discriminating against another person, this is preferably considered to amount to an instruction to discriminate.

Secondly, the word 'instruction' implies some degree of intent on the side of the instructor, which could cause some confusion, seeing that the concepts of direct and indirect discrimination do not involve an intent requirement.[55] In this respect it should be stressed that the intent implied by 'instruction' is not aimed at the discriminatory nature of the action envisaged by the instructor, but only at the effect of getting the other person to execute what is instructed. Since the concepts of direct and indirect discrimination do not require intent, it would not make sense to require such discriminatory intent to be present with the instructor. Take the example of an employer who instructs his subordinates not to hire persons of a particular ethnic group, because he wants to maintain a certain degree of ethnic diversity in his workforce, and not because he wants to discriminate against the particular group. He has no discriminatory intent; only the intent to get his subordinates to apply his hiring policy. Regardless of his lack of discriminatory intent, his instruction should reasonably be considered to amount to an instruction to directly discriminate – provided, of course, that none of the exceptions for direct discrimination are applicable.

PART TWO: CASE STUDY

6.4. Harassment

6.4.1. Situation prior to the RED and the changes brought about by implementation

Of all four Member States under study, the Netherlands was the only one in which anti-discrimination law protected against discriminatory harassment

53 Tyson (2004), at 118; Brown (2002), at 208.
54 Tyson (2004), at 118; Toggenburg (2002), at 231-244.
55 See section 4.2.3 and the introduction to section 5.2.2.

prior to the implementation of the RED. The GETA did not contain an express prohibition of harassment, but the ETC had developed the concept of 'discriminatory treatment', which comprised all kinds of bullying and intimidation linked to a protected characteristic.[56] The occurrence of such discriminatory treatment was considered to amount to direct discrimination on the side of the employer, school board and other principally envisaged actors, if they had not fulfilled their duty of care to prevent and end it. The RED brought about an explicit reference to discriminatory harassment in the GETA, which now provides in Article 1a(2) that harassment is constituted by:

> conduct that is connected to [the protected characteristic or direct or indirect discrimination, MB] and that has the purpose or effect of violating the dignity of the person and creating a threatening, hostile, degrading, humiliating or a hostile environment.

The ETC has adjusted to the new legal framework, in that this body now applies two concepts of harassment: one very serious form that follows the definition of Article 1a(2) GETA, and the less serious form of 'discriminatory treatment', which is still considered to be comprised by the prohibition of direct discrimination. The RED did therefore not produce any substantive changes; it simply led to the express recognition of one very serious form of harassment that was previously dealt with under the general heading of 'discriminatory treatment'.[57]

In the other Member States there was no provision for discriminatory harassment prior to the implementation of the RED.

In Hungary, the first implementation phase produced a prohibition of racial harassment in the Public Education Act. This Act defined harassment as:

> any behaviour or instigation that is aimed at humiliating or threatening a child or pupil, to violate his or her right to human dignity, as well as the creation of an atmosphere that may result in the same effects.[58]

The second implementation phase extended the reach of the prohibition of discriminatory harassment to other fields of application than education. Thus, Article 10(1) of the pre-2007 version of the HETA defined harassment as:

> conduct violating human dignity related to the relevant person's [protected characteristic, MB], with the purpose or effect of creating an intimidating hostile, degrading, humiliating or offensive environment.

[56] Gijzen (2006), at 185.

[57] Holtmaat (2007), at 30-31; Gijzen (2006), at 193.

[58] Article 4 (8), (10) and (13) of the Public Act on Education.

In applying this provision the AET found it particularly difficult to deal with cases of sexual harassment,[59] which was the reason for an amendment in 2007, adding the qualification "*of a sexual or other nature*". The most recent definition now reads as follows:

> conduct of a sexual or other nature violating human dignity related to the relevant person's [protected characteristic, MB], with the purpose or effect of creating an intimidating hostile, degrading, humiliating or offensive environment.

In Estonia, the first implementation phase introduced a prohibition of racial harassment in the field of employment only. Article 10(2)(4) of the ECA stipulated that:

> harassment shall be deemed to be a form of direct discrimination on any of the protected characteristics, MB]. Harassment shall be taken to occur where an unwanted conduct or act, either verbal, non-verbal or physical, takes place against a person in a relationship of subordination or dependency with the purpose or effect of violating the dignity of the person and of creating a disturbing, intimidating, hostile, degrading, humiliating or offensive environment, and the person rejects such conduct or tolerates it for a reason that it affects his or her access to office or employment or in order to maintain the employment relationship, have access to training, receive remuneration or have access to other advantages or benefits.

This provision added a number of requirements to the definition of Article 2(3) RED, and was criticised for not being in conformity with the RED.[60] The second implementation phase therefore brought about a less restrictive definition, and Article 3(3) of the EETA now provides that:

> [d]irect discrimination is also harassment, which is unwelcome behaviour for a person based on a [protected characteristic, MB], the purpose or actual impact of which is the violation of the dignity of the person and the creation of a threatening, hostile, disparaging, humiliating or offensive atmosphere.

Finally, in Belgium the introduction of the concept of discriminatory harassment in the ADA was preceded by the adoption of general legislation against bullying and mobbing at work in 2002.[61] From 2003 onwards employment-related harassment was regulated by this special legislation and the ADA. The ADA defined discriminatory harassment in Article 2(6) in the following way:

---

59 *Report on the activities of the Equal Treatment Authority and the experiences of the implementation of Act nr. 125 of 2003 on equal treatment and the promotion of equal opportunities*, AET, July 2006, at 14.

60 Poleshchuk (2007), at 21.

61 *Royal Decree of 11 July 2002 on the protection against violence, harassment and unwanted sexual behaviour in the workplace*, which was repealed in 2007; at the same time its substantive provisions were transferred to the *Law of 4 August 1996 on the Wellbeing of workers in the execution of their work*, MB 18 September 1996, which now in ChapterVbis provides for protection against harassment at work.

> harassment shall be considered to be a form of discrimination in the case of unwanted conduct that has the purpose or effect of violating the dignity of a person, and creating an intimidating, hostile, offensive, humiliating or damaging environment.

The Law on the Well-being of Workers (hereafter: LWW), which is still applicable, defines harassment as:

> unlawful and recurring behaviour, taking place outside or inside the organisation; which in particular can be expressed in conduct, words, threats, actions, gestures and unilateral writings; and which aims at or results in the violation of the personality, dignity or physical or mental integrity of a person, undermines his position, or creates a threatening, hostile, degrading, humiliating or offensive environment.[62]

It was considered unfortunate by scholars and the government that two regimes for harassment were applicable to discriminatory harassment in an employment context, and the second implementation phase was used to create more clarity in this respect. Article 12 of the new ARA prohibits racial harassment, which is defined in Article 4(10) as follows:

> unwanted conduct that is related to one of the protected grounds, and which aims at or results in the violation of the dignity of a person, and the creation of a threatening, hostile, insulting, humiliating or offensive environment.

Article 6 of the new ARA specifies that the provisions on harassment in this law are not applicable in cases of harassment in employment as defined by the LWW. Thus, racial harassment occurring in an employment context is regulated by the LWW; outside this field of application, the regime of the new ARA applies.

This overview shows that Member States apparently have not generously made use of the room granted to them by the discretion clause of Article 2(3) RED, and have remained rather close to the RED's definition of harassment. Still, in some areas they have developed or maintained national particularities, which will be exposed in the following sections. In view of the relative novelty of the concept of discriminatory harassment in the Member States it is unsurprising that many aspects of its application have yet to crystallise. The following discussion is therefore necessarily rather concise, and often goes no further than indicating possible routes to be taken in the future.

62 Article 32ter(2) LWW; Van Putten (2004a), at 119.

6.4.2. The definition of harassment

6.4.2.1. 'An unwanted conduct'

The 'unwanted' standard has not found its way into all four national anti-discrimination frameworks. In Hungary and the Netherlands the standard was omitted. In the latter Member State this was a deliberate choice. The Dutch government wanted to make sure that victims' passive or cooperative conduct would not backfire at them in the form of a requirement that they establish their expressed disagreement.[63] The ETC in its quasi-jurisprudence has confirmed that passive or cooperative behaviour of the victim does not preclude a finding of harassment, since such behaviour may in some cases seem to be the safest option for a victim.[64] It is unclear whether the Hungarian legislator omitted the 'unwanted' standard for the same reason as the Dutch legislator, but the choice to do so has ensured that the AET and the Hungarian courts will not require the victim to prove that he/she did not consent to the harassing behaviour.

In Belgium and Estonia, the 'unwanted' aspect does form part of the definition of harassment, but so far it does not seem very likely that it will be applied in such a way as to impose an additional barrier for the victim, at least not in Belgium. In the latter Member State, the general harassment provision in the LWW does not contain an 'unwanted' standard, which shows that it was not considered to be a necessary element of harassment by the Belgian legislator. It can be expected that the harassment provision in the new ARA will be applied in accordance with its counterpart in the LWW.

In Estonia, the 'unwanted' standard in the EETA is a much toned-down version of a condition that made up part of the old ECA's definition of harassment, and which still features in the harassment provision of the Gender Equality Act.[65] This condition required the victim to show that he/she had rejected the conduct, or had tolerated it because it would otherwise negatively affect his/her work opportunities or conditions. This condition greatly increased the burden of proof for the victim of harassment, and moreover excluded instances of harassment where the victim was too intimidated or

---

[63] *Advice and Report on the Amendment of the General Act on Equal Treatment and certain other acts in order to implement directive 2000/43/EG and directive 2000/78/EG (Implementation Act)*, TK 2002-3, 28 770, A, at 14-15.

[64] Opinion 2007-193 ETC, paras. 3.16-17.

[65] Article 3(1)(5) of the Gender Equality Act provides that harassment is present: "where, in any subordinate or dependent relationship, any form of unwanted verbal, non-verbal or physical activity or conduct of a sexual nature occurs, with the purpose or effect of violating the dignity of a person, in particular when creating a disturbing, intimidating, hostile, degrading, humiliating or offensive environment *and the person rejects or submits to such conduct as it is a direct or indirect prerequisite for getting hired, maintaining the employment relationship, participation in training, receipt of remuneration, or other advantages or benefits.*" (emphasis added, MB)

scared to express discontent. In view of this history it is remarkable that the EETA does not replicate this particular standard, and the omission could be perceived as deliberately effectuated by the legislator, which will presumably induce Estonian courts to interpret 'unwanted' in a lenient way. This optimistic interpretation needs to be confirmed in practice, however.

The interpretation of the word 'conduct' has so far not caused difficulties in the Member States, to the extent that it has come to the fore at all. In fact, to our knowledge there is not a single case in which the interpretation of 'conduct' was expressly at stake. So far, there is only Hungarian and Dutch quasi-jurisprudence on harassment, which reveals an inclusive approach as to the types of conduct that are deemed to constitute harassment.

Examples drawn from the practice of the Hungarian AET include: making obscene jokes and sexually charged remarks;[66] imposing unnecessary requirements and denying certain benefits to an employee;[67] making racist and insulting remarks and subsequently dismissing persons of Roma origin;[68] making public private and sensitive information about employees.[69] This list suggests an inclusive approach to the meaning of 'conduct'. Moreover, some decisions of the AET reveal that this body is willing to apply the qualification of harassment to single incidents, and does not require a certain pattern of behaviour or a series of events. For example, the single act of making public a list of employees who had been on sick leave was serious enough in the AET's eyes so as to constitute harassment.[70] The AET's lenient approach is supported by the Advisory Body to the AET. In its opinion on harassment the Advisory Body confirms that passive as well as active behaviour is targeted, and that a sufficiently serious single incident can constitute harassment.[71]

The Dutch ETC has so far only twice applied the label of harassment,[72] but this is not due to a restrictive interpretation of 'conduct'. The cause rather lies with the strict approach taken by the ETC to 'harassment', which is reserved for very serious forms of harassing behaviour.[73] The two successful 'harassment' cases concerned sexual intimidation, involving inter alia sexual remarks and a sexually charged workplace;[74] and the inappropriate follow-up of a complaint of sexual intimidation, which involved a humiliating confrontational conversation between colleagues.[75] In addition to 'harassment', the ETC

66 EBH 69/2006.
67 EBH 22/2006.
68 EBH 516/2007.
69 EBH 81/2008; EBH 866/2007.
70 EBH 81/2008.
71 *Position Paper of the Advisory Body on Equal Treatment on the notions of harassment and sexual harassment*, No. 2/2007(III.23.No.384/5/208(IV10).
72 Opinions 2006-65 and 2007-11 ETC.
73 See section 6.4.1.
74 Opinion 2006-65 ETC.
75 Opinion 2007-11 ETC.

makes use of the notion of 'discriminatory treatment', which is applied rather leniently. The types of behaviour that have been addressed in 'discriminatory treatment' cases so far include: making racist or degrading remarks,[76] unequally distributing the tasks in the workplace[77] and consistently ignoring a co-worker.[78] This list shows that the ETC accepts both verbal and non-verbal conduct and passive behaviour as amounting to 'conduct' and is in this respect equally lenient as the Hungarian AET. Moreover, in a similar fashion as the Hungarian AET, the ETC accepts sufficiently serious single incidents of racist abuse as constituting 'discriminatory treatment'.[79] This inclusive approach ensures a relatively high level of protection of anti-discrimination law.

There is hardly any relevant practice in the two other Member States, and interpretations of 'conduct' are therefore yet to be developed. In Estonia, one author has submitted that 'conduct' comprises "any verbal, non-verbal or physical conduct",[80] a suggestion which is preferably followed by the Estonian courts. In Belgium the situation is slightly complicated, in view of the dual structure of the anti-harassment framework. Whereas Article 4(10) of the new ARA does not provide any insight in the meaning of 'conduct', Article 32ter(2) of the LWW provides that harassment is constituted by behaviour, words, threats, actions, gestures and unilateral writings.[81] This reveals a broad interpretation of 'conduct', and there is no reason to assume that courts will be more restrictive when applying the harassment provision of the new ARA. At the same time it should be pointed out that the LWW does not apply the concept of 'harassment' to single incidents, which are separately regulated under the heading of 'violence at work'.[82] Indeed, Article 32ter(2) LWW refers to "*recurring* behaviour" in its definition of harassment, which could induce Belgian courts to apply 'harassment' in the new ARA in the same way. This would mean that very serious single events would not be covered by the new ARA, which would obviously impact negatively on the level of protection provided by this Act.[83] It is therefore preferable that Belgian courts interpret 'harassment' in the context of the new ARA as comprising also those situations that are categorised separately in the LWW under 'violence at work'. It is, however, doubtful that they will do so, in view of the fact

[76] See for instance Opinions 2008-44 ETC; 2006-75 ETC; 2006-71 ETC; 2005-167 ETC; 2004-128 ETC.

[77] Opinion 2006-71 ETC.

[78] Opinions 2006-71 ETC; 2005-167 ETC.

[79] See Opinion 2007-57 ETC, para. 4.1(d), in which the ETC considered that a single racist remark, if proven, in itself constituted 'discriminatory treatment'.

[80] Tavits (2004).

[81] Article 32ter(2) LWW.

[82] Article 32ter(1) LWW defines violence at work as follows: "each act whereby an employee of another person to whom this law is applicable is threatened or attacked physically or psychologically in the execution of his work."

[83] Foubert (2004), at 10-11.

that the Constitutional Court in a judgment on the new ARA has described harassment as constituting "illegitimate behaviour, notably by humiliations and threats, taken by a person in a malignant and *repetitive* manner in order to destabilise another person" (emphasis added, MB).[84] The words in italics make clear that the Constitutional Court does not consider single events to be able to constitute harassment."

6.4.2.2. 'Related to racial or ethnic origin'

Three out of the four national anti-discrimination Acts formulate the causal aspect of discriminatory harassment in similarly weak terms as Article 2(3) RED, and require the harassing conduct to be 'related to' the protected characteristic. Practice in the Netherlands and in Hungary reveals that causality hardly plays a part in the review process. Indeed, these bodies seem satisfied that the 'related to' aspect is present as soon as the protected characteristic has played some part in the events complained of. For instance, they apparently consider the causal link to be self-evident in cases involving racist jokes or remarks. Moreover, they do not require the victim to show that another person would not have been harassed in the same way.[85] Nevertheless, one decision of the Dutch ETC makes clear that, despite its overall lenient approach, this body does require a real link with a protected characteristic. The case involved a conflict between a disabled person and a security guard, in which the guard verbally abused the disabled person. The ETC considered that the facts established no link whatsoever with the person's disability, and thus considered that there was no prima facie case of disability-related harassment.[86]

In Belgium, the provision on discriminatory harassment has not yet been applied, but it has been suggested in literature that the causal link should be approached strictly, despite the 'related to' wording of Article 4(10) of the new ARA. According to these authors, courts should conclude discriminatory harassment only when the protected characteristic is one of the primary causes or motivations of the harassment, and where the use of the characteristic is not incidental or simply instrumental.[87] If Belgian courts were to follow this suggestion, the burden of proof for victims of discriminatory harassment would increase considerably, and the concept of discriminatory harassment would moreover be placed back in the realm of formal equality, as was

84 Constitutional Court, Case No. 17/2009, 12 February 2009, para B.53.2.

85 For the Hungarian AET see EBH 516/2007, in which superiors made racist remarks and said that they did not want to work with Roma persons, which was considered by the AET to constitute harassment. For similar cases ruled by the ETC see for instance Opinions 2008-44 ETC, 2006-75 ETC; 2006-71 ETC; 2005-167 ETC; 2004-128 ETC.

86 Opinion 2005-65 ETC, para. 5.6-5.7.

87 De Prins et al (2005), at 500; Foubert (2004), at 11-12.

explained before. Belgian courts will therefore hopefully apply a more lenient approach than the one proposed in literature. In any event, the issue would be relevant only outside of the field of employment, since the general anti-harassment framework of the LWW does not require any link with a protected characteristic.

The Estonian framework stands out among the three other Member States in that it appears to require a strict causal link: according to Article 3(3) EETA harassment is only discriminatory if it is 'based on' a protected characteristic. If this part of the definition is interpreted strictly, the concept of discriminatory harassment would be placed back in the realm of formal equality and the level of protection of the Estonian anti-discrimination framework would be lowered considerably. A strict approach might not be in contravention of the RED, however, in view of the margin of appreciation granted to Member States by Article 2(3) RED. Still, from a substantive equality viewpoint, it is to be hoped that Estonian courts will not apply the causal aspect of discriminatory harassment too strictly.

6.4.2.3. 'With the purpose or effect'

All four Member States have retained the 'purpose or effect' wording of Article 2(3) RED, and thus have at first glance opted for an objective perspective as regards the application of the dignity and hostile environment tests.[88]

In the Netherlands the need for such an objective perspective was emphasised by the government at the occasion of the implementation of the RED.[89] The Dutch ETC has indeed consistently interpreted harassment objectively, in that it qualifies the behaviour complained of according to its own standards and not that of the victim or the perpetrator.[90] However, it has so far not developed a particular approach, such as for example the American 'reasonable person' or 'reasonable woman' standards. Its practice with regard to 'discriminatory treatment' shows that it takes into account the broader context within which the harassment takes place and the relevant power relationships in society. It has for instance emphasised more than once that persons belonging to minority groups in society can perceive certain remarks and jokes differently from persons belonging to the majority group.[91] As was explained above, such a context-specific and asymmetric attitude reflects a substantive equality outlook.

[88] For Belgium, this is confirmed by Van Putten (2004a), at 120.

[89] *Parliamentary proceedings on the Amendment of the General Act on Equal Treatment and certain other acts in order to implement directive 2000/43/EC and directive 2000/78/EC*, TK 2002-3 28 770, 5, at 18.

[90] Gijzen (2006), at 194. See for instance Opinion 2006-65 ETC, para. 5.5, in which the ETC confirms that the violation of dignity and hostile environment tests are to be applied objectively.

[91] Opinion 2008-134 ETC, para. 3.22; Opinion 2002-39 ETC, para. 5.3.

Fundamental rights and freedoms of alleged perpetrators of harassment have furthermore been recognised in the Dutch framework. The government expressly recognised the need to respect these rights when applying the concept of harassment in the Explanatory Memorandum to the IA. The government also announced further research on this matter,[92] but it is unclear whether such a study has actually taken place. The harassment and 'discriminatory treatment' cases that have been examined by the ETC so far have not brought the issue up yet, so that it is still unclear how fundamental rights and freedoms will be accommodated. It is in any case positive that the issue has been recognised.

The manner in which the objective approach plays out in Belgium, Estonia and Hungary is still obscure, in view of the limited practice available so far.

6.4.2.4. 'Of violating the dignity of a person and of creating an intimidating, hostile, degrading, humiliating or offensive environment'

It is interesting to note that the dignity and hostile environment tests have not been further elaborated or exemplified at the national level, while all four Member States have included them in their definitions of discriminatory harassment. This is perhaps not very surprising for Belgium and Estonia, where the concept so far has not been applied in practice. In Hungary and the Netherlands, on the contrary, quite a number of harassment cases have come up already, but the case-law is very casuistic in nature and does not produce any meaningful benchmarks or criteria.

For instance, the Dutch ETC usually mentions the tests only to emphasise that harassment is very serious behaviour that cannot easily be established; it subsequently examines the severity of the behaviour complained of in order to determine whether the label of harassment is appropriate, but it does not apply any set of criteria in this respect. As was mentioned before, the ETC hardly ever concludes that harassment has taken place, and it far more often resorts to the concept of 'discriminatory treatment'. Thus, the occurrence of racist jokes and offensive remarks in itself is consistently considered not to cross the threshold of severity required for harassment but to amount to 'discriminatory treatment'.[93] More generally, the latter concept is applied to all

[92] *Advice and Report on the Amendment of the General Act on Equal Treatment and certain other acts in order to implement directive 2000/43/EC and directive 2000/78/EC,*TK 2002-3, 28 770, A, at 15.

[93] See for instance Opinion 2005-167 ETC, para. 6.7: "[t]he fact that discriminatory remarks have sometimes been made, that the applicant has been hurt by them and that he has complained about them a number of times is, according to the Commission's consistent opinion, not sufficient to constitute a presumption of a conduct that violated the dignity of the applicant and created a threatening, hostile, offensive, humiliating or degrading environment (Opinion 2005-65 ETC and Opinion 2005-75 ETC). The legislator intended to communicate with the prohibition of harassment that it is a qualified and severe form of discrimination, which is

kinds of undermining bullying behaviour that has some link with a protected characteristic, with no threshold of severity that has to be attained. Seeing that the ETC is very lenient in its application of the concept of 'discriminatory treatment', it actually provides a very high level of protection against discriminatory harassing conduct.

The Hungarian AET has also adopted a lenient attitude, and appears ready to apply the label of 'harassment' to any kind of humiliating behaviour. Thus, making discriminatory or offensive remarks,[94] giving unnecessary and nonsensical assignments,[95] publicising sensitive personal information[96] and unnecessarily criticising or embarrassing a person[97] are all forms of humiliation that constitute harassment according to the AET, regardless of their severity. Its approach is comparable to that of the ETC, in that it rejects any humiliating or undermining behaviour linked to a protected characteristic, regardless of its severity. Such an approach reflects a clear conviction of the immorality of using protected characteristics to put people down and can be welcomed from a minority perspective. Similarly to the ETC, therefore, the AET applies an approach that would seem to be more lenient than the regime provided by Article 2(3) RED. This should in principle be positively evaluated since it means that the HETA provides a very high level of protection against discriminatory harassment. Still, as was mentioned before, it is important that such a lenient approach remains within certain boundaries, and more particularly that it also shows regard for the interests of the alleged perpetrator.

In this respect it is interesting to note that the Hungarian framework has come up with a very original way of accommodating the perpetrator perspective, namely by way of allowing for the objective justification of behaviour that allegedly amounts to harassment, along the lines of the general objective justification test of Article 7(2) HETA.[98] The position paper on harassment of the Advisory Body to the AET makes clear that this justification possibility is not intended as an escape route for perpetrators of harassment. In other words, if the behaviour complained of is sufficiently serious and linked to a protected ground, there is no possibility of justifying this behaviour as being acceptable. The AET's practice indeed shows that the justification test is not used as an escape route, but as a means of establishing whether the conduct

so serious that no justification possibility applies to it. (..). Therefore, heavy and cumulative requirements need to be fulfilled in order for harassment to be established. A mere offense is insufficient to constitute harassment." In the same case, the ETC concluded that discriminatory treatment had taken place, because there had been some racist remarks and the employer had not adequately responded to them (see paras. 6.8-6.11).

94 EBH 69/2006; EBH 516/2006.

95 EBH 22/2006.

96 EBH 81/2008; EBH 866/2007.

97 EBH 704/2007, EBH 681/2007.

98 See section 5.5.4.6 for a discussion of this justification possibility.

complained of was sufficiently serious so as to amount to harassment.[99] For example, if an employer submits an employee to a medical assessment, and he cannot objectively justify his decision to require such a medical assessment, his behaviour is qualified by the AET as harassment. On the other hand, if the employer submits credible and valid reasons as to why he required a medical assessment, there is an objective justification and the behaviour complained of does not constitute harassment.[100]

Even though it is commendable that the Hungarian framework in this way ensures that the perpetrator perspective is accounted for, in addition to the victim perspective, it is unfortunate that it has done so in this particular way. After all, the objective justification approach raises the impression that behaviour amounting to harassment can be justified, which is not the case. The RED does not provide for any justification for harassing behaviour. It is arguably difficult for inexperienced lawyers and other persons to understand that the objective justification test is only used as a means of establishing that the behaviour complained of was indeed so serious as to constitute harassment, and not as a means of justifying behaviour that is considered to amount to harassment. It would therefore be advisable for the AET and Hungarian courts not to make use of the Article 7(2) objective justification test when assessing the seriousness of the behaviour complained of, and simply to scrutinise the explanations given by the alleged perpetrator on their own merits.

6.4.3. The duty of care implied by Article 2(3)

The liability regimes of the various national frameworks were explained in section 2.4.1.2, the findings of which will be briefly replicated here.

In the Netherlands and Hungary, principally envisaged actors are directly liable for the actions of their subordinates, and therefore have the duty to prevent and effectively end instances of harassment within their sphere of influence. Conversely, direct liability of subordinates or third persons is not possible in Hungary and the Netherlands, and both frameworks have been criticised for this lack in protection. In Belgium and Estonia the situation is still uncertain, as it is not yet clear whether anti-discrimination law only targets principally envisaged actors, or all persons acting in a particular field of application.[101]

For Belgium it is at least clear that an inclusive appraoch is taken in the field of employment, as the LWW imposes direct liability on colleagues and other third parties, which ensures that in this field the actual perpetrators of

[99] *Position Paper of the Advisory Body on Equal Treatment on the notions of harassment and sexual harassment*, No. 2/2007(III.23.No.384/5/208(IV10).

[100] EBH 450/2006.

[101] See section 2.4.1.2.

harassment can always personally be held responsible.[102] This regime could have a spill over effect in fields outside employment, where the regime of the new ARA applies, which would ensure a high level of protection against discriminatory harassment.[103]

As regards duties of care to be inferred from the probibition of harassment, the situation is as follows. The liability of principally envisaged actors in Hungary and the Netherlands means that these actors have certain duties vis-à-vis the persons under their care. To the very least this entails an incidental duty of care. In Hungary, harassment cases have so far all concerned the behaviour of employers or managers and thus involved personal liability of principally envisaged persons, so it is still unclear how the incidental duty of care will be filled in.

By contrast, the incidental duty of care is already well developed in the Dutch framework, which sets an excellent example for the other frameworks. The decisions of the ETC on 'discriminatory treatment' reveal that the ETC scrutinises quite strictly the response of employers and other principally envisaged actors to specific complaints of harassment. In view of the vulnerable position of the harassed person, the ETC requires these actors to take a proactive approach, and not to wait for the harassed person to thoroughly substantiate his accusations and to report each and every instance of alleged harassment.[104] Furthermore, in a case of racial discriminatory treatment within a school, the ETC required the school to consult an external expert, because the internal complaints procedure was not suitable in view of the strained relations within the school.[105] In another case, involving racial 'discriminatory treatment' in the workplace, the ETC considered that the employer should have investigated whether the worsened work performance of the victim, which had constituted the reason for a diminished annual pay increase, had been caused by the harassment complained of. Moreover, it considered that transfer of the victim to another team was not in itself an effective measure, because the employer should have also taken action to ensure that the harassers would not repeat their conduct in the future with regard to other persons.[106] These examples show that the ETC sets quite a high standard for principally envisaged actors and actively investigates whether they have done all that could be expected of them.

In Belgium and Estonia it is not entirely clear to which extent principally envisaged actors have an incidental duty of care. The Belgian LWW requires employers to take appropriate measures to end harassment in the workplace.[107] Similarly, Article 12 of the Estonian EETA imposes a duty on employers to

[102] Article 32bis LWW.
[103] Van Putten (2004a), at 134-135.
[104] Opinion 2008-134 ETC, paras. 3.22-3.
[105] Opinion 2008-44 ETC, paras. 3.19-20.
[106] Opinion 2006-71 ETC, para. 3.21.
[107] Article 32septies LWW.

protect their employees against discrimination in the workplace. For lack of practice it is not yet clear what these duties practially entail. We are not aware of similar duties in other fields of application, such as education or healthcare. It is to be hoped that there will be positive spill over in these fields from the duty of care in the field of employment.

In addition to an incidental duty of care, there is or appears to be some provision for structural duties of care in three out of four Member States under study. The Hungarian framework is unique in not providing for structural duties. In its 2006 annual report the Hungarian AET deplores the lack of statutory duties of care for employers as regards sexual harassment in the workplace, and thus appears to implicitly say that it cannot develop such duties by itself.[108] This presumably means that the AET will only go so far as determining the principally envisaged actor's responsibility in each particular case, and that it will refrain from developing structural duties of care.

The Belgian framework shows some regard for the structural duty of care of principally envisaged actors, which formally exists only in the field of employment. The LWW requires employers to set in place a prevention mechanism on the basis of a risk analysis for their particular workplace. This entails inter alia the following elements:

- treatment of complaints by a specifically appointed and trained person
- impartial and expedient intervention by this person
- measures for the reintegration of persons who have filed a harassment complaint
- specific protection for employees working with third persons
- specific duties for persons with management tasks
- education and training of employees.[109]

---

[108] *Report on the activities of the Equal Treatment Authority and the experiences of the implementation of Act nr. 125 of 2003 on equal treatment and the promotion of equal opportunities, AET, July 2006, at* 14: "Today there are no legal regulations prescribing or encouraging employers to take measures for the elimination of sexual harassment. While it is true that according to [*Council Directive 76/207/EEC of 9 February 1976 on the implementation of the principle of equal treatment for men and women as regards access to employment, vocational training and promotion, and working conditions*, MB] these regulations have to be created in accordance with national legal regulations and practices, unfortunately they do not exist yet. While making the code of conduct of cases enforcing the requirement of equal treatment a compulsory element of equality policies in the next amendment of the Equal Treatment Act would be a step forward, it would not be satisfactory according to the Authority (since it would not be obligatory for all employers)."

[109] Articles 32quater-32octies LWW.

This list of requirements to quite an extent conforms to the *Recommendation on the protection of the dignity of women and men at work* and the *Framework agreement on harassment and violence at work* that were mentioned in section 6.2.3. Still, it is remarkable that the LWW remains silent on the need for effective sanctions, which is a lost opportunity. In any case, the explicit and elaborate regulation of the structural duty of care of the employer is a positive asset, and it is to be hoped that this regime will provide inspiration for courts applying the harassment provision of the new ARA outside the field of employment. School boards and medical institutions could for example be required to set in place certain safeguards against the harassment of students and patients comparable to those required by the LWW.

The aforementioned duty of care for employers provided in Article 12 of the Estonian EETA could be interpreted as requiring structural measures against harassment. If interpreted strictly, this provision could provide quite a high level of protection against harassment in the field of employment.

The Dutch ETC has developed a consistent and thorough approach to the structural duty of care implied by the prohibition of harassment. This duty mainly entails the setting up of effective and transparent complaint mechanisms for harassment. According to a consistent line of quasi-jurisprudence, these mechanisms need to fulfil the following requirements:

1) complaints need to be dealt with confidentially, by an impartial person/body that preferably has expertise with regard to discrimination

2) the investigation needs to be thorough, which means inter alia that both the perpetrator and the victim need to be given the opportunity to express their own perception of the events

3) both parties need to be continuously informed about the proceedings of the investigation

4) transcripts should be kept of all conversations between the investigator and the parties and the final outcome should be laid down in a written report

5) effective measures need to be taken on the basis of the final outcome[110]

All of this makes for thorough and effective treatment of complaints. In addition to this procedural duty, principally envisaged actors have a more

[110] See for example Opinions 2007-40 ETC, para. 3.7; 2008-134 ETC, para. 3.18; 2008-44 ETC, para. 3.18; 2006-75 ETC, para. 3.20; 2006-71 ETC, para. 3.20; 2004-128 ETC, paras. 5.9-5.10. See also Gijzen (2006), at 191-192.

general duty to ensure that no harassment takes place within their sphere of influence, which could entail broader preventive measures, such as training of personnel and adopting codes of conduct.[111] The main focus of the ETC is, however, on effective complaints procedures, which receive most attention in its decisions. In all, the ETC's approach offers a high level of protection and is in line with the guidelines set out by the soft-law measures at the European level that were mentioned before.

6.5. Instruction to discriminate

In none of the Member States the instruction to discriminate was expressly regulated in anti-discrimination law before the implementation of the RED. In the Netherlands, the ETC traditionally approached instructions by principally envisaged actors to their subordinates as being covered by the prohibition of direct and indirect discrimination, but the GETA did not contain an explicit provision to this effect.[112] It now provides in Article 1(1)(a) that the "instruction to direct and indirect distinction" is a 'distinction' in its own right. The explicit regulation of the instruction to discriminate has brought within the reach of the GETA those situations in which the instruction is given to a person with whom the instructor is not in a hierarchical relationship, which was not the case prior to the implementation of the RED.[113] Interestingly, the new provision on the instruction to discriminate only applies to these new situations, because the government deemed it desirable that the ETC's approach to instructions given by principally envisaged actors to their subordinates was continued. This means that the concepts of direct and indirect discrimination will be applied in situations in which a principally envisaged actor instructs a subordinate, and not the concept of the instruction to discriminate.[114] For example, if an employer instructs his manager not to hire any persons of Moroccan origin, this is considered by the ETC to constitute direct discrimination, not an instruction to discriminate. The latter concept covers for example instructions given by the editor of a magazine to a freelance journalist and instructions given by a homeowner to the constructor company that he has contracted. Extension of the anti-discrimination provisions to these non-hierarchical relationships has increased the protective reach of the GETA and in this respect the RED has positively impacted on the Dutch anti-discrimination regime.

[111] Opinion 2001-34 ETC, para. 4.10.
[112] Holtmaat (2007), at 31; Houtzager & Bochhah (2004), para. 4.2.
[113] Asscher-Vonk & Hendriks (2005), at 66; Houtzager & Bochhah (2004), para. 4.2.
[114] *Parliamentary proceedings on the Amendment of the General Act on Equal Treatment and certain other acts in order to implement directive 2000/43/EG and directive 2000/78/EG*, TK 2002-3 28770, 5, at 28; Holtmaat (2007), at 32; Cremers-Hartman (2004), at 33.

In Belgium, the first implementation phase produced prohibitions of the instruction to discriminate in the ADA and the old ARA, which were slightly altered by the new ARA.[115] This Act now defines the instruction to discriminate in Article 4(12) as follows:

> any practice which consists of the instruction of any person to discriminate against a person, a group, a community or one of their members on grounds on one of the protected grounds.

In Estonia, Article 10(5) ECA after the first implementation phase provided that:

> [a]n instruction given to a person to discriminate against another person shall be deemed to be discrimination.

The new provision in Article 3(5) EETA now provides that:

> [a]n order to discriminate against persons based on any [protected characteristic, MB] shall be deemed to be discrimination.

In Hungary, the concept has been captured by Article 7(1) HETA from the beginning, and has not been changed by the 2007 amendments. This article provides that:

> direct negative discrimination, indirect negative discrimination, harassment, unlawful segregation, retribution, *and any orders issued therefore* mean a breach of the principle of equal treatment (emphasis added, MB).

Even though practice still needs to confirm this, a first appraisal of the various national provisions would seem to reveal that the concept of instruction is not limited to instructions of direct discrimination, but also covers instructions of indirect discrimination.[116] The Dutch ETC indeed applies the concept to indirect discrimination, in addition to direct discrimination.[117] As was explained above, such a broad approach enlarges the reach of anti-discrimination law and therefore enhances its level of protection.

---

[115] The ADA regulated the instruction to discriminate in Article 2(7), stating that: "any behaviour consisting in instructing any person to adopt a discriminatory attitude towards a person, a group, a community, or one of their members, is considered to be discrimination in the sense of this law." A similar provision was inserted in Article 1 of the old ARA.

[116] For Belgium this has been confirmed in literature see De Prins et al (2005), at 502; Vrielink et al (2003), at 370.

[117] See for example Opinion 2005-114 ETC, in which an employer had instructed an employment agency to recruit students for a particular job, which was considered to amount to an instruction to indirectly discriminate. Most cases on the instruction to discriminate concern direct age discrimination cases. See for instance Opinions 2005-88 ETC, 2005-149 ETC and 2007-142 ETC.

Practice of the ETC with regard to the instruction to discriminate furthermore reveals that this body takes an inclusive approach, by accepting implicit forms of instruction, such as expressing a preference for a particular category of persons.[118]

In Belgium, two cases that were ruled under the old ADA indicate that the concept of instruction is interpreted as covering implicit forms of instruction. In a case involving a claim of direct racial discrimination with regard to the rental of an apartment, the Ghent Court of Appeal refused to hold the owners of the apartment liable because they were not the ones who had refused to rent out the apartment: this had been done by their mother. In addition, the Court considered that the defendants had not instructed or *knowingly condoned* a prohibited discrimination.[119] This indicates that the Court would have imposed liability for knowingly condoning discrimination, which reveals a rather strict attitude towards persons who have such a hierarchical or contractual position that they can influence a decision to discriminate. A summary judgment of the Ghent Court of First Instance provides an even clearer indication of a lenient approach to the interpretation of 'instruction'. The judgement expressly mentions the ADA's provision on the instruction to discriminate, after which it points out that the applicants have not proved that the defendants have ordered*, encouraged, condoned or approved* the contested act.[120]

Interestingly, both the Estonian EETA and the Hungarian HETA approach the concept in terms of 'an order' to discriminate. The word 'order' appears to point to a slightly more formal concept than 'instruction', and could induce Estonian and Hungarian courts to accept only explicit and more or less official forms of instruction, which would be unfortunate.

The question whether discriminatory intent is required for the instruction to discriminate has only come up in Belgium so far, and has formed the object of debate among Belgian scholars. According to them, case law under the old ARA and the new ARA on direct discrimination seemed to show that discriminatory intent of instructors is required.[121] In a recent judgment, the Arbitration Court confirmed their suggestion, by stating that the concept instruction to discriminate could only be applied to persons who know that the treatment they order is not in line with the principle of non-discrimination.[122] As was explained above, such a requirement diminishes the impact of the concept of the instruction to discriminate, and it is therefore desirable that Belgian courts do not apply it when applying Article 4(12) of the new ARA.

118 Opinion 2005-88 ETC, para. 5.10.
119 *CEOOR and D. v. D. and M.*, Ghent Court of Appeal, 30 November 2005.
120 Ghent Court of First Instance, 31 December 2003.
121 De Prins et al (2005), at 502-503.
122 Constitutional Court, Case No. 17/2009, 12 February 2009, paras B.52.1-B.52.4.

6.6. Summary and conclusion

As it is one of the conceptual chapters, this chapter took the same dual approach as the chapters on direct and indirect discrimination regarding the link with minority protection. This means that the focus was on determining in which way the prohibitions of harassment and the instruction to discriminate can be interpreted as extensively as possible, as well as on conceptual soundness and consistency. The chapter made clear that the separate regulations of racial harassment and the instruction to discriminate are important additions to the traditional concepts of direct and indirect discrimination, as they target forms of discrimination that are generally less directly connected to a protected characteristic. More particularly, they envisage forms of discrimination that employ unequal power structures in society and in that regard are important from a substantive equality point of view.

Minimum baseline of protection

As regards the concept of discriminatory harassment, the theoretical part of this chapter revealed that there is hardly an identifiable minimum baseline of protection, because Member States are accorded a margin of appreciation by Article 2(3) RED, the exact implications of which are still unknown. Moreover, as the concept was not legally regulated in European equality law prior to the adoption of the RED, there are no parameters set out by the ECJ to refer to. The only minimum baseline that can accordingly meaningfully be established at this point is the condition that there must be a provision for racial harassment in the national anti-discrimination frameworks.

Unsurprisingly, the case study revealed that all four Member States have complied with this condition. In Estonia and Hungary the implementation of the RED meant the first-time introduction of the concept of discriminatory harassment in national anti-discrimination law. In both Member States there was a movement visible towards more conformity with the wording of Article 2(3) RED over time, which confirms that implementation of the RED is more appropriately described as a dynamic process than as a single event. In Belgium and the Netherlands, where national law regulated (racial) harassment prior to the implementation of the RED, Article 2(3) RED produced refinement and complementation of the existing regimes. Thus, in the Netherlands a two-tiered approach was developed, with the previously existing concept of 'discriminatory treatment' comprising less serious forms of harassment, and the newly inserted concept of 'harassment' referring to very serious forms of harassment. Similarly, in Belgium general anti-harassment law in the field of employment was maintained, and the harassment concept of Article 2(3) RED was only introduced for fields outside of employment. The Belgian two-tiered regime proved to be complex to assess, as both strands of harassment law have their own particularities, and it is not yet clear to what extent there will be cross-fertilisation between the two.

This chapter's analysis of the concept of the instruction to discriminate was very brief, in view of the ancillary nature of this concept. Again it was found that the minimum baseline of protection set in place by the RED is not easily determined, as there was no previous experience with this concept in other strands of European equality law to draw inspiration from. All four Member States have included the instruction to discriminate as a prohibited form of discrimination in the national anti-discrimination laws and in that respect have complied with their obligations under the RED. In the Netherlands this again led to a two-tiered approach, according to which the RED's concept of instruction is perceived as targeting only instructions given in non-hierarchical contexts. In accordance with the ETC's consistent practice, instructions given by superiors to subordinates are qualified as either direct or indirect discrimination, depending on the subject matter of the instruction.

Obscurities and opportunities for providing a higher level of protection

The theoretical framework pinpointed a number of aspects of the concept of discriminatory harassment that are not yet clear and that need to further crystallise in the future. These uncertainties came back at the national level, as lack of relevant practice proved to be an important obstacle in the case study part, especially with regard to Estonia and, to a lesser extent, Belgium. In Belgium the analysis could at least draw from the previously existing legislation against harassment in the field of employment. By contrast, the concept of discriminatory harassment has been applied quite a few times already in the Hungarian and Dutch frameworks, and both were found to set in place a relatively high level of protection against discriminatory harassment, in particular the Dutch framework.

First of all, the Dutch ETC and the Hungarian AET do not require the victim to prove that he or she did not consent to the behaviour complained of, and apply a generous interpretation of the types of conduct that can constitute harassing behaviour, including non-verbal forms of conduct and sufficiently serious single incidents. In Belgium, the general anti-harassment law describes harassment as comprising a chain of events, which could have a restrictive effect on the interpretation of discriminatory harassment.

Secondly, the ETC and the AET have followed the RED in applying a more generous approach to causality for harassment than for direct discrimination: any connection with a racial or ethnic ground suffices to make the harassment *racial* in nature. It is consequently not necessary to establish that a person not sharing the protected characteristic was or would have been treated differently. It was explained that this more lenient approach is appropriate, in view of the fact that persons belonging to vulnerable racial or ethnic groups are much more often harassed in a way that targets their racial or ethnic origin than persons belonging to the majority group in society, due to unequal power structures in society. Each instance of such harassment is therefore in fact rooted in the racial or ethnic origin of the victim and is appropriately labelled as discriminatory. The Estonian EETA at this point would seem to deny this reality and to require a strict causal link, according to which there is only racial harassment if the harassment can be established to have been *based on* the victim's racial or ethnic origin. In Belgium some scholars have called for a similarly restrictive approach.

Thirdly, both the ETC and the AET do not set a very high threshold as regards the severity required for a finding of harassment. It was interesting to note that this lenient approach was effectuated in the Dutch context by way of applying the concept of 'discriminatory treatment' to those instances of undermining and degrading behaviour that do not reach the high threshold of the concept of 'harassment' as defined in accordance with Article 2(3) RED. The Hungarian AET so far appears to consider all forms of undermining behaviour that can be linked to a protected characteristic as constituting discriminatory harassment. In this respect it should be emphasised that, whereas a lenient approach is welcome in principle, it should not cross the boundaries of conceptual soundness and consistency.

It was furthermore remarkable to find that the Hungarian AET has developed a peculiar way of assessing whether the threshold of severity for discriminatory harassment has been reached. The AET applies the general justification test provided by the HETA for direct non-racial discrimination and indirect discrimination to this effect. A similarly inappropriate use of the justification possibilities of the HETA was found to exist in Chapter 5, where it was pointed out that the AET makes use of the justification tests to establish causality for direct discrimination. It is unclear why the AET has opted for this conceptually inappropriate approach, but it would appear that insufficient experience with discrimination law is the primary reason.

Finally, it was found that the ETC has developed far-reaching duties of care for principally envisaged actors, such as employers and schools, in order to protect the persons under their responsibility against discriminatory harassment. The ETC has not only developed an incidental duty of care, which concerns the particular way in which a particular instance of harassment was dealt with, but also a more structural duty of care, which requires effective prevention- and complaint mechanisms. By contrast, the Hungarian AET deems itself competent only to formulate incidental duties of care. Both the Estonian and Belgian frameworks are expected to develop similar incidental duties of care. The Belgian framework furthermore provides for a structural duty of care in the field of employment; the Estonian frameworks shows some openings in this respect. The Belgian regime is furthermore unique in providing for direct liability of non-principally envisaged actors in the field of employment, which is a positive spill over effect from the general anti-harassment legislation applicable in this field.

As regards the concept of the instruction to discriminate, many aspects that were mentioned in the theoretical framework were generally difficult to assess, due to an overall lack of practice. It was positive to note that the national provisions would appear to cover not only instructions to directly discriminate, but also instructions to indirectly discriminate. The Dutch ETC has furthermore set a good example by accepting implicit forms of instruction, which so far appears to be followed by Belgian courts. By contrast, the wording used in the Hungarian and Estonian definitions of instruction points to a restrictive interpretation according to which only formal forms of instructions are covered.

In conclusion, this chapter revealed that the effectiveness of the two concepts, especially the concept of harassment, depends to a high degree on the way in which they are interpreted and applied at the national levels. The margin of appreciation granted to Member States arguably leaves it up to the Member States to interpret harassment extensively or restrictively. Similarly, for lack of guidance at the European level, the concept of the instruction to discriminate is largely to be filled in at the national level.

As the national regimes still need to be developed, it is difficult to draw conclusions as to the way in which the various Member States have approached the various issues. It is in any case clear that the single Member State that already had a firm anti-discrimination framework in place at the time of the implementation of the RED, the Netherlands, has opted for a high level of protection. Moreover, the Dutch anti-discrimination acquis that existed prior to the implementation of the RED can be said to have had a positive impact on the final outcome of the implementation process. After all, the two-tiered approaches to harassment and the instruction to discriminate build on the ETC's practice that was developed prior to the implementation of the RED. The Hungarian framework has also set in place a relatively high level of protection against discriminatory harassment, which is perhaps connected to the minority-sensitive context within which it operates.

Chapter 7

Positive Action

> With a view to ensuring full equality in practice, the principle of equal treatment shall not prevent any Member State from maintaining or adopting specific measures to prevent or compensate for disadvantages linked to racial or ethnic origin (Article 5 RED)

Part one: Theoretical framework

7.1. Introduction

Positive action is a highly relevant concept from a minority protection point of view, and complements the prohibition of discrimination in an important way. Whereas the prohibition of discrimination focuses on individual instances of discriminatory treatment, positive action applies a group-centered focus, and aims at improving their overall situation in society. The concept is therefore very useful in tackling structural inequalities and is closely connected to the goal of substantive equality.[1]

Article 5 RED, which regulates positive action, occupies a special place among the substantive provisions of the RED, as it is permissive in nature, rather than obligatory. Whereas the provisions that were discussed in the previous chapters *require* that Member States regulate some aspect of non-discrimination law, Article 5 only *provides for an opportunity* to take measures, and sets certain boundaries to that end. As was explained before, this provision is generally perceived as providing for a justification possibility of certain

[1] Henrard (2007b), at 129.

measures that would otherwise be considered to constitute discrimination.[2] Thus, Article 5 RED regulates only one portion of positive action measures, namely those that conflict with the prohibition of discrimination.

It would arguably be a missed opportunity for this chapter only to examine the extent to which Article 5 permits positive action measures that conflict with the prohibition of discrimination of the RED. Especially in view of the central importance of positive action for achieving substantive equality, it seems essential to approach this concept from a broader perspective. Thus, in addition to examining to what extent the RED allows for positive action measures that would otherwise amount to direct or indirect discrimination, this chapter assesses more generally in which way positive action could contribute to effective minority protection. Section 7.2 discusses in consecutive order: the aims that can be pursued by positive action; the various positive action measures that can be taken; the unwanted effects that are preferably avoided by positive action schemes; and the possibilities for Member States to set in place duties of positive action. Section 7.3 subsequently examines the limits set by Article 5 RED for positive action measures that conflict with the prohibition of discrimination, and pays particular attention to the jurisprudence of the ECJ in the field of gender equality law.

7.2. General overview of positive action: ends and means

7.2.1. Nature and aim of positive action

Positive action is an open-ended concept, for which no single definition exists. The large amount of literature on positive action reveals that it is a very broad notion, and that it can be more or less broadly interpreted.[3] At the same time,

[2] Formally speaking, Article 5 RED provides a justification possibility not only for potentially directly discriminatory, but also for potentially indirectly discriminatory positive action measures. However, the test of legality of potentially indirectly discriminatory positive action measures is arguably subsumed by the objective justification test, which forms an inherent part of the concept of indirect discrimination. In this respect, Article 5 RED is much more relevant for potentially directly discriminatory positive action measures than for potentially indirectly discriminatory measures. See also section 7.3.2.3 on the ECJ's approach to potentially indirectly discriminatory positive action measures.

[3] De Vos (2007), para. 6; Schöpp-Schilling (2003), at 22; Bossuyt (2002), paras. 5 and 6. A selection of definitions encountered in literature include the following: "a process to introduce a dynamic result-oriented approach that internalizes group dimensions into an equally static and individual formal equality model" (De Vos (2007), para. 5); "any form of proactive action designed to benefit a disadvantaged group" (O'Cinnéide (2006), at 354); "all measures which go beyond the prohibition of discrimination and seek to alter the composition of the workplace, institution, or so on" (Costello (2003), at 178); "a coherent packet of measures, of a temporary character, aimed specifically at correcting the members of a target group in one or more aspects of their social life, in order to obtain effective equality" (Bossuyt (2002), para. 3); "programmes

the discourse on positive action has produced a number of core characteristics that are generally agreed upon. First of all, positive action clearly has a strong group focus, since it is aimed at improving the situation of particular disadvantaged groups in society, not that of particular individuals.[4] As was mentioned before, it is thus closely linked to the idea of substantive equality, and relies on the recognition that some groups are in need of extra attention, in view of their specific circumstances.[5] Secondly, positive action is concerned with discriminatory structures and dynamics of institutions rather than with individual instances of unfair treatment. As such, positive action is capable of tackling structural or institutionalised forms of discrimination. Thirdly, it is proactive, because it is not so much triggered by individual litigation, but rather originates with policymakers or other actors that are attentive to the needs of particular groups.[6]

Some consider temporariness to be another core characteristic of positive action, and find that it should only be applied as long as the envisaged group is at a disadvantage compared to other groups in society.[7] According to this understanding, positive action is only aimed at eradicating causes and effects of discrimination, and should not aim at serving more permanent interests of minority groups. Others take a broader view and consider positive action also suitable for pursuing permanent interests, more particularly the interest to maintain a separate identity as a group.[8] The temporariness controversy is thus closely connected to the question as to which aims are to be pursued by positive action.

Broadly speaking, two visions are possible as regards the aims pursued by positive action, which have been classified in terms of backward versus forward-looking perspectives.[9] According to a backward-looking perspective, positive action aims to compensate for the past discrimination of persons belonging to disadvantaged groups, or to eliminate the consequences thereof. Relevant keywords in this regard are 'redress', 'remedy' and 'redistribution'.[10] This perspective can be associated with the first pillar of minority protection, that is, protection against discrimination, and it moreover presupposes that

designed to eliminate invisible and visible discrimination and to encourage underrepresented groups to reach a situation where they are more likely to be the best candidates for a place or post" (Pitt (1991), at 282).

4 De Vos (2008), at 302 ; De Vos (2007), at 8.

5 De Vos (2007), para. 9; Tobler (2005), at 25; Fredman (2002), at 128-129.

6 Gijzen (2006), at 207.

7 Bossuyt (2002), para. 3; Gijzen (2006), at 207; McCrudden (1986), at 242.

8 Lam (2004), at 47. Compare Raday (2003), at 44 and Freeman (2003), at 105, who make this argument with regard to positive action on behalf of women.

9 De Vos (2008), at 303; De Vos (2007), para. 5; De Schutter (2007), at 34; Fredman (2000), at 123; Wiggers (1991), at 28. This distinction is sometimes framed in a different terminology. For example, McCrudden (1986), at 237-239, speaks of compensation vs. distributive justice, and keeps a separate category for utilitarian considerations.

10 Gijzen (2006), at 214-215.

positive action measures are temporary in nature. This is not the case for the forward-looking perspective, according to which positive action is aimed at giving disadvantaged groups a proper place in society, in line with a particular conception of justice or, on a lower moral level, with particular utilitarian goals.[11] Keywords that come up here are 'participation', 'diversity' and 'inclusion',[12] which point not only to the first pillar of minority protection, but also to the second pillar, that is, protection of the right to identity. From a minority protection point of view, positive action is ideally rooted in a vision that combines forward and backward-looking perspectives, since this would ensure that the full range of minority interests is covered.

7.2.2. Types of positive action

There are innumerable possibilities as to the ways in which positive action can be pursued in practice, and scholars have tried to create some structure by distinguishing different categories.[13] The categorisation devised by McCrudden is the most elaborate one and has been taken over by other authors,[14] which is why it is replicated here. He distinguishes the following types of positive action:

1) activities aimed at identifying and eradicating discriminatory practices

2) facially neutral policies that tend to favour persons belonging to disadvantaged groups, and that are aimed at increasing their participation

3) outreach programmes specifically aimed at particular groups, encouraging persons belonging to such groups to pursue certain socio-economic activities, or offering specific support, such as training

4) preferential treatment

5) redefinition of merit[15]

---

11 See Raday (2003), at 36-37 for an enumeration of the various conceptions of justice that could play a part in this regard.
12 Gijzen (2006), at 215.
13 See for example Lam (2004), at 18-19; Raday (2003), at 38; Bossuyt (2002), paras. 72-80.
14 De Vos (2007), para. 5; Gijzen (2006), at 207-213; Costello (2003), at 178-180.
15 McCrudden (1986), at 223-225.

The different categories admittedly do not constitute watertight compartments, but the list at least gives a good overview of which kinds of actions can be taken. In this section, the five categories will be exemplified, and where possible examples of positive action measures taken at the European level will be mentioned. The examples will show that, despite the fact that McCrudden's classification was devised for the field of employment, it holds value also for other fields of social life, which makes it useful for the RED framework.

7.2.2.1. First category: activities aimed at identifying and eradicating discriminatory practices

This type of positive action is for example in play when an employer critically scrutinises his hiring policy and as a result decides to adjust the personal assessment tests he uses, in order to accommodate for cultural differences between applicants. If pursued horizontally across the whole policy spectrum of a particular actor, these kinds of activities amount to 'mainstreaming', a form of positive action that entails: 'the systematic incorporation from the outset of non-discrimination and equality of opportunity concerns into all public policies, legislation and programmes'.[16] Mainstreaming is an instrument that can be used by policymakers to check all existing and new policies for their compatibility with equality goals and can be very useful in detecting and preventing structural forms of discrimination.[17] At the EU level, Member States are obliged to pursue mainstreaming of gender equality by Article 3(2) TEC;[18] no similar duty exists as regards racial equality. The European Commission already unofficially deploys racial mainstreaming activities, as part of its general pre-legislative scrutiny in relation to the Charter of Fundamental Rights.[19] Moreover, the Lisbon Treaty contains a general duty

---

[16] *Non-discrimination mainstreaming-instruments, case studies and ways forward*, Centre for Strategy and Evaluation Services, European Commission, April 2007, at 1. See also Shaw (2005); Stratigaki (2005), at 167; Fredman (2001), at 165.

[17] O'Cinnéide (2006), at 355.

[18] See furthermore Article 1(a) of *Council Directive 76/207/EEC on the implementation of the principle of equal treatment for men and women as regards access to employment, vocational training and promotion, and working conditions as amended by Directive 2002/73/EC of the European Parliament and of the Council of 23 September 2002*, which provides that: "Member States shall actively take into account the objective of equality between men and women when formulating and implementing laws, regulations, administrative provisions, policies and activities in the areas referred to in paragraph 1."

[19] *Communication from the Commission – Compliance with the Charter of Fundamental Rights in Commission Legislative Proposals – Methodology for systematic and rigorous monitoring*, European Commission 2005, COM/2005/0172 final; Efthymiou et al (2008), at 15. See also the *Commission's Action plan against racism,* European Commission 1998, COM(1998) 183, in which it mentions mainstreaming of racial equality concerns as a general policy objective.

of mainstreaming for all discrimination grounds currently regulated at the European level, including race.[20] It is expected that this article will become binding in the near future.

Whereas mainstreaming is usually associated with the public sector, as a tool for national policymakers, a comparable strategy can be pursued in the private sector, entailing diversity management within private organisations. The 1995 *Joint Declaration on the prevention of racism and xenophobia* of the Social Partners at the European level identifies the following types of action that could be pursued by private actors in this respect: the identification and elimination of discriminatory barriers; monitoring of ethnic proportions in the workforce; scrutiny of all company procedures in order to identify discriminatory elements; provision of special training and reasonable accommodation of minority members where possible.[21] Attention for this type of positive action has increased in the private sector, especially because diversity has come to be seen as an economically valuable good, which can enhance competitiveness.[22] The European Commission has recently also taken a clear interest in the potential of diversity management as a tool for furthering substantive equality.[23]

7.2.2.2. Second category: facially neutral policies that tend to favour persons belonging to disadvantaged groups, and that are aimed at increasing their participation

An example of this type of positive action is the provision of language courses that are open to anyone, but particularly benefit ethnic and racial minorities. Examples can furthermore be found in the *Recommendation on the promotion of positive action for women* that was adopted by the Council in 1984. This document encourages Member States inter alia to adapt working conditions and develop vocational training strategies in a way that benefits women.

---

[20] Article 2(17) of the Lisbon Treaty provides as follows: "[i]n defining and implementing its policies and activities, the Union shall aim to combat discrimination based on sex, racial or ethnic origin, religion or belief, disability, age or sexual orientation."

[21] *Joint Declaration on the prevention of racial discrimination and xenophobia and promotion of equal treatment at the workplace*, European Social Partners 1995, EN/05/95/61370300.p00.

[22] Shaw (2005), at 22-23; Barmes & Ashtiany (2003); *Trends and developments 1997-2005, Combating ethnic and racial discrimination and promoting equality in the European Union*, European Union Agency for Fundamental Rights 2007, at 26-27.

[23] *Continuing the diversity journey. Business practices, perspectives and benefits*, European Commission 2008; in its 2008 *Communication on non-discrimination and equal opportunities*, European Commission 2008, COM/2008/0420 final, the Commission also expresses its intention to promote diversity management. See also *The business case for diversity: good practices in the workplace*, European Commission 2005.

It furthermore recommends taking measures to foster greater sharing of occupational and social responsibilities, which is also expected to enhance the proportion of women in the workforce.[24]

7.2.2.3. Third category: outreach programmes specifically aimed at particular groups, encouraging persons belonging to such groups to pursue certain socio-economic activities, or offering specific support, such as training

The aforementioned *Recommendation on the promotion of positive action for women* contains many examples of this type of positive action, and encourages Member States inter alia to monitor the position of women in the labour market; to diversify the vocational choice of women; to facilitate appropriate placement, guidance and counselling services for women; to encourage women candidates in sectors where they are underrepresented and to enhance the active participation of women in decision-making bodies.[25]

Comparable measures could be taken for the benefit of particular racial or ethnic minority groups. The RED itself mentions an example of this type of positive action in Recital 17, which encourages the adoption of measures that 'permit organisations of persons of a particular racial or ethnic origin where their main object is the promotion of the special needs of those persons' (emphasis added, MB). Such organisations could enhance overall participation of racial and ethnic minorities in society at large, as well as in the decision-making processes with respect to policies that are of interest to them. Participation of minorities in these decision-making processes is highly relevant in order to enhance the overall effectiveness of positive action policies and to avoid counterproductive effects.[26] Depending on whether the guiding vision is backward-looking or forward-looking, this type of positive action could furthermore include measures aimed at preserving the separate identity of minority groups in society, such as special provisions for education in a minority language, or the accommodation of religious holidays not celebrated by the majority of the population.[27]

---

[24] *Council Recommendation 983/635/EC) of 13 December 1984 on the promotion of positive action for women.*

[25] *Council Recommendation 983/635/EC) of 13 December 1984 on the promotion of positive action for women.*

[26] Shaw (2005), at 26; Fredman (2001a), at 27; McCrudden (2001), at 257-258; see for a nuanced description of the usefulness of participation as a key aspect of positive action Fredman (2005), at 379-384.

[27] McCrudden deliberately chose not to consider these types of measures as positive action (McRudden (1986), at 222). The present author sees no reason, however, for excluding these types of actions, since they have a group focus and are of a proactive nature, and thus can be seen as measures of positive action from a forward-looking point of view.

7.2.2.4. Fourth category: preferential treatment

This type of positive action entails granting a person a particular post, training place, or other good, because of his or her belonging to a disadvantaged group. Such preferential treatment can come in different forms, ranging from soft measures that set a certain target figure to be reached, to hard quotas or rules that simply determine that a particular job, opportunity or benefit should be given to a person solely on the basis of their racial or ethnic origin. Preferential treatment measures have as such not yet been taken at the European level. They have appeared, however, in requests for a preliminary ruling of the ECJ on their legality. The ECJ's jurisprudence in this regard is discussed in section 7.3.2.

7.2.2.5. Fifth category: redefinition of merit

McCrudden uses this category to designate instances in which group affiliation constitutes a functional requirement for a particular job. This particular use of group affiliation has entered the RED in the form of the GDOR, which is discussed in section 4.4.2. It can be contested that this is actually a form of positive action, however. After all, the GDOR exception is not focused on alleviating group disadvantages; it rather takes functional requirements as its point of departure.[28] This was also the position taken by the EFTA court in *EFTA Surveillance Authority v. Norway*, in which it refused to go along with the argument of the Norwegian government that a particular positive action measure constituted a GDOR, which was allowed by the ETD. According to the EFTA Court, the argument that the concept of the GDOR could be used to justify a measure that aimed to increase the proportion of women in the workforce did not 'find support in the wording of [the Equal Treatment Directive, MB] nor in the case law of the Court of Justice of the European Communities'.[29]

7.2.3. Potential unwanted effects of positive action

Practice and theory reveal that positive action does not always produce the desired effect and in some instances even undermines the very aim it was intended to achieve. This is particularly true for the stronger forms of positive action, which fall within McCrudden's third, fourth and fifth categories. By explicitly targeting protected groups, these measures risk perpetuating stereotypical beliefs and fostering essentialist thinking about persons

[28] De Vos (2007), paras. 40-41.
[29] *EFTA Surveillance Authority v. Norway*, Case E-1/02, 24 January 2004, para. 46.

belonging to certain groups,[30] not in the least as regards the way they look at themselves.[31] After all, giving particular groups special treatment can reinforce the impression that persons belonging to these groups do not have the skills and mentality necessary for achieving particular goals themselves.

Moreover, positive action measures can exacerbate divisions and tensions in society, especially if they are aimed at a few vulnerable groups only and exclude other groups that are also in need of special attention.[32] Such tunnel vision can spur competition between vulnerable groups for the favour of the particular positive action policymaker.[33] Furthermore, it is often argued that the most vulnerable persons within the target groups are the ones who are least likely to benefit from positive action, whereas they are most in need of it.[34] It is for instance usually the better educated members of vulnerable groups that benefit from preferential schemes in employment, not the ones that have not finished high school.

Finally, positive action measures can, maybe unintentionally, serve as an assimilation tool, by requiring the minority to fit in with the ways of the majority.[35] For example, language courses and integration courses offered by the state risk putting too much emphasis on the need for racial and ethnic minorities to adjust to the majority standard. For this reason, scholars have emphasised the need for the participation of minority groups in the design and development of positive action measures.[36] Such participation ensures that the voice of those belonging to vulnerable groups is heard in the process of designing policies for their benefit, which reduces the risk of assimilationist tendencies.

More generally, the aforementioned considerations make clear that positive action measures need to be based on well-balanced decision-making. This implies inter alia that there needs to be a thorough and objective factual basis for positive action, as well as careful consideration of all interests involved and adaptation to the specific context within which the measures are to be applied.

---

30 De Schutter (2007), at 52; Bagenstos (2006), at 16; Ellis (2005), at 309; Choudry (2000), at 164; Alexander (1992), at 217; McCrudden (1986), at 241.

31 O'Neil & Peron (2003), at 15; Alexander (1992), at 217; Gottesman (1991), at 1743.

32 McCrudden (1986), at 241.

33 Holzleithner (2005), at 949-950; Alexander (1992), at 217; Gottesman (1991), at 1762.

34 Bossuyt (2002), paras. 11-12; Jackson (1999), at 260.

35 *Thematic comment no. 3, The protection of minorities in the European Union*, EU Network of Independent Experts on Fundamental Rights 2005, CFR-CDF.ThemComm2005.en, at 24.

36 Shaw (2005); Fredman (2005), at 379-384, Fredman (2001), at 164. See also Article 15 of the FCNM, which requires States to ensure participation of persons belonging to national minorities on issues that particularly affect them, and the ACFCNM's *Commentary on the effective participation of persons belonging to national minorities in cultural, social and economic life and in public affairs*, 27 February 2008, ACFC/31DOC(2008)001.

7.2.4. Duties of positive action

The fact that the RED does not impose a duty of positive action should not prevent Member States from considering the option of imposing such duties in the national context.[37] After all, Article 6 RED allows Member States to provide for a higher level of protection against discrimination than prescribed by the RED. Thus, as long as the Member States remain within the boundaries set by Article 5 RED and the jurisprudence of the ECJ, they are free to take a more robust approach to positive action and to develop certain duties of positive action. Needless to say, such duties could greatly further the cause of substantive equality, by achieving a certain degree of proactive restructuring of society. At the same time it is clear that duties of positive action should be carefully delineated, especially in order to respect fundamental rights and freedoms of private actors, as was pointed out before.[38]

There are a number of ways in which Member States could realise duties of positive action. First of all, national legislation could provide for self-standing positive duties for particular actors who have a certain degree of power or responsibility, as has been done by inter alia the UK, Ireland and Canada.[39] Such duties could entail for instance a duty to promote equal treatment in the workplace, a duty to mainstream equality concerns in policy development, a duty to ensure minority group participation in relevant decision-making processes, a duty to provide for education in a minority language, etcetera. One of the great advantages of self-standing positive duties is the fact that they are effective immediately after their adoption and do not need individual litigation to come into existence. Moreover, they can be very neatly tailored to the particular context within which they are to operate, and by their specificity contribute to legal certainty.[40]

Notwithstanding these considerable advantages, Member States could consider self-standing duties to be a step too far, in which case it is perhaps more feasible to make use of existing concepts within the anti-discrimination paradigm in order to impose duties of positive action. As explained earlier, the concept of indirect discrimination is particularly useful in this respect, and provides ample opportunity for the creation of positive duties.[41]

---

[37] Tobler (2006), at 15.

[38] See section 2.2.2.2.

[39] Shaw (2005), at 32-35; Fredman (2001), at 163-167 as regards the UK and Ireland; Hepple et al (2000), at 59-65 as regards Northern Ireland. For a discussion of Canadian employment equity law, see Hucker (1999). See also *ECRI General Recommendation no. 7*, 13 December 2002, para. 8, which calls upon Member States to recognise positive duties to promote equality for public actors.

[40] See for more elaborate discussions of the usefulness of positive duties in the anti-discrimination paradigm Fredman (2005); Fredman (2005)a; Hepple (2001).

[41] See section 5.3.

Moreover, it has been suggested that the concept of reasonable accommodation, which plays a part in disability discrimination law,[42] could be used in this regard.[43] This concept would seem to be particularly valuable for the accommodation of the more permanent, identity-related interests of minority groups, as it inherently focuses on the differences between persons with a protected characteristic and the majority group in society. It actually requires that these differences are taken into account and that they are accommodated to a reasonable extent. Member States could for instance require certain actors, such as employers and educational institutions, to reasonably accommodate persons belonging to minority groups as regards linguistic requirements, dress requirements, curriculum content, religious holidays, etcetera. The ECJ has, for instance, ruled in *Vivien Prais* that the principle of equality required that European entry exams be organised in such a way that religious holidays are respected, insofar as this is reasonable.[44]

Not all authors agree on the applicability of the concept of reasonable accommodation for vulnerable groups, however. According to some, reasonable accommodation is an inherently individualised concept, which cannot be applied to groups as a whole.[45] To be true, reasonable accommodation envisages individual instances of meeting the needs of persons belonging to vulnerable groups, but this clearly does not mean that these individualised forms of accommodation in the end do not benefit the group as a whole. There would thus not seem to be any real objections to using the concept of reasonable accommodation outside the field of disability discrimination.[46]

---

[42] Article 2(b)(ii) of the FD provides that: "as regards persons with a particular disability, the employer or any person or organisation to whom this Directive applies, is obliged, under national legislation, to take appropriate measures in line with the principles contained in Article 5 in order to eliminate disadvantages entailed by such provision, criterion or practice." Article 5 of the FD provides that: "[i]n order to guarantee compliance with the principle of equal treatment in relation to persons with disabilities, reasonable accommodation shall be provided. This means that employers shall take appropriate measures, where needed in a particular case, to enable a person with a disability to have access to, participate in, or advance in employment, or to undergo training, unless such measures would impose a disproportionate burden on the employer. This burden shall not be disproportionate when it is sufficiently remedied by measures existing within the framework of the disability policy of the Member State concerned." See for the meaning and application of the concept of reasonable accommodation Henrard (2008b), p. 283; Gijzen (2006), at 394-400; Waddington (2004); Whittle (2002), at 311-315.

[43] O'Cinnéide (2006), at 363; De Schutter & Verstichel (2005), at 18-19. See for a more elaborate discussion of the potential of the concept of reasonable accommodation Henrard (2008b), at 283-289.

[44] ECJ *Vivien Prais v Council of the European Communities*, Case 130-75, 27 October 1976, paras. 12-19.

[45] Gijzen (2006), at 83; Waddington (2004), at 29-34.

[46] See for instance Henrard (2008b), at 276-281, who describes how the Canadian, American and Israeli anti-discrimination frameworks make use of the concept of reasonable accommodation for other discrimination grounds.

Another way in which positive action duties can come into play at the national level is in the form of a remedy for discriminatory practices.[47] Thus, in individual discrimination cases, courts can order the particular actor to either undo the effects of his past discriminatory behaviour, or to compensate for the damage caused by way of positive action.

Finally, Member States can opt for a pseudo duty of positive action, by requiring authors of positive action policies to act in accordance with those policies. If, for example, a company develops a positive action programme and makes this known to the public, there are strong arguments in favour of holding the company accountable for not acting in conformity with this publicly undertaken commitment to positive action.

7.3. Limits to positive action: Article 5 RED and the jurisprudence of the ECJ

Whereas the previous section proceeded from the premise that Member States have quite some liberty as to how they approach positive action in their particular national contexts, this section takes as a starting point the limits set by European law regarding positive action measures. As was mentioned before, this issue is only relevant for the stronger forms of positive action, which can mainly be found in categories three, four and five, and to some extent category two, of McCrudden's classification. Since these forms of positive action are targeted at protected groups, they conflict with the prohibitions of direct and indirect discrimination and thus raise the question as to where the boundaries for positive action must be drawn.

The permissive wording of Article 5 RED is slightly misleading in this respect, as it would seem to imply that Member States have complete freedom in devising positive action schemes. Experience with positive action in the field of European sex equality law shows, however, that in reality Member States have to respect strict limits that are set in place by the prohibition of discrimination. The ECJ has proved to be quite tough in assessing the compatibility of positive action measures with the prohibition of discrimination. It is generally expected that the principles developed by this court in the field of gender equality are also applicable in the context of the RED.[48]

At the same time, there is some speculation as to the relevance of the different wording of Article 5 RED with regard to the formulation of Article 2(4) ETD, which formed the basis for the ECJ's case law on positive action in

[47] De Vos (2007), at 6; Ambrus (2010).

[48] De Vos (2008), at 318; Parmar (2004), at 133; Tyson (2004), at 123; Skidmore (2001), at 131.

sex equality law.[49] It has been submitted that the differences in wording could lead to divergent approaches in practice, which means that it is not entirely sure to what extent the sex equality acquis is transposable to the framework of the RED. In addition, the broader material scope of the RED, as well as the particularities of the grounds of racial and or ethnic origin as compared to sex can be expected to require some fine-tuning of the sex equality acquis to the RED context.[50]

In view of these considerations, this section combines an overview of the case law developed in the field of sex equality with a discussion of the potential implications for the RED. In this latter respect, attention will be paid to the wording of Article 5 RED, the broader material scope of the RED and the particularities of the grounds of racial and ethnic origin. The analysis is preceded by a brief overview of the formulations of Article 5 RED and the relevant positive action provisions in gender equality law.

7.3.1. Formulation of Article 5 RED as compared with other positive action provisions

It is repeated here that Article 5 RED reads as follows:

> [w]ith a view to ensuring full equality in practice, the principle of equal treatment shall not prevent any Member State from maintaining or adopting specific measures to prevent or compensate for disadvantages linked to racial or ethnic origin.

The first positive action provision in the field of sex equality law appeared in the ETD and provided in Article 2(4) that:

> [t]his Directive shall be without prejudice to measures to promote equal opportunity for men and women, in particular by removing existing inequalities which affect women's opportunities in the areas referred to in Article 1(1).

The Treaty of Amsterdam subsequently inserted a positive action provision into the TEC, which now, in Article 141(4), provides that:

> [w]ith a view to ensuring full equality in practice between men and women in working life, the principle of equal treatment shall not prevent any Member State from maintaining or adopting measures providing for specific advantages in order to make it easier for the under-represented sex to pursue a vocational activity or to prevent or compensate for disadvantages in professional careers.

---

[49] De Vos (2008), at 312-313; at 317-321; Prechal (2004), at 540. Other authors have focused on the textual differences between Article 5 RED and Article 141(4) TEC, and their potential impact on the interpretation of Article 5, see Tridimas (2006), at 71; Gijzen (2006), at 225; Holzleithner (2005), at 942; Ellis (2005), at 311-312.

[50] De Vos (2008), at 319; De Schutter (2007), at 49-50; Rodrigues (2001), at 107-108.

In 2002 the original provision of the ETD was amended in order to bring it in line with Article 141(4) TEC and the positive action provisions of the RED and FD, and now reads as follows:

> Member States may maintain or adopt measures within the meaning of Article 141(4) of the Treaty with a view to ensuring full equality in practice between men and women.

The formulation of Article 5 RED largely resembles the more recent positive action provisions of Article 141(4) TEC and the amended ETD, and it is therefore regrettable that these provisions have hardly been separately interpreted by the ECJ, which could have provided more insight into the meaning of Article 5 RED. Most positive action cases that have appeared so far revolved around Article 2(4) ETD in its previous form (and the similarly worded Article 6(3) of the *Agreement on Social Policy* in *Griesmar.)*[51] In some cases, Article 141(4) TEC was invoked in addition to Article 2(4) ETD but not actually applied by the ECJ. In these cases the ECJ first found that the particular positive action measure was in breach with Article 2(4) ETD, after which it merely stated that the relevant measures could also not be justified under Article 141(4) TEC, since they were disproportionate to the aim pursued.[52] As is explained below, the proportionality principle has become the central review mechanism for positive action measures in the ECJ's case law on the old Article 2(4) ETD, and this reference to proportionality in the framework of Article 141 TEC thus raises the impression that there is no real difference between the regimes of the old Article 2(4) ETD and Article 141(4) TEC. This impression is confirmed in *Commission v. Greece*, in which the ECJ applied Article 141(4) TEC, and used exactly the same reasoning as it employed in *Griesmar* for Article 6(3) of the *Agreement on Social Policy*, which is similar to Article 2(4) ETD.[53]

Still, in *EFTA Surveillance Authority v. Norway*, the EFTA Court suggested that the differences in wording of the newer positive action provisions were relevant, and could lead to different regimes than the one developed under the old Article 2(4) ETD. It did not give any concrete examples, however.[54] As was mentioned before, the following analysis of the ECJ's case law will pay attention to the relevant differences in wording.

---

[51] *Agreement on Social Policy*, OJ 1992 C 191, at 91.

[52] ECJ *Abrahamsson v. Fogelqvist*, Case C-407/98, 6 July 2000; ECJ *Griesmar v. Ministre de l'Economie*, Case C-366/99, 29 November 2001; ECJ *Briheche v. Ministre de l'Intérieur*, Case C-319/03, 30 September 2004.

[53] ECJ *Commission v. Greece*, Case C-559/07, 26 March 2009, paras. 65-73. In this case, the ECJ decided that a pension scheme exempting certain categories of women from a minimum years of service requirement was not permitted by Article 141(4), because it did not target any specific disadvantages experienced by these women, and did not grant an exemption to men in similar situations. The Court expressly mentioned *Griesmar* in this respect.

[54] *EFTA Surveillance Authority v. Norway*, Case E-1/02, 24 January 2004, para. 56. See also the opinion of Advocate-General Maduro in ECJ *Serge Briheche v. Ministère de l'intérieur, de la sécurité intérieure et des libertés locales*, Case C-319/03, 29 June 2004, paras. 48-50,

7.3.2. Jurisprudence of the ECJ in gender equality law and its potential relevance for Article 5 RED

7.3.2.1. Overview of the positive action cases

Jurisprudence of the ECJ (and in one instance the EFTA court) on positive action in the field of sex equality comprises eleven cases. For easy reference in the remainder of this section, the relevant cases are listed here:

1. *Commission v. France*, Case 312/86, 30 June 1988
2. *Kalanke v. Freie Hansestadt Bremen*, Case C-450/93, 17 October 1995
3. *Marschall v. Land Nordrhein-Westfalen*, Case C-409/95, 11 November 1997
4. *Badeck v. Hessische Ministerpräsident*, Case C-158/97, 28 March 2000
5. *Abrahamsson v. Fogelqvist*, Case C-407/98, 6 July 2000
6. *Schnorbus v. Land Hessen*, Case C-79/99, 7 December 2000
7. *Griesmar v. Ministre de l'Economie*, Case C-366/99, 29 November 2001
8. *Lommers v. Minister van Landbouw*, Case C-476/99, 19 March 2002
9. *Briheche v. Ministre de l'Intérieur*, Case C-319/03, 30 September 2004
10. *EFTA Surveillance Authority v. Norway*, Case E-1/02, 24 January 2004
11. *Commission v. Greece*, Case C-559/07, 26 March 2009

Most of these cases concerned claims of direct discrimination, which means that the positive action measure singled out women as the beneficiaries of some measure, to the exclusion of men. The contested measures included rules of preferential treatment of women for particular posts;[55] the obligation to set binding targets of a particular proportion of men-women to be achieved

---

in which he proposes a different understanding of 'opportunities' vs. 'results' on the basis of Article 141(4) TEC.

[55] *Kalanke, Marschall, Badeck, Abrahamsson, EFTA Surveillance Authority v. Norway* involved provisions granting women priority over men for particular positions, with various degrees of strictness.

in the workforce;[56] recruitment policies targeted specifically at women;[57] more generous job requirements for women;[58] and special facilities for women, such as child care facilities.[59]

Only two cases concerned indirect discrimination. One of the positive action measures under scrutiny in *Badeck* involved a provision that allowed for adjusted job criteria benefiting women who had acquired relevant skills in their domestic and other non-job related activities.[60] In *Schnorbus,* the contested rule accorded preferential admission conditions for university places to applicants who had spent a year in military service, the beneficiaries of which were necessarily men. Both cases thus involved facially neutral measures that tended to benefit the members of a particular sex, and therefore came within the scope of the prohibition of indirect discrimination.

7.3.2.2. Positive action as an exception to the principle of equal treatment

The ECJ traditionally approaches the question of the legality of positive action from the point of view that positive action constitutes an exception to the principle of equal treatment.[61] This perspective has been criticised for being fundamentally biased in favour of the individual perspective over the group perspective.[62] In other words, the interest of the person that has allegedly been discriminated against would have a preliminary advantage over the interest of the group advantaged by the particular positive action measure. After all, stronger argumentation is usually needed for applying an exception to a norm than for following the normal application of the norm, which leans on a

56 In *Badeck*, universities were required to set a binding target for particular posts in accordance with the percentage of women with the appropriate degree of education in the particular field.

57 In *Badeck*, one of the contested measures was a rule according to which at least as many women as men, or all the women applicants, had to be called to interview if they satisfied the conditions for the particular post.

58 In *Briheche,* the contested measure was an age limit for entering public service that did not apply to particular categories of women.

59 In *Badeck*, one of the contested measures was a rule determining that half of the available training places had to be allocated to women; in *Lommers*, child care facilities were generally reserved for women, and men could only obtain a place in case of an emergency; *Griesmar* involved a pension credit for mothers at the time of their retirement; *Commission v. Greece* involved preferential pension conditions for certain categories of women.

60 See *Badeck*, para. 31 of the judgment for a full description of the measure.

61 See Costello (2003), at 183-184, who explains how this perspective permeated the draft of the Equal Treatment Directive in the mid-seventies. Originally, positive action was conceived as a necessary component of equal treatment. However, this was not accepted by the Social Affairs Council and did not make it to the final draft.

62 Prechal (2004), at 40; *Ninth Report of the European Union Committee of the House of Lords*, 16 May 2000, para. 128; Brown (2002), at 16.

presumption of legality. Indeed, the ECJ has often made clear that it interprets exceptions to the principle of non-discrimination strictly, and has explicitly applied this rule to positive action in the field of sex equality.[63]

It has therefore been submitted that it would have been preferable for the ECJ to approach positive action as an inherent component of the principle of equality. From a substantive equality perspective, this is indeed the desirable approach, because it ensures that, for true equality in practice, the interest of vulnerable groups is placed at the same level as the interest of an individual not to be discriminated against. This in turn has an important symbolic effect, since it makes clear that the goals of formal and substantive equality are equally important in the equality paradigm. The wording of Article 5 RED, according to which '[t]he principle of equal treatment shall not prevent…' certainly allows for such a perspective.[64]

The ECJ has, however, yet to be convinced by these arguments and it has so far refused to depart from its traditional approach. In *EFTA Surveillance Authority v. Norway* one of the parties suggested that the EFTA Court adopt a new perspective on positive action, which would entail treating positive action as an inherent aspect of the principle of equal treatment rather than an exception. The Court refused to do so.[65] It is doubtful that national courts have room to take a more favourable stance.

7.3.2.3. Central importance of the principle of proportionality

Throughout the case law on positive action there is a clear development discernable of increasing importance of the proportionality principle. This principle was mentioned for the first time in *Abrahamsson*, in what would appear to be more of an afterthought than part of the actual judicial assessment.[66] In *Lommers* proportionality moved to the centre, and became the central mechanism for assessing the legitimacy of positive action measures.[67] In this case the ECJ considered that: 'according to settled case law, in determining the scope of any derogation from an individual right such

63 See for example *Kalanke*, para. 21.

64 Hepple & Barnard (2000), at 576-577.

65 *EFTA Surveillance Authority v. Norway*, paras. 25 and 45.

66 *Abrahamsson*, para. 55, which comes after the substantive assessment of the legality of the contested positive action measure in the light of Article 2(4) ETD. In this paragraph the ECJ briefly considered the compatibility of the measure with Article 141(4) TEC, and stated that: "[i]n that connection, it is enough to point out that, even though Article 141(4) EC allows the Member States to maintain or adopt measures providing for special advantages intended to prevent or compensate for disadvantages in professional careers in order to ensure full equality between men and women in professional life, it cannot be inferred from this that it allows a selection method of the kind at issue in the main proceedings which appears, from any view, *to be disproportionate to the aim pursued.*" (emphasis added, MB)

67 De Vos (2008), at 314-315; Gijzen (2006), at 233-234.

as the equal treatment of men and women laid down by the Directive, due regard must be had to *the principle of proportionality*, which requires that derogations must remain within the limits of what is appropriate and necessary in order to achieve the aim in view and that the principle of equal treatment be reconciled as far as possible with the requirements of the aim thus pursued' (emphasis added, MB). This approach was repeated in *Briheche*, and in *EFTA Surveillance Authority v. Norway*.[68] It is therefore more or less settled now that positive action measures are to be scrutinised according to the three-tiered test of appropriateness, necessity and proportionality stricto sensu.[69]

It should be emphasised that the gradual move towards proportionality does not mark a substantive shift in the ECJ's approach towards positive action.[70] To the contrary, the ECJ itself considers the principles that were developed in the pre-proportionality cases still to be valid today, and sees them in retrospection through a proportionality lens. This can be inferred from the ECJ's judgment in *Briheche*, in which it first repeated the principles developed in its previous case law, and then went on to state that: ("*[t]hose conditions are guided by the fact that*, in determining the scope of any derogation from an individual right such as the equal treatment of men and women laid down by the Directive, *due regard must be had to the principle of proportionality*") (emphasis added, MB).[71] Thus, even those positive action cases that were at the time not expressly assessed in terms of proportionality can in hindsight be seen as de facto applications of this principle. This facilitates the discussion of the ECJ's case law in the following subsection, which is structured around the elements of appropriateness, necessity and proportionality stricto sensu.

The move towards proportionality would seem to be mainly relevant for those cases in which positive action measures are claimed to be directly discriminatory. After all, the objective justification test of the concept of indirect discrimination incorporates a proportionality test, and potentially indirectly discriminatory positive action measures can therefore simply be scrutinised in the framework of the objective justification. It is not yet clear whether the ECJ shares this point of view. In *Schnorbus* it did not make expressly clear which test it applied when scrutinising the legality of the particular measure, which could be either the test associated with Article 2(4) ETD, or the objective justification test of indirect discrimination. After having found that the particular measure was indirectly discriminatory, it considered that the measure was still acceptable, because it was 'objective in nature and

[68] *Briheche*, para. 24; *EFTA Surveillance Authority v, Norway*, para. 43.
[69] For a discussion of these separate aspects of proportionality, see sections 5.2.4.3 and 5.2.4.4.
[70] De Vos (2008), at 311-312.
[71] *Briheche*, para. 24.

prompted solely by the desire to counterbalance to some extent the effects of [the delay caused by military service, MB]'. It furthermore briefly stated that the measure was not disproportionate.[72]

Regardless of which test was formally applied in *Schnorbus*, the reference to proportionality raises the impression that the test for potentially indirectly positive action measures is substantively the same as the one for potentially directly discriminatory measures. Thus, in the following discussion, no attention will be paid to potential differences between allegedly directly and allegedly indirectly discriminatory measures of positive action. The ECJ's case law will be discussed through the prism of the proportionality principle. Prior to the discussion of the meaning of the components of appropriateness, necessity and proportionality stricto sensu, some consideration is given to the requirements developed by the ECJ in relation to the aim pursued by measures of positive action.

7.3.2.4. Legitimacy of the aim pursued by positive action

Existence of an actual disadvantage

The case law reveals that the ECJ requires positive action measures to be based on a proper factual basis, which means that the beneficiary group must in reality experience a disadvantage. Thus, in *Commission v. France*, a general provision that allowed special measures for women was deemed not to be legitimate, since the facts of the case did not reveal any actual instances of inequality that justified the adoption of this provision.[73] Conversely, a provision that granted conditional preferential treatment to equally qualified women for particular posts was deemed permissible in *Marschall*, because it counteracted the negative effects of prejudices and stereotypes concerning the role and capacities of women in working life. In this way, actual instances of inequality were reduced, and the measure was therefore considered by the ECJ to be legitimate.[74] This consideration for negative effects of prejudice and stereotypes arguably opens up the door for establishing the disadvantage required with the help of qualitative data. This in turn would make it easier to justify the adoption of positive action measures and is particularly relevant for the RED framework, where relevant ethnic and racial statistics are often hard to come by.[75]

---

72 *Schnorbus*, paras. 44 and 46.

73 *Commission v. France*, para. 15.

74 *Marschall*, paras. 29-31.

75 The lack of statistical data is currently a concern that has been raised by a number of NGO's and experts, since it is often very difficult to find other means of proving disparate impact. See Ringelheim (2008); De Schutter (2007), at 22-33.

In *Badeck* the ECJ again emphasised the need for a sound factual basis and took this criterion into account when considering the legitimacy of the various positive measures that were presented. It started its judgment with a brief recapitulation of its previous rulings, and repeated that 'a measure which is intended to give priority in promotion to women in sectors of the public service *where they are under-represented* must be regarded as compatible with Community law' (emphasis added, MB).[76] The first measure at stake, which required binding targets to be determined in accordance with the characteristics of the relevant sectors and departments, and provided for conditional preferential treatment of equally qualified women in sectors *in which they were underrepresented*, was therefore legitimate.[77]

The second contested measure was a national rule that prescribed binding targets for temporary posts in academia to be determined in accordance with the proportions of qualified women in the relevant sectors. The ECJ considered that the system did not fix an absolute ceiling, but fixed a ceiling by reference to the number of qualified persons, which amounted 'to using an *actual fact* as a quantitative criterion for giving preference to women' (emphasis added, MB), and was therefore justified.[78]

The third measure concerned a rule that allocated at least half of available training places to women. The ECJ found this rule to be acceptable, inter alia because it was based on the *fact* that 'in social reality women continue to be disadvantaged compared with men and that, despite formal legal equality, in particular in employment, [women] do not have equal access to qualified (...) positions' (emphasis added, MB).[79] This consideration again reveals that the ECJ accepts qualitative data as evidence of an actual disadvantage, in addition to quantitative data.

The fourth measure was a rule that stipulated that all women qualified for a particular position had to be called for an interview, or at least a number equal to the number of men called. The court accepted this rule, since it applied to sectors in which women *were underrepresented*.[80] *Badeck* thus clearly shows that the ECJ expects positive action measures to be based on factual evidence about the particular situation of the target group.

Further application of the actual disadvantage criterion can be found in *Griesmar* and *Commission v. Greece*, in which the ECJ rejected preferential pension rules for categories of women, because it did not in any way offset disadvantages experienced by women in their working life.[81] And finally, the ECJ in *Lommers* commenced its examination of a provision granting child care

76 *Badeck*, para. 23.
77 *Badeck*, paras. 26-38.
78 *Badeck* paras. 39-43.
79 *Badeck*, paras. 48-55.
80 *Badeck*, paras. 56-63.
81 *Griesmar*, paras. 64-67; *Commission v. Greece*, paras. 67-68.

facilities exclusively to women with an examination of the particular situation of women in the employer's workforce, in order to determine whether they were actually at a disadvantage.[82]

The insistence by the ECJ on an actual disadvantage makes sense and is in line with the rationale of positive action, which aims to offset certain disadvantages experienced by particular groups. Still, as was explained before, 'disadvantage' is a relative notion, and courts should not adopt too narrow a vision in this respect.[83] It is particularly important that they pay sufficient attention to the perception of the persons belonging to the group targeted by the positive action measure, which can differ considerably from the majority view. Moreover, it is submitted that the strictness with which the actual disadvantage requirement is applied should depend on the relative strength of the positive action measure at stake. In view of the potential unwanted effects of positive action, it is understandable and even desirable that the strongest forms of positive action, in particular preferential treatment, are supported by persuasive factual data that reveal a clear disadvantage experienced by the target group. On the other hand, courts could and should be more lenient with regard to weaker forms of positive action that are less harmful to the non-targeted group. For these measures, evidence of broader societal disadvantage should suffice.

The final aim of substantive equality

The ECJ has in the relatively more recent positive action cases referred to 'substantive equality' as the aim pursued by positive action measures.[84] Article 5 RED underlines this substantive equality outlook by referring to 'full equality in practice' as the aim to be pursued by positive action.[85] The explicit recognition of the relevance of substantive equality is promising, since it makes clear that the principle of equality entails more than the formally equal treatment of all persons. This offsets to some extent the disadvantageous exception-based approach to the positive action of the ECJ that was outlined before. Moreover, since 'substantive equality' is capable of covering even identity-related interests, the door has been opened for positive action measures that serve these types of rights. Thus, accommodation of religious or linguistic differences would for instance be possible, in addition to the prevention and elimination of discriminatory practices.

82 *Lommers*, paras. 36-8.

83 See section 5.2.2.2.

84 *Briheche*, para. 25; *EFTA Surveillance Authority v. Norway*, para. 43.

85 Prechal (2004), at 541.

Forward versus backward-looking perspective

The case law does not reveal any particular attention to the question as to whether positive action measures should be forward-looking or backward-looking, or both. As was mentioned before, a combination of both perspectives is preferable from a minority protection point of view. It is therefore advantageous that Article 5 RED embraces both perspectives by speaking of prevention of (i.e. backward-looking) as well as compensation for (i.e. forward-looking) disadvantages linked to racial or ethnic origin.[86]

Equal opportunities versus equal results

Article 2(4) ETD, which formed the basis for the ECJ's case law on positive action, referred to 'equal opportunity' as the aim pursued by positive action. This formulation induced the ECJ to assess the legitimacy of the aim pursued by a positive action measure along the lines of a distinction between equality of opportunity and equality of results. Equality of opportunity requires a levelling of the playing field, so as to enable persons belonging to vulnerable groups to compete on an equal footing with other persons. Conversely, equality of results guarantees a specific outcome for persons belonging to vulnerable groups.[87] In view of the wording of Article 2(4) ETD the ECJ considers only the former type of equality to constitute a legitimate aim for positive action measures. Thus, in *Kalanke* the ECJ stated that: '[n]ational rules which guarantee women absolute and unconditional priority for appointment or promotion go beyond promoting equal opportunities and overstep the limits of the exception in Article 2(4) of the [Equal Treatment Directive, MB]. Furthermore, in so far as it seeks to achieve equal representation of men and women in all grades and levels within a department, such a system substitutes for equality of opportunity as envisaged in Article 2(4) the result which is only to be arrived at by providing such equality of opportunity'.[88]

Kalanke and the subsequent cases reveal that the ECJ considers 'opportunities' in the field of employment to extend to all kinds of conditions in the labour market that influence a person's ability to perform well or to obtain a job, whereas 'results' is understood to refer to the guaranteed obtainment of a particular job.[89] Thus, any measure that unconditionally

86 De Vos (2007), para. 28.

87 See on the opportunities vs. results distinction Bossuyt (2002), paras. 30-39; Gijzen (2006), at 211; Fredman 2003, at 113-115.

88 *Kalanke*, para. 22-23.The condition that Member States should remain within the scope of equality of opportunities was repeated in *Marschall*, para. 25; *Badeck*, para. 18; *Abrahamsson*, para. 42; *Lommers*, para. 33. See also Cohn (2003), at 306-308; Barrett (2003a), at 129-130.

89 *Kalanke*, para. 19; *Marschall*, para. 27; *Badeck*, para. 45; *Griesmar*, para. 64; *Lommers*, para. 32; *Briheche*, para. 25. See also Gijzen (2006), at 225.

grants a particular post to a woman is aimed towards 'equality of results' and therefore unacceptable.[90] To the contrary, measures that guarantee particular training places to be filled by women or nursery facilities to be granted to women are in principle acceptable.[91]

Even though the ECJ's approach to opportunities versus results is relatively easily applicable in the context of employment, it is submitted that the distinction is not practical in the context of a broader material scope such as that of the RED. After all, it is a matter of argument whether something creates a result or rather an opportunity.[92] For example, being admitted to a particular school can be seen as a matter of result from an education perspective, as well as a matter of opportunity from an employment perspective. It is therefore fortunate that Article 5 RED does not refer to either opportunities or results, and simply speaks of 'full equality in practice'. It is to be hoped that the ECJ and/or national courts will indeed leave aside the opportunities versus results distinction and develop more practicable benchmarks for scrutiny of the legitimacy of the aim pursued by a positive action measure.

7.3.2.5. Appropriateness

The various judgments rendered so far have raised hardly any appropriateness-related issues. *Griesmar* and *Commission v. Greece* show how appropriateness can be relevant in the context of positive action. In both cases, more favourable pension conditions applied to certain categories of women who were considered to have built up a pension gap because they had cared for their children. According to the ECJ, in order to be legitimate the measures 'must, in any event, contribute to helping women conduct their professional life on an equal footing with men'. The contested provisions did no such thing, however, as they accorded a benefit at the date of retirement, and did not provide a remedy for problems encountered by women in the course of their professional career. The measures were therefore considered not to be legitimate and thus infringed the principle of equal pay.[93] Moreover, in *Griesmar* the ECJ remarked that the measure had been applied since 1924 and had 'still not been possible to resolve, by means of that provision, the problems which such a female civil servant may encounter in her career'.[94]

These cases reveal that a positive action measure must be rationally connected to the actual instance of equality that it is intended to tackle. In

90 *Kalanke*, para. 22; *Abrahamsson*, para. 52; *EFTA Surveillance Authority v. Norway*, para. 54.

91 *Badeck*, paras. 53-54; *Lommers*, paras. 32-34.

92 De Schutter (2007), at 44; Fredman (2005), at 376; Trelogan et al (2004), at 58; Strauss (1998).

93 *Griesmar*, paras. 62-67; *Commission v. Greece*, paras. 67-68.

94 *Griesmar* para. 66.

other words, granting a mere benefit to a vulnerable group that finds itself at a disadvantage is not enough: the measure should effectively be able to offset that particular disadvantage.

Along similar lines of thought, the reference to 'specific measures' in Article 5 RED would seem to require that positive action is effectuated by measures that have been specifically developed for the particular purpose they aim to achieve. Thus, a certain degree of tailoring to the characteristics of the particular context within which the measure is to operate appears to be necessary. Such a requirement seems justified, especially for the stronger forms of positive action, which risk producing unwanted harmful effects.

7.3.2.6. Necessity (subsidiarity and proportionality stricto sensu)

The ECJ's positive action jurisprudence shows regard for the requirement of necessity, which can be subdivided into the tests of subsidiarity and proportionality stricto sensu. It is repeated here that the subsidiarity test entails a search for less intrusive ways of achieving the aim pursued, and that proportionality stricto sensu entails an analysis of the degree to which the weight of the aim pursued by a measure is in balance with the degree of intrusion it entails for the opposing interest.[95]

An example of subsidiarity reasoning is found in *Lommers*, where the ECJ considered that a rule that reserved nursery places for women could perpetuate a traditional division of roles between men and women, and could therefore potentially breach the proportionality principle, if the aim sought after could still be achieved by extending the benefit to working fathers.[96] As was mentioned before, it is desirable that potential counterproductive effects for protected groups are taken into account, and the sensitivity displayed by the ECJ in this regard is therefore welcome.

Proportionality stricto sensu thinking comes back in the consistent line of jurisprudence according to which persons not belonging to the advantaged group should never be absolutely and unconditionally excluded and should always at least have a chance of receiving the particular advantage in play.[97] Absolute and unconditional exclusion is apparently too intrusive in comparison with the aim pursued by the particular positive action measure. The ECJ also emphasises in this context the need for the objective assessment of each individual case. In *EFTA Surveillance Authority v. Norway* the EFTA court nicely summarises the relevant case law as follows: '[n]ational rules and practices derogating from [the right to equal treatment, MB] can only be permissible when they show sufficient flexibility to allow a balance between

95 See sections 5.2.4.3 and 5.2.4.4.

96 *Lommers*, paras. 41-42.

97 *Kalanke*, para. 22; *Marschall*, para. 33; *Badeck*, paras. 23, 27 and 53; *Abrahamsson*, para. 52; *Lommers*, paras. 44-47; *Briheche*, paras. 27-28.

the need for the promotion of the underrepresented gender and the opportunity for candidates of the opposite gender to have their situation objectively assessed. There must, as a matter of principle, be a possibility that the best-qualified candidate obtains the post.'[98]

For rules of preferential treatment for particular posts, this means that a saving clause should be available, ensuring that exceptions to the rule are possible where the individual circumstances so warrant.[99] Rules of preferential treatment that do not concern the obtainment of a particular post but rather target work conditions in the broader sense are equally required to show sufficient consideration for persons not belonging to the advantaged group. Thus, reserving a number of training places exclusively for women is only acceptable if men have sufficient possibilities to acquire a training place elsewhere.[100] Similarly, a rule of preferential treatment of women as regards childcare opportunities needs to make provision for men who are primary caretakers of children, who should have a possibility of obtaining a nursery place as well.[101]

As positive action measures raise difficult questions as to how to strike the right balance between conflicting interests, it seems appropriate to require that each individual case is assessed on its own merits. This is all the more true for cases in which more than one vulnerable group is represented.[102] From this perspective, the ECJ's strict adherence to the requirement that positive action measures should always allow for consideration of individual circumstances is to be endorsed. At the same time, there is a real danger that courts will habitually value more highly the individual interest of the person disadvantaged by a positive action measure than that of the vulnerable group. This would seem to be particularly true for national contexts in which there is not much support for anti-discrimination or minority protection mechanisms. In this respect it is repeated that legal recognition of positive action as a constitutive component of the equality principle rather than an exception to it is desirable.

Another application of proportionality stricto sensu is the consistent rejection by the ECJ of rules that allow for the preferential treatment of sufficiently qualified women over better qualified male candidates. According to the ECJ, such a disregard for the merit principle is simply not permitted, and is always

---

98 *EFTA Surveillance Authority v. Norway*, para. 45.

99 *Marschall*, para. 33, *Badeck*, paras. 34-36.

100 *Badeck*, para. 53.

101 *Lommers*, paras. 44-45. See also *Commission v. Greece*, para. 69, in which the ECJ pointed out that men who were primary caretakers should benefit from the same advantages that were granted to women who were primary caretakers.

102 Compare Holzleithner (2005), at 955, who submits that the saving clause required by the ECJ for rules of preferential treatment is the entering point for the consideration of other grounds of discrimination.

disproportionate to the aim pursued.[103] This point of view is acceptable in view of the potential counterproductive effects that a merit-disregarding measure would produce, such as the perpetuation of harmful stereotypes. At the same time it should be emphasised that 'merit' is a contextual notion and can easily be applied in an ethnocentric manner.[104] Courts should thus be vigilant and critically assess the particular interpretation of 'merit' in each individual case, so as to prevent the unjustified imposition of the majority norm on minority groups in society.

It should be mentioned in this context that the ECJ condoned in *Badeck* the adjustment of job criteria in order to accommodate women who had acquired relevant professional skills in domestic and other non-job related activities.[105] This is an important step forward, since adaptation of job requirements in line with particular characteristics of vulnerable groups is a powerful instrument against structural forms of discrimination.[106] The ECJ has set some limits to this possibility in *Abrahamsson*, by requiring that the adapted requirements must be transparent and amenable for review in order to obviate any arbitrary assessment of the qualifications of the candidates.[107] This qualification seems justified in view of the principle of legal certainty.

PART TWO: CASE STUDY

7.4. Introduction

In the theoretical framework it was first examined which possibilities Member States have with regard to the instrument of positive action and it was subsequently assessed which limits are set in place by Article 5 RED and the ECJ. As the main focus of this study is on the implementation of the RED, this section will follow a reverse order, and will start with a discussion of the manner in which the Member States have implemented Article 5 RED in section 7.5, and the limits they have set in place for positive action in section 7.6. In section 7.7 a concise overview is given of the various positive action measures taken by the four Member States.

---

103 *Abrahamsson*, para. 52. See also Gijzen (2006), at 230-231.

104 Jackson (1999), at 261.

105 See *Badeck*, para. 31 for a full description of the measure.

106 See *EFTA Authority v. Norway*, para. 57, in which the EFTA Court recognises the importance of this tool for the enhancement of equality between men and women, and the reduction of actual instances of gender inequality. See also Gijzen (2006), at 229, who speaks of "an excursion to the realm of substantive justice" in this regard.

107 *Abrahamsson*, para. 49.

7.5. Implementation of Article 5 RED in the national frameworks

Prior to the implementation of the RED no statutory positive action provisions were available in the national frameworks under study, with the exception of the Netherlands. The Dutch GETA has provided for the possibility of taking positive action measures for racial and ethnic minorities since its entry into force in 1994, and the relevant provision was maintained, though slightly altered at the occasion of the implementation of the RED. Thus, Article 2(3) GETA now provides that:

> [t]he prohibition on discrimination contained in this Act does not apply if the distinction is a *specific* measure that aims to place women or persons belonging to a particular ethnic or cultural minority group in a privileged position *in order to eliminate or reduce existing inequalities connected with race or sex* and the distinction is proportionate to that aim (emphasis added, MB).

The emphasised words were added by the IA, so as to connect to the particular formulation of Article 5 RED.

The lack of any express legal provision in the other Member States does not mean that the concept of positive action was unknown or unapplied: in Belgium and Hungary the constitutional courts had acknowledged the possibility of positive action measures in their equality jurisprudence, and had formulated a number of requirements for the legality of such measures.[108] In both Member States, the implementation of the RED produced an express provision on positive action in the national anti-discrimination acts, which partially built upon the requirements formulated by the constitutional courts. In Belgium, the first implementation phase produced Article 4 of the ADL, which provided that:

> [t]he provisions of this law do not prevent adopting or maintaining measures that aim to prevent or compensate disadvantages, in order to ensure full equality in practice.

The second implementation phase produced a slightly more complex regulation of positive action. Article 10(1) of the new ARA now provides that:

[108] For Belgium, see Court of Arbitration, No. 9/94, 27 January 1994, in which the Arbitration Court determined that positive action measures are permissible if they comply with the following requirements: they should proceed from a sound factual basis; there needs to be a legislative mandate; the measures need to be temporary, and should not go further than is strictly necessary. For Hungary see Constitutional Court, Decision no. 9/1990, in which the Constitutional Court considered that, if a social goal or constitutional right could only be realised through positive discrimination, this would not be unconstitutional. It furthermore stated that the boundaries of such positive discrimination were found in the principle of human dignity and in the other fundamental rights guaranteed by the Constitution.

> direct or indirect distinction on the basis of one of the protected characteristics can never lead to the establishment of any form of discrimination if this distinction amounts to a measure of positive action,

the latter concept of which is defined in Article 4(11) as pertaining to:

> specific measures to prevent or compensate for disadvantages related to [a protected characteristic, MB], in view of ensuring full equality in practice.

The Belgian legislator furthermore decided to expressly lay down the requirements for positive action, and thus inserted Article 10(2) in the new ARA, which stipulates that:

> a measure of positive action is only permitted if there is an apparent inequality; if the elimination of this inequality has been designated as an aim to be achieved; if the measure is temporary and disappears when the inequality has ceased to exist; if it does not unnecessarily limit the rights of others."

Finally, Article 10(3)-(4) of the new ARA provides that the government will determine in which situations and under which conditions measures of positive action can be taken, and will consult with the Social Partners in that respect.

In Hungary, the regulation of positive action went through different phases, and interestingly involved not only the authorisation of positive action measures, but also provision for certain obligations of positive action. Until the 2007 amendments the HETA contained a separate section on the promotion of equal opportunities, which laid down a number of obligations and opportunities to enact measures of positive action. It required the development of a national equal opportunities programme, and it provided local governments with the opportunity to develop a similar type of programme. It furthermore required that state-funded bodies with more than 50 employees and companies of which the state was the majority shareholder devised their own equal opportunities plans.[109] At the occasion of the 2007 amendments this separate section was repealed, and the provision on the national equal opportunities programme was deleted from the text. The two provisions concerning equal opportunities plans of local governments, state-funded bodies and state-owned companies were transferred to the inconspicuous 'closing provisions' section of the HETA.[110] The reasons for these changes are obscure.

---

109 Previous Articles 31-36 of the HETA.

110 Article 63(4) and (5) HETA provides that: "[b]udgetary organisations employing more than fifty persons, as well as legal entities in which the state has a majority ownership are obliged to draw up an equal opportunities plan. […] Municipal governments may devise a local equal opportunities programme, which serves for the analysis of the state of affairs of the disadvantaged groups living in the particular settlement and in which the municipal government defines the objectives promoting equal opportunities for these groups, with a particular attention to housing, education, health care, employment and social status. The local equal opportunities programme shall define the size of funds required for the implementation of the set objectives, a schedule of implementation. The municipal government shall approve a report on the actual completion of the implementation schedule by June 30 of the year following the subject year."

In addition to the provisions on equal opportunities programmes and plans, the HETA provides for provisions that permit various forms of positive action, in line with Article 5 RED. The general provision on positive action is found in Article 11, which provides that:

> (1) [t]he disposition aimed at the elimination of inequality op opportunities based on an objective assessment of an expressly identified social group is not considered a breach of the principle of equal treatment if a) it is based on an act, on a government decree based on an act, or on a collective contract, effective for a definite term or until a specific condition is met, and/or b) the election of a party's executive and representative organ and the setting up of a candidate at the elections defined in the Act on the Electoral Procedures is executed in line with the party's fundamental rules. (2) A measure aimed at evening out a disadvantage shall not violate any basic rights, shall not provide unconditional advantage, and shall not exclude the consideration of individual circumstances.

The HETA furthermore contains a number of specific provisions on positive action in selected fields of application. For the field of employment Article 23 provides that:

> [a]n act, a government decree based on an act or a collective agreement may order an obligation for preferential treatment for a specified group of employees in respect of the labour relationship or other relationship aimed at employment.

For the field of social protection and healthcare Article 25 paragraph (2) provides that:

> [p]ursuant to or authorized by the law and based on health, disability, or a characteristic defined in art. 8, a government decree may grant additional benefits to specified groups of society within the framework of the social and health care system, in accordance with the provisions herein.

For the field of education Article 29 provides that:

> [a] government decree created pursuant to the law or the authorization thereof may order an obligation to provide preferential treatment to a specified group of participants in education within or outside the school system in respect of education or training.

Contrary to the other three Member States, the Estonian legal framework did not have any previous experience with positive action at the time of the implementation of the RED. This perhaps explains why the first implementation phase entailed very limited regulation for positive action: the ECA only allowed for special measures for women and disabled persons.[111] Only with the adoption of the EETA in 2008 did positive action for racial and ethnic minorities become legally regulated. Article 6 of this act stipulates that:

[111] Article 10(1) ECA allowed for the "grant of preferences on grounds of pregnancy, confinement, giving care to minors or adult children incapacitated for work and parents who are incapacitated for work" and the "grant of preferences to disabled workers, including creation of working environment taking account of the special needs of disabled workers."

> [t]his Act does not restrict the application of such measures, the purpose of which is to diminish or prevent the disparity resulting from a [protected characteristic, MB]. The measures applied in such manner must be in proportion to the objective to be attained.

7.6. Limits to positive action in the national frameworks

7.6.1. Positive action as an exception to the principle of equal treatment

There are some differences between the Member States as regards the manner in which the relationship between positive action and the principle of equal treatment is regarded. Whereas the Belgian and Dutch frameworks clearly approach positive action as an exception to the prohibition of discrimination, the Estonian and Hungarian frameworks have taken a less clear stance.

The Dutch perspective on positive action as an exception can be inferred from the place of the positive action provision in the GETA, since it is listed among the 'general grounds of exception'.[112]

The new Belgian ARA could at first glance be perceived as approaching positive action as a component of the equality principle rather than as an exception to it. The Act does not mention positive action next to the other justification provisions for direct and indirect discrimination, but regulates it separately. Furthermore, Article 11 of the new ARA is not framed in exception language, but rather seems to emphasise that positive action is not a form of discrimination: 'direct or indirect distinction on the basis of one of the protected characteristics *can never lead to the establishment of any form of discrimination* if this distinction amounts to a measure of positive action' (emphasis added, MB).

Still, the Explanatory Memorandum to the new ARA reveals that positive action is seen as an exception to the principle of equal treatment, which is in line with the traditional approach of the Arbitration Court towards positive action.[113] It should be mentioned that the positive action provision in the decree of the Walloon region remarkably does not approach positive action as an exception, but rather as an emanation of the principle of equal treatment. Article 10 of this decree stipulates that the Walloon government takes measures of positive action 'in order to ensure the principle of equal treatment'. This clear positioning of positive action as an emanation of the principle of equality is unique in the Belgian framework and provides a good example of substantive equality reasoning.

---

[112] See also Asscher-Vonk & Hendriks (2005), at 76-77.

[113] Doc. 51 2722/001, 23; De Vos (2008), at 326; De Schutter (2007a), at 76.

The other two national frameworks do not approach positive action as an exception, at least not explicitly, but their approaches vary in how favourably they look upon positive action as forming part of the equality paradigm. The more favourable attitude is found within the Hungarian framework. Positive action in this framework appears to be regarded as an emanation of the principle of equal treatment rather than as an exception. The Constitutional court's case law reveals that it considers formally unequal treatment sometimes necessary in order to achieve the goal of substantive equality, and would seem to consider the aims of formal equality and substantive equality to be of equal value.[114] The HETA proceeds from a similarly broad understanding of the principle of equal treatment, which is mentioned in Article 1 as the basis for the anti-discrimination framework. Article 1 HETA defines this principle not in the traditional understanding according to which equal cases should be treated equally and unequal cases should be treated unequally. Instead, it provides that:

> all natural persons abiding in the area of the republic of Hungary and any groups thereof, as well as legal entities and organizations without legal entity, shall be treated with the same respect and deliberation and *their special considerations* shall be equally respected (emphasis added, MB).

This provision, in particular the emphasised section, makes clear that substantive equality is considered to be a constitutive component of the principle of equal treatment. Unsurprisingly, therefore, positive action is not listed among the exceptions/justifications to direct and indirect discrimination in Article 7 of the HETA, but is separately regulated. Against this background it is somewhat surprising that ABET has referred to positive action as 'an exemption reason', which is at odds with the idea that positive action is an inherent component of the principle of equal treatment, and more aligns with the ECJ's exception-based perspective. This example reveals that the particular position of positive action within the Hungarian equality paradigm is not yet totally clear.[115]

Similarly to the Hungarian framework, the Estonian framework does not seem to approach positive action as an exception to the principle of equal treatment, which can be inferred from the place of the positive action provision in the EETA. This Act does not list the positive action provision among the exceptions to the prohibition of discrimination, but groups it under the heading of 'principles of equal treatment'. This could mean that positive action is approached as an inherent aspect of the principle of equality, which still needs to be confirmed in practice, however.

[114] Constitutional Court, Decision no. 9/1990.

[115] See Position No. 10.007/1/2006 TT of the Advisory Board of Equal Treatment on the division of the burden of proof, 13 January 2006.

7.6.2. Type of actor that is allowed to enact measures of positive action

There is an interesting divergence among Member States as regards the extent to which they allow for positive action measures to be taken by private actors. Both Hungary and Belgium have opted for a restrictive approach and permit positive action initiatives only if they are based on a legislative mandate or, in the Hungarian context, on a provision in a collective agreement.[116] It should be mentioned with regard to the Belgian context, however, that the Flemish and German decrees do leave open a possibility for private positive action initiatives within their limited fields of application.[117] Still, the overall Belgian approach is particularly strict, because it does not leave open any possibility for private initiative, and makes the adoption of positive action measures completely dependent on the establishment of political consensus.[118] Compared to this approach, the Hungarian HETA is more lenient, since it at least gives the social partners initiating power.

The Estonian and Dutch frameworks do not impose any requirement of public permission of positive action. In Estonia, one decision of the Gender Equality Commissioner reveals that this supervisory organ considers it permissible for private actors to take positive action measures.[119] In the

[116] See Article 10(3) of the new Belgian ARA, which stipulates that positive action must be based on and conform to a governmental decree on positive action. Some scholars have expressed doubts as to whether private actors could adopt measures of positive action at all, see De Schutter (2007a), at 76; De Vos (2008), at 327. Still, the Explanatory Memorandum to the new ARA reveals that the government did not exclude this possibility, since it explicitly mentions the possibility of positive action being taken by private actors: Doc 51. 2720/001, 23. For Hungary, see Article 11 HETA, which requires measures of positive action to be based on an act or on a collective agreement.

[117] Article 26 of the *Decree of the Flemish Community containing a framework for the Flemish equal opportunities and equal treatment policy,* 10 July 2008, provides that: "[t]his decree does not prevent, in order to guarantee full equality in practice, the adoption or maintenance of temporary specific measures to compensate for an apparent inequality connected to [one of the protected characteristics, MB], to the extent that these measures are objectively justified by a legitimate aim and the means for the achievement of the aim are appropriate and necessary." Article 12 of the *Decree of the German Community on guaranteeing equal treatment in employment do not refer to public actors as the only authors of positive action*, 17 May 2004, provides that: "[n]othwithstanding the principle of equal treatment, specific measures can be adopted or maintained that contribute to ensuring full equality in professional life by preventing or compensating for disadvantages that are connected to the [protected characteristics, MB]."

[118] De Vos (2008), at 326-327.

[119] In a case published on the Estonian part of the website of the Commissioner (at www.svv.ee, accessed August 2009), the Commissioner considers that an event that was organised for boys only, by what would appear to be a private organisation, could potentially be justified as being a measure of positive action.

Netherlands, it is generally understood that private actors may initiate positive action, provided, of course, that they fulfil the relevant requirements.[120]

7.6.3. Central importance of the principle of proportionality

Interestingly, the national frameworks have all codified the ECJ's requirement of proportionality in their legislative provisions on positive action, with varying degrees of specificity. Article 6 of the Estonian EETA and Article 2(3) of the Dutch GETA are very concise, and simply require the measure to be proportionate to the objective to be attained.

Article 10(2) of the new Belgian ARA is more elaborate, and requires that the measure:

1) is temporary and ceases to exist when the aim is achieved

2) does not unnecessarily limit the right of others

Article 11 of the Hungarian HETA is also more extensive and requires the measure:

1) not to violate any fundamental rights

2) not to provide an unconditional advantage

3) not to exclude the consideration of individual circumstances

These latter two requirements directly stem from the jurisprudence of the ECJ, and are illustrative of the intention of the Hungarian legislator to align with this court's approach to positive action.[121]

More generally, it is commonly understood in all four Member States that the various national requirements for positive action are to be applied in compliance with jurisprudence of the ECJ in the field of gender equality law.[122] Thus, the following discussion of the national applications of the proportionality principle follows the same order as the above discussion of the requirements developed by the ECJ. Due to lack of practice, it is generally not

[120] See for instance *Jaarrapport 2007*, Commissie Gelijke Behandeling 2007, at 11-12, in which it announces its intention to pay increased attention to the concept of positive action, as carried out by both public and private actors.

[121] Kádar (2007), at 56. See also the *Explanatory Memorandum to Act CXXV of 2003 on Equal Treatment and Promotion of Equal Opportunities*, specifically with regard to Article 11, which refers to the ECJ's judgments on positive action.

[122] For Belgium, see De Vos (2008), at 326. for Estonia, see the *Explanatory Memorandum to Act 384 SE III on Equal Treatment*, which points out that the EETA should be applied in compliance with the requirements of European equality law. For The Netherlands, see Gijzen (2006), at 254.

possible to determine whether indirectly discriminatory measures of positive action will be treated differently from directly discriminatory measures of positive action. Only the Dutch ETC has so far encountered an indirectly discriminatory form of positive action, and the manner in which it dealt with this is discussed at the end of this section.

7.6.3.1. Legitimacy of the aim pursued by positive action

Existence of an actual disadvantage

In accordance with the case law of the ECJ, the national frameworks all require or appear to require positive action measures to be based on sufficient factual evidence. This is visible in the requirement of an 'apparent inequality' in Article 10(2) of the new Belgian ARA, and the 'based on an objective assessment of an expressly identified social group' requirement in Article 11 of the Hungarian HETA. As regards Estonia, the Gender Equality Commissioner considered that an event organised for boys only could was only permissible if *factual data* would confirm that significantly more girls visited such events organised until now.[123] In a similar way, the Dutch ETC consistently requires proof of an actual disadvantage in practice.[124]

The ETC actually applies a more lenient approach with regard to positive action for racial and ethnic groups than for women, since quantitative data on these groups are more difficult to come by. The ETC is for instance satisfied with general statistical data on the position of these groups in the whole workforce, and does not require specific information on the particular sector within which the measure applies.[125] Quantitative evidence is furthermore not requisite in the Dutch framework, since the ETC also accepts qualitative data as proof of actual disadvantage of these groups, such as facts of general knowledge.[126]

A similarly lenient approach is found in the new Belgian ARA, which in Article 30(3) provides that indirect discrimination is present in the case of the use of 'intrinsically suspicious' criteria and can be established with the help of facts of general knowledge. The same lenient approach presumably applies in the context of positive action. According to one handbook published by a Hungarian NGO, the Hungarian framework also allows for the use of qualitative evidence in addition to quantitative data, which still needs to be

[123] The case is described in Estonian on the website of the Commissioner (at www.svv.ee, accessed August 2009).
[124] Gijzen (2006), at 255; Asscher-Vonk & Hendriks (2005), at 79; Gerards & Heringa (2003), at 125.
[125] Opinion 2008-1 ETC.
[126] Gijzen (2006), at 256; Gerards & Heringa (2003), at 133.

confirmed in practice.[127] By contrast, the Estonian framework would seem to only provide for the possibility of adducing quantitative evidence. Article 6 of the Estonian EETA refers to the prevention or elimination of *disparities*, which according to the Explanatory Memorandum are understood to point to *numerical* forms of underrepresentation.[128]

It should finally be mentioned that the Dutch framework applies a clearly asymmetrical approach, as it only permits positive action for those groups that are at a structural disadvantage in important areas of public life.[129] This means that racial or ethnic positive action is only possible for racial or ethnic minorities that are structurally disadvantaged within society, which reveals substantive equality thinking. No similar asymmetrical approaches have been discerned in the other frameworks so far.

Types of acceptable aims for positive action

Not all national provisions employ the same wording as Article 5 RED with regard to the aims to be achieved by positive action.

Article 4(11) of the new Belgian ARA is the only provision that uses wording identical to Article 5 RED. This provision refers to 'full equality in practice', and appears to accept both forward and backward-looking strategies ('prevent or compensate'). Still, the case law of the Belgian Arbitration Court, which has been laid down in Article 10(2) of the new ARA, gives reason to think that forward-looking aims for positive action might not be accepted in practice. One of the Arbitration Court's requirements is that the aim of a positive action measure should be the *elimination* of an apparent disadvantage, which would seem to allow only for backward-looking types of aims. This impression is confirmed by the temporariness criterion mentioned by Article 10(2) of the new ARA. Therefore, despite its broad definition of positive action, the new Belgian ARA would in reality seem to apply a more restrictive conception than Article 5 RED. It is interesting to note in this respect that the Walloon and German decrees refer to the 'prevention' of disadvantages, and therefore embrace forward-looking strategies. It is questionable however whether this will actually be helpful in practice, since the Arbitration Court's jurisprudence applies to the federated entities as well.[130]

---

[127] *White Booklet 2006*, Legal Defence Bureau for National Ethnic Minorities (NEKI) 2007, at 81.

[128] See the *Explanatory Memorandum to Act 384 SE III on Equal Treatment*: "The Act provides for the application of the so-called positive measures, i.e. it is permitted for the purposes of reducing certain *under-representation* to give certain persons more favourable treatment in a comparable situation." (emphasis added, MB)

[129] Gijzen (2006), at 251; Asscher-Vonk & Hendriks (2005), at 77-78; TK 2002-3, 18 770, 5, at 21.

[130] De Schutter (2007a), at 77.

As regards Estonia, Article 6 of the EETA is very brief in describing the aims to be pursued by positive action, and merely speaks of *diminishing* or *preventing* a disparity connected to a protected characteristic. It thus seemingly allows for both backward and forward-looking strategies. The Legal Chancellor, however, is of the opinion that positive action measures should be temporary in nature, which rather points to a focus on backward-looking aims.[131] The Legal Chancellor furthermore suggests a strict approach as regards the assessment of aims pursued by positive action measures, and it has stated that positive action measures need to be based on 'very grave grounds'.[132] It remains to be seen whether the Estonian Equal Treatment Commissioner and Estonian courts will display a similarly strict attitude, which would entail a relatively high threshold and thus would likely have a discouraging effect.

The Dutch framework has also been reluctant to embrace forward-looking strategies, which can be inferred from the fact that Article 2(3) GETA only refers to the *elimination* of disadvantages. The omission to mention *prevention* as a legitimate aim actually stems from a deliberate choice of the Dutch legislator. At the occasion of the implementation of the RED, the government emphasised that the inclusion of 'prevention' was neither necessary, nor desirable.[133]

By contrast, the Hungarian HETA would seem to allow for forward-looking strategies. The phrase '*elimination* of inequality of *opportunities*' in Article 11 HETA is broad enough to cover both backward and forward-looking aims, despite the lack of a reference to 'prevention'. The Hungarian Constitutional Court has furthermore formulated the aim to be pursued by positive action in terms of 'greater social equality', which clearly points to a substantive equality perspective and can be expected to influence the interpretation of 'opportunities' of Article 11 HETA.[134]

The phrase 'elimination of inequality of opportunities' in Article 11 HETA is reminiscent of the opportunities versus results distinction that is applied by the ECJ. It is not clear in which way 'opportunities' is interpreted in the Hungarian framework, and it therefore remains to be seen whether this reference will constitute an obstacle in practice.

The opportunities versus results distinction of the ECJ has clearly been incorporated in the Dutch framework, and the ETC applies the same interpretation of 'opportunities' and 'results' as this latter court.[135] The

---

[131] *Position paper on the violation of the principle of equal treatment,* 08.2007 nr 7-5/070340/00705874, Legal Chancellor 2007.

[132] *Position paper on the violation of the principle of equal treatment,* 08.2007 nr 7-5/070340/00705874, Legal Chancellor 2007.

[133] TK 2002-3 28770, 3, at 9.

[134] Hungarian Constitutional Court, Case No. 9/1990.

[135] The ETC has for instance considered that special courses for women belonging to ethnic minorities that aimed to improve their position in the labour market remained within the sphere

opportunities versus results dichotomy is relevant for the strictness with which the proportionality test is carried out, as the ETC applies less strict scrutiny in cases involving 'opportunities' than in cases involving 'results'. This approach is in line with the ECJ's jurisprudence, but could be problematic, as was pointed out before. It is still unclear how the ETC will apply the results versus opportunities distinction in fields outside the sphere of employment.[136]

Finally, an interesting feature of the Hungarian framework should be mentioned, which is its attention for identity-related interests of minorities. The HETA permits quite generously measures that aim to accommodate these more permanent minority interests. The measures are formally not grouped under positive action, but are considered to flow separately from the general principle of equality as expressed in Article 1 HETA. Article 28(2) HETA provides for the setting up of elementary and secondary forms of education that are tailored to the needs of particular religious and cultural minorities.[137] Paragraphs 30(2) and 30(3) HETA provide for the possibility of special institutions for the preservation of cultural traditions and the maintenance of a separate identity.[138] As these measures are not categorised under the heading of positive action in the HETA, it is unclear which legal requirements apply to them. The fact that they apparently justify measures that potentially conflict

of 'opportunities', see Opinion 2005-225 ETC. Conversely, preferential treatment with regard to the obtainment of posts has been treated as pertaining to 'results' (*Memo on Positive Action*, TK 2004-5, 28 770, no. 11, at 21).

[136] There has so far been one case on positive action in the field of social protection, which concerned a training course aimed at women of an ethnic minority background in order to facilitate their integration in the labour market. This measure was so closely related to the domain of employment that it was easily fitted into the traditional understanding of opportunities vs. results, and was unsurprisingly deemed by the ETC to aim for equality of opportunities, see Opinion 2005-225 ETC. The decision does not shed light, however, on the manner in which the ETC will apply the opportunities v. results dichotomy in cases that concern measures that are less closely connected to the field of employment.

[137] This article provides that: "[t]he principle of equal treatment is not violated, if a) in elementary and secondary education, at the initiation and by the voluntary choice of the parents, or b) in higher education by the students' voluntary participation, education based on religious or other ideological conviction, or education for ethnic or other minorities is organised in a way that the goal or the curriculum of the education justifies the creation of separated classes or groups; provided that this does not result in any disadvantage for those participating in such education, and that the education complies with the requirements approved, laid down and subsidised by the state."

[138] The article provides that: "[e]ntry into premises established for a group defined by the characteristics listed in article 8 for the purposes of preserving traditions or maintaining cultural and self-identity and open to the immediate public may be limited or subject to membership or specific conditions. This limitation must be obvious from the name of the establishment and the circumstances of the use of the service; and this shall not be done in a manner that may be humiliating and defamatory to individuals who do not belong to the particular group, and furthermore it must not provide an opportunity for an abuse of this right."

with the prohibitions of direct or indirect discrimination means that they will have to comply with the case law of the ECJ. Practice needs to confirm whether the European positive action aqcuis will indeed be complied with.

The Dutch ETC also shows regard for the more permanent interests of minority groups, but in a less conspicuous way than the HETA. Similarly to the Hungarian framework, measures aimed at accommodating more permanent needs of minority groups are not categorised as positive action in the Dutch framework, and are consequently not seen as constituting an exception to the prohibition of discrimination.[139] To the contrary, the ETC considers such special measures to be wholly in line with the principle of equality, which can be inferred from the fact that it sometimes encourages their adoption. For instance, in one case it encouraged an employer to take broader measures in order to ensure the full participation and integration of minorities in the workforce, and even proposed to take measures that were not temporary but permanent in nature.[140] So far, no cases have come up in which these types of measures were claimed to be discriminatory, so it is unclear how the ETC would resolve the resulting conflict of opposing equality interests.

7.6.3.2. Appropriateness

The appropriateness test formally only comes back in the Estonian and Dutch frameworks, where it consistently forms part of the proportionality test.[141] In this respect, it is not problematic that Article 6 EETA does not use the adjective 'specific' or a similar qualification in order to incorporate the tailoring requirement of Article 5 RED ('specific measures'). As was mentioned before, this requirement can be considered to constitute a particular application of the appropriateness test.

This overlap can be clearly seen in the Dutch framework, where the addition of a reference to 'specific measures' did not impact on the ETC's approach

[139] This particular understanding of positive action can be inferred from Article 2(3) GETA, which refers to measures that aim to place persons belonging to protected groups 'in a privileged position'. Similarly, the word used in the Dutch legal framework to designate positive action schemes is '*voorkeursbeleid*', which literally means 'preferential policy'. See furthermore the government's *Memo on positive action*, TK 2004-5, 28 770, no. 11, 13, in which it states that, in addition to '*voorkeursbeleid*' (read: preferential treatment), 'social policy' of public and private actors can be used in order to improve the position of the target groups. By 'social policy' the government arguably points to all kinds of measures that do not involve preferential treatment but that benefit vulnerable groups in another way.

[140] Opinion 2008-1 ETC.

[141] For Estonia, see Decision of the Constitutional Chamber of the Supreme Court, 3-1-3-10-02, 17 March 2003, para. 30, in which the Supreme Court describes the proportionality principle as comprising the three tests of suitability, necessity and proportionality stricto sensu. For The Netherlands, see Advice 2008-01 of the ETC, in which it lays out its framework for positive action, and mentions the suitability criterion in the context of the proportionality test.

to positive action, which already incorporated an appropriateness criterion.[142] The ETC interprets appropriateness as requiring that the particular measure is effectively capable of achieving its aim. For instance, in a case involving a rule that exempted female soldiers with children from serving abroad the ETC dismissed the measure as illegitimate because the effectiveness of the measure could not be established. The rule had been applied for over 15 years, without resulting in a meaningful increase in the proportion of women in the armed forces. The ETC considered that the author of the positive action rule should at least have evaluated the effectiveness of the measure over the years.[143]

Another interesting example of how the ETC shows regard for the effectiveness of positive action measures is found in a case involving a rule of unconditional preferential treatment of women. After having considered that the particular instance of preferential treatment was unlawful for other reasons, the ETC emphasised in an obiter dictum that the measure had wrongly failed to show consideration for other unrepresented groups in the employers' workforce, such as ethnic minorities and disabled persons. Seeing that these groups were officially mentioned in the employer's diversity policy, the employer should have made provision for the possibility of hiring a man of an ethnic minority background, or a disabled man.[144] Such regard for the broader context within which positive action takes place, and more particularly for potential conflicts between vulnerable groups, ensures balanced decision-making and contributes to social cohesion.

It should furthermore be mentioned that the Dutch ETC does not shy away from making recommendations on how to make positive action measures more effective, and thus has regard for appropriateness in a more positive sense than simply as a factor that determines the legality of positive action measures.[145] This attitude contributes to the overall effectiveness of positive action measures in bringing about substantive equality in practice.

Finally, the ETC applies a separate transparency requirement that can be categorised as falling under 'appropriateness'.[146] This requirement entails a duty to make public the intention of applying a policy of positive action. The transparency requirement does not directly stem from the ECJ's jurisprudence on positive action, but still should be positively assessed, since it promotes legal certainty and leads to greater awareness of the existence of positive action measures.

---

[142] Gijzen (2006), at 254; Asscher-Vonk & Hendriks (2005), at 79; Gerards & Heringa (2003), at 125.

[143] Opinion 2008-52 ETC, para. 3.33.

[144] Opinion 2004-173 ETC, para. 5.10.

[145] See Opinion 2008-1, in which the ETC gives advice to the supporting organisation of the Dutch Parliament on its intended policy of positive action. The ETC recommends the organisation inter alia to make the positive action measures obligatory and to raise awareness within the organisation with regard to the policy.

[146] Opinion 2008-1 ETC.

In the other Member States appropriateness is not a separately recognised requirement, but this does not have to be problematic. The necessity test can fairly easily be used in these frameworks to take appropriateness-related arguments into consideration.[147] After all, if a measure is not capable of achieving the aim it pursues, and thus is inappropriate, it can hardly be expected to be considered necessary or proportionate in a strict sense.

Moreover, both the Belgian and Hungarian frameworks have implemented the tailoring requirement captured by 'specific measures' in Article 5 RED, which can be used to apply appropriateness-related arguments. Article 11(1) of the Hungarian HETA requires positive action measures to expressly identify the social group they target, which in turn implies that the measure must have been specifically adopted for the particular group. The new Belgian ARA goes further and not only refers to 'specific measures' in Article 4(11), but also requires that the elimination of the particular disadvantage needs to be 'designated' as an aim, by what would logically appear to be the Belgian government. According to Article 10(3) of the new ARA this body needs to adopt a Royal Decree that stipulates the situations in which positive action measures are to be taken and the conditions that need to be fulfilled. As was mentioned before, this requirement of prior governmental consent makes it more burdensome to adopt positive action measures and thus reduces the chances of any measures actually being taken.

7.6.3.3. Necessity (subsidiarity and proportionality stricto sensu)

The subsidiarity and proportionality stricto sensu aspects of the principle of proportionality come back in all four national frameworks, albeit with variable degrees of precision.

Article 10(2) of the new Belgian ARA remains on a rather general level and goes no further than requiring that rights of others are not unnecessarily restricted, which supposedly requires the performance of a subsidiarity test and a balancing act. The temporariness requirement set by Article 10(3) of the new ARA can moreover also be seen as stemming from proportionality reasoning.[148] As was mentioned before, this requirement restricts the scope of positive action measures to backward-looking type of aims, which is unfortunate. It is generally expected that the various aspects of Article 10(2) will be interpreted in line with the jurisprudence of the ECJ, which means that the aforementioned requirements of objective assessment of each individual case and respect for the merit principle most likely also apply in the Belgian context.[149]

---

[147] For Belgium, see De Vos (2008), at 328, who submits that the requirements of Article 10(2) of the new ARA can be interpreted 'through European glasses'.

[148] De Vos (2008), at 328.

[149] De Vos (2008), at 326.

Article 6 of the Estonian EETA is rather concise, and simply requires a proportionate relationship between the positive action measure and the objective pursued by it. Case law of the Constitutional Chamber of the Supreme Court reveals that proportionality incorporates both the subsidiarity and the proportionality stricto sensu tests.[150] It is unclear to what extent the ECJ's positive action jurisprudence in the field of sex equality law will be followed in the Estonian framework.

The Hungarian HETA offers a more detailed elaboration of the proportionality principle than its Belgian and Estonian counterparts, and has more particularly codified some of the principles developed by the ECJ. Thus, in addition to the requirement that fundamental rights should not be violated, which presumably requires a balancing act to be performed, the HETA requires that no unconditional advantage is granted and that consideration of individual circumstances is ensured. As was mentioned before, these latter requirements stem directly from the ECJ's jurisprudence, and their express mention can be considered to encourage compliance with European law.

Similar regard for the European equality regime is found in the Dutch framework, particularly in the practice of the ETC. In addition to the aforementioned requirements of a proper factual basis, appropriateness and transparency, the ETC applies separate requirements of due diligence and proportionality stricto sensu.[151]

The due diligence requirement is interpreted in line with the ECJ's requirement that each individual case should be the object of separate objective assessment. For example, in a case involving a policy to invite only persons of a minority background for a job interview the ETC decided that this deprived other persons of the opportunity to be individually assessed and therefore violated the precision requirement.[152] The ETC has furthermore followed the ECJ in its insistence on upholding the merit principle, and therefore only allows for preferential treatment in the case of equal qualifications.[153] The proportionality stricto sensu requirement is interpreted by the ETC as meaning that the seriousness of the disadvantage of the group benefiting from the positive action measure should be in proportion with the disadvantageous effects of the measure on persons not belonging to the vulnerable group.[154] In other words, a balancing act of the two main interests involved in the case is required.

[150] Decision of the Constitutional Chamber of the Supreme Court, 3-1-3-10-02, 17 March 2003, para. 30 and Decision of the Constitutional Chamber of the Supreme Court, 3-4-1-1-02, 6 March 2002, para. 15.

[151] Opinion 2008-1 ETC.

[152] Opinion 2008-81 ETC, para. 3.17.

[153] Opinion 2008-1 ETC; Gijzen (2006), at 255.

[154] All of these requirements have been clearly explained in the ETC's opinion 2008-1. See also Gijzen (2006), at 257; Gerards & Heringa (2003), at 127-128.

Interestingly, the ETC has considered more than once that the proportionality principle could call for a less strict approach with regard to positive action on behalf of racial or ethnic groups than the approach developed by the ECJ in the field of sex equality law, in 'exceptional circumstances'.[155] It is not entirely clear what the ETC considers to be such 'exceptional circumstances'. So far, most positive action measures have concerned measures benefiting women, which means that the approach for racial or ethnic positive action is not fully developed yet. Still, it is clear that the grounds of racial and ethnic origin receive a very high level of protection in the Dutch equality framework, which in turn enhances the level of protection for minorities.

7.6.3.4. The Dutch ETC and potentially indirectly discriminatory measures of positive action

The ETC has so far only once encountered a case in which a positive action appeared before it as a potential instance of indirect discrimination. The case involved a draft positive action policy of the city of Amsterdam, which aimed at increasing the proportion of persons from Turkey, Morocco and the Middle-East in the workforce. The city intended to include in its job advertisements a text that specifically invited persons from Islamic countries to apply. Moreover, it intended to first select these persons for interviews and only later, if necessary, persons from another background. The ETC considered the measure not to be aimed directly at a religious group, but still constituted a prima facie case of indirect discrimination against persons that did not adhere to the Islamic religion. It then went on to apply the objective justification test for indirect discrimination, into which it integrated its normal regime for positive action in cases of direct discrimination. Thus, it applied the criteria outlined above, and first examined whether there was an actual disadvantage. In this context, it required that the city substantiate its choice for this particular target group, because the policy risked excluding other vulnerable ethnic or cultural minorities at a comparable disadvantage in the labour market. This again suggests a context-sensitive approach and heightened scrutiny for the ground of racial and ethnic origin.

As regards the intention to select only persons from the target group for interview, the ETC considered that this was not in line with the requirement of objective assessment of each individual case. Moreover, the ETC stated that it was difficult to assess the overall proportionality of the measure, since the actual disadvantage had not been established in sufficient detail. It also considered that the transparency requirement was not fulfilled, because the

155 Opinion 2008-81 ETC, para. 3.21; Opinion 2008-143 ETC, para. 3.10.

planned text did not make clear that origin from an Islamic country was applied as an actual job requirement and only invited persons with such an origin to apply.

Finally, the ETC assessed another aspect of the draft policy, which involved an intended rule of preferential treatment of members of the target group with regard to training places and internships. Since it considered that this rule involved the aim of equal opportunities and not equal results, the ETC applied a more lenient test, but still considered that unconditional preference for candidates of the particular target group seemed difficult to justify, because the less intrusive method of targeted recruitment seemed sufficiently effective.[156] This latter consideration is a clear example of the application of the subsidiarity test.

All in all, the ETC's decision makes clear that this body in substance applies similar tests for directly discriminatory positive action measures and indirectly discriminatory positive action measures. As was mentioned before, the ECJ appears to take a similar approach. The ETC's approach is clearer, however, as this body explicitly refers to its principles on directly discriminatory positive action in an indirect discrimination case, and thus unambiguously applies the same test for both types of positive action. This is fortunate in terms of transparency and legal certainty.

7.7. Measures of positive action taken at the national level on behalf of racial or ethnic minorities

7.7.1. Duties of positive action

Notwithstanding the silence of the RED and the ECJ on duties of positive action, the possibility of imposing such duties has been recognised in all four Member States. Some Member States have even already set in place certain duties of positive action.

The Explanatory Memorandum of the new Belgian ARA explicitly mentions the option of imposing duties of positive action on private actors by Royal Decree.[157] The suggestion has not yet been acted upon, however. It remains to be seen whether duties of positive action will become a reality in the Belgian context, which does not recognise any positive duties flowing

[156] Opinion 2008-143 ETC, paras. 3.1-15.

[157] *Explanatory Memorandum to the Draft law amending the law of 30 July 1981 that penalises certain acts motivated by racism and xenophobia*, Doc 51. 2720/001, 52.

from the principle of equal treatment other than the ones explicitly required by the European legislator.[158] Still, the recognition of the possibility of duties of positive action is welcome.

As was mentioned before, the Hungarian HETA contains a duty for state-funded and state-owned entities to develop an equal opportunities plan in its 'closing provisions' section. The AET monitors the extent to which this obligation is complied with, but only in a formal way. Thus, it is satisfied with the mere presence of an equal opportunities plan, and does not set any substantive requirements.[159] Articles 23 and 29 HETA furthermore permit duties of preferential treatment to be imposed by acts or collective agreements in the field of employment and education. Practically speaking, this means that one of the strongest forms of positive action in McCrudden's classification could be imposed, by the legislator or by social partners. Thus, the legitimacy of strong forms of positive action is affirmed, as is the notion that substantive equality sometimes requires special measures to be taken. Still, the provisions have not yet been acted upon. It should be mentioned that the Hungarian climate is more receptive to duties of positive action than the Belgian one, seeing that the AET and Hungarian courts have already adopted far-reaching positive duties as flowing from the prohibition of direct discrimination.[160]

The Estonian EETA imposes in Article 13 a duty on educational institutions to organise the curriculum in accordance with the principle of equality.[161] The Explanatory Memorandum to the EETA reveals that the duty entails offering special training on the meaning of the principle of equality.[162] Article 14 EETA furthermore imposes a duty on ministries to supervise compliance with the principle of equal treatment within their respective areas of competence, and to cooperate in promoting the principle of equal treatment, which would seem to

[158] See sections 4.8 and 5.4. Article 9 of the *Act of 10 May 2007 combating certain forms of discrimination* provides for the concept of reasonable accommodation of disabled persons, in line with article 5 FD.

[159] Article 14(1)(a) HETA stipulates that the AET shall conduct investigations at request to establish whether the employers obliged to do so have approved an equal opportunities plan. The article does not formulate any substantive criteria that must be applied, and the AET's practice indeed shows that it only investigates whether an equal opportunities plan exists. See for instance EBH/339/2008 (violation of the HETA for not having adopted an equal opportunities plan).

[160] See section 4.8.

[161] This article provides that: "[e]ducational and science institutions, other institutions and persons organising training will in determining study content and arranging the studies take into account the necessity to promote the principle of equal treatment."

[162] According to the *Explanatory Memorandum to Act 384 SE III on Equal Treatment*: "[o] ne of the main purposes of the draft is the promotion of the principle of equal treatment, i.e. changing the prejudices and attitudes effective in practice by education and propaganda (…). Prejudices can be eliminated and the society developed exactly by educating, propagating the idea and carrying out public briefing."

come down to a duty of mainstreaming.[163] Both types of duties can be qualified as falling into McCrudden's first category: activities aimed at identifying and eradicating discriminatory practices. Even though these duties remain quite vague and are not backed-up by a monitoring or enforcement mechanism, they at least send out the important symbolic message that sometimes special action is required in order to ensure true equality.

In the Netherlands, both the ETC and Dutch courts have developed a pseudo duty of positive action, namely the duty to act in compliance with one's own policy of positive action. Thus, if an employer adopts a policy of positive action and makes it public, he is not allowed to apply the policy at will, but should consistently adhere to it. Furthermore, if a positive action policy is applied and none of the candidates fulfil the job profile, the ETC requires that, if present, a person belonging to the targeted minority group is selected, if he is not less qualified than the other applicants.[164] This recognition of a duty to act in compliance with one's positive action policy is likely to increase the effectiveness of positive action policies, and thus enhances the quality of the Dutch framework.

It is furthermore interesting to see that the ETC applies the same quality requirements for this pseudo duty of positive action as those that are applied in the context of complaints of unlawful positive action measures. Thus, in a case in which a person of a minority background complained that a positive action policy had unjustifiably not been applied, the ETC assessed the manner in which the hiring process had been carried out in the same way that it usually scrutinises positive action measures. It concluded that there had been a lack of transparency and objectivity, causing uncertainty among applicants regarding the job requirements, and that the author of the positive action policy had therefore violated the requirements of the GETA.[165] This approach enhances the coherence of the Dutch positive action regime and thus contributes to its overall effectiveness.

7.7.2. National positive action measures

In all four Member States positive action measures for racial or ethnic minorities have been developed and applied. This section does not intend to give a comprehensive overview of all measures currently in place, but rather to point out the most remarkable features and trends.

---

163 This article provides that: "[e]ach ministry will supervise within its area of administration the compliance with the requirements of this Act and will cooperate with the other persons and authorities in promoting the principle of equal treatment."

164 Wentholt (1999), at 157, at 159. See for example Leeuwarden District Court, 4 August 1999, LJN: AA1048.

165 Opinion 2007-55 ETC, paras. 3.11-13.

Weak link with the RED

The measures taken at the national level can only to a very limited extent be linked to the adoption of the RED. The aforementioned duties of positive action provided for by the Hungarian HETA and the Estonian EETA are examples of positive action measures that can be directly linked to the RED, since they are contained in the instrument that implements the RED. The equal opportunities policy of the Flemish government in Belgium, which is regulated in one of the instruments that implements the RED, is another example.[166] In Hungary, a number of positive action measures for the Roma minority have been explicitly linked to the adoption of the RED, and are described in an official report under the heading: "The effects of measures taken to transpose the directive on the Roma, the largest minority group in Hungary".[167] The measures described in this report include a duty of mainstreaming concern for the interests of the Roma minority in all policy fields for the Hungarian ministries, and subsidy schemes for improving the situation of Roma in the fields of housing and education.

Nevertheless, the majority of the positive action measures have been developed independently of the RED, which therefore clearly has had only a limited impact on positive action activity in the Member States. Despite the general lack of a formal connection with the RED, it is useful to broadly assess which positive action measures are being deployed in the Member States. This arguably helps to rightly assess the climate for positive action at the national level and to predict in which way Article 5 RED will be used in the future.

Focus mainly on education and employment

It is noteworthy that the greater part of positive action measures in the Member States are operable in the fields of education and employment. Outside of these fields, positive action is relatively rare. Some examples are found in Hungary, where there is a general mainstreaming duty for all departments to integrate concern for the Roma minority in all fields of public policy.[168] Furthermore, positive action measures aimed at the improvement of the situation of Roma

[166] *Decree containing a framework for Flemish equal opportunities and equal treatment policy*, of 10 July 2008, MB 23 September 2008; *Decree of the Flemish Community of 8 May 2002 on the equal participation in the employment market*, MB 26 July 2002.

[167] *Report pursuant to Council Directive 2000/43/EC implementing the principle of equal treatment between persons irrespective of racial or ethnic origin, Ministry of youth, family, social affairs and equal opportunities*, Budapest, 15 July 2005.

[168] 'The effects of measures taken to transpose the directive on the Roma, the largest minority group in Hungary' of the *Report pursuant to Council Directive 2000/43/EC implementing the principle of equal treatment between persons irrespective of racial or ethnic origin, Ministry of youth, family, social affairs and equal opportunities*, Budapest, 15 July 2005.

in this Member State have been adopted not only in the fields of education and employment, but also in those of housing and healthcare. Many of these measures have been adopted within the framework of the Decade of Roma Inclusion Programme.[169] An example of positive action in the field of housing is a subsidy scheme developed by the Ministry of Youth, Social and Family Affairs and Equal Opportunities for small villages to carry out desegregation plans. These plans included strategies for the social upgrading of certain segregated neighbourhoods and assistance to Roma persons who wanted to move away from such neighbourhoods.[170] In Estonia, in addition to the duty of mainstreaming that covers all policy areas, language training courses are offered to persons belonging to the Russian-speaking minority within the framework of the National Integration Plan.[171] These courses aim at increasing the social inclusion of this minority group in Estonian society, and thus extend beyond the fields of education and employment, while being closely connected to them.

For the greater part, however, positive action measures are deployed in the fields of employment and education. For instance, in the Netherlands a diversity plan for civil servants and the national police force is operable, the aim of which is to increase the participation of ethnic minorities. The plan entails inter alia the adoption of target figures and diversity management instruments.[172] The Dutch Ministry of Social Affairs and Employment has furthermore set up various forms of cooperation with Dutch municipalities in order to enhance the participation of young and female members of racial and ethnic minority groups ('allochtones') in Dutch society. This ministry has also set up a campaign to inform and coach employers in ensuring a discrimination-free working environment.[173] Moreover, the Dutch Ministry of Education, Culture and Science has taken measures to prevent school drop-out in the lower echelons of the Dutch education system and to facilitate the integration of socially disadvantaged students in education.[174] This ministry has also set up a coordination mechanism forcing local schools to work together to counter segregation in education.[175]

---

[169] See for a detailed overview of the measures to be taken the Hungarian government's Action Plan for 2008–2009 in the framework of the Decade of Roma Inclusion Programme, to be found at www.romadecade.org (accessed August 2009). See also Kádar (2007), at 57-58.

[170] See Kádar (2007), at 58.

[171] See Kovalenko (2006).

[172] See the periodical report submitted by The Netherlands to the CERD in 2008, CERD/C/NLD/18, 14-16 and 28-9.

[173] See the website of the Ministry of Social Affairs and Employment at www.minszw.nl, under the heading '*gelijke behandeling*' ('equal treatment') (accessed August 2009).

[174] See www.minocw.nl/aanvalopschooluitval and at www.minocw.nl/achterstanden (accessed August 2009).

[175] See the periodical report submitted by The Netherlands to the CERD in 2008, CERD/C/NLD/18, 9.

In the Belgian context the majority of the measures in employment have been taken at the federated level. The federal government has adopted a few measures to ensure equal treatment in its recruitment policy,[176] and has set up a department that provides support to employers who intend to adopt a diversity policy.[177] At the federated level, the Flemish government has included in its most recent decree on equality a section on 'equal opportunities policy',[178] which entails an obligation for all departments to develop target figures and action plans to increase equal opportunities for vulnerable groups. It should be mentioned, however, that racial and ethnic minorities have not been recognised as the main target groups of Flemish equal opportunity policy, and have received less attention than women, homosexuals and disabled persons.[179] The Flemish government has furthermore adopted specific measures to assist employers in adopting diversity plans and to facilitate the integration of newly arrived immigrants in the labour market.[180]

Positive action in education is only found at the federated level in Belgium, in view of the exclusive competence of the Communities in this matter. Thus, the Flemish government has adopted a decree on equal opportunities in education, which entails inter alia the obligation for schools to participate in cooperation forms aimed at ending segregation and increasing inclusion of disadvantaged pupils.[181] The French and German Communities have adopted decrees that offer special training classes for newly arrived immigrant children, and for additional financial support for schools in order to accommodate socially disadvantaged children.[182]

The strong focus on the fields of employment and education is not surprising, since these areas are of basic importance for the social inclusion and participation of minorities. Moreover, these fields have traditionally been

---

[176] See www.selor.be, under the heading '*gelijke kansen*' ('equal opportunities') (accessed August 2009).

[177] See www.expertisepunt.be/node/378 (accessed August 2009).

[178] See Articles 6-13 of the *Decree of the Flemish Community containing a framework for the Flemish equal opportunities and equal treatment policy*, 10 July 2008.

[179] See www.gelijkekansen.be (accessed August 2009).

[180] See www.werk.be (accessed August 2009) for the policy on assisting employers in adopting diversity plans. As regards the integration policies, the following can be said: on 23 January 2009, the Flemish Parliament approved a draft decree on Flemish integration policy, the final text of which has not yet been adopted. This decree entails measures with regard to the training and coaching of newly arrived immigrants in Flanders; see www.politics.be/persmededelingen/20811 (accessed August 2009).

[181] *Decree of the Flemish Community of 28 June 2002 on equal opportunities in education(I)*. See also Overbeeke (2003), at 744-746.

[182] For the French policy, see www.enseignement.be under the headings of '*primo arrivants, classe passerelle*' ('newly arrived persons, temporary class') and '*décret discriminations positives*' (decree on positive discrimination' (accessed August 2009). For the German policy, see the *Decree of the German-speaking Community of 17 December 2001 on schooling for first-generation immigrant pupils*.

strongly regulated by the state, which facilitates the adoption of positive action measures. Still, minorities experience disadvantages also in the other fields covered by the material scope of the RED, which would ideally be tackled as well. The inclusive focus of the Hungarian framework sets a good example in this respect, although it must be emphasised that the position of the Roma in this Member State is much more serious than that of the immigrant communities in Belgium and the Netherlands, or the Russian-speaking minority in Estonia.

Preference for weaker forms of positive action

It is remarkable that the stronger forms of positive action in McCrudden's classification, more particularly *preferential treatment* and *redefinition of merit,* are hardly found at the national level. One example of the former category is provided by the Hungarian framework, where a rule of preferential treatment applies to socially disadvantaged students, who only need to meet 80 per cent of the normal qualification requirements for a place in university faculties.[183]

The majority of the positive action measures in the Member States are, however, situated in the weaker categories distinguished by McCrudden, more particularly *activities aimed at identifying and eradicating discriminatory practices*, *facially neutral policies that tend to favour persons belonging to disadvantaged groups* and *outreach programmes specifically aimed at particular groups*. The mainstreaming duties in Hungary and Estonia are an example of the first category, as is the awareness raising campaign among employers with regard to discrimination in the workplace, organised by the Dutch Ministry of Social Affairs and Employment. The Dutch, Flemish and Hungarian measures aimed at ending school segregation are furthermore a good example of positive action of the first category. An example of the second category is provided by the campaign against early school-leaving of the Dutch Ministry of Education. The diversity policy for public servants and measures supporting employers in carrying out a diversity policy of the Dutch Ministry of Social Affairs and Belgian federal government also fall within the second category.

Many measures of the third category, *outreach programmes*, can furthermore be found in the Member States. For example, the measures developed for newly arrived immigrants by the Belgian Communities fall within this category, as do the language courses offered within the framework of the Estonian Integration Program. The various measures to support socially disadvantaged students also belong to this category, just as the many measures developed by Hungary to support the Roma minority within the framework of

183 This is determined in Article 19/A of *Government Decree 268/2000 on the General Rules of Admission Procedures of Universities*. See Kádar (2007), at 57.

the Decade of Roma Inclusion. Finally, the special measures developed by the Dutch Ministry of Social Affairs in cooperation with the local municipalities to improve the participation of immigrant youth and women in the labour process can be grouped in this category.

It is interesting to note that racial and ethnic minorities are mostly indirectly targeted by these measures, as target groups are often defined in terms of social disadvantage rather than of ethnicity. In view of the difficulty in obtaining racial or ethnic data in many Member States and the risk of stigmatisation, this practice can be considered to enhance the effectiveness of positive action measures. Furthermore, the preference for weaker forms of positive action is understandable, because the stronger forms produce conflict with the prohibition of direct and indirect discrimination and are generally less popular in societies. Moreover, the stronger forms of positive action are more risky in terms of perpetuating harmful stereotypes, which calls for prudence. Still, in cases of grave disadvantage, preferential treatment may be the only measure that works effectively. The possibility of adopting this form of positive action should therefore not be absolutely dismissed.

Some identity-focused measures

Only in the two newer Member States, Estonia and Hungary, can measures aimed at the preservation of the separate identity of minority groups be found. In both Member States, special acts have been adopted in order to accommodate the identity interests of minorities, as was mentioned in Chapter 1.[184] Both acts allow for the instalment of forms of local minority self-government and special institutions or schools aimed at preserving the minority identity. In Estonia these special provisions have hardly been made use of, whereas in Hungary many minority self-governments have been installed.

In Estonia, there has furthermore been some activity with regard to minority education. In 2006 a special department of Ethnic Minority Education was launched; its main aim is to shape and monitor the education of ethnic minorities, address the interests of minorities and support inclusion of their linguistic and cultural identity in education.[185]

The Hungarian government has adopted a number of measures aimed at supporting the Roma minority in preserving its identity within the framework of the Decade of Roma Inclusion. Moreover, as was mentioned before, the Hungarian HETA accommodates to some extent identity-related interests, by providing for the possibility of setting up minority institutions and schools.

[184] For Estonia this is the *Act on the Cultural Autonomy of Minorities*, adopted on 26 October 1993. For Hungary, this is *Act LXXVII on the Rights of National and Ethnic Minorities*, which was also adopted in 1993.

[185] Resolution 301 of the Ministry of Education, 4 April 2006. See also Kovalenko (2006), at 15.

It should be emphasised that only this latter form of accommodation of identity interests can be linked to the RED, as the HETA is the implementing instrument of this directive.

Similar attention for the preservation of the separate identity of minority groups is not found in the two other Member States. There is rather a counteracting force visible in the relatively recently adopted measures in Flanders and the Netherlands aimed at integrating immigrants into mainstream society.[186] Whereas these integration policies can be considered to produce greater social participation and inclusion of minorities in society, they also risk fostering assimilationist tendencies, which calls for prudent implementation.

7.8. Summary and conclusion

The analysis in this chapter differs from that of the previous chapters in a number of respects. First of all, whereas the previous chapters relied on a fairly obvious and clear-cut connection between the discrimination concepts and minority protection, the analysis in this chapter started from the position that positive action stands in a complex relationship to minority protection. On the one hand, positive action is a very important instrument for the achievement of equality for vulnerable racial and ethnic groups in Member State societies. On the other hand, positive action measures can harm the cause of minority protection in various ways, for instance by reinforcing negative stereotypes or disempowering minority groups. In view of this ambiguous relationship between positive action and minority protection, this chapter took a balanced position, according to which positive action measures are only beneficial if they are appropriately tailored to the context within which they are to operate.

Secondly, whereas the previous chapters dealt with the various obligations that Member States have under the RED, this chapter could only go so far as to examine which opportunities they have to enact measures of positive action, and which restraints they have to take into account. This is due to the particular nature of Article 5 RED, which permits and circumscribes the adoption of positive action measures in the Member States. In other words, the article provides for a justification possibility of positive action measures that would otherwise be considered to constitute discrimination.

In view of these particular features of the positive action provision of the RED, this chapter took a dual focus. On the one hand, it examined which opportunities, pitfalls and legal limitations are relevant for effective and

[186] See for a detailed description of the Dutch policy in this regard *Integratienota 2007-2011: zorg dat je erbij hoort!* ('Memo on Integration 2007-2011: make sure you participate!') of the Ministry of Public Housing, Environmental Planning and Environment, to be found at www.minvrom.nl (accessed August 2009). The Flemish decree on minorities was transformed in January 2009 into a decree on integration; see for more details at www.marinokeulen.be/mod_cat/inburgering (accessed August 2009).

legitimate positive action schemes. On the other hand, it explored the outer limits of the playing field that Member States have. These latter limits can be seen as constituting the minimum level of protection required by the RED with regard to positive action, as they are not optional, but have to be complied with by the Member States.

Opportunities and pitfalls for positive action

The first part of the theoretical framework explored the playground available to Member States as regards positive action and identified the different goals and forms of positive action that can be pursued. It was explained that there are weaker and stronger forms of positive action: the weaker ones not singling out any vulnerable groups while still benefiting them, and the stronger ones expressly targeting particular groups. It was furthermore pointed out that the risk of counter productivity increases with the stronger forms of positive action. As these aim at particular groups, they especially risk perpetuating stereotypes, exacerbating group tensions in society, and benefiting the relatively privileged group members instead of the more vulnerable ones.

In view of these risks, combined with the general perception that strong forms of positive action are not terribly popular in Member State societies, it was not surprising to note in the case study part that the Member States have preferred to pursue the relatively weaker forms of positive action. After all, these measures are easier to justify to the broader public. Thus, many forms of general measures were found, which in an indirect way benefit vulnerable groups, such as language training courses, measures to support employers in carrying out a diversity policy, desegregation measures in education, and awareness raising campaigns. Moreover, only in the two newer Member States, Hungary and Estonia, measures that accommodate identity-related interests of minority groups were found. Both Member States have in place specific Minority Acts that allow for some forms of autonomy, and have provided for possibilities of education tailored to minority identities. Still, the Estonian Minority Act is generally perceived as a dead letter that does not substantively alter the position of minorities in society. The Netherlands and Belgium have not adopted any comparable measures that serve the second pillar of minority protection.

It was furthermore remarkable that the RED had a very modest impact on Member State practice as regards positive action: only a handful of measures could be identified that were adopted on the basis of the RED. This can perhaps be explained by the general preference among Member States for weaker positive action measures, which do not need any express legal legitimisation, since they generally do not come into conflict with the prohibition of discrimination.

The case study part furthermore revealed that the possibility of imposing duties of positive action have been recognised in all four Member States, which was an interesting finding, in view of the lack of any provision for such duties in the RED. Still, in practice this possibility has been made use of to a limited extent. The Estonian EETA requires Ministries to mainstream the principle of equality in their policies, and requires Estonian educational institutes to provide training on the principle of equality, but these duties are not monitored in any way. In Hungary, certain state-funded and state-owned actors are required to set in place an equal opportunities plan for their employers, which is monitored in a formalistic way by the AET. In the Netherlands, there is a pseudo-duty of positive action for actors who have publicly committed to a positive action policy: they are required by the ETC and Dutch courts to act in accordance with this policy.

Limits to positive action: minimum baseline of protection

In the second part of the theoretical framework the minimum level of protection against potentially discriminatory forms of positive action as required by Article 5 RED was examined. The analysis revealed that the limits that need to be respected by Member States only apply to the stronger forms of positive action, that is those that target a protected group. It was explained that the exact contours of the minimum baseline are not yet fully outlined, since the ECJ has not yet had the opportunity to interpret Article 5 RED. Still, the ECJ's jurisprudence on positive action in the field of sex equality law is most likely transposable to quite an extent to the framework of the RED, and was therefore used for the analysis.

The case study part confirmed this impression and revealed that the four Member States under study have to a considerable degree transposed the sex equality acquis to the field of racial discrimination. It was shown that the tendency of the ECJ to approach positive action as an exception to the equality principle has found resonance at the national level. This holds particularly the Netherlands and Belgium, which have unambiguously retained a similar perspective; in Hungary and Estonia it is less clear whether positive action is seen as an exception to the equality principle. The exception-based perspective would seem to deny the reality that positive action furthers the aim of substantive equality and accordingly is wholly in line with the equality principle. Still, to the extent that it is not coupled with overly strict scrutiny of positive action measures, its effects are mostly symbolic in nature.

It was furthermore pointed out in the theoretical framework that the ECJ has developed a distinction between equality of opportunities and equality of results in the field of sex equality law, and has permitted only equality of opportunities as a legitimate aim to be sought after by positive action measures. As this distinction is not practical in the context of as broad a material scope as the RED's, it was suggested that this distinction is preferably not copied by Member States. So far only the Dutch framework has clearly followed the ECJ in this respect; the Hungarian HETA uses the notion of 'opportunities', but it is not certain that the ECJ's particular understanding will be followed. It is unclear whether Belgium and Estonia will apply the opportunities versus results distinction in the future.

The case study made clear that the Member States have all followed the guidelines developed by the ECJ in the field of gender equality law for the test of legality of positive action measures. All four Member States have accepted the proportionality-based model of review of the ECJ as the mechanism to determine the legality of a particular positive action measure. The Dutch ETC was found to be the only national body that has further elaborated the regime set in place by the ECJ. It has for instance made expressly clear that potentially indirectly discriminatory positive action measures are to be scrutinised by the same set of requirements as potentially directly discriminatory measures. Furthermore, the ETC has set in place a transparency requirement, according to which the author of a positive action measure must make public his intention of using it.

It was remarkable to find that the Member States have in some instances set even stricter limits for positive action than those required at the European level. For instance, whereas Article 5 RED recognises both the elimination and prevention of disadvantages as legitimate goals of positive action, three out of four Member States apply a backward-looking perspective and only permit measures that aim at eliminating discrimination. Only Hungary allows for taking preventive positive action measures. It was explained that a backward-looking perspective is less sensitive to the need for pro-active restructuring of society and accommodating identity-related interests, and therefore contributes to a lesser degree to substantive equality than does a forward-looking perspective. It was moreover shown that both Belgium and Hungary require public actor initiative and/or approval for the stronger forms of positive action, which makes it much harder for private actors to initiate such measures. In a different way, the Estonian framework appears to have set in place an additional barrier for positive action measures, by requiring quantitative evidence of the disadvantage targeted by a particular positive action measure. Case law will need to show whether disadvantages that can only be established by qualitative evidence will actually be refused as legitimate causes for positive action measures in Estonia.

On the other hand, the Dutch and Hungarian frameworks each facilitate or encourage positive action in a way that is not required by the RED. The Hungarian framework provides for possibilities of initiating positive action aimed at identity interests of minorities, which is a unique feature of this framework and allows for taking positive action measures that serve the second pillar of minority protection. The Dutch framework is clearly based on a substantive equality outlook, as it applies an asymmetric approach to positive action, which means that only structurally disadvantaged groups in society can be targeted by positive action. The Dutch ETC, moreover, displays a proactive and encouraging attitude vis-à-vis positive action measures. It does not shy away from making recommendations to make positive action measures more effective, and has used the appropriateness test as a tool to apply certain quality requirements for positive action measures. Practice has furthermore revealed that the ETC intensely looks for the right balance to be struck between the need for proactive measures to improve the situation of vulnerable groups in society, and the need to avoid negative effects for the group, as well as for individuals not belonging to the protected group.

In conclusion, positive action has clearly proved to be unsuitable for a 'black or white'-type of analysis. It holds great minority protection potential, but, if applied in an imprudent way, risks undermining the very aims it intends to achieve. From this perspective, the strict limits set in place for the stronger forms of positive action by both the ECJ and the national frameworks are understandable and, for the most part, even desirable. Still, the limits set in place by the Member States in addition to the requirements of the ECJ are unnecessary and overly restrictive. These limits would seem to point to a hesitant attitude vis-à-vis the stronger forms of positive action, which is also reflected in the limited number of such positive action measures currently operating in the Member States. On the other hand, the general recognition of the legitimacy of positive action duties in all four Member States would seem to indicate that positive action is understood to be an important tool in the anti-discrimination framework. These seemingly contradictory approaches should perhaps be seen as underscoring the complexity of the relationship of positive action with the overall principle of equality.

Notably, only in Hungary and the Netherlands the hesitant attitude towards forward-looking positive action measures was offset by a number of positive features that encourage the adoption of certain forms of positive action. This finding adds weight to the argument that a strong historical focus on non-discrimination and minority protection can positively impact on the quality of implementation. Moreover, it is clear that the traditional priorities of the national paradigms clearly come back in the way in which they approach positive action. Thus, the Dutch framework is clearly geared towards achieving substantive equality, whereas the Hungarian framework puts much emphasis on serving identity-related interests of minorities.

Chapter 8

Conclusion

8.1. Theoretical analysis: the potential of the RED for minority protection

As the first decade after the adoption of the RED draws to a close, there is quite some reason for optimism as regards the impact of this instrument on the level of minority protection in the Member States. As was explained in Chapter 1, an effective minority protection regime is generally considered to rest on two pillars: a pillar of effective protection of general human rights with special relevance for minorities, particularly the right to non-discrimination, and a pillar of special minority rights for minority groups. The theoretical sections in this study therefore examined the extent to which the RED could set in place effective mechanisms in order to serve these two pillars of minority protection. This meant an assessment on different levels: attention was paid not only to conceptual clarity, consistency and overall effectiveness, but also to the manner in which substantive equality and identity-related interests of minority groups could inform the application of the RED.

From the theoretical sections in this study it can be concluded that the RED provides Member States with an appropriately equipped toolbox to set in place an inclusive and effective anti-discrimination regime. It was shown that the broad scope of the RED and its extensive set of discrimination concepts allow for an effective and inclusive response to racial and ethnic discrimination as it manifests itself today in Member States' societies. The emphasis on horizontal application of the non-discrimination principle in addition to vertical application, the extensive material scope of the RED, the provision for four separate and complementary concepts of discrimination and the provision for positive action measures together make for a solid foundation for a powerful anti-discrimination framework.

Moreover, it was shown that the RED to a high degree can be applied in accordance with a substantive equality perspective: a number of opportunities were identified to take into account the special position of vulnerable racial and ethnic groups in society when implementing the RED's provisions. The concept of indirect discrimination was shown to be particularly relevant in this respect, as its application inherently entails consideration of the situation of vulnerable groups in society. The possibility of inferring positive duties vis-à-vis protected groups is a very valuable asset of this concept, which can therefore have a far-reaching impact on Member States' societies, depending on how progressively it is applied. In addition, the concept of positive action was put forward as an essential tool for furthering substantive equality in society, in particular because this concept is can be used in a pro-active way and is not dependent on individual litigation.

In theory, therefore, it is possible to implement the RED in such a way that the first pillar aspect of minority protection is adequately served.

In addition, a number of possibilities were identified for serving the second pillar aspect of minority protection, that is, identity-related interests of minority groups. It was for instance pointed out that certain aspects of the material scope, such as non-economical social advantages that comprise inter alia linguistic rights, are of special relevance for minority groups seeking to maintain a separate identity. It was furthermore explained that identity-related interests could inform the application of concepts such as indirect discrimination and positive action, and could even call for certain positive duties that actively accommodate identity-related interests of protected groups.

It should be emphasised that quite a portion of the minority protection potential of the RED can only be realised by interpreting the provisions of this instrument in a particular, minority-sensitive fashion. It was shown that there are still many questions as regards the exact position of the minimum baseline of protection set in place by the RED, and the theoretical sections identified a number of uncertainties and obscurities as to the proper interpretation of the RED.

It was furthermore shown that the European equality acquis as developed by the ECJ shows a number of lacunae and inconsistencies, which means that this Court's jurisprudence can only be drawn from to a limited extent to interpret the RED in an effective and minority-sensitive way. The ECJ has so far applied an ad hoc approach to equality law, dealing only with the matters that rise before it, and not necessarily paying much attention to overall consistency and stability of the developing acquis. One serious deficiency in this respect is the inconsistent and conceptually inappropriate way in which the ECJ has approached the delineation of the concept of direct discrimination vis-à-vis indirect discrimination. In addition, the ECJ has so far refrained from developing clear guidelines for the application of indirect discrimination, which is generally perceived to be a complex concept. It should be mentioned that the jurisprudence on positive action admittedly provides an exception in this respect, as the eleven judgments on this topic have apparently set in place a coherent and balanced regime for positive action.

In view of the relative inexperience with anti-discrimination law on the Member State level, it would be greatly beneficial if the RED would be given more substance at the European level. The theoretical analyses in the foregoing chapters provide some insight into the way in which this can be done in such a way that increases the level of minority protection. The most important matters will be summarised here. Thus, from a substantive equality-oriented, minority-sensitive perspective, the 'to do' list as regards the interpretation of the RED would be as follows:

Personal scope

1. Provide for direct liability of all potential actors in the fields covered by the material scope, or require well-functioning systems of personal/vicarious liability or positive duties for principally envisaged actors.

2. Provide for flexible and context-sensitive definitions of racial and ethnic origin, in line with international law and modern understandings of which proxies are nowadays used to perpetrate racism, such as religion and language.

3. Make provision for intersectional discrimination, by way of expressly recognising this particular type of discrimination and applying the concepts of discrimination in accordance with this understanding. If different regimes apply for the different grounds implicated in a case of intersectional discrimination, apply the regime that offers the highest level of protection.

4. Recognise that differences in treatment based on nationality are covered by the RED to the extent that they constitute indirect racial discrimination.

MATERIAL SCOPE

5. Make clear that the 'within limits' clause of Article 3(1) RED cannot be used to set in place additional delineations of the material scope of national anti-discrimination law: all aspects mentioned in this article should be fully covered.

6. Apply non-market based interpretations of 'employment' (abandon the remuneration factor) and 'goods' and 'services' (abandon the profit aim and include public services).

7. Apply a clear, transparent and narrow interpretation of the 'available to the public' clause in Article 3(1)(h) RED: only those goods or services that objectively belong to the sphere of the right to privacy or the freedom of association are to be excluded from the scope of anti-discrimination law. In addition, make clear that the clause should be applied on a case-by-case basis.

DIRECT DISCRIMINATION

8. Develop a clear, transparent and conceptually meaningful distinction of direct versus indirect discrimination. Direct discrimination should cover only those actions for which the direct cause or reason was a person's racial or ethnic origin, including covert direct discrimination and discrimination by proxy. No effects-based approach should be applied, and no claims for special provision for particular needs should be accommodated in the context of direct discrimination.

9. Recognise the possibility of direct discrimination manifesting itself in a collective fashion, and allow for statistical evidence of direct discrimination.

10. Reject any justificatory use of the comparison for direct discrimination; abandon the comparability test.

INDIRECT DISCRIMINATION

11. Adopt an inclusive approach for the first phase of the model of review: make clear that both qualitative and quantitative evidence is permissible; do not put much emphasis on the disadvantage requirement; do not impose additional requirements of the establishment of a formal difference in treatment or a causal link.

12. Develop clear benchmarks for the comparison to be carried out: which tests to apply, how to draw the pool of comparators. Make use of the comparability test only in order to draw the pool of comparators, and not to bring justificatory reasoning into the first phase of the model of review. Take into account historical discrimination, which has potentially tainted the pool of comparators.

13. Develop more sophisticated criteria for the objective justification test, and expressly include a proportionality stricto sensu test as part of the necessity test.

14. Recognise the possibility of inferring positive duties from the concept of indirect discrimination, and set in place appropriate parameters in order to protect the interests of the potential duty-bearers. There is in particular room for developing further-reaching positive duties for public actors, who have a duty under international law to make an active effort to improve the situation of vulnerable racial and ethnic groups in society.

HARASSMENT AND THE INSTRUCTION TO DISCRIMINATE

15. Provide more guidance as to the meaning of the various tests to be carried out for the concept of harassment: reject any requirement of proof of non-consent; set in place benchmarks for duties of principally envisaged actors, which preferably entail a structural duty in addition to an incidental duty of care.

16. Accept implicit forms of instruction as forming part of the concept of the instruction to discriminate and make clear that no discriminatory intent is required.

POSITIVE ACTION

17. Make clear that positive action emanates from the equality principle, and is not an exception to it.

18. Encourage Member States to adopt effective and useful positive action strategies. Make for instance use of the appropriateness test to set in place certain quality requirements.

This list reveals that no legislative changes are necessary, and that the RED can be made more effective simply by making use of the technique of interpretation. The ECJ can therefore play an important role in leading the way towards realisation of the RED as a more effective instrument in tackling discrimination, ensuring substantive equality and accommodating identity-related interests of minority groups. To be true, the ECJ cannot take on this role without the help of national courts, on which it is dependent for questions for preliminary rulings. Still, the ECJ could take on a more proactive attitude, by maximising the opportunities offered by questions for preliminary rulings to further develop the equality framework. So far, the ECJ has displayed a minimalist attitude, answering only those questions posed by national courts that it deems necessary, and moreover answering them in a cursory manner. The court could make much better use of the room provided by preliminary questions to progressively fill out those aspects of the European anti-discrimination framework that are still obscure, and to push the agenda of substantive equality further.

8.2. Case study sections: implementation at the national level and implications for minority protection

As the present study examined only four Member States, the conclusions presented here only concern these four countries. However, as was mentioned before, these four Member States make up a representative sample of the 27 EU Member States, and it is expected that the findings in this study are valid more generally and provide a good indication of the overall implementation process of the RED in the EU.

The case study sections of the previous chapters revealed that the implementation of the RED has had a clear impact at the national level and has undeniably aligned the national levels of protection against discrimination. The most obvious effect of the RED in this respect is the adoption of comprehensive, horizontally applicable anti-discrimination laws in those Member States in which there were only a number of anti-discrimination provisions in the national constitution and/or general civil and criminal law.

Prior to the implementation of the RED, the Netherlands was the only Member State that had a general act on equal treatment in place. At present, such acts exist in all four Member States.

Even at a more substantive level, the RED has had a converging effect, by producing to a considerable extent similar terms and concepts in national anti-discrimination law. Thus, whereas prior to implementation there were many sectors of public life not covered by national anti-discrimination provisions, the material scope of national anti-discrimination law is now the same for all four Member States, with minor differences. Moreover, in three out of four Member States there was a single concept of discrimination prior to the implementation of the RED, i.e. unjustified unequal treatment, whereas now all four have incorporated the more sophisticated system of four discrimination concepts of the RED. In addition, all Member States now apply the closed system of justification for direct discrimination of the RED instead of the open-ended justification possibility of their national constitutional systems. Finally, whereas an express provision for positive action was only present in the Dutch framework prior to the implementation of the RED, all four Member States now have in place such provisions.

All of this makes for a higher level of minority protection in the Member States: the first pillar of minority protection is much better served as a consequence of the RED, since the national anti-discrimination provisions now in place are much more comprehensive than before, and have more force.

Nevertheless, in spite of the undeniable harmonising and quality-enhancing effect of the RED, national frameworks still show a number of deficiencies, and there are moreover still many differences between them, reflecting national particularities.

It was interesting to see that compliance with those aspects of the minimum baseline that are already sufficiently clear was not complete. In some instances, unsatisfactory compliance can be attributed to lack of experience and knowledge of European law and equality law, as is for instance clearly the case in Hungary. The Hungarian AET has on a number of occasions displayed a misunderstanding of the systematics and the concepts of the RED. As this body is committed to complying with European law and the jurisprudence of the ECJ, it is expected that the deficiencies noted in this respect will evaporate over time.

Other deficiencies would seem to be attributable to the wish of the national legislator to maintain certain particularities of the existing national anti-discrimination paradigm. This was for instance clearly visible in the Netherlands, which already had a comprehensive anti-discrimination framework in place prior to the RED. The intricate web of justification possibilities of the Dutch GETA and the particular 'distinction'-based definitions of discrimination were greatly appreciated features in the national context and were therefore not altered in accordance with the RED. Only now, after having received a letter of notification from the European Commission, the Dutch government is taking steps to amend some aspects of the GETA that are not in line with the RED. Similar developments were visible in Hungary and Belgium, which initially maintained the Constitutional Courts' justification system for the equality principle, and only after a number of years amended it to bring it in line with the system of the RED. Hungary still maintains quite a peculiar justification system for indirect discrimination which can be traced back to the constitutional framework. These examples show that previous experience with anti-discrimination law is not invariably a factor that enhances the quality of implementation and can sometimes hamper full compliance with the RED.

Unsurprisingly there was found to be quite some divergence at the national level with regard to those aspects of anti-discrimination law that are not (clearly) regulated by the RED. Thus, Member States greatly differ in the way in which they have regulated matters as diverse as liability schemes, positive duties and discrimination based on nationality. Interestingly, the two Member States that have a strong traditional commitment either to anti-discrimination law (the Netherlands) or to minority protection (Hungary), have often preferred those options that entailed higher levels of protection. For instance, in both Member States positive duties of principally envisaged actors have been recognised, even though these are still underdeveloped in the Hungarian framework. Both Member States have furthermore included the ground of nationality in their anti-discrimination laws, and have therefore effectively sailed round the problematic exception of Article 3(2) RED. Furthermore, in Hungary the strong commitment to minority protection has produced specific provisions that accommodate second pillar minority interests, while in the Netherlands a clear emphasis on substantive equality can be identified in the ETC's quasi-jurisprudence, which has led to a relatively high level of protection in practice. These two examples illustrate how particular national interests and priorities can give a certain colour to implementation legislation and can enhance the level of protection beyond the requirements of the RED.

By contrast, Belgium and Estonia, the two states with sensitive minority issues (and as regards Estonia a complete lack of experience with anti-discrimination law), have generally opted for maintaining the level of protection required by the RED and have not exceeded it. Belgium does show one exception in this respect, as the new Belgian ARL protects against nationality discrimination, which goes beyond the requirements of the RED. The explanation lies probably in the fact that nationality discrimination has traditionally been categorised under racial and ethnic discrimination in Belgian criminal anti-racism law. This is thus an example of how previous experience with anti-discrimination law can favourably impact on the quality of implementing legislation. Furthermore, even though Belgium has generally not opted for a higher level of protection than required, it has set in place a rather robust anti-discrimination framework that is better designed in some respects than the RED. For instance, the material scope has been further exemplified, and matters of proof have been further elaborated than in the RED. The relatively high quality of Belgian implementation is explained by the fact that the government consulted a number of highly qualified anti-discrimination experts in the process of designing the new ARA, and in this way confirmed its commitment to setting in place an effective anti-discrimination framework.

Estonia, to the contrary, has set in place a very basic framework that is hardly any more specific than the RED, and does not offer a higher level of protection, save perhaps for the few unmonitored duties of Estonian ministries and educational institutions with regard to the promotion of equality. Moreover, the Estonian EETA provides for an overly broad justification possibility for direct discrimination, which is not permitted by the RED. This very basic track record is probably due to the fact that Estonia does not have much experience with European law, and that it is moreover the Member State with the least favourable national context for anti-discrimination law, as became clear in the course of the interviews with numerous experts and officials. The RED and other European equality instruments were not very favourably received in Estonia, as discrimination was generally perceived as a non-issue. According to popular Estonian mentality, individuals are themselves responsible for their success in life and should not try to hold others accountable for their misfortunes under the guise of 'discrimination'. Despite this unfavourable background, a first step has been taken, and the regime set in place by the EETA is revolutionary for Estonia in many ways. The Estonian example shows that the quality of implementation greatly depends on the national context, and that the top-down imposition of anti-discrimination law has its limits. It also highlights the importance of developing a sophisticated and high quality framework at the European level by the ECJ, which will force Member States such as Estonia to follow suit, as they will not easily make improvements on their own initiative.

The case study sections in this study revealed that many aspects of the national anti-discrimination frameworks are still in their infancy and need to further crystallise in the future. Moreover, many of the inconsistencies and flaws that were identified at the European level were also found at the national level. The Netherlands provided a very positive exception in this respect, and the practice of the Dutch ETC is in many ways exemplary for other national courts and bodies. It should not be overlooked, however, that this body has had many years to develop its sophisticated and coherent approach to discrimination, and it is therefore not very surprising that the other national frameworks still lag behind.

The recommendations that were outlined above for the European level are also valid for the national frameworks to the extent that they have not yet been followed up. In addition, the case studies revealed a number of country-specific steps that could be taken in order to make national anti-discrimination law as effective, clear and consistent as possible, which is bound to have positive repercussions for minorities. The most important recommendations are recapitulated here.

BELGIUM

1. Endeavour to come to a better alignment of the new federal ARL and the various federated instruments.

2. Abandon the notion of 'intentional indirect discrimination' and accept covert direct discrimination as a form of direct discrimination.

3. Apply a more lenient approach to the causal link required for discriminatory harassment than for direct discrimination.

4. Abandon the requirement of prior public consent for positive action initiated by private actors.

ESTONIA

1. Make clear that the open-ended justification possibility in Article 9(1) EETA does not apply to direct racial discrimination.

2. Make clear that differences in treatment based on nationality should be scrutinised under the EETA to the extent that they constitute indirect racial discrimination.

HUNGARY

1. Align the circle of private actor addressees of the HETA with the requirements of the RED.

2. Abandon the use of the GDOR as an open justification possibility in disguise.

3. Align the justification scheme for indirect discrimination with the requirements of the RED.

4. Abandon the practice of allowing for a justification for harassment.

5. Abandon the requirement of prior public consent for positive action initiated by private actors.

THE NETHERLANDS

1. Endeavour to make Dutch courts more familiar with the GETA anti-discrimination framework as developed by the ETC.

2. Interpret 'services' as comprising public services.

3. Align the GETA's system of justification possibilities with the requirements of the RED.

Again most of these recommendations can be followed up by making use of the technique of interpretation, and national courts and supervisory bodies therefore have a big responsibility: their interpretation can make the difference between a dead text that does nothing more than offer formal equality, or a living instrument that furthers the aim of substantive equality and radically alters society into a more stable and coherent community of groups and individuals of equal worth. As was mentioned before, it is highly desirable that the ECJ takes the lead in this process and makes use of every opportunity it gets to increase the effectiveness of the RED by way of providing clear and coherent interpretations in line with the suggestions that were mentioned earlier. The case studies have revealed that the Member States generally make an effort to comply with European law, which means that a strong and progressive approach by the ECJ will probably find resonance at the national level. In this respect, the future looks bright.

In fact, the true bottleneck for the coming of age of the RED as "the most efficient minority protection tool in the EU"[1] is perhaps not so much inadequate implementation, but rather a lack of initiative on the side of the beneficiaries of anti-discrimination legislation. Estonia provides an excellent example of this challenge. Even though the RED was not very welcome in this Member State and was clearly imposed from the top down, it did eventually lead to the adoption of an act that mostly complies with the RED. However, very few discrimination cases have come to the surface so far in Estonia, none of which concerned racial or ethnic discrimination. This is mainly due to the aforementioned public mentality according to which discrimination is a non-issue and individuals are themselves responsible for their success in life. The

1 See section 1.1.

Estonian example makes clear that, in addition to clear and high-quality rules, it is necessary that people know about them and that lawyers know how to apply them. Moreover, awareness-raising and publicity as regards the problem of discrimination is essential. In this respect, the second part of the RED, which deals inter alia with awareness raising and support mechanisms, is an essential component of the RED, without which the first part cannot be truly achieved.

One Hungarian proverb claims that "one acre of the land of performance is worth twenty acres of the land of promise", which seems particularly suited for the RED. This study made clear that the 'land of promise' of the RED is very wide and fertile, and offers great potential for minority protection. At the same time, the 'land of performance' was found to be underdeveloped and not yet fully explored. It is to be hoped that the 'land of performance' will be much better cultivated in the second decade of the RED's existence, which is about to commence.

Jurisprudence and Quasi-Jurisprudence

A. International Supervisory Bodies

1. Committee on the Elimination of Racial Discrimination (CERD)

Individual complaints

Diop v. France, CERD 2/1989, 10 May 1991
GAC Enkelaar v. France, CERD 2/1989, 18 March 1991

Concluding Observations

Concluding Observations on Albania, 2003, CERD/C/63/CO/1
Concluding Observations on Estonia, 2006, CERD/C/EST/CO/7
Concluding Observations on Ghana, 2003, CERD/C/62/C)/04
Concluding Observations on Guyana, 2006, CERD/C/Guy/CO/14
Concluding Observations on Morocco, 2003, CERD/C/62/CO/05
Concluding Observations on Slovenia, 2003, CERD/C/62/CO/09
Concluding Observations on Turkmenistan, 2003, CERD/C/TKM/CO/5
Concluding Observations on the United Kingdom, 2003, CERD/C/63/CO/ 11
Concluding Observations on Uzbekistan, 2006, CERD/C/UZB/CO/5

General Recommendations

CERD General Recommendation No. 19, Racial segregation and apartheid (Art. 3), 18 August 1995

CERD General Recommendation No. 25, on Gender related dimensions of racial discrimination,

20 March 2000

CERD General Recommendation No. 29, on Descent, 1 November 2002

CERD General Recommendation No. 30, on Discrimination Against Non Citizens, 1 October 2004.

2. Committee on Economic, Social and Cultural Rights (CESCR)

GENERAL COMMENTS

General Comment No. 13 on the right to education, E/C.12/1999/10

General Comment No. 14 on the right to the highest attainable standard of health, E/C.12/2000/4

General Comment No. 7 on forced evictions, E/1998/22 Annex IV.

General Comment No. 19 on the right to social security, E/C.12/GC/19

3. Human Rights Committee (HRC)

INDIVIDUAL COMPLAINTS

Gueye v. France, Human Rights Committee (HRC), 6 April 1989, Communication 196/1989, CCPR/C/35/D/196/1985

GENERAL COMMENTS

General Comment No. 23, The rights of minorities (Art. 27), 8 April 1994.

General Comment No. 15, The position of aliens under the Covenant, 11 April 1986.

B. European Courts and Supervisory Bodies

1. Advisory Committee on the Framework Convention for National Minorities (ACFCNM)

COUNTRY OPINIONS

Second Opinion on Estonia, 24 February 2005, ACFC/OP/II(2005)001

Second Opinion on Germany, 1 March 2006, ACFC/OP/II(2006) 001

Second Opinion on Norway, 5 October 2006, ACFC/OP/II(2006)006

Second Opinion on the Russian Federation, 11 May 2006, ACFC/OP/II(2006)004

COMMENTARIES

Commentary on the effective participation of persons belonging to national minorities in cultural, social and economic life and in public affairs, 27 February 2008, ACFC/31DOC(2008)001

2. European Committee on Social Rights (ECSR)

INDIVIDUAL COMPLAINTS

Autism Europe v. France, complaint no. 13/2002, 4 November 2003

ERRC v. Bulgaria, complaint no. 31/2005, 8 October 2006

ERRC v. Italy, complaint no. 27/2004, 7 December 2005

3. European Court of Human Rights (ECtHR)

D.H. and others v. the Czech Republic, No. 57325/00, 7 february 2006

D.H. and others v. Czech Republic, no 57325/00, 13 November 2007

Gaygusuz v. Austria, no. 17371/90, 16 September 1996

Niedzwiecki v. Germany, no. 58453/00, 25 October 2005

Sampanis and others v. Greece, no. 32526/05, 5 June 2008

Timishev v. Russia, no.'s 55762/00 and 55974/00, 13 December 2005

4. European Court of Justice (ECJ) and the EFTA Court

Abrahamsson v. Fogelqvist, Case C-407/98, 6 July 2000

Allonby v. Accrington & Rossendale College and others, Case C-256/01, 13 January 2004

Allué and Coonan v. Università degli studi di Venezia, Case 33/88, 30 May 1989

Angelika Helmig and Waltraud Schmidt v. Deutsche Angestellten-Krankenkase a.o., Joined cases C-399/92, C-409/92, C-425/92, C-34/93, C-50/93 and C-78/93, 15 December 1994

Badeck v. Hessische Ministerpräsident, Case C-158/97, 28 March 2000

Bartsch v. BSH, Case C-427/06, 22 May 2008

Bickel and Franz, Case C-274/96, 24 November 1998

Bilka Kaufhaus v. von Hartz, Case 170/84, 13 May 1986

Birds Eye Walls Ltd v. Friedel M Roberts, Case C-132/92, 9 November 1993

Blaizot v. University of Liège, Case 24/86, 2 February 1988

Briheche v. Ministère de l'intérieur, de la sécurité intérieure et des libertés locales, Case C-319/03, 29 June 2004

Briheche v. Ministre de l'Intérieur de la sécurité intérieure et des libertés locales, Case C-319/03, 30 September 2004

Brown v. Rentokil, Case C-394/96, 30 June 1998

Burton v. British Railway Board, Case 19/81, 16 February 1982

Caballero v. Fogasa, Case C-442/00, 12 December 2002

Caisse régionale d'assurance maladie de Lille (CRAM) v. Diamante Palermo, née Toia, Case 237/78, 12 July 1979

Centrum voor gelijkheid van kansen en racismebestrijding v. Firma Feryn NV, Case C-54/07, 10 July 2008

Chacón Navas v. Eurest Colectividades, Case C-13/05, 11 July 2006

Coleman v. Attridge Law and Steve Law, Case C-303/06, 17 July 2008

Coloroll Pension Trustees Ltd tegen James Richard Russel a.o., Case C-200/91, 28 September 1994

Commission v. France, Case C-318/86, 30 June 1988

Commission v. Greece, Case C-559/07, 26 March 2009

Commission v Italy, Case 7/68, 10 December 1968

Commission v. UK, Case 165/82, 8 November 1983

Constance Christina Ellen Smith and others v. Avdel Systems Ltd, Case C-408/92, 28 September 1994

Defrenne v. Societe Anonyme Belge de navigation aerienne Sabena, Case 43/75, 8 April 1976

Dekker v. Stichting Vormingscentrum voor Jong Volwassenen, Case C-177/88, 8 November 1990

EFTA Surveillance Authority v. Norway, Case E-1/02, 24 January 2004

Elsner-Lakeberg v. and Nordrhein-Westfalen, Case C-285/02, 27 May 2004

Enderby v. Frenchay Health Authority and Secretary of State for Health, Case 127-92, 27 October 1993

Erika Steinicke v. Bundesanstalt fur Arbeit, Case C-77/02, 11 September 2003

Félix Palacios de la Villa v. Cortefiel Servicios SA, Case C-411/05, 15 February 2007

Félix Palacios de la Villa v. Cortefiel Servicios SA, Case C-411/05, 16 October 2007

Françoise Gravier v. City of Liège, Case 293/83, 13 February 1985

Gabriele Gruber v. Silhouette International Schmied & Co. KG, Case C-249/97, 14 September 1999

Griesmar v. Ministre de l'Economie, Case C-366/99, 29 November 2001

Habermann-Beltermann v. Arbeiterwohlfahrt, Case C-421/92, 5 May 1994

Helga Kutz-Bauer tegen Freie und Hansestadt Hamburg, Case C-187/00, 20 March 2003

Helga Nimz v. Freie und Hansestadt Hamburg, Case C-184/89, 7 February 1991

Hilde Schönheit v. stad Frankfurt am Main Case 4/02 and 5/02, 12 November 2001

Ingrid Rinner-Kühn v. FWW Spezial-Gebäudereinigung GmbH & Co. KG, Case 171/88, 13 July 1989

Jackson and Cresswell v. Chief Adjudication Officer, Cases C-63/91 and 64/91, 16 July 1992

Johnston v. Chief Constable of the RUC, Case C-222/84, 15 May 1986

Jørgensen v. Foreningen af Speciallæger, Sygesikringens Forhandlingsudvalg, Case C-226/98, 6 April 2000

Julia Schnorbus v. Land Hessen, Case C-79/99, 7 December 2000.

Kalanke v. Freie Hansestadt Bremen, Case C-450/93, 17 October 1995

Katharine Rinke v. Ärztekammer Hamburg, Case C-25/02, 9 September 2003

K.B. v. National Health Service Pensions Agency, Case C-117/01, 7 January 2004

Kuratorium für Dialyse und Nierentransplantation v. Lewark, Case C-457/93, 6 February 1994

Larsson v. Dansk Handel & Service, Case C-400/95, 29 May 1997

Lawrence and others v. Regent Office Care Ltd and others, Case C-320/00, 17 September 2002

Liefting v. Directie van het AZA, Case 23/83, 18 September 1984

Lindorfer v. Council, Case C-227/04, 27 October 2005

Lommers v. Minister van Landbouw, Case C-476/99, 19 March 2002

Maria Nelleke Gerda van den Akker and others v. Stichting Shell Pensioenfonds, Case C-28/93, 28 September 1994

Marschall v. Land Nordrhein-Westfalen, Case C-409/95, 11 November 1997

Marshall v. Southampton and South-West Hampshire Area Health Authority, Case 152/84, 26 February 1986

Maruko v. Versorgungsanstalt der deutschen Bühnen, Case C-267/06, 1 April 2008

Meyers v. Adjudication Officer, Case C-116/94, 13 July 1995

Ministère Public v. Mutsch, Case 137/84, 11 July 1985

National Pensions Office v. Emilienne Jonkman and others, joined cases C-231-233/06, 27 June 2007

Netherlands v. European Parliament and Council of the European Union, Case C-377/98, 9 October 2001

Netherlands v. Reed, Case 59/85, 17 April 1986

Nikoloudi v. Organismos Tilepikinonion Ellados AE, Case 196-02, 10 March 2005

O'Flynn v. Adjudication Officer, Case C-237/94, 23 May 1996

Omega Spielhallen- und Automatenaufstellungs-GmbH v. Oberbürgemeisterin de Bundesstadt Bonn, C-36/02, 14 October 2004

Othmar Michaeler a.o. v. Arbeitsinspektorat der Autonomen Provinz Bozen, Cases C-55/07 and C-56/07, 24 January 2008

R v. Secretary of State for Health, ex parte Richardson, Case C-137/94, 19 October 1995

Regina and Secretary of State for Employment, ex parte Nicole Seymour-Smith and Laura Perez, Case C-167/97, 9 February 1999

Richards v. Secretary of State for Work and Pensions, Case C-423/04, 27 April 2006

Sari Kiiski v. Tampereen kaupunki, Case C-116/06, 20 September 2007

Schnorbus v. Land Hessen, Case C-79/99, 7 December 2000

Silke-Karin Mahlburg v. Land Mecklenburg Vorpommern, Case C-207/98, 3 February 2000

Specialarbejderforbundet i Danmark v. Dansk Industri,/Royal Copenhagen, Case C-400/93, 31 May 1995

Stamatelaki v. NPDD Organismos Asfaliseos Eleftheron Epangelmatioi, Case C-444/05, 19 April 2007

Société Arcelor Atlantique et Lorraine e.a. v. Premier Ministre e.a., Case C-127/07, 16 December 2008

Sotgiu v. Deutsche Bundespost, Case 152/73, 12 February 1974

Tadao Maruko v. Versorgungsanstalt der Deutschen Bühnen, Case C-267/06, 6 September 2007

Tadao Maruko v. Versorgungsanstalt der Deutschen Bühnen, Case C-267/06, 1 April 2008

Tele Danmark v. Handels- og kontorfuntionaerernes Forbund, Case C-109/00, 4 October 2001

The Queen v. Secretary of State for Social Security, Case C-243/90, 4 February 1992

Ursula Voß v. Land Berlin, Case C-300/06, 6 December 2007

Vivien Prais v. Council, Case 130/75, 27 October 1976

Watts v. Bedford Primary Care Trust, Case C-372/04, 16 May 2006

Webb v. EMO Air Cargo, Case C-32/93, 14 July 1994

Werner Mangold v. Rüdiger Helm, Case C-144/04, 22 November 2005

Worringham and Humphreys v. Lloyds Bank, Case 69/80, 11 March 1981

C. National Jurisdictions

1. Belgium

COURTS

Court of Arbitration, no. 23/1989, 13 October 1989

Court of Arbitration, no. 18/1990, 23 May 1990

Court of Arbitration, no. 9/1994, 27 January 1994

Court of Arbitration, no. 106/2003, 22 July 2003

Judge of the Ghent Court of First Instance, summary procedure, 31 December 2003

Court of Arbitration, no. 157/2004, 6 October 2004

Court of Cassation, 9 November 2004

Ghent Correctional Tribunal, 10 May 2005

MRAX v. S.A. IMMO MDH, Brussels Court of First Instance, 3 June 2005

A.e.a. v. Provincie Limburg, Antwerp Court of Appeal, 14 June 2005

CEOOR and D. v. D. and M., Ghent Court of Appeal, 30 November 2005.

T.S.T. v. F.W.A.G., Tongeren Labour Court, no. 199/2005, 6 March 2007

Ghent Labour Court, 26 March 2007
Brussels Labour Court, no. KG-284, 6 April 2007
Charleroi Correctional Tribunal, 26 September 2008
Constitutional Court, Case No. 17/2009, 12 February 2009
Brussels Labour Court, 28 August 2009

2. Estonia

COURTS

Decision of the CRC of the Supreme Court, 3-4-1-1-02, 6 March 2002
Decision of the CRC of the Supreme Court, 3-4-1-2-02, 3 April 2002
Decision of the CRC of the Supreme Court, 3-1-3-10-02, 17 March 2003
Decision of the Supreme Court, 3-2-1-37-05, 24 May 2005
Decision of the CRC of the Supreme Court, 3-4-1-33-05, 20 March 2006

GENDER EQUALITY COMMISSIONER

'Boys only' case, mentioned on www.svv.ee (Estonian)

3. Hungary

COURTS

Constitutional Court, Decision no. 9/1990
Constitutional Court, Decision no. 61/92
Constitutional Court: Decision no. 45/2000
Constitutional Court: Decision no. 71/2002
Pest Central District Court, 20.P.85.346/2003/10, 1 July 2003
Metropolitan Court, 19.P.21.788/2004/10, 8 October 2004
Supreme Court, Pfv. IV.20.678/2005/5, 8 June 2005
Szabolcs Szatmár Bereg County Court, 1.p.21.752/2004/26, 13 June 2005
Debrecen Court of Appeal, Pf.II.20.513/2005/4, 28 October 2005
Debrecen Court of Appeal, Pf. l. 20.683/2005/7, 9 June 2006
Metropolitan Court, 8.K. 33.297/2006/5, 11 December 2006
Hajdú-Bihar County Court, 6.P.20.341/2006/50, 2 May 2007
Miskolc Labour Court, 19 June 2007, 6.m.755/2006/22
Supreme Court, Kfv.IV.37.450/2006/5, 11 July 2007
Supreme Court, Pfv. IV.20.936/2008/4, 19 November 2008

Authority on Equal Treatment (AET)

EBH/82/2005
EBH/37/4/2005
EBH/13/5/2005
EBH/10/2006
EBH/22/2006
EBH/69/2006
EBH/314/2006
EBH/450/2006
EBH/516/2006
EBH/553/2006
EBH/29/27/2006
EBH/23/2007
EBH/30/2007
EBH/46/2007
EBH/56/2007
EBH/226/2007
EBH/271/2007
EBH/278/2007
EBH/418/2007
EBH/419/2007
EBH/516/2007
EBH/681/2007
EBH/700/2007
EBH/704/2007
EBH/866/2007
EBH/142/3/2007
EBH/44/14/2007
EBH/81/2008
EBH/188/2008
EBH/231/2008
EBH/339/2008
EBH/476/2008
EBH/384/4/2008

4. The Netherlands

COURTS

High Council, 13 February 1998, NJ 1999/58
Leeuwarden District Court, 4 August 1999, LJN AA1048
High Council, 12 April 2002, NJ 2002/411
High Council 13 June 2000, NJ 2000/513
Central Appeal Council, 17 May 2001, LJN AB1704
Rotterdam District Court, 20 July 2001, LJN AD3775
High Council, 17 September 2002, NJ 2002/548
High Council 23 April 2004, NJ 2008/393
Injunction Judge of the Utrecht District Court, 15 November 2005, LJN AU6168
Utrecht District Court, 24 May 2006, LJN AY4333
The Hague District Court, 26 July 2006, LJN AY5005
Amsterdam Court of Appeal, 19 October 2006, LJN AZ0509
Utrecht District Court, 10 January 2007, LJN AZ7462
Rotterdam District Court, 6 August 2008, LJN BD 9643

EQUAL TREATMENT COMMISSION (ETC)

1997-29 ETC
1997-69 ETC
1997-99 ETC
1998-57 ETC
2001-34 ETC
2001-70 ETC
2001-78 ETC
2002-39 ETC
2002-84 ETC
2002-157 ETC
2002-159 ETC
2002-204 ETC
2003-18 ETC
2003-104 ETC
2003-132 ETC
2003-142 ETC
2003-149 ETC
2004-77 ETC
2004-116 ETC

2004-128 ETC
2004-173 ETC
2005-08 ETC
2005-25 ETC
2005-52 ETC
2005-65 ETC
2005-75 ETC
2005-88 ETC
2005-90 ETC
2005-91 ETC
2005-114 ETC
2005-144 ETC
2005-149 ETC
2005-167 ETC
2005-189 ETC
2005-190 ETC
2005-225 ETC
2006-5 ETC
2006-11 ETC
2006-18 ETC
2006-20 ETC
2006-53 ETC
2006-55 ETC
2006-61 ETC
2006-65 ETC
2006-71 ETC
2006-75 ETC
2006-110 ETC
2006-153 ETC
2006-202 ETC
2006-204 ETC
2006-206 ETC
2006-222 ETC
2006-256 ETC
2006-257 ETC
2006-258 ETC
2007-2 ETC
2007-4 ETC

2007-11 ETC
2007-12 ETC
2007-14 ETC
2007-40 ETC
2007-55 ETC
2007-57 ETC
2007-61 ETC
2007-73 ETC
2007-83 ETC
2007-85 ETC
2007-91 ETC
2007-92 ETC
2007-93 ETC
2007-96 ETC
2007-109 ETC
2007-126 ETC
2007-127 ETC
2007-132 ETC
2007-137 ETC
2007-142 ETC
2007-156 ETC
2007-157 ETC
2007-173 ETC
2007-193 ETC
2008-1 ETC
2008-2 ETC
2008-40 ETC
2008-44 ETC
2008-52 ETC
2008-81 ETC
2008-87 ETC
2008-102 ETC
2008-107 ETC
2008-109 ETC
2008-122 ETC
2008-127 ETC
2008-134 ETC
2008-143 ETC

D. Other Jurisdictions

1. Australia

Australian Iron and Steel PTY v. Banovic [1989] 168 CLR 165 FC 89/052

2. South Africa

Government of the Republic of South Africa v. Grootboom 2001 (1) SA 46 (CC)

3. United Kingdom

J.H. Walker Limited v. Hussain, 1996 ICR 291
Mandla v. Dowell Lee and Others 1983, IRLR 209
Nagarajan v. London Regional Transport ,1999 ICR 877
R. (ERRC) v. Immigration Officer at Prague Airport, 2004 UKHL 55.
Showboat Entertainment Centre Ltd v. Owens, 1984 IRLR 7 EAT
Weathersfield Ltd v. Sargent, 1999 IRLR 94, CA

4. United States of America

Brown v. Board of Education of Topeka, 347 U.S. 483 (1954)
Oncale v. Sundowner Offshore Services, Inc., 523 U.U. 75, 118 S. Ct. 998, 140 L. Ed.2d 201 (1998)

Selected General Bibliography

Books, articles and reports by author

Abrams (1998)
K. Abrams, 'Equality and impasse. Mobilizing group-based perspectives in an era of group-blindness', N. Devins, D.M. Douglas (eds.), *Redefining equality*, Oxford: Oxford University Press 1998, p. 13-28.

Adams (2003)
M. Adams, 'Vrijheid of gelijkheid? De nieuwe Belgische antidiscriminatiewet en de soevereiniteit in eigen kring', *Nederlands Tijdschrift voor Rechtsfilosofie en Rechtstheorie* 2003, p. 89-96.

Ahtela (2005)
K. Ahtela, 'The revised provisions on sex discrimination in European law: a critical assessment', *European Law Journal* 2005, p. 57-78.

Alexander (1992)
L. Alexander, 'What makes wrongful discrimination wrong? Biases, preferences, stereotypes and proxies', *University of Pennsylvania Law Review* 1992, p. 151-219.

Alexy (2001)
R. Alexy, 'Põhiõigused Eesti põhiseaduses', *Juridica eriväljaanna* 2001, p. 73-87.

Alkema (2003)
E.A. Alkema, '*Artikel 1 Grondwet in de Nederlandse constitutionele orde en de relatie met andere grondrechten en internationale gelijkheidsgeboden', Het discriminatieverbod van artikel 1 Grondwet: nationale en internationale perspectieven*, Leiden: NJCM Boekerij 2003.

Alofs & De Becker (2004)
E. Alofs, A. De Becker, 'De antidiscriminatiewet en het bestuursrecht', *Nieuw Juridisch Weekblad* 2004, p. 586-93.

Alves (2008)
J.L. Alves, 'Race and religion in the United Nations Committee on the Elimination of Racial Discrimination', *University of San Francisco law review* 2007/08, p. 941-982.

Arai-Takahashi (2002)
Y. Arai-Takahashi, *The margin of appreciation doctrine and the principle of proportionality in the jurisprudence of the ECHR*, Antwerp: Intersentia 2002.

Armour (2005)
J.D. Armour, 'Toward a tort-based theory of civil rights, civil liberties, and racial justice', *Loyola of Los Angeles Law Review* 2004-5, p. 1469-1482.

Arnardóttir (2003)
O.M. Arnardóttir, *Equality and non-discrimination under the European Convention of Human Rights*, The Hague: Martinus Nijhoff 2003.

Arnull (2006)
A. Arnull, *The European Union and its Court of Justice*, Oxford: Oxford University Press 2006.

Ashford (2006)
E. Ashford, 'The inadequacy of our traditional conception of the duties imposed by human rights', *Canadian journal of law and jurisprudence* 2006, p. 217-235.

Asscher-Vonk (1999)
I.P. Asscher-Vonk, 'Towards one concept of objective justification', T. Loenen, P.R. Rodrigues (eds.), *Non-discrimination law: comparative perspectives*, The Hague: Kluwer Law International 1999, p. 39-51.

Asscher-Vonk (2001)
I.P. Asscher-Vonk, 'Gelijke behandeling, richtlijnen, de bomen en het bos', *SMA* 2001- 4, p. 191-195.

Asscher-Vonk & Hendriks (2005)
I.P. Asscher-Vonk, A.C. Hendriks, *Gelijke behandeling en onderscheid bij de arbeid*, Deventer: Kluwer 2005.

Bacik (2003)
I. Bacik, 'Harassment', C. Costello, E. Barry (eds.), *Equality in diversity, the new equality directives*, Dublin: ICEL 2003, p. 151-176.

Bagenstos (2006)
S.R. Bagenstos, 'The structural turn and the limits of antidiscrimination law', *California Law Review* 2006, p. 1-48.

Bagenstos (2007)
S.R. Bagenstos, 'Implicit bias, science, and antidiscrimination law', *Harvard Law and Policy Review* 2007, p. 477-493.

Baker (2008)
A. Baker, 'Proportionality and employment discrimination in the UK', *Industrial Law Journal* 2008, p. 305-328.

Bamforth (1996)
N. Bamforth, 'Limits of anti-discrimination law: legal and social concepts of equality', J. Dine, B. Watt (eds.), *Anti-discrimination law: concepts, limits and justifications*, Addison, Harlow: Wesley and Longman Limited 1996, p. 49-62.

Banton (1996)
M. Banton, *International Action Against Racial Discrimination*, Gloucestershire: Clarendon Press 1996.

Baquero Cruz (1999)
J. Baquero Cruz, 'Free movement and private autonomy', *European Law Review* 1999, p. 603.

Barmes (2003)
L. Barmes, 'Promoting diversity and the definition of direct discrimination', *Industrial Law Journal* 2003, p. 200-213.

Barmes (2007)
L. Barmes, 'Constitutional and conceptual complexities in UK implementation of the EU harassment provisions', *Industrial Law Journal* 2007, p. 446-467.

Barmes & Ashtiany (2003)
L. Barmes, S. Ashtiany, 'The diversity approach to achieving equality: potential and pitfalls', *Industrial Law Journal* 2003, p. 274-296.

Barnard (1996)
C. Barnard, 'Gender and commercial discrimination', J. Dine, B. Watt (eds.), *Anti-discrimination law: concepts, limits and justifications*, Addison, Harlow: Wesley and Longman Limited 1996, p. 63-76.

Barnard (2001)
C. Barnard, 'The changing scope of the fundamental principle of equality?', *McGill Law Journal* 2001, p. 955-977.

Barnard & Hepple (1999)
C. Barnard, B. Hepple, 'Indirect discrimination: interpreting Seymour-Smith', *Cambridge Law Journal* 1999, p. 399-412.

Barrett (2003)
G. Barrett, 'Re-examining equality in EC law', *Yearbook of European Law*, Oxford: Oxford University Press 2003, p. 117-153.

Barrett (2003a)
G. Barrett, 'The concept and principle of equality in the European Community: pouring new wine into old bottles?', C. Costello, E. Barry (eds.), *Equality in diversity, the new equality directives*, Dublin: ICEL 2003, p. 99-134.

Barrett (2006)
G. Barrett, '"Shall I compare thee to…?" On article 141EC and *Lawrence*', *Industrial Law Journal* 2006, p. 93-101.

Barrett (2006a)
B. Barrett, 'Vicarious liability for harassment by an employee', *Industrial Law Journal* 2006, p. 431-438.

Batselé (2001)
D. Batselé, 'Racisme et liberté d'expression dans la législation et la jurisprudence Belges', *Revue Trimestrielle des Droits de l'Homme* 2001, p. 321-342.

Bayart (2002)
C. Bayart, 'De opmars van het discriminatierecht in arbeidsverhoudingen', *Journal des Tribunaux du travail* 2002, p. 309-329.

Bayart (2003)
C. Bayart, 'Discriminatie in de arbeidsverhoudingen, De ras- en kaderrichtlijn: technieken en potentiële gevolgen', D. Cuypers (ed.), *Gelijkheid in het arbeidsrecht, Gelijkheid zonder grenzen?*, Antwerp: Intersentia 2003, p. 3-63.

Bayart & Bosmans (2008)
C. Bayart, I. Bosmans, 'De federale antidiscriminatiewetten en arbeidsbetrekkingen in de private sector: algemeen overzicht', C. Bayart, S. Sottiaux, S. Van Drooghenbroeck (eds.), *De nieuwe federale antidiscriminatiewetten*, Bruges: Die Keure 2008, p. 537-596.

Bayart & Deiteren (2008)
C. Bayart, C. Deiteren, 'Direct en indirect onderscheid', C. Bayart, S. Sottiaux, S. Van Drooghenbroeck (eds.), *De nieuwe federale antidiscriminatiewetten*, Bruges: Die Keure 2008, p. 172-225.

Beaton & Tougas (2001)
A..M. Beaton, F. Tougas, 'Reactions to affirmative action: group membership and social justice', *Social Justice Research* 2001, p. 61-78.

Bell (1999)
M. Bell, 'Equality and diversity: anti-discrimination law after Amsterdam', J. Shaw (ed.), *Social law and policy in an evolving European Union*, Oxford: Hart Publishing 1999, p. 157-170.

Bell (2000)
M. Bell, 'Article 13 EC: the European Commission's anti-discrimination proposals', *Industrial Law Journal* 2000, p. 79-84.

Bell (2001)
M. Bell, 'Meeting the challenge? A comparison between the EU racial equality directive and the Starting Line', I. Chopin, J. Niessen (eds.), *The Starting Line and the incorporation of the racial equality directive into the national laws of the EU member states and accession states*, Brussels: Commision for Racial Equality & MPG 2001, p. 22-54.

Bell (2002)
M. Bell, *Anti-discrimination law and the European Union*, Oxford: Oxford University Press 2002.

Bell (2002a)
M. Bell, 'Combating racism through European laws: a comparison of the racial equality directive and protocol 12', I. Chopin, J. Niessen (eds.), *Combating racial and ethnic discrimination: taking the European legislative agenda further*, Brussels: Commission for Racial Equality & MPG 2002.

Bell (2004)
M. Bell, 'Equality and the European Union Constitution', *Industrial Law Journal* 2004, p. 242-260.

Bell (2004a)
M. Bell, 'A patchwork of protection: the new anti-discrimination law framework', *Modern Law Review* 2004, p. 465-477.

Bell (2008)
M. Bell, *Extending EU anti-discrimination law: Report of ENAR Ad Hoc expert group on anti-discrimination law*, Brussels: ENAR 2008.

Bell & Waddington (2001)
M. Bell, L. Waddington, 'More equal than others: distinguishing European Union equality directives', *Common Market Law Review* 2001, p. 587-611.

Bell & Waddington (2003)
M. Bell, L. Waddington, 'Reflecting on inequalities in European equality law', *European Law Review* 2003, p. 349-369.

Benvenisti (1999)
E. Benvenisti, 'Margin of Appreciation, Consensus, and Universal Standards', *Journal of International Law and Politics* 1999, p. 843-854.

Bernard (2008)
N. Bernard, 'Les lois anti-discrimination et le secteur du logement (privé et social)', C. Bayart, S. Sottiaux, S. Van Drooghenbroeck, *De nieuwe federale antidiscriminatiewetten*, Bruges: Die Keure 2008, p. 797-843.

Bertrand, Chug & Mullainatthan (2005)
M. Bertrand, D. Chug & S. Mullainathan, 'Implicit discrimination', *American Economic Review* 2005, p. 94-98.

Bitskey & Gyulavári (2004)
B. Bitskey, T. Gyulavári, 'Az anti-diszkriminációs szabályozás reformja', *Acta Humana* 2004, p. 13-40.

Bitskey & Gyulavári (2005)
B. Bitskey, T. Gyulavári, 'The Hungarian Equal Treatment Act: a new Member State's perspective', unpublished, 2005.

Blank et al (2004)
R. Blank, M. Dabady, C. Citro (eds.), *Measuring racial discrimination*, Panel on methods for assessing discrimination, Washington: National Academies Press 2004.

Blank (2005)
R. Blank, 'Tracing the economic impact of cumulative discrimination', *AEA Papers and Proceedings* 2005, p. 99-103.

Boelaert-Suominen (2005)
S. Boelaert-Suominen, 'Non-EU nationals and Council Directive 2003/209/EC on the status of third-country nationals who are long-term residents: five paces forward and possibly three paces back', *Common Market Law Review* 2005, p. 1011-1052.

Bossuyt (2002)
M. Bossuyt, *Report of the Special Rapporteur: Prevention of discrimination. The concept and practice of affirmative action*, Economic and Social Council 2002, E/CN.4/Sub.2/2002/21.

Bossuyt (2003)
M. Bossuyt, 'The concept and practice of affirmative action', I. Boerefijn, A.P.M. Coomans, J. Goldschmidt, R. Holtmaat, M.W. Wolleswinkel (eds.), *Temporary Special Measures - Accelerating de facto Equality of Women under Article 4(1) UN Convention on the Elimination of All Forms of Discrimination Against Women*, Antwerp: Intersentia 2003, p. 65-74.

Bowers & Moran (2002)
J. Bowers, E. Moran, 'Justification in direct sex discrimination law: breaking the taboo', *Industrial Law Journal* 2002, p. 307-320.

Bowers, Moran & Honeyball (2003)
J. Bowers, E. Moran, S. Honeyball, 'Justification in direct sex discrimination: a reply', *Industrial Law Journal* 2003, p. 185-187.

Brems (2004)
E. Brems, 'Nieuwe discriminatiegronden in de Wet Bestrijding Discriminatie', M. De Vos, E. Brems (eds.), *De Wet Bestrijding Discriminatie in de praktijk*, Antwerp: Intersentia 2004, p. 37-68.

Brennan (2003)
F. Brennan,'The race directive: recycling racial inequality', *Cambridge Yearbook of European Legal Studies* 2002-2003, p. 311-331.

Brown (2002)
C. Brown, 'The race directive: towards equality for *all* the peoples of Europe?', *Yearbook of European Law*, Oxford: Clarendon Press 2002, p. 195-227.

Brubaker (2004)
R. Brubaker, *Ethnicity without groups*, Cambridge: Harvard University Press 2004.

Bulmer & Solomos (1998)
M. Bulmer, J. Solomos, 'Introduction: rethinking ethnic and racial studies', *Ethnic and Racial studies* 1998-5, p. 819-837.

Burri (2001)
S. Burri, 'Bouwstenen voor gelijke behandeling. De EG richtlijn voor gelijke behandeling in arbeid en beroep', *SMA* 2001, p. 434-443.

Burri (2006)
S. Burri, *How to interpret the concept of genuine occupational requirements?*, Presentation held at the Academy of European Law in Trier, 31 October 2006, available at www.era.int (accessed July 2009)

Burri & Dorssemont (2005)
S. Burri, F. Dorssemont, 'The transposition of the Race Directive (2000/43/EC) and the Framework Directive on Equal Treatment in Employment (2000/78/EC) into Dutch and Belgian law', *The International Journal of Comparative Labour Law and Industrial Relations* 2005, p. 537-570.

Cabral (2004)
P. Cabral, 'A step closer to substantive equality', *European Law Review* 1998, p. 481-487.

Carasco (1993)
E. Carasco, 'A case of double jeopardy: race and gender', *Canadian Journal on Women and the Law* 1993, p. 142-152.

Caruso (2003)
D. Caruso, 'Limits of the classical method: positive action in the European Union after the new equality directives', Boston University School of Law Working Paper Series, Working Paper no. 03-21, accessible at http://www.bu.edu/law/faculty/papers (accessed October 2007).

Chalmers (2001)
D. Chalmers, 'The mistakes of the good European?', S. Fredman (ed.), *Discrimination and human rights. The case of racism*, Oxford: Oxford University Press 2001, p. 193-250.

Charpentier (1998)
L. Charpentier, *The European Court of Justice and the rhetoric of affirmative action*, European University institute, Working Paper RSC 98/30.

Cholewinski (2002)
R. Cholewinski, 'The Community non-discrimination principle and its potential application to the EU rules on borders and visas', *Borders of discrimination in the European Union*, Brussels: MPG 2002, p.39-49.

Cholewinski (2005)
R. Cholewinski, 'Migrants as minorities: integration and inclusion in the enlarged European Union', *Journal of Common Market Studies* 2005, p. 695-716.

Choudhry (2000)
S. Choudhry, 'Distribution v. recognition: the case of anti-discrimination law', *George Mason Law Review* 2000, p. 145-183.

Christensen (2001)
A. Christensen, 'Structural aspects of anti-discrimination legislation and processes of normative change', *Legal perspectives on equal treatment and non-discrimination*, A. Numhauser-henning (ed.), Deventer: Kluwer 2001.

Clarke (2006)
L. Clarke, 'Harassment, sexual harassment and the employment equality (sex discrimination) regulations 2005', *Industrial Law Journal* 2006, p. 161-178.

Closset-Marchal & Van Drooghenbroeck (2008)
G. Closset-Marchal, J-Fr. Van Drooghenbroeck, 'L'action en cessation an matière de discriminations', C. Bayart, S. Sottiaux, S. Van Drooghenbroeck (eds.), *De nieuwe federale antidiscriminatiewetten*, Bruges: Die Keure 2008, p.361-413.

Cohn (2003)
Y. Cohn, 'Affirmative action for women in the workplace at home abroad: a comparison of Johnson v. transportation agency and Abrahamsson v. Fogelqvist', *Columbia Journal of Law and Social Problems* 2003, p. 277-328.

Cook (2003)
R. Cook, 'Obligations to adopt temporary special measures under the Convention on the Elimination of all forms of Discrimination against Women', I. Boerefijn, A.P.M. Coomans, J. Goldschmidt, R. Holtmaat, M.W. Wolleswinkel (eds.), *Temporary Special Measures - Accelerating de facto Equality of Women under Article 4(1) UN Convention on the Elimination of All Forms of Discrimination Against Women*, Antwerp: Intersentia 2003, p. 119-141.

Costello (2003)
C. Costello, 'Positive action', C. Costello, E. Barry (eds.), *Equality in Diversity. The new equality directives*, Dublin: ICEL 2003, p. 177-212.

Craig (2007)
R. Craig, *Systemic discrimination in employment and the promotion of ethnic equality*, The Hague: Martinus Nijhoff 2007.

Craig & De Búrca (2003)
P. Craig, G. De Búrca, *EU Law*, Oxford: Oxford University Press 2003.

Cremers-Hartman (1999)
E. Cremers-Hartman, 'Werkingssfeer AWGB', I.P. Asscher-Vonk, C.A. Groenendijk (eds.), *Gelijke behandeling: regels en realiteit*, The Hague: SDU 1999, p. 29-88.

Cremers-Hartman (2004)
E. Cremers-Hartman, *Gelijke behandeling bij de arbeid in zes wetten*, Deventer: Kluwer 2004.

Cuypers (2003)
D. Cuypers, 'There will never be equality in the servant's hall. Gelijkheid in het arbeidsrecht', M. Adams, J. Velaers (eds.), *Vrijheid en gelijkheid. De horizontale werking van het gelijkheidsbeginsel en de nieuwe antidiscriminatiewet*, Antwerp: MAKLU 2003, p. 445-488.

Dambre (2004)
M. Dambre, 'De Wet Bestrijding Discriminatie en het huurrecht', M. De Vos, E. Brems (eds.), *De Wet Bestrijding Discriminatie in de praktijk*, Antwerp: Intersentia 2004, p. 321-347.

Davidovic & Van Walsum (2009)
M. Davidovic, S. K. Van Walsum, 'Ras en nationaliteit', *Gelijke Behandeling: oordelen en commentaar 2008*, Nijmegen: Wolf Legal Publishers 2009, p. 29-48.

Davies (2002)
G. Davies, *Nationality discrimination and free movement law* (Doctoral thesis Groningen RUG), 2002.

Davies (2005)
G. Davies, 'Should diagonal discrimination claims be allowed?', *Legal Studies* 2005, p. 181-200.

Davies (2006)
G. Davies, 'Subsidiarity: the wrong idea, in the wrong place, at the wrong time', *Common Market Law Review* 2006, p. 63-84.

Davies & Costello (2006)
G. Davies, C. Costello, 'The Jurisprudence of the Court of Justice in the field of sex equality since 2000', *Common Market Law Review* 2006, p. 1567-1616.

De Boeck (2003)
A. De Boeck, 'Doorwerking van het gelijkheidsbeginsel in het contractenrecht', M. Adams, J. Velaers (eds.), *Vrijheid en gelijkheid. De horizontale werking van het gelijkheidsbeginsel en de nieuwe antidiscriminatiewet*, Antwerp: MAKLU 2003, p. 413-444.

Decker (2005)
C.D. Decker, *Status of national minorities digest: a thematic look at five national laws*, Flensburg: ECMI 2005.

De Fey et al (2004)
C.C. De Fey, A. Kellermann, J.W. Nieuwboer, *Met recht discriminatie bestrijden*, The Hague: Boom Juridische Uitgevers 2004.

De Kluiver (2006)
H.J. de Kluiver, Gelijkheid in vereniging, S.D. Burri (ed.), *Gelijke behandeling, oordelen en commentaar 2005*, Nijmegen: Wolf Legal Publishers 2006, p. 167-180.

Demeter (2006)
J. Demeter, 'Az egyenlő bánásmódról és az esélyegyenlőség előmozdításáról szóló törvény – az Egyenlő Bánásmód Hatóság által lefolytatott eljárások tükrében', *Acta Humana* 2006, p. 49-66.

De Prins (2003)
D. de Prins, 'De verhouding tussen verenigingsvrijheid en antidiscriminatie naar Belgisch, Nederlands en Amerikaans recht. De toegang tot politieke partijen als toepassingsgeval', M. Adams, J. Velaers (eds.), *Vrijheid en gelijkheid. De horizontale werking van het gelijkheidsbeginsel en de nieuwe antidiscriminatiewet*, Antwerp: MAKLU 2003, p. 511-539.

De Prins et al (2005)
D. De Prins, S. Sottiaux, J. Vrielink, *Handboek Discriminatierecht*, Deventer: Kluwer 2005.

De Schutter (2003)
O. De Schutter, 'La loi Belge tendant à lutter contre la discrimination', *Journal des Tribunaux* 2003, p. 845-856.

De Schutter (2004)
O. De Schutter, *Report on measures to combat discrimination. Directives 2000/43/EC and 2000/78/EC. Country Report Belgium*, Brussels: MPG 2004.

De Schutter (2005)
O. De Schutter, *The prohibition of discrimination under European Human Rights Law*, Brussels: European Commission 2005.

De Schutter (2005a)
O. De Schutter, *The protection of minorities in the European Union*, Thematic Comment No. 3, EU Network of Independent Experts on Fundamental Rights 2005.

De Schutter (2005b)
O. De Schutter, 'EU Roma Integration Directive – Filling the Gap in the Equality Legal Regime', *Roma Rights Quarterly* 2005, p.27-30.

De Schutter (2007)
O. De Schutter, 'Three models of equality and European anti-discrimination law', *Northern Ireland Legal Quarterly* 2007, p. 1-56.

De Schutter (2007a)
O. De Schutter, *Report on measures to combat discrimination. Directives 2000/43/EC and 2000/78/EC*, Brussels: MPG & Human European Consultancy 2007.

De Schutter (2008)
O. De Schutter, 'Ethnic profiling: a rising challenge for European human rights law', *Modern Law Review* 2008, p. 358-384.

De Schutter & Verstichel (2005)
O. De Schutter, A. Verstichel, *The role of the Union in integrating the Roma: present and possible future*, EDAP 2005-2, at www.eurac.edu/edap.

De Vos (2003)
M. De Vos, 'Worden Europese arbeidsrelaties Amerikaans? Kritische rechtsvergelijkende perspectieven bij de discriminatieverboden in het arbeidsrecht', in D. Cuypers (ed.), *Gelijke arbeid zonder grenzen*, Antwerp: Maklu 2003, p. 241-264.

De Vos (2004)
M. De Vos, 'De bouwstenen van het discriminatierecht in de arbeidsverhoudingen na de wet bestrijding discriminatie', M. De Vos, E. Brems (eds.), *De Wet Bestrijding Discriminatie in de praktijk*, Antwerp: Intersentia 2004, p. 69-106.

De Vos (2007)
M. De Vos, *Beyond formal equality, positive action under directives 2000/43/EC and 2000/78/EC*, Brussels: European Commission 2007.

De Vries (2006)
K.M. de Vries, 'Inburgeringseisen en het gelijkheidsbeginsel', P.R. Rodrigues, S. van Walsum, 'Ras en nationaliteit', J.H. Gerards, B.P.Vermeulen, P.J.J. Zoontjens (eds.), *Gelijke behandeling: oordelen en commentaar 2006*, Nijmegen: Wolf Legal Publishers, 263-277.

De Witte (1999)
B. De Witte, 'The past and future role of the European Court of Justice in the protection of human rights', P. Alston, M. Bustelo, J. Heenan (eds.), *The EU and human rights*, Oxford: Oxford University Press 1999, p. 859-898.

De Witte (2004)
B. De Witte, 'The Constitutional Resources for an EU Minority Protection Policy', in G. N. Toggenburg (ed), *Minority Protection and the Enlarged European Union: The Way Forward*, Budapest: Local Government and Public Reform Initiative 2004, p. 107-124.

Dhami et al (2006)
R. Singh Dhami, J. Squires, T. Modood, *Developing positive action policies: learning from the experiences of Europe and North America*, Research Report no. 406, Department for Work and Pensions 2006.

Diggs Mange (2007)
M. Diggs Mange, 'The formal equality theory in practice : the inability of current antidiscrimination law to protect conventional and unconventional persons', *Columbia Journal of Gender and Law* 2007, p. 1-42.

Dine & Watt (1995)
J. Dine, B. Watt, 'Sexual harassment: moving away from discrimination', *Modern Law Review* 1995, p. 343-363.

Dobe & Chokar (2000)
K. Dobe, S. Chokar, 'Muslims, Ethnicity and the Law', *International Journal of Discrimination and the Law* 2000.

Doyle (2007)
O. Doyle, 'Direct discrimination, indirect discrimination and autonomy', *Oxford Journal of Legal Studies* 2007, p. 537-553.

Driessen-Reilly & Driessen (2003)
M. Driessen-Reilly, B. Driessen, 'Don't shoot the messenger: a look at community law relating to harassment in the workplace', *European Law Review* 2003, p. 493-507.

Drijber & Prechal (1997)
B.J. Drijber, S. Prechal, 'Gelijke behandeling van mannen en vrouwen in horizontaal perspectief', *Sociaal Economisch Weekblad* 1997, p. 122-167.

Dummett (2004)
A. Dummett, 'Implementing European anti-discrimination law', in Niessen & Chopin (eds.), *The development of legal instruments to combat racism in a diverse Europe*, The Hague: Martinus Nijhoff 2004.

Ehrenreich (1999)
R. Ehrenreich, 'Dignity and discrimination: toward a pluralistic understanding of workplace harassment', *Georgetown Law Journal* 1999, p. 1-64.

Ellis (1994)
E. Ellis, 'The definition of discrimination in European Community sex equality law', *European Law Review* 1994, p. 563-580.

Ellis (1998)
E. Ellis, *EC sex equality law*, Oxford: Oxford University Press 1998.

Ellis (2003)
E. Ellis, 'Social advantages: a new lease of life?', *Common Market Law Review* 2003, p.639-659.

Ellis (2005)
E. Ellis, *EU anti-discrimination law*, Oxford: Oxford University Press 2005.

Emiliou (1996)
N. Emiliou, *The principle of proportionality in European Law*, Deventer: Kluwer 1996.

Farkas (2003)
L. Farkas, 'Will the groom adopt the bride's unwanted child? The Race Equality Directive, Hungary and its Roma', *Roma Rights* 2003-1/2, available at www.errc.org (accessed 9 May 2008).

Farkas (2005)
L. Farkas, 'A miskolci deszegregációs per első felvonása', *Fundamentum* 2005, p. 157-164.

Farkas (2007)
L. Farkas, *Segregation of Roma in Education. Addressing structural discrimination through the Race Equality Directive*, Luxembourg: Office for Official Publications of the European Communities 2007.

Farkas et al (2003)
L. Farkas, A. Kádár, J. Kárpáti, 'Néhány megjegyzés az egyenlő bánásmódról szóló törvény koncepciójához', *Fundamentum* 2003-2, p. 121-130.

Farkas et al (2006)
L. Farkas, A. Kádár, J. Kárpáti, *Az egyenlő bánásmódról és az esélyegyenlőség előmozdításáról szóló 2003. évi CXXV. törvény magyarázata*, Budapest: Másság Alapítvány 2006.

Fernandes-Mendes (2004)
H. Fernandes Mendes, 'Is voorkeursbeleid van minderheden nog van deze tijd?', *NJCM-Bulletin* 2004, p. 624-628.

Fineman (2004)
M.A. Fineman, 'Equality across legal cultures, the role for international human rights', *Thomas Jefferson Law Review* 2004-5, p. 1-14.

Finlay (2003)
M. Finlay, 'Indirect discrimination and the article 13 directives', C. Costello, E. Barry (eds.), *Equality in Diversity. The new equality directives*, Dublin: ICEL 2003, p. 135-150.

Flynn (1999)
L. Flynn, 'The implications of article 13 EC – After Amsterdam will some forms of discrimination be more equal than others?', *Common Market Law Review* 1999, p. 1127-1152.

Foblets & Velaers (2006)
M-C Foblets, J. Velaers, 'De hoofddoek, het onderwijs en de anti-discriminatiewet', *Rechtskundig Weekblad* 2006-7, p. 122-132.

Ford (1994)
C.A. Ford, 'Administering identity: the determination of race in race conscious law', *California Law Review* 1994, p. 1231-1285.

Foubert (2004)
P. Foubert, 'Basisconcepten van de wet bestrijding discriminatie en haar verhouding tot andere antidiscriminatieregels', M. De Vos, E. Brems (eds.), *De Wet Bestrijding Discriminatie in de praktijk*, Antwerp: Intersentia 2004, p. 1-36.

Fredman (2000)
S. Fredman, 'Affirmative action and the European Court of Justice: a critical analysis, J. Shaw (ed.), *Social Law and Policy in an evolving European Union*, Oxford: Hart Publishing 2000, p. 171-195.

Fredman (2001)
S. Fredman, 'Equality: a new generation?', *Industrial Law Journal* 2001, p. 145-168.

Fredman (2001a)
S. Fredman, 'Combating racism with human rights: the right to equality', S. Fredman (ed.), *Discrimination and human rights. The case of racism*, Oxford: Oxford University Press 2001, p. 9-44.

Fredman (2002)
S. Fredman, *Discrimination law*, Oxford: Oxford University Press 2002.

Fredman (2003)
S. Fredman, 'Beyond the dichotomy of formal and substantive equality: towards a new definition of equal rights', I. Boerefijn, A.P.M. Coomans, J. Goldschmidt, R. Holtmaat, M.W. Wolleswinkel (eds.), *Temporary Special Measures - Accelerating de facto Equality of Women under Article 4(1) UN Convention on the Elimination of All Forms of Discrimination Against Women*, Antwerp: Intersentia 2003, p. 111-118.

Fredman (2005)
S. Fredman, 'Changing the norm: positive duties in equal treatment legislation', *Maastricht Journal of Comparative and European Law* 2005, p. 369-397.

Fredman (2005a)
S. Fredman, 'Providing equality: substantive equality and the positive duty to provide', *South African Journal of Human Rights* 2005, p. 163-190.

Fredman (2005b)
S. Fredman, 'Double trouble: multiple discrimination and EU law', *European Anti-discrimination Law Review* 2005, p. 8-13.

Fredman & Szyszczak (1992)
S. Fredman, E. Szyszczak, 'The interaction of race and gender', B. Hepple, E. Szyszczak (eds.), *Discrimination: the limits of law*, London: Mansell Publishing 1992, p. 214-226.

Freeman (2003)
M. Freeman, 'Temporary special measures: how long is temporary and what is special?', I. Boerefijn, A.P.M. Coomans, J. Goldschmidt, R. Holtmaat, M.W. Wolleswinkel (eds.), 2003, *Temporary Special Measures - Accelerating de facto Equality of Women under Article 4(1) UN Convention on the Elimination of All Forms of Discrimination Against Women,* Antwerp: Intersentia 2003, p. 97-110.

Friedman (2003)
G.S. Friedman, 'The European transformation of harassment law: discrimination versus dignity', *Columbia Journal of European Law* 2003, p. 241-274.

Flauss (2001)
J. Flauss, 'L'action de l'Union Européenne dans le domaine de la lutte contre le racisme et la xénofobie', *Revue Trimestrielle des Droits de l'Homme* 2001, p. 487-515.

Forshaw & Pilgerstorfer (2008)
S. Forshaw, M. Pilgerstorfer, 'Direct and indirect discrimination: is there something in between?', *Industrial Law Journal* 2008, p. 347-364.

Gardner (1992)
J. Gardner, 'Private activities and personal autonomy: at the margins of anti-discrimination law', B. Hepple, E. Szyszczak (eds.), *Discrimination: the limits of law*, London: Mansell Publishing 1992, p. 148-171.

Gear Rich (2004)
C. Gear Rich, 'Performing racial and ethnic identity: discrimination by proxy and the future of Title VII', *New York University Law Review* 2004, p. 1136-1270.

Gearty (2000)
C. Gearty, 'The Internal and the External 'Other' in the Union Legal Order: Racism, Religious Intolerance and Xenophobia in Europe', P. Alston (ed.), *The EU and Human Rights,* Oxford: Oxford University Press 2000, p. 327-359.

Gerards (2002)
J.H. Gerards, *Rechterlijke toetsing aan het gelijkheidsbeginsel*, The Hague: SDU 2002.

Gerards (2003)
J.H. Gerards, 'Het toetsingsmodel van de Commissie Gelijke Behandeling voor indirect onderscheid', D.J.B. De Wolff (eds.), *Gelijke behandeling: oordelen en commentaar 2002*, Deventer: Kluwer 2003.

Gerards (2004)
J.H. Gerards, 'Kroniek oordelen Commissie Gelijke Behandeling 2000-2003. Multiculturaliteit en botsing van grondrechten', *NJCM-Bulletin* 2004, p. 629-650.

Gerards (2005)
J.H. Gerards, *Judicial review in equal treatment cases*, The Hague: Martinus Hijhoff 2005.

Gerards (2006)
J.H. Gerards, 'Implementation of the article 13 directives in Dutch equal treatment legislation', *Maastricht Journal of European and Comparative Law* 2006, p. 291-309.

Gerards (2006a)
J.H. Gerards, Note on case 2006-20, J.H. Gerards, B.P. Vermeulen, P.J.J. Zoontjens (eds.), *Gelijke Behandeling: Oordelen en Commentaar 2006*, Nijmegen: Wolf Legal Publishers 2006, p. 311-320.

Gerards & Heringa (2003)
J.H. Gerards, A.W. Heringa, *Wetgeving gelijke behandeling*, Deventer: Kluwer 2003.

Germain & Eyben (2008)
J-F Germain, C. Eyben, 'Les sanctions civiles. La nullité et les dommage et intérêts forfaitaires', C. Bayart, S. Sottiaux, S. Van Drooghenbroeck, *De nieuwe federale antidiscriminatiewetten*, Bruges: Die Keure 2008, p. 333-359.

Gijzen (2004)
M. Gijzen, *Report on measures to combat discrimination,* European Network of Legal Experts in the non-discrimination field 2004.

Gijzen (2006)
M.H.S. Gijzen, *Selected issues in equal treatment law: a Multi-layered comparison of European, English and Dutch law*, Antwerp: Intersentia 2006.

Gill & Monaghan (2003)
T. Gill, K. Monaghan, 'Justification in direct sex discrimination law: taboo upheld', *Industrial Law Journal* 2003, p. 115-122.

Goldschmidt (2001)
J.E. Goldschmidt, 'De hete adem van Europa; Implementatie van nieuw gelijke behandelingsrecht in Nederland', *Nederlands Juristen Blad* 2001, p. 983-990.

Goldschmidt & Hendriks (2003)
J. Goldschmidt, A. Hendriks, 'Gelijkheid anno 2003. Het gelijkheidsbeginsel en andere grondrechten in een veranderende samenleving', *Nederlands Juristen Blad* 2003, p. 1277-1284.

Goldston (2006)
J. Goldston, 'Holes in the rights framework: Racial discrimination, citizenship, and the rights of noncitizens', *Ethics and International affairs* 2006, p. 321-347.

Goodman-Delahunty (1999)
J. Goodman-Delahunty, 'Pragmatic support for the reasonable victim standard in hostile workplace sexual harassment cases', *Psychology, Public Policy and Law* 1999, p. 519-555.

Gottesman (1991)
M.H. Gottesman, 'Twelve topics to consider before opting for racial quota's', *Georgetown Law Journal* 1992, p. 1737-1767.

Gratia (2001)
M. Gratia, 'The effectiveness of anti-racism legislation in Belgium', *From principle to practice. Evaluation of legislation dealing with racial and ethnic discrimination in certain EU member states*, Brussels: ENAR 2001, (http://www.enar-eu.org/en/publication/index.shtml).

Gratia (2004)
M. Gratia, *Rapport alternatif d'ENAR 2004 Belgique*, Brussels: ENAR 2004.

Griffiths (1992)
J. Griffiths, 'The social working of anti-discrimination law', B. Hepple, E. Sczysczak (eds.), *Discrimination: the limits of law*, London: Mansell Publishing 1992, p. 313-330.

Groenendijk (2006)
K. Groenendijk, 'Citizens and TCN: different treatment or discrimination?', J.Y. Carlier, B. Coulie (eds.), *The future of free movement of persons in the EU: Analysis of Directive 2004/38 of 29 April 2004 on the right of citizens to move and reside freely*, Brussels: Bruylant 2006.

Guild (2000)
E. Guild, 'The EC directive on race discrimination: surprises, possibilities and limitations', *Industrial Law Journal* 2000, p. 416-423.

Guild (2000a)
E. Guild, 'The European Union and article 13', G. Moon (ed.), *Race discrimination, Developing and using a new legal framework*, Oregon: Hart Publishing 2000, p. 65-79.

Gutek & O'Connor (1999)
B. Gutek, M.A. O'Connor, 'The utility of the reasonable woman legal standard in hostile environment sexual harassment cases: a multimethod, multistudy examination', *Psychology, Public Policy and Law* 1999, p. 596-629.

Gyulavári (2006)
T. Gyulavári, 'Előnyben részesítés', *Fundamentum* 2006, p. 67-71.

Gyulavári (2007)
T. Gyulavári, 'Három évvel az antidiszkriminációs szabályozás reformja után', *Esély*, 2007-3, p. 29-61.

Halmai (2005)
G. Halmai, 'Third party effect in Hungarian Constitutional Adjucation', A. Sajó, R. Uitz, (eds.), *The Constitution in private relations,* Utrecht: Eleven International Publishing 2005, p. 99-114.

Hannett (2003)
S. Hannett, 'Equality at the intersections: the legislative and judicial failure to tackle multiple discrimination', *Oxford Journal of Legal studies* 2003, p. 66-108.

Harris (2000)
A.P. Harris, 'Equality trouble: sameness and difference in twentieth century race law', *California Law Review* 2000, p.1923-2014.

Hendriks (2003)
A. Hendriks, *Wet gelijke behandeling op grond van handicap of chronische ziekte*, Deventer: Kluwer 2003.

Henrard (2000)
K.A.M. Henrard, *Devising an adequate system of minority protection. Individual human rights, minority rights and the right to self-determination*, The Hague: Martinus Nijhoff 2000.

Henrard (2005)
K.A.M. Henrard, 'Ever-increasing synergy towards a stronger level of minority protection between minority-specific and non-minority-specific instruments', *European Yearbook on Minority Issues* 2003/4, Leiden: Martinus Nijhoff 2005, p. 15-41.

Henrard (2006)
K.A.M. Henrard, 'The latest recommendations endorsed by the HCNM on ethnic policing: a new development in relation to minority protection?', *European Yearbook of Minority Issues* 2005-6, p. 67-98.

Henrard (2006a)
K. Henrard, *The Impact of International non-discrimination norms in combination with general human rights for the protection of national minorities: the European Convention on Human Rights*, DH-MIN(2006)020.

Henrard (2006b)
K. Henrard, *The Impact of International non-discrimination norms in combination with general human rights for the protection of national minorities: several United Nations Human Rights Conventions,* DH-MIN (2006)021.

Henrard (2007)
K.A.M. Henrard, *Equal rights versus special rights? Minority protection and the prohibition of discrimination*, Brussels: European Commission 2007.

Henrard (2007a)
K.A.M. Henrard, 'Botsende grondrechten en het EHRM: een pleidooi voor meer zorgvuldige argumentatie en minder 'margin of appreciation' voor staten', E. Brems, R. de Lange, K.A.M. Henrard (eds.), *Botsing van grondrechten*, Den Haag: Boom Juridische Uitgevers 2007.

Henrard (2007b)
K.A.M. Henrard, 'Non-discrimination and Full and Effective Equality', M. Weller (ed.), *Universal Minority Rights: A Commentary on the Jurisprudence of International Courts and Treaty Bodies*, Oxford: Oxford University Press 2007, p. 75-147.

Henrard (2008)
K.A.M. Henrard, 'Een zoektocht naar een beter begrip van en een adequaat toetsingsmodel voor indirecte discriminatie' (note on D.H. a.o. v. Czech Republic, ECtHR, no. 57325/00, 13 November 2007), *NJCM Bulletin* 2008, p. 234-250.

Henrard (2008a)
K.A.M. Henrard, *Mensenrechten vanuit internationaal en nationaal perspectief,* The Hague: Boom Juridische Uitgevers 2008.

Hepple (2000)
B. Hepple, 'Freedom of expression and the problem of harassment', J. Beatson, Y. Cripps (eds.), *Freedom of expression and freedom of information*, Oxford: Oxford University Press 2000, p.177-196.

Hepple (2001)
B. Hepple,'Equality and empowerment for decent work', *International Labour Review* 2001, p. 5-18.

Hepple (2004)
B. Hepple, 'Race and law in the fortress of Europe', *Modern Law Review* 2004, p. 1-15.

Hepple & Barnard (2000)
B. Hepple, C. Barnard, 'Substantive equality', *Cambridge Law Journal* 2000, p. 562-585.

Hepple et al (2000)
B. Hepple, M. Coussey, T. Choudhury, *Equality: a new framework*, Report of the Independent Review of the Enforcement of UK Anti-discrimination Legislation, Oxford: Hart Publishing 2000.

Heringa (1991)
A.W. Heringa, 'De AWGB: is iets beter dan niets of is het zelfs iets al te veel?', A.W. Heringa, A.K. Koekkoek, L. Mulder (eds.), *Gelijk behandelen*, , Zwolle: W.E.J. Tjeenk Willink 1991.

Hofkens & Demeestere (2003)
J. Hofkens, S. Demeestere, *Discriminatierecht in de arbeidsverhoudingen*, Mechelen: Ced-Samson 2003.

Hofman et al (1995)
J.A. Hofman, J.W. Sap, I. Sewandono, *Grondrechten in evenwicht*, Deventer: Kluwer 1995.

Holmes (2005)
E. Holmes, 'Anti-discrimination rights without equality', *The Modern Law Review* 2005, p. 175-194.

Holtmaat (2003)
R. Holtmaat, 'Stop de inflatie van het discriminatiebegrip', *NJB* 2003, p. 1266-1276.

Holtmaat (2006)
R. Holtmaat, 'Discriminatie of onderscheid', M.L.M. Hertogh, P.J.J. Zoontjens (eds.), *Gelijke behandeling: principes en praktijken. Evaluatieonderzoek Algemene wet gelijke behandeling*, Nijmegen: Wolf Legal Publishers 2006, p. 3-116.

Holtmaat (2007)
R. Holtmaat, *Report on measures to combat discrimination, Country report: The Netherlands*, Brussels: MPG 2007.

Holzleithner (2003)
E. Holzleithner, 'Faces of discrimination: the case of sex equality', *Protection against discrimination and gender equality: how to meet both requirements*, Report of the second experts' meeting, Brussels: MPG 2003.

Holzleithner (2005)
E. Holzleithner, 'Mainstreaming equality; dis/entangling grounds of discrimination', *Transnational Law and Contemporary Problems* 2005, p. 928-957.

Horspool & Humphreys (2006)
M. Horspool, M. Humphreys, *European Union Law*, Oxford: Oxford University Press 2006.

Houtzager & Bochhah (2004)
D. Houtzager, N. Bochhah, 'Onderscheid op grond van ras bij de arbeid: nieuwe ontwikkelingen', *Sociaal Recht* 2004, p. 272-278.

Howard (2004)
E. Howard, 'The EU Race Directive: its symbolic value – its only value', *International Journal of Discrimination and the Law* 2004, p. 141-163.

Howard (2005)
E. Howard, 'Anti-race discrimination measures in Europe: an attack on two fronts', *European Law Journal* 2005, p. 468-486.

Howard (2006)
E. Howard, 'The case for a considered hierarchy of discrimination grounds in EU law', *Maastricht Journal of European and Comparative Law* 2006, p. 445-470.

Howard (2008)
E. Howard, 'Race and racism – why does European law have difficulties with definitions?', *International Journal of Comparative Labour Law and Industrial Relations* 2008, p. 5-29.

Hucker (1999)
J. Hucker, 'Affirmative action Canadian style: reflections on Canada's employment equity law', T. Loenen, P.R. Rodrigues (eds.), *Non-discrimination law: comparative perspectives*, The Hague: Martinus Nijhoff 1999, p. 265-277.

Hunt (2002)
M. Hunt, 'Human rights review and the public-private distinction', G. Huscroft, P. Rishworth (eds.), *Litigating rights, perspectives from domestic and international law*, Oxford: Hart Publishing 2002, p. 73-88.

Jackson (1999)
D.W. Jackson, 'Affirmative action in comparative perspective: India and the United States', T. Loenen, P.R. Rodrigues (eds.), *Non-discrimination law: comparative perspectives*, The Hague: Martinus Nijhoff 1999, p. 249-264.

Jans (2007)
J.H. Jans, 'The effect in national legal systems of the prohibition of discrimination on grounds of age as a general principle of Community law', *Issues of Economic Integration* 2007, p. 53-66.

Jans et al (2007)
J.H. Jans, R. de Lange, S. Prechal, R.J.G.M. Widdershoven, *Europeanisation of Public Law*, Groningen: Europa Law Publishing 2007.

Jolls (2000)
C. Jolls, 'Accommodation mandates', *Stanford Law Review* 2000, p. 223-300.

Jolls (2001)
C. Jolls, 'Antidiscrimination and accommodation', *Harvard Law Review* 2001, p. 642-699.

Jones (2003)
T. Jones, 'The Race directive: redefining protection from discrimination in EU law', *European Human Rights Law Review* 2003, p. 515-526.

Jones (2004)
J. Jones, '"Common constitutional traditions": can the meaning of human dignity under German law guide the European Court of Justice?', *Public Law* 2004, p. 167-187.

Kádár (2007)
A. Kádar, *Report on measures to combat discrimination. Directives 2000/43/EC and 2000/78/EC. Hungary*, Brussels: MPG 2007.

Kellerman (2004)
A. Kellerman, 'Begrippen en definities', C.C. de Fey, A. Kellerman, J.W. Nieuwboer (eds.), *Met recht discriminatie bestrijden*, Den Haag: Boom Juridische Uitgevers 2004, p. 19-32.

Kelman (2001)
M. Kelman, 'Market discrimination and groups', *Stanford Law Review* 2001, p. 833-896.

Kilpatrick (1998)
C. Kilpatrick, 'Community or communities of courts in European integration? Sex equality dialogues between UK courts and the ECJ', *European Law Journal 1998*, p. 121-147.

Kimber (2003)
C.J.M. Kimber, 'The directive on race discrimination in Ireland: reform or radical change?', C. Costello, E. Barry (eds.), *Equality in Diversity. The new equality directives*, Dublin: ICEL 2003, p. 243-268.

Knook (2005)
A. Knook, 'The Court, the charter, and the vertical division of powers in the European Union', *Common Market Law Review* 2005, p. 367-398.

Koekkoek (1991)
A.K. Koekkoek, 'Grenzen aan grondrechten', A.W. Heringa, A.K. Koekkoek, L. Mulder (eds.), *Gelijk behandelen*, Zwolle: W.E.J. Tjeenk Willink 1991, p. 29-54.

Kollonay-Lehoczky (2005)
C. Kollonay-Lehoczky, 'The significance of existing EU sex equality law for women in the new member states. The case of Hungary, *Maastricht Journal of European and Comparative Law* 2005, p. 467-493.

Kollonay-Lehoczky (2006)
C. Kollonay-Lehoczky, 'Előnyben részesítés', *Fundamentum* 2006-4, p. 71-78.

Kovács (2002)
P. Kovács, 'The legal status of minorities in Hungary', *Acta Juridica Hungarica* 2002, p. 207-217.

Kovács (2005)
K. Kovács, 'Az igazságos kvóta', *Fundamentum* 2006-4, p. 5-16.

Kovalenko (2006)
J. Kovalenko, *Racism in Estonia, ENAR shadow report 2006*, Brussels: ENAR 2006.

Kusters (2003)
J. Kusters, 'Discriminatie ten opzichte van allochtonen op de private huurmarkt', M. Adams, J. Velaers (eds.), *Vrijheid en gelijkheid. De horizontale werking van het gelijkheidsbeginsel en de nieuwe antidiscriminatiewet*, Antwerp: MAKLU 2003, p. 541-571.

Kusters (2006)
J. Kusters, Note on the Case of the Ghent Court of Appeal on 30 November 2005, *Rechtskundig Weekblad* 2006, p.148-152.

Labuschagne (1999)
B.C. Labuschagne, 'Accommodating religious diversity in employment', T. Loenen, P.R. Rodrigues (eds.), *Non-discrimination law: comparative perspectives*, Deventer: Kluwer 1999, p.133-142.

Lacey (1992)
N. Lacey, 'From individual to group?', B. Hepple, E. Szyszczak (eds.), *Discrimination: the limits of law*, London: Mansell Publishing 1992, p. 99-110.

Laurent (2003)
P. Laurent, 'Les directives des 29 juin et 27 novembre 2000 et la loi du 25 février 2003 contre les discriminations: nouvelles compétences, nouvelles procédures', *Actualités de Droit* 2003, p. 611-672.

Lee (2005)
A. Lee, 'Unconscious bias theory in employment discrimination litigation', *Harvard Civil Rights - Civil Liberties Law Review* 2005, p. 481-503.

Lerner (2003)
N. Lerner, *Group rights and discrimination in international law*, The Hague: Martinus Nijhoff 2003.

Liegl et al (2005)
B. Liegl, B. Perchinig, B. Weyss, *Combating religious and ethnic discrimination in employment*, Brussels: ENAR 2005.

Loenen (1992)
T. Loenen, *Verschil in gelijkheid*, Zwolle: W.E.J. Tjeenk Willink 1992.

Loenen (1999)
T. Loenen, 'Indirect discrimination: oscillating between containment and revolution', T. Loenen, P.R. Rodrigues (eds.), *Non-discrimination law: comparative perspectives*, London: Kluwer Law International 1999, p. 195-211.

Loenen (2003)
T. Loenen, 'Het gelijkheidsbeginsel en andere grondrechten in de multiculturele samenleving – ontwikkelingen sinds 1983', *NJCM Bulletin* 2003-4, p. 259-276.

Loenen (2006)
T. Loenen, 'Noot bij CGB 2006-55', *NJCM Bulletin* 2006, p. 823-33.

Lustgarten (1992)
L. Lustgarten, 'Racial inequality, public policy and the law: where are we going?', B. Hepple, E. Szyszczak (eds.), *Discrimination: the limits of law,* London: Mansell Publishing 1992, p. 455-471.

Lynch (2005)
C. Lynch, *Racism in Europe*, *ENAR Shadow report 2005*, Brussels: ENAR 2005.

Lynch & Baker (2005)
K. Lynch, J. Baker, 'Equality in education: an equality of condition perspective', *Theory and Research in Education* 2005, p. 131-164.

Majtényi (2004)
B. Majtényi, 'Minority rights in Hungary and the situation of the Roma', *Acta Juridica Hungarica* 2004, p. 131-148.

Majtényi (2005)
B. Majtényi, 'Mi lesz veled "bezzeggyerek"? Változóban a kisebbségi jogi szabályozás', *Fundamentum* 2005, p. 109-120.

Makkonen (2002)
T. Makkonen, *Multiple, compound and intersectional discrimination: bringing the experiences of the most marginalized to the fore*, Institute for Human Rights, Abo Akademi University 2002, accessible at http://www.abo.fi/instut/imr/norfa/timo.pdf (accessed at 19 June 2009).

Makkonen (2004)
T. Makkonen, 'Is multiculturalism bad for the fight against discrimination?', M. Scheinin, R. Toivanen (eds.), *Rethinking non-discrimination and minority rights*, Turku: Åbo Akademi University 2004, p. 155-177.

Manknell (2003)
D. Manknell, 'Discrimination on grounds of sexual orientation, harassment and liability for third parties', *Industrial Law Journal* 2003, p. 297-309.

Marshall (1985)
S. Marshall, 'Reversing discrimination', S. Guest, A. Milne (eds.), *Equality and discrimination: essays in freedom and justice*, Stuttgart: Franz Steiner Verlag 1985, p. 61-76.

Masselot (2004)
A. Masselot, 'The new equal treatment directive: plus ça change…', *Feminist Legal Studies* 2004, p. 93-104.

McColgan (2005)
A. McColgan, *Discrimination law*, London: Hart Publishing 2005.

McColgan (2007)
A. McColgan, 'Reconfiguring discrimination law', *Public Law* 2007, p. 74-94.

McCrudden (1985)
C. McCrudden, 'Changing notions of discrimination', S. Guest, A. Milne (eds.), *Equality and discrimination: essays in freedom and justice*, Stuttgart: Franz Steiner Verlag 1985, p. 83-91.

McCrudden (1986)
C. McCrudden, 'Rethinking positive action', *Industrial Law Journal* 1986, p. 219-243.

McCrudden (1992)
C. McCrudden, 'Regulating discrimination: advice to a legislator on problems regarding the enforcement of anti-discrimination law and strategies to overcome them', B. Hepple, E. Sczysczak (eds.), *Discrimination: the limits of law*, London: Mansell Publishing 1992, p. 295-312.

McCrudden (2001)
C. McCrudden, 'International and European norms regarding national legal remedies for racial equality', S. Fredman (ed.), *Discrimination and human rights. The case of racism*, Oxford: Oxford University Press 2001, p. 251-307.

McCrudden (2003)
C. McCrudden, 'Theorising European Equality Law', C. Costello, E. Barry (eds.), *Equality in Diversity. The new equality directives*, Dublin: ICEL 2003, p. 1-38.

McDougall (2008)
G. McDougall *Promotion and protection of all human rights, civil, political, economic, social and cultural rights, including the right to development,* Report of the Independent Expert on Minority Issues, A/HRC/7/23 2008, Geneva: United Nations 2008.

McInerney (2000)
S. McInerney, 'Equal treatment between persons irrespective of racial or ethnic origin: a comment', *European Law Review* 2000, p. 317-323.

McInerney (2002)
S. McInerney, 'The Charter of Fundamental Rights of the European Union and the case of race discrimination', *European Law Review* 2002, p. 483-491.

McInerney (2003)
S. McInerney, 'Legal protection against discrimination based on racial and ethnic origin under European Union law – necessary but not sufficient?', *International Journal of Discrimination and the Law* 2003, p. 3-43.

Medda (2008)
R. Medda, *Old and New Minorities: Reconciling Diversity and Cohesion a Human Rights Model for Minority Integration*, Baden-Baden: Nomos Verlagsgesellschaft Mbh & Co, 2008.

Meiknecht (2002)
A. Meijknecht, *Towards International Personality: The Position of Minorities and Indigenous Peoples in International law*, Antwerp: Intersentia, 2002.

Mitchell (2004)
B. Mitchell, 'Unfair discrimination or necessary for equal opportunity? The ECJ upholds positive action in Lommers v. Minister van Landbouw', *Loyola of Los Angeles International and Comparative Law Review* 2004, p. 469-481.

Modood (1992)
T. Modood, 'Cultural diversity and racial discrimination in employment selection', B. Hepple, E. Szyszczak (eds.), *Discrimination: the limits of law*, London: Mansell Publishing 1992.

Monaghan (2007)
K. Monaghan, *Equality Law*, Oxford: Oxford University Press 2007.

Monster et al (1999)
W.C. Monster, B.P. Vermeulen, K. Waaldijk, 'Uitzonderingen', I.P. Asscher-Vonk, C.A.Groenendijk (eds.), *Gelijke behandeling: regels en realiteit*, The Hague: SDU 1999.

Moon (2006)
G. Moon, 'Multiple discrimination - problems compounded, or solutions found?', *Justice Journal* 2006, p. 86-102.

Moon & Allen (2007)
G. Moon, R. Allen, 'Dignity discourse in discrimination law: a better route to equality?', www.justice.org.uk/images/pdfs/dignityfinal.pdf (accessed June 2009).

Morawa (2002)
A.H.E. Morawa, 'The evolving human right to equality', *European Yearbook of Minority Issues*, London: Kluwer Law International 2002, p. 157-205.

Morris (1999)
A.J. Morris, 'On the normative foundations of indirect discrimination law: understanding the competing models of discrimination law as Aristotelian forms of justice', *Oxford Journal of Legal Studies* 1995, p. 199-228.

Muda (2002)
M. Muda, 'Regulation of gender equality as a fundamental right in Estonia', *Juridica International* 2002, p. 106-116.

Mulder (1991)
L. Mulder, 'De wetgever en het voortvluchtige gelijkheidsbeginsel', A. W. Heringa, A.K. Koekkoek, L. Mulder (eds.), *Gelijk behandelen*, Zwolle: W.E.J. Tjeenk Willink 1991.

Mulder (1999)
L. Mulder, 'How positive can equality measures be?', T. Loenen, P. Rodrigues (eds.), *Non-discrimination law: comparative perspectives*, The Hague: Martinus Nijhoff 1999, p. 65-75.

Mullender (1998)
R. Mullender, 'Racial harassment, sexual harassment, and the expressive function of law', *Modern Law Review* 1998, p. 236-244.

NicShuibhne (2003)
N. NicShuibhne, 'Article 13 EC and non-discrimination on grounds of nationality: missing or in action?', C. Costello, E. Barry (eds.), *Equality in Diversity*, Dublin: ICEL 2003, p. 269-294.

O'Cinnéide (2003)
C. O'Cinnéide, 'Making use of positive equality duties: the UK experience', C. Costello, E. Barry (eds.), *Equality in Diversity*, Dublin: ICEL 2003, p. 75-98.

O'Cinnéide (2004)
C. O'Cinnéide, 'Goods and services: setting the scene', J. Cormack (ed.), *Combating discrimination in goods and services*, Brussels: MPG 2004, p. 4-8.

O'Cinnéide (2006)
C. O'Cinnéide, 'Positive action and the limits of existing law', *Maastricht Journal of European and Comparative Law* 2006, p. 351-364.

O'Connell (2008)
R. O'Connell, 'The role of dignity in equality law: lessons from Canada and South Africa', *International Journal of Constitutional Law* 2008, p. 267-286.

O'Donovan (1985)
K. O'Donovan, 'Affirmative action', S. Guest, A. Milne (eds.), *Equality and discrimination: essays in freedom and justice*, Stuttgart: Franz Steiner Verlag 1985, p. 77-82.

O'Hare (2001)
U. O' Hare, 'Enhancing European equality rights', *Maastricht Journal of European and Comparative Law* 2001, p. 133-165.

O'Leary (1999)
S. O' Leary, 'The free movement of persons and services', P. Craig, G. De Búrca (eds.), *The evolution of EU law*, Oxford: Oxford University Press 1999, p. 377-416.

O'Neil & Peron (2003)
T. O'Neil, L-H. Peron, *Rights based approaches to tackling discrimination and horizontal inequality*, Background Paper, Poverty and Public Policy Group, London: Overseas Development Institute 2003.

O'Nions (2007)
H. O'Nions, *Minority rights protection in international law: the Roma of Europe*, Aldershot: Ashgate Publishing Ltd. 2007.

Overbeeke (2003)
A. Overbeeke, 'Non-discriminatie en gelijke kansen inzake schoolkeuze in het Vlaamse onderwijs – requiem voor het toelatingsbeleid van identiteitsgebonden instellingen?', M. Adams, J. Velaers (eds.), *Vrijheid en gelijkheid. De horizontale werking van het gelijkheidsbeginsel en de nieuwe antidiscriminatiewet*, Antwerp: MAKLU 2003, p. 707-753.

Pager (2003)
S. Pager, 'Strictness and subsidiarity: an institutional perspective on affirmative action at the European Court of Justice', *Boston College International and Comparative Law Review* 2003, p. 35-76.

Pap (2005)
A.L. Pap, 'Ethnic discrimination and the war against terrorism – the case of Hungary', *Fundamentum* 2005, p. 31-46.

Parekh (1992)
B. Parekh, 'A case for positive discrimination', B.Hepple, E. Szyszczak (eds.), *Discrimination: the limits of law*, London: Mansell Publishing 1992, p. 261-280.

Parmar (2004)
S. Parmar, 'The European Court of Justice and anti-discrimination law; reflections on gender equality jurisprudence for the future interpretation of the Race Directive', J. Niessen, I. Chopin (eds.), *The development of legal instruments to combat racism in a diverse Europe*, The Hague: Martinus Nijhoff 2004, p.131-154.

Pentassuglia (2003)
G. Pentassuglia, *Minorities in International Law*, Strasbourg: Council of Europe, 2003.

Pincus (1996)
F. Pincus, 'Discrimination comes in many forms: individual, institutional, and structural', *American Behavioral Scientist* 1996, p.186-194.

Pincus (1999)
F. Pincus, 'From individual to structural discrimination', F. Pincus, H. Ehrlich (eds.), *Race and ethnic conflict*, Boulder USA: Westview Press 1999, p. 82-87.

Pitt (1992)
G. Pitt, 'Can reverse discrimination be justified?', B.Hepple, E. Szyszczak (eds.), *Discrimination: the limits of law,* London: Mansell Publishing 1992 p. 281-299.

Pogány (2004)
I. Pogány, 'Legal, social and economic challenges facing the Roma of Central and Eastern Europe', *Queen's papers on Europeanisation*, Belfast: School of Politics and International Studies, 2004, No. 2.

Poleshchuk (2003)
V. Poleshchuk, *Report on measures to combat discrimination in the 13 candidate countries, Country Report Estonia*, Brussels: MPG 2003.

Poleshchuk (2004)
V. Poleshchuk, *Non-citizens in Estonia*, Tallinn: Legal Information Centre for Human Rights 2004.

Poleshchuk (2005)

V. Poleshchuk, *Report on measures to combat discrimination. Country Report Estonia*, Brussels: MPG 2005.

Poleshchuk (2006)
V. Poleshchuk, 'Estonia: media, ethnic discrimination and anti-discrimination legislation', *Media against intolerance and discrimination: Estonian situation and international experience*, Tallinn: Legal Information Centre for Human Rights 2006, p. 9-52.

Poleshchuk (2007)
V. Poleshchuk, *Report on Measures to combat discrimination. Country Report Estonia*, Brussels: MPG 2007.

Popelier (2003)
P. Popelier, 'Laten we allemaal vriendjes zijn! Over de antidiscriminatiewet en wetgevingsmethoden.', M. Adams, J. Velaers (eds.), *Vrijheid en gelijkheid. De horizontale werking van het gelijkheidsbeginsel en de nieuwe antidiscriminatiewet*, Antwerp: MAKLU 2003, p. 246-286.

Poulter (1998)
S. Poulter, *Ethnicity, Law and Human Rights*, Oxford: Oxford University Press 1998.

Prechal (2004)
S. Prechal, 'Equality of treatment, non-discrimination and social policy: achievement in three themes', *Common Market Law Review* 2004, p. 533-551.

Preedy (2000)
K. Preedy, 'Fundamental rights and private acts: horizontal direct or indirect effect? – a comment', *European Review of Private Law* 2000, p.125-133.

Raday (2003)
F. Raday, 'Systematizing the application of different types of temporary special measures under article 4 of CEDAW', I. Boerefijn, A.P.M. Coomans, J. Goldschmidt, R. Holtmaat, M.W. Wolleswinkel (eds.), *Temporary Special Measures - Accelerating de facto Equality of Women under Article 4(1) UN Convention on the Elimination of All Forms of Discrimination Against Women*, Antwerp: Intersentia 2003, p. 35-44.

Réaume (2002)
D. Réaume, 'Discrimination and dignity', *Louisiana Law Review* 2002, p. 645-696.

Réaume (2005)
D. Réaume, 'Comparing theories of sex discrimination: the role of comparison', *Oxford Journal of Legal Studies* 2005, p. 547-564.

Réaume (2006)
D. Réaume, 'The relevance of relevance to equality rights', *Queen's Law Journal* 2006, p. 696-730.

Reddy (2006)
K. Reddy, 'The horizontal application of the equality guarantees and race discrimination by the business sector', *Tydskrif vir die Suid Afrikaanse Reg* 2006, p. 782-801.

Rich (2004)
C.G. Rich, 'Performing racial and ethnic identity: discrimination by proxy and the future of Title VII', *New York University Law Review* 2004, p. 1134-1199.

Ringelheim (2006)
J. Ringelheim, *Diversité culturelle et droits de l'homme: la protection des minorités par la Convention Européenne des Droits de l'Homme*, Brussels: Bruylant 2006.

Ringelheim (2008)
J. Ringelheim, 'Recueil de données personnelles et lutte contre les discriminations. Une tension nécessaire entre non-discrimination et vie privée', C. Bayart, S. Sottiaux, S. Van Drooghenbroeck (eds.), *De nieuwe federale antidiscriminatiewetten*, Bruges: Die Keure 2008, p. 63-100.

Roberts (2001)
P. Roberts, 'Employers' liability for sexual and racial harassment: developing the reasonably practicable steps defense', *Industrial Law Journal* 2001, p. 388-395.

Rodrigues (1997)
P.R. Rodrigues, *Anders niets? Discriminatie naar ras en nationaliteit bij consumententransacties*, Lelystad: Koninklijke Vermande 1997.

Rodrigues (2001)
P.R. Rodrigues, 'De betekenis van de Europese antidiscriminatierichtlijnen voor de Nederlandse rechtsorde', E.R. Brouwer, C.A. Groenendijk (eds.), *Derdelanders in de Europese Unie, Europees migratierecht vanuit Nederlands perspectief*, Utrecht: Forum 2001, p. 101-132.

Rodrigues (2005)
P.R. Rodrigues, 'Ras en nationaliteit', S.D. Burri (ed.), *Gelijke behandeling, oordelen en commentaar 2005*, Nijmegen: Wolf Legal Publishers 2005, p. 19-33.

Rodrigues & Van Walsum (2006)
P.R. Rodrigues, S. van Walsum, 'Ras en nationaliteit', J.H. Gerards, B.P. Vermeulen, P.J.J. Zoontjens (eds.), *Gelijke behandeling: oordelen en commentaar 2006*, Nijmegen: Wolf Legal Publishers 2006, p. 21-40.

Romain (2002)
J.J. Romain, 'Des principes d'égalité, d'égalité de traitement et de proportionnalité en droit privé, en particulier dans la théorie des troubles de voisinage et l'abus de droit (plus précisément dans le cas du refus individuel de contracter)', *Revue de Droit de l'Université Libre de Bruxelles* 2002, p. 185-255.

Rorive & Van der Plancke (2008)
I. Rorive, V. Van der Plancke, 'Quels dispositions pour prouver la discrimination?', C. Bayart, S. Sottiaux, S. Van Drooghenbroeck, *De nieuwe federale antidiscriminatiewetten*, Bruges: Die Keure 2008, p. 415-461.

Rosas (2004)
A. Rosas, 'The European Court of Justice: sources of law and methods of interpretation', G. Sacerdoti, A. Yanovich, J.Bohanes (eds.), *The WTO at ten: the contribution of the dispute settlement system*, Cambridge: Cambridge University Press 2004, p. 482-489.

Russel & O'Cinneide (2003)
M. Russel, C. O'Cinneide, 'Positive action to promote women in politics: some European comparisons', *International and Comparative Law Quarterly* 2003, p. 587-614.

Rutherglen (2006)
G. Rutherglen, 'Disparate impact, discrimination, and the essentially contested concept of equality', *Fordham Law Review* 2005-6, p. 2313-2339.

Safran (2008)
W. Safran, 'Language, ethnicity and religion: a complex and persistent linkage', *Nations and Nationalism* 2008, p.171-190.

Sasse (2004)
G. Sasse, 'Minority rights and EU enlargement: normative overstretch or effective conditionality?', G. Toggenburg (ed.), *Minority protection and the enlarged European Union: the way forward*, Budapest: LGI Books 2004, p. 61-83.

Schiek (1999)
D. Schiek, 'Freedom of contract and a non-discrimination principle – irreconcilable antonyms ?', T. Loenen, P.R. Rodrigues (eds.), *Non-discrimination law: comparative perspectives*, Deventer: Kluwer 1999, p. 78-89.

Schiek (2002)
D. Schiek, 'A new framework on equal treatment of persons in EC law?', *European Law Journal* 2002, p. 290-314.

Schiek (2005)
D. Schiek, 'Broadening the scope and the norms of EU gender equality law: towards a multidimensional conception of equality law', *Maastricht Journal of European and Comparative Law* 2005, p. 427-466.

Schiek et al (2007)
D. Schiek, L. Waddington, M. Bell (eds.), *Non-discrimination law*, London: Hart Publishing 2007.

Schöpp-Schilling (2003)
H.B. Schöpp-Schilling, 'Reflections on a general recommendation on article 4(1) of the Convention on the elimination of all forms of discrimination against women', I. Boerefijn, A.P.M. Coomans, J. Goldschmidt, R. Holtmaat, M.W. Wolleswinkel (eds.), 2003, *Temporary Special Measures - Accelerating de facto Equality of Women under Article 4(1) UN Convention on the Elimination of All Forms of Discrimination Against Women,* Antwerp: Intersentia 2003, p.15-33.

Schultz (2001)
V. Schultz, 'Talking about harassment', *Journal of Law and Policy* 2001, p. 417-430.

Sewandono (2001)
I. Sewandono, 'De rassenrichtlijn en de Algemene Wet Gelijke Behandeling', *Sociaal Econoisch Weekblad* 2001, p.218-226.

Shaw (2005)
J. Shaw, Mainstreaming equality and diversity in European Law and policy, 2005, available at www.law.uvic.ca/demcon/documents/Shaw_Jo (accessed August 2009)

Shoenfelt et al (2002)
E.L. Shoenfelt, A.E. Maue, J. Nelson, 'Reasonable person versus reasonable woman: does it matter?', *Journal of Gender, Social Policy and the Law* 2002, p. 633-672.

Sierra (2002)
M.M. Sierra, *Towards equal treatment. Transposing the Directive – Analysis and proposals*, Brussels: ENAR 2002.

Simon (2007)
P. Simon, *"Ethnic" statistics and data protection in the Council of Europe countries*, Study Report for ECRI 2007.

Sinclair (1998)
A. Sinclair, 'Harassment: discrimination in interpretation', *Web Journal of Current Legal Issues* 1998, p. 1-16.

Sjerps (1994)
I. Sjerps, 'Het concept van indirecte discriminatie', *In Concreto, bijdragen over rechtsvorming gelijke behandeling*, C.E. Van Vleuten (ed.), Den Haag: Ministerie van Sociale Zaken en Werkgelegenheid 1994.

Sjerps (1999)
I. Sjerps, 'Effects and justifications, or how to establish a prima facie case of indirect discrimination', T. Loenen, P. Rodrigues (eds.), *Non-discrimination law: comparative perspectives*, London: Kluwer Law International 1999, p. 237-247.

Smits (2003)
J. Smits, 'Constitutionalisering van het vermogensrecht', *Nederlandse Vereniging voor Rechtsvergelijking*, Deventer: Kluwer 2003, p. 1-164.

Sottiaux (2008)
S. Sottiaux, 'De rechtvaardigheidsgronden in het federale antidiscriminatierecht', C. Bayart, S. Sottiaux, S. Van Drooghenbroeck (eds.), *De nieuwe federale antidiscriminatiewetten*, Bruges Die Keure 2008, p. 227-256.

Sólyom and Brunner (1999)
L. Sólyom, G. Brunner, *Constitutional Judiciary in a new democracy. The Hungarian Constitutional Court*, Michigan: University of Michigan Press 1999.

Spiliopoulou Åkermark (1999)
A. Spiliopoulou Åkermark, 'Minority women: international protection and the problem of multiple discrimination', L. Hannikainen, E. Nykänen (eds.), *New trends in discrimination law – international perspectives*, Publications of Turku Law School 1999-3, p. 85-118.

Steele (2005)
I. Steele, 'Tracing the single source: choice of comparators in equal pay claims', *Industrial Law Journal* 2005, p. 338-344.

Stratigaki (2005)
M. Stratigaki, 'Gender mainstreaming vs positive action. An ongoing conflict in EU gender equality policy', *European Journal of Women's Studies* 2005, p.165-186.

Strauss (1998)
D. Strauss, 'The illusory distinction between equality of opportunity and equality of result, *Redefining equality*, N. Devins, D.M. Douglas (eds.), Oxford: Oxford University Press 1998, p. 51-64.

Swenden (2003)
W. Swenden, 'Personality versus territoriality: Belgium and the Framework Convention for the Protection of National Minorities', *European Yearbook of Minority Issues* 2002-2003, p. 331-356.

Szajbély (2005)
K. Szajbély, 'A magyar antidiszkriminációs szabályozás fogalomrendszere', *Romániai Magyar Jogtudományi Közlöny* 2005, p. 43-52.

Tavits (2004)
G. Tavits, 'Muudatused töölepinguliste suhete õiguslikus reguleerimises: kaitse otsingul Euroopa Liidu abiga', *Juridica* 2004, p. 550-559.

Taelman (2004)
P. Taelman, 'Het handhavingsrecht van de Wet Bestrijding Discriminatie', M. De Vos, E. Brems (eds.), *De Wet Bestrijding Discriminatie in de praktijk*, Antwerpen: Intersentia 2004, p. 203-260.

Terlouw (2005)
A. Terlouw, 'Discriminatie op grond van nationaliteit', *NJCM-Bulletin* 2005, p. 119-127.

Thüsing (2003)
G. Thüsing, 'Following the US example: European Employment discrimination law and the impact of Council Directives 2000/43/EC and 2000/78/EC, *International Journal of Comparative Law and Industrial Relations* 2003, p. 187-218.

Theunis (1997)
J. Theunis, 'Het gelijkheidsbeginsel', A. Alen, J. Theunis (eds.), *Publiekrecht. De doorwerking van het publiekrecht in het privaatrecht*, Gent: Mys en Breesch 1997, p. 81-129.

Theunis (2001)
J. Theunis, 'The principle of equality in the Belgian Constitution and in the European Convention of Human Rights, J. Vande Lanotte, J. Sarkin-Hughes, Y Haeck (eds.), *The principle of equality. A South-African and a Belgian perspective*, Antwerp: MAKLU 2001, p. 115-137.

Thiery (2007)
Y. Thiery, 'Gelijkheid, dienstverlening en verzekering: een herontdekkingstocht', *Tijdschrift voor Belgisch Handelsrecht* 2007, p. 747-772.

Thornberry & Estebanez (2004)
P. Thornberry, M.A. Martin Estebanez, *Minority Rights in Europe*, Strasbourg: Council of Europe, 2004.

Tison (2002)
M. Tison, 'L'égalité de traitement dans la vie des affaires sous le regard du droit Belge', *Journal des Tribunaux* 2002, p. 697-710.

Tobler (2002)
C. Tobler, 'Rechtsgelijkheid en voorkeursmaatregelen in het EG Recht', *NJCM Bulletin* 2002, p. 360-374.

Tobler (2003)
C. Tobler, 'How to Use the Experience With Sex Discrimination for the Other Grounds', in: *Protection against discrimination and gender equality: how to meet both requirements*, Second Expert's Seminar, Brussels: MPG 2003, p. 14-27.

Tobler (2005)
C. Tobler, *Indirect Discrimination*, Antwerp: Intersentia 2005.

Tobler (2006)
C. Tobler, *Substantive equality and positive action in EC sex equality law: can the EU oblige the Member States to provide for positive action measures?* (Paper presented at the ISL Workshop 'Equality as a social right'), Oñati - Spain 2006.

Tobler (2008)
C. Tobler, *Limits and potential of the concept of indirect discrimination*, European Commission 2008.

Toggenburg (2002)
G. Toggenburg, 'The race directive: a new dimension in the fight against ethnic discrimination in Europe', *European Yearbook of Minority Issues* 2002, p. 231-244.

Toggenburg (2003)
G. Toggenburg, 'Minorities (...) the European Union: is the missing link an "of" or a "within?"', *European Integration* 2003, p. 273-284.

Toggenburg (2005)
G. Toggenburg, 'Who is managing ethnic and cultural diversity in the European Condominium? The moments of Entry, Integration and Preservation', *Journal of Common Market Studies* 2005, p. 717-738.

Tojerow (2008)
J. Tojerow, 'La réforme du 10 mai 2007: motifs et orientation', C. Bayart, S. Sottiaux, S. Van Drooghenbroeck (eds.), *De nieuwe federale antidiscriminatiewetten*, Bruges: Die Keure 2008, p. 1-30.

Tridimas (2006)
T. Tridimas, *The general principles of EU law*, Oxford: Oxford University Press 2006.

Tyson (2004)
A. Tyson,'The negotiation of the Race Directive', J. Niessen, I. Chopin (eds.), *The development of legal instruments to combat racism in a diverse Europe*, The Hague: Martinus Nijhoff 2004, p. 111-130.

Vande Lanotte & Haeck (2005)
J. Vande Lanotte, Y. Haeck (eds.), *Handboek EVRM: Algemene Beginsele*n, Antwerp: Intersentia 2005.

Van der Mei (2005)
A.P. Van der Mei, 'Het verbod van onderscheid op grond van ras bij sociale bescherming en sociale voordelen', S.D. Burri (ed.), *Gelijke Behandeling: oordelen en commentaar 2005*, Nijmegen: Wolf Legal Publishers 2005, p. 181-195.

Van der Pot (2006)
C.W. Van der Pot, *Handboek van het Nederlandse staatsrecht*, revised by D.J. Elzinga, R. de Lange, Deventer: Kluwer 2006.

Van Dijk (1988)
P. van Dijk, 'De conventie inzake de uitbanning van alle vormen van rassendiscriminatie', T.C. Van Boven, P. van Dijk, J. Hoens, P.J. Kuyper (eds.), *Bestrijding van rassendiscriminatie*, Nijmegen: Ars Aequi Libri 1988.

Van Dijk et al (2006)
P. Van Dijk, F. Van Hoof, A. Van Rijn, L. Zwaak (eds.), *Theory and practice of the European Convention on Human Rights*, Antwerp: Intersentia 2006.

Van Dooren (1997)
M.I. Van Dooren, *Recht op arbeid vrij van rassendiscriminatie*, Leiden: NJCM 1997.

Van Dooren (2006)
M.I. Van Dooren, *Aandacht voor het rassendiscriminatieverdrag in het wetgevingsproces*, Rotterdam: Landelijk Bureau ter bestrijding van Rassendiscriminatie 2006.

Van Drooghenbroeck (2003)
S. Van Drooghenbroeck, 'La loi du 25 février 2003 tendant à lutter contre la discrimination : les défis d'une <<horizontalisation>> des droits de l'Homme', *Administration Publique* 2003, p. 208-252.

Van Drooghenbroeck (2004)
S. Van Drooghenbroeck, 'La non-discrimination dans les rapports entre particuliers: de nouvelles données', M. Pâques, J-C. Scholsem, (eds.), *L'Egalité: nouvelle(s) clé(s) du droit?*, Brussels: Editions Larcier 2004, p. 79-185.

Vanheule (2003)
D. Vanheule, 'De antidiscriminatiewet en de Antiracismewet', M. Adams, J. Velaers (eds.), *Vrijheid en gelijkheid. De horizontale werking van het gelijkheidsbeginsel en de nieuwe antidiscriminatiewet*, Antwerp: MAKLU 2003, p. 389-409.

Vanheule et al (2005)
D. Vanheule, S. Bouckaert, M-C. Foblets, 'Grondrechten van vreemdelingen: de toepassing van artikel 191 van de Grondwet door het Arbitragehof', *Tijdschrift voor Bestuurswetenschappen en Publiekrecht* 2005, p. 319-333.

Van Putten (2004a)
M. Van Putten, 'Regelgeving ter bescherming tegen intimidatie op het werk: Juridische grenzen en mogelijkheden', *Tijdschrift voor Sociaal Recht* 2004, p. 99-192.

Van Putten (2004b)
M. Van Putten, 'Regelgeving ter bescherming tegen intimidatie op het werk: Juridische grenzen en mogelijkheden. Naschrift', *Tijdschrift voor Sociaal Recht* 2004, p. 407-417.

Vékás (2006)
L. Vékás, 'Egyenlő bánásmód a polgári jogi jogviszonyokban?', *Jogtudományi Közlöny* 2006, p. 355-364.

Velaers (2003a)
J. Velaers, 'De horizontale werking van het discriminatieverbod in de antidiscriminatiewet. Enkele constitutionele beschouwingen', M. Adams, J. Velaers (eds.), *Vrijheid en gelijkheid. De horizontale werking van het gelijkheidsbeginsel en de nieuwe antidiscriminatiewet*, Antwerp: MAKLU 2003, p. 287-326.

Velaers (2003b)
J. Velaers, 'De antidiscriminatiewet en botsing van grondrechten', M. Adams, J. Velaers (eds.), *Vrijheid en gelijkheid. De horizontale werking van het gelijkheidsbeginsel en de nieuwe antidiscriminatiewet*, Antwerp: MAKLU 2003, p. 327-387.

Velaers (2004)
J. Velaers, 'Het arbitragehof en de antidiscriminatiewet', *Tijdschrift voor Bestuurswetenschappen en Publiekrecht* 2004, p. 601-614.

Veldman (1999)
A. Veldman, 'Preferential treatment in European Community law: current legal developments and the impact on national practices', T. Loenen, P. Rodrigues (eds.), *Non-discrimination law: comparative perspectives*, The Hague: Martinus Nijhoff 1999, p. 279-291.

Veldman (2001)
A. Veldman, 'De nieuwe Europese arresten over voorkeursbeleid', *Nemesis* 2001-17, p.116-120.

Veny (2004)
L.M. Veny, 'De Wet bestrijding discriminatie in de ambtenarij', M. de Vos, E. Brems (eds.), *De Wet bestrijding discriminatie in de praktijk*, Antwerp: Intersentia 2004, p. 107-149.

Verhelst & De Wilde (2003)
I. Verhelst, I. De Wilde, 'De gevolgen van de anti-discriminatiewet voor het arbeidsrecht', *Nieuw Juridisch Weekblad* 2003, p. 438-450.

Verloo (2006)
M. Verloo, 'Multiple inequalities, intersectionality and the European Union', *European Journal of Women's Studies* 2006, p. 211-228.

Vermeulen (2005)
B.P. Vermeulen, 'De toelaatbaarheid van spreidingsbeleid en aanverwante maatregelen in het onderwijs', S.D. Burri (ed.), *Gelijke behandeling, oordelen en commentaar 2005*, Nijmegen: Wolf Legal Publishers 2005, p. 217-229.

Vermeulen (2006)
B.P. Vermeulen, 'Kerkgenootschap en geestelijk ambt', M.L.M. Hertogh, P.J.J. Zoontjens (eds.), *Gelijke behandeling: principes en praktijken. Evaluatieonderzoek Algemene wet gelijke behandeling*, Nijmegen: Wolf Legal Publishers 2006, p. 217-248.

Vickers (2006)
L. Vickers, 'Is all harassment equal? The case of religious harassment', *Cambridge Law Journal* 2006, p. 579-605.

Vierdag (1973)
E.W. Vierdag, *The concept of discrimination in international law: with special reference to human rights*, The Hague: Martinus Nijhoff 1973.

Volokh (1992)
E. Volokh, 'Freedom of speech and workplace harassment', *UCLA Law Review* 1992, p. 1791-1872.

Volokh (1994)
E. Volokh, 'How harassment law restricts free speech', *Rutgers Law Review* 1994-5, p. 563-578.

Voogsgeerd (2000)
H. Voogsgeerd, 'The approach of the EC Court of Justice towards the concept of indirect discrimination: a unique approach?', P.C. Westerman (ed.), *Non-discrimination and Diversity*, The Hague: Boom Juridische Uitgevers 2000.

Voorhoof (2004)
D. Voorhoof, 'De antidiscriminatiewet als beperking op de expressievrijheid: ultieme realisatie van het gelijkheidsbeginsel of veelkoppig monster?', M. De Vos, E. Brems (eds.), *De wet bestrijding discriminatie in de praktijk*, Antwerp: Intersentia 2004, p. 151-202.

Vrielink (2003)
J. Vrielink, 'De Belgische antidiscriminatiewet: een kritische bespreking', M. Adams, J. Velaers (eds.), *Vrijheid en gelijkheid. De horizontale werking van het gelijkheidsbeginsel en de nieuwe antidiscriminatiewet*, Antwerp: MAKLU 2003, p. 189-245.

Vrielink et al (2003)
J. Vrielink, S. Sottiaux, D. De Prins, 'De anti-discriminatiewet. Een artikelsgewijze analyse', *Nieuw Juridisch Weekblad* 2003, p. 258-75 and p. 294-302.

Waaldijk (2004)
K. Waaldijk, 'The Netherlands', *Combating sexual orientation discrimination in employment: legislation in fifteen EU member states*, European Group of Experts on combating sexual orientation discrimination, The Hague: Asser Press 2004, p. 341-375.

Waddington (1999)
L. Waddington, 'Testing the limits of the EC Treaty Article on non-discrimination', *Industrial Law Journal* 1999, p. 133-151.

Waddington (2000)
L. Waddington, 'Tweede generatie richtlijnen gelijke behandeling: de nieuwe richtlijn inzake gelijke behandeling ongeacht ras of etnische afstamming en de kaderrichtlijn gelijke behandeling in arbeid en beroep', *Sociaal Recht* 2000, p. 357-362.

Waddington (2003)
L. Waddington, 'The new equality directives: mixed blessings', C. Costello, E. Barry (eds.), *Equality in Diversity. The new equality directives*, Dublin: ICEL 2003, p. 39-54.

Waddington (2004)
L. Waddington, *Implementing and interpreting the reasonable accommodation provision of the Framework Employment Directive: learning from experience and achieving best practice*, Brussels: European Commission 2004.

Waddington & Bell (2001)
L. Waddington, M. Bell, 'More equal than others: distinguishing European Union equality directives', *Common Market Law Review* 2001, p. 587-611.

Waddington & Bell (2003)
L. Waddington, M. Bell, 'Reflecting on inequalities in European equality law', *European Law Review* 2003, p. 349-369.

Waldron (1985)
J. Waldron, 'Indirect discrimination', S. Guest, A. Milne (eds.), *Equality and discrimination: essays in freedom and justice*, Stuttgart: Franz Steiner Verlag 1985, p. 93-100.

Weis (1979)
P. Weis, *Nationality and Statelessness in international Law*, Alphen aan den Rijn: Sijthoff and Noordhoff 1979.

Wentholt (1999)
K. Wentholt, 'Het verbod onderscheid te maken', I.P. Asscher-Vonk, C.A. Groenendijk (eds.), *Gelijke behandeling: regels en realiteit*, The Hague: SDU 1999, p. 89-130.

Weyts (2004)
B. Weyts, 'Verzekeraars en de Antidiscriminatiewet', *Nieuw Juridisch Weekblad* 2004, p. 1082-1091.

White (1996)
R.H. White, 'Vicarious and personal liability for employment discrimination', *Georgia Law Review* 1996, p. 509-562.

Whittle (2002)
R. Whittle, 'The framework directive for equal treatment in employment and occupation: an analysis from a disability rights perspective', *European Law Review* 2002, p. 303-326.

Wiggers (1991)
J.H. Wiggers, *Recht doen aan gelijkheid*, Nijmegen: Ars Aequi Libri 1991.

Winant (2006)
H. Winant, 'Race and racism: towards a global future', *Ethnic and Racial studies* 2006, p. 986-1003

Woltjer (2003)
A.J.Th. Woltjer, 'De CGB en onderscheid naar ras of nationaliteit: waar haalt ze het vandaan?', D.J.B.Wolff (ed.), *Gelijke behandeling: oordelen en commentaar 2002*, Deventer: Kluwer 2003, p. 121-127.

Zoontjens (2006)
P.J.J. Zoontjens, 'Moet de CGB al het eenzijdige overheidshandelen toetsen?', P.R. Rodrigues, S. van Walsum, 'Ras en nationaliteit', J.H. Gerards, B.P. Vermeulen, P.J.J. Zoontjens (eds.), *Gelijke behandeling: oordelen en commentaar 2006*, Nijmegen: Wolf Legal Publishers 2006, 291-307.

Zoontjens (2006a)
P.J.J. Zoontjens, 'Eenzijdig overheidshandelen', M.L.M. Hertogh, P.J.J. Zoontjens (eds.), *Gelijke Behandeling: principes en praktijken. Evaluatieonderzoek Algemene Wet Gelijke Behandeling*, Nijmegen: Wolf Legal Publishers 2006, p. 117-176.

Zoontjens (2006b)
P.J.J. Zoontjens, 'Gelijkheid, verenigingsvrijheid en privacy', M.L.M. Hertogh, P.J.J. Zoontjens (eds.), *Gelijke behandeling: principes en praktijken. Evaluatieonderzoek Algemene wet gelijke behandeling*, Nijmegen: Wolf Legal Publishers 2006, p. 175-216.

Zoontjens (2006c)
P.J.J. Zoontjens, 'Noot bij oordeel 2006-110', H. Gerards, B.P. Vermeulen, P.J.J. Zoontjens (eds.), *Gelijke behandeling: oordelen en commentaar 2006*, Nijmegen: Wolf Legal Publishers 2006, p. 330-335.

REPORTS AND OTHER POLICY DOCUMENTS BY TITLE

Aandacht voor het rassendiscriminatieverdrag in het wetgevingsproces, Landelijk Bureau ter bestrijding van Rassendiscriminatie: Rotterdam 2006.

Action plan against racism, European Commission 1998.

Analytical Report on Legislation, RAXEN National Focal Point Belgium, Brussels: Centre for Equal Opportunities and Opposition to Racism 2004.

Artikel 1 Grondwet, Commissie Rechtsgevolgen non-discriminatiegronden, 12 April 2006

Bakens voor spreiding en integratie, The Hague: Onderwijsraad 2005.

Beleidsbrief Inburgering, Flemish Parliament, 1387 no. 1, 2007-2008

CERD country report Hungary, 2002, CERD/C/431/Add.1.

Combating discrimination in goods and services, Report of the fifth experts' meeting, hosted by the British Commission For Racial Equality, 29-30 January 2004, p. 15-22.

Combined sixth and seventh periodic reports of the Republic of Estonia to the Commission on the Elimination of Racial Discrimination, 1 April 2005, CERD/C/465/Add.1.

Concluding observations of the UN Committee on Economic, Social and Cultural Rights with regard to the state Report of Hungary, 22 May 2007, E/C.12/HUN/CO/3.

Council Recommendation on the promotion of positive action for women, European Commission 983/635/EC, of 13 December 1984.

ECRI General Policy Recommendation no. 7 on national legislation to combat racism and racial discrimination, 13 December 2002.

ECRI Report on Hungary (fourth monitoring cycle), ECRI, 2008.

ENAR General Policy Paper no. 3, November 2006, on Third Country Nationals, http://www.enar-eu.org/en/policy/GPP_3_EN.pdf (accessed 28 December 2006).

Ethnic minorities in the labour market. An urgent call for better social inclusion, Report of the High Level Advisory Group of Experts on the Social Integration of Ethnic Minorities and their Full Participation in the Labour Market, December 2007.

European Roman Rights Centre, *Shadow Report on Hungary to the United Nations committee on the Rights of the Child,* September 2005 , available at www.errc.org (accessed 15 May 2008).

European Roman Rights Centre, *The impact of legislation and policies on school segregation of Romani children*, February 2007, available at www.errc.org (accessed 9 May 2008).

European Union anti-discrimination policy: from equal opportunities between men and women to combating racism, European Parliament, DG for Research, Working Document, Public Liberties Series, LIBE 102 EN 1997.

Explanatory Memorandum, European Commission 1999/0253, 25 November 1999.

Het verschil gemaakt. Evaluatie AWGB en werkzaamheden CGB 1999-2004, Commissie Gelijke Behandeling 2005.

Integratienota 2007-2011: zorg dat je erbij hoort! ('Memo on Integration 2007-2011: make sure you participate!'), Dutch Ministry of Public Housing, Environmental Planning and Environment, www.minvrom.nl (accessed July 2009).

Jaarverslag Commissie Gelijke Behandeling 2006, available at www.cgb.nl (accessed July 2009).

Jaarverslag Commissie Gelijke Behandeling 2008, available at www.cgb.nl (accessed July 2009).

Joint Declaration on the prevention of racial discrimination and xenophobia and promotion of equal treatment at the workplace, European Social Partners EN/05/95/61370300.p00, of 28 October 1995.

Linguistic minorities in Estonia: Discrimination must end, Amnesty International 2007.

Media against intolerance and discrimination: Estonian situation and international experience, Tallinn: Legal Information Centre for Human Rights 2006.

Muslims in the European Union: Discrimination and Islamophobia, European Union Agency for Fundamental Rights 2006.

Ninth Report of the European Union Committee of the House of Lords, *The new European equality directives*, of 16 May 2000, accessible at http://www.publications.parliament.uk/pa/ld199900/ldselect/ldeucom/68/6801.htm (accessed on 31 October 2006).

Non-discrimination mainstreaming-instruments, case studies and ways forward, Centre for Strategy and Evaluation Services, for the European Commission, April 2007.

On national legislation to combat racism and racial discrimination, ECRI General Policy Recommendation no. 7, 13 December 2002.

Ontario Human Rights Commission, *An intersectional approach to discrimination: addressing multiple grounds in human rights claims*, at http://www.ohrc.on.ca/english/consultations/intersectionality-discussion-paper.shtml (accessed on 6 October 2006).

Opinion on Possible Groups of Persons to which the Framework Convention for the Protection of National Minorities Could be Applied in Belgium, Venice Commission, March 2002, CDL-AD (2002) 1.

Position No. 10.007/1/2006 TT of the Advisory Board of Equal Treatment on the division of the burden of proof, Equal Treatment Authority 2006.

Position No. 10.007/2/2006 of the Advisory Board of Equal Treatment, Equal Treatment Authority 2006.

Position No. 10.007/3/2006 TT of the Advisory Board of Equal Treatment on the obligation of providing accessibility, Equal Treatment Authority 2006.

Position No. 1/2007 TT of the Advisory Board of Equal Treatment on the questions eligible to be asked by employers at job interviews, Equal Treatment Authority 2007.

Promotion and protection of all human rights, civil, political, economic, social and cultural rights, including the right to development, Report of the Independent Expert on Minority Issues A/HRC/7/23 2008.

Putting equality into practice. What role for positive action?, European Commission, March 2007.

Racism in Estonia, ENAR 2005.

Resolution ResCMN(2005)10 on the implementation of the Framework Convention for the Protection of National Minorities.

Resolution on non-discrimination and equal opportunities for all, European Parliament, P6_TA(2006)0261, 2006.

Report of the Special Rapporteur on contemporary forms of racism, racial discrimination, xenophobia and related intolerance, E/CN.4/2003/23.

Report of the Special Rapporteur on contemporary forms of racism, racial discrimination, xenophobia and related intolerance, E/CN.4/2005/18/Add.4.

Report of the Special Rapporteur on contemporary forms of racism, racial discrimination, xenophobia and related intolerance, E/CN.4/2006/17.

Report on Estonia in 2005, EU network of independent experts on fundamental rights, CFR-CDF/Rep[EE]2005.

Report on the activities of the Equal Treatment Authority and the experiences of the implementation of Act nr. 125 of 2003 on equal treatment and the promotion of equal opportunities, Equal Treatment Authority 2006.

Report on the proposal for a Council directive on implementing the principle of equal treatment between persons irrespective of racial or ethnic origin, European Parliament, Committee on Citizen's freedoms and rights, A5-0136/2000.

Roma: Discrimination starts with primary education, Amnesty International, 2006, EUR 05/004/2006.

Second Report on Estonia, ECRI, June 2001.

Tackling Multiple Discrimination. Practices, policies and laws, European Commission, September 2007.

The business case for diversity: good practices in the workplace, European Commission 2005.

Thematic Comment No. 3 of the Network of Experts on Fundamental Rights on the protection of minorities in the European Union, April 2005.

The Netherlands: Discrimination in the name of integration. Migrants' rights under the Integration Abroad Act, Human Rights Watch 2008.

Third Report on Belgium, ECRI, June 2003.

Third Report on Estonia, ECRI, June 2005.

Trends and developments 1997-2005, Combating ethnic and racial discrimination and promoting equality in the European Union, European Union Agency for Fundamental Rights 2007.

Verschil moet er zijn. Bestuur tussen discriminatie en differentiatie, Raad voor het Openbaar Bestuur, April 2006.

White Booklet 2003, Legal Defence Bureau for National Ethnic Minorities (NEKI) 2003.

White Booklet 2006, Legal Defence Bureau for National Ethnic Minorities (NEKI) 2007:

Fehér Füzet 2006. A Nemzeti és Etnikai Kisebbségi Jogvédő Iroda beszámolója, Másság Alapítvány 2007.